Donated by Kerry Diotte
Member of Parliament 2015-2021

City Politics, Canada

City Politics, Canada

James Lightbody

broadview press

Copyright © 2006 James Lightbody

All rights reserved. The use of this publication reproduced, transmitted in any form or by any means, electronic, mechanical, photocopying, recording, or otherwise, or stored in a retrieval system, without prior written consent of the publisher—or in the case of photocopying, a licence from Access Copyright (Canadian Copyright Licensing Agency) One Yonge Street, Suite 1900, Toronto, Ontario M5E 1E5—is an infringement of the copyright law.

Library and Archives Canada Cataloguing in Publication

Lightbody, James, 1945–
    City politics, Canada / James Lightbody.

Includes bibliographical references and indexes.
ISBN 1-55111-753-3

    1. Municipal government—Canada—Textbooks. I. Title.

JS1708.L53 2005   320.8'5'0971   C2005-905945-1

Broadview Press, Ltd. is an independent, international publishing house, incorporated in 1985. Broadview believes in shared ownership, both with its employees and with the general public; since the year 2000 Broadview shares have traded publicly on the Toronto Venture Exchange under the symbol BDP.

We welcome any comments and suggestions regarding any aspect of our publications— please feel free to contact us at the addresses below, or at broadview@broadviewpress.com / www.broadviewpress.com

North America
PO Box 1243,
Peterborough, Ontario,
Canada K9J 7H5
Tel: (705) 743-8990
Fax: (705) 743-8353
customerservice
    @broadviewpress.com

PO Box 1015
3576 California Road,
Orchard Park, New York
USA 14127

UK, Ireland, and
Continental Europe
NBN Plymbridge
Estover Road
Plymouth PL6 7PY
United Kingdom
Tel: +44 (0) 1752 202301
Fax: +44 (0) 1752 202331
Customer Service:
cservs@nbnplymbridge.com
orders@nbnplymbridge.com

Australia and New Zealand
UNIREPS
University of
New South Wales
Sydney, NSW, 2052
Tel: + 61 2 96640999
Fax: + 61 2 96645420
info.press@unsw.edu.au

Broadview Press Ltd. gratefully acknowledges the financial support of the Government of Canada through the Book Publishing Industry Development Program for our publishing activities.

Edited by Betsy Struthers.

Cover design, photograph, and typeset by Zack Taylor, www.zacktaylor.com

Printed in Canada

contents

list of abbreviations

AAMDC Alberta Association of Municipal Districts and Counties
ACRA Alberta Capital Regional Alliance (Edmonton)
AMO Association of Municipalities of Ontario
AUMA Alberta Urban Municipalities' Association
BCMC Big City Mayors' Caucus
BMR Bureau of Municipal Research (Toronto)
BRZ business revitalization zone
C4LD Citizens for Local Democracy (Toronto)
CAO chief administrative officer
CAVE Citizens Against Virtually Everything
CCCD Citizens' Council on Civic Development (Vancouver)
CCF Cooperative Commonwealth Federation
CDEC corporations de développement économique communautaire (Montreal)
CFMM Canadian Federation of Mayors and Municipalities
CGA Civic Government Association (Edmonton)
CMA Census Metropolitan Area
CHBA Canadian Home Builders Association
CIVAC Civic Action Committee
CMHC Canadian Mortgage and Housing Corporation
COG Council of Governments
COPE Coalition of Progressive Electors (Vancouver)
CORRA Confederation of Resident and Ratepayers Association (Toronto)
CTF Canadian Tax Foundation
CUP Calgary Urban Party
CUPE Canadian Union of Public Employees
ERD Emergency Response Department (Edmonton)
FAUI Fiscal Austerity and Urban Innovation (United States)
FCM Federation of Canadian Municipalities
FOIPP Freedom of Information and Privacy Protection Act (Alberta)
GDP gross domestic product
GNP gross national product
GTA Greater Toronto Area
GVRD Greater Vancouver Regional District
GVTA Greater Vancouver Transportation Authority

HUD Housing and Urban Development (United States)
ICEC Independent Citizens' Election Committee (Winnipeg)
IT information technology
LAC La Ligue d'Action Civique (Montreal)
MCM Montreal Citizens Movement
MLA member of the Legislative Assembly (provincial)
MP member of Parliament (federal)
MPP member of provincial Parliament
MSUA Ministry of State for Urban Affairs
NCC National Capital Commission (Ottawa)
NDP New Democratic Party
NGO non-governmental organization
NIMBY not in my back yard
NIP Neighbourhood Improvement Program
NML National Municipal League (United States)
NPA Non-Partisan Association (Vancouver)
NPC new political culture
NPM new public management
OECD Organization for Economic Cooperation and Development
OGTA Office of the Greater Toronto Area
OMB Ontario Municipal Board
PPP public-private partnerships
PQ Parti Québécois
QUANGO quasi-autonomous non-governmental agency
RAG Resident Advisory Groups (Winnipeg)
RMOC Regional Municipality of Ottawa-Carleton
SMSA Standard Metropolitan Statistical Area (United States)
SOPC Save Our Parks Committee (Edmonton)
SPD special purpose districts
SPO strong party organization
SSSOCCC Stop Spadina Save Our City Coordinating Committee (Toronto)
TEAM The Electors Action Movement (Vancouver)
TQM Total Quality Management
UBCM Union of British Columbia Municipalities
UCA United Citizens' Association (Calgary)
UDI Urban Development Institute
UMC upper middle class
UN United Nations
UNSM Union of Nova Scotia Municipalities
URGE Urban Reform Group of Edmonton

preface

This is a work focused on the politics of public policy-making in the major cities in which most Canadian citizens have chosen to live. It is intended, in the first instance, for post-secondary students in the social sciences and their teachers. But it is also for other citizens who, with little concrete information about what city councils do, still pay their taxes and are directly subject to the everyday consequences of council work, works, and caprice.

City politics are interesting in and of themselves; in the matrix of governments and agencies that exists in Canada, it is a game in which a good bluff matters more than grand strategy, the luck of the throw more than clearly defined tactics. City politics are more poker than chess, "Snakes and Ladders" not "Chinese Checkers."

Any science in the study of political life tries to discern recurrent patterns in the cascade of current events. The art occurs when the commonwealth of ideas and feelings in these patterns is harnessed to some purpose greater than simply holding office. In these pages we will study city politics backwards through the lens of the public policy choices that have been enacted. It is my general conclusion that public policy innovation remains most frequently accomplished as the result of street level experience; even our largest cities are still local and intensely personal.

This book is divided into four sections. We begin by defining Canada as the metropolitan nation which it today is, then we reflect upon the nature of public policy and its practical applications in this urban setting. The beginning ends with some notes about formal institutions and the history that works them. Like other levels of the state, cities are the creatures of their own past, yet, not being bound by constitutional autonomy, their structures are easily adapted. The seldom recognized but accompanying danger is that fresh institutions are presented as a quick fix for far more fundamental policy issues. This is one of the recurrent issues confronted here.

Part II examines the process dimension of city politics, specifically elections, partisanship, overt lobbying, and the new influence of social movements, many with international frames of reference. Part III investigates the working of intergovernmental relations not only between central governments and cities but also among governments of the same sort within city-regions. Here I include a discussion as to why the governments of Canada's three central provinces chose to pursue, across the past political generation, a common strategy in consolidating municipal governments within their principal metropolitan areas.

Finally, the book concludes with a look at selected policy pressure points for Canadian cities that have resulted from the economic, social, and political integration of the global community, with some consequences for those who today hold office. It is in this context that I am reminded of a quip by acerbic wag Steven Wright: "It is the early bird which gets the worm; it is the *second* mouse which grabs the cheese." It has been my oft-frustrated hope that leadership at city hall stops playing the role of first mouse! I remain confident that better informed citizens, especially as participants, can help.

Key terms are emphasized in bold in the text. Definitions for these can be found in the Glossary at the end of the book.

Over the course of a long career, I have worked as a journalist, ministerial aide, and university teacher. It has been my good fortune to witness, first-hand, municipal administration from the *harambee* of Kenya to the resolution of metropolitan servicing problems in Tel Aviv and Mumbai, as well as in Winnipeg and Toronto. I have served on the national executive of one of Canada's political parties, planned and successfully executed strategy in mayoralty election campaigns, and acted as paid consultant to city and provincial governments with respect to metropolitan consolidations. As to this last, my position, both academic and applied, is well known: in the normal course of events a city-region is best governed by a single city government. Along this path, many people have freely provided their insights, and I thank them all without reservation.

Special thanks are particularly due my colleagues Terry Nichols Clark, Randall Hatfield, Tom Plunkett, Tom Pocklington, Allan Tupper, and David Walker for their unflagging curiosity and unstinting support. I also would like to acknowledge the many students who provided insights through their questions and amazing patience with my occasional sardonic assessments of city administrators and their political herders. It is also appropriate to acknowledge a debt to Mary Louise McAllister who has recently published an excellent work, *Governing Ourselves?: The Politics of Canadian Communities* (2004). Her assiduous research and writing reassures me that the work of cities is just as directly important to those who really matter—their residents—as I also believe it to be. Generous thanks are also due to several researchers over the past few years; I wish specifically to mention Melanie Lau, Jay Makarenko, Mike Wagner, and Daniel Webb.

The team at Broadview Press was enthusiastic, supportive, and thoroughly knowledgeable about serious publishing in the social sciences. For me, the experience began at the top with, first, Donald LePan, who initially invited me to consider working with Broadview, and then, Michael Harrison, whose gracious encouragement helped more than he may know. I further appreciate the gently competent professionalism at the press, especially from those with whom I worked most closely—Greg Yantz, Barbara Conolly, and Betsy Struthers, whose diligence in copy editing was a wonder.

Most importantly, I attest to the fortitude of the brightest lights in my life, my joyously thoughtful partner Lisa Kline, and my daughters Tanya and Teresa, each of whose patience and unstinting support over the long haul made the crafting of this text possible.

Last, whatever problems Irish philosopher George Berkeley (*c.* 1720) may have had with concepts of reality, I am reasonably persuaded that I do exist. If correct in this, I am ready and willing to respond to student questions about city politics; consider e-mailing me: jim.lightbody@ualberta.ca

James Lightbody
Edmonton

introductory note

The best place to start any examination of city politics in Canada is to under-stand that this country is a federal political community. This means that political authority is divided between a central government and ten prov-inces. All federal states must have a written constitution that clearly specifies what each level of authority may do. Canada's Constitution is found in two British statutes, the British North America Act (1867) and the Constitution Act (1982).

Both documents operate under the assumption that Canada is to be both a parliamentary democracy in the Westminster (UK) tradition and a federal political system. This means two things. First, the political executive will be chosen from among the elected members of the respective parliaments or legislatures and will be accountable on a continuous basis to them. Second, specific and exclusive functions of government are assigned to each—federal and provincial—level of authority (Malcolmson and Myers 2005: 33-38). For the purposes of this book, the two most important sections of both Acts are section 91 and 92, which list the exclusive powers assigned, respectively, to the federal and provincial governments.

Section 92 begins with the preamble "In each Province the Legislature may exclusively make Laws in relation to Matters coming within the Classes of Subject next hereinafter enumerated ..." Sixteen powers are then listed; the eighth is "Municipal Institutions in the Province." Local governments in Canada, including its largest cities, are entirely under the legislative control of provincial governments. While on the surface the forms and powers of all cities may appear generally similar, in reality there are ten different provin-cial sets of rules governing what they may do, what they must do, and how they are to pay for it all.

So we may begin the study of major Canadian cities in the twenty-first century with a statement of what they are not. They are not the independent city-states of Greece during its classical period. Nor are they the autonomous city corporations which began to emerge in Europe during the twelfth century as economic associations of merchants trying to establish a sanctuary from feudal nobles or absolute monarchs. Canadian cities are not the small towns of New England which practice a form of direct democracy through which all citizens have the power to assemble and to decide all important town matters. They also do not have the legal security of **home rule** enshrined in most American state constitutions and which guarantees cities (and other municipalities) the right to exist without direct interference from any other governing body.

All 3,500 Canadian local governments exist as bodies incorporated under the statutes of their respective provinces. As legal corporations, all municipal governments must abide by the legal provisions of those statutes and any other regulations the provincial governments may choose to enforce. Even the most powerful among Canada's 250 cities are thus told by provincial governments what their boundaries will be and what their range of policy-making authority is to be. In general terms, city government services are of three sorts: hard, soft, and financial. The first group includes basic utilities—potable water, sewage treatment—roadways, and public transit. The second embraces the protective services (police, fire, bylaw enforcement, and ambulance), planning and zoning, and a range of services directly for people like parks and recreation, social services and housing, and cultural programs. The last group handles the financial affairs common to all large corporations from management of personnel and insurance for the corporation to revenue collection and debt management. The minimum policy requirements in each of these areas will vary from province to province.

In the rapid period of urbanization following the Second World War, Canada's population began to concentrate in a relatively few very large city-regions. By the 2001 census of Canada almost 80 per cent of us lived in an urban setting, and there were 27 census metropolitan areas (CMAs), defined by Statistics Canada as a population centre of 100,000 or more people. In this book our interest is with the bigger Canadian cities because over half of us (57 per cent) now live in the 15 largest.

It quickly became evident in large city-regions that policy action was required to supply certain kinds of services required by the entire urban area, such as providing water, collecting and treating sewage, building freeways, and establishing public transit. But, because in the 1950s the people in major CMAs were still governed by numerous cities and towns as a legacy of the past, policy development and coordination, particularly in the hard service policy areas, proved difficult. The solution was to create an area-wide type of government, a second level or tier over and above the existing municipalities. At the outset only one function was assigned to these authorities—for example, to build and operate a water treatment facility—and thus they became known as Special Purpose Districts (SPD).

As the SPDs proved their value, provincial governments sought to bring a greater coherence to the policies of their major metropolitan regions by creating a second-tier governing authority that could coordinate the services provided through SPDs with a more comprehensive land-use plan. These new bodies were to be known as Metropolitan Governments and the first was Toronto in 1954, followed by Winnipeg in 1961 and Montreal in 1969. No existing local governments were ever dissolved at this time; indeed, in most cases the Metro-level council was made up of delegates from the region's existing cities.

The Metro idea worked adequately for a time; the greater Vancouver region still employs it. Beginning in Winnipeg in 1971, however, provincial authorities became aware of serious shortcomings in both policy development and delivery in their major urban regions. The legislated response was to amalgamate all municipalities, to dissolve the second-tier Metro level, and to create one new city government for the entire city-region. The media needed a shorthand term to describe these proposals, so Winnipeg's consolidation was known as "Unicity," and Toronto's (1997) was labelled "Megacity." Of course, many suburban councillors objected to the changes, but the Westminster model concentrates authority in the hands of the majority party in the provincial legislature and, since the Constitution places municipal institutions under the exclusive power of these provincial legislatures, there existed no real means for these councillors or their citizens to challenge the dramatic changes to institutions. Consequently, and unlike the United States, Canada's city-regions tend to be governed by very large operations.

The purpose of this book is to try to help the reader understand why all of these developments came about and, more importantly for citizens, who influences how the public policy in our cities is now made.

PART I

An Introduction to Canadian
Metropolitan Politics

one | The study of urban politics

At one and the same time, Canadians are citizens of the federal union, of their individual province, of their specific **city-region**, and of their own distinct neighbourhood community. To each is owed a particular allegiance which varies in intensity and commitment over time and which is often dependent upon whatever political issue is at stake. Political scientist Norton Long once reminded his readers that Thomas Jefferson viewed the hierarchy of citizen loyalties in the United States as going from town, to state, to the federal government, and yet that "Today it is clearly the reverse" (1968: 260–61). An Environics poll for the Association of Canadian Studies in January 2003 reported that 46 per cent of respondents rated provinces first, 32 per cent rated the federal government first, and 13 per cent rated municipalities first. Thus, in Canada today the provinces stand paramount "as the most important level of government in their lives." At the same time, 63 per cent of respondents agreed that municipalities "showed leadership" in their policy priorities, compared with 59 per cent for the provinces, 56 per cent for ethnic and religious leaders, and 53 per cent for federal authorities (Baxter 2003: 1).

However informed by these citizen perceptions it may be, any inquiry into the public policy-making capabilities of Canada's cities must begin with the clear understanding that they develop within an interrelated federal political system. In broadest terms, the central theme of this chapter is that in Canadian city politics everyone believes they have a say, decisions are made, but still no one is ever clearly, precisely, accountable for what has been done.

The earliest struggles for municipal institutions in nineteenth-century Canada were in part a quest for sufficient decentralized local authority to provide for local needs. The twenty-first century opens with an eerily similar globe-wide quest for institutions to realize what has been termed by some a **new localism**—basically, governing mechanisms that come complete with democratic means for genuine local self-control over community development. It is in this context, then, that part of our purpose here is to assess just how democratic and effective are Canadian city governing institutions.

Underpinning the emergence of the study of urban politics, as differentiated from the more traditional field of local government in political science, is the well-observed urban crisis of the late 1960s and the 1970s. This was triggered in the postwar United States by a dual migration: as white, and relatively affluent, residents abandoned the central city to live in exclusion behind suburban boundary lines, they were replaced by poorer migrants comprised of southern blacks, Mexicans in the southwest and other Hispanics elsewhere, and Appalachian whites. By 1970, 70 per cent of American blacks lived in urban areas. A snowballing city-suburb social and economic pattern of differentiation was matched by serious service and revenue discrepancies.

This urban "crisis" was not artificial for the city's residents. In the United States, it was marked by the fiscal collapse of several large cities, such as Cleveland, where it was made manifest by the inability to meet the public payroll. It was largely rooted in the failure of the city's social—and, more importantly, political—institutions to adapt to and provide for the demands generated by rapid and inexorable urbanization. The "urban crisis" phrase was for a time championed in Canada to justify several symbolic policy initiatives such as the short-lived federal Ministry of State for Urban Affairs (MSUA), created in 1971, which was internally sabotaged by the Canadian Mortgage and Housing Corporation (CMHC), and finally disbanded in 1979 shortly after the 1976 election of the Parti Québécois (PQ) in Quebec (Higgins 1986: 109-12). While we will chart the now familiar dimensions of urbanization in a moment, the point must be made that the large-scale urbanization of Canada was still a relatively recent phenomenon by the end of the last century. Its impressive take-off was a product of this country's engagement in the Second World War (1939-45), and it occurred roughly a generation after the United States had weathered somewhat similar changes. The point must also be made that the jurisdictional fragmentation of Canadian city-regions *did not* justify social and economic discrimination as it had south of the border.

The political structure and processes that attempted to accommodate the inevitable attendant pressures of urbanization were direct products of the mid-nineteenth century's dominant theory of governing, which was rooted in **laissez-faire** liberalism. Despite the absence of any constitutional guarantees for democratic autonomy, local practices have proven markedly resistant to change over the years. In large measure, this is the result of widely shared notions among powerful local elites in the municipal community that these practices are appropriate for a caretaking role. The elites, or urban political regimes focused on capital accumulation, can live adequately with social institutions intended originally to service an agrarian economy, even when that economy has moved well into a post-industrial, information-technology phase, as long as the streets are repaired, the garbage removed, and the protection of person and property appear to be maintained in the best managerial fashion. Indeed, even ancient physical structures can be made to work. Today, 9.5 million Parisians and 7.5 million Londoners cope with city core street plans whose original design purpose was not to accommodate SUVs but the mediaeval ox–cart.

Urbanization emerged as a direct consequence of industrialization and the resulting decline in individual self-sufficiency. The dramatic change in women's roles in the work force from a private to more public focus has had at least three consequences: the extension: of the franchise first to women and then to minority groups despite the reluctance of the male, property-owning electorate; an intensifying quest for more equitable representation in public office; and an expectation that the realm of government most immediately involved in the private lives of citizens—the municipal—extend its operations well beyond the traditionally limited service to property.

1.1　Canada as a Metropolitan Nation

The small size of this country's population spread across a wide continent produced an instinctive strategy of spot concentration. Largely in order to maximize commercial and industrial locational efficiencies, a small number of relatively large population centres emerged. Each of these has some regional significance and an historically important trading hinterland. This skirt of cities across Canada means that the greatest number of her citizens live in an "urban system" with an east–west axis and within 300 kilometres of the American border. This demographic reality has come to have considerable importance for the commercial and cultural public policies of provincial and national governments.

Of even greater potential importance to Canadian national public policy is that, since the 1990s, Canada's population growth has been concentrated

Table 1.1: Urbanization of Canada, by Province, 2001

Province	Population	% Urban[1]	% in CMAs	CMAs[2]
Ontario	11,410,046	84.7	74.8	11
Quebec	7,237,479	80.4	77.6	6
British Columbia	3,907,738	84.7	62.6	3
Alberta	2,974,807	80.9	63.5	2
Manitoba	1,119,583	71.9	60.0	1
Saskatchewan	978,933	64.3	42.8	2
Nova Scotia	908,007	55.8	39.6	1
New Brunswick	729,498	50.4	16.8	1
Newfoundland and Labrador	512,930	57.7	33.7	1
Prince Edward Island	135,294	44.8	0	0

Source: Statistics Canada.
Notes:
   1. This includes CMAs and Census Agglomerations (CA). The CA is a large urban area and adjacent urban and rural areas with a high degree of social and economic integration with the urban core. The urban core population must be at least 10,000.
   2. This column totals 28, not 27, because the separate portions for the Ottawa-Hull CMA are tabulated within their respective provinces.

into a handful—four, in fact—of urban growth corridors. While virtually all significant growth has occurred within the country's 27 **Census Metropolitan Areas** (CMAs), by 2001, 57 per cent of us lived in the 15 largest and over 42 per cent in just the six largest urban areas (which captured two-thirds of all population accretion during 1991-2001). The four large city-regions now account for just over half of Canada's population—15.3 million people—and have experienced a 7.6 per cent population increase since 1996 while the rest of the country has had 0.5 percent growth. These four corridors are:

   1. the "Golden Horseshoe," centred on the city of Toronto, with 6.7 million people, representing a 9.2 per cent increase from 1996, due mostly to 445,000 foreign immigrants, roughly the equivalent of adding a city the size of Hamilton to the area's population;
   2. the basin centred on Montreal, which has 3.7 million people, 12 per cent of Canada's population and over half of Quebec's, with a growth of 2.8 per cent with 126,000 new immigrants since 1996;
   3. Vancouver's lower mainland and Victoria, population now 2.7 million (growth rate of 7.3 per cent), with the Vancouver CMA absorbing immigrants at Toronto's rate by adding 180,000 in the last five years;

Table 1.2: Canada's 12 Largest Cities, 2001

City	Population	CMA Pop'n	% in City	% Growth[1]
Toronto	2,481,494	4,682,897	51.39	4.0
Montreal	1,039,376	3,426,350	30.34	2.3
Calgary	878,866	951,395	92.38	14.4
Ottawa	774,072	1,063,664	72.77	7.3
Edmonton	666,104	937,845	71.02	8.1
Winnipeg	619,544	671,274	92.29	0.2
Mississauga	612,925	4,682,897	13.09	12.6
Vancouver	545,671	1,986,965	27.46	6.2
Hamilton	490,268	662,401	74.01	4.8
Halifax	359,111	359,183	99.98	4.7
Surrey	347,825	1,986,965	17.51	14.2
Laval	343,005	3,426,350	10.01	3.8

Source: Statistics Canada 2002a.
Note:
    1. The measurement of CMA growth is taken from the 1996 to 2001 censuses.

    4. the Alberta metropolitan corridor from Calgary to Edmonton with a population of 2,150,000 (up 12.3 per cent since 1996, based largely on in-migration from other provinces), which now accounts for three-quarters of the province's population and 7 per cent of the country's.

1.1.1 The urban political geography of Canada

Because of the apparent necessity to centralize in cities, Canada has become one of the most urbanized countries (80 per cent) in the world. This migration of population from the rural to the urban occurred with such rapidity and unpremeditated design following the Second World War that both governing and many other social institutions of the city have yet to adapt well to changed circumstances. Today about 25 million Canadians live in 139 urban places (over 10,000 population). Thus, the focus in this text is with the political behaviours of those Canadians who reside within such a **metropolis**.

    For census purposes Statistics Canada has defined a CMA as a built-up central urban core plus its working-day commuter-shed of at least 100,000 population. A CMA is normally *not* governed by a single city administration as is shown in the discrepancy in Table 1.2 between central city size and that of the wider census area. Some scholars now refer to these urban environs as city-regions, a term more in vogue in the international community. Some French urbanologists use "megalopolis" to describe those major cities which lie close together. British geographers tend to use "conurbation" when they speak of city-regions that transcend a single major municipality. In Canada, the Toronto-centred urban corridor from Oshawa through Hamilton may very well fit this latter term.

Hidden in all these numbers is the reality that a matrix of governments—federal, provincial, and regional as well as municipal—all works politics within this same urban space. Christopher Leo notes the essential roles played by all levels of government in fuelling the postwar suburbanization of Canada. While the federal government provided incentive financing, the provinces detailed municipal responsibilities through statutes and regulations, and municipalities themselves defined the precise planning legislation while providing infrastructure support in the form of roads and water pipes (1995b: 31). Caroline Andrew has questioned the existence of any overall coherence in what turned out to be both a complex and substantial state intervention in support of the private economy (1995: 137-38). One consequence of this multi-government response was such an overlapping of authority that everyone had a say (and most officials found frequent opportunities for media events), but no one ever had the final word over an appropriate strategy for Canada's overall urban growth.

In the Canadian context, this is where Clarence Stone's well-known analysis of American **urban regimes** can help us answer some obvious questions. To him (as discussed in the next chapter), urban regimes are informal arrangements which manage friction points between groups while enabling public bodies and private interests to work in tandem to make and then put into practice governing priorities (1989: 231). The urban regime is, then, a loosely knit, city-regional coalition of community leaders that is somewhat differently constituted in each city and whose particular access to various resources supports the efforts of elected leaders to build economic growth. The extra-community professional and commercial linkages of these intellectual and commercial entrepreneurs enable them to transcend municipal boundaries to import ideas as well as capital. If there is a genuine regional voice for the city-region governed through many municipalities, it will first be sourced in its urban regime, secondly in the **policy communities** for separate service and functional arenas, and only lastly in its plainly visible political structures.

Even city-regions divided by only a few local governments find that their metropolitan local governments never have quite the same boundaries as their CMAs. For instance, on the eve of the consolidation era in 1996, the

ten largest Canadian city-regions were governed by just under 300 municipalities altogether, quite exclusive of school boards, hospital districts, and the
numerous other instrumentalities of the modern state. Since 1998 Toronto
has been both Canada's largest city *and* city-region; in that year and just
prior to its legislated **amalgamation**, the second largest city-region, Montreal,
had 99 local governing bodies within the CMA, and only 30 per cent of
that population could call the city proper its home. Similarly, the Vancouver
CMA operates through 23 municipal jurisdictions, while around 28 per cent
live in the central city. In one Canadian CMA, Ottawa-Hull, the city-region
encompassed some two dozen cities split between two different provinces.

The best assessment in 2002 was that somewhat over 3,500 front line,
directly elected, municipal governments existed in Canada. Quebec alone
had 1,451 (including 196 towns and cities); Ontario's 416 municipalities
represented a reduction of 400 due to provincially ordered consolidations
in the years since 1998. There are approximately 29,500 municipal councillors across Canada, and the largest 12 cities had 267 of them plus, of course,
the 12 mayors. There are just under 250 cities of various sizes. Reflecting
its populist history, Saskatchewan has the second largest number of local
governments at 813, four times the figure for neighbouring Manitoba (197).
None of these sums include the many independently elected school and
hospital districts or the many other partially autonomous local decision-
making bodies such as library boards and police or planning commissions.
Local governments alone employed 886,983 Canadians in 2002, a decline
in number of 17,270 from 1992 (Treff and Perry 2004: 6-7). This decline
itself represents **ideology** in concrete terms: it is the direct consequence of the
recent **neo-conservative** trend to municipal consolidation and privatization
of service delivery. In Ontario, municipal staff were reduced by 23,000 over
this period, while in Quebec, 19,125 staff positions were eliminated. The
result has been an offloading of traditional service obligations to quasi-private
agencies for soft services like recreation and to other, usually non-unionized,
commercial operators for hard services such as waste collection. CMA core
cities, on average, now employ one worker for every 70 residents.

Certain patterns emerge from information on the city-regions within
which the cities numbered in Table 1.2 are situated. In 2001 three CMAs
were essentially unitary in their governing (with one municipality for most
of the CMA). Six of the cities were in city-regions that were "bipolar" in
that they possessed two relatively large city centres. The remaining three
cities and city-regions had a central hub that accommodated roughly three-
quarters of the total CMA population, with the rest distributed among a
variety of suburban local governments. The Edmonton CMA fits none of
these patterns. Ottawa, then in the Ottawa-Hull CMA, is unique in its inter-

provincial straddling of two provinces. In general, this fact of urban geography has frustrated planning of any area-wide policy initiatives in that CMA, except for the autonomous activities of the National Capital Commission, a federal agency. A final small anomaly is Lloydminster, which straddles the Alberta-Saskatchewan border and which exists under separate charters from both provinces but is, for statistical purposes, considered a Saskatchewan city.

1.1.2 For how much does the reality really count?

This urban concentration of living patterns has had direct policy consequences for federal governing. Since half of all Canadians live in the central corridor between Windsor in the southwest and Quebec City in the northeast (about one-third directly in the Montreal and Toronto CMAs), as long as representation is largely determined on the basis of population, for any party to form a federal government it will of necessity have to capture the greater number of these votes. Platforms, programs, and policies will be formulated in response to issues defined by the facts of city life. In plain language, there are more federal constituencies in the urban realm of Toronto than there are on the ranch lands and oil fields (and cities) of Alberta. Even in that province, over half the residents themselves live in the metropolis. The real politics of a metropolitan nation means that a federal policy of strict gun control, anathema to the citizens of Red Deer, may very well be applauded in suburbs like Mississauga.

Another city-federal policy arena is housing. As shown in Table 1.3, over 60 per cent of urban Canadian residents outside Quebec endeavour to own and operate their own households. Over the long term, urban electors will demand, with varying degrees of intensity, adequate provision of serviced land and programs to support home financing to meet this expectation. Even the proportion of renters versus home owners may have policy impacts, such as rent controls of some sort in cities and federal monetary programs to assist in home ownership.

This simple matter of housing can also be divisive nationally because of the social cleavage apparent in home ownership. The Clark Progressive Conservative federal government in 1979 performed a short policy dalliance with a proposal for tax deductibility on mortgage interest payments without apparently carefully calculating in advance the negative political fallout in Quebec's metropolitan areas where some francophone politicians immediately decried the plan as an anglophone benefit. Such fundamental problems as servicing with potable water, sewage removal, keeping roads in good repair, and the protection of residential streets (through parking controls, adequate lighting, and community policing) can become issues asked

Table 1.3: Home Ownership in 2001, by Percentage, 12 Large Canadian CMAs

Toronto	63.2	Quebec City	55.5
Montreal	50.2	Winnipeg	65.5
Vancouver	61.0	Hamilton	68.3
Ottawa-Hull	61.7	London	62.8
Edmonton	66.3	Kitchener	66.7
Calgary	70.6	St. Catharines	73.2

Source: Derived from Statistics Canada 2002b.

of all candidates for public office at all levels—municipal, provincial, and federal—regardless of the specifics in what the constitution permits. At the same time, despite higher ongoing costs and new program commitments, "hold-the-line" public pressures on the residential property tax load rose in electoral salience as provincial and federal governments of all political stripes sought to balance their own budgets and reduce deficits by withdrawing from long-standing shared-costs operations that once fuelled city expansion.

Complementing this background stress is the further reality that the face of that urban electorate has itself changed in many significant respects. In the 1956 census, arrivals to Canada came mostly from Europe, and only the Chinese ethnic group registered as visibly distinct among the top ten countries of origin. By 2001, of Canada's 5.4 million residents not born in the country, nearly one-quarter still came from the United Kingdom (UK) or northwestern Europe, but one-fifth were from eastern and southeast Asia, and another 7 per cent arrived from south Asia. While another quarter (23.4 per cent) had been born in southern and eastern Europe, over 10 per cent came from Central and South America. By 2001, the census data reveal (Table 1.4b) the many new identities in the nationality of Canada's major city regions, many of which create policy problems in addition to new opportunities for innovation.

It is important to note that Statistics Canada reports show that 94 per cent of all new arrivals to Canada for the period 1991-2001 settled in an urban centre, and of these almost 73 per cent chose to live in Toronto, Vancouver, and Montreal (in that order). By 2001, while only 56 per cent of native-born Canadians lived in the metropolis, 85 per cent of all foreign-born residents did. As have other newcomers to North America in the past, and for a package of similar reasons, visible minorities have chosen to live in central cities. Newcomers have initially, and understandably, wished to live in close proximity to relatives and to people like themselves; there is also the practical need for the affordable accommodation and access to public transportation

Table 1.4a: Canadian CMA Residents by Ethnic Origin (by %)

CMA	*1971*			*1996*		
	European	Asian	Other	European	Asian	Other
Toronto	84	1.4	14.6	70	16	14
Montreal	90	0.4	9.6	66	8	26
Vancouver	89	3.8	7.2	74	18	8
Ottawa–Hull	95	0.5	4.5	86	4	10
Edmonton	93	1.1	5.9	87	5	8
Calgary	93	1.2	5.8	86	8	6
Quebec City	99	–	–	93	0.8	6.2
Winnipeg	90	0.7	9.3	86	3	11
Hamilton	92	0.6	7.4	92	3	5
London	94	0.4	5.6	92	3	5

Source: Derived from Statistics Canada 1971, 1999.

that central cities provide. The census of 2001 confirms that the Toronto CMA attracts the largest number of newcomers and that 41.4 per cent of the population is immigrant, an increase of 4 per cent from 1991. Before 1961 virtually all of Toronto's immigrants (92 per cent) came from Europe, but today only 30 per cent originate there. Of the top ten immigration sources, only Poland (with 3 per cent) constitutes a European source. The significance of this for Toronto is that the city has become a multi-ethnic community of a size and racial diversity unknown elsewhere in the world: for the period 1991–2001, 78 per cent of immigrants were considered members of a visible minority group, while in Vancouver—a city with one-quarter of Toronto's population—the number was 83 per cent. For the City of Vancouver, 37.5 per cent of its residents are foreign-born, and ten times as many have arrived from Hong Kong as from the UK. Eighty per cent of arrivals between 1991 and 2001 were Asian-born. Even a much less heterogeneous Montreal has felt similar pressures as its immigrant population has expanded at twice the rate of the non-immigrant over this same period. But here, the size of the overall migrant community means that it still constitutes only a small fraction in the city.

The impact of constant international migration upon Canada means that both policy issues and appropriate state action are constantly being reformulated. What levels of government, for instance, ought to burden its taxpayers with the costs of expanded English or French as a second language instruction? City councils are still feeling their way on specific services required

Table 1.4b: Canadian CMA Residents by Ethnic Origin, 2001 (by %)

CMA	UK	France	EU	Arab	West Asian	South Asian	East Asian	Sum%
Toronto	27.4	4.7	35.6	1.5	1.9	10.8	14.7	96.6
Montreal	9.3	26.6	18.2	3.7	1.1	1.8	3.6	64.3
Vancouver	36.8	6.5	31.8	0.6	1.5	8.3	25.1	110.6
Ottawa-Hull	36.0	26.0	21.5	3.4	0.8	2.3	4.7	94.7
Calgary	44.9	9.9	41.9	1.3	0.6	4.1	9.8	112.5
Edmonton	39.9	12.2	47.2	1.3	0.3	3.3	7.9	112.1
Quebec	5.2	34.6	3.2	0.4	0.01	0.01	0.5	43.5
Winnipeg	37.4	13.7	49.7	0.4	0.2	2.0	7.7	111.1
Hamilton	45.8	8.1	41.6	1.1	0.8	2.3	3.6	103.3
London	51.9	9.2	36.2	2.0	0.7	1.3	3.0	104.3

Source: Derived from Statistics Canada 2002c.
Note: The percentages reflect totals of "single" and "multiple" responses. The data do not include the category of "Canadian." As a result, note the consequence in the low summary percentage of the francophone cities, for instance.

by visible minority populations. Andrew, especially, has noted that race relations, civil liberties matters, and particularized crime prevention have all become new priorities in policing (1995: 155). In 2000, the low income residents of Canada's CMAs were 35 per cent from recent immigrants, 18 per cent from other immigrants, and 42 per cent Aboriginal peoples (Heisz and McLeod 2004: 66). Of course these rates vary across the country; as Aboriginal numbers are higher in the west, the immigrant proportion of the low income population increases in the east (to 68.3 per cent in Toronto and 33.7 per cent in Montreal). These findings point to a secondary policy issue: recent immigrants seek out low income housing at a rate slightly less than Canada's Aboriginal people, 10 and 12 per cent respectively. Toronto Public Health, for example, has taken on staff "to provide culturally and linguistically relevant services (such as family home visiting and tuberculosis prevention), and to locate services to address the needs of traditionally excluded groups" (Kwong 2004: 107). As the policy picture is evolving, it appears that municipal staff who deliver front-line services, those who are out on the streets, will have to lead in the adaptation of traditional practices. Subsequent city council initiatives will test new practices in turn and carve out new possibilities for their citizen-centred public policies. Municipal governments may inadvertently perform the function of innovation in the overall federal political system.

While it is international migration that bags the headlines, some aspects of internal in-migration constitute an almost invisible policy world. About half of Canada's Aboriginal peoples now live in urban areas (Graham and Phillips 1998: 188-90). By 1999, Winnipeg accommodated the most with 43,500 (7 per cent of population), but Edmonton stood second with 25,300 (4 per cent). More so than international arrivals, these people tend to be unemployed and living in poverty. In urban areas, the 1996 Royal Commission on Aboriginal People observed, the incidence of poverty (as measured by annual family incomes beneath $10,000) was 26 per cent, but was at about 35 per cent for Aboriginal peoples. Their disproportionate rate of criminal incarceration was also highlighted by that Royal Commission: in 1997-98, Aboriginal peoples in Saskatchewan constituted 10.8 per cent of the overall population but accounted for 72 per cent of persons sent to provincial jails. And, in Alberta, the respective data were 39 per cent in jail from a population share of 4.2 per cent. The numbers show that Aboriginal peoples are more likely than non-Aboriginal people to be denied bail, to be held in pretrial detention, to plead guilty, to receive sentences of incarceration, and to be jailed for defaulting on fines, especially in Saskatchewan (Griffiths and Verdun-Jones 1994: 638-45).

Furthermore, by 1999, about one-third of the urban Aboriginal community was under the age of 14, and, unsurprisingly given the overall combination of factors faced, this community draws inordinately upon social support services. For example, around 40 per cent of the Alberta case load in family social services now involves Aboriginal children. Pressures also build on the obvious policy areas of preventive and reactive policing, on public health officials, and for community housing programs, as well as on the specialized services delivered by quasi-private support agencies like the Young Women's Christian Association (YWCA). Community stereotyping rooted in historic lower economic and subsequent social standings has produced not-so-genteel discrimination against an already marginalized community that is, moreover, absolutely unrepresented among councillors at any city hall. Debates over questions of "assimilation" are not relevant for persons who have left the traditional community behind but have found themselves unacceptable to their new hosts. It is but a matter of time, certainly very early in this twenty-first century, before Canadian city governments will be abruptly awakened by this unobserved, slumbering problem on their doorsteps.

But this is social politics, and the urban regime in the twentieth-century Canadian city chose to define itself almost exclusively by the economic. In the broadest policy terms, Canada's CMAs, and the municipalities within them, are at one and the same time in competition with each other for external investment and development funds. One policy consequence is seen clearly in the United States. There, the local governments of the metropolis are numerous, land-use controls are strictly local, and property taxes are central to local governing. Most local administrations have been highly receptive to business pleas for tax exemptions, usually bolstered by the competitive blandishments of other cities, some of which will be in the same census district. Sustained growth becomes the measure of successful cities, usually at the expense of the living environment as well as of less fortunate residents and neighbourhoods. Harvey Molotch (1976), a prominent American exponent of the view that the city acts principally as a growth machine, argues that those with substantial landholdings in business, and the development industry itself, are easily able to enlist willing allies among the mass media, utilities, and cultural institutions such as universities and sports franchises to present a united front endorsing continued growth because these interests all share the same physical place. This explanation of long-term city political behaviour has been labelled a "political economy of place" (Harding 1995: 41-46).

In Canada, an approach like Molotch's easily explains the dominant twentieth-century city policy style with its associated year-to-year economic growth measures for the business and commercial sectors (sometimes labelled the **boxcar loadings** approach) which were almost always the test of a productive city administration. As will be discussed in Chapter 2, such an approach is sometimes styled **boosterism** and encompasses the activities of all those whose unbridled support for a community's sustained growth is assessed exclusively by successful commerce. For these people, the role of local government is to support expansion of the community's entrepreneurs at the expense of any and all other social, cultural, or environmental objectives (Lightbody 1995: 8-9, 271, 303). The governmentally fragmented city-region is compelled to spur internal competition while at the same time its lead actors cannot extol any real difference in community or service levels as an attraction for external capital sources. The modern burgher's battle cry has become "More of the same but at less tax burden." The divergent points in this discussion will be considered later.

1.1.3 To understand public policy is the quest

Most citizens see city government by what it does: for instance, garbage is picked up, pot holes are repaired, clean water flows from taps, parks are maintained, and the police arrive when called. Generally, the minor consequences of urbanization have been reasonably benign. In each of the major provinces, for instance, associations of municipalities have been formed to lobby provincial governments on procedural and financial matters. As will be discussed in Chapter 9, these associations are usually organized with one for the cities and one for the rural municipalities and small towns. Policy differences between these two opposing factions become important when priorities in bartering with the provinces for cash clash. Rural municipalities consistently affix a very high importance to support for the costs of the construction and maintenance of secondary roads. While asphalt is obviously also important to city councils, other priorities for social service or diversified policing undertakings and community housing also rank highly. Such city-specific programs tend to be neither understood nor seen as core responsibilities by the more numerous rural politicians. To the extent that the provincial budgeting for municipal activities is perceived as a **zero-sum game**—especially where provincial governments believe they must treat all municipalities, but not citizens themselves, on an equal footing—cities tend to be shorted both in absolute amounts and in distributive formulae. For example, provincial grants for local transportation expenditures tend to be deployed not on a per capita but on a per kilometre basis.

The important point here is neither stylistic nor symbolic. Who is represented will affect questions in caucus and at the cabinet table. Where the continued imbalance favouring rural members in legislatures persists, as will be noted in a moment, the formulation of general policies in areas such as transportation will in all likelihood favour secondary highways at the expense of urban rapid transit. Social service block funding will discriminate against cities if it is based on per capita to municipalities, since people in need have naturally gravitated to where they can be accommodated. Not so curiously, even provincial election dates themselves follow the farm seeding and harvesting schedule; June, for example, seems especially propitious in Saskatchewan. Wherever provincial policy-makers must seek out the lowest common denominator to purchase policy peace, it is more often to be found in agrarian pastures than city parks.

Still, policy issues such as transit and transportation (streets), police and fire protection, ambulances, housing, and many of the most immediate aspects of social services, recreation, culture, and libraries usually fall within the municipal bailiwick. These are central to the good urban life, but secondary to the traditional core responsibilities of proper planning (and environmental design) and public health. The larger political problem emerges when there are insufficient funds to meet public expectations from locally generated revenues. The broader issue of public finance is considered in more detail in Chapter 9, but here it is important to note that a strict constitutionalist interpretation of the division of powers between Canada's central government and the provinces has seriously inhibited even the possibility for a national urban development strategy. The Canadian pattern diverges quite markedly from the role played by Housing and Urban Development (HUD), a federal cabinet level office, in the United States. So, as the Canadian state grapples with global interconnections in the years ahead, and notwithstanding the obvious conclusion that many of the core issues about which policy decisions will have to be reached are urban both in their initiation and resolution, our federal system as a whole cannot yet embrace any coherent metropolitan strategy.

Regardless of what the political architects of Confederation may have intended, in the twenty-first century those policy arenas that most directly have an impact upon individual citizens, their standards of living, and their most intense inter-human relationships, have evolved within provincial jurisdiction. The various provinces may, and have, designated specific matters under **section 92** to their local governments for program development, administrative delivery, and cost-sharing. Separately elected school boards have been delegated specific responsibilities for education for a century and a half. Yet, Long reaffirms Peter Rossi's observation that local politicians "just cannot take themselves and are not taken by others sufficiently seriously to do much" (1968: 250). They are too many. And their political pursuits are so piecemeal, and so necessarily pragmatic in so many ways, and in so many grand villages, that cumulatively they are quite accurately dismissed as practicing the "low politics" of Canada.

The simple theme of rural angst still constitutes a formidable political barrier to urban centripetal reorganization. Municipal district leaders have consistently expressed to ministers and governing caucus members their suspicions of the consolidation of provincial capital regions. As one step in this policy polka, they have drawn upon their own past experience in watching big city leaders directly lobby senior bureaucrats and their ministers, with some success, for program adaptations that are beneficial to urban citizens literally on the doorsteps of provincial capitals. In the second step, more skilful rural politicians play to the apprehension of provincial elected leaders over the potential political competition were one mayor "able to speak for half the province's population." Indeed, in 1970, Manitoba Premier Ed Schreyer was able to persuade his New Democratic Party (NDP) caucus to accept Winnipeg Unicity only after he assured them of continuing provincial control through the dual mechanisms of attaching conditions to grants and using provincial regulatory agencies. In 1997, it might well be argued that the passing of the balance of voter power from the City of Toronto to the ring of suburbs around it (sometimes called the "905 region" for its common telephone area code) enabled the provincial minister's design for city-region unification insofar as suburban voters held more core values in common with the rural members of the governing caucus than did their city counterparts.

In a small ironic twist of *fin-de-siècle* rethinking, urbanist Jane Jacobs appeared in 1997 as a prominent opponent of Toronto's **Megacity** legislation,

Bill 103. Long a self-confessed foe of "big-city" government, Jacobs argued against what she saw to be "standardization" because "it precludes innovative and creative approaches to problem-solving" (1997: 7). One of her major themes was that diversity always lies at the heart of urban energy and that neighbourhood sameness, be it of housing or in commercial activity, subtracts from the urban gusto that acts as a magnet to future investment. This post-industrialist view of a widely diversified economy combined with dispersed urban political authority played well to public choice theorists who predictably decried the Toronto amalgamation (Graham and Phillips 1998: 12, 78).

One problem for the Jacobs point of view, however, was the mistaken equation of city administrative boundaries with distinct communities holding particular needs. Before amalgamation for instance, four of the six cities to be combined were each already among the 12 largest in Canada. There was also no evidence that any of the suburbs varied much in its treatment of, or response to, residents. Nor had the metropolitan level failed the test of innovation if the argument against it were confined to those functions it had actually the power to provide. Still, the justification of the CMA as best governed by a discrete series of small villages played well to rural angst while sustaining misbeliefs about the true nature of autonomous towns within city-regions these days. The Jacobs contentions subsequently became part of the mantra for the case against city-region centripetal reorganization elsewhere in Canada nonetheless.

1.2 Do Local, Democratic Municipalities Matter?

It is important to begin by acknowledging that, for a variety of pre-Confederation circumstances, Canada is today a *federal* political community. All federal polities require a written constitution at the heart of which is an assignment of exclusive responsibilities to both the central government and to the regions, states, or provinces. The framers of the Canadian Constitution had hoped to devise a reasonably centralized model for they saw in the just concluded American Civil War the folly of too great regional autonomy. Indeed, many had hoped for a unitary form for their new state (as in the UK) and, failing that, perceived provinces with powers somewhat akin to those of very large municipalities. This is so hinted by the last enumeration in section 92, the specific grant of power to the provinces, which reads "Generally all Matters of a merely local or private Nature in the Province." But those were simpler times, and the meddling of the British Law Lords ensured that this vision was not to prevail.

1.2.1 The constitution and the city

In practical terms, sections 91 (federal) and 92 (provincial) define the heart of the Canadian division of powers. The court system has become an integral part of the living Constitution as it has been called upon to decide whether or not a specific national or provincial government law fits within the authority given. If the particular legislature is found indeed to have the power to have passed the law, the court will find it *intra vires*, or within the competence. If the legislature is found to be offside, the court as umpire will declare the specific law to be *ultra vires*. As will become quite clear, the question of *vires* is rather important to the everyday functioning of all municipalities.

So, how much do municipalities matter today? The constitutional position of local government in Canada is very clear. Section 92 of the Constitution Act (1982) establishes that "In each Province the Legislature may exclusively make Laws in relation to Matters coming within the Classes of Subject next ... enumerated," and at subsection 8, just after the establishing and management of hospitals and asylums (92.7) and just before the licensing and regulation of saloons and taverns (92.9), we find "Municipal Institutions in the Province." Local governments thus know where they stand, in law, and this means at least three important ground rules have been unmistakably established.

1. Municipalities in Canada have *no* autonomous, local, and democratic constitutional standing. They have a constitutional position within the realm of provincial omnicompetence.

2. Local governments, as incorporated statute creatures of provincial legislatures, exist precisely as defined by provincial statute law. Also, as provincial subordinates, they are bound to provide services only within the classes of governing provided for the provinces themselves under section 92.

3. The federal government has no direct power in relation to Canadian municipalities and cannot intervene in their affairs. The federal role has thus been both cautious and difficult, and, often to the chagrin of federal interventionist politicians, there has never been involvement to parallel the American HUD Secretary.

Canada is also a parliamentary democracy, based on the Westminster model, at both the federal and provincial levels. For the real world of politics, this means that two powerful constitutional doctrines prevail. The first is that each parliament is supreme in its own time. In other words, no parliament can pass a law that will bind the hands of a future parliament because it, too, is supreme for its term in office. For local government, this means that there is no statute guarantee of perpetual existence. As the citizens of Metropolitan Toronto discovered in 1997, a determined provincial government has the power, if it possesses the will, to abolish any or all units of local government within its borders. This introduces the second doctrine: the rule of law. Essentially, this requires that any action of the state, no matter how odious to the many, must be founded in statute law. Even strict provisions of the Charter of Rights and Freedoms may be taken by the end run of the notwithstanding clause (section 33 of the Constitution Act, 1982), a form of legislative override by statute intervention. By statute, then, the ten provincial legislatures of Canada must, can, and do define very precisely what Canadian municipalities may, may not, and must do.

1.2.2 The politics of metropolitan Canada are important

The study of the politics of major population areas is important in its own right for three reasons. First, political units of a half-million people or more are important instruments of policy determination. We must understand the nature of these policy-making operations not only because most Canadians have chosen to live in them but also because the decisions made by cities directly affect the quality of our everyday lives. Choices concerning water and waste, police and fire protection, traffic bylaws and zoning regulations, libraries, parks and recreation, and social programs are all essential to the effective pursuit of the good life in this new century.

City governments will increasingly be large scale in and of themselves. Toronto's city budget is now four times larger than the annual budget of the UN's core operations worldwide. The UN budget, in turn, is more than $1 billion less than that set aside for Tokyo's fire department. The New York headquarters of the UN employs but 10 per cent of the people employed by the City of Toronto (45,000) or Stockholm (59,000). Total municipal budgeting in the larger provinces of Canada tends to be the equivalent of about one-fifth of any provincial budget, but it is usually raised and spent in a system dominated by **citizen-amateurs**, without ministry or opposition. These practices raise several potentially substantial questions about the possibility for consistency and open accountability.

Second, the large scale of the Canadian local government operation spills over into important considerations about social problems. By 2002, local governments across Canada raised revenues from their own taxation sources of about $26.7 billion. By comparison, in 2002-03 the federal government spent $134.5 billion on programs, while the provinces together shelled out $217.8 billion. Local governments cumulatively spent $47.4 billion for a combined deficit of $20.7 billion (Treff and Perry: 2004 Appendix A).

Since by statute, and unlike their federal and provincial counterparts, local administrations cannot accumulate an annual deficit for operations, this difference has to be met by other sources. Sales of local goods and services, as well as investment revenues, now meet about two-thirds of this difference, and intergovernmental **transfer payments** make up the other 37 per cent. Although transfers from other governments, mostly the provincial, have decreased by 31 per cent since 1994, this gross figure hides variations among the provinces' municipal systems that reflect provincial priorities. As Treff and Perry comment, "Every province except Saskatchewan experienced a decrease in transfers to local governments over the period, ranging from a decline of 69 percent in Nova Scotia, 63 per cent in British Columbia [to] almost 12 percent in Alberta, and almost 4 percent in Quebec. Saskatchewan local governments experienced an 18 percent increase in revenues from transfers …" (2004: A-9). Even so, to meet demand pressures, expenditures by local governments over this time frame increased in all provinces but Newfoundland and Labrador: in New Brunswick by 31 per cent, in Alberta by 27 per cent, and in Ontario by 26 per cent. It is important to note that over these nine years the actual proportion of municipal revenues within the national economy, even across the ten-province board, has not budged. Total municipal expenditures today equal about 9 per cent of Canada's gross national product (GNP), which compares to that of the combined provinces at about 14 per cent and the national government at 16 per cent.

Especially over the past generation when citizens have expected more in the way of public services than their local governments can reasonably afford to provide, the major provinces have consistently responded by frustrating any nascent federal financial relief initiatives as intrusions into matters of provincial jurisdiction. We will discuss the details in Chapter 9, but typically the provinces compensate with modest shared-cost options, the federal government with the use of its **spending power** to transfer limited funds directly to individual citizens. Provinces then reply by claiming interference in their constitutionally based mandate to set regional priorities sensitive to regional needs and demand a transfer of federal taxing capabilities directly to *their* treasuries. Since the 1970s, municipal leaders have persistently petitioned for either predictable provincial grants not linked to specific programs or for a cut of the "growth taxes" related to rising incomes. Simply put, until the Liberal government found itself heading into the tough election campaign of 2004 and sought to widen its citizen support, they have been ignored by the constitutionally autonomous levels of the state. What is the end result? Survey evidence suggests that informed citizens have become cynical about all this political posturing, have rejected the established representative policy structures, and have begun to turn instead to more immediately productive direct action through private operations often outside the ambit of state agencies. These matters we consider in Chapters 7 and 8.

The third reason why the study of city-regions is important is that they and their legally defined and spatial communities of cities and towns possess certain advantages for the investigations of social scientists. For some time, political scientists in particular have sought to develop generalizations about the political behaviour of individuals as such and when they are grouped into political parties, pressure groups, and private or public bureaucracies. Inquiry of this sort begins with comparison, and cross-community comparison provides the key test for hypotheses generated in one city. The barrier to this work has often been one of scale, for national political systems are comprised of millions of individuals and thousands of specific groups and associations with varying degrees of political awareness. In addition, diffuse, large-scale political parties and, on occasion, social movements, as well as enormous bureaucracies in both the public and non-governmental sectors, present further obstacles. And, at the end of the research, an uncountable number of influences from beyond the boundaries of the political system come into play. Accurate surveys of electoral behaviour are also extremely costly, usually prohibitively so even for teams of investigators.

But the study of the city, as a political system, reduces or eliminates most of the research problems relating to scale. Another advantage lies in the high probability that the city system is less influenced by external environmental pressures because its low politics tend to be very functionally specific (concerning roads, for example) on the one hand, while on the other it is protected by the borrowed legitimacy of the province. This latter is somewhat ironic in that the much-decried large dosage of provincial political control may actually create a heightened sense of autonomy from outside meddling within the range of powers granted. The point is that once problems of scale become manageable, an astute investigator may be able to generalize about some aspect of human behaviour within one city system. In the larger provinces, one might then be able to test such findings, while holding important variables such as tax and statutory regimes, general policy requirements, and perhaps even **political culture**, as constants. One quite recent example is the assessment of the comparative costs of governing the Calgary (unitary) and Edmonton (polycentric) metropolitan regions (Lightbody 1998).

As Aristotle once did, by using the city as an explanatory laboratory we may actually be able to begin to learn why people in politics behave as they do, while studying that which causes worse or better government. It is hard to tell if your community is in any way distinct until you begin to compare it with others which may be similar. In the process we may learn something of how better to govern the cities in which we live.

1.2.3 Why equitable urban representation is overdue

One political reality retarding Canada's emergence as a metropolitan nation has been the constant of **rural angst** about urban intentions. Those who have not chosen to migrate into the city have held an unrequited passion for the life on the land. Reinforced by the curious notion that urban life is inherently wicked and that city dwellers have set aside their naturally existing social and economic cleavages to form a policy conspiracy against them, rural electors have fiercely countered metropolitan planning and growth designs at every turn. Indeed, there is an asymmetry to Canadian city policy priorities between what an integrated urban social and economic system might require and what is permitted by provincial legislatures still controlled by members disproportionately accountable to voters in little towns and rural areas. To a large degree, modern cities are limited in realizing more favourable overall public policies by their ex-urban fellow citizens.

In applied terms, rural angst is provided *bona fide* political power by the reticence of provincial authorities to update their constituency boundaries. Once in power, politicians have a natural reluctance to take into account subsequent population drift to urban centres by adjusting an electoral system which has rewarded them with government. All legislatures in Canada have subsequently been more or less skewed to considerable rural advantage, the provincial invariably more so than the federal. Inattention to redistribution meant that by 1965 the federal member of Parliament (MP) for York-Scarborough represented 178,300 electors while his counterpart for the Îles de la Madeleine represented but 8,300. In plain language, this means that the islanders each held 21.5 times the voting power of a suburban Torontonian, giving us a mathematical indication of the prevailing bias.

Pastoral virtue appears to be a more deliberate principle provincially. For instance, the Manitoba redistribution in 1956, at the dawn of Canada's urban age, was considered to be the fairest among the provinces at that time. It was legislatively directed to count five rural voters as the equivalent of seven urban. In other words, the urban dweller was 30 per cent less a person than the rural resident. One direct policy consequence of this should be noted: until 1969 the Manitoba minister of municipal affairs was exclusively a rural portfolio despite the demographic reality that over half of the province's population lived within greater Winnipeg and 18 of the province's 24 most important municipal governments were also in that area. In Alberta, for the entire period of Social Credit government (1935-71) no municipal affairs minister ever represented a city riding. Even today, in that legislature, the over 60 per cent of provincial population living in the province's two large CMAs is entitled to only 48 per cent of legislature representation. On the other hand, the Ontario decision to contest the provincial general election of 1999 on the basis of federal constituency lines has enhanced urban representation substantially, if not absolutely equitably.

Since rural angst finds solace in the comfortable imbalance of provincial legislatures, any suggestion that representation on the basis of population be assigned a higher priority is viewed with something akin to horror. For example, in 1999, delegates to the Alberta rural municipalities' annual general assembly (meeting in Edmonton) placed cause and consequence into perspective as they "feared the province's current review of the size of the legislature could make it harder for them to lobby for funding" (*Edmonton Sun*, 1 April). Neither atypically nor unreasonably, this association argued for a larger per municipality block grant for roads maintenance regardless of the community's population size.

Similar representation problems still persist at the federal level. By the 2004 election, about 140 of the 308 ridings elected MPs from entirely within Canada's CMAs, and a further 10 or so were mostly included therein. While almost half the federal House of Commons was thus city-oriented, any fair sort of strict proportional representation would have added another 50 or so ridings to this national geographic concentration at the expense of rural communities. Even subprovincial regional governments face imbalances (as considered in Chapter 5). Andrew Sancton once summed up the situation for Ontario, showing, for example, that Sarnia with 58 per cent of the Lambton County voters was entitled to only 15 of 37 county council positions and Mississauga with 63 per cent of Peel Region had but 10 of 21 councillors at that level (1992: 287). Generally, such failure to exhibit representation by population has not generated much in the way of popular rebellion. Even where regional local administrations are not representative and have demonstrated a persistent inability to provide central city services adequately, the provinces are ultimately on the hook to provide back-up. Of this, Harold Kaplan made the essential point (and it affects all Canadian municipalities): "No one need worry about weak integration leading to the collapse of local systems, since these systems borrow the legitimacy and stability of the [provincial] systems" (1967: 19).

The argument against equal "rep by pop" is based on matters of geographic distance and is sometimes misleadingly labelled "effective representation." Here the claim on behalf of rural interests is that urban residents find it easier than their ex-urban counterparts to contact their member of the Legislative Assembly (MLA) or member of the provincial Parliament (MPP) in the closely interconnected urban space; therefore, city ridings can easily be four times more populous than rural. This idea of the representative's primary role as problem-solver is quaintly reflective of the agrarian culture of a century ago. Incongruence with modern circumstances means that the truly important policy questions concerning urban issues are dealt with by policy-makers who are disproportionately rural representatives.

The transformation of the Canadian community from frontier and farm came quickly over a short period of time; this may in part explain a lag in the adjustment of popular social images. This outlook also has gained a curious legitimacy through shared nostalgic sentiments of something romantic having been lost in the journey from agrarian roots to the thrust and bustle of urban modernity. The word itself, **nostalgia**, is derived from the ancient Greek root *nostos*, a melancholic longing for the home village. Some social institutions early in the last century—for example, the Catholic Church in the province of Quebec—did indeed view the movement away to city life and work as tantamount to a desertion of family and faith. Even in the 1970s and 1980s, several of the larger western provinces endeavoured to pursue policies to decentralize their own operations and to attract private capital to small town and rural areas in order to preserve the rural "way of life." These proved largely futile in the face of individual pursuits of personal social objectives as well as broader international economic imperatives.

Still, mirrored in Hollywood imagery, a considerable segment of the social science of the city until well into the late twentieth century was coloured by a stubborn sense of the city as evil, debilitating, and corrosive of the soul. The study of the city's political institutions, until at least the post-Korean War generations, was thus an exercise in **urban pathology**, an endeavour to provide diagnosis and institutional prescription for the malady of city living. What is overlooked is that much of the mythical "good life" of the collective agrarian past also meant poor roads, limited communications, few educational opportunities, and difficult access to all aspects of public health programs.

But nostalgia can be a commanding force in political debates since perceptions, not forgotten realities, govern values. For instance, struggles by central cities (as in Winnipeg in 1971) to amalgamate institutions with their suburbs quickly come to grief as those who have fled the urban core advance shrill exclamations that they are being asked to sacrifice their new-found—and normally evenings and weekends only—quasi-rural qualities-of-life. Edmonton's suburban amalgamation attempt in 1979–80 failed in part because the voters in suburban communities advanced state-of-siege fears that, if local boundaries were to be obliterated, rapists from the core city would surge outward to ravage their now unprotected neighbourhoods.

The silliness of symbols as representations of what we believe true of our community can be seen by a quick glance at the obverse sides of our currency—crooning loons, noble polar bears, children playing hockey on an icy lake—or city telephone directory covers of the mid-1990s in which Montreal has featured a meadow of pink foxtails, Calgary an elk overlooking kayaks swirling through white water, and Victoria a farmer's field. This is the case notwithstanding the reality that several of our cities are now relatively large political units. Calgary, Edmonton, and Winnipeg are each four times the size of Prince Edward Island, Montreal ten times, Toronto 20. The Toronto and Montreal city-regions are, by population alone and not even taking into account their economic prowess, the third and fourth largest Canadian provinces.

The fact of the matter is that nearly 80 per cent of Canadians, by the 2001 census, live in urban centres. For this country, it was the Second World War and the time immediately following that launched the substantial urban in-migration. For this period, all social and economic variables seemed to work in a similar direction; more usually the social scientist will find at least some variables which work as counter-pressures to temper the general trends. The requirements of the war machine led Canada to enlarge industries such as steel manufacturing and to establish entirely new enterprises for the production of synthetic rubber, combustion engines and their component parts, and petroleum processing. The emergence of a demand for skilled labour pools easily enticed the rural underemployed to relocate to the cities where factories were located, a trend which, after the war, was further reinforced by the mechanization of agricultural production. Hence, the postwar decade marked the heaviest decline for Canada's agriculturally dependent work force.

After the war, urban-centred industrial developments—for instance, the automotive manufacturing complex and the mobility it facilitated—dramatically fuelled the metropolitan growth of Canada. The emergence of petroleum processing capabilities, for example, quadrupled the size of the Edmonton city-region's population in the 30 years following 1947. New developments in transportation (air passenger) and communications likewise contributed to this growth. Finally, whereas prewar immigration to Canada had, until the Great Depression, largely bolstered the agrarian population, postwar migrants were at first displaced European workers and bourgeoisie. Not unnaturally they were, and are, drawn to Canada's urban corridors. How, then, have scholars tried to make sense of these policy consequences?

1.3 The Social Science of the City

Although most citizens are unfamiliar with the results of urban research, some among the opinion-molding elites with professional and cosmopolitan interests and their media contacts will habitually tap into "current thinking" about local practices in Canada and elsewhere (usually this means the United

States). This shapes media reportage in the first instance or, in the second, sharpens beliefs in the need for, practicality of, and alternatives available for civic adaptation to changed circumstances. So, in the same manner that the victors in any war, domestic or foreign, shape history through words, the intellectual elite is important because it determines what activities were and are legitimate, and, where change is anticipated, it also prescribes in advance what institutional patterns are socially condoned.

The role of urban-centred social science research is, of course, to expand our understanding of human behaviour in cities by asking three basic questions: What do we know? How do we know it? And why is it important? For instance, we know from poll numbers that fewer citizens vote in city elections than provincially or federally. Through survey research, several factors can be identified that consistently appear to deter a more active, across-the-board interest in local campaigns; as discussed in Chapter 5, these are bound together by the common denominator of insufficient knowledge of city hall. The curiosity in explaining this voter boycott is important in that those parts of the community that do turn out to vote appear the more likely to be rewarded with councillors and policies that please them. At another level, some among the local urban regime's leadership who can identify specific institutions as probable barriers to more desired ends, and are aware of better options, may become electorally active for a time sufficient to target these structures for change. Hence, knowledge and its interpretation become the starting blocks for most action.

There are essentially two epochs in the study of the Canadian city, one preceding and the other following the assassination of President Kennedy in 1963. This event led to a large Democratic majority in the American Congress in 1964 that endorsed President Johnson's "Great Society Program." The massive injection of federal funds directed toward defining and resolving city-centred policy shortcomings in that country was to have a considerable impact upon Canadian social scientists as well as urban activists of this period.

1.3.1 In the Crawford tradition

Until Canada entered the third reform era of the 1960s, there were few Canadian political scientists who paid even scant attention to local government. Their focus was neatly uniform and directed towards the institutions and legal structures of municipalities. In this, the scholarship followed closely in the footsteps of Aristotle, who collated 158 city constitutions because he thought that ethics and politics were practical sciences to be studied not only for understanding but also with an eye toward changing the manner in which people choose to live.

For those scholars studying local government, the Canadian city itself was not understood as being complex and its operations even less so. It was reasonably easy to discern a common purpose or mission for local administration when its operations were the more or less exclusive preserve of several hundred or so male, property-owning electors. Beyond Toronto, and leaving aside the curiosity of Montreal for the moment, the socially homogenous electorates of Canadian cities before the end of the First World War were very small business indeed. The common point of the analysis of such early writers as Grant Crawford (1954), Rowat (1969), Plunkett (1968), and the first edition of Tindal and Tindal (1979) was to make clear the constitutional, institutional, and procedural rules that formally structured local decisions and not to appreciate the politics of process or the source of power, which brought certain kinds of issues to the decision tables and denied others. Where there is any hint of ideology at all, it struggles to define how "common sense" might best be applied. Some few on city councils and their retained consultants, usually in a city's suburbs, yearn still to rekindle these nostalgic golden days of a town council "in which members sit around a common table or horseshoe, making eye contact with each other and fully engaged in a common discussion" (Sancton 1997: 17).

But if there were one set of conditions that defined the social science of the North American city in the early twentieth century, especially in the development of the metropolis of the eastern and midwestern parts of the United States, it found its source in the **machine politics** under **boss rule**. No American city politics text book is complete without a thorough assessment of this period, and, on the eve of the Great Depression in 1929, Harvard Professor W.B. Munro delivered an influential public lecture series at the University of Toronto. It was his assessment of public currents that "[o]f all branches of government in Canada, the government of cities has proved the most susceptible to American influence. In the form and spirit of their government Canadian cities have been steadily moving away from English standards and veering toward the organization and methods of municipalities in the United States" (1929: 99).

He was correct to note the two influences in conjunction. For its earliest roots, the Canadian inspiration in municipal affairs was British, but, from 1900, the primary impetus for study and prescription became American. The continuing American influence since is surprising only if it is forgotten that four out of every five political scientists in the world are American and that many among the remainder hold their most senior degree from an American university. Americans are both our closest neighbours geographically and also a migrant dependent new society, so their growth problems initially appeared to bear a superficial resemblance to Canada's. Even at the turn of this new century, Canadian city politicians and bureaucrats have continued to emulate American role models for their internal administrative improvements. So it is that these days some variant of **Total Quality Management (TQM)** as practiced in Madison, Wisconsin or Indianapolis, Indiana, provides the latest and best benchmarks for assessing either quality of life or the measurement of Canadian municipal performance.

1.3.2 Boss rule as the shame of the cities

Because it constitutes such a bogeyman hovering over many if not all landscapes of twentieth-century city reform, it is important to understand a few of the precise details of boss rule. It was first described in detail by James Bryce, later British ambassador to Washington, in his *The American Commonwealth* (1888). His scathing indictment of party political behaviour not only played well to the predominantly rural, small town values which still stood as the fulcrum for the realization of any American's dream,[1] but also legitimated a strand of reformers who came to be labelled "muckrakers." Whereas the earlier *Democracy in America*, Alexis de Tocqueville's splendidly romantic but confused romp written in 1835, had but 35 pages considering state and municipal government, Bryce devoted 255 to the subject. To Bryce, great cities were a desirable end, but, in his time, they seemed to embody all that was wicked or could be corrupted, and the boss system with its rings of cronies lay at its diabolical heart.

What constituted American boss rule? The political machine emerged in the 1840s and remained a potent force for roughly a century, the whipping-boy for many generations of North American reform. It was a partisan operation and an urban phenomenon. Its systematic operations were tightly controlled from the top down by a small coalition of ward or borough leaders even though it was often personified by a single, usually non-elected boss. It was a methodical, highly disciplined hierarchy of authority right down to the level of the polling station. It gave the appearance of a permanent social organization in which individuals who performed their tasks well could find promotion upwards through the ranks. The machine had many dimensions, but its primary focus was on the winning of public office and the rewards of the public treasury.

The machine's source of power lay in its ability to control votes, which it did as long as people placed less value on the vote than on what they knew the machine could provide in exchange. Where the citizen was generally indifferent to issues or personalities, and where little harm to him could be seen coming from city hall in any case because of his low income or social status, then his ballot was indeed up for grabs. In exchange for his favourable vote, he was offered by the low-ranking machine politician, or ward–healer, small material incentives such as a gift of food or a favour of employment or health care which were not insignificant to the recipient in the period before the extension of social welfare. Even a small bit of help in dealing with an impersonal city bureaucracy built loyalty.

More importantly, the medium of exchange was "friendship," in the spirit of Martin Scorsese's 2003 film *Gangs of New York*. New migrants suffering dislocation trauma discovered an apparent connection to others in the machine along with a sense of attachment or belonging, even a sense of access to power and authority, as well as finding someone to whom to turn in a moment of duress. Facing discrimination from the older established community, newcomers also found the machine to be an agency of almost perfectly open upward social mobility. Invariably, the evidence demonstrates that the lower the income and the higher the number of new arrivals (either from abroad or from poorer areas within the country) in a ward the more dependable it became for the political machine (Winter 1969: 276-79; Banfield and Wilson 1963: 116 ff).

The daily grind and pattern of activity of New York City's Tammany Hall district leader is well captured in the 1903 memoir of Boss Plunkitt. Here is a person who has no life but politics:

> Everybody in the district knows him. Everybody knows where to find him, and nearly everybody goes to him for assistance of one sort or another, especially the poor of the tenements. He is always obliging. He will go to the police courts to put in a good word for the "drunks and disorderlies" or pay their fines, if a good word is not effective. He will attend christenings, weddings, and funerals. He will feed the hungry and help bury the dead. A philanthropist? Not at all. He is playing politics all the time. (Riordan 1903: 90-91)

And this local boss was corrupt, of course.

Even though the key factor in all of the great machines' survival was their ability to reward friends, they were never able to afford to buy enough votes to capture city hall completely. Still, patronage became important not only for the material benefits granted but also for the social recognition it sometimes conferred to those sensitive about their origins. At the top, graft was large-scale; elements of its practice are further discussed in Chapter 5. It was this large harvest that infuriated the reformers, but the fury was sustained by their overall contempt for the machine's supporters. The bosses were generally dismissive of episodic, and city-specific, reform initiatives. Plunkitt's view of one such occurrence was that it cost only $42.04 to manufacture a clean government movement for newspaper consumption (Riordan 1903: 60). His point was that the machine endured because it not only gave protection and modest prosperity to the immigrant newcomer from the moment of arrival but also produced a kind of professional politician who "looks after his own interests, the organization's interests, and the city's interests all at the same time" (1903: 29). Thus, the institutionalized racket that was New York City's Tammany Hall, for instance, was a benevolent form of blended corruption. Even during Prohibition in the 1920s, the price to obtain a job on the city payroll was one year's salary.

The one last gasp of boss rule came in 1944 when the Bronx Democratic machine, under boss Edward Flynn, placed Harry Truman onto the Democratic Party ticket as vice-presidential candidate. Ironically, it may also have been the behind-the-scenes influence of Flynn, who had been one of President Roosevelt's closest advisers in assembling the social legislation of the New Deal, which caused the machine's own demise. After this championing of social reform proved successful, the machine's former constituents could now at last turn to the modern state for relief from the squalid stability of the original point-of-entry neighbourhood. In leaving, they also abandoned traditional voting behaviours.

1.3.3 Reform aftermath and consequences

Machine politics did not take hold in the Canadian city for several reasons. The cities themselves were smaller, and the rewards of office were consequently fewer. Civil service reform came early in the twentieth century and insulated municipal institutions from subsequent abuse of appointment and tender. Even the early pattern of immigration was not into urban space but mostly to the rural landscape, as newcomers were largely banished to the Canadian prairies by the British and French ethnic charter groups. Potential voting recruits were thereby not available to "wannabe" bosses until after the Second World War. Even in the late 1940s, Toronto was a small city with a virtually homogenous society (Kaplan 1967: 214).

In the Canadian context, then, machine politics were denied the role of social integration until minorities challenged the Anglo elite establishment for political control in the 1950s.[2] These activities bred some collateral damage. For example, Edmonton's Mayor William Hawrelak took unregulated personal access to public goods and piecemeal graft, an approach which contrasted sharply with the past systemic application of the entire city enterprise in support of an economic expansion which benefited the city's entire commercial claque. It must be added that graft was in no way disproportionately reserved for newer Canadians. Abuse of office-holding, usually related to land profiteering, led some social scientists in the last years of the twentieth century to consider new rules to govern the conduct of office-holders and to establish procedural codes of ethics. However, the old standards of Canadian establishment gentility were not effectively challenged until almost a half-century after ethical brinksmanship had empowered sweeping municipal reform south of the border.

In Canada, more importantly, the electoral system was itself a barrier to boss rule. In the United States, every office from local inspectors through state assemblies up to the federal presidency and Congress were elected on the Tuesday after the first Monday in November in even numbered years. Coherent party organization was essential, focused, and intense in an "all for one" sort of way. Canadian elections have been held at separate times from Confederation and thus have denied putative Tammany operations the great rewards that could come from simultaneous multi-level victories. The system simply did not work to institutionalize the structured collective behaviour that sustained the boss operation.

Still, those individuals with an interest in civic reform might very well have taken the British lead and used the municipal corporation as a collective public enterprise with which to challenge not only the natural environment but also dysfunctional social and economic constellations of power. They did not, for reasons to be discussed later (see Chapters 4 and 6). In hindsight, their greatest positive contribution to civic policy-making at the time was undoubtedly the introduction of "new standards for accounting and financial management" (Magnusson 2002: 332). What else was tried?

The urban reform movement as it took shape in the United States was based on a number of fundamental assumptions. Such turn-of-the-century (1900) reformers as Seth Low, Frank Goodnow, Lincoln Steffens, and James Bryce were very pessimistic about urban society and genuinely believed that the city itself had a strongly debilitating impact on the human spirit. For the native-born, it was relatively easy to blame recent immigrants (the Irish mostly, but Okies and southern blacks later on) as being at the root of perceived governing pathology. Since the political machine was the logical outcome of partisanship effectively realized, reform became strongly anti-party; and because bosses had abetted state legislators' awards of lucrative municipal monopoly franchises like electricity, water, gas, and transit to sundry friends and cronies, reformers also sought a means by which to build municipal autonomy.

The attack of the urban reformers culminated in the formation of the National Municipal League (NML) and the publication of its *A Municipal Program* in 1900. This included a model city charter which, like the modern baseball cap with its plastic size adjusters, was fit for all municipalities (see Chapter 4, p. 145). Around the end of the nineteenth century, this program was introduced widely through various publications (Sayre and Polsby 1965: 120-21) and was in turn urged on Canada by community leaders of that era. For example, in a 1909 speech to the Union of Alberta Municipalities, Red Deer's ex-mayor H.H. Gaetz argued that "[i]n drafting an Act for Alberta our Legislature could not do better than follow it [the model city charter] closely in determining the nature and form of the powers which should be vested in Alberta municipalities" (Masson and Anderson, 1972: 29). Some form of this speech was ubiquitous at every municipal convention across Canada during this period. For quite a while, these assumptions and proposed institutional changes came quickly to stand as *the* basis for analysis, and their realization became a primary objective for social science writing.

Just as, from 1947, Kenneth Wheare influenced the worldwide direction of debate respecting federal institutions, so too have many students of the Canadian city dwelt in the shadow of Bryce-style pessimism concerning its citizens, their appetites, and their politics. Even today, some prominent Canadian academic writers colour their assessments of institutional change with an eye to its compatibility with machine politics. For instance, appearing on behalf of the suburbs in their losing challenge of the constitutionality of the Toronto Megacity legislation in 1997, Sancton argued that the changes could well lead to the ominous specter of bossism. Although "a return to machine-style politics of the nineteenth century is not inevitable," in his bleak landscape, the alternative to the machine may be even worse: "Cliques, factions, secret deals, and ongoing chaos would characterize the local political process" (1997: 23, 33). In short, citizens of large cities cannot be entrusted with their own governing.

A more proactive line of response than the preventive, almost negative, prescriptive medicine of the Brycian line of thinking lay in the idyllic world of the "City Beautiful" in town planning. The City Beautiful movement had its genesis in the 1893 Chicago Columbian Exposition which emphasized a grand aesthetic design rooted in the appropriate development of public space. Writing during the 1920s era of urban sprawl, Lewis Mumford called the urban region "a special place created by people interacting with their environment. The natural region could be a bulwark against massive urbanization and the standardization of culture" (Hodge 1991: 278-80). By 1906, city-wide planning under these influences was undertaken for Toronto (for example, the University Avenue redevelopment), Calgary (1914), Edmonton (1915), and Vancouver (1929). McAllister, however, also observes the fundamental cynicism of these operations: "Aesthetic considerations were not ignored in the early 1900s, but such elements of city planning as the preservation of distinctive landscape features and the creation of forested park areas were designed primarily to draw people to the community ..." (1995: 272).

One offshoot of this thinking that was to have serious implications for metropolitan governing was the notion of the dispersed and autonomous suburb.

Social scientists of this period became advocates of the reform movement's singular path, and the segregation of "politics" from "administration" became so central and embedded a doctrine that it is still advocated in city halls today (Price 1995: 196-98). In theory, a numerically small council of about seven individuals elected at large and freed from the day-to-day management of administrative detail, would grandly formulate broad policy initiatives; a politically neutral city manager could then implement and administer such program decisions without favour or partisan bias. In practice, as we shall see later, it is not at all easy to contain these two worlds in separate and watertight compartments.

The seminal text of Banfield and Wilson (1963) was important because it marked a general return to an older tradition of studying the observed behaviour of people as political animals. Urban politics had been rediscovered by social science scholarship and returned to prominence in the years immediately after the Second World War. Political scientists, in particular those interested in the study of political parties, interests, and voters turned their attention to urban organizations and processes as clinical data for the study of humanity and away from an opportunity to indict citizens for either malaise or evil intent.

This turn away from the generalized attack on the process side of city politics in a ham-fisted attempt both to neuter them and to reserve the activity for the expert led to an appreciation that politics and power were a normal part of the democratic world. Boss rule and the image of the big city machine were reassessed as imperfect but serviceable agencies both for representing certain kinds of citizens (low income and ethnic minorities), which were intentionally disregarded by the "clean government" reformers, and for integrating newcomers into a complex, unfamiliar society. The classic medium of exchange for migrants was friendship, access, and a sense of belonging into the new community. Classic work by sociologist Robert Merton (1957 and 1968) and political scientist Samuel Eldersveld (1964) rehabilitated the boss system as an integrative device, somewhat as Boss Plunkitt had seen it. As to assessing the 1880-1915 reform movements, as American Congressional leader Tip O'Neill, borrowing from Benjamin Franklin, put it so well, "Where you stand depends upon where you sit!"

Large-scale urbanization in the United States during the interwar period produced, as it did a generation later in Canada, very complex metropolitan regions, with their own distinctive patterns of stress related to population expansion that paid no heed to traditional city boundary lines. The tangled intergovernmental patterns of city-regions were initially approached by

NML reformers in 1926 and 1940 as yet another problem for their social engineering, but they were defeated in attempts to bring order for two reasons. The first was simply that each city-region was so markedly unique in all conditions that they collectively defied any universal formula for improvement (Sayre and Polsby 1965: 123-24).

The second, more serious, issue came as an unintended consequence of the original municipal program set out in the NML's 1900 publication of that name. **Home rule**—enacting constitutions for autonomous communities to thwart the meddling of state legislature in municipal contracts—became an ideological and strategic barrier to wider integration of metropolitan governing. Whenever a referendum asked the question, electorates were quite unprepared to surrender local control of local institutions. In crude terms, suburban whites would not submit to inner city black and Hispanic voters control of their police; inner core residents would not dilute majority political power over city institutions by admitting suburban Republicans. By the mid-1950s, this pragmatic impasse opened the window to scholarly *ex post facto* theoretical rationalization in the form of public choice theory, which has enjoyed a resurgence since the late 1980s as a justification of the new localism.

Not to put too fine a veneer on it, public choice theory seeks to justify the pattern of multiple city-region municipalities in light of the conspicuous American failure to provide wider area governing cohesion. It does not simply explain the failure but, far more than its predecessors who employed international relations modelling to examine intergovernmental relationships, chooses to beatify the context. In brief, public choice theorists acknowledge the existence of a clear separation, for governments, of service production from service delivery, promulgating the axiom that functional and political consolidations need not be congruent (Ostrom, Tiebout, and Warren 1961). The particularized metropolis is then understood to promote efficiencies in the interplay among contending providers of public services (Savitch and Vogel 1996: 12; Keating 1995: 123-27). Efficiency, in the nut-and-bolt accounting sense, becomes the paramount pursuit, and very localized democratic units are seen as the best to serve the interests of competition, the marketplace, and citizens as service consumers (Bish 1971: 150-53). This thinking, by the way, is where the odious notion of citizen as customer finds its source.

Of course, a wide variation in local service levels, taxation rates, and indeed the very social composition of cities will result, but this is considered desirable purely from the perspective of publics being able to choose their personally preferred basket of public goods (Long 1968: 244-48). Even today, **neo-liberal** offshoots of the public choice thesis persist in Canada (Sancton 1994), but, as will be noted (see Chapter 12), their struggle with the redistributive policy advocates of the consolidated city and the realities of metropolitan reform in Canada has in most instances proved to be ineffectual.

1.3.4 New models help understand city complexity

Such study as Key's (1949) in the United States opened up an academic debate over the distribution of power within the urban community. Thus, by the 1950s, social science research had been directed from concerns with the administration of services to the management of conflict, from "how" government works to "who governs" and, in Canada, from a description of the formal arrangements in the Crawford style into an examination of extra-legal distributions of influence. Power, not function, had become the central theoretical concept by the 1960s.

Knowing that not all citizens were able to participate equally in political life, the question at the local level became defined as what sort of elite structure made public decisions. Basically by taking a formal policy choice and endeavouring to uncover the strategic and tactical influences and conditions that produced its explicit formulation, the debate about *community power* produced two schools of thought, depending on which category of political science they represented. Sayre and Polsby (1965: 127-34) note that political scientists largely found a pluralistic power arrangement in which different groups exert influence in specific policy worlds. Sociologists came generally to the conclusion that a more narrowly defined power elite cut basic deals across the board. Some practical consequences for public policy of these approaches are specifically considered in the next chapter.

Happily, not much Canadian social science ink was ever spilt over the structure of local community power, probably because expert and citizen alike share an understanding of the concentrated authority of Westminster parliamentarianism, which has fostered a **political culture** that incorporates a calculated deference even to municipal authority. Such deference, or spectator political culture, well serves those in the commercial community who associate local administration with beneficial public improvements and economic concessions. At best, community power studies have pointed to the focal points where, for the system to be understood, analysis of public policy choices should be made.

In Canada, Donald Higgins's *Urban Canada* (1977) represented a breakthrough for its appreciation of the politics of decision-making at city hall. Even a decade later, Higgins felt obligated to remind his audience that, in his judgement, this approach was necessary because "it avoided positing one 'right' approach to analyzing local and urban political phenomena" (1986: x). His first book was written in the heyday of the highly politicized third urban reform period of neighbourhood communities in the 1970s. After tracing the history of the emergence of local governing institutions, Higgins broke from Crawford's lingering influence to study their political implications and consequences. For instance, his notes on the politics of planning understand that it includes much more than any final written document and must focus on process as being equal in weight to the importance of any policy which eventually results. Consequently, to open up city hall necessarily meant an examination of all aspects of the city politic, from the conduct of elections to the predispositions of professional planning staff (1986: 249-53).

In an almost tangible sense, Higgins made clear that legitimate conflict existed within city politics. Since then, and notwithstanding a great wealth of case studies by city, region, and, in particular, functional areas (for example Bunting and Filion 1991; Frisken 1994), at its core the modern period has rediscovered the concept of the city as a social and political association of enclaves and neighbourhood communities. New assumptions about citizenship in the city produced a realization of the competitive interests in each of whose diversities was permitted a particular break with the long prevailing homogenized reform orthodoxy of 1900.

To make sense of this profusion of writing—and there is no need to list it all here—we need to recognize that the root concerns remain the three classic questions of city politics: (1) what exactly constitutes the urban community, (2) who is to exercise what authority, and (3) what is the definition of an appropriate role for citizenship within a period of newly emerging and constantly adapting social movements. The first outlines the framework for the second which, in turn, must demonstrate appropriate willing responsiveness in the face of the third. The research findings raise a number of important issues.

1.3.4.1 THE DEFINITION OF COMMUNITY

Two basic questions are central to the definition of community: to what extent is the Canadian city-region defined and confined by its local administration? Second, how is it to be governed?

Finding the appropriate governing mechanisms for Canada's city-regions has bedevilled observers and government ministers since the 1950s. American studies of metropolitan governing options may well have set the stage for a successful introduction of urban regional structures across Canada if only by sensitizing the urban regime to the nuance of problem areas. There is an irony for Americans in the relative success of these structures in Canada in light of their failure at home, since the original Articles of Independence of the United States were the form's direct model. In Canadian scholarship, the one important throwback to an earlier period of reflection about structures is Kaplan's functionalism (1967, 1982). But, even here, his analysis took place in the context of new structures in flux, of innovation and adaptation by people in varying contexts, of who tries what to make the operation work.

The foremost student of the Canadian city-region, Andrew Sancton (especially 1994), notes that the unique dimension of each city-region defies any singular approach. But there are basic models. The best exemplar of the **polycentric metropolitan system** is the Greater Vancouver Regional District (GVRD) while Winnipeg Unicity (1971) epitomizes the **unitary metropolitan system**. Indeed, the wording of Bill 103 for Toronto's 1997 consolidation is nearly identical to the Winnipeg legislation. Each of these approaches is grounded in theory. In the case of the polycentrists, it is public choice; for unitarists, it might awkwardly be labelled liberal redistributive interventionism. I have argued in recent years that area-wide functions like environmental protection or sanitation may not best be fulfilled by local administration at all. because such functions should be shifted onto the shoulders of that government which has the fiscal resources and geographic authority to be able to respond effectively (i.e., the provinces) and the city should be entrusted with only the most purely local and discretely bounded of services, as in the Australian model (Lightbody 1997b). The critical question for students of the Canadian city-region (and for students of the British situation) is this: is there actually a provincial ministry strategy on urban matters? As will be seen in Chapter 13, little in the way of citizen protest or academic study will have any impact if a provincial ministry is determined on a specific course of action.

The new problem for social scientists of the city in this new century is that the new borderless global economy has implications that are nearly impossible to know. Community leaders in some nascent **world cities** like Toronto, Montreal, and even Vancouver try to forge a "world status" for their particular urban environments. Their activities range from targeted tourism initiatives to Olympic games and venues. Some city-regions even devise their own "paradiplomacy" through foreign investment policies and trading linkages. In Canada the best-known student of this phenomenon is Patrick Smith (1992, 1995, 1998), who concludes that "while such municipal internationalism may produce more intergovernmental conflict [over development], the more interdependent world is also likely to limit the capacity of senior governments to impose their jurisdictional wills so easily" (1992: 50). The ancillary problem for city, provincial, and federal political authorities is that there will also be losers in the race by national cities to achieve world standing (Andrew 1995: 156-57; Garber 1997: 39), necessitating a political accounting of some sort. Thus far, the only real lesson is the lessening relevance of local boundary as an artifact delimiting urban space even as the municipality itself becomes the very foundation of modern national economies (Smith 1998: 72-73).

1.3.4.2 THE OBLIGATIONS OF LOCAL POLITICAL AUTHORITY

The recent study of the politics of the demographic city as an integrated field of research has focused attention on linkages of many sorts among disciplines and across local, substate regional, and international political boundaries. Most of these contacts and contracts are economic in nature and do anything but enrich the small cache of local authorities' political power.

This suggests that the new role for the city public official must include the quest for greater world status within and beyond local borders. Local activists in international social movements present an equally legitimate local perspective, which has now been raised to the status of public good, assuming some form of the axiom that "local livability through sustainable economic development contributes significantly to urban solutions to global problems" (Smith 1998: 70). Movements with global outlooks in issue areas such as ecology, disarmament, fair trade, and Third World development now command recognition at city hall. To look outside one's own city, even if forced, puts pressure on local officials to expand traditional agendas to embrace options from world experience. For instance, to restrict reliance on automobiles requires serious consideration of alternative public and private transportation modes in planning the future for the entire city-region's future development.

Public demands of officials during the last reform period of the 1960s, and the concomitant social science of direct participation and neighbourhood government, tended to be reactive, neighbourhood protective, and conservative. This experience was not based on the ideas of the City Beautiful but reflected power focused on preserving the stakeholders' own proximate environments. During this period, sometimes elaborate social science paradigms, generally in sociology, sought to explore and validate the various techniques deployed to reincorporate citizen-amateurs into the policy process. Most influential was Sherry Arnstein's "ladder of participation" (1969), which produced four models of possibilities ranging from developing a more informed electorate to types of "citizen control" such as the plebiscite (BMR 1975: 46). But even added together, the combined campaigns of generally isolated groups was a struggle predestined to collapse if only because of the sheer weight of the opposing and integrated political and economic forces (Leo 1995b: 28-30).

Bemusedly gazing on, other students in the political economy tradition, informed by Marx, had long realized that while the system itself was powerful, individuals operating within it were largely autonomous (Magnusson 1990, 1992: 69-93). Such work extended well beyond the classic Marx and his certain knowledge that the capitalist system would fail because it could not plan (Long 1968: 253-54). Indeed, the initial task for the leadership of local social movements was to identify publicly some local hegemony to confront.

Political science has yet to come to grips with the basic problem that local officials are obliged to plan even as they know they cannot do so for a bundle of external factors. The discipline is still surprised that citizen cynicism with the promises and promulgations of local city governments grows apace. This may be so especially where both neo-conservatives and social democrats share a common but unrealizable ambition:

> The ambition, clearly, is to free [Vancouver] from its dependence on the pro-
> vincial resource base and ultimately to make it a relatively autonomous centre
> of global capital—connected to Hong Kong, Singapore, Tokyo, Los Angeles,
> and Toronto, but subordinate to none of them.'" (Magnusson 1990: 174)

There still remains, in the urban-centred disciplines, far too much attention to "official" leaders in city politics. For instance, throughout their essay on "the public's role in Winnipeg's economic future," the authors, who are city planners, turn to professional homilies in which public participation and definition of political authority still mean private business managers in the symbiotic service of town councillors (Graham and Phillips 1998: 27-30). Indeed, throughout that text there appears to be a need to analyze conventional leadership roles even where there is no observable citizen following.

In broader response to this shortcoming, and in the tradition of scholarship which examines the "second face of power," the last new gasp in making sense of city political operations draws from the urban regime concepts of Clarence Stone (1989). The best current Canadian representation of these ideas lies in the work of Judith Garber (Garber and Imbroscio 1996). Importantly, she recognizes that changes internationally to the structure of economic opportunities must yield a new appreciation of the local vulnerabilities of any urban regime (Garber 1997: 39). Still, Stone's work encourages attention to the means by which the human capital of the core city can receive public reinvestment. This may occur when urban regimes try to become more inclusive so as to broaden the traditional governing coalitions away from the earlier alliance of public officials with land-focused commercial interests.

1.3.4.3 THE NATURE OF CITIZENSHIP IN AN ERA OF NEW SOCIAL MOVEMENTS

One reaction to participation reformers of the 1960s was the "end of citizenship" model as it was incorporated in the mercantilist views of Osborne and

Gaebler (1992). This "Whig," or pre-democratic, liberalism is somewhat reminiscent of the 1900 epoch of social engineering in that the citizen is seen as a customer who may look for choice from alternative service providers. The citizen becomes a less than active public participant and is expected to signal market preference only as the proverbial box store shopper seeks the best price. Local government is under pressure to adapt, to move away from its traditional obligations and monopoly over universal service delivery. Adherents to the Osborne and Gaebler line have legitimized innovation in the provision of public services by city managers who themselves face stringent conditions of fiscal austerity.

In one way or another all studies of this last sort are rooted in the American public choice formulation of the separation of service *provision* from service *production*. The argument out of necessity is that somehow governments which do less may accomplish more; it usually takes on the cliché formula of dividing the bad oarsmen from the good helmsmen:

> Steering requires people who can see the entire universe of issues and possibilities and can balance competing demands for resources. Rowing requires people who focus intently on one mission and perform it well. Steering organizations need to find the best methods to achieve their goals. Rowing organizations tend to defend 'their' method at all costs. (Osborne and Gaebler 1992: 35)

Thus, "good" organizations are those which innovate, while "bad" ones stagnate with past practices. The good is imaginative; the bad is focused. The bad is bureaucratic and probably unionized; the good is flexible, non-hierarchical, and low cost through minimal wage.

But the very resource scarcity which caused the quest for alternative service delivery in the first place also limits the collection of political information about its public impacts. Hence, ironically, councils come to depend on the interest group pressures of cohesive policy communities and, more generally, traditional urban regime guidance. For a wider range of ordinary citizens to behave genuinely as active participants in governing, they must be expected to play a tripartite role. They would evaluate programs; in formal groupings they might offer partnership in service administration; as informed individuals they might propose alternatives for existing programs, drawing from their cosmopolitan professional or work experience to question the expertise of city hall professionals and their traditional partners among developers' planners and the building professions (engineers, architects, etc.). Furthermore, new technology has been applied to assist citizens to deal with city hall to a limited degree and to still limited access. All major cities now have website home pages that permit a limited type of individual response through e-mail on policy issues and piecemeal problem-solving.

Opportunities to expand this involvement remain. Perhaps reflecting the influence of the stronger lines in feminist inquiry and of the feminist movement with its emergent global linkages generally (which usually means from the United States outwards), recent scholarship of women in particular has stipulated new policy avenues for cities and new requirements for engaging citizens in **private-public partnerships**. As Judith Garber summarizes, "efforts to open up local democracy to diverse groups have linkages to social movements with global visions" (1997: 41). In this, we think of feminist, environmentalist, anti-racist, and gay rights activists, individuals who are turned on and tuned in—but not to everything. They are still policy specific, so cross-disciplinary research needs to be done to determine both catalysts to action and the conditions which promote and permit engagement. Finally, even the investigation of the increased voice of women on Canadian city councils may come to mean a renewed consequence, and relevance, for the role of *all* elected officials (Trimble 1995).

Finally, what one surely hopes to uncover is a good—by which is meant fair for the many—democratic system of political institutions. At its heart is an appreciation that good citizens cannot be expected to do the impossible, nor all of the work. But they can, and will, choose competently between reasonably presented competing policy alternatives when and where they are offered.

Notes

1. Bryce was very precise in his targeted concern: "Now the Spoils System, with the party machinery which keeps it oiled and greased and always working at high pressure, is far more potent and pernicious in great cities than in country districts. For in great cities we find an ignorant multitude, largely composed of recent immigrants, untrained in self-government; we find a great proportion of the voters paying no direct taxes, and therefore feeling no interest in moderate taxation; we find able citizens absorbed in their private businesses, cultivated citizens unusually sensitive to the vulgarities of practical politics, and both sets therefore specially unwilling to sacrifice their time and tastes and comfort in the struggle with sordid wire-pullers and noisy demagogues. In great cities the forces that attack and pervert democratic government are exceptionally numerous, the defensive forces that protect it exceptionally ill-placed for resistance. Satan has turned his heaviest batteries on the weakest part of the ramparts" (1888: I, 577).

2. Local governments tend initially to be more open to minority group electoral success than broader area governments. For example, the first black elected official in Canada was Victoria's councillor Mifflin Gibbs in 1866; the first councillor without French or British descent was A. Skaleter (Icelander) in 1892 in Winnipeg; and the first Ukrainian-Canadian to hold elected office anywhere in Canada was Theodore Stefaniuk, who was elected Winnipeg city councillor in 1911.

two | The policy-making system of the Canadian city

The purpose of this chapter is to define basic concepts, processes, and structures in public policy-making and to outline a simple model of how the components work together. The apparently complex bones of state institutions are bound by the sinews of personal interaction into a body politic in which real opportunities may exist for citizens to have a say in the ongoing political process. The model suggests various practical ways in which these opportunities may be exploited; we will consider later how this happens through political parties (Chapter 6), interest groups (Chapter 7), and social movements (Chapter 8), or by a fundamental reorganization of the city-region's governing structures themselves (Part III).

While active practitioners profess that the target of governing, municipal or otherwise, is to provide basic public services, this objective has from time to time been subjugated to particular initiatives directing city services largely to economic development and the growth of the private sector economy in the community. North American cities especially have tended to score the success of their urban existence by growth measures, more so than have older cities in Europe where plans for sustainable communities are accorded greater merit. The label for specific civic policies meant to result in continuous growth and city expansion, best measured by the number of factories,

---

2.1 Cutting Through the Policy Maze

   2.1.1   A note about public policy analysis

   2.1.2   The political system

   2.1.3   The need for political resources

   2.1.4   Making policy choices

   2.1.5   Decisions and non-decisions

   2.1.6   Impacts and consequences

2.2 Power and the Fixing of Priorities

   2.2.1   State intervention and local control

   2.2.2   An initial word about leadership in authority

boxcar loadings, and other GDP (gross domestic product) monetary units, is boosterism. In this thinking, goals for public sector initiatives become easily integrated with private, growth-machine interests at the expense of meting out broadly based public service for all residents. How can this occur?

Traditionally, the social science of city politics has focused on studying what formal constitutional arrangements guide governing, or *structures*, and how decisions are made within these formal institutions, or *process*. Such studies almost always presumed that improved institutions could be engineered and hence felt a need to advance a set of realizable prescriptions that would presumably result in better city governing. Usually unasked was the corollary question: "Better, but for whom?" The point is not to make a normative assessment as to whether one governing formula is desirable or not. Rather, it is that the student of city policy-making must be able to discern, by the consequences, why and how policies which favour particular claques or clienteles come to be written into budgets and the law.

The word "reform" means change. All reformers claim that change along their proposed path is beneficial. So, the short answer to "for whom is the city best governed?" is that those who introduced new ideas, be it in 1900 or 1970, always understood that these would work to their own supporters' immediate advantage. They also believed, strongly, that although their work might momentarily disadvantage a few of their fellow citizens, over time it would also improve the lot of all. Such is revolutionary zeal, and it emerges even in the business community. Thus, studies like those in the political economy of the city led to the identification of the "movers and shakers" who get things done by building working coalitions out of a series of marginal policy wins—social, economic, and political—for all involved. As noted in Chapter 1, the compact space and smaller scale of the Canadian city operation has permitted sustainable urban regimes to emerge behind the scenes of the political front stage reported in the daily media.

It may be that the regime in a particular city preferred a concentrated political authority such as that which exists in both corporations and institutionalized pressure groups and which facilitate the emergence of a legitimate leader. For this reason, in the early part of the twentieth century, businessmen who understood the corporation model favoured the emergence of the council-manager, board of control, and **at-large election** arrangements combined with anti-partyism and "clean government" arguments. They themselves worked well in such a system, genuinely believed that the city operation was only a business and should be run and evaluated as such, and accepted the burden that they should be its natural political leaders. No competing models were any more value-free. Any group—even the 1960s counter-culture rebels, who advocated change under the banner that their proposals were objective or value-free—inevitably falls into the "reform trap": claiming that their way is value neutral when in fact it is meant to impose their *own* objectives. So, during municipal elections, we must realize that any local candidate who asserts "common sense" as a platform for governing is relying on his or her own belief package. Why not "good sense" in any case? The important point is that any form of organization carries its own bias within it and that some structures create more openings for particular groups than do others.

Presently, the local politics of the Canadian city is pure "brokerage" on its operational side just as political party leadership in federal politics has sometimes been said to act as "the grand brokers and mediators of a fractious society" (Van Loon and Whittington 1996: 348). This means that the ideology of anti-partyism forces individual councillors to consider important policy issues on their own, without guidance from a party direction. In theory, floating alliances not bound by the artificial manacles of partisan difference, and giving everyone imaginable a chance to have their say, write **public policy** to accord with majoritarian views. Although this ideology is dominant, there is also considerable corporatist-style delegation of operational authority to agencies within the various policy communities of the city.

The task of this chapter is to present an abstract model suggesting the usual relations among all of these policy-making pieces.

2.1 Cutting Through the Policy Maze

Metropolitan and city hall policy-making can be rather confusing for even the best informed citizen without something of a guide to its operation. However it is dressed up theoretically, political life remains a series of interrelated and more or less integrated activities that work through a set of formal institutions to make choices affecting citizens. All institutional arrangements, and the political processes which work them, can thus be considered a **political system**. In the rather large public operation that a city represents, interactions are structured, demands are voiced (with greater or less support from other individuals and groups), choices are made, and conflicts are worked through to take one or another form of public policy. Theoretical and applied social scientists aim to provide the necessary guide to these processes by explaining the dependent variable of public policy. Especially for ideologues—Marxists and public choice neo-liberals alike—the purpose of their analysis must be explaining what, or if, any difference in policy conditions will come about as the result of their reasoning.

What do people do politically and what results from such behaviour? We may well ask: Does the low voter turnout, which we will discuss in Chapter

5, produce a group of city councillors from a particular category of citizens who then favour their voters with, say, better streets and more frequent garbage collection? Whatever the answer may be, and it is probably "yes," does not invalidate the investigation. It is in this sense that analysis of policy systems is more oriented to explaining *what* people in public positions do, rather than describing the constitutional platforms from which they do it. It is nonetheless well understood that legal and structural features in local governing continue to be important. These create power centres and instill operational authority. For instance, that Canadian provinces operate with the Westminster parliamentary method means a premier can order dramatic metropolitan government reorganization or dismiss a locally elected school board or city council whereas an American state governor, operating within a legislative system of strict checks and balances, could not remotely dream of doing so.

Structures and institutions must be considered in their social, economic, and cultural contexts and not be restricted to the rare and immaculate models of Bryce-style reformers. Rather than a quest for an ideal form of city governing, the relevant questions become: Why do certain forms emerge in a given context? What impacts can we identify in resulting local policies that may work towards the larger public good? Let us dispense with any necessary *a priori* anathema towards party politics, which is just another way of freely ordering the collective public life. It is appropriate to query why certain methods of conflict resolution emerge in one community and quite distinct patterns in another. Then, if our observations reveal potentially more beneficial policy packages in the former than in the latter, we may choose to become prescriptive ourselves.

This study of political and policy systems is descriptive of condition rather than diagnostic, if by the latter a prescription is deemed necessary. Indeed, the policy system approach is subject to the critique that because it endeavours to understand and relate how fundamental conflict is resolved, it also attempts to explain, justify, and forgive the status quo. What is here overlooked, often in ideological haste, is that understanding necessarily precedes amending. Comparative assessments can well lead to our arguing for processes that promote citizen involvement, or economic administration, or the political voice of generally less powerful neighbourhoods and collective interests. Always the primary question must be: How do different governing structures affect the development of public policy?

2.1.1 A note about public policy analysis

Although most political scientists have inquired in one way or another into the sources of public policy, during the latter part of the twentieth century a specialized subdiscipline emerged that was directly interested in the analytic aspects of the process. Through it, four analytical approaches to the examination of public policy have evolved. The first generic type of policy study is descriptive research into a particular program or functional pursuit, such as reports on the history of property taxation and the patterns of its commercial-residential ratios.

A second, related school evaluates policies with an eye to their social or physical setting, producing, for instance, work about environmental impacts. Such study often leads to prescription in that it is predictive: if you do X, then Y will result; but, if you were to do A instead, then you would likely wind up with a far more desirable B result. The many studies of watershed conservation provide cases in point.

The third approach shares an empirical focus with the others in that propositions are formulated, evidence is accumulated, and hypotheses are tested. Its roots are in early studies of budgeting in the public sector. Here, by the 1960s, public money management tools became highly evolved even if not highly effective instruments for control. Such analysis of the making of governing policy quickly moved from Charles Lindblom's "science of muddling through" in 1959 to Thomas Dye's ground-breaking synthesis *Understanding Public Policy* (1972). Paradigms to manage public programs more practically towards objectives generated a plethora of acronyms and managing fads, producing what one scholar once labelled a "new evaluation industry" (Pal 1997: 252). Based on the presumed rationality of policy actors, these so-called systems relied upon refined program measurement techniques, the bases of many of which were no more sophisticated than the surmises behind the Pentagon's SWAG.[1] Of course, it is also true that some policy-makers may be brilliantly intuitive or lucky.

In the 1970s, the Canadian federal government entered into multi-year planning centred on program areas and with an eye to realizing stipulated objectives by deploying PPBS (Planning, Programming, Budgeting System) with a vengeance. In the 1980s, it moved to PEMS (Policy and Expenditure Management System) and in the 1990s, PS2000. This last thrust encapsulated then contemporary neo-liberal ideology as reflected in state downsizing and offloading, program delivery restructuring, and resource-driven financial allocations. In other words, the government's philosophy became "do less and pass the responsibility to other governments or private contractors whenever feasible and pay-as-you-go." By the demonstration effect reported through sympathetic business and academic circles and by variously supportive media, these ideas spilled quickly into the provinces and those metropolitan cities eager to emulate the purported successes of federal authorities (as reported by variously supportive media). The nasty reality in this great circle of rationality was that not much really changed since over 90 per cent of federal expenditures were targeted to existing, politically-approved, ongoing programs.

Note that the focus so far has been on governing and state action. Policy analysis can, of course, be applied to the operations of any large organization. So, a fourth school of policy analysis works directly with private clients, with the purpose of influencing individuals in the political process to produce outcomes which favour that client's interest. It is aided in this by the reality that while *public* policy-making must, at least theoretically and in **liberal democracies**, operate in the clear fish-bowl of open accountability, the *private* sector can behave in more closed and secretive ways (Weimer and Vining 1999: 43-57).

For example, in soliciting taxpayer support for economic development projects, proponents will often resort to the public relations pseudo-science of **economic multipliers** when concocting probable community benefits but then frequently cite provisions for client confidentiality when pressed for mathematical details. Professional sports entrepreneurs and their spokespersons are especially adept in this numerical twilight zone. In Canadian city politics the classic example is certainly Montreal Mayor Drapeau's persistent claim, based upon his rosy fiscal projections, that the 1972 Olympics would never indebt city taxpayers: "The Olympics can no more have a deficit than a man can have a baby" (Purcell 1989: 169). Sancton assesses the actual aftermath of the "most extravagant games ever held" by noting that even with federal and provincial help in reducing the $1 billion deficit, Montreal's taxpayers wound up paying a special Olympic tax levy for over 20 years (1983: 74). Considering this sort of manipulation, a standard text observes that "The analysts' predicament, however, becomes much more complicated when their clients do not actually try to force them to cook up results, but rather misrepresent what they have already done" (Weimer and Vining 1999: 55).

Policy analysis of public affairs, the approach taken here, focuses on activities, on decisions taken in sequence within complex institutional arrangements, among many possible choices, which may yield social and economic problem-solving initiatives. The advantage of looking at policy as an integrated process is that "it facilitates the understanding of public policy-making by breaking the complexity of the process into any number of stages and sub-stages, each of which can be investigated alone or in terms of its relationship to any or all other stages of the cycle" (Howlett and Ramesh 2003: 13-14). This also includes those important instances when public policy refers to the conscious choice of policy-makers *not* to take action (Pal 2001: 111-13). We shall begin our study with a look at how the overall operation shapes up.

Figure 2.1: The Environment of the City Policy System

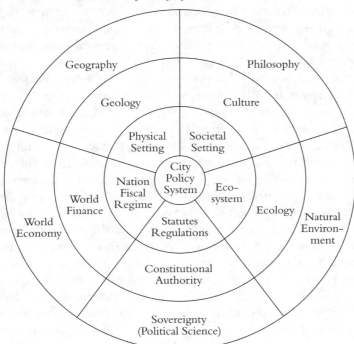

2.1.2 The political system

The first step is always, arbitrarily, to determine the boundaries of the urban policy system by defining the primary task of political life and, thus, the role of the political system. Some political scientists, even Robert Dahl (1961), defined a political system so broadly as to include virtually any persisting human pattern that included some focus on "power, rule, or authority." We are more exclusive here, defining it as that complex of public institutions and processes that frames the authoritative allocation of scarce resources and that locates values in the community. In other words, we will inquire into all matters that may lead directly or indirectly to public policy. The caution in this for politics in a global age is that a preoccupation with political conflicts only at the national or subregional level masks the new reality that political power is now always in conflict with other active cartels of power from outside the system. Globalization dilutes the real meaning of historic, spatial boundaries for the Canadian city system, because financial operations, as well as social and cultural movements, today apply internationally derived expectations and standards to what were once purely local operations.

Despite the complexities of the many conflicting webs of beliefs, economics, or social structure in which any city government may be located, we will assign any activity or influence that does not impinge directly upon the invention of specific public policy into the general environment of the city political system. That is, any matter that is neither directly political as defined, nor local, is consigned for the moment to a relatively large dustbin. Hence, the many politically important social and economic policy choices of the federal government, for example, are not considered relevant until they have a direct and discernible impact on city policy choices. These distinctions are not always clear and easy, however. If, say, the federal monetary policy were such that interest rates were to rise dramatically, then the costs of borrowing for public works (roads, bridges) by local authorities would rise and potentially squeeze out spending on possibly more desirable public goods. Or, to take a different tack, if an international union, or the Catholic Church, were to decide that its Canadian locals, or priests, were not to engage directly in electoral politics (as both have) this would clearly prevent union officials and clerics from seeking council seats. And, so forth.

At this point, it is sufficient to acknowledge that the city governments of the metropolitan system function within a diverse and interconnected policy universe, which is continuously and tremendously vulnerable to many sorts of unanticipated external pressures. It is also one in which it can be extremely difficult to forecast the local consequence from even the foreseen choices taken at some distance from the local community.

To try to unravel this complexity, to make some sense of the policy operation, it seems helpful to consider its separate compartments in the abstract. But, to use the words of the constitutional courts, these are not "watertight compartments," and in its continuous operations in real life, the policy system witnesses much interaction and adaptation among them at all stages of policy development. Among the various subprocesses, or stages of applied problem-solving, five broad categories present important analytic features to consider; each will be considered in detail below:

1. demand initiation;
2. political supports;
3. the conversion arena (including demand reduction and elaboration);
4. results; and
5. impacts and consequences.

Still, from the outset, it is necessary to be mindful that "the public policy process is not nearly as tightly sequential or goal-driven as the cycle model makes it appear" (Howlett and Ramesh 1995: 198). In the final analysis,

Figure 2.2: City Public Policy System

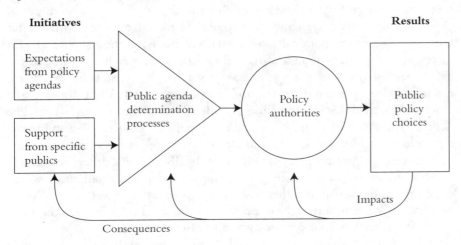

Adapted from: David Easton, *A Systems Analysis of Political Life* (New York: Wiley, 1965).

politics simply provides an avenue whereby society can evaluate and choose among competing demands for collective decisions.

2.1.2.1 DEMAND INITIATION

Although citizens' experience of the policy process is always in continuous evolution in the real world, if we were able to freeze-frame that process in time, the system could be said to start up when a set of demands for policy change originates. This abstracted representation differs from exceptional moments of calamity, for, by definition, crisis management is extraordinary in public life as well as in personal experience. Time is short, pressure is abundant, the usual rules often do not fit. But the means to handle timely policy response for even the abnormal case can still be routinized if we bear in mind the model's probable linkages.

Normally, individuals or, more often, organized groups with implicit agendas challenge political authorities to adapt the status quo to conform more closely with their expectations. It is conceivable, but not the usual case, that political authorities can also be confronted directly, or through their reading of the majority opinion in the community, to turn back the clock by overturning adjustments made in the past.

Naturally, the reason why we have a political operation in the first place, why citizens divert their time, talents, and energy to political pursuits, is that demands are constantly being made by persons and groups in the metropolis that cannot all be fully satisfied. Not all demands require an expenditure of public money either. Demands may be made for citizenship claims or for fairer access into the political system itself. Women and their supporters, for instance, had to fight long and hard for suffrage (the right to vote) in the early years of the last century. A property franchise existed for municipal elections until relatively recently, and it was not until 1958 in Toronto and 1962 in Montreal that the franchise became universal for persons of age. The democratic expectations built into differing political cultures play an important role here; New York City had already extended the franchise to white male voters without property qualification by 1822. For a different example of a non-financial demand, one person's hope to expand a small business—to open up a billiard parlour in her basement, say—may very well intrude upon a neighbour's reasonable right to privacy and peace. For such a reason, most Canadian cities today have noise **bylaws** in place.

The financial resources available to governing authorities to provide and sustain state operations are finite if not downright scarce. It is in this sense that societies delegate responsibility to the political system to make the evaluation of needs and expectations and to allocate resources to meet these as judged appropriate *authoritatively*. This last notion, of acquiescence to authority, is important. It confers legitimacy to municipal council decisions. In plain terms, political scientists mean by it that people will come to accept even decisions with which they may not agree to be binding upon them: we pay our taxes; we stop our vehicles at red lights.

Many group and individual actors, appearing in various forms, wield different kinds of power around politics. Large businesses may seriously curtail any council's general freedom to choose among sensible but competing policy options, and religious principles establish close guidelines for personal behaviour even as they might affect political choice. Still, in our system of governing, the final word, after all moral and economic consequences are fully appreciated, is believed to belong to the officials we have elected.

In small towns and isolated or otherwise freestanding municipalities, the politics of initiating a demand still tends to come informally from among neighbours and friends. Often the only effort required to make the demand heard is a little time and energy. But metropolitan cities are more institutionally developed, and the process becomes more impersonal as larger scale bureaucratic procedures prevail in public life (political parties, state agencies and departments, lobbyists) and private administration (corporations, cultural and religious organizations, and other policy interested groups). Some of this complexity is suggested below in Figure 2.3 (p. 79) in which the relative size of the balls, lines, and shapes do not always indicate the relative importance of the formal authority. It is only by assessing what was decided when that we may be best able to decipher who prevailed on what and, in that instance, why.

2.1.2.2 POLITICAL SUPPORTS

Two basic ideas should be considered here. A bedrock principle sustaining our liberal democratic representative form of government holds that as a community we have conferred the power to make decisions on our behalf upon others we have elected into public office. Because of this inferred authorization, we as citizens largely enforce the decisions made by those representatives upon ourselves. In essence, citizens have entered into a kind of social contract among themselves to set the conditions by which they will create both a civil community out of a state of nature and a pattern for its governing.

At one extreme, Jean-Jacques Rousseau (1712–78) saw sovereignty as an inalienable right of citizenship and believed that all citizens should participate directly in the making of laws. To him, representative forms of government corrupted the idea that legislatures are subservient to citizens by usurping individual participation in the articulation of the general will. His arguments still provide a foundation for advocates of direct democracy and might cause some thought about the calculations a rational person could make of the potential gains or losses from entering into any contract between citizen and state.

For example, agrarian pioneers on the Canadian plains lived in a harsh natural environment that caused them to shrewdly calculate the potential benefits of **incorporation**. Even despite pressure from the newly formed provincial governments to establish municipal institutions, the settlers refused to do so. For them, living essentially a subsistence life, municipalities constituted a tax-costly redundancy of services they were already providing for themselves. The benefits of education were more highly valued, and miniscule school districts were quick to pop up as soon as these same people could collectively afford a school building and a teacher. The point is that common agreement led to the creation of quite specific governing units.

Many in the social sciences are now interested in the broader propositions of community, legitimacy, and a general granting of implied authority, the combination of which some earlier writers labelled *diffuse support*: a general acceptance of the political operation applied in a blanket fashion as opposed to piecemeal approval of some decisions and rejection of others. In a fashion, this is another way of presenting Aristotle's conviction that constitutional government required the exercise of a political authority, rooted in law, over willing subjects, and in the common interest. As a rule, in Canada today, few questions exist about municipal legitimacy since all local governments are, theoretically, legally, and financially reliant upon the legitimacy of their provincial creators. Nonetheless, there remains an inherent tension for local government institutions because they are so easy to reform. Put another way, the local political operation does not have to hold a constitutional convention or ratify a formal constitutional amendment in order to make fundamental change. Even for important realignments, only a bylaw need be passed by council, and citizens may, or may not, be consulted about it.

When, however, citizens withdraw their support or the municipality loses government salience for them (perhaps in the aftermath of some conflict-of-interest scandal), pressure may build to adapt local institutions to new realities. So, for instance, intolerable pressures on the local tax base produced the last major annexation on Montreal Island when Pointe-aux-Trembles was annexed into the City of Montreal in 1982. Similarly, in Alberta since the 1990s, a number of villages and towns outside the metropolitan core have reverted to unincorporated hamlet status (six in 1996, two in 1997, and three the following year), dissolving their civic contract in order to take advantage of the broader assessment base of their surrounding municipal districts and counties. Citizens in these instances understood that their own local taxes would be too steep to sustain services under their immediate local control.

In theoretical terms, the withholding of citizen support for local institutions leading to a voluntary loss of status is not at all the same as that which occurs when a provincial government forcibly dissolves a municipality for provincial purposes in the context of a broader, systemic reorganization. For example, Ontario on 1 January 1998 consolidated 129 major school boards into 66 new districts, reducing the number of school trustees in the process from around 1,900 to 700. That same day, the newly legislated City of Toronto government (the Megacity) replaced six previously autonomous municipalities and the metropolitan, or city-region, corporation. In a somewhat intermediate category, this particular Ontario provincial government so strongly "encouraged" municipal consolidation by its restructuring propositions that, by June 1998, the number of self-governing local municipalities in Ontario had shrunk, with purported citizen consent, from 815 to 590.

2.1.3 The need for political resources

The second aspect of supportive behaviour, and a very different matter altogether, is the idea of *specific* support. Not all potential, or latent, demands in a community are ever exerted upon its political system. For a set of expectations to become so substantial as an issue that they must be dealt with in one way or another by political authorities, they must be considered salient, worthy, and observable. Significance is thus key if the matter of expectations is to move very far beyond a stage of wishful thinking. Demonstrable specific support enhances a latent claim and transforms it into a matter with which the political powers must deal. Types of support will vary, but generally they may be thought of as a resource to be mined, smelted, deployed, and sometimes sold in the marketplace of politics.

In his very practical world of the politics of influence, Dahl defines a **political resource** as "anything that can be used to sway the specific choices or the strategies of another individual. Or, to use different language, whatever may be used as an inducement is a resource" (1961: 226). By this definition most attributes and chattels of any individual can be deployed to political purpose. These resources for influence are neither zero sum nor permanently fixed at any particular point in time. In fact, the capacity of an individual or group to pyramid resources lies at the heart of any experience with party machine-style politics, in recent memory best exemplified at city hall by the American boss operations of Chicago Mayor Richard J. Daley, Sr. (Royko 1971).

Dahl provided a list of examples he acknowledged to be illustrative and suggestive, not exhaustive, but which suggest three basic classifications of political resources. First are resources directly related to the individual, such as control over one's time, access to credit, cash or wealth, degree of education or professional training, social standing or level of esteem in the community, native intelligence, level of energy and productivity, and possibly gender.

Second, resources may be attributes of one's formal position. A person may have leverage over jobs and contracts, command specialized information and control its flow, or enjoy the legal rights that stem from holding a public position. As to this last, for instance, city councillors have an office, phones, and support staff that challengers for their positions do not. Elected members of legislative assemblies hold a position of privilege that conveys immunity from legal prosecution for things said during debates and proceedings inside that legislature.

Third are matters about social and economic groupings themselves. The right to vote is one; for instance, where property still has the "right" to cast a ballot, partners in downtown law firms who own their own office tower but who may all reside in the suburbs still have the legal opportunity to vote in the city election. The level of solidarity in a group—that is, all subleaders in the group are working toward the same general objective—is important as is ethnic or religious definition or standing. For instance, citizens who are members of visible minorities have yet to break through the glass ceiling of city elections in proportion to their number. A group's social status also has an impact; panhandling derelicts are neither a group nor respected, but they acquire an immediate cachet if they are labelled street performers.

Central to Dahl's analysis, and essential to note, is that he holds to a concept of "dispersed inequalities" (1961: 227-28) through which he recognizes that not all persons are equally influential and that kinds of inequities in political resources do abound. But, he argues, many different kinds of resources and influence are available to democratic citizens, though some have more of one but fewer of another, not all resources are equally effective in every policy arena, and each citizen has access to at least some sources for influencing. This is *pluralism*. To reject this thesis is to argue the case for the existence of some kind of narrowly constituted hegemony of social, economic, and political power likely rooted in class differentiation. Such indeed is the legitimate stuff of power elite theory, as exemplified in this much quoted verdict of E.E. Schattschneider: "The flaw in the pluralist heaven is that the heavenly chorus sings with a strong upper class accent. Probably about 90 per cent of the people cannot get into the pressure system" (1960: 35). Or, as David Truman put it somewhat differently, "Being more influential, [the elites] are privileged; and being privileged, they have, with few exceptions, a special stake in the continuation of the political system on which their privileges rest" (1959: 489). Still, to Truman, a consensus of elites was invaluable as a weapon to defuse demagoguery.

Clearly, different resources may be applied in different combinations, at different times in the policy cycle, on different people in different positions of authority. Many are substitutable. But, speaking generally and not to the exception, the more political resources we find behind a particular demand, including the measure of skill in their practical application, the more likely a specific grievance or proactive concern will become a political issue and, in time, be satisfactorily resolved. As political sociologist Stein Rokkan once quipped, "Votes count but resources matter."

All political systems must filter the full menu of possible demands through the performance of a function called *aggregation and articulation*. No set of authorities, no matter how well intentioned, or how sophisticated their technology and public service, can ever respond appropriately to the personal policy agendas of hundreds of thousands of individuals. Sometimes labelled the function of "demand reduction," this process groups together individuals with generally similar sets of policy preferences and expresses their demands in policy manageable terms—just as a liquid may be reduced to become clearer. Political parties, interest groups, and the city's permanent bureaucrats (through their relations with clients and other citizens in the ongoing administration of programs) have traditionally played pivotal roles in this process.

The complex policy operations of Canadian cities, as will be discussed further in Chapter 7, consist of sophisticated private and area-wide policy-

oriented groups often organized in particular realms of government functions such as recreation or several aspects of social services. In federal politics
Paul Pross has written extensively about such policy communities: "Society
permits specialized publics to dominate decision-making in sectors of policy
where they have competence, interfering only when larger concerns must
take precedence, when systemic or technological change within the special
public spills over into the larger political arena" (1992: 118-19). In the environmental field, for example, and arguably because of their single-minded
policy focus, many recycling societies have access to better technological
information and innovative thinking than the officials employed in municipalities. Given both the high stakes such specialized publics have defined
for themselves and their linkages beyond subregional states like a city, it is
certainly to be anticipated that their important actors will have access to
powerful political resources. Indeed, it would be surprising if policy communities did *not* try to bring to bear some kind of external political pressure from the provincial realm, if not from special interests with national
or international standing like the Sierra Club. In Part III we will observe
that some city-regions still governed with multiple local governments face
consolidation pressures, initially in single policy fields, so as to create at least
some sort of functional agency that will be able to formulate coherent wide-
area policy responses. There might, for example, be hard lobbying to set up
a special district to manage a river valley which courses through multiple
adjacent cities.

This brings us to another point which will also be considered further.
Elected officials, and their appointed public servants, are responsible for only
a slice of the authority pie. Other influential actors in the community create informal arrangements, often through invisible hands well behind the
scenes, which make public policy possible. Unlike Pross's policy communities, which exercise a virtual quasi-delegation of authority, these are better
thought of as fluctuating networks of persons in the city who have earned
or inherited social standing, economic advantage, professional authority,
backroom political clout, and so on, all of which resources they combine as
necessary to create openings for policy decisions. This is Clarence Stone's
urban regime in action, and he argues that

> Regimes involve arrangements through which elements of the community
> are engaged in producing publicly significant results and providing a variety
> of small opportunities. The latter task often overshadows broader questions
> and makes it possible for governing coalitions to gain cooperation even
> though their larger goals enjoy only weak or even unpopular support. (1989:
> 235)

In short, urban regimes filter broad expectations and provide specific support, sometimes logistical in nature, to maximize immediately realizable, widely shared, but small gains in order to make larger social adaptation for the community possible.

Finally, specific support may come from policy **stakeholders** who are defined as a group of individuals who have identified a common interest in a portion of the more general public interest. They may consider themselves as having a shared, sometimes proprietary interest in a specific policy arena. Some stakeholder groups may exist by virtue of inhabiting a common physical space such as a residential neighbourhood or business district. Others are constituted from the clientele and contracted service delivery professionals of city departments like social services. Still other stakeholder groups are more nebulous, coming together only as a particular proprietary interest may be threatened, such as those who reside by or use, recreationally or industrially, a particular watershed. Some interest clusters within the urban regime, perhaps in many instances the Chamber of Commerce or Board of Trade, may be said to constitute a **veto authority**: their specific support is vital if a political demand is to proceed towards any sort of positive resolution. Such veto groups tend to be institutionalized directly into the policy pipeline and can decisively turn "thumbs down" at very early stages of any official consideration of new ideas.

2.1.4 Making policy choices

2.1.4.1 THE CONVERSION ARENA

For purposes of analysis, once basic demands for policy initiation or adaptation have been reduced in number, tagged with support and elaborated in such terms that they may be evaluated and political authorities may be able to respond to them, then the systems or policy cycle model targets them as being within the conversion arena. This means that the demands have reached the point at which they are fashioned into public policy choices.

This critical arena is at the heart of the policy business, for it is the crucible in which all political communities determine the management of policy choice. Individuals are chosen to fill the various roles of mayor and council, managers and civil servants. In a representative liberal democracy, some of those role incumbents are designated by election and others will subsequently be appointed by those elected. It is important to observe that while these roles assign an individual authority, they also set limits on the exercise of that power. A city mayor in Canada, for instance, is formally entitled to chair council meetings but is not, usually, provided the formal

Figure 2.3: Active Elements in the City Policy System

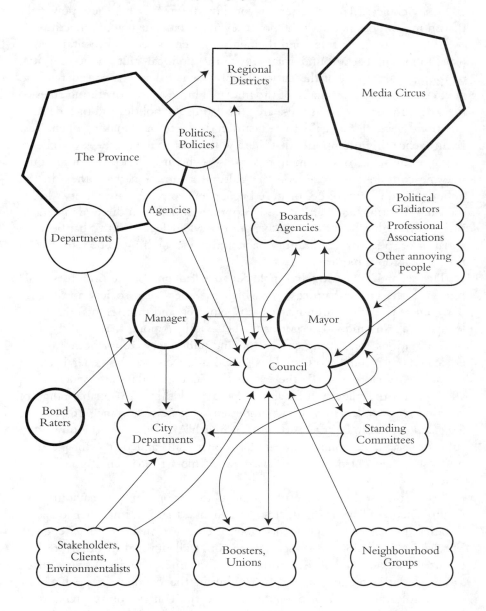

power either to hire or fire senior managers independently or to veto council policy choices. An American mayor quite frequently has these powers; a British mayor does not have the power even to chair the council meeting.

As decisions are refined and defined, two general environmental factors play important background roles. First, the political culture of the city-region, as a fragment of the national fabric (which we will consider in the next chapter), provides many of the informal but essential operating rules of the game. In some respects these are "the givens" of politics and include such questions as who is normally to be heard in the customary making of choices. By inference this also implies that there will routinely be those—even clients of important social development programs—who are overlooked or left outside the consultative process on the cultural assumption that others in the policy community will be, or have been, their voice. A community's long-standing traditions further dictate appropriate limits upon direct democracy, such as through referendums or corporatist-style delegation; this has become a matter of collective community habit and not something to be settled each time a decision is required.

The second factor involves **political socialization**. By definition, socialization is the cultural process by which members of a society instill into newcomers to their community (that is, children and immigrants) their collective goals and individual norms for behaviour. Among these will be a set of expectations concerning citizenship and public service, for both ratepayers and those in public office. This socialization creates the general setting for policy development. To the extent that its core values are widely held, all actors on the stage will be able to predict, within a reasonable range of certainty, how others may behave under any given circumstance. If all share, for example, in the bourgeois realism of North America, then the unwritten rules of acceptable conduct are understood by all, and first principle sorts of questions do not have to be raised each time a fundamental policy issue arises.

As to this second point of socio-political normative behaviour, role incumbents will have learned, at least in theory, that it is improper to accept bribes as appropriate inducements when it comes to making policy choices. Yet *baksheesh*, or tipping for service, is not at all unusual in other political cultures (Mexico and Kenya come to mind) and is, indeed, experienced as a necessary cost and *normal* behaviour in the conduct of public business. While the matter of public ethics and the contemporary pressure for codification of conduct appropriate for municipal public officials is directly addressed in Chapter 5, one consequence of large-scale immigration into the Canadian metropolis has been the import not only of new citizens but also of their learned values. The opportunity window provided for the more entrepreneurial among the arrivistes and the more venal among the home-grown has meant that first generational cultural incongruence will sustain real flashpoints and short-term controversies.

Consequently, the internal functions of the conversion arena operate with a sort of built-in political shorthand learned from the home, school, peers, and a variety of other social institutions including mass media. Frankly, most of us remain unaware that we, and they, are so behaving. Code words, for instance, carry mega-meanings within them and will indicate that a person is going to behave in such-and-such a way. In cities, individuals on both sides of a serious economic or social distinction (class, race, language, or religion), for example, will understand to whom the phrase "those people" refers. Similarly, in policing, a "rat" is not a rodent but either a noun or verb describing a person or behaviour that betrays illicit activity within the force to internal authorities; to be such is not highly valued. Perhaps the important point here is that those within the policy conversion arena of the modern metropolitan city perform as well as they do because predictability has become an underlying component.

2.1.5 Decisions and non-decisions

2.1.5.1 RESULTS

As noted, public policy is the dependent variable which, in one way or another, all of the social sciences endeavour to explain. At the city level specifically, policies may take one of several quite distinctive forms. They may be considered as decisions and non-decisions, including possible decisions that are never contemplated.

2.1.5.2 DECISIONS

Most commonly, a public policy is thought of as the conscious decision of the legislative body, in this case the city council, and it may take one of several generic forms. At city hall, the operational form for decisions made is most likely to be a bylaw. Here, as when a bill passes through the federal or provincial legislature, three readings are required before it can be enacted and made law. The term "bylaw" comes through mediaeval English from Danish conquerors who employed it to describe a "lawe" made for a "bye," which was their term for an English "tun" or township. For less important matters such as internal administrative reorganizations or symbolic gestures, city councils may choose to take a single vote to pass a simple resolution.

Figure 2.4: Possible Policy Choices

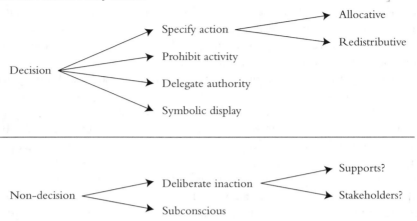

Such policy decisions may specify particular action that the local government is to undertake. These policies are, in turn, labelled *allocative* when they apply to all residents of the municipality or *redistributive* when they are directed towards specific categories of persons. Allocative policies are often contained in major documents like the annual budget bylaw, which dictates taxation and expenditures for all citizens, or the city's longer term General Municipal Plan, which in broad strokes lays out the general ways in which land within the city's boundaries may be used. Spraying against mosquito infestation probably benefits almost all citizens and thus is an allocative policy. Redistributive state activities use general revenues to provide public support for designated categories of persons. It is easy to think of various social service programs right off the bat, but examples also include targeted funding for people with disabilities, for those who yearn for a municipal cricket pitch, for stadiums for professional sports teams, or for concert halls. Where the distinction is not particularly clear, loud controversy over state support will be perennial and intense; for instance, is public transit a redistributive subsidy to those who ride or, like roadways and traffic management themselves, an allocative public work?

City councils also *prohibit* both widely, and specifically, certain sorts of behaviour on the part of all their citizens. In this category we might place parking regulations, traffic ordinances, and any number of the licensing bylaws. Bylaws determine the size and shape of permitted outdoor advertising and where signs may be placed. Are, for example, large, inflatable, interior-lit, plastic beer bottles necessarily a desirable downtown street feature or not? Historically, provisions for public health inspections are an integral *raison d'être* of local administrations. The General Municipal Plan itself, through the various steps in zoning, both permits and limits what might be built and where and for what purpose. Under its everyday application, local restaurants might, for instance, be told precisely how many tables and chairs over how much square space may be set on the public sidewalk adjacent to premises during the summer months. While it is difficult to be precise, it is generally the case that somewhat between two-thirds and three-quarters of any council agenda will be concerned more or less directly with issues that involve land management and servicing.

Thirdly, councils may choose to *delegate* authority over the detailed administration of policy to its permanent or quasi-bureaucracy. In this instance, the council will set forth the broad direction it wishes to establish and then entrust the precise application to professional administrators or **arms' length authorities**. The federal government, for example, has laid out loosely defined broadcast standards in statutes, but the responsibility for setting precise Canadian content requirements and who will be entitled to hold a broadcast licence is delegated to the Canadian Radio and Telecommunications Commission (CRTC). In the same vein, the provinces have found little that is more politically controversial than municipal **annexation** issues, which is why they have created quasi-judicial bodies like the Ontario Municipal Board (OMB) to hear the protagonists and render a verdict based on purely "technical" grounds. Most major cities have similarly devised an agency variously called a Municipal Planning Commission or Development Appeal Board with responsibility to give detailed life to the General Municipal Plan and its area structure subcomponents.

Legislative bodies want to control the basic policy thrust without the burden of day-to-day administration, perhaps also believing that a specialized oversight will breed consistency in the application of rules for discrete policy worlds. This is also the basic principle underpinning the council-manager system and its council-commission board variant in Western Canada. With this model, a small council, much like a corporate board of directors, sets very broad policy guidelines and then retains a professional administrator to develop appropriate regulations, to supervise the detail of program delivery, and to hire and fire the city's various other senior managers. Except in the case of municipal executive committees, councils cannot generally delegate policy-making powers to their standing committees. Nor may councils, as legislative bodies, surrender their law-making status. But they can delegate to a subordinate the power to make regulations that have legal force. The field of administrative law specializes in the relatively autonomous authority of such subordinate legislation, especially along such avenues as equity in appeals, due process and fairness in policy application, and degree of public control over the non-elected policy custodians.

A final sort of policy choice, normally accomplished by a council *resolution* (which only requires one reading before council to be passed), is called *symbolic*. This frequently entails little in the way of public expenditure and occurs when folkloric heroes, civic pioneers, or even special events are honoured by the naming of public spaces such as parks, roads, or bridges. These actions should not be dismissed as entirely unimportant. To honour sports heroes is thought to confer good feelings of accomplishment on all citizens and a sense of community in praising the achievements of a fellow citizen. Symbolic acknowledgement of a particular person, even a long dead champion, is often understood by the participants as the conferring of official recognition on the special public with whom he or she was identified. As a rule, symbolic policies are integrative in building diffuse support and, due to their general unimportance to citizens outside the recognized population, rarely controversial. Where, however, a symbolic choice touches upon a more underlying social cleavage—for instance, whether or not a new Chinatown Gate must be inclusive of newcomers in the Canadian Vietnamese community as well as those with a more long-standing tradition in Canadian culture, or a deeper cultural division over putative values, as with the official declaration of a Gay Pride Day—councillors may face some considerable, occasionally unanticipated, public controversy. These are, nonetheless, conscious policy choices made.

2.1.5.3 NON-DECISIONS

Policy choices may also take on a different guise: they may be *non-decisions*. As indicated in Figure 2.1, the non-decision may assume one of two quite separate personalities, either one of deliberate inaction or of subconscious avoidance.

In the first instance of *deliberate inaction*, councillors as policy-makers may be unprepared to decide on an issue due to a lack of information concerning political supports. Political authorities, especially city councillors, may be unaware of or uncertain if the public support behind, or generated for, a particular new or innovative set of demands is sufficient to justify committing community resources to it. They may be unclear as to the position of the official leadership within the relevant policy community. They might not know the position, if indeed there is one, of key leaders in the urban regime; this is especially important when those persons are widely understood to constitute a veto group over new policy in this particular field.

Consequently, if council believes it has insufficient information available along these political lines, or if councillors are uncertain if the city administration has access to the personnel or other technical capacity for effective program delivery, then council will decide *not* to decide! In this very frequent case, the decision is deferred or put off by referring it to committee "for further hearings and study," to the administration "for review and recommendation," or to task forces or commissions of inquiry "for full public investigation."

As to these last, city governments in the metropolitan region may choose, from time to time, to create policy explorations that may be more, or less, independent of council direction. The more independent style is some kind of commission or committee of inquiry. These may often be free-wheeling, publicly accessible, and politically uncontrollable after the original commissioners themselves are selected. Councillors, just like cabinet ministers, seem to like these operations because the "political heat" is taken away from them while the subject matter "is under study." Elected councillors are as wary as coyotes of them because the results and recommendations are not predetermined, and, unlike cabinet ministers, their city bailiwicks are too local to allow them to ignore the findings forever.

Less autonomous, and thus more popular among city politicians, are **task forces**, which focus on a quite specific question or public policy initiative. They may be either an *ad hoc* committee of council or a commission of interested members of the public, selected usually from the affected policy community. They are required to answer: "What should we do and how can we do it?" The ideal task force consists of wide representation from any in the community who might feel impacts from policy change as well as policy specialists who will find themselves on an even footing with ordinary but interested electors. But if the task force has been substantially representative, open in process, and consensual in its findings, its members will likely live to see some of their recommendations implemented. In this instance, for this policy area, they will have done the political work for the politicians.

To refer a matter to some subordinate body "for further study" is a very different matter from delegating a policy decision that actually goes forward to someone to administer, since making a choice is deferred. Whatever the reasoning behind the non-decision may be, it is important to remember that even when a decision not to decide is taken, a public policy choice has been made, and that is not to tamper with the current status quo. Inaction is a *choice* that has been consciously made, not just some item that policy authorities never considered as one that had to be addressed (Pal 2001: 21-22).

Sometimes even the decision not to decide is not made. In other words, a subconscious choice has been reached by the responsible authorities without benefit of any public airing. The theoretical refinement of the notion itself arose in the community power debate between political scientists and sociologists during the 1950s to late 1970s. This debate, which ended in something of a draw before disengagement, focused on who exercised either pluralist influence or elite power over decisions taken for the local community. The idea of decisions subconsciously not taken, power struggles not entered into publicly, became best known through the work of Peter Bachrach and Morton Baratz and their comments about "the second face of power" (1962). They pointed out that certain issues or potential allocative choices are thought not to be within the domain of the political system so that possibilities for policy action do not reach the point of being considered and public inattention is taken as a given.

In some Canadian metropolitan areas with multiple local governments, local social services, for instance, have been an entirely discretionary matter. Even if service costs are funded mostly through intergovernmental transfer programs, many rural and upper-middle-class suburbs will not initiate them because such policies would stand in conflict with "their own community values." And since these municipalities can bar entry into their communities by those in need of such programs through the legal expedient of restrictive zoning practices, no demand for them is ever heard. As an example, the Edmonton CMA today sees a discrepancy of over 30:1 in the ratio of social services spending between the core city and some of its suburban enclaves.

This situation would be familiar to Bachrach and Baratz: "When the dominant values, the accepted rules of the game, the existing power relations among groups, and the instruments of force, singly or in combination, effectively prevent certain grievances from developing into full-fledged issues which call for decisions, it can be said that a non-decision-making situation exists" (1963: 641). In these circumstances, even if professionals in program delivery are aware of deficiencies, they are unlikely to raise the matter in the public policy arena if they know in advance that their idea would be, at best, a minority one, that even minor recommendations would be permanently pigeon-holed, and that their actions might be considered disloyal by their employers with career consequences. Power is thus exercised through the creation of subconscious barriers to the airing of policy options. Although spared the severe race and urban **underclass** divisions of the American metropolis, one result of the fractious governing of the Canadian city-region has been considerably divergent service packages among the separate cities which, in turn, reflect the locally centred dominance of particular groups.

Through the simple institution of government boundaries, this mobilization of bias in Canadian metropolitan areas can organize some issues into open policy conflict and suppress others. Thus, the virtually unnoticed "second face of power" is made real, as we shall see.

2.1.6 Impacts and consequences

2.1.6.1 IMPACTS AND CONSEQUENCES

In the normal case, the political processes of the policy cycle do not end with the enunciation of a concrete policy decision. Choices made have impacts on the community, many of which are intended of course, but others of which will turn out to have been unintended and unexpected. On very rare occasions, policy decisions will produce pretty much precisely the results that the decision-makers originally wished. More usually however, there will be some slippage between the policy objectives of the ideal and what has actually been realized.

This is understandable considering the innumerable limiting pressures and constraints that impose their semi-sovereign wills on both elected councillors and their support and advisory staffs. Indeed, **satisficing**—combining the words "satisfy" and "suffice"—was a word coined by Herbert Simon to describe circumstances in which public policy-makers have to get by with less than optimum options and results. What this word describes in the real world is a quest for those minimum common denominators that any given policy choice *can* fulfill. For most city councillors, this rapidly cascades into a quick series of quite down-to-earth matters: What is the minimum dollar charge to implement this change within a fixed and finite budget? Since we do not have the luxury of being able to delete any ongoing program because each represents a past political commitment to groups making demands, must we find new money from higher taxation or fees? Does the administration have the organizational resources to administer the plan? Do we have the specialized technological or professional expertise to operate in a new area? Might it be possible, or necessary, to farm out responsibility to a non-governmental agency or contractor? What is the minimum response that the key players in the policy community will accept? What political compromises must be worked to accommodate the most vocal stakeholders?

The one responsibility of city councils is to rank the relative weights among these conflicting variables. Often it is because they are unsure of how to weigh, say, demand support for a small but new program against the cost of taking on new staff or technology that councils refer matters so frequently back to standing committees or to their administrators. Once the councillors have found the minimum response that satisfies the conditions they collectively value the highest, they move on to their next problem, for it is believed there is neither time nor information nor experience enough to seek out the one best or absolutely rational policy option. Such less than rational, under par policy choices out of supposed pressing necessity were once labelled the "art of muddling through" by Charles Lindblom (1959).

City halls in Canada universally deploy an approach of graduated **incrementalism**, which depends on precedent and builds on past limited successes, or what Lindblom also, and aptly, labelled "successive limited comparisons." The prevailing attitude seems to be that "what worked in [the] past can, with minor tinkering, be made to work in [the] future" (note Pal 2001: 21-22; Howlett and Ramesh 2003: 170-72).

Put another way, decisions do not vary much from the track record because all participants find it politically easier than starting fresh and because the standard operating method of any bureaucracy is more comfortable with adaptation than innovation. This policy style describes a cautious response to most issues and much that passes for reasonable thought at city hall. Both councillors and their bureaucrats evaluate closely the positive and negative political fallout from any policy innovation in other similar metropolitan cities before venturing on a similar tack. For instance, in July 2000, Halifax Regional Council resolved a highly contentious policy debate by voting to phase in a graduated ban on lawn pesticides over a four-year period. Well down in the Canadian Press story about this is the observation that "The Halifax bylaw is being reviewed by dozens of Canadian municipalities, including Toronto and several in Quebec, looking to introduce similar legislation."

Moreover, the programs elaborated by authorities are not likely to be precisely those which were originally advocated by either stakeholders or other influential voices in the relevant policy network, if only because of satisficing pressures. Often, it is initially enough for the policy community to enter the issue into the **political gateway** as a legitimate item for authoritative debate and possible resolution. Recognizing that there is little likelihood of any sunset provision or a definite end put to their initial program, policy advocates will be satisfied with almost any first toe over the incremental threshold.

Nor do individuals, once chosen as political authorities, ever appreciate fully that they must behave as the makers of those ideal choices that any model of rational policy-making requires (Howlett and Ramesh 2003: 167-69). Still, the policy model does tell us what factors may have directly influenced the choices which are made. Because some policy consequences are very much unintended or yield side-effects that are quite surprising—the sort of thing that economists happily label "slippages"—any political model need envisage some reintroduction of demands.

For instance, if one travels up the Mombassa coastal highway north to Malindi, a road similar in construction to provincial secondary highways in Canada and hence atypical of east Africa, one crosses the Kilifi Creek inlet near Takaungu. Until recently, small ferries traversed the gap, but European foreign aid replaced these with a bridge to facilitate tourism at Italian–owned Malindi hotels. However, this action also permitted an increase in gross vehicle weight for trucks, which have wreaked havoc on the roadway surface and base. There are no Third World budgets for roadway maintenance, so these are not repaired. Similar situations also arise in more industrialized countries. The San Francisco Bay Area boasts the BART subway system. Built to state-of-the-art specifications, it was efficient and clean for many months after opening—due in part to the absence of riders. This latter fact rather surprised policy leaders since the heavy capital costs of subway construction had been supported through borrowing approved by plebiscites. Post-vote surveys revealed that citizens had approved of BART because they "knew" their neighbours would ride the rails, thus leaving the freeways clear for their own personal drive to work.

Somewhat closer to home are urban examples of similar unintended consequences familiar to most Canadians. For example, most metropolitan cities have undertaken to construct sidewalk ramps at intersections to ease street access for people in wheelchairs. Now mindless twits on 20-speed bikes can terrorize normal pedestrians by cruising sidewalks at breakneck speed without any need to slow at the curbs. Municipal liability is but one example of the undesirable outcomes.

Such examples illustrate the reverse flow of policy intelligence from actual consequence to incremental improvement. It can carry positive (where ideas work) or negative (when they fall short) nuance. Much of the data gathering necessary to determine policy impact is done by civic administrators during their direct work with clientele, and up to 80 per cent of any council's observable policy work will likely be in the nature of incremental tinkering based on staff recommendations. Impact intelligence also works through the policy community and leads to the reintroduction of incremental demands, the accumulation of supports behind them, and the mediation of grievances.

Finally, and theoretically, positive results may build diffuse support for authorities to the extent that they can reconcile expectations positively. However, system legitimacy requirements don't matter all that much when provincial governments are the ultimate authority. On the other hand, this also implies that the provinces may intervene to protect their own standing.

2.2 Power and the Fixing of Priorities

2.2.1 State intervention and local control

Provincial authorities may at times come to the conclusion that the bundle of allocative and redistributive policies flowing from the metropolitan municipal operation does not live up to their own rough assessment of constituent expectations. However justified this general reasoning, provincial governments, in order to fulfill their particular political agendas, may assume that specific patterns in demand have been shut out by municipal authorities in the local policy arena. The province determines that established institutions have created barriers either to the first airing of an issue, or to the equitable deployment of competitive political resources, or to the establishment of a target authority with appropriate decision-making competence. As a result, the province must undertake a systemic and possibly democratizing reform of local institutions, such as advocated by the reformers of 1900.

Two practical examples of this process spring to mind. In 1971, social democratic reformers of the third urban reform period were elected to the NDP provincial government of Manitoba, and some senior cabinet ministers had first-hand experience with the frustrations of municipal governing. They saw in Metro Winnipeg's multiple municipalities a municipal system that had become distant, remote, and unaccountable to neighbourhood and lower income electors partly because of the two-tier metropolitan arrangements then in effect, large wards for metro-level and City of Winnipeg elections, and at-large elections generally in the suburbs (a detailed discussion of the bias of electoral arrangements is in Chapter 5). At base, the desire to clarify accountability by reducing the number of authorities and to empower local neighbourhoods was the impetus for unifying all of these jurisdictions into one Unicity government.

For Toronto and the amalgamation of the densely urban core of that city-region in January 1998, the ideological neo-liberal (i.e., very conservative) provincial Progressive Conservative government used virtually identical wording to the 1971 Winnipeg Act. Municipal institutions were perceived to be incongruent with the policy targets of the "big players" in Toronto's urban regime. A further incentive was a desire to reduce the number of tiresome city councillors. Different from the Winnipeg case was the Ontario cabinet's choice to empower wider area actors through creating a wide-area structure with a strong administrative cluster of authority at its centre.

2.2.2 An initial word about leadership in authority

The recurring problems of metropolitan city politics are that everyone seems to have a say, decisions seem to be made with little durability, and, concurrently, no one seems to be accountable for either specific choices or for the general condition of the city. In large measure, our task is to find and define leadership in authority.

Leadership in authority has the ability to be innovative, to enter new ideas, new means, and new categories of people into the system. This may take the minimal guise of adapting procedural rules to produce conflict-of-interest guidelines, for example. Innovation may change structures (for instance, to wards in elections so that minorities may possibly gain guaranteed representation), and it may ultimately change policy itself, dramatically, to enhance or firm up the social security net at the local level. New thinking breeds new policy in the ways that environmentalism has led, at a minimum, to widespread practical recycling and that feminism has encouraged equity in employment for much wider sectors of the community.

Seldom has the call to innovate by challenging vested authority been more clearly presaged than by sociologist John Porter who wrote of a need for a new style of "creative politics" that would be able challenge existing social structure and public ideology. According to him,

> By mobilizing human resources for new purposes, it has the initiative in the struggle against the physical environment and against dysfunctional historical arrangements. Creative politics requires a highly developed political leadership to challenge entrenched power within other institutional orders. It succeeds in getting large segments of the population identified with the goals of the political system and in recruiting their energies and skills to political ends. (1965: 369)

This is not city politics as it exists in Canada today.

Porter was arguing the case for reorienting the Canadian federal party system from its very conservative sustenance of the status quo as defined in the pursuit of national unity. He believed that to seek only the reconciliation of cultural particularism would erect barriers to the pursuit of something more meaningful or substantive such as, perhaps, distributive justice or social development. Forty years on, the national political system does not seem to have progressed much, by Porter's own measure. Implicit in his analysis is the existence of a second face of power, a trap baited with national unity questions, which diverts attention from a politics that has any real hands-on meaning for modern citizens.

Canada's metropolitan city councils have been too easily suckered into a somewhat similar trap. Spared the high politics of national reconciliation, councillors fixate on the low politics of the daily amelioration of, for instance, the garbage collecting operation. They will peek into the open end of political gateways after they are well ajar. But who sets the gate fixture and inaugurates any entry? If basic, large, adaptive capabilities have been abrogated by existing political authorities, then this leadership vacuum will, over time, be occupied by other active interests. In the early years of the last century, the political machine of the boss era worked city hall's backrooms in the United States. Along the same lines as Porter, Robert Merton makes this entirely valid assertion: "By this centralized organization of political power, the boss and his apparatus can satisfy the needs of diverse subgroups in the larger community which are not adequately satisfied by legally devised and culturally approved social structures" (1957: 72).

These days the politics of small opportunities yielding large ends involves what has been labelled the rule of urban regimes. Put simply, policy is accomplished through the actions of public figures and private individuals working in tandem to reduce conflict and to cut deals on small advantages for all concerned. Private conversations arrange the possible, public officials make the law. In the abeyance of authoritative public leadership validated by elector choice among genuine alternatives, councils have abdicated direction in order to muddle along with *pro forma* decisions and increasingly symbolic choices. They have chosen to leave to influential private actors the basic task of adapting the community to work within a complex, challenging new world order.

Note

1. "Scientific Wild-Ass Guess." The term was attributed by William Safire to Colonel John Stuart (in 1984) as the basis for his estimates to General William Westmoreland of enemy troop strength during the Vietnam War. Safire observes that, "The Army web page warns readers 'to avoid using these terms in official correspondence, at formal briefings, when dealing with outsiders'" (Safire 1999: 27).

three	# Urban political culture and the limits to policy choice

While the local evening news and daily papers happily reveal fractious personality differences between public figures, the rich pattern of city politics within which these take place is, in reality, established by continuing broad currents and underlying themes. This basic context is called political culture. In urban areas, its study reveals the environment in which all activities leading to public policy decisions are undertaken. The concept is normally used by social scientists to compare the relationship of citizens to authority in larger political units like national states or important regional governing arrangements. If it is agreed, however, that cities fall into this latter category, then the idea of political culture can help to explain why specific patterns in governing institutions and political relationships emerge in particular contexts and not in others.

3.1 Political Culture Structures Urban Political Debate

To examine political culture is to extract from the total social life of the community all of those particular factors which colour how people think about political authority, what things they know about it (true or not), and why they feel the way they do about the entire operation. Technically, political culture refers to the pattern of orientations toward political objects held by members of a political community (Kaplan 1967: 209-11; Van Loon and

Whittington 1996: 91-108). So, a country's urban political culture consists of the thoughts and feelings of all individuals within its urban spaces about political actors, structures, events, and permanent institutions. We want to know how these ideas and attitudes have an impact on the individual's subsequent political behaviour. Is there, for example, a widely shared belief that civic government represents a unique opportunity for citizens to influence public policy through direct participatory grassroots democracy? Ought people then to hold feelings of guilt for betrayed obligation and responsibility if they are not themselves in the game? Or, if one accepts the idea of the general importance of elected representatives making decisions on the people's behalf, is it reasonable for one to be able to deflect all responsibility onto these elected representatives when nobody ever seems to be accountable for wrong choices made?

Importantly, even the collective political setting of Canada's largest cities constitutes but one part of the national political culture. In this sense, cities may be referred to as a political subculture. This does not imply inferiority but, just as with the position of Quebec in Canada, it describes some portion of the whole. Equally, the subculture of cities within the regions of Canada like the Maritimes or prairies may be expected to reflect the variation of their region from the national mean. Finally, it must be observed that the sum of the political subcultures of a nation's communities helps to shape, but never equals, that of the national community itself.

3.1.1 The resolution of public policy issues

Because we are trying to capture a picture of the sum total of the feelings of many tens of thousands of people about governing, any statement generalizing about one city's political subculture must be somewhat nebulous. So, why should we bother? Let us consider three answers to this question.

3.1.1.1 RECALLS AND INITIATIVES, PLEBISCITES AND REFERENDUMS

First, a community's political culture involves a common understanding of the means by which fundamental political disputes among citizens and politically significant individuals over the distribution of goods and services—indeed, over public resources of all types—will be settled with clinching authority. In earlier times, common agreement among male property owners might be expected to generate a consensus over the construction of, for instance, a school house. For Canadian liberal democracy in the twenty-first century, the hard choice at the municipal level is whether basic political divisions are to be deferred for resolution by some elected representative body such as the city council or school board. Or is it expected that major matters, as defined by the community, are to be ratified "by the people" through referendum or plebiscite? Whether a community naturally does one or the other each time an issue of substance comes along is not much debated. The expectation is long engrained as precedent, practice, and culture.

While Canadian political culture has borrowed conventions from both British and American custom, it has proven difficult to reconcile the essential incompatibility of two traditions rooted in considerably divergent concepts of political sovereignty. The British tradition, however modernized, still vests sovereignty at the top, in the person of a monarch, and all rights and freedoms of her subjects are those which have been wrested from the Crown by law and by convention since the time of absolute monarchy and the Magna Carta. To the considerable extent that Canada operates under a constitution similar in principle to that of the UK, its cultural traditions have also been inherited. The executive operation is conducted in the sovereign's name by her agents who are, for the most part, elected. And yet vestiges of Crown privilege persist, one of which is that local governments do not have the power to tax any Crown property. In this tradition, citizens do not have the right to a *direct* voice in the making of the law (Lipset 1985).

The American Revolution established a new direction in which sovereignty resides at the bottom, as spelt out in the first paragraphs of the Declaration of Independence: "governments are instituted among men, deriving their just powers from the assent of the governed"; it further declared "the right of the people" to alter or abolish any governing form that did not seem likely "to affect their safety and happiness." In practical terms this means that the authority exercised by the modern state executive in the United States consists only of those powers which, in theory, citizens as sovereign have assigned to it. For American Progressives in the twentieth century, citizens-as-sovereign retained the powers both to dismiss office-holders who had in some way betrayed the public confidence and to write measures directly into law as they themselves saw fit. These measures, flowing out of the traditions of Jacksonian direct democracy, are the two activities known respectively as "the recall" and "the initiative."

In both instances, the state constitution permits petition by some small proportion of the electorate (now around 10 per cent) either to declare a state or local office vacant or to put a measure directly to the electorate. In the first case, the office-holder is out of a job and must seek re-election in a subsequent vote. This delegate democracy implies that the elected individual must faithfully represent directly the will of constituents or face the consequences. For example, in 2003 in California, actor Arnold Schwarzenegger was elected governor in the recall vote which terminated the term of Governor Gray Davis. Alberta's 1936 Recall Act required 66 per cent of electors to recall their MLA at a time when American states commonly used a number between 20 and 30 per cent. The act was repealed retroactively in 1937 after organizers found enough signatures to recall Premier William Aberhart in his own riding of High River–Okotoks.

In the case of the initiative, voters have the opportunity to vote yea or nay on the law itself. If the majority is in favour, the initiative is deemed to be law, and elected representatives are out of the decision loop entirely. For instance, on 6 June 1978, a California initiative, Proposition 13, reduced property taxes as a source of municipal funding by one-half. Today about half the American states permit the initiative possibility.

The legal difference between a referendum and a plebiscite is that, whereas the latter is merely an expression of the public's opinion on an issue, the referendum is a binding decision and, in some instances, a citizens' vote on a bylaw itself. The root word of plebiscite is the Latin "plebes" or commoner, that part of the community that was not among the "gentes" or patrician class.

By the 1990s the rules governing the conduct of referendums in Canada, perhaps inevitably, had been structured to the advantage of elected office-holders. This is because, as with the recall, legislators are distinctly unenthusiastic at having their judgement open to such direct public question. Procedural obstacles always, and in equal measure, accompany lip-service favouring direct democracy precepts. In the Alberta 1995 comprehensive revision to municipal governing statutes, greater autonomy was pledged to local governments; at the same time, the percentage of electors required to force a referendum on a bylaw was doubled from five to ten, and the period for signature collection reduced to 60 days. For a further example, in British Columbia a plebiscite in conjunction with the October 1991 provincial election indicated that 81 per cent of voters favoured a recall possibility and 83 per cent favoured the ability to propose referendum questions. The subsequent act (1993) required signatures equal to 50 per cent of those who had been *eligible* to vote in the past election, and the petition had to be collected within a 60-day period. For a binding referendum to be held, 10 per cent of voters in each of the province's 75 ridings had to sign up; passage required 50 per cent plus one of all voters *and* of voters in two-thirds of the constituencies. Jack Masson observes that direct democratic possibilities have been eroded in Alberta over the last 30 years, an attack led by municipal politicians fearful of diluting their authority (1994: 6), but such an assessment applies much more widely across Canada as a whole.

To all intents and purposes, the British tradition does not allow plebiscites, so the Canadian experience with them has been mixed; the west has been far more amenable to municipal decisions by plebiscite on major issues than either Atlantic or central Canada (Higgins 1986: 322-24). This geographic difference is largely the result of the migration of ideas across the North American plains during the American Progressive era of the 1920s. Moreover, local governing institutions in the west were not only more recent introductions than those "back east" but also were subject to quick adaptation and drastic structural change in response to harsh climatic and cyclical economic circumstances. They were also forged in response to the sheer burden of impossible distance. Particularly on the prairies, **populist** roots in the political culture set before the Great Depression linger on and find current expression at all levels. They are to be seen in the rejection of historic political parties; the rise of the cooperative movement, the suspicion of traditional hierarchical "big business" corporations and private-sector trade unionism, and the acceptance of individual accomplishment as representing the singular benchmark for successful standing. That these characteristics persist to some degree elsewhere in the country, or that they tend to be more pronounced in rural areas, is not at issue. It is their heightened salience as predictors for the local processes in western Canadian cities that should be noted here.

Some important general policy consequences of differences in political culture can be found in the restructuring of city-regions. In the UK in 1986, the abolition of the Greater London Council—the area-wide government for the 32 boroughs of that city-region—and six other metropolitan boroughs elsewhere was initiated by central government fiat. Indeed, until the vote on the future unification of London in 1998, there had never been a binding referendum on metropolitan restructuring in any country that was directly modelled on Westminster parliamentary government, and this includes Canada. In the United States, any significant change to metropolitan governing institutions has been subject to referendums. In virtually every instance, the success rate for centripetal change being about 15 per cent, electors have chosen to reject academic and economic elite advice in order to stick with the familiar in governing arrangements. Such decision-making by plebiscite is one reason why the average city-region in the United States finds itself with 117 units of local government.

In short, political culture dictates how such basic choices about institutions, and their subsequent policy redistributions, will be made.

3.1.1.2 THE RELATIONSHIP OF CITIZENS TO POLITICAL AUTHORITY

Second, political culture generally establishes the relationship of citizens to political authority, by structuring the basic behaviours of individuals and groups in politics. Compared to that of the United States, Canadian political

culture includes a wider deference to political authority, so citizens are relatively less likely to engage in direct political action and confrontation (Van
Loon and Whittington 1996: 109-11). Even with the collapse of trust in
traditional hierarchical authorities of all stripes over the last decade or so,
Canadians appear to be less likely than Americans to integrate into the body
politic through membership in any one of numerous formal organizations
which in turn might advance their collective interests. The political action
committee format (for labour, or gun ownership, or pro-life or pro-choice
camps on the issue of abortion) that has become so influential in individual American Senate and House elections is not much of a factor during
Canadian votes.

Popular sovereignty in Canada, such as it is, is traditionally and culturally
focused on representative institutions. As a result, minorities on any policy
position need to be prepared to defer to official judgement as expressed in
the majority choice of any properly constituted representative body. In this
dominant style, there is a strong tendency not to question political leadership too closely on a day-to-day basis between elections. The corollary is
that broad segments of any city's population appear to be unaware of, and
uninterested in, official decision-making. Referring specifically to municipal
politics, the Bureau of Municipal Research (Toronto) once observed that,
"Direct, intensive, wide-ranging participation characteristics of American
politics contrast sharply with the Canadian experience of restricted participation and deference to political leadership" (BMR 1970: 6). This difference
in emphasis between actively democratic participation and enduring democratically chosen leadership has public policy consequences.

Kaplan, among others, has written of the relatively passive urban political culture of Canada. Outside of cathartic single issue moments, formal
groups even as democratic watchdogs do not exist. Of the normal routine of
Metro Toronto policy-making (1954-66), for instance, he documented that
private pressure groups in the Toronto area were most conspicuous by their
generally weak interest in issues coming before council as compared to his
observations of American city politics (1967: 172-78). The only significant
source of influence he noted were the few reporters in the local press gallery whose most important role was to sort issues by placing them into the
broader context of a pervasive cultural consensus. None of the "hopeful"
reforms to increase institutionalized citizen activism within local government policy development that were suggested a generation ago by another
observer, Christopher Leo (1977), has materialized. The limited individual
participation in the process of city elections is discussed later in this chapter.

This sort of passive spectator politics has practical consequences. It may
be assumed that for any major policy choice—the extension of a freeway, for

instance—city councillors must seek out two very general kinds of information. They need to know many sorts of *technical* data relating to present and projected traffic volumes, construction and design, and financing implications. But, importantly, they should also have at least crude *political* information about community assessments of the project, because any freeway will have dramatic consequences upon neighbourhoods. Even borrowing to build one may subtract worthy possibilities from any short list of alternative priorities. But, in the absence of an actively participatory and continuously attentive local political culture, decisions tend to be guided by the technical line because the costs (primarily measured as time) of acquiring reliable political knowledge are considered too high. Given their own experience of deference to official positions, councillors may also factor in the probable willingness of their electors to forgive and forget anything negative.

Such a democratic deficit may produce an assumption that broad consensus over the ends and objects of city government exists. This kind of culture led to the city freeway building frenzy of the 1960s, all of whose basic designs, from Toronto through Winnipeg and Edmonton to Vancouver, were remarkably similar from city to city (Leo 1977: 22). The original design documents progressed so far towards implementation only because of the apparent dearth of citizen attention. When such a plan as the Metropolitan Edmonton Transportation Study was first advanced in 1965, for instance, council asked the city commissioners to compile a list of those objecting to its MacKinnon Ravine freeway component; the list comprised three individuals and one community organization. Even in 1971, only 22 groups and individuals appeared before council to submit opposition to any plan to divert city resources into massive highway projects. Similarly in Vancouver, the Chinatown freeway and connectors were squelched only after over 800 citizens joined with the Board of Trade and Downtown Businessmen's Association to invade city council chambers in protest. Still, the plans were shelved only for the time being. Metro government freeway designs for Toronto similarly mobilized a new conservatism among multiple residents' groups whose mass confederation through the Stop Spadina Save Our City Coordinating Committee (SSSOCCC) in 1968, along with public confrontations, ultimately induced the provincial government to terminate Metro's freeway construction ambitions in 1971. The point is that officials could contemplate building such freeways because the political culture was largely a spectator one.

Finally on this point, for councillors to argue that they rely mostly on technically qualified information as the basis for decision on a subject covers up a deflection of important normative questions into the world of administration. Leo has noted that in the late 1960s Canadian city freeway debates were hustled by councils into details of "transportation planning." Councils could thus claim that "road-building was a largely administrative matter, which would not benefit by extensive exposure to the political process" (1977: 30). This, in turn, leads to a situation in which choice degenerates into a purportedly value-neutral arena, thus becoming a means to impose the decision-maker's own values by using putative scientific assessments in an atmosphere both impersonal and detached.

An even more democratically fraudulent aspect of this behaviour develops when senior professional administrators devise an agenda rooted in their own version of the public good without evident council knowledge. When the Vancouver Transportation Study was first unveiled to city council in June 1967, it provided little public clue as to the variety of integrated projects then in the commissioners' heads (Gutstein 1983: 201-02). Edmonton's Commission Board kept all transportation design documents "internal" and launched a major interrogation investigating the one instance when a critical assessment was leaked to the media and, presumably, to councillors (Lightbody 1983: 274-75). And so it goes, even today. The larger issue here is that bureaucratic continuity ensures that not even politically trumped plans ever die. Reworded, but not reworked, roadway plans in particular—being the most noticeable due largely to their disruptive shock-and-awe construction activities—retain the attention of observant non-elected stakeholders and other specialized policy communities.

3.1.1.3 LIMITS TO THE MUNICIPAL ENTERPRISE

Third, the political culture of a community also sets broad limits to the scope of the municipal enterprise. Through "common agreement" it may be understood that not much is to be undertaken in the world of social services, say, and that provision for recreation entails only the building and maintenance of the local hockey rink. This notion of the applied face of power and political gateways has been considered in Chapter 2. At its heart it covers such fundamental questions as a person's place in society and, in turn, that society's obligations and responsibilities to the citizen.

Some policy possibilities never become the object of debate at a given point in time. For instance, local political culture legitimizes institutions that may themselves serve to neuter certain potential policy demands. In the United States, it is well documented that cities that have adopted the core essentials of the 1900 reform package also have consistently lower levels of tax-supported expenditures; similarly, councils elected at-large spend less *per capita* than those chosen by smaller block or neighbourhood wards (Dye 1972: 180-82). Non-partisan councillors who are elected city-wide tend toward a managerial style and devise policies that are applicable across the city.

These are substantiated by a widely shared melting-pot cultural expectation which overrides any precise "on the ground, in your neighbourhood" policy formulation. Council members who are chosen to represent neighbourhoods, on the other hand, must satisfy more sharply defined street level demands rooted in cultural distinctions from the whole. The city as a community is viewed through the prism of the home ward, and area-specific benefits are expected. These politicians bargain and cut deals until enough find benefit to create a voting coalition majority.

One question that tends to be excluded from the city policy agenda when "common agreement" on city-wide objectives seems dominant is the extent to which city governments should invest their energies in subsidized lower income housing. It was not until 1987 that the City of Ottawa moved to establish a land trust program (supporting 175 housing units), a direction followed in 1993 by Vancouver (493 units) and by Edmonton in 1997. Any city government must reach the stage at which a majority of its council is prepared to acquire property and then, in partnership with volunteer agencies and using federal rehabilitation funds, find the cultural justification to revitalize inner city neighbourhoods by selling the homes to lower income families. Such cases change the traditional sphere of municipal action, and the first moves are both ideologically and politically laden with conflict, in consequence becoming fractious and protracted. This is especially so since this specific city activity was unthought-of in the early postwar decades when federal and provincial efforts were focused on middle-class home ownership while municipalities restricted their endeavours to the hard servicing (water, sewer, roads) of large tracts of privately owned land. Once over the threshold of serving a new class of municipal clientele, these joint housing initiatives appear to have penetrated the incrementalist policy spiral, and the core issue of intervention itself stands publicly non-debatable.

3.1.2 Foundations of ideology and public ethos

Canada's dominant political ideology is liberal democratic. Liberal ideas are pervasive and embrace such basic operational political values as popular sovereignty, political equality, and majoritarianism. That is, the final political authority is held to be citizens as electors, whose individual rights and freedoms ensure that they are politically equal in the polling booth. Representatives periodically elected are understood to be sensitive to majority opinion just as the minority on any issue assumes that it must not always endure such status (Van Loon and Whittington 1996: 97-108). Throughout the twentieth century in Canada, this liberal bedrock of consensus, unlike that which exists in the United States, has also experienced strong exposure to viable socialist and genuine conservative ideological expression, which has prevented the emergence of a monolithic belief system.

In short, notwithstanding the importance of agrarian dissent in the early part of the twentieth century, Canada has had a history of dissenting ideologies centred in the cities. So prevalent is the liberal world view, however, that its basic values have become our shared normality. This means that citizens are more aware of the ideologies which dissent than they are of their own. For example, when speaking of the 1970s reform era in Canadian cities, Higgins defines ideology only in the form of "radical socialism" or "libertarian anarchism," the point being that each constituted radical dissent from prevailing ideological conventions (1986: 148-49). It was precisely because they presented a challenge to what was seen as normal that these views were considered ideological. Indeed, so extensive is the prevailing sense of what is natural that, curiously, the word "ideology" is not even mentioned in the index of most standard texts, one exception being *Canadian Metropolitics* (Lightbody 1995).

Matters of ideology have deep roots in communal political culture. As the concept is most widely understood today, ideological thought began to capture wider popular expression only about three centuries ago. In a sense, it is the riptide beneath the shoreline current of ideas. An ideology is a shared, comprehensive, internally consistent association of ideas through which people make sense of the world. It provides an explanation of both existing circumstances and future policy direction. Belief both sustains and justifies events. Like ethnicity, it wields a pejorative sword in that it is usually applied to others who are seen to be "ideological" while the viewer is not. In this thinking, the dominant ideology of any community becomes its "common sense" and a justification for the status quo against any demand for policy adaptation.

At some point in time, a single pattern of shared beliefs asserts such dominion that it becomes a community's **public ethos**, which stands alone as the conventional belief system of a people or period. In this vein, Nigel Harris once wrote of the long period of Conservative party dominance in British politics by noting how well that organization had tapped into the country's beliefs: "Conservative ideology is British public ideology, its precise nature depending upon which groups are dominant in British society at any given time and what is the nature of the radical attack upon the British status quo" (1971: 99). He concluded by observing that if the radical attack were so marginal as not to offer any serious electoral threat, "then Conservative ideology becomes 'common sense.'" Looking into the mirror closely, one might similarly conclude that there is such a shared ideology for most

Canadian city councillors, and it is expressed in concrete policy terms by what, in fact, they do while in office.

A community's political culture may accept considerable diversity in ideology as it establishes the dimensions within which policy debate may range. In Chapter 6, we will consider ideology specifically as a valid basis for partisan alignments in civic elections. But because the social and economic demographic of the city is so integrated and the legislative range so precisely described, the many possible ideologies of city politics tend to be condensed into a single, programmatic package. Reasonable contrary positions when they do emerge are diluted from extreme expression by the attempt to integrate electoral platforms into the public ideology.

There thus appears to be a large dose of agreement about what a local political operation ought to do in generic terms about police, fire, water, and roads. There are still fundamental questions to ask about how many, how soon, who is to be permitted to share in the public good, and who pays how much and for what. But on these matters public ideology permits superficial, not fundamental, differences, and victories of style over substance are accepted as public virtues. The focus on questions of service diverts attention from what would constitute an ideological division in other settings, and common sense diverts ideology from its primary purpose of clarifying what is meant and for what individual leaders stand. The relationship of citizen to elected governors is also pretty much set. Leo saw this during the 1960s freeway debates in Vancouver so much so that "When the political authorities did make a decision, they sometimes sought a way of making it without taking full responsibility for it. They engaged in 'kite flying,' allowing momentary popular pressures to fill the vacuum of leadership. Or they let their officials bear the brunt of responsibility" (1977: 30). Generally, though, passive acquiescence from citizens and timid representative leadership are the expected public norms rather than more sharply defined, keenly debated, and narrowly majoritarian choices with immediate practical consequences. Ideology helps divide choices into camps, clarifies the stakes through focus, and gives grounding and validity to policy debates.

The Canadian tradition disproportionately encompasses the values, myths, and ideas of liberalism, which incorporates in its heart a belief in individual achievement. Even economic or social inequality in the liberal's world is an individual's burden insofar as the role of the state is but to provide an *equality of opportunity* allowing each to attain their personal best. Radical challenge today, when it is couched in ideological terms and is not a specific-issue social movement, comes mostly from social democrats. The common aim of their progressive programs is to deploy the power of the state in some redistributive policy fashion to embrace a more *equal social condition* for all. This usually focuses on wealth but in the 1970s also embraced the political empowerment of neighbourhoods and particular social groups. The occasional ideological conservatives at city hall stand so clearly alone that they can be identified by their support of programs based on notions of *noblesse oblige*: those with superior standing must aid the less fortunate as an obligation and not through any liberal sense that individuals may ultimately be enabled to improve themselves. The extreme individualism of **radical libertarians** remains of little relevance to Canadian city politics.

A convenient shorthand by which journalists capture and provide social context to any ideological moment is to try to place people and their positions on a **left to right spectrum**. This notion originated in the physical seating plan of the National Assembly of post-revolutionary France where the leadership of the most conservative factions sat to the Speaker's right. Today, "the right" is taken to characterize the most status quo associations and "the left" the challenge to established ways of doing business. The right places a strong commitment on unbridled free enterprise and the market economy, individualism and private property, and corporatism in order to offload state responsibilities and to limit the state's role in the community. The left advocates social welfare, progressive taxation, state intervention and regulation, redistributive public policies, and state economic management (Gibbins and Youngman 1996: 11–16).

The centre of this spectrum depends upon political culture and traditions and will naturally vary from one community to the next. But, generally, the left symbolizes more rapid and drastic change, the right stability. The complication for these old understandings in this new century is that a combination of global and modernizing pressures has thrust traditional ideologies against the shoals of an emergent new political culture (NPC) globally and has collapsed older means of categorization. One of the NPC's central distinguishing characteristics, as identified by Fiscal Austerity and Urban Innovation (FAUI) project teams in 36 countries, is that leaders now immersed in post-materialist ideas clearly discriminate between social and fiscal or economic positions so much so that a person's stance on one no longer automatically confers a stance on any other (Clark and Inglehart 1998: 15–33). Marxist mayors in Marseilles may privatize municipal services, while younger fiscal conservatives elsewhere embrace an interventionist ecological agenda. The basic importance for the new political movements to be considered in Chapter 8 is that social concerns today hold greater salience in electors' agendas.

From the ideological friction of twentieth-century North America, municipal reformers forged a public ideology sometimes styled as the **bourgeois ethic**. Although not usually presented for what it was, a class theory of politics, Banfield and Wilson spelt out the "middle-class ideals for local government" at various points throughout their text *City Politics* (1963). What they described was the public ideology for that period, and it was a full cruise package complete with ship of state, crew, preferred passengers, and destination.

Forty years ago, local politics was seen to be a cooperative search for the *concrete implications* (i.e., specific policies) of an *objective public interest* (i.e., no competing alternatives are legitimate for conflict in the city), identified with the *community as a whole* (Banfield and Wilson 1963: 38-44). The logic behind this thinking required that authority be exercised by those who were "best qualified" as technical experts and not politicians. These ideas also produced the City Beautiful planning movement. To realize community objectives, the public virtues expected of leaders were honesty, efficiency, and impartiality (Banfield and Wilson 1963: 123). Characteristically for this period of municipal reform, these were qualities more usually associated with a professional bureaucracy and not a skilled political leadership. The normal governmental arrangements required by the ideal were, logically, non-partisanship, at-large elections, the city manager, master planning, and metropolitan area government (Banfield and Wilson 1963: 151). Community leaders in this tradition were also inclined to build public works such as museums, libraries, aquariums, convention centres, and physical education toys in the form of stadiums and arenas.

For reasons considered elsewhere (see Chapters 1 and 4), Canadian reformers for the first half of this century widely subscribed to this package. But while incorporating important elements of this American bourgeois ethic, the public ideology of the Canadian city is also defined by three distinctive experiences with both structure and process.

First, and rather like American community leadership but without the divisive encumbrance of racial distinction, the Canadian urban regime shared the perception of the city as essentially a socially homogenous enterprise. This belief was sustained partly by the small scale of even major cities, partly because the history of rapid urban expansion was recent so social images had not adjusted, and partly because of the apparently wide consensus within the regime in support of economic growth for the city, equated earlier with industrialization and more recently with global competitiveness and positioning.

For instance, Alan Artibise wrote about Winnipeg's interconnected social and economic elites at the turn of the last century (1874-1914). For this regime, the role of local government and municipal politics was very clear indeed: "Measuring progress in material terms, Winnipeg's businessmen directed their efforts toward achieving rapid and sustained growth at the expense of any and all other considerations ... the common outlook of

Winnipeg's businessmen that the expansion of economic enterprise should be the prime concern of the local government is a dominant theme throughout the period ..." (1975: 23). Land development hustlers sustained this pressure, and councils mostly bought into boosterism notions that the city's best interests paralleled those of the business lobby. To attain unrequited growth required a grand design, and any nonconforming public policy demand tended to be summarily dismissed as coming from an out-of-step ideologue. In this context, the role of the city councillor was only to arbitrate among the various space- and interest-specific pluralist requests for servicing supports. Since the city was not seen to be riven by any sort of class division, there needed to be no larger vision than this.

Secondly, complementing this pattern of thought was the dominant perception that city government ought to be about local housekeeping. This view has been variously described as "the caretaker" function of municipal administration in direct contrast to any thought of care-giving. The scope of the municipal enterprise was seen in and of itself to preclude dividing policy positions on the basis of ideology. Indeed, the outright thrust of the 1900 reformers was that the city was in the business of service and that politics of any stripe, but especially ideological divisions, were to be eradicated because they were not relevant. This meant non-partisanship, and the homily became "there is no Liberal or Conservative way to pave a street." In the UK, as in Canada, those community leaders who advocated local anti-partyism—mostly rural, suburban, and more conservative political activists—began their argument with the statement that partisanship "is superfluous since most decisions at the local level are 'technical' decisions and as such ought not to be 'distorted' by party politics" (Bulpitt 1967: 1). In theory, if what local governing is about is thought by citizens to be only the proper administration of pipes, police, and potholes, then the city councillor ought to have no more positivist societal role to play than apportioning these services among the very specific interests demanding them.

Thirdly, the political operation sustained by the public ideology of Canadian cities is best described as disjunctive or, in other words, divisive and ill-organized. This is evident both in council's formal executive arrangements and in its political practices. As to the former, despite the substantial American influences elsewhere apparent in city governing since 1900, the Canadian municipal executive is drawn more along British lines where the position is virtually symbolic. In Canada the office of head of council, or mayor, is largely ceremonial and, with few exceptions, is just another vote among the many. Crawford, for example, concluded that, "Such power and influence as [the mayor] may appear to have is based more upon prestige and personality than upon legal authority" (1954: 90). The most optimistic observers can credit the mayor only with a limited power to coordinate the various committees in city hall's ambit (Plunkett 1968: 22-25). It is only from time to time that the personal appeal of a particular mayor, such as Jean Drapeau in 1960s Montreal or Al Duerr in 1990s Calgary, will so tap into the political expression of the city's ethos that massive electoral pluralities result. This in turn empowers that mayor's informal suasion over the choices, but only on significant issues, of the more narrowly elected ward councillors. This is the exceptional circumstance, not the general rule.

The Canadian tradition diverges considerably from the American model, which concentrates authority in the person of a **strong mayor** with extensive budgetary, personnel, and autonomous agenda-setting and veto powers for and over council. Even though British practice determines the role of the Canadian mayor, our cities have not developed its supporting system of disciplined party organizations that command decision-making in those urban settings. That is, to discover the policy agenda for Westminster City Council (in London), influential people in the community need only to have a chat with the leader of the majority Conservative Party caucus; the figurehead mayor would never be consulted. Canadian municipal anti-partyism is legitimized by American reformers' arguments, but the power in the American mayoral system to make enforceable policy choices has not been replicated. In fact, Canadian cities have inherited the weakest elements of both systems.

When everyone seems to have an equal say, no one is ever directly accountable. A public ideology is dominant because it apparently satisfies the greatest number at least well enough on most occasions. It is the subconsciously accepted means of defusing and resolving issues. As will be noted later, periods of economic, social, or political stress can create conditions that will permit the leadership for structured challenges to develop. But the Canadian experience is that too few of these challenges, fronted by strong protagonists, have exhibited sufficient cohesion and endurance over time for viable local party systems to emerge. The two successful types of local party are either long-standing coalitions which encode the operational face of the public ideology, like the Independent Citizens' Election Committee in Winnipeg (1921-86), or more narrowly specific and episodic parties of a type which would be called "third parties" in federal and provincial politics, such as the Urban Reform Group of Edmonton (1972-83) or the Montreal Citizens' Movement (1984-94).

Whenever a political system finds itself without a consistently effective and politically balanced expression of the genuine social and economic divisions in its community, it will respond with specific, directed, interest group bargaining. Non-elected policy communities who claim hegemony within idea territories will be instrumental in directing council's "common sense" voting and administration. Active citizenship is not required since the process becomes a politics of limited and specialized access. Federally, a similar strategy of divide and prevail has been labelled an "elite accommodation" based upon regionalism and its resulting pluralistic consequences (Presthus 1973: 20-21). At the municipal level, this non-ideological style implies that council is little more than a public opinion weather gauge which writes public policy in response to political actors and demands it recognizes as significant. But it is not as inclusive as its advocates and brochures allege.

3.1.3 Robert Baldwin's legacy

Trying to understand why so many in city politics appear to have a say, why no one ever seems directly accountable, and why no decision is ever final, is to tap into the historic groundwater sustaining political culture. Ontario's nineteenth-century record is central in this not only because the province lurks so large in Confederation but also for the tangible impact of its early institutions. These stamped heavily across the prairie west and, to an extent, shaped the mindsets of practitioners in the provinces of both coasts.

Advocates of comprehensive municipal governing improvements have been active across Canada since the early 1820s. Municipal reform gained considerable legitimacy through the Report of Lord Durham's Royal Commission following Canada's 1837 Rebellion. Municipal institutions were not provided for in the subsequent Act of Union in 1840. The Municipal Corporations Act (the Baldwin Act) of 1849 was, however, part of the wider struggle for responsible government within the British North American colonies, and it was formulated within that liberal reform mindset. Long known by the surname of government leader, Durham's informal adviser, and the bill's sponsor, Robert Baldwin, this comprehensive restructuring initiative brought blanket, or systemic, changes to rural municipalities along the lines of Lord Sydenham's existing Ordinances for Lower Canada; thus, Baldwin's provisions were in keeping with the more democratic aspects already in operation in the colony's urban realm. The institutional details of its design to establish responsible local control in order to raise funds for municipal services are considered in Chapter 4.

The act's passage did not settle separate and conflicting ideas about what role municipalities were to play in society. Kaplan is insightful in observing that all municipal reformers in the nineteenth century shared one piece of common ground: "Municipal government would be a refuge from political conflict and rancour, a haven for unadorned common sense" (1982: 64). The belief that there were no "major issues" to be resolved meant there was no need for politicians to resolve conflict, nor for ministerial government or political party competition. Leo notes that Canada's first reformers believed that efficient, honest management was the central key to good local administration: "Politics, they were fond of saying, had its place at the provincial and federal levels, but at the local level it was little more than an invitation to graft and inefficiency" (1977: 7). The difficulty was, and is, that at least three distinct and contradictory missions were seen for municipalities, and this inherent tension in political culture set the stage for continuing conflict (Kaplan 1982: 55-112).

The first basis for decentralized local administration was found in the county courts of quarter sessions presided over by appointed justices of the peace. Their initial responsibilities as judicial authorities gave them powers to ensure public order and safety, but an Ordinance of 1785 extended limited civil jurisdiction to them. Municipal functions were split from judicial purview only with the Districts Council Act of 1841. Local councils continued, and continue today, to mete out justice piecemeal to individuals. Still, a mayor is often addressed as the city's "chief magistrate" or "your worship"; more potently, councils as legislative bodies remain distinct in their dealing with even the most specific personal grievance of citizens. In this role, their decisions are evaluated on the basis of explicit judicial fairness and not breadth of any political vision.

The second basis derived in large part from the roughly 15,000 United Empire Loyalists, mainly from New York State, who settled the shores of Lake Ontario from Kingston to Niagara. They knew both the importance of the corporate form and the foot-dragging of colonial authorities in granting it (Isin 1995: 62). They also had experience with direct democracy in the New England town meeting. For many of their leaders, municipal governing was distinct from other political realms because the popular will could be expressed directly through small units of government and open assemblies of citizens. In the liberal thinking of the time, local government would be a training ground for citizenship of both citizens and the representatives they might send to other legislatures. Thus was born the cliché of the town meeting as the "indispensable cornerstone of democracy," a comment first made by Alexis de Toqueville (1946: 57). By the 1960s these concepts were re-adopted in North America as "neighbourhood democracy" and became, in 1971, the foundation for the Winnipeg Unicity institutional reforms. For process democrats who subscribe to these views, city policy is primarily evaluated on both how open and participatory the policy process has been and on how widely majoritarian (or popular) the preferred decision is.

Kaplan also recorded a third strand within the local governing political culture. This set of views, with long British roots, saw local administration as a **public corporation** with its separate **Crown charter**. Engin Isin argued that the corporation became that vehicle for governing by which local communities could manage their own most immediate affairs directly, balancing central authority with municipal necessity. Thus, in a calculating manner, the Westminster system could stave off any further rebellion from local sources by offering them some autonomy. This kind of incorporation circumscribed any more directly democratic practices (Isin 1995: 80-83). The image of the municipality as corporation was a living reality since local governments in British North America had status as incorporated bodies through the actions of wider area legislatures. Thus, the council was a subordinate agency limited in its undertakings to those activities that were clearly spelt out for it under the statute by which it was incorporated.

Over time, and specifically after American municipal reform's new direction took hold in 1900, it became increasingly elementary to apply measures of private productivity to public undertakings. This was in large measure because the local public ethos had led Canadian municipal reformers not to follow the late nineteenth-century British movement into municipal corporate socialism. Canadian local leaders subscribed to a belief that such goals were better pursued through the "high politics" of federal and provincial action and instead chose to follow American attempts to emulate private enterprise throughout city institutions. This easily translated into efforts to measure council actions on the basis of provision of maximum local improvements at lowest per unit costs. Such evaluations may today be seen both in "user fees" attached to public services and in tendered competitive costing of service provision between public employees and private contractors. A belief in businesslike efficiency thus comes to govern governing.

Each of these three cultural strands holds some salience for city electors today. Each makes virtually anything possible at city hall by an appeal to its particular tradition. Any decision may be continuously questioned by invoking a long line of legitimate but conflicting belief in one or both of the other justifications. Even the cornerstone concept of representation retains an element of remoteness to local democratic traditions, providing for cynicism in its wake. In all, the dominant ethos that sustains Canadian city government is vibrant but diminished in comparison with that of the national system in its failure to build an overall and widely shared coherence in public purpose.

3.2 Small Roots, Tall Grass: Participation Possibilities

At the height of the classical period in Greece 2,400 years ago, Aristotle presumed that to lead a good life necessarily implied participation in the life of the state. There are two possibilities for active citizen participation within local governing today: elected representation and, less commonly, direct democracy. Both are entrenched in competing, but not mutually exclusive, views of democratic fundamentals. At one time Toronto's Bureau of Municipal Research argued that "There is no absolute limit to which citizens should participate in government" (BMR 1970: 5). Sadly, however, very serious cultural, philosophical, and procedural limitations restrict the capacity of individual citizen-amateurs to become involved directly in a continuous and effective fashion.

The concept of participation by citizens is fundamental to liberal democratic theory. Especially in policy-making at the level of local government, citizens expect to be consulted whenever anything out of the ordinary is being considered, particularly when the issue directly affects their neighbourhood. Thirty-five years ago, as today, the BMR found the emphasis on involvement both "pervasive" and an integral feature of community disputes: "[citizens] insist in participating in the decisions that affect them, and the [authority] assures them that they are [so participating]" (1970: 5). At the heart of this apparent conundrum lies a cultural conflict between the relative power of its twin representative and direct democracy traditions. In the normal flow of the policy cycle, and thus outside of solicitations from the especially powerful, any city council's records reveal that elected councillors usually strive to preserve the appearance of autonomy through, (1) proclaiming allegiance to some sort of objective public interest, (2) rejecting what they perceive to be more narrow and self-interested demands, or (3) eventually denying that group spokespersons are representative of the areas or positions they purport to represent. As Kaplan (1982) has elsewhere demonstrated, group leadership, particularly from neighbourhood communities, will ultimately and in frustration argue that elected officials are too power hungry and ought to abandon their own interpretations of constituents' best interests and to accept those interests as they are directly expressed. This critique can be traced back to Rousseau and, in England, to G.D.H. Cole's theory of guild socialism (Pateman 1970: 35–42). In this tradition, democratic participation is most effectively exercised by individuals through community associations or very local organizations.

Indeed, contemporary notions of citizen involvement collapse when faced with a cultural context that emphasizes the necessity for elected representatives. As has been noted earlier, the direct participatory traditions of Jacksonian democracy did not find especially fertile soil in Canada's political culture. With exceptions, and with indifference still too often interpreted as deference, the Canadian experience with local governing assigns paramount standing to persons in official capacities. Such as it is, "majority rule" is premised upon voter turnouts (of one-third) every three to four years, with those elected as representatives usually winning fewer than half, but one more than anyone else, of the votes cast. These representatives may, or may not, choose to involve policy communities and their interested networks in ongoing policy development. But such public participating is not the public governing (i.e., making real choices). With the limited exception of specifically permitted plebiscites, most often on issues of public borrowing, there is no formal stipulation or guarantee that authorities must ever consult their constituents.

If one looks precisely at those who actually govern, Canada can be seen to be constituted as an *oligarchy*, even though it can be argued that the governing clique has reasonably broadly based social attachments. Social scientists define oligarchy as a state in which power over policy is exercised by relatively few individuals and in which not all citizens are expected to share equally. That many of the 1970s arguments for "citizen control" were either supported, or dismissed, as radical attacks upon "the system" is ironic in that the case being advanced was not the overthrow of the establishment but only that a different and presumably wider range of groups be institutionalized into the established policy process. Lorimer (1972), for example, assaulted the hegemony of property development and real estate interests and called for the vitalizing of neighbourhoods and *their* groups' penetration into corridors of policy determination.

Liberal pluralism is premised upon the idea that group organization is central to an individual's ability to hold politicians accountable. This democratic façade is defensible if free and open competition among groups ensures that the public policy concerns of all significant communities are voiced. In addition to groups, dispersed power, and the quintessential liberal notion of competition, this world view also requires representative government institutions. Part of the problem with realizing direct democracy ideals in Canada lies in the practical applications and with the impossibility of subjecting existing representative forms to more direct democratic controls (Macpherson 1953: 53-55). Central to most modern debate in liberal democratic theory is a fundamental division of opinion over the relative autonomy of the representative once chosen (Pitkin 1972: esp. 144-67). At one extreme stand those populists who advance a *delegate theory* in which the legislature member is an agent to be guided in all critical decisions by the expressed wishes of constituents. In its most familiar form, Pitkin notes, this means that "the representative must do what his principal would do, must act as if the principal himself were acting" (1972: 144). At the other end are those espousing a more *detached theory*; they would agree with Edmond Burke who, in his 1774 speech to his electors of Bristol, argued that parliamentarians ought to exercise maximum discretion to act independently, based upon their own assessments of best public interest after careful reflection and informed legislative debate. (Burke was not on this occasion re-elected.)

Because it is somewhat taken for granted that elected representatives are essential for modern democracy, governing becomes more remote from citizenship. Even at the municipal level, the inability of local councillors to define the importance of their policy debates in terms that directly engage residents creates a sense of policy distance which, in the regular routine and not only the extreme instance, sets city hall policies as more distant from the personal political agendas of residents than those emanating from Ottawa. This in turn makes it more difficult for citizen electors to hold their local councils to consistent accountability. So, in the larger cities of Canada, the phrase "government closest to the people" is more an empty shell than practical reality.

Over the last political generation, little serious effort has been directed to setting traditional forms aside to craft an up-to-date type of citizen-based direct democracy modelled on the popular assemblies of the classic Athenian period. Even academic commentators find their apologia reduced to technical obstacles such as that policy matters are too complex; or that they require too prompt a response; or, in the final analysis, that there are simply too many citizens to permit modern assemblies. Beginning in the 1960s, a spectrum of social science research also suggested that modern voters were no longer citizens in the classic sense either, inasmuch as they tended to be uninformed, uninvolved, disinterested, and inactive, at least electorally (Bachrach 1967: 32-35). Election data of recent years indicating a consistent decrease in voter turnout at all levels can be cited in support of this proposition. Is this a good thing? Some American political scientists, like H. McCloskey (1964), argued that passivity was essential to system survival, that its decision avenues would otherwise be overloaded by continuous demand pressures. Critic Carole Pateman summarized this approach: "in the contemporary theory of democracy it is the participation of the minority elite that is crucial and the non-participation of the apathetic, ordinary man lacking in the feeling of political efficacy, that is regarded as the main bulwark against instability" (1970: 104). Others, like those within the social communications tradition of Karl Deutsch (1953), added the touch that citizen apathy also permits benevolent, educated, cosmopolitan political elites to arrange complex but mutually beneficial policy compromises which more strident and closely instructed delegate representatives could not possibly achieve. Democratic participation is thus stood on its head.

The inevitable critical response to these musings has usually begun with the assertion that whenever citizens become indifferent, it is because the policy system itself discourages non-manipulated direct involvement. Such criticism enervates arguments for specific ways to resurrect an active and continuous role for citizens in their own governing. As we have seen, the ideal of direct democracy persists as defining the unique character of Canadian local government. Drawing upon this, many students of, and activists within, local government presume that a more participatory democracy is both possible and desirable. They argue that individuals ought to be able both to participate *and* to govern (Higgins 1986: 24-27). But because this tradition has not been central in the dominant (and thus socialized) world view in Canadian cities, precise applications have consistently been hard to implement as they always appear to run against the practical grain.

For some time the generic term for direct participatory policy citizenship has been **grassroots democracy**. Grassroots was the term used in mining operations in the 1870s for the soil just under the surface. William Safire notes that "The phrase began with a rural flavor, implying simple virtues of the land as against city-slicker qualities" (1968: 171). It first came into more popular political use in the United States at the Bull Moose Convention in Chicago in 1912. Grassroots concepts also lift pragmatic ideas from both representative and direct democracy theoretical traditions (Masson 1994: 16-18). After the Second World War, political campaigners from all ideological persuasions used it to imply that they had drummed up wide elector support for their positions, and it was then adopted by Canadian anti-party activists. The rhetoric is now so enshrined as both totem and test of democratic proceedings that it is invoked, even by city hall administrators, to legitimate almost any populist behaviour. But without stronger cultural foundations, almost all local grassroots-styled institutions of recent years have quickly become both fraudulent and manipulative: the saddest example of unrealized grand ambitions along these lines was the Resident Advisory Group (RAG) experiment associated with Winnipeg Unicity in 1971 whose failure is discussed below. Even so, local government officials still appeal to such philosophical icons of the nineteenth century as Alexis de Tocqueville and John Stuart Mill in advocating the rebirth of the town meeting of colonial British North America.

Nostalgia for New England town gatherings has created a reference point and symbolic measure of success for any grassroots governing initiative. During the formative years of colonial settlement in the six New England states, town and township gatherings met local needs for basic public services (Bryce 1888: I, 532-36). The communities were socially homogenous, church and state distinctions were less clear, and political assemblies were social occasions. In practice, all male settlers of age within a roughly half-mile radius of the central meeting house—church, school or town hall—were eligible to participate, speak, and vote. Both the town and its immediate rural areas were thus involved. Meetings were called at least once a year, but more typically met three or four times annually. Budgets were passed, accounts approved, and proposed taxes agreed upon. A group of three to nine "select-men" were chosen each year to oversee municipal works between town sessions, but their decisions had to be sanctioned by their fellow citizens. Direct accountability was clear and immediate. A school committee was always separately selected.

As the form evolved, it was Bryce's assessment that "no better school of politics can be imagined, nor any method of managing local affairs more certain to prevent jobbery and waste, to stimulate vigilance and breed contentment" (1888: I, 534). Just as Mill had mused, local self-government seemed to provide a suitable training ground for citizenship with a potential for inculcating democratic behaviours on a wider scale. Bryce added the footnote, however, that the whole business failed if it became too large or was adulterated by the Irish or French-Canadians whom he considered too easily susceptible to demagoguery. Nonetheless, the basic success of the form is generally recognized: in Rhode Island, it was the towns which created the state; in Massachusetts, towns were the only politically corporate bodies until 1821; and throughout New England, the form is still recognizable today.

In Canada, the town meeting dates back to its practice in Nova Scotia for a few months in 1795. Lord Durham noted that in the early nineteenth century similar gatherings often ran in parallel with the quarter sessions operation, both of which accepted the notion of local initiative to construct local public works. These informal town meetings in the local regions around Niagara and Kingston were not, strictly speaking, legal, but were not disallowed by the Crown. This governing by town meeting was rather intermittent, and the common weal was small enough in those times that all participants could be consulted. Forms of direct democracy persisted well into the twentieth century in the rural communities of Canada. S.M. Lipset, in his *Agrarian Socialism*, observed that in Saskatchewan in the 1950s available local offices in school boards, municipalities, hospital, and other districts meant that "there is one position available for every two or three farmers" (1950: 200) if you added in various cooperatives and so forth. About 15 per cent of the rural population held elective posts exclusive of church, community organizations, fraternal lodges, and the like.

Mill and de Tocqueville both believed that local self-government was desirable in, but not a necessary condition for, a national democratic state. Both also recognized, as did Bryce, that large cities presented different criteria that detracted from possibilities for direct participation. Higgins later observed that liberal democrats have been "muddled" in their appreciation of the potential for city democracy, noting that Mill shared with de Tocqueville the view that "the magnitude of needs in an industrial age for government services in large cities is such that units of government there must be relatively large, and large size mitigates against participatory, representative, [sic] local government" (1986: 16).

The ideal of the town meeting as a democratic model for today's society is something of a deceit for, as E.E. Schattschneider put it: "Primitive democratic theorists never tire of telling us that democracy was designed to work in New England town meetings, not in a modern national state. The analysis is fatuous. We might as well attempt to return to a handicraft economy" (1960: 138). Even Bryce developed, upon reflection, serious reservations about de Tocqueville as theorist and as student of practice, calling him one who "soars far from the ground and is often lost in the clouds of his own somber meditations" (1888: II, 1547). Yet such models drawn from historic antecedents serve a valid purpose for evaluating existing institutions and pointing to a path for their betterment.

Let us now explore some of the participatory possibilities in the conventional processes of elected representation by examining direct opportunities for institutionalized citizen participation that is more continuous than casting a yea or nay vote for incumbents every three or so years. We reject as insufficient Joseph Schumpeter's familiar mid-twentieth century concept of democratic process: "Democracy means only that the people have the opportunity of accepting or refusing the men who are to rule them" (1943: 285). Of course Schumpeter also thought that "bombarding" representatives with letters was a noxious practice instead of seeing it as one way in which citizens can make their voices heard.

3.2.1 A ladder of electoral participation

For individual participation in the electoral process, the act of voting is the greatest exertion to which most people will commit. We will note, in Chapter 5, the many factors which have led to a situation in which, in the normal course of events, two-thirds of citizens choose not to vote in city elections or to participate in electoral activities. By these measures, elections seem to constitute something of a democratic fraud. Table 3.1 provides a Guttman scale of possible municipal campaign involvement, which shows that anyone who performs a higher level of task (such as raising money) will in all probability have undertaken all lower ranked activities.

This model identifies three classes of involvement above apathy (as measured by non-voting). At the highest rank are the **political gladiators**, a group comprising fewer than 5 per cent of the population and for whom electoral politics is a consummate passion and an almost full-time avocation. Especially in the limited territory of one city, most will be well-known to each other from partisan struggles federally and provincially. Under non-partisan

Table 3.1: A Ladder of Local Electoral Participation

Highest Activities: The Political Gladiators (3 to 5 per cent)
  1. Holding a public (or party) office.
  2. Being a candidate for public office.
  3. Soliciting party funds.
  4. Attending a strategy meeting or caucus.
  5. Becoming an active member in a political group.
  6. Contributing time in a political campaign.

Midway Activities: The Intermediaries (5 to 9 per cent)
  7. Attending a public rally or political meeting.
  8. Making a monetary contribution to a local candidate or party.
  9. Contacting a public official or political candidate.

Lowest Activities: The Spectator-Participants (25 to 40 per cent)
  10. Wearing a button; putting up a lawn sign.
  11. Attempting to convince someone to vote a certain way.
  12. Initiating a political discussion about the election.
  13. Voting.
  14. Being aware of electoral politics.

Non-participant (50 to 75 per cent)

Sources: Adapted from Milbrath 1965: 18; Mishler 1979: 39-64; Van Loon and Whittington 1996: 420-22.

conditions, they may well sign up as a team for local purposes; certainly, an officially non-partisan local candidate will turn first to those persons who are known to have political experience and a track record. Boss Plunkitt put it best: "Me and the Republicans are enemies just one day of the year—election day. Then we fight tooth and nail. The rest of the time it's live and let live with us" (Riordan 1903: 38).

The next small cohort is the intermediaries, individuals whose activities are sufficiently important to suggest that they may be in transition from political spectators to activists. Most of us are such spectator-participants, whose interest waxes from knowledge that there may be an election underway to identifying ourselves openly with a campaign or cause by button, lawn sign, or car bumper sticker. By the way, one proof of the Guttman scale is that anyone with a lawn sign is virtually certain to vote on election day.

The evidence for this hierarchy in city elections comes from the best available data supported by ballpark calculations. For instance, we know that no more than 5 per cent of Canadians belong to a political party at any level of government in Canada. Survey evidence also suggests that less than one-quarter of respondents during a federal campaign try to convince someone to vote a particular way. Only one in 30 is a financial donor, and only 5 per cent recall being asked to give to political parties (see Milbrath 1965: 18;

Mishler 1979: 39-64; Van Loon and Whittington 1996: 420-22). The difference in the hierarchy for municipal politics from the federal and provincial is that the pool of intermediaries shrinks dramatically.

Electoral participation is positively related to income and other measures of higher social status. In this sense, the real world of democracy is also somewhat of a demographic fraud. The gladiators are those men and women in business and the professions who have sufficient control over their own time and access to enough wealth to indulge their personal passion for elections nearly full time. They are also more cosmopolitan in interpersonal contacts and outlook, and their interest in elections tends to encompass all levels of the body politic. They have increasingly become able to transfer their attention from federal to provincial to city elections as the stakes of the latter two arenas of governmental policy have become so much more important. In this process, they have inverted Mill's hope that the local would serve as the training ground for national statesmen. However, at the local level the voters have not followed along.

This is only a record of electoral activities and does not take into account other important involvement in local policy arenas, such as, at the extreme, protest demonstrations. However, were one to march against city hall to protest flagrant disregard for sound environmental practices, but did not bother to vote because "It doesn't matter, they're all the same," then one would be classified as apathetic in this particular political hierarchy. Such skepticism about voting has been countered by efforts to generate a style of more directly accountable self-government.

3.2.2 Direct citizen democracy

3.2.2.1 POPULISM

Support for direct democracy in Canada's major metropolitan areas results from the merger of several trends. The logic defining North American participatory demands derives from populism which, as a political movement, gains credence as traditional hierarchical forms of organization lose unquestioning public allegiance. The difference between current and past pressures for populism is that private as well as public forms of it are under the hammer. As an ideology, populism appears to be as well explained by its targets as by its own basic principles. The target is virtually any identifiable pattern of privilege, set of elite beliefs, or large-scale hierarchical organization. It will be noted later that populism both describes an integrated set of beliefs and defines a more widely based social movement. To be the latter implies that a rather plump assemblage of economic, social, or political preconditions have generated disruptive stress upon the political community (Gibbins and Youngman 1996: 196-224). These conditions produce coincident, but often individually packaged, sets of grievances which, when taken together, produces what Americans like to style as the revolt of the grassroots.

As we have seen, legitimacy for more direct democratic forms is the legacy of eighteenth-century town meetings both in Canada and the United States. The modern problem, as predicted by de Tocqueville and Mill, lies in size: the bigger the community, the less the reasonable chance for fair and open public participation. Community leaders during the third reform period of the 1960s and 1970s tried to apply variations of direct democracy to general policy-making by modifying the *structures* of governing. Generally these efforts failed, and the movement fizzled off into concentration on reform of the policy *process*, ultimately into forms of individual direct action on specific issues resulting sometimes in success in particular cases. The recent response by government officials to such process demands has been to treat individuals as consumers—as clients not citizens.

The combination of structural failure with achievements through process on individual issues has two consequences. First, the size of the future city has become less relevant, except perhaps for matters of economy of scale, division of labour, and the acquisition of professional specialists and their technologies. Second, elected and appointed office-holders will be forced to respond to the well-articulated, often narrow demands made by expertly qualified, politically skillful and quickly mobilized issue movements. As these networked communities develop competency in defining specific issues so as to win priority on the wider public agenda, very real grassroots democracy may begin to express itself.

The distinguishing themes of any populist revolt are always suspicion and then rejection of large-scale organization in the form of political parties, "big business" corporations, private-sector trade unions, or traditional religious denominations. Even conventional news media, the newspapers, lose their cachet as sources of primary information as they become just another part of massive conglomerates which reduce journalism to entertainment. Individuals can now find their own primary information on the Internet. Populists value individual accomplishment, usually in the face of some considerable adversity, as the mark of success. And, because any populist challenge to conventional lines of authority is rooted in the individual, it follows that traditional democratic political avenues must also be recast to accommodate direct personal participation, control, and accountability. So, populists combine a nostalgia for rugged frontier-style individualism—you're only what you make of yourself—with a reliance on direct action to build a more utopian community.

The essential problem for any attempts to recreate the populism of the New England town meeting in urban Canada is the practical matter of community size. Concerning the town meeting mythology, Peter Bachrach argued that "viable democratic theory can hardly be built upon a dream that has not the remotest chance of being realized" (1967: 6). Even the great optimist Robert Dahl concedes that the "modern city cannot be a polis" (1967: 969). Any modern reformer must directly confront the fundamental problem of size as a barrier to more participatory democracy. Professor and town councillor L.J. Sharpe (1981) theorized that a threshold community size of about 50,000 is the largest that will permit direct citizen involvement, and Dahl (1967; Dahl and Tuft 1973) estimates the optimum to lie between that number and around 200,000. This may be, but the reality is that there is no single optimal maximum, nor for that matter minimum, size (apart from one) for a direct democratic unit of governing.

A balance must always be struck between any value associated with direct participation and what that involvement is able to influence. In other words, large cities have more powers, greater resources, and wider functional diversity at the same time as their governing representatives may seem more remote and influencing them is more costly in time and money (Keating 1995: 119-21). The capacity to make decisions directly has been found to diminish once a community is larger than about 8,000 residents; yet, if the representative processes of larger cities can be shown to be comprehensible and genuinely accessible to residents, their citizens will continue to legitimize those processes by participation in them. The corollary is also true, even for smaller communities: democratic decentralization does not necessarily mean effective citizen control if representatives unaccountable for their actions or long-standing elitist power structures remain intact. David Rayside discovered that even in an Ontario community of under 3,500, for example, "the agenda of local politics excludes anything that might be construed as interfering in the business of business" (1989: 117). Being smaller does not necessarily guarantee having sway over matters of local substance.

3.2.2.2 THE THIRD PERIOD OF MUNICIPAL REFORM

During the third period of municipal reform in Canada in the 1960s and 1970s, some community leaders tried to realize direct democracy through modifying the structures of governing. These efforts to pioneer methods of organizing the citizen into direct involvement arose out of, and in reaction to, the apolitical "local management for commercial ends" form engineered in 1900. Essentially—and not at all radical except as so defined by prevailing public ideologies—the aim was to attain responsible individual control over decisions most affecting everyday living. Some of these procedural stabs at direct democratic forms took legitimacy from the town meeting, but the mechanism in reality came from the progressivism of the post-First World War era. Thus, neighbourhood democracy was based on ideals of administrative decentralization, community organization, and participatory politics (Higgins 1986: 261-67). In this sense, the structure of the democratic state was rethought so as to resemble the democratic equivalent of Ukrainian *matroshka*, or stacking dolls. Each level from the smallest was progressively larger, but each was legitimate and possessed a more or less expansive realm of authority while the whole itself maintained an overall integrity.

Practical applications of such progressivism found their fullest expression in town planning and community development (P.J. Smith 1995: 234-37; Draper 1971). More than most public officials, professionally trained urban planners confront a fundamental gap between their readings of objective community interest—the broader public whom they serve—and of the elected councillors who represent that interest for a time and who seem determined to hold on to the power to decide the precise application of the public interest. As P.J. Smith puts it, "Where planners were once defined as experts on future urban forms, today it is just as important that they bring the skills of mediators, facilitators, and *animateurs* to the community-planning process. That may blur the boundary between 'administration' and 'politics'" (1995: 237). Any public interest is by definition broadly shared and thus subject to conflicting interpretation. Moreover, it is in the nature of political power to shift its locus from time to time. Therein lies the ethical dilemma for urban planners.

For a short cycle in the 1970s, in opposition to such specifically neighbourhood intrusive projects as new freeways into Chinatown, Mill Creek, and Spadina respectively, citizen advocacy and community activism enjoyed wider, but still social elite, support in major cities like Vancouver, Edmonton, and Toronto. It was possible then to envisage a range of possibilities for direct citizen participation, brightly described in such writing as Sherry Arnstein's *The Ladder of Participation* (1969) and subscribed to enthusiastically by Toronto's Bureau of Municipal Research (BMR 1975: 46). This brief flirtation with a democracy sculpted along lines of classic citizenship depended upon citizens who were well informed, constantly attentive to public issues, and actively engaged. In theory, direct citizen participation in local governing ranged along a continuum from acquiring information, through consultation and partnership, into full citizen control, and from sustained listening to specific institutionalized choices. This could be achieved through traditional public hearings and the use of aldermanic ward offices; to written briefs or formal petitions and the appointment of citizens to functionally specific boards and commissions; to task forces and advisory committees; and, finally, to citizen control *via* plebiscites or some form of ward council.

At this last extreme, Milton Kotler, in his *Neighbourhood Government: The Local Foundations of Political Life* (1968) represents those who planned to decentralize the city into partly autonomous neighbourhood corporations with direct local control over some community services. The only *genuine* attempt to realize such an ideal as this last in Canada was the **community committee** concept associated with Winnipeg Unicity through which libraries, parks, and limited planning controls were to be decentralized to neighbourhood assemblies. The 50-person council was divided geographically into 12 communities of three to five wards with roughly the same boundaries as the previous municipalities. As subcommittees of council, these communities were to have formal standing over services deemed "purely local" and to facilitate links between citizens and their councillors (Brownstone and Plunkett 1983: 68–69). There would be at least annual assemblies which all residents might attend and at which these residents would elect advisers, the RAGs, to assist councillors on a more-or-less ongoing basis.

As it turned out, over the course of a brief political generation, this ideal plan—as others on the "participatory ladder"—became nothing more than a participatory fraud. The idea of appointing prominent citizens to boards in functional areas such as parks, planning, libraries, or policing, for example, had been an intrinsic element in the late nineteenth-century reform envelope. It was thought that panels of blue ribbon citizens, being themselves beyond reproach, would both remove specific functional matters "from politics" and apply only objective expertise to policy matters. Elected officials, given the power of appointment, quickly took to the concept as ducks to water and in assessing who might be considered a responsible citizen used a measure similar to that of the prime minister in appointing persons to serve in the Senate. Boards were used as patronage plums, for status ends if not for gratuities. They also proved useful as devices to diffuse the accountability of councillors, especially in difficult matters of zoning variance. Neighbourhood government and ward offices were subverted for largely propaganda ends; further, when acting in an ombudsman capacity, they inevitably enhanced the reputations of incumbent officials.

Even plebiscites may be distorted in their application. For example, in 1977 the very pro-development council of the Edmonton suburb Spruce Grove was in a quandary when residents voted 58 per cent against an annexation of lands to be serviced for development. The developer assuaged council's angst and assured a majority vote not to oppose his annexation initiative before the provincial board when he noted that public opinion against annexation had mellowed "because the last annexation had been more strongly opposed by citizens" (*Edmonton Journal*, 2 March 1977). Over the years, most recently in 1996, the Vancouver Non-Partisan Association (NPA) council tried to defuse a plebiscite favouring the establishment of wards by drafting an intricate package of alternatives among which residents had to choose one. If voters were first to choose to abandon the city-wide vote by 60 per cent, then 60 per cent would have to agree on the same system from among four options. Needless to say, this did not happen.

Sadly, city politicians publicly supportive of 1970s grassroots concepts have also systematically "redefined grass-roots democracy in such a way that they could claim it was being practiced in their community and then carried on as usual" (Masson 1994: 17). In Canada, the boldest attempt to codify citizen involvement on a more permanent basis was the ideal of the community committee RAGs program proposed for Winnipeg Unicity. All area residents attending an annual general meeting were to choose RAGs "to advise and assist" councillors; the method of selecting the RAGs was intentionally left to each city neighbourhood itself. However, the provincial government found itself situated between those who strongly supported total unification and those concerned with preserving "local identity" (Brownstone and Plunkett 1983: 72-75). Furthermore, the MLAs did not trust citizens to behave wisely; the legislation permitted the newly elected city councillors to reduce the few powers assigned to the community committees, and they did so quickly. By 1977, the Unicity Act was also amended to a council of 29—today, it is 15—and the number of community committees to six—and, today, they are gone.

Experience in the United States has shown that district councils can work well when cities are prepared to subsidize at least an office and an organizer (Osborne and Gaebler 1992: 74-75). In Winnipeg, the barely token commitment to RAGs and community committees by authorities soon dissolved into cynicism and disenchantment for citizens as they became "the preserve of the local councillors, small groups of activist-minded citizens, and developers and builders who must appear in such forums to gain a zoning variation or a subdivision approval" (Axworthy 1980: 118). Even the original legislation's principal authors conceded that by eliminating smallness and the capacity of community residents to get to know one another, "the system's participatory potential was reduced" (Brownstone and Plunkett 1983: 140). Just as students do not find it necessary to attend lectures that have no bearing on final exams, citizens found no time to participate in meetings without consequence. Grassroots democracy was proven incompatible with the façade of administrative decentralization used by councils to assuage and manipulate citizen demands for greater involvement.

In the United States, Saul Alinsky (1971) moved further to the last logical rung or extension of the ladder in the form of episodic confrontation with, and direct action against, community power centres within the urban regime. Problems with Alinsky-style radicalism developed with the flattening of traditional hierarchies in organizations in the latter part of the twentieth century and the lessening salience of their influence. As hierarchies of power diminish, so too does the political importance of those for whom they have provided a target. By the turn of this century, these crusades in North American local communities were few, and debates from the third reform phase remained only reminders of possibilities. While some still see potential in local government as a laboratory for innovation in public participation, and label such opportunity as citizen engagement, to describe council assemblies as meeting any criteria for "open public forums" while relishing the joyless routinization of organized participation smacks rather of cheerleading from the public officials' bleachers (note Graham and Phillips 1998: 94, 114, 136–37).

3.2.2.3 DIRECT ACTION ON SPECIFIC ISSUES

So, the institutionalization of direct democracy having failed, in time the reform movement splintered into the process of direct action on specific issues. In part this was because, as Leo wrote, "Unfortunately, the tradition of the reform movement has left us with a system of municipal government which, for the most part, is neither adequately representative of the electorate, nor genuinely accountable to it" (1977: 64). As did other 1960s reformers concerned with structural changes, he foresaw "far-reaching institutional reform" as the only possible corrective to this inveterate dual predicament. But, on the process side of politics, trying to persuade those in authority to amend the very procedures which have established their authority in the first place so as to include applications of popular democracy has proven difficult. The early optimism of third-wave reform academic theorists was crushed within a generation.

Although impressive electoral gains were accomplished by third-wave reformers in the 1970s in Vancouver, Toronto, and Edmonton, their tenuous hold on majority power, when combined with the pressing necessities of daily policy decisions, gave little latitude for procedural radicalism. The reform movement's most impressive victory arguably came, as a last gasp, in Montreal in 1986. While in opposition to the regime of Mayor Jean Drapeau, the Montreal Citizens Movement (MCM), formed in 1974 with a loosely socialist focus, highlighted grassroots mass organizing rather than traditional electoral politics. The leadership's avowed intent was "to decentralize administration by dispersing decision-making powers throughout the city's neighbourhoods" (Thomas 1995: 123). In 1986 the party won all but three council seats. However, once in power, and under Mayor Jean Doré's leadership, the caucus gradually discouraged participatory forms apart from instituting a question period for citizens prior to formal council meetings. Abandoned was "the development of processes to incorporate the views of its grass roots into its policy" (Thomas 1995: 126). As Thomas precisely documents, the focus drifted into organizational success, and that was increasingly measured by re-election prospects at the expense of democratizing initiatives. In 1994, a ragtag coalition of ideological misfits labelling itself "Vision Montreal" defeated the MCM by winning 39 of the 51 council seats, leaving the MCM with six and Mayor Doré defeated.

The experience in Montreal and in Winnipeg's community committees and RAGs reveals that, to no surprise, locally elected politicians in Canada have persistently tended to hoard control. One lesson is that it seems far easier to disperse accountability than authority. Where local parties have existed, Canadian electors have found it better to condemn the whole lot for broken trust.

3.2.2.4 THE FAILURE OF REFORMING STRUCTURE AND PROCESS

Multiple failures of even modest official efforts to structure continuous direct participation in city-regions across Canada resulted in reduced trust in such initiatives and, ultimately, a decline in demand for them. As established institutions reverted to chronic habits of inertia, vested hierarchy, and the exploitation of process by office-holders, citizens simply disengaged. The lack of transparency in process from both elected representatives and their bureaucrats and procedural sabotage—such as shortening time lines to disadvantage those seeking alternatives to "official" plans, programs, or projects—gave citizens ineradicable lessons in futility. To the surprise of very few, active interest in local public policy structures was replaced with cynicism and a sense of distance. Even in national politics, two-thirds of Canadians surveyed "have little or no confidence in their political leaders" and rate elected representatives as only slightly more worthy of trust than used car dealers (Zussman 1997: 239-41). The federal general election survey of 1997 found that 88 per cent of respondents agreed with the statement that "politicians are ready to lie to get elected." More than half "strongly agreed" and 57 per cent believed that "quite a few people running the government are a little crooked" (<http://www.isr.yorku.ca/ISR>). Indeed, the trend against identifying oneself with a traditional party actually began late in the third reform period and gained significant momentum by the late 1980s. The

Canadian experience in this is not unique: in 17 of 21 industrialized countries, the percentage of people surveyed who supported the proposition that "more respect for authority would be a good thing" weakened significantly after 1981, and ties to historic and centralized political institutions declined apace (Clark 1994a: 32-59; Zussman 1997: 243-48).

Municipal politics in particular appear to have grown more individual. This partially explains the paradox mentioned by David Zussman: Canadians have greater personal capacity to participate more fully in politics in that they have never been more educated or interested in political issues, but, at the same time, their attachments to traditional vehicles for participating has never been lower. He writes: "citizens are choosing different avenues, mechanisms and styles for their political participation" (1997: 234-35). Sustained by cynicism with their representatives, attempts to resurrect more direct democratic forms by the current generation of electors focus on specific policies at the community level in issues networks. Structure may still be tangentially important; for instance, in 1999, Los Angeles voters rejected a larger city council and supported the placing of key zoning approvals at the neighbourhood level, and in 1997 neighbourhood leaders tried to rally residents against the Toronto Megacity initiative (as also happened in Montreal three years later). People may be less likely to vote but be more willing to protest city hall or to boycott private corporations for political motives.

Concerns from new agendas now sustain active intervention. Quality of life issues—schools, policing, the safety of drinking water—are the most local policies of all. In this new political culture of micro-control, the issues are in the general policy worlds of environmentalism, ecology, urban growth management, feminism (and abortion), gay and lesbian rights, "and other consumption and life-style concerns" (Clark 1994a: 23). It is the important finding of Clark and his 38-nation international research team that increasingly people's salient interests no longer rest in party or class but in their identification with highly personalized issues, such as day care or recycling garbage. When grouped around an identifying axis—environmentalism or feminism, for instance—multiple parallel activities may be described as a new social movement, a more complex set of phenomena to be described and discussed in Chapter 8. Established local authorities have found it increasingly difficult to respond because coalitions are constantly reforming and new leaders emerging from issue to issue.

3.2.3 New theories defuse direct participation

At the peak of the third reform period, Leo wrote that "If the demand for greater citizen involvement in the making of local government decisions continues to grow as it has in the past decade, it may become necessary to establish a regularized, on-going process of citizen participation and make it one of the formal institutions of local government" (1977: 64). Neither part of this equation ever materialized. What the state at all levels has done is to treat particular communities as clients and individual citizens as customers.

Civic political leadership interpreted diminished public interest in the wider issue arenas of the councils' own political lives (such as budgets or General Municipal Plans) as justification to decelerate further democratic decentralizing. Councillors and their closest advisers retreated to the corporate enterprise strand of urban political culture (and public choice theory) to regard citizens as individual purchasers of services. This allowed specific issue policy networks to bully the discussion in the precise matters that interested their clients. The main catalyst for these developments has been the fiscal austerity now embracing local governments internationally and which has forced a redefinition of citizenship to fit conditions of persistent revenue shortage.

The **governance** concept so fashionable lately is American in origin and contends that citizens are "customers" and that governing itself is an exchange and needs to be "customer-driven" (Osborne and Gaebler 1992: 166-94). Some apologists cultivate the illusion that demand pressure has been alleviated through the selective application of "user fees" and the so-called **co-production of services** both with private agencies and for-profit enterprises. The 1990s notion of co-production implies that government works in a public-private partnership (PPP) with neighbourhood associations, service clubs, private agencies, and even business corporations to provide or maintain a facility or service (such as a hockey rink, neighbourhood park, drop-in centre, or a preventive social service like visiting seniors) at lower cost and with a presumed greater sensitivity to consumer need (Tindal and Tindal 2000: 354-56). Service consumers pony up capital and operating costs, in cash or kind, by working fund-raising bingos and casinos or volunteering construction and maintenance labour. In a rather real sense, communities have been forced by exigency to return to a style reminiscent of the nineteenth century, even for road building and public health. But, to be very clear as to language, co-production today is not a form of direct citizen participation since it is not the product of devolved authority and the alternative would be no service at all. As well, continuing accountability tends to be defused through co-production activities: in the event of policy collapse, if everyone is implicated, then no one can be directly responsible.

Fees are not, strictly speaking, user-based if *everyone* must pay, as in the case of garbage collection, or if they are to be ideologically applied, as in the case of public roadways funded 100 per cent through general revenues at the same time as public transit is only partly subsidized. The new governance ideas, by separating out, identifying as users, and separately charging individual groups in the community, directly confront a long-standing virtue of public institutions by which they present a kind of non-discriminatory policy blindness through their universalism.

This increasingly fractured view of democratic governing as a benign style of paternalism is only possible given a view of the urban community as being so fragmented into particular population identities that representative government is essentially an umpire, rising over the fray so as to sort and spread, sparingly, the public largesse. The downside to such particularist treatment of client groups is that each identity must be defined by needs as distinct and somehow unequal, which coincidentally frustrates that mixing of economic classes and ethnic communities that could constitute a stronger locus for the whole Canadian democratic identity. The stoking of possible resentments arising out of inequitable policy treatment reduces efficacy within the system by undermining any sense of objective public trust and by eroding the capacity of public institutions to offer the minimum common denominator programs that we call the safety net.

What is overlooked in the enthusiasm to reinvent governing is that the "spirit of entrepreneurialism" is not a monopoly of corporate enterprise. The central claim is that "participatory democracy" should be an important component of entrepreneurial governing (Osborne and Gaebler 1992: 15, 74). Yet, local politicians appear to have accepted the business efficiency line while rejecting the idea of involvement. As Osborne and Gaebler, the authors of *Reinventing Government*, very carefully note, privatization is only one answer, one arrow in the quiver of governing possibilities; it is not the sole solution (1992: 45). Their point is that while business usually does some things better in the delivery of specific services, it is not the only way to run even such a profoundly service-oriented government as the municipal. Public service may well be judged by assorted business performance measures and be the better for it. But, as an essential *caveat*, Tindal and Tindal approvingly cite the city administrator of Rossland, British Columbia as observing that "the people are neither clients nor customers ... they are the owners" (2000: 366).

One recent practical application of the new entrepreneurial spirit is community policing (for example, Neighbourhood Watch) in which citizens become "the eyes and ears" of the force. It has been effective in major American inner cities like Houston, New York, and Tulsa because it is grounded in widespread citizen self-help and neighbourhood patrol interventions. The concept has become more than a little defrauded when transferred to Canada where it is used mainly as a budget alternative to sustained street patrols; the police increasingly prove unable to respond quickly to duress, and citizens as service shoppers must hobble to police mini-stations with their complaints. Another application is the newly established "resource centres" for urban Aboriginal people in Calgary, Winnipeg, or Saskatoon where they at least may receive sensitive moral support, if little more. Similarly, there are overnight sanctuaries for those seeking refuge from spousal abuse in city cores (though not usually their suburban fringes), with possible openings for those from across the metropolitan region. The rule becomes that potential consumers of these services must anticipate their futures and choose their domicile location with an eye to municipal boundaries.

Ideas for customer-centred government may cause the public itself to measure government performance only against private-sector companies. This perception, reinforced from the top, forgets that different rules exist for public operations; these include open accountability, equity in operations, and equitable service for the voiceless many. The private bureaucracy of the corporate world is not congenitally superior to that of the public sphere, nor is it universal. By their own niche choices and quest for profitability, corporations target preferred customers who are never expected to participate directly in determining corporate direction. Even politically articulate elites may overlook the reality that the state, even at the local level, is a universal enterprise and, by definition, must serve a public interest that includes service to various minorities which may be screened from consideration by private operations. Still, and to the good, even the perception of a customer-sensitive public operation can hold positive outcomes. Osborne and Gaebler list in their "governance bible" some 17 ways in which American local governments have formally heard the voice of "the customer" through complaint tracking and the use of ombudspersons to focus groups and customer councils (1992: 177-79). Given the demonstration impacts of social science fads, most of these are now already deployed with limiting degrees of belief and enthusiasm across all of Canada's city-regions.

3.2.4 New communications and the metropolitan agenda

Past experiences with local democratic practices are today given texture by new realities. Within the last generation a new global culture has emerged, one that has opened national political cultures to significant cross-polity influences. Although the wider impacts of the globalization phenomenon will be discussed in Chapter 14, it is important to note here that the emergence of a new, worldwide, and in some respects widely shared political culture centred in city-regions has placed positive stress on established governing arrangements.

The integrated economy of the world has encountered frustrations with conventional local governing arrangements and the incongruence between structure and culture. As globalization becomes synonymous with persistent activity, instant knowledge, dramatic experience, and constant change, its new educated work force, familiar with information technologies (IT), will apply new standards to city management. In this hurly-burly environment, institutionalized activities that do not offer changing choices for self-expression will lose out.

Because of their experience with managing and adapting under constant pressure, new and specific-issue social movements do not fit conveniently onto any left to right spectrum. The new metropolitan agenda of city-regions is now not only internationally derived but focused on matters under local control. Thus, conventional media are often befuddled, reporting the same group orchestrating the same event on the same day as being both radically reactionary and belligerently progressive.

The universalism of electronically disseminated world culture does not necessarily represent uniformity of thinking, however. It does mean that political culture is more susceptible to a variety of outside influences. The corollary is that it also opens a wider audience for individual excellence. Just as the custodians of the Latin-rooted languages have found contamination by the ubiquitous use of English on the Internet, a similar contagion extends to previously insular national public policies when they are subjected to external standards in judging performance and outcomes, often at the most local of levels.

The new international political culture is grounded in a style of populism, which means that citizens as individuals may apply more universal standards to their lifestyles, while activist organizations gain the shape-shifting spontaneity of quicksilver. In Canada specifically, the organization of province-wide local governing institutions foundered early in the twentieth century due to problems of distance, poor transportation, and weak or delayed lines of communication. Today, use of contemporary communications to demand rapid policy responses may overwhelm the structures devised to cope with those very different early barriers. More generally, the social identities of the past which grew out of race, nation, class, religion, and even gender are today confronted by new collective identities rooted in immediate experiences. Personal consciousness has evolved into an increased awareness of what persons who are generally similar but living elsewhere are doing and feeling. The power of such knowledge is obvious. When electronic images of natural disasters such as the 2004 tsunami in southeast Asia or of the terrorist attack on the World Trade Center in New York were immediately spread on the Internet, this fostered a sense of world engagement with the plight of the victims.

The new language of **citizen engagement** that describes these phenomena captures old ideas and their application with new words and an optimistic liberal jargon. The behaviour of engaged citizens, though, is central to modern populist expression in urban areas (Clark 1994a: 23-28). In practical terms this means that social class has been removed as an organizing principle, leaving only individuals and their personal choices. The democratic struggle is no longer between socialism and market capitalism, but has been redefined as a new alignment of self-expressed egalitarianism based on what people directly want from life versus any established hierarchy's orthodoxies. In this new language of identity (and echoing Arthur Bentley in 1908), one frequent assertion is that the individual personality is a complex compendium of many attachments from any of which a political identity may emerge. Political action may be required of each person in certain circumstances, and individuals will respond on the basis of personal experience. For example, a student so preoccupied with his or her studies as to be politically unaware and inactive may find it necessary to join others in confronting authority should draconian fee increases be unexpectedly announced.

Stuart Hall has written expressively of these new political identities and argues that the more profound expressions of "the local" come from within the cultural revolution fostered by IT. Groups formerly at the margins of power in social life now fight for recognition of their identity. Formerly subordinate communities in the arts or identified by gender, ethnicity, or shared space, "have acquired through struggle, sometimes in very marginalized ways, the means to speak for themselves for the first time" (Hall 1991: 34). The fluidity of this new discourse means that established urban regimes are threatened by new local communities as these latter can now, at last, see new ways to define themselves to others. Even Osborne and Gaebler have gingerly noted "What Americans *do* hunger for is more control over matters that directly affect their lives: public safety, their children's schools, the developers who want to change their neighborhoods" (1992: 74). These activities involve what in the UK is labelled the hands-on work of the "low politics" that shapes daily lives and local communities. It is in this context that Osborne and Gaebler (1992), among many other observers, note how many long hours individuals now devote to improving their community organizations while eschewing conventional party politics. While the enormity of the scale of global issues may appear overwhelming, citizenship stemming from the personal need to make a difference has opened new possibilities in communities without borders of such smaller scale that direct participation appears to matter.

For individual political behaviour, the common expression has increasingly been opposition to any form of tightly structured institutions as being politically appropriate. This has meant more direct personal action and expectation of immediate accountability. Zussman writes that "Information technology has in fact contributed to many of the decentralizing and democratizing tendencies we have witnessed over the past few years. It has been widely remarked that the electronic media have contributed to the fall of tyrannical regimes, including the Marcos dictatorship in the Philippines and communist rule in East Germany and in the former Soviet Union" (1997: 251). Information technologists readily argue that technology is deadly to all forms of hierarchy; information cannot be censored and is equally accessible to all. Osborne and Gaebler have also noted that "People and movements that were seen only a few years ago as hopelessly isolated and idealistic are now leading revolutions and governing nations" (1992: 330).

The existence of the World Wide Web has also changed the face of election campaigning in First World countries. In 1998, Jesse Ventura won the Minnesota gubernatorial race as an anti-establishment independent candidate by side-stepping the major parties by campaigning on the Internet. He had a most unconventional and non-hierarchical background as a professional wrestler, B-movie star, and mayor of Brooklyn Park, a small suburb of Minneapolis. His campaign circumvented traditional gatekeepers and any real need for well-financed party support, labour or business endorsement, or sympathetic media. Electors sized up his message personally, and so many of them chose to spread the word (just as word of mouth can propel an unlikely movie to box office success) that Ventura had to open a physical location for his campaign headquarters "because he needed a place to store 'Jesse for Governor' T-shirts" (Francis 1999). By 2000, three-quarters of American Senate candidates had an Internet site, as did nearly all gubernatorial candidates. Even in local elections, all British Labour candidates are provided with laptops to link them instantaneously to party headquarters for research. The use of the Internet in 2004 permitted a national Green Party campaign for Canada's 308 constituencies; to most voters, local candidates were names only, a spot on the ballot for voters who had informed themselves about platform positions through the websites.

By the turn of the century in 2000, Angus Reid Group research of Internet access among school children across 16 countries concluded that Canada placed second to Sweden with 74 per cent having access at school and 71 per cent at home: Sweden's results were 78 and 80 per cent respectively (Foss 2000). Data for young people in the United States showed 59 per cent with Internet access at school and 68 per cent with access at home. The growth in usage was rapid: in 1999, for example, surveys revealed that 55 per cent of Canadians used the Internet; in 2000 that number surpassed 70 per cent. The common direction of the data is clear, and the results are global.

Possibilities for direct action are now knowable, the data bases from which to query authority are available, and they are now individually accessible in the home.

In conclusion, it should be noted that the political culture of the new localism is now expressed in urban locales, operating with more information yet less certainty of outcome. An ironic consequence of global connections, it has grown out of a perception that the only tangible democratic control lies in self-governing. Citizenship means influence, influence requires direct participation, and direct participation occurs most likely when making choices whose outcomes can have an immediate impact on daily lives. Whether or not traditional nation-states are downsized to skeletal patriotic exercises under the force of globalization, the democratic urges to control the immediate environment for living that sparks demands for municipal governing appear to be strengthening.

While people everywhere may be less interested in using such traditional political means as voting, democracy itself may have become more realizable. If the test of a democratic state is micro-control over quality-of-life matters, and if the consequence of a given policy process is not preordained before it begins, then participation in social associations that will pay off in lifestyle improvements has validity. Put simply, globalization has enlarged the arena in which people with a demonstrated competence can act and can win results.

The intellectuals who are legitimating the new entrepreneurial tilt to American governing have a rather limited view of the "global revolution" as essentially confined to any governing policy change that emulates American-style, and business-oriented, initiative (Osborne and Gaebler 1992: 328-31). What should be noticed, importantly, is that the ideology of the party in power no longer constrains choice in the policy agenda. Even in the late 1980s, Social Democrats in Sweden and Labour in the UK embraced stricter performance measures and service provision approaches rather than traditional state-run interventions. Local government institutions may now find themselves playing out any number of distinct roles in direct participation in the marketplace, through facilitating economic activity, by regulating the tax system and monitoring the private market, or in ameliorating the negative social consequences of free market economies (Goetz and Clarke 1993: 203-05). A mix of all roles is typically found in advanced industrialized societies. It is the instantly available shared knowledge of these distinct possibilities and practical applications that provides an opportunity structure for local developments globally.

four | The development of locally accountable organizations

Canadian municipal administration is more directly concerned with tangible service provision to citizens than are other levels of the state. The historic evolution of relatively autonomous authority and immediate local accountability has been grounded by this basic distinction. Even more so than other governing levels in Canada, modern municipal practices are highly conditioned by their past carried forward. In this chapter, we will explore the basics of today's local institutions in this general light.

The purposes here are two-fold. The first is to pull together the glimpses of the development of municipal institutions provided in previous chapters into a concise statement of their historical foundations by focusing on themes of wider responsibility (in area and function) and direct and open accountability to those governed. The second is a discussion of the practical shape, or institutionalized structures, for city governing which have resulted.

A productive way to look at the emergence of Canadian democratic structures is through themes and the issues that illustrate their current relevance, marking the points at which controversy was resolved. Institutions and practices, once they are engrained into a local community's political culture as the established order of business, usually endure well after their original and, at the time, reasonable purpose is forgotten.

The latter part of the twentieth century was a stressful time of adjustment for Canada's cities with movement away from themes of access towards public accountability and from efficient administration of allocative and redistributive styles of public services to the view that citizens were "customers."

4.1 Setting the Roots for Local Autonomy

In his essay, *The Life of Reason* (1905), George Santayana famously observed that "Those who cannot remember the past are condemned to repeat it" (1905: 284) and that progress is not so much rooted in absolute change but "depends on retentiveness" since an absolute discard of past practices leaves nothing to improve upon. So, a brief look at the history of municipal governing will help us understand the current situation.

A natural pattern of local authorities gradually emerged in the UK out of the jumble of manor house, charities, church parishes, guilds, and self-help groups that characterized the feudal era (Byrne 1994: 13–17). Local leaders naturally arose (or were appointed by the king) in "shires," or counties, many of whose boundaries extended back to Anglo-Saxon times. These men were known as reeves, or justices of the peace, and among their tasks were maintenance of roads, nuisance control, a little poor relief, and the administration of local justice. (The title of our modern sheriff is derived from "shire reeve.") The oldest city charter in British history, that of Winchester in 1185, was one source for the "conferred rights and freedoms" referred to in the Magna Carta of 1215. By the middle of the fourteenth century, five basic rights that denoted the firm incorporation of a borough under royal charter were codified. These were the right of perpetual succession, the right to sue and to be sued in the name of the corporation, the right to hold land in *mortmain* (in its own possession), the right to a common seal, and the right to make bylaws. In practical terms, the principal power of the smallest boroughs lay in their right to appoint their own justices of the peace to adjudicate less important matters autonomously.

Incorporation of urban communities was not a matter of any pressing public policy interest in eighteenth-century British North America. Local urban communities as trading and economic entities preceded the first attempts at providing them with even rudimentary governing institutions. Interest in local municipal structures grew, however, because of their value in providing infrastructure support for local marketing. The first incorporation of a city in the remaining British North American colonies was St. John, New Brunswick, on 30 April 1785. Its royal charter provided for a mayor and six aldermen and was issued in response to demands from "prominent men" in the community, Loyalists who had migrated north three years earlier and who were familiar with the New England style of town meetings (Isin 1995: 61-63). The British colonial office was reticent to extend local democratic forms to colonists, essentially because the ruling elite perceived that direct democracy had played an important role in fostering the American Revolution. Therefore, no further city incorporations were granted for the next half century.

The quest for a locally accountable, or responsible, system of municipal government in Canada began in the towns of Lower (Quebec) and Upper (Ontario) Canada well before the Rebellion of 1837-38. In 1828 William Lyon Mackenzie, a member of Upper Canada's Assembly and a resident of the town of York (later Toronto), asked: "Would it not be of the greatest advantage to our townsfolk if an act for the incorporation of this town (after the most approved principle now in operation in towns in Great Britain) could be passed into law?" (Isin 1995: 70). Mackenzie became the first mayor of Toronto on its incorporation in 1834 and subsequently a principal in the Rebellion. In Lower Canada, both Montreal and Quebec were granted charters in 1832, but both were dissolved in 1836 during the early troubles of the Rebellion and were not renewed until 1842. Also in 1832, Brockville, Ontario, became the first of nine communities to elect a Police Board "to prevent vice and preserve good order." The board's powers were limited; it was strictly supervised; and its primary role was to pay through local taxation for policing costs which the senior level of government found burdensome—thus setting a precedent for the 1990s provincial practice of "downloading" service responsibilities onto local governments.

The British response to the short-lived Rebellion was to appoint a royal commission under John Lambton, Lord Durham, to investigate the colonists' complaints. Durham, nicknamed "Radical Jack," was one of the leaders in the struggle to produce the British Reform Act (1832), of which he was a principal co-author. Being somewhat imperious, and a potential leader of the opposition in the British Parliament, he was a prime candidate for export to the colonies. Durham's Report addressed the issues that led to the Rebellion, especially the lack of local institutions. Speaking of Lower Canada, he wrote that "The utter want of municipal institutions giving the people any control over their local affairs, may indeed be considered as one of the main causes of the failure of representative government, and of the bad administration of the country" (Craig 1964: 67). He specifically addressed practical problems arising from the absence of city governments in Quebec and Montreal: "the disgraceful state of the streets, and the utter absence of lighting, are consequences which arrest the attention of all, and seriously affect the comfort and security of inhabitants" (Craig 1964: 69).

In Upper Canada, rural residents were still permitted only a semblance of local control under the Parish and Town Officers Act (1793), which assigned them the power to regulate the height of fences. They were still subject to the arbitrary provisions of quarter sessions where centrally appointed justices of the peace not only administered justice but also managed such municipal business as they thought necessary; their powers included the ability to dismiss locally elected officials. The rural municipal operation was also called into question by the close association of the justices of the peace with the "Family Compact," the coterie of urban social and economic elites who advised the governor and guided his patronage. (The "Chateau Clique" was a similar group in Quebec.) The settlers, many of whom were Loyalists, disliked this system intensely; accordingly, support for the Rebellion in Upper Canada came largely from rural areas, not from town residents. Having been personally and politically involved in the struggles to restrict privileged autocrats in the UK, Durham believed (like John Stuart Mill) that a vital local democracy brought liberty. Further influenced by one of Canada's greatest reformers, Robert Baldwin, Durham devoted considerable attention to the pressing need for autonomous local institutions: "The establishment of a good system of municipal institutions throughout these Provinces is a matter of vital importance.... The establishment of municipal institutions for the whole country should be made a part of every colonial constitution ..." (Craig 1964: 145).

The Act of Union (1840), which resulted from the recommendations in Durham's Report, created one large Province of Canada, replacing the former divisions with subordinate entities called Canada West (Ontario) and Canada East (Quebec); it made no mention of local government. But the new governor, Charles Thomson, later Lord Sydenham, also believed in the necessity for local self-government. Under his influence, the District Councils Act of 1841 extended self-governing powers over functions other than judicial into the rural areas of Canada West; Canada East produced similar measures in 1845–47 after the restoration of city status to Montreal and Quebec in 1842. This was followed by the Municipal Corporations (Baldwin) Act of 1849, a comprehensive reform bill which consolidated the municipal system within a single act and, outside of the cities, established the province-wide two-tier form of county government for Canada West, a form that still exists in Ontario today (Plunkett and Betts 1978: 53–56; Higgins 1986: 48–49).[1] Central government intervention was restricted to two general areas: the protection of civil rights from arbitrary acts and the protection of the municipality's credit. The latter was necessary because of fears that popular democracy would lead to spending costs which would have to be borne by property owners. These two controls, incidentally, remain central to the provincial-municipal relationship in the twenty-first century, as will be discussed in Chapter 9. The general reform acts in the two provinces of Canada were ground-breaking; it would take the UK another 50 years to move so far.

The men of property who were enfranchised by the 1849 reforms ensured that provincial legislatures would always be able to override local governments so that service would be delivered to a standard appropriate in their eyes. "Although liberal writers give the impression that Canadian municipal government was conceived as somehow autonomous and democratic, actual legislation such as the Baldwin Act embodied a restrictive, calculating, and centralized mode of municipal government" (Isin 1995: 82). Throughout the nineteenth and well into the twentieth century, the brake (seldom the accelerator) on the expansion of local powers and the democratic effectiveness of local structures was in the hands of small cadres of "prominent men," their families, and commercial entities with local interests with behind-the-scenes political influence on provincial ministries (Higgins 1986: 61).

Confederation itself, a generation later in 1867, was not exactly a revolutionary democratic victory. Only about 15 per cent of the population were enfranchised because of property and gender; in the cities the electorate was not more than a few percentage points greater. The property qualification for senators—that they must possess assets worth more than $4,000—was intended to enshrine this liberal doctrine. John A. Macdonald observed that the Senate would serve to protect the rights of minorities and that "the rich have always been fewer in number than the poor" (MacKay 1963: 47-48). In 1867, the provinces were widely understood to be rather large municipalities, as expressed in section 92.16 of the British North America Act 1867, which set their jurisdiction as being over "Generally, all Matters of a merely local or private Nature."

On the prairies, outside the cities established in the wake of the railroads, certain common patterns were set early. The first was to emulate the Baldwin package. Both Manitoba and the Northwest Territories took a paper initiative to create a two-tier county form in 1883, only to abandon the non-existent institutions within three years as too elaborate for the population and geography. In British Columbia in 1872, the year after the province joined Confederation, the legislature passed a Municipal Clauses Act, which was based on the Baldwin form. Manitoba in 1873 and Saskatchewan and Alberta in the first years of the twentieth century produced legislation *enabling* residents to incorporate themselves as single-tier rural municipalities. Not many did. Hence, the provinces of Saskatchewan (1908) and Alberta (1911) set up departments of municipal affairs to oversee, direct, and control the establishment of systems of municipalities despite the reluctance of their respective rural populations. It was not until the Great Depression that Ontario and Nova Scotia (1935) and New Brunswick (1936) found it necessary to start similar ministries to avert debt default by resorting to the protection of the credit rationale embodied in the 1849 legislation.

Foot-dragging sabotaged first efforts to facilitate the creation of local governments by permissive legislation in the west for three reasons: (1) there were too few people who were too focused on personal survival, and thus there was insufficient revenue and interest; (2) distances were too great, and most transportation routes were undeveloped; and (3) the farmers were deeply suspicious of potential taxation by any new level of government. By the end of the First World War, the three prairie provinces had mandatory legislation on the books. But the two-tier—regional and township—county form that was entrenched in central Canada never successfully emerged on the prairies and did so only in British Columbia in the late 1950s with the introduction of regional districts centred on cities.

To place the historical evolution of Canadian local government into broader perspective then, we must consider the themes which have persisted from the outset. These are fourfold:

1. an attempt to achieve local control, which is not to be confused with any sort of struggle for genuinely democratic local practices;

2. local decentralization, which would permit quick and easy institutional adaptations to fit local circumstances and their residents' own standards for efficacy and efficiency;

3. the model for municipal governing, which was widely understood *never* to exist as any direct replication of the provincial and federal parliamentary model;

4. the diffusion of concentrated political authority, which might emerge at the local level in the general campaign for decentralization of specific powers.

That basic package continues to this day as city governments continue to wrestle with two broad policy issues. The first is internal: how continuously—and how extensively—should those responsible for city operations be held directly accountable by electors? The second is external in nature, focusing on the city's relative autonomy in its relations with constitutionally superior authority. The enduring general problem, present even in the newest legislation in Alberta and Ontario, has always been to strike the appropriate balance between central control and local autonomy; provincial governments have never surrendered *their* right to make that decision (see Chapter 9).

4.2 Canada's Reform Periods and Lingering Consequences

In Chapter 3 we observed that the reformers of 1820–49 could not reconcile their different perceptions concerning the central purpose of municipalities. Each of the three divergent streams noted then produced a lingering influence on institutions, legitimating later local political practices. In its own fashion, each stream provided a source for the first, second, and third reform eras. The first reform period democratized the two-tier structure of the county court operation. Leaders of the second period tried to emulate corporate structures in municipalities (albeit from the private sector, not the Victorian public corporation); and those during the third, often without self-awareness, endeavoured to resurrect the tradition of direct participatory democracy. All these structures and political norms, even in shadowy form, are present today.

4.2.1 Emergence of the classic committee model

Direct democracy has little precedent in the Canadian experience. The New England town meeting was regarded as a revolutionary aberration; when it appeared in Nova Scotia for a few months in 1760-61 after 8,000 New Englanders immigrated there, it was quickly disallowed by the Crown. In 1770 the colony's legislative council (which represented only its small ruling oligarchy) approved a resolution to outlaw town meetings entirely. Lord Durham was later to offer his own caustic observations about such actions when he observed of central Canada: "The settlers in the eastern townships ... can contrast the state of things on their own with that which is to be seen on the other side of the line, have a serious and general cause of discontent in the very inferior management of all their own local concerns.... The Government appears even to have discouraged the American settlers from introducing their own municipal institutions by common assent ..." (Craig 1964: 68). Thus, Durham urged the speedy introduction of responsible government at all levels in order to avoid unfavourable, and perhaps revolutionary, comparisons to the American experience of self-governing.

Canada's urban areas were the first to be "democratized," a term coined by James Bryce in 1888. St. John was incorporated in 1785, Montreal and Quebec in 1832, Toronto in 1834, Halifax in 1841, Kingston and Hamilton in 1846, and Ste Hyacinthe and Jonquière in 1857. In the west, railroad development encouraged the growth of cities, which emulated the familiar central Canadian forms and functions. Regina and Moose Jaw became cities in 1883; Calgary, which had been established as a town in 1884, incorporated in 1893; and Edmonton, founded as a town in 1892, followed in 1904. New

Westminster was the first city in British Columbia in 1860, followed by Victoria in 1867, and Vancouver in 1886, after the colony joined Confederation and the Canadian Pacific Railway (CPR) chose it as its western terminus. Saskatoon became a city in 1906; it had originally been founded as a colony of the Temperance Colonization Society in 1882 (Higgins 1986: 53).

Political leaders of the 1820-30 reform period nearly all agreed that the municipality would have a unique mission, even as they could not agree as to what, precisely, it was. But, because of this general understanding, its structures could not mimic those of the senior levels; party politics and ministerial government were anathema. The legislative and executive functions of governing were combined in one body (Crawford 1954: 58) in an approach that appears closer to American congressional concepts than to the Westminster system. Although elected at-large like American governors and presidents, the Canadian mayor was given few formal powers (no veto, no power to appoint or dismiss, little budget influence) and was never considered "first among equals." By merging the British **weak** (ceremonial) **mayor** with American anti-partyism, Canadian reformers accepted the least concentrated form of political authority from both systems, including that the position of chairs of standing committees would not be analogous to ministers in any parliament. As a more contemporary activist put it, "deliberate selection of the congressional form suggests a conscious effort to establish and maintain a non-partisan—and by extension, a non-policy-oriented—local government structure" (Fish 1981: 91). Fixed election dates and relatively short terms in office also meant that councillors almost always were either rookies or hardened incumbents hell-bent on re-election, which was not that hard a task in non-partisan elections if controversy was avoided. The model, by its nature, diffused conflict and prevented political mobilization around large issues

In addition, the anglophile oligarchy in cities east of the prairies adapted the familiar British **council-committee model** to their new surroundings. In the British model, members of the public served as committee members along with elected councillors (this practice, however, has been largely abandoned in the UK since the local government reforms of 1993). In Canada, however, councillors kept their committees to themselves, largely because many specific functions (like overseeing libraries, parks, planning, and policing) were assigned to special purpose, elite citizen authorities in the wake of the 1900 reform period (Crawford 1954: 108). By 1967, the Maud Committee's report on *The Management of Local Government* in the UK reported that even major local authorities were trying to operate with 30 or more standing committees. After enumerating the advantages and shortcomings of this situation, the committee recommended that no more than six committees were helpful (Byrne 1994: 225). Canadian city council operations were not

Table 4.1: Comparing Advantages with Shortcomings of Councils with Committees

Probabilities	Political		Administration	
	strength	*weakness*	*strength*	*weakness*
1. Political accountability		buck-passing		deference
2. Coordination city-wide		attainable		silo thinking
3. Control over policy	powerful		persuasive	
4. Control over budget	powerful			compliant
5. Public access	good			considerable
6. Transparency	high		occasional	
7. Responsive to public		pandering	potentially	
8. Policy community influence	welcomed		consequential	
9. Operational efficiency		diluted	potentially	
10. Policy innovation		precedent		seldom

usually so fractured—again because of the delegation of specific functional realms to quasi-autonomous special purpose boards (the sort of thing which the British label **QUANGO**, or quasi-autonomous non-governmental organization). One exception was Vancouver where by the mid-1950s, 70 committees and other bodies had emerged under Vancouver's council-committee system, an uncoordinated jumble "that made efficient government virtually impossible" (Gutstein 1983: 198).

Table 4.1 portrays the probable consequences for the political and administrative leadership of the council-committee model. It summarily presents a picture of heightened probability for access by citizens but policy control by councillors at the expense of overall operational coordination and efficiency as measured by budget controls and a city-wide organizational view.

The positive aspects of this form holds that committees expedite general business by working through contentious details outside council chambers; that councillors develop a kind of specialized knowledge and issue familiarity through long service on particular committees; and, finally, that administrators can interact with councillors more openly, and private citizens are more easily given voice than in a rule-managed council meeting.

The negatives are also easily compiled. The existence of standing committees reinforces the natural non-decision inclination for as long as possible through buck-passing by referring matters for "further study" or for an "administrative report to committee." Having to attend too many committee meetings complicates councillors' "busy schedules" especially since many of the arguments will be repeated in the televised council chamber.

Councillors come to view any issue through the periscope of their own committee's operations and are on the alert to expand or at the very least protect its budget envelope. Finally, it encourages the councillors' natural inclination to meddle tirelessly in routine service delivery. Others provide similar checklists (Tindal and Tindal 2004: 266-68; Higgins 1986: 148-51; Crawford 1954: 109-12).

Fifty years ago, the great frequency of council and committee meetings compensated for the absence of municipal "ministers" since "It is thus possible for the elected representatives to give almost continuous supervision of administration" (Crawford 1954: 58). But by the 1970s, it had become clear that neither councils nor individual councillors in major cities could closely supervise the daily activities of many thousand civic employees (Lightbody 1998). Today, the councillor's role is to represent constituents, establish policy direction, enforce compliance with directives, and accept accountability for the broad consequences. The sheer number and weight of the policy issues comprising the agenda of today's large city councils renders anachronistic the natural tendency to any overuse of committees since councillors do not have time for special meetings to consider specific delegated obligations. It is precisely these shortcomings which caused almost all of Canada's major cities to move away from the council-committee model by the end of the last century; Vancouver, for instance, had replaced its decision-making committee multiplex with a **commission board** by 1956.

But this approach still remains the *modus operandi* of some towns and smaller suburban cities which ring the Canadian city-region even as it has been rejected as appropriate for larger cities. Standing committees can satisfy the administrative and policy needs for those socially homogenous communities where in excess of 80 per cent of council decisions are normally taken unanimously. Thus, the classic model may operate at its limited best in small town and rural district management.

4.2.2 American bosses; consequences for Canada

Canadian cities have never been insulated from external influences, especially from the United States: "Municipal reform, like agrarian protest, was a continental movement, and Canadian reformers linked their organizations with their larger American counterparts. They naturally looked south for guides to action ..." (Magnusson 1983a: 16). While only three American cities (New York, Baltimore, and Philadelphia) were incorporated by 1820, within a single political generation the urban east of the United States was both formally organized *and* under the political sway of machine politics, as discussed in Chapter 1. Thus, for late nineteenth-century civic reformers the problem of the cities was fundamentally a problem of bosses and party politics.

By the 1890s reform was in the air. By drawing extensively from the Report of a New York reform commission in 1876, as well as from sources within his own, very eclectic, social circles, Bryce clarified what he saw as a pressing need to "clean up" city government.[2] As we saw in Chapter 1, this call was taken up by the NML, a progressive coalition of experts and community leaders, whose *A Municipal Program* was designed to be appropriate for any and all units of local governing.

The NML program, and its model city charter, may best be paraphrased under its three general objectives; only the first and third concern us here. The second deals with relative city autonomy and will be considered later (pp. 171-72).

1. Political parties have no place in city government.

- City elections should be separate from state and national elections.

- The ballot should be shortened to elect only the mayor and council.

- Candidates should be nominated by petition of electors (no more than 50 signatures required) to avert the party primary system.

- Candidates should be listed alphabetically to make the ballot non-partisan.

- A merit system should be established for public service appointees, and works and operations contracts should be opened to public tender.

3. Concentrate power and responsibility in chief executive.

- Adopt the general model of the business corporation.

- Develop a system in which a strong mayor has the power to hire and fire, prepare budget documents, and veto council decisions.

This basic municipal model became the unquestioned guidebook for city government reformers across North America at least until the Great Depression.

In 1915 the NML suggested replicating the private corporation model by concentrating executive authority not on an elected mayor but in the person of a professional city manager. In the extreme, and as practiced in the American southwest, the manager implemented the broad policy choices made by the city's "board of directors," the elected council. Good government civic reformers in urban Canada readily adopted the main elements of this American prescription. "Almost like a tidal wave, these ideas spread rapidly across Canada and were implemented in large numbers of municipalities" (Higgins 1986: 245). The city of Westmount appointed Canada's first city manager in 1913, the year that Dayton, Ohio became the first in the United States to do the same. The city manager/council arrangement remains typical of contemporary local government today.

This reform package was not neutral, and both held and continues to hold an ideological bias in favour of exploiting certain kinds of conflict. "The modernization of administrative structures that occurred as a result of this wave of municipal reform had the effect of increasing the capacity of the local authorities, but not of changing their basic orientation" (Magnusson 1983a: 19). To enact this model is to maximize the influence of specific political resources—money, expertise, social standing—while deflating the worth of others—community organization, local leadership, neighbourhood reputation. Thus, it is not surprising that it was introduced to Canadian cities by local business leaders. Alan Artibise has concluded, for example, that "the purpose of reform was not to remove a corrupt or dishonest group from political power and replace it with another, more acceptable group. There was never any doubt as to who would control the government" (1975: 58). He notes that a franchise restricted to male property owners, coupled with property owners' ability to vote in each polling subdivision in which they owned property plus a form of governing that centralized power in a board of control, assured businessmen that "their conception of desirable public policy would prevail." In another case at the beginning of the twentieth century in Montreal, businessmen used a form of this model to limit the number of local "gratuity seekers" (Kaplan 1982: 149).

The business community wanted a powerful, centralized municipal executive that would control council and stage-manage a façade of popular participation in city public affairs. City "management" worked through a structure of board of control, or centralized administration, or commission board, staffed by full-time experts whose decisions and actions could not be questioned seriously by a council with neither time, nor information, nor alternative resources. For any city's commercial elite, this arrangement was not only practical but also had the fashionable cachet of "cutting-edge" reformism that other city cosmopolitans wished to emulate.

Once promoted on the grounds that the form would protect cities and citizens "from the evils of politics," city management has today become the standard orthodoxy across North America, employed by almost half of American cities larger than 2,500 people. Sustaining the movement is "the new public management," a phrase given popular currency in 1992 by David Osborne and Ted Gaebler in their book *Reinventing Government*; Gaebler, incidentally, is himself a former city manager. The contemporary mantra is Total Quality Management (TQM) which derives from recent efforts to develop a "new public management." The TQM concept implies that the public service should emulate the innovative and cost-conscious practices of private-sector entrepreneurs, including business plans, a customer service orientation, and benchmarks by which to assess performance. But while the media love the rhetoric and managers the concepts, "a substantial number of 800 suburban governments surveyed 'reported zero reforms'" (England 2003: 210-11; see also Lightbody 2003: 76-82). Fifty years ago there were 35 city managers in Canada (28 in Quebec); by the end of 1969 there were 100 (78 in Quebec), and, as in the United States, the form was typically to be found in mid-size (under 100,000 population) cities. Vancouver's first TEAM (The Electors Action Movement) council replaced its two-man commission board with a city manager in 1972-73; Edmonton similarly replaced its four-man commission board in 1983-84. Today all 12 major Canadian cities use this managerial style.

The operational basics were in 1900, and are in 2005, simple enough. Like a private corporation's board of directors, a small council, elected city-wide through preferential balloting and operating without standing committees, sets broad policy guidelines. In the United States, usually the mayor is selected from among his peers, whereas in Canada, the mayor is elected city-wide. The council appoints a skilled professional manager whose task is to implement the detail of their directives with efficiency and effectiveness. In smaller cities the manager usually becomes the dominant civic leader (England 2003: 202-03). The original Quebec enabling legislation is illustrative: a manager is "declared to be the executive officer to supervise and direct, under the control of the mayor and council, the affairs of the municipality and the work the council orders to be carried out" (Crawford 1954: 172). The manager performs the routine stuff of approving payrolls, accounts, contract specifications, and looking into citizen complaints, but he also does such major work as preparing the budget, hiring and firing submanagers, and recommending policy on any bylaw proposals. Surveys of American managers discovered that they spent half their time "managing" and one-third on policy issues; the rest was spent forging external relations with other governments (England 2003: 201).

England notes that the concept of civic management was founded on a myth—"the politics-administration dichotomy" which means that administration can be kept clear of politics. This "was a very important myth, as it allowed the fledgling discipline of public administration to distance itself from the fraud, corruption, and inefficiency associated with party politics and political machines ..." (2003: 200). Canadian cities have melded city management onto their classic arrangements, keeping all their larger councils, ward elections, council committees, and mayor (elected city-wide). So here the form does not enact the separation of powers of the administrative (or executive) from the legislative. Councils frequently label their newly minted official a Chief Administrative Officer (CAO), not a manager. Higgins observed 20 years ago, in a comment still valid today, that it is not uncommon in Canada to have department heads deal directly with councillors and not work only through the CAO (1986: 152). What such "reforms" have effectively done overall is to adopt weaknesses from both models, resulting in delay, conciliation, and hierarchical inefficiencies.

Most managers in North America today are men (88 per cent, down from 99 per cent in 1974), and about half are 46–55 years of age. Ninety per cent have a university degree; 2 per cent are lawyers. Larger cities tend to employ more educated personnel (Renner 2001), who are almost always better educated than most of the elected councillors. A career in municipal management can also pay well. The satirical magazine *Frank* "revealed" that in Ottawa, based on the March 2003 public salary disclosure by the province, 200 city employees earned over $100,000 (more than in London, Hamilton, and Mississauga combined). The city manager was paid $245,458; his deputy $212,322; the general manager of human resources $182,333; the general manager of corporate services $177,874; and the chief information officer $163,478 (*Frank* 2004).

The clarity of any summary table is fudged by the operational realities of any one city, but what the picture portrayed in Table 4.2 reveals is the probability that, under city management, while councils are accountable for the broad scope of city-wide policy, they defer to the city manager in the normal course of selecting options and tend to avoid responding to public demands. At the same time, the manager, who controls the budget, basic policies, and personnel moves, can potentially run a reasonably efficient, closed and, where obliged, innovative, service-oriented bureaucracy. Power is rooted in expertise and control over information flow, especially where pressure on councillors' time means they can be overwhelmed by detail.

Table 4.2: Comparing Advantages with Shortcomings of Chief Administrative Officers (City Managers)

	Political		Administration	
Probabilities	*strength*	*weakness*	*strength*	*weakness*
1. Political accountability	clear			slight
2. Coordination city-wide	high		powerful	
3. Control over policy		one preferred option	powerful	
4. Control over budget	reasonable		powerful	
5. Public access		slight		naught
6. Transparency	big picture			slight
7. Responsive to public		pandering		uncertain
8. Policy community influence		substantial	substantial	
9. Operational efficiency	unimpeded		high	
10. Policy innovation		unlikely, except marginal ideas	potential	

Rather like deputy ministers in the Westminster model, city managers can, in Higgins's phrase, "intentionally or inadvertently" affect the flow of information to council through being selective (1986: 154).

In any organization chart, people work in and around the frames; in the small policy community of Canadian city management, there is considerable blurring of roles. For one thing, since councils often require more administrative details (if only to explain decisions to constituents), the data show that managers have become more central to broader range, longer term policy development. While councillors, with relatively short political lives, come and go, and managers of city departments are focused on the daily details of their operations, it is only the manager with permanent tenure who can plan for the longer term from a city-wide perspective (Crawford 1954: 172). This central shortcoming in the dichotomy myth has been noted by all (for example, Tindal and Tindal 2004: 278). Plunkett and Betts put it like this: "The impossibility of completely separating policy and administration in practice has, of course, been one of the main difficulties affecting the operations of the manager system" (1978: 113). They also note that where fundamental issues set the community into conflict, forcing the manager to decide is also forcing him to take sides. Ergo, as the centre of political controversy, the manager is placed in the public spotlight in conflict with councillors and sometimes with the mayor. At least any short-term controversy ends when the manager moves on.

4.2.2.2 COMMISSION BOARDS

Few large, diverse American cities (over 500,000 population) outside the southwest employ the city manager style. This is not the case in Canada, but there are currently questions about whether the managerial "span of control" has now become too much for one individual. The result is the rediscovery and application of another management mode, the almost anachronistic style of civic management by non-elected commission boards. This was a peculiar western Canadian variant of the city manager program, with Winnipeg in 1998 the last to abandon the form. It is important to know a bit about the approach if only because of Ontario's recent innovations with municipal bureaucracies headed up by "management committees."

The board form was introduced into prairie cities during the early years of the twentieth century, usually because booster city councils were anxious for rapid economic development while private entrepreneurs proved too timid to be entrepreneurial and to invest in the supportive infrastructure of power, phones, and street cars. As councils themselves chose to make these investments, they also sought out professional managers and a collective-style management team to direct the new enterprises in the corporate style of the times. Because of the focus on utilities, the councils normally hired managers with professional training as engineers. So, this form predated, by roughly a century, the more recent efforts by the larger, now amalgamated Ontario cities for collaborative city management. These latter efforts are not so much "ironic" (Tindal and Tindal 2004: 281) as verdant proof that organizational restructuring is often a surrogate for any real change in the substance of policy itself. Experience with the commission board operation in the west is also a portent of future shortcomings.

As it evolved, the commission board format brought out into the open a number of advantages and shortcomings which confounded clarity in policy accountability at the level of city politics. This form of city management replaced a single professional with a small team of professional managers, usually three or four. Typically, one commissioner was concerned with hard services, such as utilities and transportation, another with social and protective services; and a third with finance, personnel, and long-term planning. Each commissioner was charged with supervising and coordinating the activities of the departments within their separate jurisdictions; by the 1980s, for example, the city of Edmonton had around two dozen line departments. Department heads and managers were accountable to their

Table 4.3: Comparing Advantages with Shortcomings of Commission Boards (a.k.a. Collaborative Management)

	Political		Administration	
Probabilities	*strength*	*weakness*	*strength*	*weakness*
1. Political accountability		indirect		slight
2. Coordination city-wide	potential		powerful	
3. Control over policy	indirect		powerful	
4. Control over budget		ciphers	powerful	
5. Public access		slight		naught
6. Transparency		on the trivialities		naught
7. Responsive to public	go-betweens			slight
8. Policy community influence	expected		credible	
9. Operational efficiency		unimpeded	high	
10. Policy innovation		seldom		vetted out

respective commissioners and not to council committees. Additionally, the commissioners acted as a board with responsibility for the management and coordination of the overall municipal operation. Usually the head of council was also a member of the board; at times, there was also an additional official entitled chief commissioner.

Although expanded in Table 4.3, the four arguments sustaining this kind of administrative arrangement are always these:

1. council focuses on policy-making and representation, leaving the administrative detail to the commissioners;

2. where commissioners specialize in functional areas the potential for knowledgeable advice to council is enhanced;

3. the existence of the board permits a broad overall coordination of administration within the corporation;

4. the presence of the mayor on the board creates a vital link between policy-making and its implementation.

The arguments against the board concept accumulated during the 1970s:

1. the presence of the head of council may curtail honest, thorough administrative assessments among the board;

2. commissioners rummage into too much managerial detail at the expense of planning and organizing (especially when they were promoted from "within the ranks");

3. the relationship among the commissioners, managers, the council, and its standing committees was always in flux and far from clear, often with the result that lines of authority were smudged;

4. internal bureaucratic struggles over realistic options in public policy never found the light of public opinion, so that councils were too often presented with the "single preferred option" choice;

5. commissioners had a tendency to react negatively to any intrusion of the citizen–amateurs on council into their professional direction of policy.

Table 4.3 reveals a tight, closed bureaucratic hierarchy with authority where it matters within the city-wide operation and over policy development, budget, and who is to be heard—which usually means the more, not less, institutionalized policy communities. The council exercises influence as a sounding board but seldom has any veto capacity.

Above all else, the problem with the commission board structure, which led to its demise in the west, was that it was, and was widely perceived to be, a closed shop that brooked outside interventions with thinly veiled contempt. Commissioners were understood to think of themselves as the city government, and council was lightly tolerated as an ineffectual opposition. This bizarre understanding of democratic accountability had come into wide public question by the end of the 1980s. Still, Ontario's new and enlarged amalgamated cities of this century have seemingly of necessity adopted a style of collaborative city management that is very reminiscent of the commission board form abandoned in the west.

4.2.3 The reaction to corporate rule and the façade of participation

Any significant period of municipal reform has focused debate on matters of *accountability*. In practical terms three issues have been considered: (1) that those administering programs have appropriate levels of autonomous authority so that they may be held accountable; (2) that those making policy choices have sufficient information to choose intelligently among alternatives and then to delegate the detail of program administration responsibility wisely; and (3) that the citizen, not only the expert, has sufficient clear knowledge to be able to affix blame or assign credit to those who are responsible for choices taken.

To renew interest in these questions almost always serves the public good by contrasting current practices with theoretically better alternatives. The preceding discussion suggests that all current forms leave some room for improvement; that no structure will be ideal; and that each will reflect the public ideology of place, period, and people.

The third reform period, impelled by reaction to large-scale urban redevelopments and city public works, resulted in some dramatic changes in council personnel for a time from the mid-1970s to mid-1980s. Much of this change in people and approaches, as will be considered specifically in later chapters, was grounded in the theory and rhetoric of direct citizen participation. Herself involved in the fray, Susan Fish put the dogma plainly: "The citizen participation movement ... carried with it, however, the notions that: City Hall and its administration are the enemy; the City administration is filled with experts, people whose careers are devoted to a particular specialty; therefore, all experts and career civil servants must be the enemy and wrongheaded" (1981: 98; also Magnusson 1983a: 34).

Quite apart from its narrow association with persons prominent in the business community, one shortcoming in the application of the city management model lay in its central premise that the separation of policy development from actual policy application was the best way a city ought to be run. Unintended consequences, or **policy slippage**, meant that much "policy-making" necessarily flowed out of ongoing policy administration. Yet leaders of citizens' movements active during the third reform period critically observed that, in the corporate model, much of this routine bureaucratic choice-taking was closed to direct public participation.

In all major Canadian cities, but most especially Toronto, Vancouver, Winnipeg, and Montreal, urban activists challenged the closed authority and previously unrivalled expertise of city halls. The initial policy focus was usually on freeways or large, inner city redevelopments. Municipal politics was to be all about neighbourhoods, just as it was in the "good old days." In celebrated cases, citizens "took back their communities" in Toronto and Vancouver. Edmonton's Light Rail Transit system was one such policy victory for citizens opposing integrated arterial roadway mega-projects. Urban political parties like TEAM in Vancouver, the MCM, Toronto's Civic Action Committee (CIVAC), and the Urban Reform Group of Edmonton sensitized their communities to broader social concerns than streets and sewers at the local level and, more importantly, de-deified the whole process of bureaucratic decision-taking for a time.

But the brief history of control by citizen movements is one of momentary triumphs with a sorry legacy of achievement, especially when measured by the institutionalizing of changes to the policy process. This is mostly because citizens lost faith in structures without teeth, and councillors quickly lost interest in any decentralization of authority (from them) over neighbour-hood planning. Those in this planning policy community who were con-tinuously attentive to process changes were land developers whose constant access and abundant resources under the traditional forms were threatened for a brief period. The most significant reform codification lay in the 1971 Winnipeg Unicity package and was intended to realize the participatory rhetoric of third reform leaders; it wound up being long on faith and short on angels. The RAG and community committee plans were shell initiatives which collapsed within a decade (note Higgins 1986: 269-74); any similar faint vestiges associated with Toronto Megacity (1997) were taken seriously by no one, including the legislation's authors. When the federal government first became interested in cities for a short time (1973-78), it worked through the CMHC to preserve nearly 500 central city communities through upgrades to housing. Its Neighbourhood Improvement Program (NIP) used the federal spending power and tri-level implements like Winnipeg's core city initiative to require the involvement of committees of neighbourhood residents from initial concept approvals through implementation. Many of these neighbourhood leaders later took to the electoral waters, notably Jan Reimer (as councillor and mayor) in Edmonton.

In Montreal in 1986, the newly elected MCM introduced a public question period in council (with the occasional appearance of a hippy guitar player), but no genuine devolution of council's authority down to the neighbour-hood level as promised. Although nine RAG-style District Advisory Com-mittees were required to hold public hearings, they had no power other than to advise the council's powerful executive committee: "the MCM executive committee argued that the requirements of everyday practical politics left little latitude for the implementation of many basic MCM policies" (Thomas 1995: 131). Montreal also provides an early example of an attempt to real-ize community empowerment when, in 1984, 1985, and 1986, three pub-lic-private partnership *corporations de développement économique communautaire* (CDEC) were established by social activists and community organizations to alleviate poverty in central neighbourhoods. Financial exigencies, however, led the CDEC to approach the state for support, and by 1990, when the city and federal governments came on board, the operation was enlarged to the *arrondissement* (boroughs of 150,000+ people) level. Such co-option required accountability for funds received, gradually lessening local autonomy and initiative in the process. The mandates were also institutionalized so as to include, for example, operating employment centres. Whether they will survive, even in this form, as instruments of wider political engagement under the remains of the amalgamated island city remains problematic. What seems clear is that even limited mechanisms of direct democracy cannot function without a sustained ideological base both in political culture and represented on council.

Magnusson has recently offered this gloomily accurate assessment of the consequences of this hopeful period in Canadian city politics: "In the end, the new reformers had limited impact. If anything, their criticisms of existing government activities provided a spur to privatization" (2002: 336). Beginning in the 1980s in Canada, the failure to institutionalize citizens directly into the process of making binding neighbourhood decisions contributed to an ideological drift into the forced downsizing of the state at the municipal level and the privatizing of many of its previously central operations. Why is there such fatalism about direct involvement here when 5 per cent of municipalities are still able to govern by town meetings in the United States? In large measure, this is because, as municipalities become little more than major shopkeepers, civic politicians have led the vanguard of changing expectations and requirements of citizenship in the city. Now public policy priorities have become confused with product testing, consumer response, "time and motion" efficiencies, and brand awareness (thus we see municipal "branding" campaigns in which a city logo becomes ubiquitous). The tools deployed by "policy consultants" for each major city department are those of soap manufacturers—focus groups and marketing assessments—to gauge public opinion, a twenty-first century form of policy satisficing, if you will. It is to be noted that these superficially objective corporate policy tools are, by their nature, a form of passive citizenship focused on reactions and seldom permissive of anything verging on initiative or innovation.

4.3 Power and Accountability at City Hall

The head of any Canadian urban council, or mayor, is typically elected at-large and not from and among the council. This is more in keeping with the American way than the British in which the mayor is often chosen by council from outside their number to occupy a symbolic "head-of-state" formal position. In practical political terms, the Canadian system has both strength and weakness. Being elected by all citizens presumably provides a moral suasion for the mayor's platform among the council, and the mayor can, as a result, speak for the entire community on most issues of consequence. Yet the mayor's vote is only one, equal in power to each of the other council-lors. To accomplish anything like an innovative policy agenda, the mayor must be an astute political leader who devotes time to coalition-building and personality politics. This individual must be prepared to sacrifice the optimal policy (as he or she sees it) to win broader acquiescence for more incremental actions. Otherwise, the mayor will have to be satisfied with occupying the moral high ground while not actually accomplishing anything.

To be elected from and among the councillors has seldom been seriously contemplated in recent years. The original Winnipeg Unicity White Paper in 1970 presented such a proposal, but it was diluted by the provincial cabi-net to provide for a mayor who might balance the projected suburban power base within the city council. The idea was again broached in the Taraska Unicity Committee of Review Report (1976) and was again ignored by the provincial government. Apparently, the idea of a unicity was enough origi-nality for provincial ministers to bear, and neither the Toronto nor Montreal megacities—which directly emulated so many of the original Winnipeg Unicity concepts—included internal mayoralty election. It is evident that the provinces have proven too timid to intervene in such bold internal struc-turing. Or perhaps, provincial governments can see a longer term political advantage for themselves in the diluted political competition from city coun-cils so fractured as to be unable to speak with a single voice united behind one of their own as civic first minister.

4.3.1 Formal limits on leadership authority

A model describing the leadership patterns of the more successful Canadian big city mayors bears an uncanny parallel to that of the better anti-party Canadian premiers. Ramsay Cook once described the ideology of Manitoba's Progressive premier, and first leader of the federal "Progressive" Conserva-tive party, John Bracken, in these terms: "For the next twenty years he led a 'Progressive' government that pursued extremely conservative policies and was therefore suspected of being a Liberal government in disguise ..." As to his style of policy-making as relevant for city councils, Cook continues: "Everything was to be solved by administration, which for Bracken was not only separate from politics, but best kept that way" (Cook 1979: 78).

In this vein, it is wise to remember that the prime minister would be starved of power according to a strict interpretation of the Constitution or statute books of Canada. There is no reference to the office in the former, and the latter refers to the prime minister only in connection to the Official Residences Act and in the Election Expenses Act, as the prime minister is the recognized head of a registered political party. In reality of course, and

Table 4.4: Mayors, Managers, and the Capacity for Executive Direction

		Mayor	
		++	− −
Manager	++	1	2
	− −	3	4

Note: Each of the four numbered quadrants represents a situation; that is, quadrant one represents a case where there is both a strong mayor and a strong manager.

by long-standing convention, the position of premier or prime minister is the single most powerful office in the Westminster parliamentary form of government. Early municipal reformers quite consciously wanted none of this power for the head of their councils.

The mayor has few formal powers defined by statute, these usually being limited to chairing council and serving *ex officio* on all standing committees. These have seldom been adjusted over the years; in Alberta, for example, the powers are those set out in the 1870 Ontario legislation. Unlike first ministers, however, there are few informal mechanisms to solidify a power base for the mayor. As is so often the case, it is the exceptions—Vancouver with a long tradition of local parties and Montreal with the power to appoint the executive committee—that demonstrate the validity of this general rule.

With all these limitations, any potential for authentic innovation through executive leadership in Canada's cities tends to be focused on both the mayor and city manager and their ability to devise a teamwork approach (England 2003: 202–3). In my own assessment using a strength-weakness quadrant (as noted in Table 4.4 where ++ indicates strength and − − weakness), the capacity for innovation appears highest with both a strong mayor and a strong manager (Lightbody 2003). The power of the mayor may be calculated by that individual's political capacity to provide stability by consistently winning critical policy votes In his assessment of council workings, for instance, Masson implies that the more effective mayor *has* to be able to work around the fickleness factor inevitable on council because, having limited official powers, he or she *must be* prepared (and somewhat proficient) to wheel and deal to confirm leadership in council (1994: 183-88, 72-77). In Vancouver, Gutstein sums up the council's history with this note covering the third reform era: "As long as the mayor has a voting majority, council functions smoothly (this was to occur in 1973-4 and 1979-80, but when the mayor is in the minority, council seems almost directionless (1977-8 and 1981-2)" (1983: 207). Another good example is Edmonton under the aforementioned Mayor Jan Reimer (1989-92) where, hobbled by a hung council (which was evenly divided in ideological terms), she accomplished little of substance beyond periodic affirmations of virtue (Lightbody 1997a: 116-7).

The manager must be skilled in presenting due "deference to council's leadership" while still wielding the initiative over policy development within the organization, especially during the preparation of the budget. Any manager's relative strength is assessed by the usual measures of organizational cohesion and absence of policy sabotage, by the organization's effective and rapid implementation of politically taken policy choices, and by its capacity to introduce innovative options (that is, policy that is community sensitive) in program initiation and subsequent management. Any ongoing city operation can put up with a situation where, for a time, one or the other office-holder is weak (situations 2 and 3). Such weakness may stem from ideological rigidity, such as in the case with Mayor Reimer who, although a competent mayor in most respects, was prepared to lose policy votes on council rather than dilute her ideologically "optimal" positions. This had the sorry consequence of abandoning senior managers and their considered policy advice to council's whim.

In situation 4, executive direction becomes little other than a quest for management adequacy because leadership on both sides of the equation is missing. Quite simply, "when the mayor is politically distracted *and* the manager is ineffectual, authority founders, leaving lower level officials and councillors to struggle to gratify policy community clienteles" (Lightbody 2003: 83). The usual contemporary arrangement in larger cities of city manager-mayor-council works best when a powerful mayor or a strong manager can operate adequately when one or the other is weak. Authority collapses when both mayor and manager are inept. A general discussion of the power and shortcomings of democratic leadership is presented in Chapter 8.

Individual Canadian mayors are exposed too often for their silliest behaviours, partly because of the informal cheerleading requirements of the job description. For instance, the Canadian Press reported in November 2003 that, nine days after his election on a platform "of being a people's mayor," Saskatoon Mayor Don Aitchison, owner of a men's clothing store, instituted a dress code for meetings in the mayor's office. He noted that "It's respect for the position, not Don Aitchison ... I've always said, 'Casual dress, casual thoughts.'" He further observed that "When we're discussing things to do with the city, I think we need to be in a business-like mode" (*Edmonton Journal*, 5 February, 2004). Perhaps it is to the good that there is no national inventory kept of ridiculous hats or foolish costumes worn by mayors in any given year.

4.3.2 The roles of elected representatives

Let us begin an assessment of what councillors can face with a real case. In the spring of 2003, some Edmonton drivers involved in car accidents received a bill from the city's Emergency Response Department (ERD, or fire and ambulance service) for costs of "environmental cleanup." The minimum bill was $600; some were for accidents that had occurred up to 24 months earlier; and insurance companies refused to pay them. Councillors heard, loudly, from their constituents, a circumstance senior managers half-heartedly apologized for in a September memo to council: "we had intended to give you a 'heads-up' on this—that we were going to be doing this, and that you might get a response as result—but we overlooked that, and we apologize for that oversight" (Edmonton 2003: 47; quotations in this case study are from this source). The apology was not, of course, for the action but for failing to alert council that their voters might be aggrieved by this hidden administrative initiative.

How did this come to pass? The ERD, under new public management (NPM) pressure from senior managers, sought in its 2002 budget "to identify several aggressive revenue strategies based on existing authority, which included Dangerous Goods billings ..." (2003: 29). This sounded good on paper, and the source document was indeed a 1991 council policy decision for cost recovery after a "Dangerous Goods or Hazardous Chemical Spill." At that time, however, council's executive committee specifically exempted auto accidents. Various changes to fee schedules were made over the intervening ten years, but the central policy was not altered politically. Financial exigencies after 2000 prompted council (as in other cities across Canada) to direct senior management to explore cost recovery options in all operations. Unexpectedly using their imaginations, ERD managers took this as the green light to target drivers, even though "their new computer system" would not be able to process the billings for 18 months. The ERD was still able to report to council that it anticipated "new revenues" of $750,000+ per annum to result.

The administrative justification in response to one councillor's inquiry represents the NPM at its unbridled worst in the form of revenue gouging (the bills were for a minimum $588, plus $440 per additional half hour, plus mileage, expenses, and 15 per cent handling), double-dipping (since ERD was already tax supported), arbitrary (all were presumed guilty, and unpaid bills were to be placed against individual property tax), marginal illegality (they represented probable violation of provincial Freedom of Information and Privacy Protection legislation), and the viewpoint that the citizen is generally irresponsible and thus subject to appropriate punishment. While the first three of these concerns have sadly come to be expected, the last two merit special comment.

First, Alberta's Freedom of Information and Privacy Protection Act (FOIPP) does not permit information collected for one purpose to be applied for another. In Edmonton, the ERD requisitioned accident reports from the separate police service (whose bill to ERD for this was included as a service charge on the invoice to drivers) and arbitrarily determined that the person identified by police as "Driver No. 1" was at fault and to be billed. Incidentally, police estimate that fault lies with Driver No. 1 only 80 per cent of the time, but to council ERD confidently reported "The Dangerous Goods bill is forwarded to the owner of the at fault vehicle" (2003: 29), even where charges were never filed. The ERD allowed that there was an internal appeals process to correct for errors but implied that all citizens identified as Driver No. 1 were presumed guilty.

To view the citizen as perpetrator has become a second problem. Justifying its approach to council, the ERD concluded a weary trail through the Municipal and Traffic Safety Acts with the observation that "at common-law, a person whose negligence has resulted to damage to property is liable for that damage, and pursuant to the MGA [Municipal Government Act], the City is owner of most roadways within a municipality." Ergo, that city's ERD, as judge and jury, could wring any tariff it deemed necessary from one class of accident participants. In its apologia to council, ERD management declared that their whole approach had "been based upon a philosophy that negligent, careless or deliberate acts resulting in a response of emergency services personnel should be cost recoverable from those individuals that have caused the event rather than Edmonton taxpayers as a whole" (2003: 30).

Although council ultimately bowed to citizen outrage and good sense in this instance, the episode reveals how hard it is to separate broad policy direction from its precise application: in her September 2003 memo to council, the senior general manager wrote "that ERD is pursuing various avenues of what *we see* as legitimate sources of revenue—in order to reduce our dependence on the tax levy" (2003: 48, emphasis added). It also reveals both how insensitive to good sense municipal administrators can become (the same senior management team initially cancelled Canada Day fireworks in 2003 so as to save $70,000) and how isolated from and desensitized to their fellow citizens as electors they and councillors may find themselves.

Clearly, the modern city organization has become so complex that no one person, no matter how well-trained, knowledgeable, or energetic they may be, can possibly direct the operation single-handedly. Consequently, solutions have been sought on the administrative side through some fashion of teamed executive management. However, such approaches have not yet, with *ad hoc* exceptions, been matched with collegial policy-making and teamed expertise on the political side.

The new role of city councillors involves placing priority on broad policy direction, as well as three ancillary activities. They must represent spatial and general community interests in the knowledge that staff will protect more narrow clienteles. They must generally arbitrate among policy communities with city-wide views and apportion budgets accordingly. They must be prepared to override violations of the intent, not only the letter, of broad policy by those cocooned in the administrative hierarchy. Basically these questions about accountability address two concerns: (1) when everyone has a say, no one is responsible; (2) when all are responsible, no one is accountable. The quest to balance responsibility with good service comes with caveats.

4.3.2.1 THE RATIO OF COUNCILLORS TO EMPLOYEES

First, Tindal and Tindal note (as have observers since Crawford) that councillors, particularly during committee work, "tend to become overly preoccupied with matters of administrative detail and internal management of the departments under their jurisdiction. This is a common problem with councils generally ..." (2004: 268). It was sometimes thought that smaller numbers of employees leads to "the good thing" of a close working relationship between elected and administrative personnel, sensitizing each to the problems of the other. More realistically, having fewer employees per councillor (as in smaller cities) increases the probability of political interference, program meddling, and preferential treatment. Suburbs and urbanizing rural municipalities in the city-region are typified by a minute fraction (usually well less than 10 per cent) of the central office staff of core cities: "The point is that, theoretically, the larger distance should tend to make policy concerns broader, from a focus on catching cats, say, to plotting the efficacy of truck routes" (Lightbody 1998: 39). The old localism of smaller municipalities, with fewer employees for councillors to keep an eye on, was also, and remains, prone to the diversion of the time and energy of administrators into the game of accommodating internal "council ideological feuds and personality differences" (Masson 1994: 192; Lowy and Taylor 1990: 313).

4.3.2.2 THE ROLE OF COUNCILLOR AS REPRESENTATIVE

Second, the councillor's role in large cities is clearly more to represent constituents than to usurp administration chores. What does this mean? For over 400 years, liberal democratic political philosophers have sought practical clarity in the continuing tension, manifest in all legislatures, in the role of the elected representative between, at the extremes, status as an instructed delegate or as a general trustee of the public good. The latter thinking is most associated with Hobbes and Burke and the view that representatives constitute a superior "elite of wisdom and reason" not to be bound by the narrow views of constituents (Pitkin 1972: 211-17). The alternative belief is that those represented are not dolts, but fully capable of making judgements themselves and entitled to consultation in the fullest.

While no council can ever be an exact replica of the city it represents, it still has an obligation to accord legitimacy to the many differences therein by injecting their ideas and personnel into the policy process. Michael Fenn put the classic expectation like this: "Democratic political processes at the local level have traditionally encouraged and rewarded advocacy by municipal politicians on behalf of individuals and groups in the city" (2002: 289). By the 1980s, other representational fissures were becoming more apparent (and strident). Councillors increasingly juggled divisive tendencies of territory, diversities in social standing and lifestyle preference, the demands of business and other economic sectors, the expectations of eco-system advocates and functional policy communities, and so forth (Higgins 1986: 365-73). Moreover, few individuals, once chosen as political authorities, ever accept that they *must* behave as the makers of ideal choices as any model of rational policy-making usually requires (Howlett and Ramesh 2003: 167-69).

These pressures have not abated in this new century, and more able councillors recognize that, even when trying to act independently, their discretion and judgement are limited and that at least the appearance of genuine consultation is requisite. They appreciate that programs elaborated by authorities are seldom precisely those which were originally advocated by influential voices in the relevant policy networks, if only due to reasonable satisficing pressures. A policy system's "feedback" phase is the time when policy communities can introduce innovative concepts and approaches, and new people can enter into the political "gateway" as legitimate voices in the authoritative debate. Since there is little likelihood of any sunset provision once a program is initiated, advocates for new policies will consequently tend, for a moment or two, to be appeased by this first toe-hold.

4.2.3.3 THE COUNCILLOR'S ROLE AS FULL TIME OR PART TIME

Third, and on a related note, city councillors over the last political generation have increasingly come to believe that their positions ought to be considered as full time (Lightbody 1998: 39; Sancton and Woolner 1990: 503-04). Operationally, this has meant that a few more municipal resources (as a proportion of overall budgets) have had to be diverted into support for councillors and the senior management directly responsible to them. This probably reflects not so much false consciousness or empire-building but an ever-increasing complexity on the demand side of the policy process.

There are structural limitations on councillor ambitions for matching policy responses to expectations. Since the early twentieth century, Canadian cities have subjected themselves to a proliferation of functionally specific and quasi-independent agencies, boards, and commissions (the ABCs) that truncate local political power and tend to eviscerate clear accountability, especially in governmentally fragmented city-regions. Defeated Toronto mayoralty candidate Stephen Clarkson observed of the "aura of irrelevance and impotence" surrounding local politics that, "The candidates that the voters elect have virtually no control over such central municipal bodies as the transportation commission, police commission, harbour commission, parking authority ... These men and women are seeking office for posts which give them only partial influence ..." (1972b: 167). It is not unusual for major Canadian cities in 2004 to work with some two dozen of these council-appointed agencies over and above the separately elected school (and in Vancouver, parks) boards.

These segregated activities range from the symbolic (Place Names Advisory Committee), through the regulatory (Public Health Board, Parking Commission, or Development Variance or Appeals Board) to the operational (such as the Policy Commission or Library Board). The central point remains the same: to the degree that council has delegated its responsibilities to an "arms' length" quasi-subordinate structure, it has also absolved itself of public responsibility for that function or activity no matter how "full time" councillors think themselves to be.

The 1990s focus on internal benchmarks for service and performance left in its wake a new range of semi-autonomous agencies outside regular departmental operations to which, through negotiated contracts, the "business" of providing a government service has been delegated. In Canada, all major cities sought to realign their traditional structures over the last political generation to reduce the number of core departments and to increase their number of contracted service delivery arrangements, many to private and not-for-profit operators in costs competition with city operations. Sharpe, trying through comparative study to determine if there is a central purpose for democratic local governing any more, found a purpose he labels "functionalism" but which is really public choice theory. He suggests that local government must become the pressure group for consumers who are not also producers. Otherwise, he states, citizens would need the private sector or a public corporation to undertake functions "for responding to demand for public services that have no market" (Sharpe 1981: 31). Possibly he is on the right track for these times.

4.3.2.4 THE COUNCILLOR'S ROLE IN MAKING BUDGET DECISIONS

Fourth, councillors these days happily conclude that the primary influence in the making of hard budget choices belongs to them. But they also acknowledge that their senior officials are the most active among all sources of influence over spending priorities. Councillors concede that they are guided far more by their chief administrative and financial officers and their department managers than by any other group in the city policy system. This concession that administration runs the shop floor also indicates that city budgeting, controlled by professional staff and their clientele groups, tends traditionally to be based on a straight-line projection of new budgets based on last year's spending patterns. Is this good enough?

Today's NPM praises the efficiencies of new "post-bureaucratic" structures in contrast to the dysfunctional tendencies of the kind of bureaucratic organization that is characterized by excessive rules and regulations, red tape and empire-building, and subsequent cost inefficiencies. On the other hand, the Edmonton ERD action discussed above refutes that NPM achieves universal success. Even so, today's city management prefers to describe itself in NPM terms as attending to a mission (not rule-driven) of decentralizing their authority and control either laterally or to lower operational levels (which must, by the way, increasingly generate their own revenues) and of acting as a catalyst in driving greater self-sufficiency and innovation among other agencies (state, private, volunteer) who deliver service to the public (Pal 2001: 72-74). Incidentally, this is why Canada's cities devoted so much time in the 1990s to developing **mission statements** defining themselves and their purposes, which became so inclusive, bland, and optimistic as to defy realization.

In this brave old world made new, the general problem for city councillors is that the capacity for political direction tends to be an inverse function of decentralized decision-making authority: the more that authority is devolved to subordinates or outside agencies, the less precise is their direction. Too frequently, councillors now argue that they cannot be held democratically accountable for decisions they did not make. They *will* inquire, investigate, and report on any matter of policy slippage, of course. But the core issue remains finding *any* person responsible in the slippery coil of today's state service. The neo-liberal legacy has been the neutering of public service and the difficulty of attracting, as candidates for council, persons who are genuinely innovative and creative in their successful (and private) professions and lives.

4.3.3 A basic quest for political accountability

A short period of internal organizational disruption in Canada's cities, partially occasioned by provincial initiatives and roughly centred in the 1990s decade, resulted in a concentration of focused administrative power usually in the form of a city manager. The generally weak formal standing of the head of council in Canadian municipalities had produced an apparent need for a better means to coordinate policy development and execution. Calgary was among the last of the major Canadian cities to switch to the CAO form from the commission board model in 2000. It is to be noted, however, that management there did retain five "executive directors" as well.

This widespread changeover was somewhat unusual in that Canadian city governing systems have not been much given to radical structural adaptations. Whatever the initial form had been, it tended to accumulate legitimacy, not grievance. Kaplan put it like this: "'Other things being equal,' in the absence of obstacles or discontinuities, a system will normally expand its performance capacity with the mere passage of time. Given time, a system will naturally evolve toward a greater consensus on beliefs" (1982: 607).

Other things were not equal toward the end of the twentieth century, and both exogenous (provincially forced amalgamations, service downloads, fiscal austerity) and indogenous (new demands from diverse neighbourhoods and new clientele groups) pressures led to organizational changes that were atypical. The Halifax consolidation of 1996 was the first major municipal restructuring in Nova Scotia in over 100 years. Montreal's charter changes in 1962 repealed the appointment of one-third of council but did not alter the executive committee arrangements of 1921 until 2001. Toronto's adoption of an executive committee in 1969-70 represented its first fundamental change in 70 years, and when Edmonton moved to a city manager and executive committee arrangement in 1983-84, it jettisoned 80 years of government by commission board.

Coordination of the elected side of the policy-making equation with some style of political executive periodically emerged and evolved, only to become ubiquitous entering the twenty-first century. The **board of control** was the earliest form of a municipal executive committee in Canadian cities, turning up in Toronto in 1896, in Montreal from 1909-21, and for a short time in the west in Winnipeg after 1906 and Calgary after 1913. Even though the form was mandatory for Ontario cities with more than 100,000 residents until 1970, any resemblance to cabinet government was entirely superficial. Its strength and parallel weakness was that it was above and apart, not from and among, the councillors. The child of a late nineteenth-century distrust of popular democracy and ward politics, the board of control consisted of four controllers plus the mayor elected at-large and, by statute, was provided with enormous power in relation to ordinary councillors. The controllers wrote the budget, awarded contracts, and hired and fired senior staff (Plunkett and Betts 1978: 218-20). Since the board members were all elected city-wide, each had a city-wide legitimacy when it came to budgets and policies; each was in perpetual competition with the others; each was a "mayor in the making." Controllers, like the mayor, were also sitting members of council. Since the defeat of a board initiative required a two-thirds majority of council, if the controllers were united, the rest of the council would also have to be virtually unanimous. After a time, ward councillors tended not to regard this arrangement very highly.

In response to these problems in Ontario, and to third reform pressures across the country, a general move to executive policy committees of council became widespread. Councillors sought to widen their powers of political oversight and to provide policy direction from the political arm. Toronto and Winnipeg initiated the executive policy committee form in the early 1970s; Ottawa, Hamilton, and Edmonton followed in the early 1980s. The usual size has been about a half-dozen or so members chosen by councillors from and among their number (Table 4.5). The powers delegated to them, outside Quebec, are little more than approving the council agenda, recommending policy priorities, and coordinating council's business. They also settle low level claims and handle tenders, as well as other relatively trivial, or nuisance, administrative matters. Assessed by their functions, and exempting always the abilities of a personally persuasive mayor, these operations have not generally been strong central executives if only because the rest of council, each with a constituency to serve, has been reluctant to surrender their voices and final say.

The municipal executive format in Canada thus holds little real substance and has performed even less like a cabinet than did boards of control, excepting Montreal and, to a lesser degree, Quebec City, where local "mayor's parties" have solidified central leadership. In fact, Montreal's position of "director of services" (city manager) was abolished in the 1960s so as to concentrate the power to solve problems and coordinate activities in the hands of Mayor Drapeau's chief lieutenant, Lucien Saulnier (Kaplan 1982: 418-19). Elsewhere, the combination of few formal powers plus non-

Table 4.5: Canada's 12 Largest Cities in 2004, with Administration

City	Population[1]	Council	Executive	Management	Staff	Committees	Ratio
Toronto	2,481,494	44 (x 44)	EC (M9)	CAO	45,000	6	55
Montreal	1,039,534	73 (x 73)	EC (M11)	Dir. Gen.	20,750	7	50
Calgary	878,866	14 (x 14)	EFC (M7)	CEO	10,000	4	88
Ottawa	744,072	21 (x 21)	ESD (M7)	Manager	12,030	6	62
Edmonton	666,104	12 (x 6)	EC (M4)	Manager	9,790	2	68
Winnipeg	619,544	15 (x 15)	EPC (M7)	CAO	7,000	4	89
Mississauga	612,925	9 (x 9)	Classic	Manager	3,350	8	183
Vancouver	545,671	10 (x 1)	Classic	Manager	9,000	3	61
Hamilton	490,268	15 (x 15)	SPBC	CAO	9,730	6	50
Halifax	359,111	23 (x 23)	Classic	CAO	3,000	16	120
Surrey	347,825	8 (x 1)	Classic	CAO	1,960	3	178
Laval	343,005	21 (x 21)	EC (M4)	Manager	2,215	0	155

Notes: "Council" refers to number of councillors apart from the mayor, including (x N) the number of wards. "Executive" refers to council's main policy committee (Mayor plus X), and "Classic" is the council-committee format. "Management" is administrative head; "Staff" is the number of permanent employees. "Committees" refers to the number of permanent council committees other than its executive. "Ratio" is residents per employee.

1. Indicates use of 2001 census data.

partisanship on council means little genuine capacity for "the executive" to set conclusive policy directions. This is especially the case with larger non-party councils where accountability is more diffuse, the representative role as trustees is more pronounced, and the need to present a responsive voice in public is great. Centralized bureaucratic power in combination with the ease of incumbent re-election tends to result in councillors being entranced by expertise. It becomes increasingly easy for these individuals to let administrators' programs become their election platforms in a process buffered against serious challenge. The wonderful thing about parties is that their mutual survival instinct breeds trust within any elected caucus, a trust that can allow delegation of genuine authority to a leadership cadre.

A snapshot of the municipal systems of Canada's 12 largest cities is presented in Table 4.5. Three-quarters of the cities elect councils on the basis of single-member districts; the two in British Columbia continue with the anachronistic city-wide vote. Two-thirds (eight) of these cities employ an executive committee of very similar description comprised numerically of between one-sixth of the larger to one-half of the smaller councils. Despite the variation in their formal names, their coordinating and advisory activities are generally as described above. All cities now employ a city manager; only Halifax councillors seem to enjoy delegation and standing committee work.

A figure for the number of permanent employees is presented in the second last column of the table. There were around 887,000 persons directly employed by *all* Canadian local governments in 2002, and 134,000 by these largest 12. By the end of the 1990s, the dozen largest Canadian city-regions averaged about one employee for every 67 residents (Lowy and Taylor 1990: 307; Lightbody 1998: 37-39). In Table 4.5, that average now stands at one per 68 residents. Superficially, the higher the ratio in the last column, the more likely that municipal services are performed by fewer employees—that is, for neo-liberal addicts, they are performed more "efficiently." But these figures are simply not comparable among these jurisdictions for a number of obvious reasons. Some provinces assume larger shares of the "local burden" like social welfare, planning, assessment, and so forth. Some cities own and operate their own utilities, while others act as shareholders in trust for residents and appoint boards of directors for municipal Crown corporations; employee numbers are shed in this process. Some surrender major operating responsibilities to quasi-autonomous agencies like Vancouver's Parks Board or to a regional commission for, say, transit or water treatment.

It is worth noting at this point that the single largest source of local revenues remains the bundle of taxes on real property (further discussion of municipal budgets can be found in Chapter 9). While the precise proportions vary among the provinces, for all Canadian local governments in 2002, 41.7 per cent of total revenues came from this source, a reliance that has increased marginally from 41.0 per cent in 1994. Localities in New Brunswick (53.8 per cent) and Saskatchewan (51.8) had the heaviest dependence on this revenue source; Prince Edward Island (18.2) and Newfoundland and Labrador (21.8) the least. The second largest cumulative revenue sources were "sales of goods and services" (22.7 per cent) in 2002 and "transfers from other governments" in 1994 (25.4 per cent). Reflecting cutbacks and offloading of programs and projects, government transfers to municipalities had declined to 14.7 per cent of their budgets by 2002. The absolute amounts generated for municipalities from the property tax are relatively large, with Ontario's communities raising $17.9 billion in 2002, Quebec's $7.4 billion. The single best source for comparative information like this, updated annually, is provided by the Canadian Tax Foundation (CTF) in its *Finances of the Nation* (<http://www.ctf.ca> and following the links to "Tax 101").

The CTF observes that the tax on real property is "one of the oldest taxes in Canada and is levied as an annual charge paid by the owners of real property ... The tax rate, also known as the mill rate, is usually expressed in dollars (or mills) per $1,000 of assessed value" (2004: 2.2). Usually municipalities levy and collect the property tax calculated against a tax base variously defined by the provinces but basically including land, buildings, and other items considered to be "affixed to" the property. Magnusson, writing about the low cost of administration of the property tax to municipalities, says that "real property taxes are comparatively difficult to escape. Land and buildings cannot be moved about like money or other personal property" (1983a: 23). The value of property is determined through its **assessment**, and each province does it differently, using terms such as "real," "actual," "fair," or "market" (CTF 2004: 6.7–6.10). No similar two properties will be valued in the same way across the country; assessment is intensely local and can be highly political.

Although some public economists may dispute this point econometrically, Magnusson is correct when he argues that "this form of taxation also seems to be inequitable, regressive, and highly inelastic" (1983a: 23). Normally, it penalizes persons on low or fixed incomes and those whose limited wealth is tied up in the homes they own.

Being centred on the **property tax**, which is tangible to business and ratepayers in the most immediate sense, city (and municipalities generally) budgeting practices across the country have consistently been grounded in incrementalism. While all liberal democratic governments tend to begin their budget cycles by carrying past commitments forward, this proclivity is more pronounced in municipalities where there is seldom any significant change in the ideologies or agendas of governing authorities. In the city policy document that counts the most, tax rates are determined by stability and predictability, not only for business but also for general ratepayers. Gradually increasing the tax from a widely agreed baseline becomes an easy general strategy for financial officers and the councillors they advise. Tradition becomes political expediency, as predictability in tax forecasting trumps worries about revised assessment principles, better taxation methods, or any questions about economic efficiencies. There is no evidence that many citizens or business operations are all that interested in such changes, barring an atypical adjustment.

The revenue side of the budget, having an established objective, becomes a quick march through the tradeoffs necessary to avoid the unexpected. In very practical terms, financial officers in cities operate with the motto "the best surprise is no surprise." In advising councillors, a city's financial manager often uses marketing practices such as comparison with similar communities in like tax and assessment regimes—so as to "keep in line with" the others—as they gauge what are appropriate service or taxation levels (and their own pay rates). This is always at the expense of any optimal service or taxation model.

Consequently, any city's management team most easily massages council into budget acquiescence by following tradition and not rocking the boat; that, and because councillors are possessed of so few alternate political resources, is why senior administrators have the most influence (note Chapter 7). These days, the introduction of any innovative programs—those without demonstrable precedents elsewhere and needing new money—is always contingent upon finding new revenue streams.

4.3.4 Structural reforms and the lingering quest for autonomy and new revenues

Beginning in the mid-1990s, the provinces from east to west disrupted the governing of Canadian cities. The Halifax CMA was consolidated in 1996 by a Liberal government. The Progressive Conservative government in Ontario forced the consolidation first of Toronto in 1998, then the province's other CMAs. Montreal, Longueuil, Quebec City, Levis, and Hull-Gatineau were consolidated in 2002 by the PQ. And in 1998 the provincial NDP government of British Columbia ceded control over transit and some arterial roadways to the GVRD.

These tumultuous *fin-de-siècle* consolidations imposed across entire provincial municipal systems had seemingly politically palatable goals, which were normally espoused in terms that equated efficiency with territorial aggrandizement. The political groundwork and precedents were laid 60 years earlier in the Depression-era transformation by Alberta of its municipal and schools systems from 1936-44 and by the similar introduction of regional government across Ontario following the (Smith) Committee on Taxation Report in 1967. None of the recent systemic overhauls, though, appears to have been based on past experience or on any **institutional memory** of the impacts of earlier reforms within, nor consultation among, the officials in what remains after the neo-liberal downsizes of provincial municipal affairs departments. As will be discussed later, city-region consolidations are the consequence of particular ministerial initiatives occurring normally after a change in provincial governments.

Consolidations like those that reduced the number of Ontario's municipalities from 815 to 445 from July 1996 to 2004 were never about reducing costs or enhancing local autonomy, except in the public speeches of ministers. For one example of this posturing, in a January 26, 2000 press release, the Minister of Municipal Affairs (Ontario) made this assertion: "The government established the new City of Ottawa to reduce the number of politicians and improve local government, making it simpler, more efficient, and more accountable. The goal is fewer politicians and lower taxes." Today, there are indeed fewer municipal councillors in Ottawa. This is also the case in the new Toronto Megacity, but by 2003 its operating budget of $6.4 billion had grown by one-third after five years of consolidation even as the capital budget remained static. The Megacity does, however, directly employ one-third fewer employees per capita than is the average for Canadian core cities. The major city-region consolidations of the 1990s were far more about other policy issues such as booster-style economic promotion (in the case of Montreal to keep pace with Toronto), regional planning, and modest redistributive policies than with post-unification cost savings; they were also premised on a scarcely veiled contempt from provincial politicians for their municipal counterparts and the jobs they held.

This whole process ought to have squashed dreams of the autonomous neighbourhood as a city in Canada. However, anti-urbanism remains active today; note, for example, the always informative, and aggressively opinionated, website maintained by 1970s reform activist and former Toronto mayor John Sewell (<http://www.localgovernment.ca>). Given what has been discussed previously in this chapter, bucolic world views such as this are no longer at one with reality.

We must raise the matter of home rule at this point only because its absence from the Canadian tradition has become an irritant for some of Canada's larger city mayors of late. Aspects of the American reforms of 1900, as discussed in Chapters 1 and 3, struck a responsive chord among those who would redraft the intergovernmental position of the Canadian city. The second tenet of the Model City Charter would have granted limited home rule to city governments. In 1900, it included these directions: (1) restrict the powers of state legislatures to enact special legislation affecting cities (especially as regarding utilities franchises); (2) restrain city governments by general legislation; and (3) set tax and debt ceilings to restrain expenditures. Only the first of these appeals to Canadian mayors today.

The granting of constitutional autonomy to municipalities, or home rule, proved popular in the United States a century ago. In 1868 Judge John Dillon of the Iowa Supreme Court congealed prevailing understanding about municipal powers when he ruled that municipal corporations were creatures of legislation: "As it creates, so may it be destroyed." By 1875 American states were under pressure to enhance cities' powers, and, in that year, amendments to the Missouri Constitution assigned autonomy, through municipal charters, in all areas not designated to be of state-wide interest. This was largely intended to curb the patronage powers of political partisans in state legislatures over cities' operations; in Boston, for instance, the governor of Massachusetts had been able to appoint the regulators for the licensing and sale of liquor. Over time, however, constitutional standing became the single most powerful weapon against amalgamation for suburbs surrounding a core city, a means to protect their special status as separate and unequal. Today, 47 states have a home rule provision in some form, usually not for fiscal matters like the ability to raise revenues but rather for the city's own basic structures and functions. As part of the ideological shifts of the past two decades though, states have become more interested in municipal financial and personnel management.

With respect to home rule in this country, no province has ever countenanced surrender of its constitutional supremacy. The power over cities is defined in section 92.8 of the Constitution Act 1982, although the basic idea of subordination was codified in the mid-nineteenth century with Baldwin Act controls over municipal borrowing and in the twentieth-century controls over expansion through annexations, both under the guise of protecting the credit of the local authority and its property-owning ratepayers. Although the administration of these powers is usually delegated to quasi-autonomous regulatory agencies (discussed further in Chapter 9), the hierarchical position of the province as a central government is a non-debatable proposition.

Because of this general setting, the very recent quest of Canada's self-labelled "hub city" or C-5 mayors (Toronto, Montreal, Vancouver, Calgary, and Winnipeg) for a "Model Charter" granting them newly entrenched realms of autonomy and revenue, launched in May 2002, appears somehow quixotic. In October 2001, the "big city mayors caucus" (BCMC) persuaded the Federation of Canadian Municipalities (FCM) to advance a proposal for a new deal based, for the short term, on much more federal cash for their infrastructure repairs and development. The longer term goal was also clear, at least to the mayors: "Formal constitutional change to recognize local government on an equal footing with the provinces and the federal government." It was evident then that "legal charter or home rule status that would give Canadian *cities* ... far more independence" was on their minds (<http://www.canadascities.ca/news.htm>; emphasis added). A handy draft of a city charter was included with their proposals. Four subsequent media opportunities on the subject (i.e., "cities summits") from October 2001 through June 2003 followed.

In this roughly two-year period of euphoria leading into the 2004 federal election, the BCMC launched a particularly aggressive (for them) national campaign for recognition, policy agenda priority, and cash. While neither the federal government nor the provinces showed any interest other than a provincial warning that any new federal monies would have to be worked through their good offices, the mayors' initiative did result in both symbolic and distributive policy changes.

The only solid results have been significant on recognition, but limited in the resetting of fundamentals. The Chrétien federal government, revisiting the party's 1972 history, initiated Liberal House and Senate caucus committee investigations into urban issues in the 18 months before the last election. Prime Minister Chrétien also set up a task force in the nonpartisan Privy Council Office. All of these pretty much foundered on the shoals of one or all of at least three kinds of questions, centred on issues of policy for the public good, responsibility in philosophical terms, and, not least, practical political matters.

What has not been thought through in advocacy for the C-5 Charter by mayors speaking only for, and to, their own constituents, is the policy question of why Canadian citizens as a community would be better served by *a static concept* of constitutionally enabled and preserved municipalities in this new century. The track record in the United States of the very similar 1900 reform package for city-regions is one of confused authority, protection of private privilege, service deficiencies, tax and growth expenditure discrepancies, and policy deficits at the level of city-region development. The broader philosophical questions are at least three:

1. with enshrined rights come permanent obligations, hence, liberties relative to others breed commensurate responsibilities;

2. with entrenched fiscal autonomy (i.e., specific revenue sources) is attached abandonment to city self-reliance and self-sufficiency by other levels of the state in the future;

3. with formal recognition, boundaries are defined with a permanence that defies future population shifts and evolving economic conditions.

The real politics implied in the C-5 Charter appears innocent of Santayana's admonition with which we began this chapter. The practical political questions not specifically addressed by the BCMC are: Why would Canadian municipalities, who were not invited to the table during the 1982 patriation discussion or to any tri-level conference since, be welcomed to some new constitutional carousel by any provincial government today? Who is to define *which* local authorities would be invited onto the playing field? On this matter, Canada's C-5 mayors and friends have devised a bit of a "50–50 stew, one horse and one rabbit" for their recipe. It raises the practical constitutional problems of empowering only a few cities to receive transfer funding and not the other thousands of local governments, which are included in section 92.8 of the Constitution which details matters of unquestionably exclusive provincial responsibility.

Leading into the June 2004 federal election, Liberal Prime Minister Paul Martin introduced a full rebate of GST paid by local governments and promised a "new deal for cities" based on a 5 cent per litre fuel tax rebate. In the first month after the election, it became clear that it would take several years to finalize the deal. The federal Department of Finance feared "a claw-back" by the provinces and, the new Minister of State for Infrastructure and Communities minister added, wanted flexibility to meet "the needs of com-munities large and small, from the largest cities to the smallest hamlets, but also not to lose sight of our national objectives such as the implementation of Kyoto" (*Edmonton Sun*, 21 July 2004).

In the immediate aftermath of the 2004 federal election, which produced a minority Liberal government, several cities quickly contributed their own special brand of clarity to any debate over their future fiscal standing by squabbling publicly as to whether the proposed federal fuel tax rebate should be distributed on a per capita basis or per litre sold within their boundar-ies. Some major cities preferred the latter; others the former. Toronto added that the money should be dispersed based on transit ridership so as to meet "national objectives" such as limiting greenhouse gases. Provincial govern-ments, led by Alberta, reminded all that any deal would have to be negoti-ated with the provinces in any case, and that its model based on sales was ideal: "it's very simple and doesn't need to involve a large bureaucracy" (*Edmonton Journal*, 30 July 2004). Trying to win support for his government, Martin pledged the fuel tax rebate for the cities in his spring 2005 budget based on a per capita basis. While NDP support permitted the June 2005 budget to pass, federal officials still had to negotiate precise terms of the transfers with each province, and some mayors harboured suspicions because the arrangements had not come with longer term guarantees.

Notes

1. The two-tier (or level) model normally is based on smaller, directly elected, general municipal governments with responsibility for immediate local needs (like fire or public health) and a wider area regional government over and above a number of these. The regional, or county, government has authority over area-wide needs (courts, policing, regional roads); its council is comprised of delegates chosen from among councillors already serving on lower tier councils (i.e., "indirect election"). This approach served as a template for the new institutions of Metropolitan Toronto in 1954.

2. "There is no denying that the government of cities is the one conspicuous failure of the United States. The deficiencies of the national government tell but little for evil on the welfare of the people. The faults of the state governments are insignificant compared with the extravagance, corruption and mismanagement which mark the administration of most of the great cities ... there is not a city with a population exceeding 200,000 where the poison germs have not sprung into a vigorous life, and in some of the smaller ones, down to 50,000, it needs no microscope to note the results of their growth" (Bryce 1888: I, 572).

PART II

The Politics of City Governing

five | Elections and voters

If the representative process so critical to modern liberal democracy is to be taken seriously by citizens, then the conduct of elections must not only be fair but also appear to be equitable. For participation to be thought meaningful, it must also be seen to exert some reasonable control over those in political authority by tempering behaviours between votes. Even were Canadians 35 million Aristotles, if their participation was limited only to choosing one representative in one small territory every three or four years, their wisdom would be seriously circumscribed. The three critical questions to be explored in this chapter are these: Are Canadian city elections organized to be fair in that voters' names will be on lists at the polls and that votes are tabulated honestly? Who votes and why do others boycott elections? Why do persistent problems of immorality, ethical transgression, and illegality recur, and what does this reveal about the shortcoming of the modern electoral system?

5.1 Organization and Conduct of Elections

For federal and provincial elections in Canada, independent electoral commissions are required by law to strike boundary lines that, with some considerable slack of 25 per cent larger or smaller, pretty much carve the country or province into equal population units for voting purposes. These are called electoral constituencies, or ridings, a name inherited from Old English for the third part of a shire (or county) as in "East" Yorkshire. The issue of distance and geography—of representing fields, moose, and muskeg rather than people—has still not been well worked through; the consequence, as noted in Chapter 1, is a heavy imbalance in the federal and all provincial legislatures to the advantage of rural interests. Except where cities have been required by agreement to establish guaranteed representation to newly annexed towns or territories for a specified time period, councils have consistently provided for greater equality—by population count at least—among their electoral divisions than either the federal or provincial systems.

An **electoral system** defines the framework for the selection of legislators within a representative democracy. The procedures entail two related activities. Decisions about territory must first determine the size, number, and number of representatives for each division, which are called wards at the municipal level. Second, there must be rules about who may vote and for the casting and tabulating of the votes. Although seldom a hot topic in coffee shops anywhere, political gladiators are well aware that exploiting these rules effectively is central to their primary mission. Strategists well understand the prevailing "rules of the game," including those from the underlying political culture. Then, by often sophisticated competitor analysis, and within the broad fabric of that political culture, they endeavour to counteract the tactics of opposing candidate teams. Almost by tacit agreement, and acting somewhat as an informal syndicate, these gladiators seldom question the purely technical and consequently inconsequential—to the majority of voters—election rules.

The illusion that rules do not encapsulate any pattern of bias or systemic exclusion is occasionally challenged by non-dominant groups or movements who seek to upset dramatically the tea carts of those always in power. In their classic *City Politics*, Banfield and Wilson were not at all surprised "that efforts to change fundamentally the distribution of power within a city are often directed towards changing the electoral system" (1966: 87). Such local power tussles occurred in Toronto in the late 1960s, continued in Vancouver well into the 1980s, and lay at the very heart of the Winnipeg Unicity reforms of 1971. Curiously, one of the invariable rules in all these debates is that the players never speak of power and ideology but of democratic values and good government. To claim for your own position the high ground of democratic principle is a deceptively neutral way to try to impose your own beliefs. There are no democratic principles that lead to an optimal system of election.

5.1.1 The gerrymander: affecting power in theory

No democratic guidelines conclude that the good city can be governed only by a council entirely chosen by all electors, nor is it written that a specific number of wards is ideal. No electoral oracle has spoken with sufficient clarity about the superiority of plurality or proportional voting. What we do know is that different electoral systems yield different consequences.

In municipal elections, it is *not* usually the case that any sort of independent body strikes electoral divisions for the community. While the essential format is set forth in some variant of a provincial municipal elections act and the election date is specified, within these broad terms of reference the actual activating bylaw is passed by the council itself. The apparent reason for this lies in the political culture dominant in English-speaking Canada: the operational assumption that, once they have been chosen, councillors govern in the best interest of the entire community. Past divisions are set aside, theoretically, and choices, including those governing the conduct of elections, are targeted towards an objective interest utilizing the best in the way of skilled technical advice. The *political* realities of the electoral system are minimized or, better yet, ignored. If the electoral instruments are widely understood neither to reflect nor to affect the distribution of influence, then there is no need to create an autonomous election commission to remove such matters from the crass world of politics.

This sunny view comes not without caveats. "The way electoral boundaries are drawn," wrote Lorimer, "has a lot to do with who can win elections. So there is nothing closer to the hearts of a group of politicians than a discussion about how the boundaries of the constituencies they represent should be changed ..." (1970: 37). This raises the matter of the **gerrymander**. The word itself comes from American history. In 1811 Governor Elbridge Gerry of Massachusetts, a signer of the Declaration of Independence and later Madison's vice-president, signed into law a redistribution of voting districts for his state that favoured his Democrats even though the Federalists won over 60 per cent of the votes. Because Essex County, in which Boston is situated, loosely resembles the silhouette of a salamander on a map, the *Boston Centinel* coined the new word (Safire 1968: 161-62). Since then, it is used to describe the drawing of electoral boundaries so as to favour one party by spreading its electors in a plurality position across a number of ridings on the assumption that past voting behaviours will carry forward. Opposition support is lumped in only a few districts, where they would win by huge margins. The passive gerrymander presently practiced by Canadian provincial governments fails to account for the migration of population from rural into urban areas.

The idea of the gerrymander is best illustrated by a simple model adapted from T.H. Qualter (1970: 115-16). Let us assume an urban community of 100,000 electors divided by the CPR main line. South of the tracks, living nearest the waterfront, are 40,000 working-class citizens who vote for social democratic candidates. A similarly homogenous territory north of the tracks is made up of 60,000 middle-class conservative voters. This space is to be divided into three equally populated districts of 33,333 persons. We will assume that voter turnout is 100 per cent for elections and that each person votes exactly as he or she did in the past.

As Qualter has noted, there are three possible ways to do this which do not violate any electoral law. First, to carve the space from north to south produces three districts, in all of which the conservative candidates would win by 20,000 to 13,333 votes. If the region is split from east to west, the conservative and social democratic candidates would win the top and bottom districts respectively 33,333 to nil, and the remaining central district would go to the conservative on a vote of 26,667 to 6,667. But there is a third option: a north district could be drawn from east to west—which the conservative would win 33,333 to nil—while the residual space could be split into two north-south districts each of which would be won by the social democrats with the vote of 20,000 to 13,334.

Which one of these is right? Each changes the outcome of the vote; moreover, in the third option, the minority wins more representation than the majority without violating any principle of democratic equity. Political gladiators make these calculations carefully, then argue when they appear before any impartial electoral commission that, while they enthusiastically endorse democratic principles, they must strenuously advocate the protection of neighbourhood lines or historic community ties of interest—in other words, their own electors. The lesson is that every pattern of drawing boundaries for constituencies confers some advantage to one social group at the expense of another. Hence, any elected official who argues for a system of representation based on a natural community of interest that may be reflected in some kind of traditional political division is, at heart, a politician advocating a gerrymander. In Edmonton, for instance, most recently in November 1996, in a colloquy typical of the ward restructuring game, two councillors revealed their philosophic sophistication when they enthused with the very epitome of cliché to argue "If it ain't broke, don't fix it." Their basic understanding in this case was that "it weren't broke because it elected us."

Because it is so important to the assumption and retention of their authority, political gladiators will by nature try to corrupt any electoral system as best they can.[1] For instance, the term *rotten borough*, an epithet from nineteenth-century British reform history, described incorporated spaces so small that one person or family actually controlled the selection of the member of Parliament, until the Reform Act of 1832 abolished 56 of them. Incidentally, the now familiar idea of a secret ballot, introduced in Australian state elections in 1856, first came to Canada in British Columbia in 1873 and was only a country-wide practice after Prince Edward Island accepted it in 1913. A series of reform acts in the UK up to 1918 extended the franchise and reformed the single-member districts, but that country still uses, as does Canada, the plurality method of vote tabulation—the first-past-the-post system—notwithstanding its many distortions of elector preference. Such a system always gives disproportionately more seats than actual vote percentages confer to those who have the power to change the system. Reform urgency is therefore somewhat diluted and the prevailing view maintains that the system "ain't broke."

5.1.2 Election format: by wards or city-wide

There are three basic ways to create electoral constituencies in cities (see Table 5.1). Voters may be allowed to vote for all positions in what is called the general vote, city-wide, or at-large elections. This format is most common among smaller cities in Canada's CMAs. More usually, larger cities are carved into electoral districts, or wards, with Vancouver and Surrey being the only exceptions of significance. Each ward, in turn, may return one or more councillors. The wards themselves may be drawn to cut through natural community boundaries and run from city boundary to boundary. Because of their horizontal or vertical appearance, these are called strip wards; they emulate at-large elections in their consequences but at some fraction of the cost. Block wards, on the other hand, are designed to capture neighbourhoods as voting units, and their boundaries pay attention to geographic matters, physical dividers such as railway tracks or freeways, and social and economic communities.

In the politically practical terms of representing their interest well, even leaders of Canadian community groups may not be sure which districting strategy would best maximize their group's political resources. If one opts for the block ward, then the group guarantees itself at least a single representative on council. If strip wards become the gambit, then the community would have an impact on questions raised, policies debated, and votes cast

Table 5.1: Elections in Canada's 12 Largest Cities, 1999

City	Population	Ward	Council[1]	R/Wd[2]	Wn[3]	Vs[4]	Hd	Term[5]
Toronto	2,385,421	28	56	85,194	16	6	M	3
Montreal	1,016,376	51	51	19,929	13	2	M	4
Calgary	786,082	14	14	54,863	6	0	M	3
Winnipeg	618,477	15	15	41,232	3	0	M	4
Edmonton	616,306	6	12	102,718	2	0	M	3
Mississauga	544,382	9	9	60,487	5	1	F	3
Vancouver	514,008	1	10	514,008	3	2	M	3
Laval	330,393	21	21	15,733	3	0	M	4
London[6]	325,340	7	18	46,521	5	1	F	3
Ottawa	323,340	10	10	32,334	3	0	M	3
Hamilton	322,352	8	16	40,294	3	0	M	3
Surrey	304,477	1	8	304,477	5	0	M	3

Notes:
1. Number does not include the mayor or head of council.
2. Average of residents per ward.
3. Number of women on council.
4. Members of visible minorities.
5. Term in office (number of years).
6. London retained a four-person Board of Control elected city-wide.

for a number of representatives. In Canada, since the late 1960s, the greater numbers of community activists have opted to pursue block wards.

The stratagem works this way (Hough 1970). Again, let us assume an urban setting of 100,000 voters. This time the CPR divides the community in half, with the conservatives living in the north and the social democrats below the tracks. The objective is to create two wards of equal size. Block wards could be drawn east to west along the tracks to encompass the income ghettos and would be of equal size. But if council were to decide on strip wards north to south across the tracks, then that boundary would also produce electorates with equal numbers of richer and poor people. One thing that councillors do know well, however, is that voter turnout on election day is not the same for all groups. Let us assume here that this ratio means the richer vote at twice the turnout of the poor. Thus, there will be twice as many voters in the richer area. Strip wards work to the advantage of candidates who primarily focus on the policy concerns of those richer residents; after the vote, the elected councillors will be those most likely living in the richer areas. On the other hand, block wards would negate the differential impact of turnout because no matter how many vote in the poorer district, 100 per cent of them would be from less well-to-do homes, and candidates in this area would have a real inducement to address equalities in city servicing.

Is this the way the real world operates? Yes. Before being intercepted by neighbourhood activists, Toronto city councillors tried to pull off just such a strip ward gerrymander in 1969. After an appeal to the OMB, they were ordered to implement neighbourhood wards. In the election that followed, these block districts stacked from the waterfront to the city's northern boundary, from poorer through richer, produced turnouts of 29, 38, and 48 per cent respectively. The two representatives from the first of these (Ward 6) argued effectively for some modest sensitivity towards residents in centre city urban renewal initiatives, the first time such arguments had been made on city council.

It is well understood by expert, gladiator, and informed citizen that any move from city-wide to small neighbourhood ward elections of council-lors produces fallout. Three general consequences for policy-making and any existing loci of power are especially prevalent if formal partisanship is absent. First, power is more widely distributed within the council, and it is less likely that councillors will be able to act unanimously because dispersed citizens' groups have gained institutionalized access through ward repre-sentatives. Typically, small ward councils also have more members. Second, these defined particularist groups will be officially recognized, whereas the at-large system tends to reinforce views of the city as an homogenous collec-tive, and will be more likely to be represented on council. Third, councillors will want to do overt favours for the constituents in their neighbourhoods, and policy will be made through bargaining among the councillors, with inaction the result when satisfactory deals cannot be cut (Banfield and Wil-son 1966: 90–91).

If only to bring some kind of order to their proceedings, larger councils seem conducive to at least minimal party-like organizing. This leads to the critique that to overcome stalemate, and similar to what happens in federal and provincial legislatures, controversial policy deals are worked out in the privacy of caucus, and subsequent council meetings are but shows for public consumption.

The real test is whether, after electoral system adaptation, policy choices change. They seem to. The newly elected Winnipeg Unicity small ward council (of 50, plus the mayor, in 1971) undertook no major city-wide pub-lic works expenditures, but "there was an immediate inclination for log-roll-ing in expenditures for the direct personal credit of councillors, particularly among the previous suburban representatives" (Lightbody 1978b: 502). The majority Independent Citizens' Election Committee (ICEC) party met in caucus to allocate the building of recreation facilities for their own districts at the expense of other areas and city-wide benefits.

So, while parties can work around the naturally divisive institutional tendencies of non-partisanship and small wards, as happened in Winnipeg, they actually thrive where elections are city-wide. The policy consequences are seen in the at-large cities of British Columbia. In Vancouver, for example, where the NPA held all seats on council and on school and parks boards in 1999, council touted a new scheme to implement a flat fee for garbage collection and sewerage for all homes regardless of size or value as an "environmental awareness" operation. But, by removing the charge from the slightly more progressive property tax base, the real impact was to increase taxes in lower income areas by an average of 20.7 per cent and to decrease taxation in wealthier neighbourhoods by about 4.5 per cent. The councillors were quite well aware of which citizens had been the more likely to vote. It is improbable that a neighbourhood ward council would have entertained similar policies since half of the population resides in the less wealthy area east of Main Street. It is too soon to report on the initial operations of ward elected and not overtly partisan new councils in recently amalgamated Toronto, Ottawa, or Halifax. It is to be noted that the new Toronto wards had the same configuration as the federal (as of 1998) and provincial electoral districts (since 1999). One can only speculate whether this will yield clarity or confusion about representation and authority in the minds of electors.

Finally, unlike rural municipalities where the heads of council are typically chosen from and among the ward councillors, all mayors for Canadian cities are elected city-wide. Exceptionally, the city of London, Ontario, continues with the now archaic practice of also electing four controllers at-large who, together with the mayor, constitute a Board of Control with greater formal authority.

5.1.3　Power and space: reform periods and elections

However cloaked in argument, election reform is always about ideology and power, not efficiency or good administration. This is what E.E. Schattschneider argued when he stipulated that "All forms of political organization have a bias in favor of the exploitation of some kinds of conflict and the suppression of others because organization is the mobilization of bias" (1960: 71). By its very definition, politics is rooted in conflict. So the only real question is: Who is going to win by playing on the field, and who is not? It is useful to note that "to reform" means only to replace.

During the two important reform periods of 1900 and the 1960s, the segment of the urban regime that sought to manage the city "as a whole" politically found themselves in opposition to any electoral system which, in their judgement, failed to provide a single point of focus for all of council. This not unusual quest for advantage had the incidental but salutary effect for the upper-class reformers of decreasing the electoral participation of working-class groups whose leaders and advocates, in turn and in reaction, pressed for smaller scale electoral districts.

At-large elections to give political expression to the entire space of the city were central to the NML's reform package, which was pressed upon local communities in Canada by business leaders as a value neutral means to de-politicize municipal administration, especially in western Canada and by the board of control format in Ontario and Montreal (Lightbody 1978a: 309-12). Those who most strongly favoured at-largeism in Calgary (1914), Winnipeg and Saskatoon (1920), and Vancouver (1936) pretty much represented those cities' small, entwined business and social leadership as exemplified by institutions like the Winnipeg Grain Exchange and all the cities' chambers of commerce. Banfield and Wilson once observed that, typically, businessmen, professionals, and self-identified upper-class civic leaders have consistently opposed neighbourhood wards. "Such people are invariably placed at a disadvantage by [small wards] ... because they are minority groups ... because the resources they command (social status, expertise, corporate wealth) are not effective in influencing small-district councilmen, and in part because they feel that a politics of personal influence and neighborhood interests is wrong and inefficient" (Banfield and Wilson 1966: 92).

This last and classic liberal reform position was well captured by Crawford when he stated, "Those elected at large can afford to take a community rather than a sectional view, for they are compelled ... to support measures designed to benefit the greatest number; dividing the city into sections ... is detrimental to the best community spirit" (1954: 84-85). Like other early postwar reformers in Canada, Crawford also believed that the general vote provided better and "more efficient" government. However, the reason that city regimes in Canada adopted at-largeism was widespread paranoia within the male propertied classes engendered by the 1919 Winnipeg General Strike. It was only two years after the Russian Revolution and, with Canadian troops still in Russia to combat the Bolsheviks, near hysteria combined with xenophobia to divide western cities. In the United States at this time several major cities, believing they had been targeted "by the Reds" for overthrow, had quietly deployed flying platoons of riot police during Fourth of July festivities. In Canada, victorious local business candidates changed election rules quickly and to their continuing advantage. By 1920, a number of "good government" parties had mobilized in cities from the Lakehead west, and these were "all formed by business men fearful of socialist, communist and other extremist elements" (Joyce and Hossé 1970: 17). They were ready to install American municipal reform as a tactic to defuse an anticipated labour coup at city hall. Even the large strip ward form in Winnipeg increased the costs of political information and campaigning sufficiently to guarantee sustainable business cartel victories into the late twentieth century.

By the 1960s, however, urban reform had a different face. Whatever its flower-child idealism, it was also about "real politick" and power. It began with a conception of the urban space as an amalgam of different social and economic sectors and then proceeded to the claim that their existences ought to be institutionalized on council. All available evidence indicated that the existing at-largeism only elected one class of person. For example, of 27 people elected at-large in Vancouver in the mid-1990s, only four lived in the less affluent half of the city; none of Edmonton's at-large school trustees resided in its poorer eastern half. Even Crawford (1954) had noted, and applauded, that the general vote removed "neighbourhood" representatives. The new reformers were genuinely opposed to those in urban regimes who, because of the very high city-wide costs, had used their political resources to manipulate elections.

Most importantly, the new reformers targeted electoral malaise by claiming electors had insufficient information about the numerous at-large candidates to vote in their own best interests. In consequence, voters boycotted local elections. For an example of this, in Edmonton in 1986, Richard Woodward received 4,500 school board votes to finish fortieth in a field of 57 names. This wasn't bad considering that he quit campaigning a few days after nomination, attended no forums, gave no speeches, had no posters, and had "disconnected his phone so voters couldn't bug him about his stand on the issues" (*Edmonton Journal*, 20 October 1986). In 1978 Harry Smith, a candidate for the London Board of Education, managed to glean 8,000 votes with a similar effort and finished ahead of three candidates who had run full campaigns (*Globe and Mail*, 16 November 1978).

For these reasons, reformers in the 1960s campaigned for neighbourhood wards in Toronto (Higgins 1986: 333), produced the 50 districts of 11,000 residents for Winnipeg in 1971, and clamoured in Vancouver for a return to the 12 single-person wards which the city had from 1929-36. Their arguments partially explain Calgary's move in 1977 to replace six dual-member districts with 14 single-person wards and were also the reason behind the Saskatchewan NDP government's move to bring wards into Saskatoon and Regina in 1973. This also indicates why that government's successor Progressive Conservative ministry abolished wards in 1987: the gladiatorial class understands system bias.

The tactical course of the neo-liberals of the 1990s is still being set. The priority matter has been structural redefinition of Canada's city-regions rather than questions about representation. The long inertia marked by a succession of provincial investigations into governing Ottawa-Carleton and the suburban diaspora which is Edmonton were both the result of neo-liberal provincial governments being transparently unwilling to upset their suburban supporters too greatly. At the two-tier regional level, representation was always left as a system of **indirect election** with considerable voter inequity. In its Capital Region Alliance, Edmonton with 73 per cent of the population is still entitled to only 8.2 per cent of the votes, if votes are ever taken. One policy consequence of this is that, in dire times, non-elected regimes boot their policy concerns to a higher plane, the provincial ministry, to which they have easy access and which, if it has the inclination, possesses the authority to act.

New pressures to change representation at the end of the twentieth century were somewhat similar to those at its beginnings—to smaller councils and larger wards. The aim for the old urban regime remains the same, that being to devise institutions with sufficient focused authority to facilitate economic growth in the face of anxieties over global competition. One difference has been that more women have been able to win elected roles where at least some official decision power resides.

5.1.4 Collateral consequences

It is now taken for granted that Canadian municipal elections are conducted on a first-past-the-post, or plurality system, which means that the candidate(s) who receives the most votes wins. One consequence is that usually a *majority* of electors, sometimes a quite sizable one, will have voted for someone else—the popular vote a party receives and the number of seats a party wins are usually quite different. In federal and provincial politics, some rather unusual results have come about from the combination of strict party voting with single-member plurality systems. In British Columbia in 1996, the NDP (39.5 per cent) formed the government with 39 MLAs while the Liberals received more votes at 41.8 per cent but six fewer seats. In 1998, the Liberals won the Quebec election (popular vote of 43 per cent) but the PQ (with 42 per cent of the popular vote) formed the government with 62 per cent of the seats. In the most grievous case, the federal election of 1979, the Liberals (with 40.1 per cent of the popular vote) defeated the Progressive Conservatives (with 35.9 per cent), but that party's leader Joe Clark became prime minister with an advantage of 136 to 114 MPs.

The plurality method has not always been the norm in Canadian municipal elections, nor is it usual in much of the non Anglo-American liberal democratic world. To correct for the arbitrary misrepresentation of voters' real
choices under plurality voting, any number of artificial majority-producing
arrangements have been attempted. Proportional representation systems try to
equate representation on councils to the actual distribution of tabulated votes.
The single transferable ballot by which an elector ranks individual candidates
by order of preference was widely used in western Canadian cities after the
First World War until the late 1950s. During this period, Calgary, Winnipeg,
and Edmonton also had multi-member constituencies which used this voting
mechanism to elect their provincial legislators. But because it was too complex to operate easily, only partially intelligible to the ordinary elector, and
quite cumbersome to tally in a pre-computer age, the system was abandoned.

The blending of a plurality system with non-partisanship has led to a
number of observable consequences. On municipal election day, the elector is often faced with a ballot paper with a vexing complexity of voting
options. This is especially compounded in at-large elections where there
are additional boards as in Vancouver, or a Board of Control as in London,
and school district elections. Many citizens choose simply not to vote for
the unknown on the school trustee ballot, and it is not uncommon for the
schools tally to be eight to ten percentage points lower than even the 35 per
cent voting for the mayor and councillors. The process weakens the legitimacy of the boards.

The second and more important consequence is the well-recognized
power of incumbency in non-partisan elections where name recognition and
public visibility are enormous political advantages. Kaplan calculated the re-
election of Metro Toronto level councillors at 86 per cent from 1953 to 1965
(1967: 186). Over the last two decades, across western Canada incumbents
seeking re-election are returned at a rate of 84.6 per cent. In Ontario the
figure is just a little lower at slightly over 80 per cent (Kushner *et al.* 1997:
520, 543-44). Nonpartisan elections do not feature the massive party turn-
overs that are found in Europe or in the UK. In the 2004 British local elections, Labour finished third (26 per cent) and lost 479 seats in local elections
widely viewed as a referendum on the national government's support for
the Iraq war; Conservative candidates received 38 per cent support, and the
Liberal Democrats 30 per cent. In Canada, though, an incumbent's apparent issue knowledge (based usually on procedural familiarity) is combined
with even more knowledgeable access to campaign funding, and these two
become tough resources for any challenger to overcome.

Third, curiously enough, since candidates are listed alphabetically by
surname, those in at-large elections whose surnames begin in the first half

of the alphabet, from A to M, have about a 15 per cent advantage, as voters work down the list to look for anyone who sounds familiar. One such accidental alderman was Edmonton's David Leadbeater who, in 1974, won 8.9 per cent of the total votes cast in a three-member strip ward contested by no incumbent. A young, politically unknown leftist and otherwise obscure university sessional lecturer in economics, Leadbeater no doubt benefited from surname location and his father's prominence as the city's popular Anglican archbishop.

Of course, this all presumes that the matter of elected representation is important, and, if it is important to policy choices made, then the matter of glaring inequities in representation by gender must be addressed. City politics is a white, middle-class, middle-aged, male sport. It is dominated by persons from Canada's founding European groups, although neighbourhood wards have permitted some second-generation penetration by earlier migrant communities (including those from around the Mediterranean) and episodic visible minority successes. Councils are, moreover, controlled by those who can manage their own time, not infrequently the otherwise underemployed, unemployed, and unemployable. Owners of smaller businesses (especially insurance and real estate) and others more or less retired from careers in professions like journalism, teaching, public administration, and other community work greatly predominate. Blue-collar workers cannot take the time to play the game and are only represented on councils by their unions' organizers.

Given this imposing roster, women are surely not less qualified than men to serve. At least they are no less represented at city hall than in either federal or provincial legislatures, but they are still not equally represented. Recent federal elections have returned women as about 20 per cent of the House of Commons, a slightly higher measure than on all of Ontario's local councils. Around 15 per cent of provincial legislators are women. By 1994, the number of women presenting as local candidates in Ontario equaled 20 per cent of all candidates, with a success rate that was slightly higher at 21 per cent, better than among the men (Kushner *et al.* 1997: 546-47) and twice as high as women's success rates in federal politics. Just under one-third of all *city* councillors were women. In Quebec, about 21 per cent of councillors were women in 1995 (Gidengil and Vengroff 1997: 524). For 88 cities across Canada in 1993, Linda Trimble calculated that 24 per cent of councillors were women, that they held at least one-quarter of the seats in half the cities, and that 36 per cent of councillors in Canada's 14 largest cities were female. She estimates that about one-third of women candidates are successful (1995: 94-101). Although her subsequent work focuses on provincial and federal legislatures, her general conclusion that "electoral progress for women in Canada appears to have stalled" (2003: 44) is accurate for cities as well. At its annual convention in 2004, the FCM received a report that 21 per cent of municipal politicians in Canada are female, compared to 27 per cent in the UK and 42 per cent in Sweden (<http:www.fcm.ca/English/policy/women.html>).

Some aspects of this information are presented in Table 5.1. The data suggest that women have more success in cities with larger electoral districts of 50,000 or more (33.9 per cent) than small (22.9 per cent), but the size of city itself (500,000 or more) produces no statistical difference. This is notwithstanding the recent, more detailed findings for Quebec indicating that in that province the larger the city the smaller the chance that women can have a significant impact. There were no women on the first 23-member city council for the newly amalgamated Halifax Regional Community in 1995, as all nine female candidates were defeated, including six who had previously held seats on the four former councils. In Ontario, women seem marginally to be more successful in elections in larger (26.3 per cent) than smaller (22.6 per cent) municipalities. By the way, members who are visibly from minority communities fare better where there are large wards than small, but that percentage is not yet at 10 per cent (8.3 per cent) of council representatives.

All studies across the country reveal a growing willingness for women to run, with a higher probability of winning, since the breakthrough of 10 per cent council representation in the early 1980s. Consistently more women serve in representative roles locally than in the wider area legislatures; the average for the 350 or so positions in the 27 core cities of CMAs in 2001 averaged 25 per cent. In 2004, for instance, Toronto voters returned women as just under one-third of councillors (13 of 44), and Edmonton 40 per cent (five of 12). Why are women finally so involved? It is easy to claim that less travel makes local government more easily accessible and compatible with family obligations. Trimble is more insightful, however, when she argues that women possess access to a combination of resources that may be effectively applied (such as direct local knowledge and skills in community organizing) and that personal experience with shortcomings in policy applications breeds a level of interest in city policy problems. The bottom line for Trimble is that women's participation in politics matters: "it reflects a political strategy which is cognizant of the overlap between public and private spheres and which recognizes community policies as a useful arena for political change" (1995: 110). Women choose city politics precisely because it has power over those policies that count most directly to many people.

Can it be argued that more equitable representation will make any policy difference? Some may claim there is a feminist City Beautiful with a claim to all aspects of peace, order, and good government (Graham and Phillips

1998: 31-33), but such exclusionary claims are mostly silly. Feminist activism has indeed played an important role in leading us to assess public policy not by universal precepts but by its differential impacts as defined by the person on the receiving end. Even as candidates have learned that issues of importance to women are also "men's issues," they have struggled to develop a greater sensitivity to nuance. For instance, support for a stronger economy may be interpreted differently as job security versus economic opportunities. Or safe streets may mean better lighting and community-based policing, not a SWAT (Special Weapons and Tactical) unit in full body armour.

5.1.5 Conducting actual campaigns

Most of the growing availability of published work on successful campaigns is still about federal and provincial operations, so a short comment on the conduct of city campaigns is necessary. Everyone closely associated with city politics knows when the next vote is going to be, and that is three years (four in Quebec) after the last (Lightbody 1997a). In the federal and provincial parliamentary system, the government leader may consult pollsters or focus groups before choosing to have the writs for election issued. However, the civic date is absolutely fixed by a general Municipal Election Act in each province.

From their first day in office, incumbents have a target: re-election. Of course, this has an impact on city business! Longer term policies, if any, must be begun in Year One, for in Year Three the focus is on short-term gratification. Taxes, and council salaries presumably, may be increased at the beginning of the term but not near the end. Status projects with prolonged cost lines and big-ticket items like computer system upgrades will be pushed by senior staff in Year One as will controversial hard policy choices. In this, activists scent an electorate attention span of about a half-year, barring the growth and sustenance of some strong anti-government grudge. Prestige items will be slated for Year Three, especially if they are international sporting events such as world track and field championships or university games to be held during the summer before the vote with bundles of trophies and ribbons to be presented by the mayor and councillors. The policy strategies of office-holders, such as they are, are intuitively influenced by this pattern, which is also well appreciated by the adept bureaucrat. Conversely, bureaucratic sabotage of current political "masters" for program refusal or mismanagement can be a potent resource for almost any challenger during the election period.

The larger city campaigns have evolved a natural rhythm over the years, some practical aspects of which are suggested in Table 5.2, which contrasts the

Table 5.2: Political Resources as Applied to City Election Campaigns

Activity	Incumbent	Challenger
1. Policy	What has been done	What needs be done better
	Conservative (status quo)	Radical (adaptation)
	City bureaucracy	Under-served clienteles
	Institutionalized policy groups	New social movements
2. Fund-raising	Business tied to city hall	Aggrieved developers
	Development industry	Smaller businesses
	Other client groups	
	Mayor's dinner	Fund-raising brunches
	Campaign bankroll	Surrogate political parties
3. Media	Official functions	Critical attacks
	Evening newscasts	Paid commercials
	Press conferences	Staged events
	Name recognition	Status outside politics
4. Poll Organization	Previous workers	Senior level political friends
5. Attachments	Rolodex of favours done	Friends, cultural groups
	Political supporters	Business, professional confreres
	Regime leaders	Sports associates
	Status seekers	Partisan cronies

applied political resources of mayoralty candidates under non-partisan conditions. It is always the case that incumbents want to be noticed, since name retention by the public is the mandatory resource in non-partisan politics. One fascination for those attending council meetings is to observe the mad dash to stand first with comment in front of the dinnertime news cameras.

Elections are primarily a game for the gladiators. These are a small group, probably no more than several dozen or so in a major city, who are willing to transfer their interests to the municipal level. Such gladiators and political professionals from other realms can apply hands-on knowledge of focus groups, poll organization, and opinion survey techniques. They bring skills and contacts. Experienced fund-raisers with their lists of past donors (and amounts for each) are essential, for it now costs from $250,000.00 to $1 million dollars—a minimum of $1 a household—to mount a reasonable city-wide campaign. When they can be afforded at the city level, polls are most helpful in confirming and assigning priorities to the campaign leaders' own appreciation of electorate concern, thus helping to set the tone and pace of any challenge or stay-the-course effort. Many campaigners from other political levels now view the mayor's office as a surrogate to holding power elsewhere, especially if the candidate is identified with a particular party. While this identity strengthens the call to the faithful, the corollary is that it weakens any appeal to strong partisans of other parties.

The general strategy is set around the predetermined voting date. Every time-line for policy, fund-raising, media events, commercial airing, and voter contact are worked backwards from that. For the challenger, the principal strategy is to be identified as the only credible opposition candidate by the relatively small press gallery. This serves to focus coverage on a two-person contest out of the general stampede and reduces the complexity of the ballot paper to a "yes" or "no" choice separating the two contenders. Simplifying the public education process in this way also tends to increase voter turnout somewhat. During the course of the campaign, especially before official nomination when candidates file their papers, incumbents can manipulate public policies. In response, their challengers must plot special stunts, media moments, and announcements. The harsh reality is that not much of substance differentiates the protagonists, caught as any city is in a web of provincial legislation, regulation, and financial administration. Issues of perceived differences in leadership style become paramount, and, even here, the rule of thumb is that any important message must be repeated at least three times during a campaign before all in the politically significant audience will have heard it.

Recognizing that office-holders will have public occasions, such as festivals and fairs, to exploit, challengers devote their summers to tapping every connection, from college fraternity or service club to identifiable ethnic and religious leaders, for endorsement and volunteers. To campaign for mayor is a full-time job. In the campaign itself, money and labour will *always* be in short supply.

The tactics are thus applied quickly, and fund-raising is usually paramount. A politically astute incumbent will have leftover dollars from the last campaign stashed away, likely augmented over intervening years by the proceeds from an annual mayor's dinner for supporters. For the challenger, money is a greater concern, especially if the incumbent has been generally inoffensive. However much it is, the largest donations will probably come "in kind" with a gift of TV time or studio availability to tape commercials. The campaign headquarters, with copious parking, will be squeezed from some compliant realtor. Food and venues where even brunches as well as dinners can become a policy event for media consumption and consumables on a daily basis for volunteers need to be sought. Cash will also have to be raised in small increments continuously, and this can become a participatory device identifying the small donor closely with the candidate. Oversize buttons, T-shirt sales, key-chains, and big balloons (beads and trinkets) become part of modern voter linkage.

Historically, much hoopla surrounds nomination day, which usually comes a month before the vote, when candidates and many of those who have signed the nomination papers troop down to city hall to file officially. Reflecting nostalgia for the small scale, even large city campaigns still emphasize some semblance of a personal connection with electors. For the serious city-wide candidate, the election quickly descends from eight months of grand strategy into two months of tactics—grinding, one-day-like-the-last meetings with voters. Public forums become a necessary evil, often every night, even though they are usually only attended by relatives, workers, and others already persuaded. Traditional endorsements are sought from the Chamber of Commerce or District Labour Council and from the editorial board of all major local dailies. It has, though, become more important in today's cities to elicit a public statement from religious leaders, a letter from the professional and businesswomen's clubs, or word-of-mouth endorsement among other smaller particularized communities, specifically including the gay and lesbian. Election signs remain a very important device for municipal campaigns where there are no party labels to link the voter to the names on the ballot. In labour intensive work, lawn signs must be put up and maintained. Private locations are preferred to public space eyesores because they build brand loyalty through that good neighbour's endorsement.

The media follow the news. To be set apart from the swarm, the serious challenger must stage photo-opportunities, media events, and community stunts to offset the natural media promotion of the mayor. Even the best mayoralty candidate cannot knock at the doors of each of a quarter-million households. Even phoning is difficult, notwithstanding mechanical dialing devices and phone banks, because the scale is very large for the available budget. Websites are now mandatory for all; hence, they tend to have a neutral impact as just another flake in the blizzard. By default, television becomes the friendly, if costly, medium. Free coverage through reportage is optimum. But the essential problem for any contender is institutional, for members of the press gallery tend subconsciously to provide support for the status quo. Over time, they become a part of the system on which they report and view newcomers, as do incumbents, with suspicion and a little fear. Among other things, the novice will find it difficult to penetrate the familiar language shorthand employed by councillors, their staff, and media alike. In another context, David Taras made the following astute observation: "For a strong thinker and debater, the news conference is always an opportunity; for a less able politician it can degenerate into a nightmare" (1988: 40). A bumble in trying to interpret city hall terminology during a news conference can be easily or deliberately misconstrued by reporters and subsequently portrayed as representing a more general incompetence.

The major outstanding issue here is the matter of election financing, a question in which some problem areas are considered below as an ethical matter. That city politics is not taken seriously is best demonstrated by the fact that civic elections are captive financially to those who equate city policy choices directly to personal or corporate well-being. This thinking reflects more the small town mentality of past generations rather than current complex urban settings. Simple fairness in democratic competition today requires a better minimum standard against which city elections should be measured, and it is time that regulations similar to federal requirements are set. In short, donations should be disclosed, tax receipts for deductions from provincial tax payable should be provided, free broadcast time should be apportioned, reasonable spending limits cognizant of scale should be set, and enforcement should be strictly applied. No city in Canada presently meets these conditions, and this undoubtedly contributes much to the democratic malaise which attends city hall. Quebec cities fall under the *ex post facto* eye of that province's chief electoral officer. Ontario, since 1990, has required that candidates file a statement of expenditures and contributions, requiring disclosure of sources over $100.00 and limiting any one source to $750.00. Other cities must make do with their own less formal and less easily enforced expense bylaws. There is room for improvement in all these areas.

5.2 The Citizenship of City Elections and Voting

Liberal democratic political culture opens many opportunities for personal involvement in politics. For most citizens, though, interest in public affairs tends to be focused on elected representatives and the processes which put them into public office. Occasionally one might ponder writing a letter or sending an email about a particularly egregious policy failure, but very few citizens go much beyond that thought. While responsible liberal democracies expect citizens to be involved with government, such interaction requires effective communication between the governors and those governed, a test often failed. A profound irony of our democracy is that its survival seems to hinge on the reluctance of most citizens to partake in the process as other than intelligent spectators.

Direct public involvement is not an unduly complex business until efforts are made to develop new institutions which are both representative and participatory. This was certainly one of the more important practical lessons to be learnt from the failed Winnipeg Unicity experiment (1971). Built into any representative political system are very practical limitations on the occasions in which individual citizens are welcomed to participate in the formulation of decisions whose outcomes directly affect them. In the normal case, it is the elected representative body itself that has the exclusive authority to determine whether the accordion of citizen participation is to be opened or shut. Too frequently, and notwithstanding the genteel manner of its accomplishment, it is the learned experience of municipal citizens that they have been organized out of the public policy process by their own neighbours elected into public office.

Voter participation in local elections is our concern here. Let us assume an extreme representative form of democracy in which public participation is restricted to voting every few years. This form assumes that councillors will make policy choices largely on the basis of best available technical information. Local elections are still important because voter participation provides the whole operation with an aura of legitimacy and a tacit affirmation of delegated authority.

Those social scientists who devote time to the study of elections largely do so because the act of voting provides them with one of the very few quantifiable and comparative indices of *direct* participation in politics. What they find is a considerable boycott of city elections where up to three-quarters of electors choose to stay home. Schattschneider observed that "Abstention reflects the suppression of the options and alternatives that reflect the needs of the nonparticipants" (1960: 105). Put another way, politics has to be about something that is relevant, that motivates the citizen to feel a need to choose between genuine options, and the true pathology of the city is that its political rhetoric is empty of such meaning.

About three-quarters of Canadians have historically voted in federal elections (61 per cent in 2004), and about two-thirds turn out to produce provincial results. A "good" city voter turnout is around one-third. Whenever any of the actual results deviate significantly from what we might reasonably predict from past experience, then the social scientist must ask why, and the answers reveal quite a lot about the community, the campaign, the candidates, and the local issues of importance. Because Canadian local elections are not like those in the UK and Europe where local branches of national parties are involved in the campaigns, they are also not conducted as a series of regional referendums on national issues. Another by-product of this cultural difference is that there is not so large a turnover among our councillors as occurs frequently in those jurisdictions. In Canada, local by-elections (to replace a dead, resigned, or removed councillor) and plebiscites held separately from the normal election date tend to produce voter turnout closer to 10 than 20 per cent.

5.2.1 Why is voting important?

The important questions are not about the values inherent in the relatively low levels of elector turnout and whether or not this is desirable in a free and democratic community. The frequent admonition of local newspapers to "vote as you please, but please vote" is misguided, when it can be demonstrated that only those who see themselves as having a direct stake in the outcome of an elected council's decisions have, in fact, participated. It may well be argued that an ill-informed vote by an otherwise reasonably conscientious citizen is disruptive to the process by which those better qualified to exercise public judgement should decide winners.

The important question for social science is whether those who participate are more or less evenly spread across all significant cleavages in the community. That is, do equal numbers of men and women, all income and occupational groups, newcomers and old-timers, and socially defined groups (i.e., defined by race, religion, and/or sexual orientation) turn out in roughly equal measure, be it 10 per cent or 60 per cent? The assumption is that those segments of the community which are more electorally active will stand in a better position than those who stay at home to make their influence felt in the public arena. They will have chosen persons sensitive to their agendas both to determine specific and general taxation and redistribution policies and to resolve occasionally divisive issues. Even local politicians are generally calculating enough to respond to voters in the first instance and not to residents as a whole. If the non-participants are disproportionately concentrated in certain socio-economic groupings (as we, and the councillors, know them to be), then, over the longer term, these communities will be more vulnerable to inequitable treatment by the municipal system. Such leadership as may represent non-participants in the ongoing operation will have to be more alert, more continuously observant, and better prepared to react, publicly and quickly, to the governing initiatives of representatives from the mobilized electorate.

It is in this sense that the relatively low levels of voter turnout locally assumes an important dimension, and the matter of "who votes" provides us with one measure to assess the relative openness and responsiveness of municipal democracy. Alternative plausible explanations for low levels of electoral involvement also reveal the ways in which local public decision-makers view existing institutions and processes. If, for instance, it can be shown that low voter turnout means that citizens are generally well satisfied with the direction of civic politics, then there is clearly no need to change access through institutional or procedural modifications. The evidence suggests that Edmonton through the 1950s, with its annual turnouts usually well below 20 per cent, is such a case in point. On the other hand, if political authorities are persuaded that low voter participation reveals instead that people are unprepared to involve themselves in a system that they believe is loaded against them from the get-go, then there may be compelling ammunition for a major restructuring of the operation. Powerful members of the Manitoba provincial cabinet after their 1969 election, drawing upon their personal local governing experiences, fully believed that this was indeed the case for voters among Winnipeg's multiple municipalities. The radical restructuring into Winnipeg Unicity thus became a high-level priority even in the otherwise busy agenda of a newly elected reform administration.

So the explanation for lower levels of voter participation is important for those contemplating possible reforms. There are three schools of thinking about this. First, the *satisfaction explanation* holds that most citizens generally appear to be relatively satisfied with the public policy package from their council; there is no need to rock the vote by either nominating or supporting opposition to the status quo. Low voter participation is thus to be interpreted in an affirming light. This is probably the case in the smaller, socially homogenous bedroom suburbs of a metropolitan core where there is likely to be either many acclamations to office or few serious challengers if the vote is conducted at-large. This explanation is most comfortably held by politicians representative of bourgeois interests, and they will claim that "our City is a business and the citizens are satisfied with council's management of it." If they are correct, then there is no need to seek reform of either institutions or process.

Second, a package of *technical explanations* argues that electors do not see themselves as having enough at stake in either material or ideological gains or losses to desert the comfort of their armchairs. The technical matters of zoning designations, traffic densities, and program budgeting are seen to be too complex for ordinary citizens. It is in this vein that some American scholars once argued that city hall is psychologically more distant than the national capitol (see, for example, Lineberry and Sharkansky 1974: 150ff; Banfield and Wilson 1963: 231-34). Individuals opposed to the large-scale amalgamations of Halifax or Toronto certainly claimed that size directly produces such feelings of great distance. Even the more congressional style of arrangements for the conduct of city business noted in Chapter 4 can be seen to detract from an easy familiarity for citizens more accustomed to the focused accountability of parliamentary operations.

Other critics have raised questions about inclusion, importantly and specifically about visible minorities and women. It is understood that those people in the development industry, real estate, and contracting trades who pay taxes on the basis of business assessment will identify the municipality as an immediate and intelligible process that commands their attention. Only home-owners, who pay property taxes directly, in any way approximate this level of interest. Pluralist reform academics and higher income community groups buy into these explanations to argue for reform of the process, not the political structures, to permit local political parties and neighbourhood interest groups to present a more consistently open and effective expression of policy demands during and between elections.

Finally, a more radical concern with low voting levels finds explanation in **political efficacy**. It contends that people do not choose to become involved because they hold a low expectation that such participation will in any way influence the political course of events. This is often summarized in the cliché "You can't fight City Hall." Low levels of political efficacy are fuelled by a perception of the distribution of power and influence in the community such that any electoral contribution is inherently manipulative and ultimately meaningless. To accept the validity of this assessment is to yield to the proposition that basic institutions must be fundamentally realigned so as to guarantee that popular participation in the process has consequence. The Winnipeg Unicity reforms are an example of this. These introduced small neighbourhood wards (50 of them, with about 10,000 people in each) as one step towards maximizing the value to the process of each individual's vote.

5.2.2 Structural influences on voting turnout

The likelihood of higher or lower voter turnout in any given community is a product of certain factors about the community itself. The dominant socio-economic and governmental characteristics of the municipality play an important role; any factor that diminishes people's belief in their own personal knowledge about local politics decreases the probability of their voting. Three general hypotheses thus present themselves.

A first look at a *community's social structure* considers its degree of stability as measured by the numbers of newcomers. Communities characterized by a largely static population base have, as a rule, social institutions (church, community clubs, volunteer sports groups, neighbourhood organizations) with longer continuity and shared history. Such communities have established communication lines between private leaders and public officials. Political patterns are familiar to potential voters, and ready information about civic affairs is only a coffee cup away. Back-fence gossip quickly sorts out the able candidate come election time. More qualified neighbourhood leaders move quickly and with sure support into public office. Rapidly growing suburbs of the metropolis, on the other hand, have new populations with fewer ties to the established community and its leaders. For example, a survey of Edmonton's two major and burgeoning suburbs in 1979 found that about 60 per cent of residents could not name a single member of council other than the mayor; in the city proper, that number was 14 per cent (Axworthy and Reid 1979). When knowledge of local public business is less easy to acquire, elections bear the consequence in lower voter turnout. Yet outside city-regions, as in the smallest category of Ontario localities, voting may become a communal social activity, and voter turnout tends to be in a strong, inverse correlation with community size (Kushner *et al.* 1997: 542).

Second, students of Canadian politics generally understand that the magnitude of social conflict from the nation's longstanding patterns of social cleavage spills over into politics. City politics is no different. The extent of *community homogeneity* or, conversely, its degree of racial, ethnic, social class, and cultural differences directly affect local political activities and elections. An homogenous community, be it entirely composed of white-collar insurance salespersons or blue-collar industrial workers, generates fewer differences among citizens, giving them less imperative to vote. There will be numerous acclamations to office. In a more heterogeneous community, religious leaders (be they mullah, priest, rabbi, or pastor) are not averse to providing political guidance along with the spiritual. As presumed knowledge grows, so too does the willingness to get out and vote.

Third, and as we have discussed, the *structure of political institutions* has a direct bearing on electoral participation. The reformers of 1900 sought to sterilize the municipal business from the poison germ of boss politics. They were successful, in removing not only the worst excesses of nepotism, cronyism, patronage, and graft, but also broader public interest. City management purges public division over controversial policy alternatives, and elections at-large eliminate ward and neighbourhood leaders as anchors of knowledge. Formerly contentious by virtue of its authority, the mayor's office has become essentially a titular symbol, and the public face of civic activity is hidden behind anonymous, albeit effective, bureaucracy. Having little to vote for, or at least against, citizens tend to register their massive indifference by not voting at all.

The intervention of anti-partyism can hold considerable consequence for voting independent of political structures. Political parties frame issues in order to separate their positions from those of their opponents. In advertising this is known as product differentiation: the advertiser claims that one soap has better, more antibacterial cleaning power than another. Parties engage in direct personal contact during campaigns and, by the medium of party label, link candidates to voters. To put it another way, a voter may not be acquainted with an individual candidate but will still have clear knowledge of what his or her political position is because of party affiliation. In federal and provincial elections, a competitive party contest substantially increases voter turnout by 10 or more per cent; voter participation has been found similarly to increase under comparable local conditions. Parties provide cues as to how to vote by reducing issues to comprehensible dimensions; as assumed knowledge on the part of the elector increases, so does the willingness to play in the game. In short, the presence of local political parties increases voter turnout.

5.2.3 Determinants of individual and neighbourhood voting

Working in tandem with community-wide conditions are three sets of variables at the level of individual and neighbourhood. The first of these relates to age. Younger people, and those who have retired from the labour force, are not as likely to vote as individuals in the intervening age bracket. In the federal general election of 2000, turnout for those aged 18 to 24 was 25.4 per cent; this is not unusual: in the UK a year later, that rate was 39 per cent, compared to 59 per cent overall. Younger people tend to be highly mobile, concerned more with employment prospects than mayoralty speeches, involved in the preoccupations of establishing families and homes, and consequently less likely to be embedded in neighbourhood networks. Many older individuals have a tendency to withdraw from interest in low-level public life.

As with national and provincial elections, a person's income and education have a direct correlation with voter turnout (Higgins 1986: 313). Those with greater incomes, higher status jobs, and more formal education—and these all tend to be linked—are more likely to believe themselves informed about public affairs and to have a larger stake in policy outcomes. They also tend to feel more politically efficacious. The data consistently reveal that income and education are both directly correlated with voting and with the other activities toward the gladiatorial end on the hierarchy of participation. This is somewhat tautological insofar as participation by this class produces elected officials who tend to be both from it and sympathetic to its demands.

In each urban region, a small elite group, many of whom are part of the urban regime, might accurately be labelled **community cosmopolitans**. These are persons whose professional and employment activities and connections make them swiftly aware of policy initiatives and institutional developments in other places somewhat like their own cities. They are quick to share their expertise and to borrow from the experience of others. It is they who will apply extra-territorial knowledge to the local enterprise. They will also be the principal source for innovation in city governing. One caution for public policy born out of global interconnectedness is that these groups often have agendas more in common with status and professional counterparts abroad than with non-elite neighbours at home.

Finally, and especially for municipal politics, home-ownership has a major impact on probable voter turnout. Length of residence in a particular place, which enhances knowledge of public affairs, and the higher the assessed value of a home (because property taxes are calculated directly against this) become consistently powerful stimulants to interest. Home-owners are vested stakeholders and, unlike apartment dwellers for whom the local tax bill is normally hidden in the rent, receive an annual notification (and motivation) to participate in city elections. Voter turnout by apartment tenants is always very low in most communities.

The act of voting is neither the only activity nor the most important exercise that occurs in the course of an election campaign. As we have seen, electoral participation includes all of the gladiatorial and tactical activities from campaigning for candidates to putting up lawn signs (as well as removing those of opponents or those that are found to be environmentally offensive). But for most Canadians, voting in city elections is about as active as they are likely to get, and the level of indifference as measured by low voter turnout is quite high relative to federal and provincial elections. To repeat, the urban political culture of Canada can be accurately described as spectator-participant. One question that remains is how much this voter boycott has been fuelled by a growing cynicism about those in public office (Zussman 1997).

5.3 Election Finance and Other Small Problems with Ethical Behaviour

Can politicians be trusted? This is a question that has bedevilled students of the political craft from antiquity. Plato, for example, mused about the possibilities of citizens receiving any direct benefit from politicians' actions and concluded that while this might indeed happen, it would be only to further the politicians' own best interests. He wrote that cowherds and shepherds who fattened and cared for their flocks were not looking only for the betterment of the cattle and sheep: "The actual ruler or governor thinks of his subjects as sheep, all right, but his chief occupation, day and night, is how he can best fleece them to his own benefit" (Plato 1985: 343b).

Most political scientists today are not as amoral as to advocate what Machiavelli did: that continuing power is the one true and ascendant measure of a politician's ability, regardless of ethical considerations. One very good recent study notes a common critical conclusion that, for our times, "The problem is the system, not the quality of the officials or the rules that govern their conduct" (Langford and Tupper 1993: 15). Just to be minimally effective, legislators feel that they must work with their fellows, and, over time, they become collegial. By going along to get along, by keeping company with others who also serve more narrow interests than an objective public standard, politicians' behaviours are conditioned to the manifestly unfair by the very democratic institutions that stand at the heart of liberal self-governing. Once elected into positions with authority, decent individuals learn collegial corruption from mentors who were also once plain dealers. Bryce, who was so critical of machine politics, was moved to observe that, "members of rings, or the great boss himself, are [not] wicked men. They are the offspring of a system. Their morality is that of their surroundings" (1888: II, 785). Can it thus be argued that it is democratic structures themselves that corrupt the prototypical "good person?"

Langford and Tupper assert that their investigations reveal that "serious public misconduct is more often organized and systemic than freelance and individual" (1993: 14). If they are correct, the important practical question in this issue area is one of **procedural ethics**: concern over the fairness of the democratic process becomes paramount when we assess elected officials, overriding longer term governing effectiveness, social and economic redistribution, or institutional innovation. Rules for ethical conduct, such as conflict-of-interest guidelines, should be stringently applied, their enforcement by the unimpeachable open and absolute, and sanctions swift and severe. Presumably, new process rules will enshrine more integrity into decision-making.

But can procedural rules, conflict-of-interest guidelines, and ethical codes actually enshrine probability for fair treatment at city hall? It is the frailty in human behaviour that suggests a high degree of difficulty: "Experience leads … to the conclusion that no matter how comprehensive and well-conceived they may be, codified reforms may be manipulated, subverted, or ignored" (Lightbody 1993: 213). Ethical codes are still most susceptible to easy trespass in city governments, where capital is loose and political authorities are pliable to any economic endeavour linked to community boosterism.

The low politics at city hall are intensely personal and encompass small worlds in which individual livelihoods are immediately on the line. These are the politics of personal choice, where the blandishments of realtors, speculators, construction companies and their unions, neighbourhoods, and organized groups can sway votes. Process violations are unlike the systemic dealings which thrive in federal and political operations for, in the absence of the organized political management that parties provide, freelancers can blossom. Individual transgressions are sometimes noticed, but the silent collusion of kindred individuals all engaged in roughly similar promotion makes the enforcement of morality legislation elusive. Perhaps it is the minor nature of it all that condones it.

Sharon Sutherland shares the view that the patronage system in federal politics has served party, but not public, life (1993: 127). People are drawn into public service not from a selfless sense of duty but to gain a share of the public pot for their own place and person, just as the early union of Canada was held together by a mutually beneficial and politically calculated self-interest, what Mallory once labelled a "shaky coalition of strange bedfellows" (1971: 196). The modern federal system still engenders a sense of localism and provincialism through a constant sizing-up of the relative value of the spoils distributed. The situation has not changed much since colonial days. Lord Durham, arriving in Canada in the midst of an election campaign, wrote back to the British colonial secretary that "although I have taken some pains to ascertain what may be the questions likely to divide public opinion at the Hustings, I cannot detect any that are not of a personal, municipal, or local character ..." (noted by Mallory 1971: 196).

In cities with ward systems, the neighbourhood representative is at least partially evaluated on the ability to bring home the bacon either in the form of public goods and plunder or forestalled public evils (such as landfill locations). With few exceptions, the difference from national and provincial regimes is the absence of governing party coalitions to override unobstructed freebooting. In the city-region stuck with multiple autonomous municipalities, the overall framework for governing does not even exist! Sancton, commenting on the webs of patronage within Montreal's suburbs which provided their councillors a common goal of *survivance* in the form of resistance to any city initiative, argued that suburbs anywhere could subscribe to this behaviour because suburban "leaders have no desire to lose power over local systems which have proven to be valuable sources of political influence, patronage or even personal profit" (1979: 248).

Urbanologist Scott Greer once noted how under-observed the patronage game of the American suburb had been, primarily because it was thought to be so small scale with so little in the trough. He concluded "The assumption is that small municipalities, controlled by 'friends and neighbours,' (assumed to be middle-class also) perform honestly and legally. In point of fact, nobody knows whether this is true or not" (1963: 11). John Porter, on the first page of *The Vertical Mosaic* (1965), asserted that when a community's image-creators had essentially similar social and economic backgrounds, and were a relatively small "closely linked" group, they would project a common world-view that seems true only because it is consistent overall. The

Canadian suburb is not **Pleasantville** and only seems to be so because no one chooses to pose the necessary questions. The determined investigator, serious journalist, or diligent citizen would be well rewarded by considering an alternative hypothesis: that suburban political action is a development lucrative, mutually beneficial, and personnel-rewarding operation.

5.3.1 Shaping of elections

We have learned in this chapter that any voting system holds a bias favouring one particular set of voting resources or another. Left to their own devices, elected politicians will not embrace enthusiastically any form that stands in the path of their own re-election; the main issue for citizens is how far politicians are to be left alone in designing the representation rules.

From time to time, provincial governments have intervened not in order to benefit all citizens but to further the advantage of their own closest municipal allies: "Friends don't let friends campaign impaired." The NDP's 1971 Winnipeg Unicity legislation introducing 10,000-person neighbourhood wards sought to reverse the effects of the business-farm gerrymander which installed strip wards in 1920. In 1991, the provincial Progressive Conservatives produced a system of 15 pie-shaped strip wards with an eye to swamping inner-city electors. In 1973, the Saskatchewan NDP provincial government brought wards to Regina and Saskatoon, although this was opposed by the cities' boards of trade; in 1987, a provincial Progressive Conservative government reintroduced elections at-large. Vancouver's 1929 neighbourhood wards were eliminated in 1936 by the anti-socialist provincial legislature. Successive Social Credit (conservative) governments throughout the 1970s consistently refused pressure from neighbourhood progressives for wards in the city, with a large eye on maximizing the resources of its ideologically like-minded municipal allies in the civic NPA (Lightbody 1993: 203; Higgins 1986: 325-31).

A second matter quite apart from ward alignments, but nonetheless important, is the financing of city elections. These days, big city at-large elections are an expensive proposition. In Toronto, mayoralty candidates must campaign across a territory that sends 28 members to the House of Commons, the same number as the entire province of Alberta. The Calgary area is represented by seven MPs and 21 MLAs. Winnipeg elects eight MPs and Edmonton 19 MLAs. Due to this scale, it has been reasonably estimated that, on average, successful mayoralty candidates spent an average of $200,000 on their campaigns by the end of the 1990s. The successful Toronto mayoralty race in 1997 cost in excess of $267,000. Even excluding fringe contestants, candidates for council in larger Ontario centres now spend an average of nearly $11,000 (Kushner *et al.* 1997: 549). In the Calgary mayoralty stampede of 2001, winning candidate David Bronconnier paid out in excess of $1 million while his challenger, Bev Longstaff, spent just a fraction less (*Edmonton Journal*, 17 October 2001).

Not atypically, Ontario law still allows candidates to keep money raised but not spent on election. One-time Toronto mayor Art Eggleton legitimately used part of his surplus "to pay for his wife's attendance at official functions" (Lightbody 1993: 200). Calgary Mayor Al Duerr, who hosted annual fundraisers for up to 400 guests, "could legally take the $10,000 now sitting in a blind trust for his reelection and buy a golf club membership or pay down his mortgage" (*Calgary Herald*, 21 June 1991). By the mid-1980s, the *Globe and Mail* estimated that some incumbent City of Toronto councillors easily raised two or three times from the development business what it had cost them to be re-elected (11 December 1987; Greene and Shugarman 1997: 109-10). Only half of those councillors would go on public record by *voluntarily* disclosing the source and amounts of their decisions and expenses.

Where investigation has been undertaken, it consistently finds that the real estate development industry dominates, by up to three-quarters of funds raised, the campaign contributions in the major municipal races (Graham and Phillips 1998: 103-04; Higgins 1986: 352; Greene and Shugarman 1997: 107-11). Winnipeg's Dave Brown was called "the developer's candidate" for mayor, because the development industry raised $350,000 for him to run as head of council (Greene and Shugarman 1997: 109). He lost, not only for this but for previous conflict-of-interest problems surrounding his own subcontracting operations. What is curious is that such development funds go not only to booster candidates (as would be expected) but also to almost every major candidate with any real prospect of winning.

The research also discloses that incumbents find it easier to raise money than challengers do, which means that gladiators recognize how powerful a resource incumbency itself is and, through donation, help to fulfill the prophecy. In their study of Ontario municipalities, Kushner and his colleagues reported that incumbents outspent challengers at a rate of two to one (1997: 549). As an example confirming both these observations, nearly half of the campaign donations to "socialist" Edmonton Mayor Jan Reimer's re-election in 1992 came from developers and from other free enterprisers who had significant past business contracts with city hall (Lightbody 1997a: 126-28). In the 1996 elections in Vancouver, where there were (and are) no expenditure limits, the development-friendly NPA reported spending $959,566 to elect all of its candidates, while its opponents in the Coalition of Progressive Electors (COPE) were able to spend only $360,473.

Historically, city elections in Canada have been of little interest to national corporations. According to the proxy documents appended to its 1998 *Annual Report*, an undisclosed part of the quarter million dollars or so spent by the Bank of Montreal on political donations that year went into the first Toronto Megacity elections. No other city campaign was so mentioned (it is to be noted that Quebec prohibits such contributions). To whom the money was paid, as well as the precise amount, was not disclosed. Still, the importance of that city to the bank's corporate activities could not be more graphically illustrated. In Vancouver during the middle third of the twentieth century, campaign donations from the CPR and BC Electric fuelled the coffers of the dominant NPA campaigns (Gutstein 1983: 210).

Manitoba has had provincial conflict-of-interest legislation for municipalities since 1983. A City of Winnipeg bylaw restricts mayoralty campaign expenditures to $200,000 and councillors to about $40,000. In Ontario in 1990, because non-NDP local candidates' were at a disadvantage because that party issued *provincial* tax receipts for donations to municipal campaigns, the Progressive Conservative government changed the rules, requiring that a statement of municipal contributions and expenditures must be filed and full disclosure made of all donations over $100. However, those candidates who spent less than $2,000 need only make a statutory declaration of this, not provide a detailed accounting. Usually all candidates in smaller communities (less than 10,000) will find themselves in this fiscal position.

Quebec election finance law requires that contributions of more than $100 must be paid by cheques and that companies may not contribute to municipal parties. However, during the last week of February 1999, local news television cameras captured a businessman, "peeling off five $100 bills to attend the fund-raising dinner of [Team Bourque/Vision Montreal]" (*Globe and Mail*, 8 March 1999). The provincial Chief Electoral Officer sent a team of auditors to party headquarters after the news reports. In the 1994 Montreal election when Mayor Bourque's Vision Montreal first seized control of council, the Chief Electoral Officer brought 212 charges of illegal fund-raising against the party, including money-laundering. None were personally against Mayor Bourque who was quoted at the time as saying, "the mistakes were those of a young party and won't be repeated." In an unusual twist to the arms'-length concept, the mayor added that "he had associated with some people who were not worthy of the trust and may have even abused it" (*Globe and Mail*, 21 January 1997).

The typical candidate's response to requests for transparency about the sources of their funds was given by Winnipeg Mayor Bill Norrie in 1980. Refusing to disclose his campaign donors, he argued that only his campaign fund-raisers knew the donors and that he "did not want to know" (*Winnipeg*

Free Press, 10 October 1980). in the event that donors might subsequently try to influence him. Such proclaimed ignorance for a desire to maintain an arms'-length relationship is of course not at all likely in so closely knit a community as city politics. It is unsurprising that one-quarter of the news stories between 1979 and 1990 concerning undue influence at Canadian city halls pertained to election contributions (Greene and Shugarman 1997: 139, 148). Candidates *have* to know whom their bagmen should approach for cash; this is the first skill learned in the political arts. As the interest of political gladiators in the stakes at city hall heightens, and as the relative importance of urban policies and their consequences themselves grow, it is natural to expect that behaviours and contacts from other political realms will also be transferred (Lightbody 1997a: 112-17, 129-30). This will necessitate refinement of conflict-of-interest and campaign expense codes.

In the last years of the twentieth century, there was limited public pressure to bring greater transparency into campaign finance. Quebec and Ontario (since 1996) have put provincial legislation in place governing local elections, the latter requiring candidates to disclose donor names (over $100) and to file a list of fund-raising source categories if they spend over $10,000. Elsewhere across Canada, provinces force disclosure and any limits set on expenditures and contributions onto the municipalities' own bylaws. In Alberta this is set forth in section 118 of the Local Authorities Election Act. Scofflaws easily manipulate local rules as, for example, in Edmonton, where numerous supporters in 1992 wrote cheques for $299 so as to slip under the $300 threshold for public disclosure (Lightbody 1997a: 127).

Punishments remain puny, usually a fine well under $1,000; enforcement is lax; and, unlike federal and provincial campaign finance, no deductible tax receipts are yet issued to contributors to civic campaigns. Even in Ontario in 2004, interested citizens had to contact their city clerks to uncover candidates' statements; only the city of Calgary today has an accessible and comprehensive Internet listing of campaign contributions. Widespread public participation is thus minimal, and those who most immediately benefit from policy choices remain the most enthusiastic donors. One matter that is of passing interest is how little demonstration effect there has been among local governments in clearing up these matters, arguably because it is primarily politicians themselves who must spread the message to cleanse their own behaviours.

5.3.2 Patronage

Patronage as a modern concept dates back to England in 1412 where, according to the OED, the word referred to protection for the rights of the church.

The idea grew to encompass protection and support by the church and nobility as patrons for artists and authors. Hence, the historic basis of the notion is "support received" from some more wealthy or powerful benefactor. Today, it generally means appointment to, and advancement in, public office by reason of political affiliations and not necessarily for any reason of merit. It may also refer to the granting of contracts for public expenditures, without any tendering process, on the basis of personal connections. This latter may also include an exclusive franchise, public licence, or operating permit to offer or control the provision of a public service for personal or corporate profit. Only limits to the imagination restrain the possibility for pillage.

Persons who favour procedural ethics first target overt patronage. As noted before, such institutionalized favouritism became a mainstay of the American boss system. A reforming clergyman once attacked Mayor John "Honey Fitz" Fitzgerald of Boston (1906-07; 1910-14) by claiming he "had the distinction of appointing more saloon keepers and bartenders to public office than any previous mayor" (Fraser 1984: 123). About a generation earlier in 1886, Canada's first great crusading anti-patronage mayoralty candidate, William Holmes Howland of Toronto, also campaigned against booze, Tory patronage cronies, and high taxes, mostly in that order (Higgins 1986: 236). The moral imperative still held considerable salience in 1913, when Edmonton Mayor W.J. McNamara was defeated by councillor "Fighting Joe" Clarke largely on the basis that the city's chief magistrate was in cahoots with the police chief in tolerating prostitution and gambling. The two had previously duked it out to bring one 1912 council meeting to a climax. More serenely, in 1911, J.S. Woodsworth, who was later to help found and lead the national Cooperative Commonwealth Federation (CCF), the predecessor to the NDP, also attacked municipal corruption, patronage, and the awarding of local utilities franchises to a select, and to him unsavory, gang (Higgins 1986: 242). This kind of attack was to lead indirectly to municipal ownership of the major local utilities of water, sewerage, transit, electricity, and so forth, although the stated purpose of this state capitalism was not to alleviate the requirements of municipal residents but rather to facilitate, through publicly funded services, the quick and easy booster expansion of the city-centred local economy.

As a consequence of the continental drift of municipal reform in reaction to the abuses of American machine politics, honesty and efficiency quickly became the catch phrase for the basic city model in Canada. City management, a professional bureaucracy, and contracting through tender were well entrenched as practice in the Canadian municipal culture by the end of the 1920s. The lingering problem was that all sorts of normal democratic practices came to represent sinister shades in public life.

In his later study of new reports from 1979 to 1990 in the *Canadian News Index* concerning undue influence, Ian Greene (1991) found only 23 relating to city governing, one-third of which concerned the expectation of some kind of favour returned. Still, the political class continues to provide smoke and fire. One blatant form of patronage common to all city councils is appointment to agencies, boards, and commissions. In the 1990s, Edmonton's city council devoted only one morning to the appointment of over 80 individuals to 21 boards and agencies, about half of whom could be identified as election gladiators (*Edmonton Journal*, 3 November 1980). Also not uncommon these days is the creation of a formal multicultural advisory council to which campaign organizers are appointed. They have, after all, demonstrated their commendable citizenship by working on elections and were likely chosen for that purpose in the first place because of their connections and prominence within particular enclaves. City councillors can thus kill two birds with one appointment: a small political reward and a symbolic recognition of community diversity. More established elites are still satisfied with such entities as the Exhibition Board, which usually has little in the way of honourarium but great field trips. Patronage also comes through *corporatism* by which leading members of policy communities find appointment to the police commissions, library or public health boards, and parks and recreation committees, all of which make policy choices.

In the smaller suburban cities on the periphery of the CMA, such preferential behaviour may carry over into actual municipal personnel practices. David Siegel has put his observations about such smaller centres this way: "hiring is done by the old boys' club, which leads to favoritism and nepotism. While most councils avoid excesses, the lack of a formal hiring process leads to an emphasis on a candidate's connections and viewpoints" (1993: 223). In such circumstances, employees also have little protection against arbitrary treatment, and so a defensive political lesson quickly learned is to sustain a common front against any and all challenges.

Nor is patronage to be overlooked when it comes to the press gallery. The suburban print media rely very heavily on the municipal public for their survival. It is unkindly true to observe that they become sycophantic due to council policies which provide free subscriptions to ratepayers, job printing, and advertising contracts (Masson 1994: 268). In this general pattern, latent possibilities for public outrage will be muted simply by a non-observant print media or one with a wider range of tolerance for low-level malfeasance. Editors and their few reporters easily collaborate in a collusion of silence, justified by a kind of lifeboat syndrome in which they identify themselves with the local government as being "all in this together," tossed against the common enemy of the big city ocean.

5.3.3 Self-promotion, honest graft, and aggrandizement

Sutherland views "conflicts of interest as patronage you give yourself" (1993: 130). Graft requires, as the starter, that people be in public positions so as to be able to do favours for self or others. This, then, is where procedural reform can and must be targeted.

We have discussed in the previous chapter the basic elements of boss politics. Small shadows of machine political behaviour lingered well into the urban politics of twentieth-century Canada. A few city politicians, and their administrative advisers, have been known to operate under a kind of **honest graft**. This was once best described in his memoir by Boss George Washington Plunkitt of Tammany Hall when he wished for an epitaph which summed his career as, "He seen his opportunities and he took em." In practice this meant that his party cronies would advise him of planned future civic developments, and Plunkitt would buy the appropriate properties for a song before any official announcements were made. Naturally, as the city had planned to proceed, and as his friends were the powers that be, the boss's new properties would be acquired at the newly inflated market values. This is how a backroom boy like Plunkitt could later boast that he had never stolen a dime:

> most politicians who are accused of robbin' the city get rich the same way. They didn't steal a dollar from the city treasury.... That is why, when a reform administration comes in and spends a half million dollars tryin' to find the public robberies they talked about in the campaign, they can't find them. The books are all right. The money in the city treasury is all right. Everything is all right. (Riordan 1903: 3-6)

Canadian city politics reveals some similar tales (Magnusson and Sancton 1983; Levine 1989), and much of the fun in studying city politics stems from their exposure. Among the many instances, the executive committee chairman in Montreal Mayor Drapeau's "clean government" administration had his country house built for him, without payment, by a 1976 Olympics contractor (Sancton 1983: 74). The best documented example of honest graft in Canada was William Hawrelak of Edmonton (mayor 1951-59, 1964-65, 1974-75). He wildly exemplified brash opportunism and inability to differentiate between public and private business activities. Hawrelak used his knowledge as mayor for personal and family gain. A judicial inquiry in 1959 reported that "sitting side by side with the [the commissioners] everyday so they could together serve the city's interest, the mayor while serving his own made no disclosure to his colleagues." He exploited his public position to work on retainer for other land developers, and he intervened personally to have favourable zoning changes made to family properties. Forced to resign in 1959 but re-elected in 1964, he violated the provincial planning statute governing conflict of interest in a personal land deal and was again judicially dismissed from office. Re-elected again in 1974, he appointed a disbarred lawyer as his personal aide to advise him on ethics (Lightbody 1989; Lightbody 1993: 207–08; Greene and Shugarman 1997: 108). Hawrelak did see his opportunities, and he certainly took them.

Today, many civic officials (either elected or in senior planning positions) will only wait for a short time after leaving their term in office before accepting more lucrative positions in private real estate businesses where, like retired military personnel working for the war industry, their first-hand knowledge of the public decision process is a valuable commodity. As noted, the suburban cities of the metropolis differ in that that they typically enjoy fewer procedural rules and less unfriendly media scrutiny, even though provincial statutes governing conflicts of interest do apply to them. Wherever there is a rapid economic and spatial expansion of a community, we may also expect to witness spectacular opportunities for personal growth by officials.

5.3.4 Land and lobbying

Much of the central business of the typical city council meeting agenda lies in issues involving the management and servicing of land. While any number of authors develop the thesis that, at heart, city politics are all about land, Lorimer puts the point most brutally: "City politicians generally do whatever is best for the property industry at all times, and then say they are acting for the good of the city as a whole" (1972: 96). City government *is* about property. It would be quite extraordinary if such honey did not draw a few bees.

Greene and Shugarman detail one developer's business-related "entertaining" expenses of $190,000, one-third of which was provided to city politicians and which he understood was the normal cost of doing business in and around Toronto (1997: 109–10). In the early 1990s, several Metro Toronto and suburban councillors were sentenced to lengthy prison terms for accepting bribes to favour bylaws supporting the developer's projects. Councillor Mario Gentile accepted $170,000 between 1988 and 1992 and was sentenced to two years with a fine of $92,000. Even so, he still seemed to believe that it was "natural" for an elected politician to be motivated by inducements to do favours for those helping improve the city's assessment. People from backgrounds in small business in particular have naturally brought to politics the activities that made them modest successes there. They like to give contracts to friends and relatives, and manufacturers woo them with gifts to push a particular brand of merchandise.

The desire to entertain the political industry by the land industry has solid American roots where it is more likely to be played to the extreme. Mike Royko in his biography of Chicago Boss Richard Daley observes that Daley gained his political education in the Illinois state legislature in the 1940s. Money was around for any who wanted it: "Lobbyists expected to pay for votes. Their generosity was matched by the legislators' greed." Sometimes the legislators would create a spurious "fetcher bill" that might require relaying all railway tracks six inches further apart; this would "fetch" a lobbyist bearing a gift, and the bill would fade away. "For the squeamish, there was the lobbyists' card game. The limit varied, but some nights a legislator was guaranteed winnings of up to one thousand dollars. After that, he was on his own, but the thousand dollars was a cinch. He did not have to tell his wife he was a grafter, just a lucky poker player" (Royko 1971: 48).

Even today the game plays on. In urban development, land without water and sewerage connections is just mud. During the 1980s in the York suburban region of Toronto, town engineers, municipal councillors, and millionaire developers gathered to play a little poker after a few rounds of golf. They met in town offices, law partners' board rooms, and the developers' own restaurants. Investigative reporters subsequently quoted one former associate of the developers as saying, "I used to think they were very smart to guess where the pipes were going. But I realized that where they buy land is where the pipes will go." Somehow the poker players not only moved very quickly and smartly through the development regulation process which others found capricious, but were also lucky enough to win access to 60 per cent of new sewerage allotments for their properties (Ferguson and Taylor 1987, 1988).

Smaller suburbs have to deal with the same development pressures, and the same professionally competent and diversified developers, as do core cities. But, with fewer personnel and less professional and specialized planning operations, they must usually borrow expertise from one of three sources here listed from least to very least desirable: the city-region government, contracted planning consultants (who also have other present or future clients and may find themselves in a situation of conflict), or the developers' own staffs. Even for communities not experiencing rapid population expansion, these activities quickly become a high stakes game.

Development representatives believe they must play hard and fast. An unusual example occurred in Vancouver in 1972, when the builders' party on Vancouver council, the NPA, was decimated and elected only one councillor. The group had nominated as their mayoralty candidate Bill

Street, the large developers' lawyer of choice, paid lobbyist at city hall, and NPA fund-raiser. Street had handled rezoning cases in the city hall labyrinth instead of the developers' own lawyers doing so. This expertise with "special considerations" had been honed by serving one two-year term on council in the early 1960s. Street withdrew from the race after a media uproar over his raising of money for, then openly lobbying for a decision from, the NPA council (Gutstein 1975: 140; Gutstein 1983: 206).

In 1975, Justice William C. Morrow undertook an inquiry into Alderman Alex Fallow's claim that one of the Ghermezian brothers, the family who built West Edmonton Mall, had attempted to bribe him to vote for land rezoning. In his report, Justice Morrow found that Raphael Ghermezian had indeed extended a $40,000 gift "for past service to the family." This did not constitute a bribe under the criminal code, but he "recommended the code be amended to consider such an offer a bribe, noting the Ghermezians were well aware their actions weren't technically illegal" (Beazley 1999). In 1990, a city Auditor-General's report into that family's business development of the Eaton Centre in downtown Edmonton concluded, in the words of one councillor, "the project received $110 millions in concessions from the city, approximately equal to the capital cost of the project itself" (Beazley 1999). The unbreakable 40-year lease-backs were negotiated by a committee of council itself, and the Auditor-General concluded that there had been "political interference." Reminiscing, Councillor Mason, who was not on the negotiating committee, observed: "There were no direct accusations, but everybody wondered why the council had voted narrowly for the lease. Nothing further was ever done about it" (Beazley 1999).

Realizing that the technicalities are intricate, lobbyists are often quite prepared to help guide the way. During the final vote on the complex Edmonton Eaton Centre development, the developer sat in the council's public gallery and so frantically gestured as to how to vote to his supporters on council that Mayor Purves inadvertently tried to summon "alderman Ghermezian" to order. In Toronto in 1997, developers' representatives so disrupted council deliberation with their gesticulations that one opposition councillor suggested they might as well sit right at the table (Lightbody 1993: 206). No newspaper reports reflecting on behaviours at the already quite informal council proceedings in the suburbs are available.

Kenneth Gibbons has made the case that those concerned with basic issues of political system legitimacy must quickly address conflict-of-interest questions for, over the longer term, their irresolution fuels a general public cynicism about the political behaviours of all authorities (1976: 231-50). And yet, 20 years later in 1996, the Harris government in Ontario chose not to proclaim the 1994 Disclosure of Interest Act on the pretext that its application to the officers of the province's then 800 or so local governments was too large and costly an operation.

5.3.5 Working with the multi-community city

The examples given above raise longer term structural concerns than just the momentary possibilities of bribery itself. There appear to be three interrelated questions about how rules must adapt when a community with established but often unwritten standards of conduct encounters the introduction of new behaviour patterns.

5.3.5.1 THE QUESTION OF CULTURAL PRACTICE VERSUS ETHICAL CODES

There is the general issue of accommodating transplanted old country practices. Over the past 30 years of so, Canada's city-regions have tried to adapt to a large influx of new minorities, some of whose cultural roots may sustain moral standards for personal behaviour that stand at variance with those of citizens who were born into Canada's dominant European identities. At the heart of multicultural communities is complexity, with any universal standard subject to interpretation from the distinct perspective of religions, communities, and cultures. This means, for example, that what worked in a traditional culture steeped in *baksheesh* may also be thought reasonable for Canadian city politics.

The difficulty in open societies is that the wider cultural and historical customs that normalize practices elsewhere are not ingrained habit in the recipient community. Issues of political morality run deeper than what persons in public office, and those trying to influence them, should do. For instance, it has sometimes been advanced that under-developed societies engender a cultural tolerance of a style of corruption based on family need that maximizes short-term family advantage in order to survive (Gibbons 1976: 234-35). This builds a belief in the particular community that office-holders will accept bribes whether or not they actually have in the past. So, does the immediate evidence of being caught in wrongdoing really matter?

What exists is incongruence between "accepted" personal behaviour and "expected" ethical process, in which private activities may suborn public office. In particular, city councillors may be receptive to non-official guidance when they are not well-educated, where there is no collective party-like vehicle for moral anchor, when final decision authority is widely dispersed, and where morality issues are made to appear very complex.

However, if a particular culture expects the extended family to be rewarded when one member makes good, what are the likely consequences for *any* personal rules based on universal codes? For instance, as with the consequences of any successful hunt wherein sharing was expected by the family, Aboriginal office-holders today face moral dilemmas when individual obligation clashes with more widely held moral precepts. For the Aboriginal person holding public office, the matter is very practical: "A person is deemed to owe to kin not only special affection but also partiality" (Pocklington and Pocklington 1993: 51). For a cultural tradition grounded by scarcity, relatives must come first, and nepotism is obligatory. By this measure, if individualism is out as a standard for personal responsibility, what happens when family obligations clash with codes of conduct?

The obvious point must be made that violations of traditional ethical standards respecting bribery or nepotism are no more the exclusive province of recent immigrants or the urban Aboriginal community than chaste behaviour is for all native-born. But newcomers into any community face a difficult adjustment period, and there will be friction points as the operational features of the bourgeois ethic of cities, considered in Chapter 3, are assimilated.

5.3.5.2 THE QUESTION OF WHAT CONSTITUTES UNACCEPTABLE BEHAVIOUR

The matter of what precisely constitutes unacceptable behaviour continues to be an issue. During the Hawrelak case in Edmonton 40 years ago, there were certainly two countervailing sets of community standards at play at the same time. One was an unwritten code of agreements "among gentlemen," and British "fair play," subscribed to by the city's old Anglo-Ontario elite, in public at least, but accompanied in private by genteel barriers to entry into the charmed club. The second, also traditional, was embraced among many in the city's cultural minorities led by the Slavs. For the second group, resentments with past discriminations fuelled the attitude, "so what if he made a buck, we all got rich and, in any case, he was one of us." Public judgement on election day twice narrowly confirmed this view.

Is it, then, enough to say that when complex and clouded issues are involved "Ethical behaviour is promoted by an electorate that holds the municipal council accountable for what it does" (Sypnowich 1991: 147)? Municipally, this would happen in a plurality vote, with low turnout, and presumably on many policies and personalities. Can issues be so resolved? By historic convention, yes, and students of federal politics would certainly point to the King-Byng crisis and the subsequent election of 1926. It is presumed that those for whom specific ethical standards are important will make the effort to vote. But if citizens narrowly support self-serving leadership, such as happened in Edmonton in the Hawrelak era, then are there not serious questions of universal import to reconsider? Some philosophical traditions claim that *all* individuals occupy a public office as "citizen" and, as such, hold duties with an ethical obligation to make informed moral rulings. When they have made such a ruling collectively and contrary to objective standards of public morality, should the malefactor be let off the hook?

Mayor Hawrelak's supporters wielded enough power in his community to re-elect him twice precisely because of their widely held feelings that old British standards were intended to bar those with non-Anglo genes from playing a powerful role in governing. It can be argued that "When the rules are broken, or when they are changed or not understood, or when they are challenged by an outsider, [only] the players are punished" (Lightbody 1993: 212). Hence, codification to prevent unfair influence must involve more than just a clique out of power trying to curtail the ambitions of those who wield it. However, the relative severity of the reprimand may be linked closely to underlying conflict in the city's culture. Legal codes may require that council members not vote on matters from which they can derive direct personal benefits, but to how many family members and kin should this collective extension reach? For argument at the extreme, urban Aboriginal citizens would presumably be unlikely, if asked, to surrender their individual Charter protections for the collective good of Aboriginal self-governing (Pocklington and Pocklington 1993: 53).

The use of the criminal code to censure elected officials is still a somewhat ambiguous proposition. If a councillor pleads guilty to the summary offence of assaulting an estranged spouse and receives a suspended sentence and 12 months' probation, should he or she be required to relinquish public office? There is no general legislation governing cities in any province, and no provincial legislature would so penalize its own members for any offence punishable by under five years' incarceration. Old-style civil disobedience, including legitimate picket-line duty, may provide guidelines. As one social democratic councillor once put it, "There could be times when people of conscience would find it better to go to jail to stand up for what they believe in" (Lightbody 1993: 211). What is to be accepted as a violation of acceptable public office-holding may differ very much in circumstance, in culture, and in law. For instance, civil disobedience should be just as subject to ethical evaluation as the policies that provoked it should be. But who should decide this: the courts, the moral suasion of peer groups, or citizens by vote?

5.3.5.3 THE QUESTION OF THE RIGHTS OF NEW POLITICAL COMMUNITIES

New political communities expect no less than equity in employment, promotion, and their treatment at public hands. Where, for instance, very specific gay concerns differ from those of fellow citizens, it will probably be a local matter concerning fair treatment. New political resources may be mobilized to sway the specific strategies of other individuals as new groups achieve a measure of respectability commensurate with abilities and earned status. New cultures may very well expect affirmative actions to break glass ceilings previously unacknowledged.

Actually, meeting the novel with practical applications is less a problem for diverse core cities than their homogenized suburbs where exclusion of anyone unconventional has long stood as a fundamental *raison d'être*. Whenever a social stigma is applied to particular groups—and this is easiest in smaller communities—persons identified as a part of that group may choose to flee their home towns to find refuge in the comforting social anonymity of the city. The safe harbour can be menacing to those without livelihood: young people end up living on the street or prey to prostitution. Central cities must also lead in dealing with the public health detritus of addictions: "In Ontario, as elsewhere, suburban and rural local governments have abdicated their responsibilities to their own young citizens and have allowed the problem to be exported to the nearest large urban centre" (Thomlinson 1997: 126). Innovations in all dimensions of street safety and the sensitizing of police agencies to the fundamental humanity of new groups entering the mainstream are direct consequences of the applied ethics of fair treatment.

Ongoing city policies require constant application of nuance. In this, city elections become rather less important than city politics themselves. As they come to grips with newly vocal communities, city councillors have found it more difficult to exist as null politicians, performing purely representational roles without any other action agenda. By default, city governments play an important innovative function in the Canadian intergovernmental arrangement. It was Canadian cities that provided sometimes reluctant policy leadership in the practical extension of equality rights during the 1990s as the judicial process struggled with clarification of what was legal equality as contrasted with "special treatment." Toronto, for instance, barred discrimination in hiring on the basis of sexual orientation in 1973, 13 years before the province of Ontario acted (Thomlinson 1997: 129). In Alberta, whose Individual Right's Protection Act provides no such guarantees against exclusion, the City of Edmonton followed Toronto's lead. Other cities' employees have subsequently been able to argue for judicial clarification of "equality" principles for the purposes of spousal benefits from a position of relative employment security. Wider scale tolerance can never be legislated, but such equity regulations may dispel many remaining stereotypes.

Politics is an arena in which appearance is everything. As councillors are increasingly elected from diverse backgrounds, they may bring their experience in complex conflict resolution with them. Equality, not singular privilege, becomes applied ethics when it comes to the opening of publicly controlled housing to those who are HIV-positive or to same sex couples. The local media easily focuses on the avoidance of official proclamations for Gay Pride Day, the flamboyance of its parades, or the more boisterous elements of "camp" events such as the Gay Rodeo in Calgary, but this trivializing misses the broader reality that ethical issues surrounding acceptance have passed through the political gateway to become small problems in managing logistics.

In sum, central city population diversity produces sometimes dramatic public clashes over ethical concerns. But the irony is that once the dimensions of the differing expectations are widely acknowledged to exist, they can be worked into public policy solutions. Cities have learned that equality does not mean exceptional treatment. We might end by noting that no level of Canadian politics has yet dealt acceptably with the new worlds of pending ethical violation which are emerging as personal privacy evaporates in the information age. Unresolved issues elusive of easy response—cell-phone intercepts, Webcam exposés, misdirected faxes, unanticipated e-mail diffusion, and, broadly, criminality on the Internet—are all on the doorstep of each municipal office-seeker today.

5.4 A Last Word

As a last word, do we expect the only good city politician to be a person who essentially embodies the behavioural traits of the ideal public servant? Many traditional democratic practices, even internal party matters like leadership conventions, have become objects for cleansing of any indicators of partisan favours. Langford and Tupper comment that "the good democratic politician now resembles our idea of an excellent civil servant under cabinet government. That is, he or she is neutral, technically competent, and predictable in habit and decision" (1993: 16). To accept this change surely eliminates that element of fundamental choice that lies at the very heart of democratic politics. Fairness does not mean sameness, nor should basic honesty require the elimination of stark contrasts in position.

Blatant anti-partyism is not the one obvious and genuine panacea, and conflict codes are but guidelines toward principles. Dumping overt partisanship is meaningless and gives false hope for strictly ethical behaviour, since personal ties among the interested gladiators will persist. And no matter how well-conceived or comprehensive they may be, reform checklists can be manipulated, subverted, or ignored. This is especially true in city politics where elites are closely intertwined; money can have an immediate impact;

other political resources donated "in kind" are difficult to define, let alone cost; and the strict idea of conflict of interest remains malleable when major economic development activity is on the line. Only when cheating is generally seen to be bad for community business will the anticipation of being ostracized by the urban regime constitute better deterrence.

Individual looting and personal graft has not evoked much beyond episodic outrage in Canada. As Higgins noted, not all illegal actions are considered to be corrupt enough by enough members of the political community to be condemned as immoral, nor are all unethical activities necessarily illegal (1986: 391-94). Because so few citizens appear to care deeply, some people in authority may make personal choices at the moral margin, which are strictly speaking unethical, and these actions can persist with little question. It takes the apprehension of systemic pillage by some gang or claque to sustain enough citizen energy for long enough to accomplish more in the way of sustainable correction.

The "clean government" reform of North American cities was a twentieth-century phenomenon coinciding with the urbanization of population. In the United States, Greer wrote of these as "Purification Rites" (1963: 8-9) that began with an indictment of particular corrupt villains and concluded with attempts to cauterize the operation, remove the corrupt, and invent an untouchable bureaucracy. Only then, would the "just" be tempted to present themselves for public office. Greer used as one example the 1957 Miami-Dade County governmental consolidation, which had been preceded by an anticorruption campaign as subscript to arguments for better economic growth and solid capitalist management of operations. Such a dramatic exposé of illegitimacy has never preceded any Canadian metropolitan reform.

Democratic politics creates opportunities for service, promotion, policy innovation—and corruption. Which office-holder follows which of these paths, and whether singly or with others, cannot be legislated absolutely in a pluralist, liberal democratic community if cultural tolerance of ethical malfeasance and grafting persists. Seldom are other ethical lodestones present; this seems especially so with new stress on our city systems from historic but divergent practices of new migrant cultures. Stress is compounded with the technically competent new agendas of narrowly issue-oriented citizen groups and the communication of a technological age that produces and supports the effectiveness of narrow policy networks. How to sort the significant from all else remains the important policy concern, but it is overlaid today with new questions. If basic rights of citizenship imply process equity, then applying fairness requires some sort of legal guarantee. If particular citizens find basic equality somehow transgressed by another part of the community, how far can clear regulation go to protect against even unintentional grievance? If one end for citizenship is equitable representation fairly arrived at, not only during elections but also throughout policy deliberations, must procedural ethics anticipate as well as proscribe? What actions are appropriate for city hall?

Note

1. The "cemetery vote" is the enumeration of the deceased for the ballot; in 1844 in New York, 41,000 people were qualified, but 55,000 actually voted, prompting one spoilsport to criticize, "The dead filled in for the sick" (Safire 1968: 70). In the 1858 provincial election, *Le Journal de Quebec* recounted a similar enthusiasm and noted that votes had been cast "in the names of the living and the dead of all nations" (*The Canadian Encyclopedia* 1985: Vol. I, 555). The "telegraph vote" is voter impersonation at the polling station, and its most exuberant exercise came federally in 1963 in St. Lawrence-St. George when a Jewish tailor impersonated Bishop Fading. "Plumping the ballot" is more sophisticated and requires parties operating under a transferable vote system to educate their supporters to vote only for a lesser number than permitted so as not to diminish the proportionate power of their ballot when second and third choices are being tabulated. That is, electors "fatten" their votes.

six | Political parties and theories of local non-partisanship

Unlike other local governing systems in the world, most Canadian cities are not governed by systemic party operations. In this chapter we consider the consequences of both anti-partyism and party-like behaviour, with an eye to the role of each in augmenting the direct accountability of locally elected officials. This chapter does not provide a comprehensive history of formal political party involvement in Canadian city politics. It is, instead, an argument, with appropriate examples, for more transparency in party activities. It concludes that greater accountability for public policy would ensue if parties locally were more coherent and more continuously active.

One mechanism in federal and provincial politics that both increases innovation and provides accountability has been the organized political party. That this means of focused authority is traditionally denied city electors weakens the legitimacy of municipal government generally and of its elected leaders in particular. Virtually alone among First World industrialized communities (with the exception of the United States and Australia), Canada's political gladiators have tried to insulate major cities from the clarity which comes from election campaigns organized along partisan lines: "the United

States, Canada, and Australia are world outliers with their weak parties. In these three former British colonies, the Victorian tradition is alive and strong in institutions like non-partisan elections and the professional city manager" (Clark and Hoffmann-Martinot 1998: 111). The political process remains like that of the smaller towns and municipal districts that cities now tower over. Indeed, of Canada's 12 largest cities today, only those in Quebec and the two in British Columbia see their elections divided along party lines.

During the two-tier metropolitan government period in Canada (1954–2000), no pan-metropolis party except the Metro Election Committee (Winnipeg) ever emerged for the structural reason that elections to the city-region levels were always indirect. Policy and issue coalitions consistently appeared but were usually based on suburban versus central city interests.

Perhaps three dozen Canadian cities might be large enough as important subnational political systems to lend themselves to formal political party organization. But, from the time of Baldwin and now into the twenty-first century, Canadian city elections have been conducted under invisibility cloaks of anti-partyism. Municipal councils have stood not so much as vehicles for "unadorned common sense" but as conduits for semi-official policy networks and specific interests who run their own shows. This style of operation is what is meant by politicians at senior levels when they give speeches about "community control." The massive restructuring of Canada's city-regions in the 1990s by the provinces of Ontario and Quebec had a perhaps unintended consequence. By focusing on who does what to whom in Canadian cities, both provincial governments inadvertently drew unwanted attention to those policy communities which have been operating with municipal agendas. This may yet cause urban electors to reflect very seriously upon *who* should be entrusted with the local political business.

In the twenty-first century, Canadian city politics have not matured, as citizens in most other postindustrial societies have come to expect, as a clear electoral struggle between more or less progressive elements. In Canada's recent small discussion about "the democratic deficit," "citizen-centred government," and "citizen engagement," this obvious reform avenue is seldom heard. In fact, Graham and Phillips dismissed the idea of formal parties in local elections with but two sentences (1997). The new councils of Toronto—56 elected in 1997 and 44 in the reconstituted system of 2003—have, without public debate or gladiator interest, twice produced a fractious cacophony of disparate opinions without any organization electors can hold to public account.

Although the track record of political party organizations in Canadian cities is episodic, it still poses questions of interest. Can citizens justly feel empowered if the political process does not present genuinely and well-organized competitive choices based on underlying ideological divergence? If informed sources about the particulars of civic issues remain illusive for the casually interested citizen, apart from council incumbents, city bureaucrats, and their clientelist policy communities, then will electors continue to boycott elections because there is so little to vote for other than the status quo? And, finally, is the non-partisan old-gang style characteristic of the patriarchal, homogenous, slow-moving, bourgeois city of even the mid-twentieth century still good enough for a tough new and globally focused world? These days, the growth in extra-legislative sources of pressure on the formerly languid decision pace focus on: (1) quality professional administration in senior management positions but outside government, (2) managerially experienced and coherent specific policy communities, and (3) emergent new social movements who have access to reliable information sources and expertise beyond local boundaries. Attempts to internalize the potential conflict from each of these three into traditional public debates yield serious skepticism concerning just how able Canadian city governing really is.

Without parties, politics becomes the province of upper-class policy elites. Research into gladiators' perceptions in the anglo-democracies, from British Columbia to the UK and from Australia to Austin, has revealed repeatedly that anti-partyism *is* class politics. The ideological bias of non-partisanship lies in its appeal to a status quo in which the debate is more around how well run the process of governing is than into normative questions as to what public policies that process should be about. Gidengil and Vengroff add another dimension, claiming that the "old boys" networks reinforce existing barriers to women as successful candidates: "… it could actually be that non-partisan elections handicap women because they put more of a premium on name recognition and personal financial resources" (1997: 520-21). In the perhaps well-run but arguably ungoverned cities that anti-partyism permits, Stein Rokkan's dicta prevails: "votes count but resources matter."

The predominant anti-partyism of Canadian city elections is reminiscent of the style of Manitoba's long-standing Liberal Progressive provincial government (1931-58) during which one of its leader referred to the province itself as but a "king-size municipality" (Donnelly 1963: 65). While this view reflected the political culture of the province's rural areas, it was a kind of behaviour that large cities in the west and of this period easily mimicked, especially in the anti-socialist coalitions like the Citizens Election Committee in Winnipeg and the NPA in Vancouver. W.L. Morton summarized the provincial ministry views in Manitoba:

> Parliamentary and responsible government had been seriously, if not fatally, impaired by the persistent confusion of government with administration.

> The task of democratic government, to lead, inform and inspire, had been deliberately neglected by ministers who bound themselves to their desks, doing the administrative work which should have been left to their departments. And the same ministers, largely trained in municipal affairs, reduced provincial government to municipal administration. (1967: 464)

The only task set by this government was to effectively manage a limited governmental role in the social and economic life of the community. Such agrarian liberalism, in this case imported with the earliest Ontario settlers, required a down-playing of any partisan attachments. This model easily retained its legitimacy for larger city governments long after its utility for provincial purposes had passed.

While Canadian municipal coalitions *have* contested local elections at various times and in numerous locales, too few have exhibited sufficient cohesion and endurance, or confronted similarly endowed opposition, for viable party systems to emerge. Those organizations enjoying the most success have been either widely based coalitions with modest reform programs or claques of local Liberal and Progressive Conservative gladiators mobilized to counteract the perceived municipal ambitions of more narrowly based parties of principle. These latter have been characterized by electoral success coupled to restricted memberships. In 1953, for instance, the published membership list of the Civic Election Committee in Winnipeg totalled only 30 names, and over its entire history activists recall that no more than 100 and likely closer to 50 people were active members (Stinson 1975: 253). Similarly in Edmonton, the Citizens Committee which controlled city council from 1934 until well into the 1960s, and held *all* council seats between 1945 and 1959, was never a large group, variously estimated at about three dozen business and professional men (Lightbody 1983: 265). Winnipeg's municipal process was characterized by a rudimentary party system with contests between a succession of socialist-labour parties and their Liberal-Progressive Conservative opponents under a variety of organizational guises from before the 1919 General Strike until roughly 1986 (note Taylor 1974). Although the 1919 strike did produce an immediate challenge to the institutional and political status quo, one Labour candidate accurately observed of the prevailing sentiment of anti-partyism that "All representation to date has been class representation ... [it has simply] not been working class representation" (McKillop 1970: 55). Winnipeg's 1921 civic election produced victory for the anti-labour coalition and entrenched the anti-party belief system for the remainder of the twentieth century.

6.1 What is the Point of Political Parties?

One probably unintended policy result of Canadian anti-partyism for the city political process has been little evident voter-enforced budgetary direction and policy coherence. It has long been known that, by eliminating structured choice, non-partisanship removes the one organized component of the electoral process that permits persons not closely associated with particular interest or clientele groups to influence the general policy direction of their city's councillors (Lee 1960: 176). This raises the question of what exactly ideology *is* in Canadian city politics.

6.1.1 The idea of party

Parties evolved in the twentieth century as public policy instruments permitting the non-violent articulation of citizen demands for policy change. In modern liberal democracies, political parties at all state levels have themselves become political systems in miniature. As such, they have evolved constitutions, representative and internal electoral systems for the choice of leaders and party officials, and authority structures to establish patterns in internal power dispositions. Some modern political parties are also possessed of strongly coherent belief systems. In practice this becomes **partisanship**, the active identification by an individual with a party (or cause) which, in turn and the more strongly it is felt, guides that person's participation in all aspects of political life. Partisanship in the widest sense becomes a prism through which all public policies, political leadership, media reports, and public involvement can be assessed and assigned priorities for action.

The modern political party is thus a social group, and as it brings its partisans together, it also serves to define them as being something separate from either other political attachments or purely individual existence (Eldersveld 1964). Like other social groups, parties are sets of individuals in our society who occupy particular roles and who behave as members of an identifiable community. This does not mean that they are required to wear a uniform, but rather that individuals will react to political stimuli in life in concert with other members of "their" team. All social groups establish broad objectives, intermediate goals, and quite specific tasks for individual members.

The role of parties in the policy system is best understood with a set of assumptions developed through structural-functionalism in the social sciences (Parsons 1971; Merton 1968; Kaplan 1967). While the functions themselves remain constant across communities, specific institutions adapt their own structures to particular environmental circumstances. That is, an electorally successful local political party in Surrey, British Columbia, may on the surface appear to be quite different from Quebec City's Civic Party, but functional analysis reveals that both operations perform generally similar tasks for their respective cities.

Two critical understandings underlie this tradition of study. First, every social institution is possessed of a *manifest function*, that being its primary goal and principal focus. All activities of persons who claim membership will be more or less focused on achieving this objective. Secondly, any endeavour that subverts, even inadvertently, this mission is said to be *dysfunctional* and is to be suppressed. If the manifest function of a public bureaucracy is, for example, to provide efficient, equivalent, and publicly accountable levels of service to all citizens regardless of their personal traits, then any behaviour (such as a discreet racism) that detracts from that performance has to be actively discouraged and suppressed, if the social institution is to persist successfully over time.

The manifest function of a party as a social institution is normally to gain power. In liberal democracies this is accomplished through the election of party personnel through the representative process to positions with specific state authority. At the municipal level, this means not only the mayoralty but also councillors, school trustees, parks board members, and, at various times and in various places, controllers or commissioners. Even quite narrowly focused parties such as the Greens which have little realistic immediate prospect of a plurality victory will exploit the electoral process as an educative means to establish a tactical beachfront for the longer term strategic end of winning.

This idea of manifest function is acutely appropriate for the study of party-like activities at the civic level in Canada where the distinction between party and pressure group is not always as clear as it is in federal and provincial politics. Particularly during the third reform period, the integration of electioneering and lobbying activities of, especially, left-progressive political activists were so entwined that it often became indiscernible even to them as to whether they were campaigning for office or endeavouring to influence those in authority positions. For example, in Edmonton, a quite loosely knit coalition of neighbourhood associations and single-issue groups fought attempts to realize the freeway ambitions of that city's Commission Board after the release of the Metropolitan Edmonton Transportation Study in 1964. They coalesced as the Urban Reform Group of Edmonton (URGE) to contest the civic election of 1974 and elected two to the 13-person council. But the groups continued to lobby council, singly and as a coalition, to attain a more environmentally friendly and open municipal planning operation. URGE elected three councillors in 1977, four in 1980, and two in 1983, until, policy energies exhausted, it disbanded as a party in June 1989

(Masson 1994: 464-65). It must be added that the activities of local boards of trade have never been much at odds with the continual campaigns of the traditional anti-party civic coalitions.

Functionalism aids with definitional clarity through its focus on human behaviour. Central to the definition of party-like behaviour is the pursuit of electoral power; if an organization is trying for this, then any other definitional problems may be relegated to the sidelines. Canadian local parties have not been neat and tidy operations like American city party organizations, some of which were founded during the boss era. Such long-standing operations, such as those in Chicago and Detroit, have exhibited autonomy from social institutions like labour unions and large business corporations, have a continuity over time, often reward supporters in material and symbolic terms, behave as machines with hierarchical organization that promotes personnel from within, and are able to offer candidates for all levels of the state.

Theory and practice alike confirm that an effective party system performs four latent, or supportive, functions of importance to the political community. These are not the primary objective of any single party but are the standard byproducts of parties in competition (Van Loon and Whittington 1996: 337-50). They have been variously described as (1) political recruitment and staffing, (2) political education and socialization, (3) the aggregation and articulation of interest, and (4) the integration of the policy system or general acceptance of the political community.

These latent functions are understood in established theory to be so essential to the persistence of any political system that each, to an extent, itself becomes the manifest function of other ongoing social institutions such as policy communities, the public bureaucracy, the information claque (media and public intellectuals), and commercial or religious organizations. It may seem obvious, but it is still deserving of comment, that in places where party politics are especially weak and anti-partyism is so dominant that city councillors appear to be elected solely on the basis of individual political merits, these necessary functions of political life do *not* also evaporate. As functionalists in anthropology quickly learned, the disruption in one part of a culture provokes a readjustment in others. Equally, apparent vacuums in political power do not persist for long. Other social institutions pick up the pace to fill the vacant spaces. The permanent bureaucracy, for instance, always has recruits and nominees available for board and agency appointments from among its own patronage networks of experts, consultants, and clients if the partisans on council do not. In fact, one triumph of effective party competition is that its more overt patronage regimes thwart the designs of this hidden quasi-professional world and open the structures to wider public participation.

So, the classic functional approach must consider how well any given party system performs the following four operations.

6.1.1.1 POLITICAL RECRUITMENT AND STAFFING

Representative forms of democratic governing establish formal leadership roles which need occupants and which parties in the competitive pursuit of power seek to fill. As noted in Chapter 5, parties recruit individuals into the process of electoral politics and encourage them to participate at higher levels. Active competition among party organizations mobilizes political resources (and often large numbers of volunteer workers) into the city electoral process. In this sense, party competition converts the agendas of demographic sectors of the community directly into power and policy.

But any democratic operation will also mandate those elected to appoint other citizens directly to various boards, agencies, and commissions which work in concert with, or in authority over, the permanent public bureaucracy. Planning or zoning variance agencies, parks boards, and police commissions all require citizen–amateurs (that is, not *elected* politicians) to set policy within the broad scope assigned by elected councillors. There has been no precise calculation of how directly participatory Canadian communities have become through any count of appointments to these parapolitical delegations.

People who have committed to participate and to serve implicitly accept that the policy system within which they are working is legitimate. This explains why suburban part-time officials as well as policy activists tend to be as hostile towards any metropolitan amalgamation as their directly elected councillors.

It is often assumed that people interested in city politics who are also identified as federal and provincial party partisans are perfectly mobile among the governmental levels. While it must be conceded that city councils have been happy hunting grounds for federal and, increasingly, provincial party organizers seeking candidates, more so for men than for women, they have still proved far less productive than either the local bar society or chamber of commerce.

6.1.1.2 POLITICAL EDUCATION AND SOCIALIZATION

In order to perpetuate its institutions, any urban society will try to provide newcomers—children and migrants from either abroad or from rural areas—with a generalized knowledge of collective goals and individual norms for behaviour. **Political socialization** is the cultural process by which a set of expectations concerning citizenship and public service is taught to all citizens. A narrow slice of this broader operation educates those holding public office about their rights and responsibilities. It is here that political parties flesh out very general cultural deterrents to such practices as bribery into viable codes of conduct and precise definitions of conflicts of interest.

By competing for public office, political parties translate the foundations of widely shared popular culture into the spot reality of how to decide upon immediate issues. Parties provide leadership on opinions and, by producing a set of reference points for the individual elector, a bridge between a list of candidates and voters. In modern liberal democracies this standard sort of political exchange has been labelled *transactional leadership* by James MacGregor Burns (1978: 18). By this he means that citizens barter votes for politicians who have promised to satisfy a set of demands, such as more effective policing. As he sees it, the ambitions of both leaders and followers are accomplished; democracy is served in that leaders are only as powerful as their electors permit.

In Chapter 5, we noted that partisanship may increase voter turnout in city elections for the simple reason that parties reduce complex issues to comprehensible dimensions. Parties also pull out the vote, often by educating electors on the process—when, where, and, of course, how to vote. If the electoral system is itself complex, as under the transferable balloting arrangement, then party leaders take great pains to explain it. This can include simplifying tactics such as vote "plumping" (making strategic choices in the polling booth). Parties also provide focal points around which peoples' attitudes may be grouped, a practice somewhat akin to product differentiation among different brands of soap. To build support, parties identify (or create) issues and give electors some concrete notion of how these issues should be evaluated. An effective party system furnishes leadership not only during the election phase of the policy process but also between elections.

6.1.1.3 AGGREGATION AND EXPRESSION OF INTERESTS

We observed in Chapter 2 that any political and policy system requires a general means to reduce the influx of potential demands by citizens. This is accomplished through social institutions which group people with generally similar sets of expectations. These possibilities are then expressed in such agenda terms that the policy-making process can kick into gear with at least some minimal response. The institutions for which this work is the manifest function are usually called interest or pressure groups (discussed in the next chapter).

But political parties in their struggle to win office play this aggregating game. After all, the election process is not that complicated. The essential formula is $S = X + 1$, in which (S) is success and (X) equals the competitor with the next highest vote total.

In their quest to tally that one extra vote necessary for victory, political parties try to varying degrees to articulate in their policy proposals or platforms the expectations of electors previously underrepresented, such as minorities or new social movements. Party gladiators may make the further tactical choice to include representative members from such communities among their candidates. Even if these moves are essentially symbolic (or pandering) when first deployed, they contribute to overall innovation over time by legitimizing the position and participation of new ideas and new people. It must be noted that for this function of party systems to work well, more than a single well-organized instrument must be continuously active. In this sense, innovation is most associated with the party that is currently out of power and plotting the strategies to gain office.

6.1.1.4 GENERAL ACCEPTANCE OF THE POLITICAL COMMUNITY

In structural-functional theory, this last activity is known as the integrative function: it is how citizens learn to accept the boundaries of their political community and the patterns in its systems of authority. At the substate government level, integration is generally most relevant at times immediately following the municipal reorganization of city-regions when political parties may help bind people to the new processes.

It can, for example, be easily argued that over the first years of its existence, Winnipeg Unicity's political parties developed more legitimacy for the system than either mayor's speeches or institutions like residents' advisory groups and community committees. Social and political integration, a "scarcely credible" acceptance, was observed almost with astonishment by the commissioners assessing the operations of the Unicity Act five years after its passage. Considering the "abhorrence" and "widespread opposition" which had accompanied the unification, the commissioners reported "Perhaps the single most noteworthy 'accomplishment' since the Act was passed is the general acceptance of unification." None of the over 100 submissions to them had "recommended the abandonment of the unified city, a return to the former two-tiered structure or, for that matter, a return to the pre-Metro situation of multiple autonomous municipalities" (Taraska 1976: 10). By privately and publicly working the new instruments during and between two city-wide elections, two competitive parties, each articulating city-wide platforms, legitimized the whole business. It was, indeed, these parties which

Table 6.1: General Characteristics of Local Cadre and Mass Parties

Feature	Cadre Party	Mass Party
1. *Origins*	Coalesces within council to preserve office.	As a policy or social movement outside council.
2. *Activities*	Focused precisely on the electoral calendar.	Continuous development of policy alternatives; lobbying.
3. *Reach*	Focused in a small core of political gladiators.	Broad membership and social organization; sustained activity.
4. *Candidates*	Drawn from community's social and economic elite.	Party members conversant with platforms and policies.
5. *Finance*	Small number of large donations (business).	Large number of donations from sustaining members.
6. *Policy*	Sustain the status quo; promise anything; often strong anti-party claims.	Coherent policy focus usually in a challenge to past practices carried forward.

had unintentionally minimized lingering rancour by demonstrating realizable opportunities.

In the election in Montreal preceding unification in November 2001, two parties—the United Citizens and Vision Montreal—competed island-wide. Gerald Tremblay, the candidate most opposed to unification, won, and his party received the largest number of seats—44 per cent—on the new council. More importantly, in observing this phenomena, Alain Faure concluded that it was surprising just how quickly the candidates had integrated the electoral game of the reformed city, proposing to use office to defend the interests of the entire island and mostly casting aside any supposed tradition of former municipal autonomy (2003: 52).

Even low levels of elector turnout for city elections—for example, 28 per cent for Toronto in 2000 after three years of Megacity—can signify a voting boycott since policies, institutions, and personalities are no longer centres of controversy but patterns of public administration. The legitimacy of municipal structures is no longer at stake, and suburban separatists have thrown in the towel so as to work the new system better. Low turnouts in city votes can accentuate further integration between the policies and actions of those who actually are attentive, the political gladiators, because these individuals see the powers focused in the new offices, and they take the operation very seriously indeed.

The performance of this function also relates to a question once raised by Kaplan: "Why do Canadians tolerate much weaker government at the city level than they would at the provincial or national level? The answer, in part, is that we don't take urban problems very seriously" (1965: 27). The answer is also that municipalities borrow legitimacy from their provincial creators as need be.

6.1.2 Two types of local parties

In his attempt to bring order to the comparative study of political party activities in western Europe, Maurice Duverger devised a basic typology which is still widely used by political scientists as a quick shorthand (1954: esp. 63–71). He labelled the most common basic types as "cadre" and "mass" parties. For our purposes, the most clearly distinguishing characteristics of these types, as they have been active in Canadian city politics, are summarized in Table 6.1.

Cadre parties, the dominant style in Canadian cities, are weakly knit caucus parties and tend to be dispersed in structure. After winning elections, they are unlikely to show much cohesion on details of policy votes unless they are confronted by significant opposition. On the other hand, **mass parties** are much more devoted to policies and principles while developing coherent hierarchical and centralized operating arms. A half-century ago, Duverger put the concept of the cadre party this way: "the grouping of notabilities for the preparation of elections, conducting campaigns and maintaining contact with the candidates. Influential persons, in the first place, whose name, prestige, or connections can provide a backing for the candidate and secure him votes; experts, in the second place, who know how to handle the electors and how to organize a campaign; last of all financiers, who can bring the sinews of war." He then adds a possibly pejorative summary comparison: "Quality is the most important factor: extent of prestige, skill in technique, size of fortune. What the mass party secures by numbers, the cadre party secures by selection" (1954: 64). This is also so in Canada.

Mass parties in Canadian cities have experienced what Roberto Michels (1949) termed the **iron law of oligarchy**. He argued that European social democratic parties displayed a consistent and frustrating tendency to be dominated by small cliques among the party executive and elected members. As a result, no matter how democratic and participatory the founding rhetoric or principles of any well-developed social organization, there is an inherent tendency to hierarchy and social control from the resulting apex of authority. Sadly, even mass political parties with strong populist roots acquire a logistical immunity from operational control by the membership. The prerequisites of mounting electoral warfare inherently militates against much other than a façade of participatory involvement.

These observations mean a number of things for municipal politics in Canada. First, the requirements of modern state management appear to impel social organizations like parties toward less internal democracy and a focus on central executive leadership skills. A recent example of exactly such party implosion and escape from original democratic ideals developed in Montreal within the short-lived reign of the MCM in the 1980s (Thomas 1995: 123-32). Second, it is in the nature of Canada's municipal cadre parties to embrace and personify the public ideology of their given community at a point in time. In consequence, they act as policy conservatives in defending the status quo carried forward. The corollary is that local parties which have tried, more or less, to emulate the mass party model appear to be more radical than they really are as they struggle to upset apple carts whether from the left or the right. Third, pressures to centralize and concentrate on elections leads to a focus on the personality and perceived talents of the party leader and his or her direct appeal to individual voters. Lastly, in public policy terms, increased centralization of authority empowers an antithesis in populist uprisings through new social movements, policy networks, and single issue pressure groups which *do* provide accessible and direct avenues for policy participation.

6.1.3 Ideology in action at city hall

Non-partisanship produces an incremental, non-innovative policy-making style now inappropriate for post-industrial city-regions. Succinctly said, non-partisanship is a conservative tactic, not all that surprising since by definition it does not embrace any policy sea change. The movement's active gladiators are always the most stand-pat in their world views; for instance, those in Vancouver, Canada's most completely partisan city, have seen the city as a business, an homogenous bourgeois enterprise, and somehow beyond "politics" (Easton and Tennant 1969). Similar studies for the Maud Commission (UK) found anti-partyism associated with rural, suburban, and more conservative councillors generally.

When ideology at city hall does on occasion emerge through partisan division it takes on a hue that is somewhat distinct from the other worlds of Canadian politics. Specifically, the **political ideologies** of locally organized groups appear to diverge along two dimensions. The first ideological line may be drawn between those who argue that the municipal policy world is so dissimilar to the federal and provincial that local political activity ought to be conducted by individuals and not formal parties and those for whom the local state makes important allocative decisions that are best resolved through collective actions. This axis may be considered ideological because these are essentially contrasting world views between an individual choice perspective and an organic view of the state and interpersonal relationships.

The more familiar line of demarcation is that between those who favour a larger state role in the regulation of society and of the environment, and who prefer redistributive economic practices, and those who envisage more or less unbridled free markets and societal individualism. In cities where competing parties persist, they define themselves along both axes and offer electors real choices over public policy. The central point is that citizens cannot justly feel empowered if their city political system is not genuinely competitive and if the competing viewpoints are not coherently articulated.

Ralph Miliband has argued that, while North American liberalism may support some considerable diversity in ideological positions over distributive policies of a moment, these differences are not genuinely fundamental and retain a shared, narrow, and class chauvinist view of the state (1973: 3-8, 63-67, 237-47). This is the conservative view at city hall; here conservatism is defined not as "toryism" but how Nigel Harris described it in the UK: "Conservative ideology is British **public ideology**, its precise nature depending upon which groups are dominant in British society at any given time and what is the nature of the radical attack upon the British status quo. If there is no radical attack, or if it is marginal as not seriously to impinge on public policies, then Conservative ideology becomes 'common sense' ... (1971: 99; emphasis added). Walter Young, in the Canadian context, put this nicely: "Political scientists who despair of finding a single coherent statement of the Liberal or Progressive Conservative 'philosophy' have ignored the haystack in their search for the needle. Liberalism and Progressive Conservatism are, in effect, what Liberals and Progressive Conservatives do when in office. Their behaviour reflects, by and large, the dominant values of Canadian society" (1969: 297).

Political ideology in city politics is to be found in what city council does, and does not, do. Too often the attentive public dismisses decisions of local councillors not as ideologically driven choices but as muddled when not petty. This is because Canadian cities' political campaigns have been a subterfuge which veils most councillors' federal or provincial attachments to the coherent belief systems embodied in their adherence to one or other of the established political parties.

Increasingly, well-educated citizens are denied basic opportunities for reasonable choice among distinguishable alternatives for city planning and development. For example, Vancouver's dominant political organization, the NPA, long espoused the Burkeian notion that council "should not be a congress of ambassadors from different and hostile interests" (Tennant 1981: 130). In his recent comparative study, Henry Milner has also argued convincingly that such incoherence of partisan choice across government levels, as represented by the weak political links between federal, provincial, and municipal party organizations, directly deflates municipal electoral participation (1997). Quite apart from more general concerns with appropriate representation of many categories of citizens, non-partisan behaviour has also been neither as benign nor as administratively efficient as its more ardent business apologists have claimed. As it turns out in practice, non-partisanship is a person and property exclusionary activity.

The fundamental hypocrisy of municipal non-partisanship across Canada is revealed in the covert activities of gladiators, behaviour glimpsed most often in mayoralty campaigns. As in Japan where political parties focus on parliament and governors, Canadian party activists seldom play large observable roles in mayoralty races. Mayors there, and here, tend to build personalized electoral networks—except that in Japan **clientelist**, or group patronage, expectations exist; "[Japanese] Mayors attempt to portray themselves as unifiers whose position and function are above partisan divisions" (Hoffmann-Martinot 1998: 210). Although often denied by the candidates, partisanship is a clearly relevant organizing principle in Canadian mayoral races.

In the Toronto vote of 2003, a reform-minded NDPer, David Miller, received 43.5 per cent of the vote, while John Tory, a national Progressive Conservative strategist, won 38.3 per cent. By 2003, both Winnipeg (Glen Murray) and Vancouver (Larry Campbell) also had NDPers as mayors, although the former lost as a federal Liberal candidate in the 2004 general election. Calgary's mayor David Bronconnier (Liberal) defeated former Progressive Conservative MLA Bev Longstaff in 2001; Edmonton's Mayor Bill Smith (Reform-Alliance) defeated Mayor Jan Reimer (NDP) in 1995. Quite often candidates like these, associated with one federal party, will seek the public support of prominent local gladiators from other parties to highlight their own broad appeal. These are known as **letterhead Liberals**, supporters who are valued not only for their sage strategic advice and contacts but also for the value of their endorsement.

Elsewhere in the west, 1988 city elections in Regina and Saskatoon produced a similar situation. Saskatoon Mayor C. Wright (Progressive Conservative) retired and was replaced by NDPer H. Dayday. In Regina, Mayor D. Archer, who was backed by the local NDP, was most seriously challenged by G. Dirks, a former provincial Progressive Conservative cabinet minister; Archer had replaced incumbent Mayor L. Schneider who chose to run federally for the Progressive Conservatives. Also in the west, "non-partisan" mayors moved into the provincial arena where party identification remains important. Vancouver mayors Michael Harcourt (NDP) and Gordon Campbell (Liberal) both sought, successfully, to become premier of their province. In Alberta, mayors Ralph Klein of Calgary and Laurence Decore of Edmonton, men who were distinguished more by personality traits than any single policy thought, campaigned in 1993 to become "mayor" of the entire province; the former was a Progressive Conservative following a short dalliance with the Liberals, and the latter was a Liberal (Lightbody 1999b: 173). In 1996 in Vancouver, the anti-party NPA attacked its rival COPE with large newspaper ads accusing it "of being a front for the provincial New Democratic Party which wants 'to take control of our city'" (*Globe and Mail*, 15 November 1996). The anti-NDP blitz permitted several NPA councillors who had no public visibility to adopt an anti-NDP identity. Among the industrial democracies, it has been found that "About 70 percent of U.S., Canadian, Israeli, and French mayors consider themselves close to a national party. Widespread institutional reforms did not suppress traditional parties in Canada and the United States" (Hoffmann-Martinot 1998: 210).

6.2 The Continuing Case for Non-partisanship

6.2.1 The conventional arguments against party

The case against partisanship in Canadian cities in the twenty-first century has been carried forward from the nineteenth and was heavily buttressed by the American reform initiatives around 1900. It always pivots around four points.

First is the notion of ethical behaviour and the argument, in a perversion of Lord Acton's dicta that absolute power corrupts absolutely, that party politics lead inescapably to corruption. It is argued that parties build machines, that machines evolve the boss form, and that bosses wallow in coin skimmed from the treasury. The argument reaches back to the muckrakers and the publication of *The American Commonwealth* by James Bryce in 1888. Higgins records that Vancouver's first city ward system was abolished during 1934-35 reforms as the business community campaigned to "clean up" local politics (1986: 326-27). However, no other Canadian city has ever endured such systemic corruption or anything like boss rule; the petty dipping that has occurred has hardly been sufficient to justify the full non-partisan onslaught (Lightbody 1993: 197-99).

The other side of the policy mirror is that in non-party environments no elected agency exists which can evaluate and refuse the organized power of competing group demands no matter how trivial those individual initiatives might be. In this sense, a machine-style politics of rewards may exist even where there is no ward-healing political machine. Clearly, we can have one without the other or, in other words, the symptoms without the plague.

When a **strong party organization** (SPO) does not exist, budgetary consequences reveal that it is harder to limit **clientelism**.

A second popular line of attack is that "there is no 'Liberal' or 'Conservative' way to pave a street." Such thinking stems from the period of the Baldwin Act (1849) and beliefs then current that the work of municipalities was not similar to that of Parliament and thus not appropriate for party division. This leads to today's stock phrase: "good government by common sense," which dovetails with the wish to privatize the legitimately public sphere of city government in order to pursue "business plans" of one sort or another. For the market model to prevail, there can be no legitimate role for partisan debate over issues about how public goods will be accumulated or distributed.

The third standard argument is that partisanship produces caucuses and that the real policy choices will be made in private. Stephen Clarkson, who was defeated as a Liberal mayoralty candidate in Toronto, wrote that, "One reporter told our press secretary that he personally was opposed to party politics since he was afraid that the institution of a party caucus in City Hall would reduce the amount of confidential information that he could get from the elected aldermen" (1972: 147). In such a caucus system, public discussion of public business would decline, council would become a rubber stamp for decisions already taken, and council meetings would become more theatre than they are already. Individual accountability for positions on divisive ideas debated inside caucus would be glossed over in a veneer of consensus in public, and any process for public consultation in open meetings would be reduced to pandering insofar as the real decision has been pre-empted.

One example reveals how these behaviours actually work (see Lightbody 1999b: 174-75): "Winnipeg's pro-development party, the Independent Citizens' Election Committee (ICEC, 1921-1986), did play a calculated policy game in the two terms immediately subsequent to Winnipeg Unicity which illustrates what may develop under the most cynical partisan control...." In a complex series of privately consummated trade-offs, caucus agreed to support a commercial development in ward A, whose negative spillovers were such that they would provoke residents to become more than a little hostile to the sitting councillor. While councillor B and the rest of the ICEC caucus supported the initiative, councillor A protested and voted in the negative. Later, upon a similar circumstance emerging in ward B, councillor B voted against it while councillor A and his colleagues carried the day. However one chooses to assess the policy consequences, collective choices were made, implemented, and accepted with collegial accountability. Were similar situations to arise in other cities, the same scenario would likely be re-enacted but at least there *would* be a caucus to hold to account.

These sorts of ward concerns become the primary policy influence on non-partisan election campaigns, especially where constituencies are smaller. The Winnipeg Unicity example, where 50 single-person wards had populations of roughly 11,000, is important for revealing the natural propensity in councillor behaviour. Toronto Megacity had 56 councillors in 1996 (reduced to 44 in 2003), and Montreal Megacity now has 73, numbers so large that they constitute a gateway for coalitions. However, only Montreal had competing slates in its first post-amalgamation election. So, the issue of caucusing is not over the size of city, ward, or council but whether the inevitable deal-making that will occur behind the scenes will be subject to subsequent collective accountability.

The fourth arrow in the anti-party quiver is that party organization of council work would disrupt the comfortable operations of smaller councils in lesser cities and that organization by caucus would result in procedural delays, posturing for tactical ends, and disruptive debates. Party is viewed as a device which thwarts a quicker realization of public policies in due alignment with some objective, commonly agreed-upon public good so widely shared within the community that only a few self-sustaining eccentrics are at odds.

An occasional variant along this tack is that nonpartisan councils are less likely to find themselves on the outs with a provincial government than if they were partisans of a different stripe. This point is spurious for two reasons. First, the loose integration of Canadian parties has meant that even adherents of the same party may be at odds in federal-provincial relations. For instance, Progressive Conservative Prime Minister Clark and Alberta Progressive Conservative Premier Lougheed fought vigorously over energy policy in 1979-80; equally seriously, Liberal Prime Minister Martin and Ontario Liberal Premier McGuinty disagreed about transfer payments in 2004-05. Second, provincial-municipal legislation as well as financial formulae are normally expressed in general terms, and this mitigates, where it does not preclude, the possibility of specifically targeting politically aberrant individual communities.

6.2.2 Do the classic arguments hold up?

Let us consider the arguments for the anti-party case. Where the political culture permits an opportunity for illicit or amoral behaviour, then it may be observed that politics itself corrupts. Canadian concerns with widespread patronage were once sustained by the boss-rule experience of specific American cities, but that behaviour contrasted sharply with the petty larceny of Canadian city councils like that in 1930s Vancouver. Major exposure of systemic civic corruption, such as the Pax Plante-Jean Drapeau Montreal investigations (1950-54)[1] has been notable by its rarity.

Elsewhere I have noted that "The individuals most intensely involved in major city politics may find themselves leading one of many possible triple lives of lawyer, development lobbyist and fund-raiser; small businessman, councillor and civic booster; or city planner, homemaker and careerist" (1994: 206). Minor conflicts of interest may arise out of each of these conflicted possibilities. Corruption in city-regions is relative, quite independent of the presence of local parties, and that observed is not out of line with community standards. Minor league patronage opportunities regularly emerge as councillors appoint campaign workers and fund-raisers to the various boards, agencies, commissions, and other consultative positions to which they delegate authority. Councillors even draw up the ward boundaries for the constituencies they themselves represent (i.e., gerrymandering). No anti-partyism style can effectively safeguard a city from the "honest graft" of personalities like Edmonton's mayor William Hawrelak (Lightbody 1989).

On the matter of ideological street paving, it is only a question of scale that differentiates a city street from a provincial highway, a city park from a provincial recreational area. It can as easily be argued that there is no Conservative or Liberal way to conduct federal-provincial negotiations or to administer education or health care. In a strongly convincing summary of research findings comparing provincial government expenditures, Sohrab Abizadeh and John Gray make the case that stereotypes of leftish politicians as big spenders and more conservative politicians as tight-fisted when they are in power are erroneous. The authors tested 30 governments from seven different parties in all 10 provinces during the years 1960-86 and found: "the level and growth of provincial spending is not influenced by the position of the party on the political spectrum. The big spender label attached to provincial parties of the left and the frugal label attached to parties of the right would seem to be unwarranted" (1992: 533; also, Howlett and Ramesh 2003: 80-81). Since expenditure increases occurred independent of the party in power, the authors speculate that only style issues such as public works and enhanced social programs versus forgivable loans and infrastructure support to business operations are the significant indicators of ideological differences. This is as it should be, and such collective distinctions ought also to be subject to elector evaluation in city politics.

So, what positive difference could parties make in city politics? After studying fiscal patterns in 63 large American cities, Rowan Miranda concluded that, "Cities governed by SPOs [strong party organizations] have lower expenditure *levels* and lower expenditure *growth*, especially during difficult economic times" (1994a: 95; his emphasis). Evidence from Canadian cities without strong local parties remains impressionistic even though it appears consistently to support Clark's general observation that, "Decentralized leadership in general encourages more specific, tangible projects and services, including clientelism and patronage and higher spending" (1994: 9). I have elsewhere argued that party caucuses are able to assign priorities to items and issues for partisan advantage or administrative reasoning, thus reducing the tendency for specific-issue-driven individuals to hijack council budget priorities (Lightbody 1999b: 178-79).

Another anti-party position is that parties cause councillors to agree upon policies in the privacy of caucus. All legislatures function by allowing members to settle marginal differences privately. The acceptability of such behaviour essentially becomes a test of community tolerance. While caucusing is formalized in a competitive party system, it also exists in non-partisan councils. Seldom is this activity as routinized as it was in Edmonton from 1983 to 1988 when Mayor Laurence Decore hosted "tea parties" for councillors in his chambers on Friday afternoons before the public council sessions in order to permit a private airing of opinions and positions, "His personal political intuitiveness brought a coherence to council planning that has been atypical in this city's history and which is largely impossible in a system without strict caucus discipline" (Lightbody 1999b: 176). Tim Thomas comments that when the MCM was in power in Montreal, party discipline was used to dilute any real citizen involvement, notwithstanding that such a principle constituted a central policy commitment (1995: 128-31). However, using a caucus to put party priorities into practice might yield a desirable consequence in shielding less talented councillors on the municipal equivalent of the back benches and permitting the more able to articulate positions and take the lead in debate. By contrast, in a non-partisan system, name recognition means everything in the polling booth, with the unfortunate consequence that media moments count. This is where the fine balance comes between what is said and saying anything at all.

The last question relates to whether parties would disturb smaller councils. While disruption is probable in any human conclave where personal and political differences exist, the harmony of smaller councils is in large measure a reflection of the reality that they are more uniform in their composition than the urban communities they purport to represent. Non-partisanship, especially if coupled with at-large elections, glosses over genuine differences of cultures and ideas. Nor is smooth sailing the manifest function for any legislature. Finally, the beneficial possibility that all incumbents might be defeated if there were a competitive party system, even where the opposition comes from outside the council chambers, might very well outweigh any minor inconveniences arising from party differences over principle during debates.

6.3 Assessing the Canadian Record

Even though local political elites well understand the larger stakes in big city elections, there is little indication that this group awareness requires overt partisanship to remain the dominant force in city elections. There are exceptions, principally Montreal and cities on British Columbia's lower mainland, but they are long-standing exceptions proving the general rule of anti-partyism. Different party-like activities appeared in the twentieth century, such as **slate-making** with public endorsement or pulpit exhortation. The most successful city party operations over the years have been purely local, very small cadres, often with no more than a few dozen activists in the gladiatorial roles. These successes have sustained little ideologically driven discussion among gladiators as to whether or not such behaviour is appropriate (Masson 1994: 273–85).

In Canadian cities where non-partisanship prevails, the principal candidates normally come from the same social and economic community, and there is little platform divergence on general world views. These gladiators tend to draw upon equally large networks of friends, and often pretty much the same associates, so any substantive policy differences are unlikely. Candidates either promote the same general policy drift as they struggle with credibility over any specific campaign promise or they are inclined to the simplest of political relationships—promising facilities for votes (Kaplan 1982: 155-56). Naturally, if successful, they try to deliver. This is the "transactional leadership" style discussed more completely in Chapter 8. Any public accountability is strictly between individual councillors and informed electors with first-rate attention spans.

6.3.1 The common experience of city parties

Electors probably ought to know the history of party activity in their own city, but it is more important to understand the current general situation and particular circumstances. We look here at types of organized behaviour to explore *why* each emerges when it does through examples from various city histories.

Canadian municipal anti-partyism results from weak party integration across federal and provincial lines of activities, a consequence of the constitutionally decentralized nature of the Canadian federation. Our relatively weak federal government is one cause for the difference in municipal partisan behaviour from that in western European countries, Japan, and Israel. Overall, partisan identification among voters has been decidedly weaker across North America than in other post-industrial societies (Hoffman–Martinot

1998: 200-08). By the 1990s, Canadian municipal elected officials reported the lowest SPO incidence among ten industrial democracies (followed by Australia and the United States). This behaviour correlates with the strongest policy distances of Canadian mayors from the positions of the national parties of which they are nominally members (Clark and Hoffmann-Martinot 1998: 180, 145-52).

In the absence of recognizable party labels which might otherwise band civic candidates together, define their common position, and link electors to both personality and policy, various organized interests have engaged in slate-making and other party-like activities since the early twentieth century. Typically, groups such as the Chamber of Commerce or Board of Trade, the city's labour federations, and various umbrella property industry groups (Real Estate Board, Urban Development Institute, the Homebuilders' Association) have each vetted and published a list of candidates generally sympathetic to their policy ambitions. From time to time, issue-specific fundamentalists, like the temperance movement and pro-life extremists, have joined in. In major cities today, candidates will typically be confronted by two to three dozen policy questionnaires supposedly from policy networks and designed to probe compatibility with the sender's world views and to imply blacklisting if not. More problematic is whether anyone is actually swayed by these guides to better voting.

All large city councils these days are subject to factionalism and the logic of interpersonal deal-making to some degree. Masson contends that members of the typical pro-business, slate-making operations dominant in the twentieth century behaved very much as policy independents once elected. Indeed, since the singular function of local party in Canada is precisely recruitment screening, any other potentially important theoretical functions of viable party systems are subordinated. What Masson overlooks is the restriction placed on policy debate managed through the exclusiveness of the recruitment process (1994: 284-85). Put another way, only one general world view from candidates became acceptable; as this world view—pro-business and pro-development—belonged to the council majority, the municipal budget merely constituted the operational consequence of its projects and programs.

Slates reformulated as purely local coalitions are best described by the latent functions which they did best: recruitment, screening candidates, and acting as an election mechanism for those chosen. In this role, they finessed (filtered) general policy positions but not precision platform documents; the NPA in Vancouver probably accomplished this most effectively and for the longest period. However, as in federal and provincial legislatures, to overcome stalemate and reach agreement on controversial public policy such as budgets required the private workings of a caucus or executive committee of some sort. Council meetings became outlets for public consumption via the compliant press gallery of decisions already taken. Parties of the third reform period were not much different except in their unifying policy challenge to the status quo on development issues; for instance, Toronto's "CIVAC [Civic Action Party] remained little more than an intra-legislative alliance; it developed no party structures, recruited no new candidates, and managed to vote together in council only when committee assignments were being allocated" (Kaplan 1982: 643). Many generally progressive gladiators attached themselves to third reform parties in the 1970s, but only for a short time, and their interest faded away over the course of a single political generation.

The heyday of civic party formation in Canada occurred in those times of economic or social and political stress that created the conditions necessary for new leadership to challenge the entrenched public ethos, that is, immediately after the First World War and during the 1930s and 1970s. Local coalitions emerged in response to what were seen as external threats to the stability of the dominant, ongoing urban regime. As the threats subsided, the groups dissolved into anti-partyism, and governing reverted to the managerial realization of the given community's "common sense" or public ideology. It should come as no surprise that anti-partyism always appealed to the business community not only because it believed the private corporation model would work well in the delivery of municipal services but also because its structures (like at-large elections) had the practical effect of neutering the influence of organized labour and other "disagreeable" social movements.

Local wings of fringe federal and provincial parties like Social Credit or the CCF in the 1940s saw municipal opportunities but were seldom successful beyond electing a personally popular individual councillor or two. The only overt large-scale Liberal city involvement was in the Toronto elections of 1969 (Higgins 1986: 337; Clarkson 1972). There, 16 officially identified Liberal Party and 16 NDP candidates challenged each other for the council's 22 seats. The NDP elected three, and the Liberals two; the latter's mayoralty candidate lost badly. For the first Winnipeg Unicity election of 1971, only seven of 31 NDP candidates were elected; only two additional seats were added to this caucus in 1974. In short, interventions by federal or provincial parties in city elections only came from non-dominant parties like the NDP in Winnipeg, Vancouver, and selected Ontario cities in the early 1970s. Whether these efforts were serious is questionable given the paucity of resources directed into the overall effort, and the obvious lack of attention persistently hindered NDP local efforts on the lower mainland of British Columbia.

6.3.2 The classic local coalitions

Specific conditions, usually economic and often adverse, prompted generally similar types of twentieth-century bourgeois coalitions of booster interests to mobilize in reaction to real or anticipated labour and other leftist or "progressive" civic political action. The classic civic coalitions found their electoral roots in a political world view that downplayed the relevance of social and economic cleavages and saw the city as essentially a homogenous entity, which was very like the leaders themselves. All these formations were cadre-style, in contrast to the mass tendencies of what later came to be third reform period parties. While their announced goals were efficiency and "good government," all provided not-so-subtle appeals to the public ideology that city hall was in business to serve business. Typically, party activists were disproportionately drawn from businesses directly involved in real estate and property development. All programs were rooted in dynamic booster-ism and were always unabashedly pro-growth. Civic monuments like new city halls, libraries, convention centres, stadiums, and "world-class" games or exhibitions were the legacy, providing tangible benchmarks for any who questioned these parties' vitality.

The classic parties among these, as measured purely by durability, were the ICEC in Winnipeg (formed in 1919), the NPA in Vancouver (in 1934–35), the CGA (Civic Government Association) in Edmonton (in 1920), and Montreal's Civic Party (1954). While each emphasized its detachment from federal and provincial parties, the reality is that each was a Liberal/Progressive Conservative operation in its core gladiators, especially the fund-raisers. While party "leader" is too strong a label, the city mayor was the acknowledged program spokesperson. Because they were widely known by their acronyms, Masson has labelled these reform cadres "Alphabet Parties" (1975; 1994: 283-85). But they were organized parties in name only, existing as money-raising operations to win elections in which their program was pretty much exclusively to be elected. It might be said that Canadian civic parties emerged as did the municipal wings of Japanese national parties, which have been described as being "like ghosts, they have heads but no feet." Hoffmann-Martinot notes that this characterization by a former Japanese education minister applied mostly to the more conservative parties which have traditionally had quite weak municipal organizations (1998: 213).

Major cities in Quebec were also governed by strong cadre parties. The mayors selected candidates and set the municipal agenda for large chunks of the latter twentieth century and the Montreal groupings prior to Jean Drapeau's reign more closely resembled "hunting bands" of treasure-seekers than policy or parliamentary coalitions (Kaplan 1982: 404). By the 1954 civic election, La Ligue d'Action Civique (LAC) had devised an integrated platform, a full list of candidates, and ambitions for a majority win: "LAC, its leaders insisted, was not simply a loose alliance of opportunistic cliques, like Montreal's other and earlier 'parties'" (Kaplan 1982: 359). The central point about local cadre parties in this as in other cases is that they seldom develop much in the way of an organization between election periods and, with few exceptions, no one strong leader emerges to control rivalries among the party's luminaries. Because local parties are not thought to be like their federal and provincial counterparts, there is never a party constitution that permits a leadership convention. In Montreal the LAC and its principal rival both quickly disappeared (Kaplan 1982: 364).

Although Drapeau's Civic Party began as a typical North American anti-corruption, anti-vice municipal purification exercise in the late 1950s, he consolidated his position quickly in the 1960s (Higgins 1986: 343). Drapeau cleverly wove together personal charm and a populist link to his electorate with sometimes blatant appeals to Quebec nationalism. Montreal citizens had little real public access during these years and even "Backbench councillors who were not members of the powerful executive committee had little say and were expected to vote according to the dictates of the executive" (Graham and Phillips 1998: 107). Sancton labelled this operation a pure "caucus" party or, in our terms, a cadre-style, election-focused party, whose only members were the mayor and his candidates and whose political resources were unashamedly drawn from the small business community (1983: 70-73). This "us against them" style is typical of low-level demagogues. In much the same manner Edmonton Mayor William Hawrelak (nominal head of the powerful Citizens' Committee) stressed to his voter base in the city's Slavic community his business achievements as a Ukrainian outsider up against an old Anglo establishment. Drapeau, like Hawrelak, centralized his policy and budget control while expecting block voting on council (Joyce and Hossé 1970: 44-45). He personally chose all of his party's candidates in the later years.

In Canada's other metropolitan areas, only the actions of Vancouver's NPA executive secretary in approving candidate-nominating delegates "to make certain that none of them are socialists or otherwise politically undesirable" (Joyce and Hossé 1970: 44) or the generalized pro-growth policy vetting by Winnipeg's ICEC over the years have ever suggested much in the way of strict ideological coherence in their purely local parties. By 1970, elections in 24 of Canada's largest cities saw at least one local party in the field. Tindal and Tindal note that these were normally "short-lived coalitions of local interests that display little ongoing discipline or concerted action once elected" (2000: 251-52). Joyce and Hossé found that only 46 of the 114 parties they studied were still active (1970: 70-75).

The normal pattern outside of Montreal was to exert no real caucus discipline on council because of each cohort's loose structure. Members voted pretty much autonomously on the basis of personal "common sense," and during campaigns the electorate seldom (except in Vancouver) had a choice over the competitive policies of two or more responsible groups. Even such weakly integrated local parties as Winnipeg's ICEC had initially to buy internal caucus peace during the formative years of the 50-person Unicity council by directing capital works expenditures to their own electoral base. The first newly elected Winnipeg Unicity small-ward council undertook no major city-wide public works spending, but "there was an immediate inclination for log-rolling in expenditures for the direct personal credit of councillors, particularly among the previous suburban representatives" (Lightbody 1978b: 502). The majority ICEC party (37 of the 50 seats) met discretely in caucus to decide about building, mostly recreational facilities, for their districts at a ratio of 7:1 over the former core city. In Toronto Megacity after 1998, the new councillors focused on protecting their constituents; those from North York and Etobicoke, for instance, fought to retain snow clearing from residential sidewalks and the pickup of unbagged leaves, respectively, but only for their own suburbs.

One practical consequence of anti-party coalitions in Canada's cities should be noted. In city elections when purely local parties do emerge, one party quickly tends to become dominant for a sustained period of time. They have been able to bill themselves variously as "common sense government" or "sound administration," meaning that they no longer find themselves in serious competition to bid up local state expenditures to garner votes. Thus, they have the potential to behave somewhat as an American SPO might. With office-holding longevity, the trade-offs and bargaining necessary to satisfy the "rapacious individualism" required of independents as councillors can be muted by fiscal conservatism in even a weakly integrated party, a durable direction for the city budget, and a longer time horizon in attaining objectives. As Clark has concluded, "Strong leaders, backed by a strong party, can say no to group demands, because their political base is powerful enough to let them say no. Strong parties thus contain spending and government growth" (1994b: 8). The powerful bureaucracy entrenched by such a regime may, in its policies, be well able (or at least believe that it is able) to develop and implement current best management practices in isolation from direct public interference and short-term council whimsy.

6.3.3 The third reform endeavours

The third coherent period of reform in Canadian city politics, from about 1968 (marked federally by the election of Pierre Trudeau as Liberal prime minister) into the 1980s, gave rise to a different, more mass-type style of partisanship. The movement was a child of the postindustrial economy in Canada whose growing middle class possessed the increased leisure time which permitted closer attention to the value of the environment of workplace and home. Across the First World democracies, "the second wave of civic parties wanted to implement neighbourhood assemblies and growth limit propositions to increase citizen input; they emerged in the late 1960s and included the French Groupes d'Action Municipaux. They can be considered as the precursors of the new politics of the 1980s and 1990s" (Hoffmann-Martinot 1998: 211). Its gladiators were younger, wealthier, and better educated, and the new political culture they embodied gave rise to specific issues intended to produce a better style of living. Civic business-like efficiency was insufficient as the guiding value for municipal governing, and individuals expected to be explicitly involved in the policy-making process. In tactical terms, and as noted in the next chapter, leaders in this new political culture who located in established central city neighbourhoods (the process was called "gentrification") "often joined forces with incumbent residents and their community organizations to resist … projects endangering neighbourhood livability" (Villeneuve and Séguin 2000: 556). More broadly, they shared many values in common with other social movements of the period, such as gays and lesbians, feminists, peace activists, and the nascent Greens. Each of these more narrow issue arenas produced some part of the reform coalitions' broader policy package.

The citizen activism of this movement was fertile ground for new sorts of civic parties able to pursue their new policy issues electorally with enthusiasm. The policy calls common to all were for citizen participation, environmental protection (later, recycling), community policing, better transit, affordable housing (for others), and neighbourhood conservation. The cathartic trigger in Canada's largest cities (except Calgary), as we have seen before, was often widespread citizen opposition to a council's grandiose freeway ambitions. These electoral alliances for slower paced urban growth were, for a time, more broadly based in neighbourhoods than in the gentlemen's smoking rooms of the older cadre-style coalitions of gladiators. But even as they espoused "liveable city" causes, the new urban gentry also displaced traditional lower income community residents with their ability to spend on increased property values. In Vancouver, for instance, the *Globe and Mail* described TEAM as "not a party of radicals … it is dominated by people who, if they haven't made it, are at least comfortably [well off]" (October 1974).

Villeneuve and Séguin are quite correct in observing that what set these new parties (and interest groups) apart from the traditional civic operation was "the impression they projected that they were defending idealistic causes rather than their own narrow self-interest" (2000: 556). Over a relatively short period, however, these parties, even though more akin to Duverger's mass-type than the traditional cadre claque, quickly revealed one characteristic in common: like their predecessors, they tended to be factions with little continuity.

The best known among these third reform political parties were TEAM and COPE in Vancouver, the URGE, Toronto's CIVAC and Montreal's MCM. The third reform period parties seldom gained power as such, with only TEAM (1972), the MCM (1986), and the *Rassemblement Populaire* (Quebec City, 1989) winning majorities. It is true, however, that they often were able to direct council policy-making with the aid of generally like-minded independent councillors. Supplementing community association leaders in the west, the parties' activists were largely drawn from social progressives among the Liberals, union organizers, and conservative NDPers.

In Montreal, the MCM won 18 seats in 1974 but only one in 1978. Numerous observers have noted the many discrete, informal linkages between the PQ organization and MCM gladiators during its formative opposition period (Graham and Phillips 1998: 107). It became a genuine Canadian mass party, recruiting members and candidates from the wide array of progressive social movements of the 1980s. Even in its first period of decline in 1976, the MCM as a party of the mass-type had only "shrunk to" about 800 members. Most of the leadership also had linkages to the NDP or progressive adherents in the Liberal party.

In a sense, during civic elections in both Montreal and Vancouver through this short period, electors were presented with a distinct choice between two styles of parties, two socially and economically different teams of candidates, and two divergent platforms, each drawn from the ideological coherence of two divergent reform traditions (note Higgins 1986: 346-50; Thomas 1995). Finally, in 1986, the MCM won a majority, with all but three council seats. By 1990 internal squabbling over policies and council procedure had seriously splintered the party. Typically, the constraints of budgeting and governing overwhelmed initial goals, and the movement, as party, was transformed into an election-focused crew (Thomas 1995). The seeds of defeat were sown by winning; once any of these new civic parties became closely coupled with municipal administrators, they became less innovative and lost both momentum and members. By the 1994 elections, both the MCM and the sorry remnants of Drapeau's Civic Party lost badly to a new ensemble led by retired city botanist Pierre Bourque, Vision Montreal, which won 39 of the 51 council positions.

These events had been partly presaged in Toronto where, after the election of a reform majority in 1974, there followed a splintering-off of its most left-wing members into a *real* "Reform Caucus." Although self-lauded as genuinely progressive, participant-observer Susan Fish perceived less altruistic motivations: "Working on the government side within the 'reform majority' necessitated a loss of media attention and coverage of individual 'Reform Caucus' aldermen whose actions would be subsumed within the general government thrust" (1981: 100). So, since each had to distinguish themselves from the others, caucusing would not work! More bluntly, Kaplan observed strong personality clashes; cooperation is difficult when people simply don't like each other (1982: 643).

6.3.4 Partisan vitality in Calgary and Edmonton

Both Calgary and Edmonton city councils functioned with local civic parties during the 1950s. Edmonton's Citizens' Committee, with a long history dating to the Progressive era in the 1920s, was the stronger. It dominated the local business of elections during this time; its nominees held *all* council seats from 1945 until 1959. Its platform centred on promises of "dynamic growth" under the "most efficient government possible" (Lightbody 1983: 263-65). In this configuration, the dominant personality and party leader was William Hawrelak (mayor 1951-59); as Masson notes perceptively, "During his reign as mayor in the 1950s Bill Hawrelak controlled Edmonton's city council in much the same way as a champion chess master manipulates the board pieces" (1994: 186). The Citizens' Committee dissolved in disarray after Hawrelak's scandal-initiated resignation in 1959. That Hawrelak was not the leader of a genuine SPO in the American city-county sense of having intergovernmental power during this time was clearly revealed in 1957 when he was both frustrated in his pre-election federal cabinet ambitions and defeated in the June vote. Both episodes were due to internal Liberal Party quarrels with his hubris.

Calgary's mayors were not so politically pivotal as party leaders. Don Mackay (1950-59) set about the task as a genial wagon master for the troop. His successor as mayor, Harry Hays, was introduced by the media in 1959 as having a prototypical business approach "to administer" the city. Council policy activities may have appeared less structured than the "Citizens" actions in Edmonton but, with labour both weakened and factionalized in the growth economy, the Civic Government Association (1919-55) and its direct successor the United Citizens' Association (UCA) in 1956-57 were able to exploit a proportional representation system sufficiently to tower over their opposition in electoral terms (Joyce and Hossé 1970: 47-49; Masson 1994: 466-68). The UCA in particular was championed as a universalist party, but the pretense of being "all things to all people" masked the real clout held by its leadership from business, service clubs, and institutionalized ratepayer groups. None of these Edmonton or Calgary parties was ideologically coherent in the European sense, being instead the representatives of rather narrow economic interest.

Comparative experience suggests, for Canada, that it is the very feebleness of potential municipal opposition that permits any community's commercial class to adopt the open accordion guise of the universalist non-party. Like amoeba, such groups both include and dilute potentially competitive ideological strands, while, being without much in the way of apparent structural hierarchy, they are very hard to organize against (Clark and Inglehart 1998: 41-48; Clark 1998a: 110-14). Like Bracken's wartime provincial administration in Manitoba, Edmonton's Civic Committee of the 1950s was sufficiently inclusive to embrace prominent Liberal, Progressive Conservative, and Social Credit adherents (Lightbody 1983: 266).

Edmonton entered the 1980s having elected four, left-centrist URGE councillors from their 11 candidates running and one Labour representative to the 12-person council. These numbers were reduced in two subsequent elections, and by the end of the decade pure anti-party behaviour prevailed. URGE, a third reform period party like Vancouver's TEAM, officially dissolved in June 1989. Mayor Laurence Decore, elected with 61 per cent of votes cast in 1983, explicitly chose not to involve himself in aldermanic campaigns, although during his 1986 re-election (68 per cent) he privately indicated to supporters those candidates "with whom he felt he could work" on council. Unsurprisingly, there were, in several wards, more of these than positions available. Behind the scenes he worked "to cut the deals" prior to the public council meetings, ensuring that no major policy initiative from his office was ever lost at council vote.

No parties openly contested Calgary elections during the 1980s. In 1977 the Calgary Urban Party (CUP) had tried to appeal to the city's new professional class by promising better planning and social programs but gloriously failed to elect anyone (Masson 1994: 469). CUP dissolved in the spring of 1980 to join labour, which had officially abandoned the field after total voter rejection in 1966-67, on the sidelines. By mid-decade, the council was splintered loosely into four blocs based on a combination of age with left versus more conservative approaches (McAlpine and Drabek 1991: 821). The mayor's office was a personal fiefdom, and Ralph Klein (mayor 1980-88) was twice re-elected with huge pluralities of 85 per cent in 1983 and 90 per cent in 1986. Mayor Klein, capitalizing on a policy-splintered council, exercised a kind of loosely liberal leadership with a direct popular appeal over the heads of city councillors while he "cultivated an image of himself as informal, folksy, and able to get along with almost anyone" (Masson 1994: 186). Indeed, his was the perfected image of the successfully populist politician. It would be easy to hypothesize budgetary extravagance would result were it not for the twin circumstances of a city commission board and its managerial ability to exploit Klein's own mostly latent "fiscal populism" respecting public policies. (On the latter point, note Clark and Inglehart 1998: 10-13.)

Today neither the councils in Calgary and Edmonton nor those in Toronto, Ottawa, and Winnipeg are overtly partisan.

6.4 The New Case for Open Accountability in Today's Cities

Councillors at city hall are politicians seeking election to representative positions. And, as politicians, they may be expected to exhibit certain characteristics and to engage in specific widely indulged behaviours that explains their actions in the public policy process. Intentionally or not, incumbents by definition block entrance of newcomers into the system. The case that a more overt partisan structuring of policy biases is relevant to twenty-first century city politics has two dimensions—policies and people.

6.4.1 Necessary new policies

6.4.1.1 CLEAR ACCOUNTABILITY IN POLICY CHOICE

A non-partisan council is a group in which everyone has a voice but no one is actually responsible. Candidates are elected independently, and each claims responsibility for the good choices and ducks the unhappy ones as being beyond personal control. Each councillor claims to make decisions based on "their own good sense," which is no more than that person's blend of experience, knowledge, and ideological world view. The generic problem for anti-partyism is that citizens have no "government" to congratulate or to blame either for individual policies gone wrong or for the general condition of the community, except possibly the permanent public administration. The ensuing citizen frustration has produced higher measures of public cynicism and lower voter turnout.

For example, thinking only of the budgeting process, under non-partisan conditions any fiscal document over which councillors have final sway is necessarily preceded by a complex series of log-rolling alliances, bargains, trade-offs, and compromises which work to inflate the final numbers: there has to be something for everyone. Little in the way of monetary tough love can be reasonably expected in such a system. Hard evidence from Canadian non-partisan cities remains impressionistic, but it appears that non-partisan councils are more easily intimidated by the noise of ratepayer associations and other organized sectoral interests (Kaplan 1965: 29); there is no one who can say "no" to the structured power of group demands.

On the other hand, we have noted above that party caucuses can and do assign priorities to items and issues for reasons of partisan advantage or administrative imperative. Indeed, the central theory of the SPO city is that "cities governed by strong party organizations are more successful in imposing fiscal discipline than cities without such governing arrangements because centralized parties are less responsive to interest group demands for spending" (Miranda 1994a: 80). Citizens are also able to hold the SPO to account in the polling station. In the absence of the SPO in Canada, civic expenditure increases appear not to be subject to much in the way of public controls and vary only as transactional leaders vie for elector approval.

Even for individual issues, and precisely because party caucuses do assign priorities, council agendas may be politically vaccinated against specific-issue networks and tightly wound policy communities. Procedure-conscious administrators are particularly prone to capitulate to a clientele which has a particularist voice on council, and, unless there is a political coherence such as that provided through an SPO, the city as a whole must pay the price of subamendment, referral, examination, report, reinvestigation, and delay when that clientele's expectations go unmet.

6.4.1.2 SYSTEMIC OPPOSITION

One attribute of responsible government in the Westminster parliamentary tradition is that a loyal opposition is entrenched in Parliament. Its role is to question governing policies and budgets, to hold ministers accountable, and to present themselves as an alternative "government in waiting." The anti-partyism culture in Canadian cities, however, has strongly upheld the notion that such central government institutions are either problematic or irrelevant in city affairs. This fosters an environment in which the public administration is proactive and elected representatives react.

Non-partisan councillors naturally seek name recognition since non-partisan elections generously reward incumbency. They gravitate to short-term and media-driven issues. Opposition to proposed changes in public policy tends to be specific, parochial, immediate, and focused on the most tangible and least complex of issues. On the other hand, a party system, of necessity, assigns a critic to even the least appealing civic function, recognizing that it is party performance that will be rewarded on election day. In other words, even though issues surrounding the radiation of sewerage sludge provide less fetching visuals for the dinner news than, say, planning fireworks for Canada Day, the existence of a party in opposition at city hall means that someone has to keep an eye on both.

For example, in late October 2003, the NPA opposition on council in Vancouver produced a 14-page assessment of the COPE-dominated council's first year in office (see <http://www.npa.bc.ca>). The cover depicted a city hall building split in half while two flying saucers hovered overhead. The intent was to capture the media eye, to ridicule the COPE council's opposition to the American war against Iraq and proposed militarization of outer space, and to critique specific local decisions, such as a new tax on hotel room conversions. The point is that an opposition provided a focal point, outside of elections, around which some electors were able to group their dissent. NPA councillor Peter Ladner argued that, "We've found ourselves, reluctantly, in the position of having to be an opposition, and are trying to rein in COPE a bit." COPE Mayor Campbell replied, "If you listen to the NPA … we should [only] worry about dogs and cats and sewers" (*Vancouver Sun*, 29 October 2003). A somewhat similar strategy was deployed in 1960 when Jean Drapeau and his fledgling opposition Civic Party campaigned in Montreal with a promise to fight unemployment with major investments in public works (Higgins 1986: 342).

Vigorous attention is not always appreciated by those in authority. Following the 1974 election in which opposition MCM councillors were first elected, Mayor Drapeau declared that "opposition could be a dangerous thing" and initiated a multi-faceted "campaign to make life as difficult as possible in little ways for the pesky 18 who ran successfully against the [Civic Party] establishment" (*Globe and Mail*, 17 December 1974), including threats to abolish Question Period and to withdraw secretarial support for the new opposition crew.

6.4.1.3 REDEFINITION OF BOOSTERISM IN A GLOBAL AGE

During the time when second reform period parties dominated Canada's city councils, they caught the attentive public mood by subscribing to a cluster of booster economic growth policies which Leo and Brown have labelled "the Holy Grail of city politics" (2000: 193). Canadian city councils have historically been boosters, transparently defined by policies supportive of unconstrained business development; however, after some critical analysis of implicit shortcomings, Leo and Brown conclude that a different approach could be better: "One does not have to be an entrepreneurial genius to puzzle out the consequences of stringing infrastructure to the horizon at low densities, to see that different cost structures for housing yield different policy opportunities, or to make the calculation that a massive public investment in the retention of major league sport in a marginal market is a risky proposition ..." (2000: 210). Typically, the problem in gathering public support for alternatives to rapid-growth policies has been how lonely such voices seem as they stand on the peripheries of policy debate.

Greer (1963) once labelled the booster approach the "fertility measure" of government success. Especially during times of sustained economic growth, it has been reduced to a narrow focus on the business of real estate to the point where council's policy agenda becomes almost single issue. Urban radicals like Lorimer (1972, 1978) launched forceful attacks against this supine posture, but garnered little support from either council or the wider public. Newer holistic approaches to the sustainable planning of Canadian cities have approached development from a wider perspective, in the process entering new ideological rivulets into the political mainstream (McAllister 1995). Where opposition parties in pursuit of power exist, they are inclined to embrace new ideas like these. Immediately, new concepts gain gateway legitimacy and force a broadening of the traditional booster agenda. Proposals for policies embracing more restrained growth and sustainable development, as advocated by many new social movements, are thus most likely to be welcomed within the platforms of emergent or minority parties. This is the function of innovation as performed by party systems.

6.4.2 The need for new people

6.4.2.1 RECRUITING A BETTER RANGE OF PEOPLE

It has long been the argument of the anti-party crowd that an open competition attracts persons otherwise put off by the more sordid aspects of party backrooms. "Good people" are still averse to the tough and time-devouring demands of public life. In Alberta in the 1950s, the purely local non-partisan parties of Calgary and Edmonton could be understood as a backroom bourgeois style of class politics. The decline of these anti-party coalitions as a basis for policy organization in the 1970s initially made politics in both cities more the province of better educated, specific-policy elites. This evolution of the local political culture into new patterns of behaviours was quite similar to larger changes taking place in other post-industrial societies (Clark and Inglehart 1998: 16–57). But this period passed quickly in Canada, and an age of the unimpressive is the result. Thirty-five years ago Lorimer opined that,

"The usual recourse of people who think that there is 'something wrong' with city government is to argue that what is needed is 'better people' elected to office. Instead of roofing contractors, insurance agents, and dumb lawyers, what is needed is architects, engineers, and smart lawyers" (1970: 156). He argues that this is snobbishness and that even if the conduct of council business ran more smoothly as a result, this does not in itself change the nature of the business.

To attain the name recognition non-partisanship commands, the election costs, especially where the constituencies are large (city-wide in British Columbia cities and, even if they are called wards, a larger population than Prince Edward Island in Edmonton) stand as a real barrier to many individuals. To be fair, many also have far better things to do with their money than self-promotion and, if elected, with their time than that needed for the dissection of every detail in agenda haystacks. Properly functioning parties provide a cost-cutting shorthand for electors. They will recruit, pool costs, sort, and share issues in caucus. While it may be wishful thinking, parties can also screen out those who would run on the exclusive platform of public notoriety.

6.4.2.2 RECOGNITION, ACCESS, AND REPRESENTATION FOR CITY MINORITIES

It has long been understood that the simple facts of plurality election mean that, as with new policy ideas, it is the minority party which most actively recruits new personnel from minority cultural communities. Non-partisan councils across Canada, especially those elected from large districts, work to the advantage of middle-aged white men. Consider only the matter of gender. A clear pattern has been discerned for larger cities in Quebec: "in general, the larger the city, the smaller the chances that women can have a significant impact, a finding that runs directly counter to the cosmopolitanism thesis" (Gidengil and Vengroff 1997: 527). Even though not elected through the general vote, it is largely a consequence of anti-partyism that the first enlarged council of the new city of Halifax was comprised entirely of 23 men. In Quebec, Gidengil and Vengroff suggest that "with 85 per cent of the leadership (party head and official representatives) of Quebec's municipal parties being male … the potential is there for municipal parties to serve as barriers" to the likelihood of female candidacies, a reality blunted only by the parties' own inability to persist for very long (1997: 520). Under these circumstances, cultural minorities, especially if visible, confront a bulletproof glass ceiling.

City-wide elections in Vancouver consistently discriminated on the basis of gender and class; only recently, when the growing number of minority voters made an electoral challenge possible, was this systemic flaw mediated by party gladiators. Opening the doors to Vancouver's oriental community through candidate recruitment came relatively late in the game: "The [COPE] coalition is also expected to field a candidate from the Chinese-Community this time, a failing that cost COPE dearly in the last election, when tiny lawns in the city's poorest polling areas were plastered with signs endorsing NPA candidate Tung Chan" (*Globe and Mail*, 22 September 1993). On a similar point, Gidengil and Vengroff note that in Quebec municipal elections "the presence of parties can actually help women when the dynamics of party competition reinforce pressures to nominate female candidates" (1997: 521). They offer the good example of the previously patriarchical Montreal Civic Party's being obliged to nominate women in 1978 after the MCM had managed to elect three women councillors in 1974.

These days women as councillors are not oddities, and, statistically, "gender makes no significant impact on the average probability of a candidate winning a seat on council" (Kushner *et al.* 1997: 551). Party politics can also provide a staircase and not a barrier to intergenerational social mobility. Viable parties in competition for power at city hall simply must seek out that one last vote with a calculated determination. Even if candidacies from minority groups start out as symbolic operation, the ice is broken.

6.4.2.3 ETHICAL QUESTIONS CONCERNING CAMPAIGN FINANCE

By the 1990s, city election campaigns had became as costly as those at the other levels. In big cities, area-wide campaigns cover a territory the size of at least six federal ridings—around two dozen in Toronto—so to spend "a buck a voter" is no longer out of line. Depending on ward size, serious candidates for council will reasonably spend up to $40,000, which is a lot of money for the average citizen. Even as city elections have become more expensive, extravagant campaign spending does not guarantee election. Winners have been found to spend 2.4 times more than losers, and incumbents spend twice as much as the reported average of all candidates (Kushner *et al.* 1997: 549-52).

Importantly, city campaigns are different from federal and provincial elections in that those running for office must *personally* raise the funds to do so. There are three roughly equal sources for campaign money: people who do business for city hall (consultants, architects, accountants, suppliers, etc); people who require city hall in order to do their own business (land developers, realtors, contractors, etc.); and people who are relatives, friends, and social associates (Lightbody 1997a: 126-28). In many cases all three sets of donors consider themselves to be friends and neighbours. Incumbents can raise and spend twice as much as challengers simply because they have access to all three wellsprings, while challengers have only the last. The generic ethical difficulty is that not even the best intentioned of candidates can offer believable guarantees that any complex of intermediaries on the campaign team provides an "arms' length" distance between donor and subsequent policy choices should they win. In provincial and federal politics, party pooling of fund-raising efforts and centralized spending clouds the direct *quid pro quo* potential for any single path of cash or kind. Party institutions impose a substantial psychological distance between solicitation and later policy choices.

The ingenuity of municipal campaign gladiators coping with the higher costs of non-partisan electioneering has easily circumvented, as necessary, the diluted disclosure bylaws that have been passed by councils themselves. Provincial statutes like those in Ontario and Quebec now require disclosure well after the vote and set penalties for noncompliance, but even good efforts can be dodged by ardent scofflaws. In Ontario, for example, the NDP in the 1980s initially employed the good offices of provincial MPPs, candidates, and constituencies to channel money through the provincial tax receipt process, normally losing a small cut of about 20 per cent along the way. The time is now right for provincial statute intervention across the country to devise clear financial rules for local elections with respect to the raising and expenditure of campaign funds, to provide tax relief equivalent to that of other governing levels, and to require conflict-of-interest protocols for all of their municipalities.

6.5 What Lies Ahead?

Is less of the same going to be good enough in the coming decade? Not likely.

The political reality of the Canadian cityscape has changed to become more widely diverse in ideas, clientele, and policy requirements, but the political processes accommodating these forces have adapted neither quickly nor well. New cultures, new issues, and new agendas have entered the process, and expectations, especially among the young, more educated, and affluent individuals and communities, have become more complex. Voter turnout has become less stable, and lower, as voters have become more cynical with respect to traditional leadership. Those most likely to be actively involved have turned to new movements whose issues are specific to ecology, gender, and person (privacy, access to information, equity, *etc.*). Their leaders employ new communications technologies to organize rapidly around issues of importance to individuals. It should be of little surprise that traditionally detached non-partisan councillors are perplexed, struggling as one-armed jugglers to balance the search for leaders and spokespeople to assuage, administrators to provide policy guidance, and means to attain name recognition.

McAllister suggested whimsically a decade ago that local councillors might more easily master Lewis Carroll's "Lobster Quadrille" than the new policy dance floor (1995: 286). Citizens seek both to be actively involved in the development of policy alternatives and to be a part of their administration. In the policy area of city-region land-use planning, for example, it might be expected that many reasonable, more holistic alternatives exist for the integrated development of rapidly developing metropolitan areas. Citizens appear increasingly to expect their involvement to be active, continuous, and not accomplished through delegation of authority as was the case with the blue ribbon co-option of 1950s-era planning boards.

In the absence of clear political direction, many professional city bureaucrats have become as flummoxed as the elected. Public service concerns with quality management and productivity measures, such as cost management or unit or activity costing, have little significance if the output objective of the budget exercise is a political harvest weighed by votes. Nonpartisan councils have encouraged clientele groups to behave actively as policy gold-diggers, and Miranda is firm in his conclusion that, in the United States, clientelist cities have more expansionary fiscal policies than their "reformed" counterparts (1994a: 95).

The new policy culture confronts an established policy-making style in which councillors who are non-partisan are unable to just say "no" to coherent policy communities and networks working through the city administration. Indeed, and as will be further considered in Chapter 7, Canadian councillors concede, when asked, that the greatest influences over their budgeting choices are their own finance staff, departmental heads, and chief administrative officers (Lightbody 2003). Recent calls for "more professional" conduct by elected representatives from those stuck with the administrative consequences of council decisions is in reality little more than a plea for coherent political action (Lowy and Taylor 1990: 310-13; Lightbody 1996).

Wider global commitments to new lifestyle causes produce the very personal policy areas which will be of most importance in the days ahead. This new political culture *is* focused in urban centres. Major problems in making policy arise out of the uneasy collaboration of the new ideologies with councils still subject to neighbourhood pressure as ward representatives. There is no evidence that a coherent alternative agenda will emerge out of these issue coalitions like that which sustained the third wave of Canadian urban reformers in the early 1970s. Thus far, the limited evidence suggests that informal caucusing will have to suffice as a way to moderate differences by sensitizing traditional neighbourhood interests to wider area concerns and by tempering the more strident of the issue-driven networks. Part of the intractability stems from the fears of sectoral interests that any institutional change, such as a significant expansion in council size, could erode their access to, and power over, individual members. Much of the gusto in the protests over Toronto Megacity, for example, was rooted in particular policy communities fearing absolute loss of policy gains and secure working relationships wrested from their ideologically diverse but not partisan central city council. While the protestors assumed that a new council majority would collegially skew the budget to favour only the suburban bourgeoisie, what has emerged in Toronto, along lines discussed above, is seemingly indiscriminate approvals as most existing programs and services have been "harmonized" to highest levels.

So if the lobster quadrille were accurately to characterize policy-making as society has grown increasingly complex and particularized, then local leadership cartels, in order to survive, may well try to coalesce around a nucleus of tactically smart lifestyle policy networks and endeavour to institutionalize them into the policy process. The ancient vehicle of party may not be obsolescent but a viable means to debate, devise, and implement practical, albeit satisficing, measures.

What is important to electors, then, are the policy issue areas where the substance *is* style. That is, if overall expenditures are independent of party in office, then what matters are lifestyle issues. Even as city councillors fret over matching neo-liberal expectations by providing government "on the cheap" with "user payment for services," their citizens have stampeded past them to expect decisions on approaches and process on issues like employment accessibility and equity, or simply fair treatment. For example, a recent landmark decision by the Ontario Superior Court in September 2004 completely cleared a man of drug trafficking charges when it was found that the accused had only been apprehended "because of racial profiling, because he was a black man with an expensive car." The innocent man afterwards observed, "As a black man, there is always the feeling that this can happen." Toronto police referred the decision to its own internal affairs for "whatever action is appropriate" (CanWest News Services, 17 September 2004). The attentive public will be watching.

But such a bureaucratic non-response can come about only because the anti-party council provides a political opportunity for senior administrators to make and implement their own public policy, especially when the policy community is tightly knit and closed to outside scrutiny as is policing. When councillors are absolute independents, with an 80 per cent probability of re-election, there is as little political pressure to initiate comprehensive program evaluation as there is autonomous capacity to follow through. The political sophistication of Canadian city politics has not achieved anything resembling competent oversight. For comparison sake, one could look to western European countries like France and Italy, which have strongly partisan local elections and where governing councils that cannot keep up with new realities are simply replaced.

New pressures have indeed led to new city-region structures in Montreal, Toronto, and even, through functional shifts, Vancouver. The central issue, though, is not structure but whether there will be governors with a mandate. The unresolved question remains: How will gladiators respond? So far they have proven reluctant to change any practices that, in their assessments, would compromise their own electability. Will some sort of urban regime take charge? Will clienteles rule through the permanent bureaucracy? For the public service, the question which lingers is: What public to serve?

Regardless of any normative policy impact assessments, the least "efficient" model as measured by long-standing business school standards and least "effective" as assessed by democratic expectations of responsibility are what Canadian cities have: the non-partisan council, weak mayor, and neighbourhood wards. In the absence of any hierarchically powerful administrative centre to discipline wayward budget expansion, spending levels have blossomed, citizen access remains episodic, and the overall policy agenda is incoherent.

Note

1. In a classic "Purification Rite" of big city politics (see Greer 1963: 6-18), young lawyer Jean Drapeau entered his public career in 1950 as assistant to Pacifique (Pax) Plante, dismissed assistant police director and, subsequently, investigator to the Caron Inquiry into police corruption. Caron uncovered a systemic network of police officers, public officials, and organized crime figures that had conspired to create a "sewer-world" of sex, liquor, and gambling (McKenna and Purcell 1980: 86-93; Sancton 1983: 68-69). Using the publicity as a base, Drapeau was elected mayor by a landslide in 1954.

seven | Interests and lobbying at City Hall

Over a decade ago, Linda Trimble noted that, "The fact that city *elections* are seen as less important does not necessarily mean that city politics are so seen" (1995: 104; emphasis in original). The continuing significance of actors in non-official centres of power to policy decisions and effective outcomes merits specific mention. This chapter and the next are about city-region policy communities, their role in public policy innovation, and their potential in enforcing accountability in representative democratic institutions.

Pressure groups, lobbyists, and special interests have traditionally constituted one of the more interesting yet uncertain areas of inquiry in political science. One body of thought, beginning with the American muckrakers in the early years of the twentieth century, can be traced from the work of Pendleton Herring (1936) to that of modern activists such as Ralph Nader. It has been obsessed with the secrecy and avariciousness of various deals between lobbyists and state legislators whose influence was rooted in the dispersed power of the American system. At the municipal level, machine politics and their bosses provided ample fuel for righteous indignation a century ago; home rule was originally designed to prevent cities in the United States from being violated by utilities franchises and their good friends in American state houses. We will note the basic issues in conflicts of interest in Canada as well as questions about codes of conduct towards the end of the next chapter.

While the American experience with legislators' transgressions is both sadly amusing and instructive, in Canada, as a general observation, provincial and federal parliamentarians have not been so susceptible to a systemic and direct pillaging of the public purse. To ascribe to this historic pattern of behaviour a higher ethical station for Canadian politicians would be a folly no matter how satisfying. The sorry reality is that the concentrated power enforced by the Westminster parliamentary model accompanied by party discipline in the legislatures diverts lobbying efforts to the real apex of authority. In consequence, when uncovered, national and provincial scandals have been at the senior ministerial levels and rather large scale indeed (Langford and Tupper 1993: xx). While non-partisan local councils may provide luminous opportunities for Canadian malfeasance, especially in the policy world of real estate development, careful observation indicates that such still remains the exception and not the general pattern (Greene and Shugarman 1997).

The intent in this chapter is to discuss the general concept of interests and policy communities and to assess the role of well-established groups in theory and in reality.

In the modern world, each citizen belongs to many groups representing a potential shared interest. Contemporary society is itself splintered into multiple special roles for the various aspects of work, play, and home, each of which may from time to time occupy a greater or lesser importance to an individual personality. It is in this sense that we may say that any community is **particularized**, split into special publics reflecting these separate personae. Such a community is one in which cleavages in social and economic identities may divide citizens into quite distinct groupings, or coalitions of groups, on particular policy issues. Many of these differences are voluntary. However, one of the analytically interesting aspects of ethnicity that separates its attachments from the social class divisions characteristic of western Europe or American voluntary associations is that citizens cannot choose the cultural identification into which they are born. Especially in a strongly particularist national political culture which identifies persons primarily by their group attachments, there is little else that so precisely defines who citizens are as their ethnic origins.

The concept of shared interests within society is largely a psychological phenomenon. People belong to, or share, a singular interest whenever they *feel* that they do. However, and naturally, individuals are not always aware of their potential for group attachments. A myriad number of latent communities of interest exists within modern society. Some are occupationally derived (lawyers, school teachers, or small business owners); some are demographic (pensioners, students, or those with disabilities); and some are rooted in older divergences in language, religion, or ethnicity. But all these are only potential sources of shared interest and for division in the political system. As far back as 1908, Bentley argued that an individual personality was no more than the sum of his group interests and that society itself is no more than the complex of groups comprising it. Refined and enhanced, these ideas still sustained the later pluralism of Latham (1952), Dahl (1961), and Truman (1964). In this world view, everything about a person creates a possibility for an interest that is shared with others who possess the same attributes, or who fulfill the same general position in the workforce, or who view particular public policy items similarly.

That is, there exists in cities the possibility that policy communities may form around all those who commute, or those who require subsidized housing, or even those who depend upon the general policies of specific city departments (like social services, libraries, or recreation). Yet, frequently, no formal association or continuously effective public voice will emerge either to advance or to safeguard this latent **policy community**. In theoretical terms, this situation may lead to the psychological-sociological appearance of a policy community with the fundamental assumption being the self-awareness of its members as constituting a distinct group. It is at base a question of belonging—and of being set apart from the rest of society because of that identifiable attachment.

In other words, as the common attributes shared by certain individuals in society begin to draw them together as they appreciate their own differentiation from others, they become aware of themselves as an interest, a group that may necessarily become politically active because, inherently, their collective world view embraces a set of policy priorities. Clearly, the fact that the group possesses a common interest implies that it has also developed a shared set of preferences, even if only reactive, about the direction of public policy. Similarly, attentive citizens may emerge as policy networks of generally like-minded professionals, clients, educators, and journalists organized around specific issue areas. The decisive stage comes with the transformation of latent awareness into direct action or lobbying.

By definition, a **political pressure group** may be considered as any organization that attempts to influence public policies through the application of political resources. Put differently, a pressure group is the politically significant expression of a group's interests in society by which it attempts to apply power through the mobilization of wealth, information, the time and expertise of volunteers, bureaucratic contacts, public relations, and so forth. At times, more than a single formal group will claim to represent a given policy community, with the result that councillors are conflicted about whom to include in their processes of decision-making. Similarly, where various issues claim the attention of a policy community at one point in time, a number of distinct policy networks may also be active simultaneously.

It should not be thought that "pressure" implies insidious activity or purpose, or any perversion of the democratic process. The sustaining world view of twentieth-century liberal democratic apologists insists that it is the very multiplicity of vibrant group interests which ensures that no one segment in any community prevails in every functional public policy arena forever. This is the democratic heart of pluralist thought. While the party competition of elections may not produce dramatically divergent alternatives for citizens, it is the fundamental openness and accessibility of the policy process, coupled with dynamic and competing policy communities, that holds office-holders both representative and accountable between periodic votes. Elections become referendums on office-holding; policy choice lies in the processes of the intervening years.

What pluralist analysis would have us believe is that the agency of the state is relatively neutral—not ideologically inclined—in its policy administration, and through the competitive interplay among "equally powerful agencies," policy decisions are mediated. In theory, the consensus attained will represent the necessary balance among countervailing interests (Clement 1975: 357-66). Those scholars implicitly employing a liberal pluralist analysis (such as Tindal and Tindal 2000) would argue that the probability exists that a multiplicity of pressure groups is easily able to form in order to represent effectively all the latent policy communities in city-regions. When this presumed balance is coupled with the public interest, or common good that municipal decision-makers see themselves as representing, councillors become no more than ideologically neutral policy arbiters intent upon producing generally fair and widely equitable public policies out of the competitive group interplay. Thus, the central thrust of the representative democratic process will be assessed as having been well served.

We are provided occasional glimpses into this normally subconscious mindset of councillors, and of the active reality of the underlying pluralist theory, during inadvertent instances of frankness during intense community conflicts. On one such occasion in Edmonton, in April 2003, ward councillors tried to resolve a long-standing quarrel between the expansiveness of West Edmonton Mall and its residential neighbours with respect to late-night noise, traffic, garbage, and vandalism spilling out from the mall's exceptionally large nightclub sector, by "improving communications" among the parties through the usual task force tactic. Ward councillor K. Leibovici offered this insight into councillor behaviour: "We, being neutral, can bring together all the different stakeholders, getting their issues on the table and developing short, medium and long term action plans to deal with issues that have been there for 20 years" (*Edmonton Journal,* 8 April 2003). In other words, policy responsibility is diverted from elected representatives to the residents and their corporate antagonists. Successful negotiation becomes city policy; blame for any failure to forge consensus and a comprehensive action plan can be assigned to the participants. In such a process as this, the council, curiously enough, has in reality taken a rather large step away from the actual politics of city governing.

For some time, though, neo-Marxist critics have contended that the policy processes of Canadian city-regions are not constructed as this ideal model of the pluralist ideal requires (Lorimer 1972). Policy communities opposed to the consistently well-organized voices focused on the business of land and property ownership and management and development are marginalized, and the multiple groups which seem to be interested in municipal policies tend to be so overlapping in their memberships as to represent, essentially, roughly the same slice of bourgeois community interest. In this world view, the most non-partisan councillors are understood to be anything but autonomous and enjoy sycophantic if not symbiotic ties to the policy interests which lobby them.

So, the broad lines are drawn as to how we are to look at groups within the public policy process. Persistently, analysis of formal pressure groups most openly effective in city politics in North America has demonstrated the economic roots of their interest in commerce and industry (Lineberry and Sharkansky 1974: 67-81). The veneer of this "competition" among well-organized, economically rooted groups, combined with the specialized access available to particularly well-placed local individuals and businesses, complemented with the resolutely narrow bourgeois class bias of Canadian city councillors, paints a picture of the municipal public policy process as being of, by, and for dominant business interests. Over the years, Vancouver has been a particularly noticeable and incestuous case of direct linkages among dominant groups, individuals and corporations, and civic politicians (Gutstein 1975: 25-58, 138-50). As is to be seen in Part III, it is only in circumstances where the municipal hegemony is effectively challenged by a program of exogenous authorities like provincial ministries with the determination and power to act that local governments tend to shed their semblance of neutrality to take a position in defence of the community's status quo.

In the policy processes of larger cities, formal pressure groups seeking to speak for policy communities press both elected and appointed officials for specific policy decisions. In theoretical terms, each person possesses his or her own policy agenda even if it is only reactive. Were each of these to be expressed simultaneously, the policy resolution channels of virtually any **policy system** beyond that of a small summer village would become overloaded. Conceptually, then, the policy system embraces those social institutions that group persons with generally similar policy expectations and who express them before representatives in such a manner that some policy response is required. In structural-functional terms, these constitute the twin functions of *demand reduction* and *demand articulation*. In short, the policy system is presented by groups with a more restricted number of demands, more clearly and practically expressed, and accompanied by the support of mobilized political resources.

In the policy systems framework detailed in Chapter 2, it is clear that the manifest function of policy communities and their pressure groups is political influence. In short, their members do not themselves, as a rule, seek positions as elected officials but rather try to press their case upon those who have been elected. In practical terms, this basic difference in activities clearly and easily distinguishes them from formally organized political parties at the national and provincial levels. Especially during election periods at the national (and often provincial) level, political parties endeavour to become expansive vehicles as they strive to indicate to each sector and community in the broader public that they represent their special aspirations. To the degree that citizens buy this, the party is successful in electoral terms. This approach differentiates parties from the well-established or institutionalized pressure groups in these larger systems; the groups are rather more exclusively reserved for quite specific policy groupings insofar as they work to provide information for membership and to service member needs while shielding the budgetary, legislative, and regulatory priorities of primarily a *single* shared-interest policy community.

But, as discussed in the preceding chapter, interest group operations at city hall cannot always be distinctly and easily separated from party-like behaviours especially during times of social and economic turmoil. This analytic difficulty exists even when parties and pressure groups are clearly thought-of in the structural-functional terms of their manifest functions (i.e., primary objectives). During episodes of serious policy stress—for example, the third reform period of the late 1960s and the 1970s—many pure lobbying activities were transformed into local party-like ventures. Vancouver is an excellent case in point. Here, in 1967, to facilitate large-scale property developments, the city council and Board of Administration devised an initiative to construct a freeway and new bridge approaches which would raze Chinatown and the lower east side of the city. Citizen opposition was swift and widely constituted. Paul Tennant notes that a "non-political forum for public discussion," the Citizens Council on Civic Development (CCCD), emerged for citizens generally opposed to the existing direction of city policies (1980: 22-27). Frustrated, more election-oriented individuals transformed aspects of this social movement into party-like action with TEAM. In 1968, a more radical socialist grouping, COPE, emerged independently. So, while some citizens lobbied for council support against the expressway development, their close friends and colleagues, and often the lobbyists themselves, were mobilizing to defeat the councillors in the next city election.

Closely analogous behaviour was observed in several prairie cities during this reform period. For instance, in Edmonton, under the general aegis of the Edmonton Social Planning Council, a network of local neighbourhood and community groups coalesced in opposition to the Metropolitan Edmonton Transportation Study which proposed a freeway network through the city's lush ravines and river valley. By the late 1970s, over four score groups were active and networking through this broadly based system of generally like-minded residents (over 55 per cent of persons in leadership positions were active in three or more groups). This activity led to a lobby both to oppose the new transportation chapter of the city's General Municipal Plan and, by the same people, to more overt election planning. The lobby which grew out of the loose coalition of community groups, the Save Our Parks Committee (SOPC), was successful (as in Vancouver) in derailing the paving of great swaths through the river valley ravines of the city. The more broadly focused political party, URGE, endeavoured to elect its members in civic elections from 1974 until it effectively faded away in 1989, never winning more than one-third of the council seats (Wright and Lightbody 1989: 394-96). However, SOPC continued to lobby councillors and the planning bureaucracy even as it constituted the backbone of the vote-seeking group. As occurred in Vancouver, by the end of the 1980s, with the energies of their volunteers exhausted, the political parties (even though they long outlived the advocacy coalitions) faded away, and their members' policy activities moved into the networks and communities focused on the emerging lifestyle issues of the 1990s (e.g., environmentalism).

These two examples (and similar behaviour in Montreal and Toronto) are exceptional due to the intensity, wide-spread participation, and strength of policy conviction; they are not the rule for the established policy process. The generally unquestioned acceptance of liberal pluralism, or consensus-building, which has been characteristic of Canadian city politics, has often led many observers to miss seeing the genuine relationship between specific interests and local governments. Low levels of electoral involvement also reveal how effective the de-politicizing of municipal government has been for the general population. In his evaluation of policy-making at the Metro Toronto level for example, Kaplan, mistaking a widely shared agreement that that government was mostly about building roads and sewers, argued that the "low temperature of Metro politics reflected a large degree of social consensus" (1967: 158). He continued that, at that time: "One reason for the weak involvement of general purpose groups was their satisfaction with Metro policies ... all general purpose groups agreed with more than two-thirds of policy outcomes" (1967: 173).

The lobbies noticed at the height of the third reform period were those through which citizens boycotted the consensus and de-politicization of process. These groups, like the SOPC described above, noisily emerged as *issue-specific* efforts, then typically either dissolved or reconstituted their focus, depending upon the particular circumstance, once that issue had passed through the policy gateway or been otherwise laid to rest. The best studied, and historically most significant example of this behaviour, is the SSSOCCC, which arose in Toronto in 1969 to contest the Metro government's fixation with arterial roadways. The rapid growth and influence of the SSSOCCC as well as its fate is well described by Higgins: "Perhaps exhausted by the struggle, the SSSOCCC faded out of existence, but its task of coordinating groups opposing the expressway was taken over by the Confederation of Resident and Ratepayers Association [CORRA]" (1986: 287). CORRA was both more focused on municipal elections and more widely aware of policy than its predecessor had been.

The SSSOCCC emerged in the specific context of postwar urbanization pressures and the area-wide, upper-tier, metropolitan governing model which, for Toronto (as for Winnipeg), was designed to facilitate immediate urban expansion by overwhelming political obstacles in order to spend on capital projects such as expressways and waterworks. As one of its first tasks, Metro Toronto devised a 20-year roadways project in 1953-54. In this, the two-tier model tended to diffuse direct responsibility to local electors through the tripartite tactics of functional specialization, larger area governing, and a system of indirect election. The earliest freeway stages were approved with wide consensus, and impacted neighbourhoods were easily marginalized. The opposition groups were small and geographically dispersed, and easily dismissed by Metro council as narrowly self-interested when it came time to make a decision (Kaplan 1982: 706).

Plans for expressway penetration of the Toronto city core had been on the city and suburban council agendas since 1947. The new Metro Toronto strategy in the 1960s was to create arterials by stealth—that is, piecemeal—and by employing a conscious tactic of dividing and conquering any neighbourhood opposition. Kaplan observes that the Spadina roadway could be specifically separated out, as it was built a little at a time, always beginning with the least contentious part (1982: 707; see also Nowlan and Nowlan 1970: 61-71). This approach worked to isolate and defeat citizen opponents.

The upper echelons of the Metro Toronto public service pursued roadway capital works with continuity, determination, and single-minded purpose as they saw them as the "triumph" of progressive technical expertise. Their basic "scientifically planned" objectives were not to be trifled with for "political ends" by mere elected councillors. Segments of the construction were approved in 1955, 1960, and 1963; the last vote brought the penetration of the William R. Allen (Spadina) Expressway to the City of Toronto's boundary. As an issue-specific group, the SSSOCCC was remarkable for both strategy and tactics. For the former, it recognized that the politics of freeways depended on provincial support and so focused its energies on the Progressive Conservative provincial cabinet and its relevant quasi-independent agency, the OMB, which approves municipal planning and borrowing in the province. In tactics, in 1970 it coordinated the 220 submissions opposed to the expressway, lobbied the cabinet directly, and raised funds sufficient to hire the city's most publicly prominent barrister (a Progressive Conservative) to argue their brief. While the OMB affirmed the project in 1971, sustained political pressure and pending provincial election persuaded Premier William Davis in 1975 to cede, to the City of Toronto whose council was now opposed to the project, a three-foot wide swath of land directly across the arterial's path. This promise effectively finished the roadway, even though the deed was not formally signed over until shortly before Davis's retirement in 1985 (Higgins 1986: 285–87).

A second type of local lobby in municipal politics has been *geographically specific*. Most of these lobbies are the classic neighbourhood or ratepayer associations, which persist to protect the community's interest in the status quo. In western Canada, especially, the focus through much of the twentieth century was on "community leagues," which cooperatively provided amateur sports for youth. More widely and quite frequently across the country, territorially grouped businesses form a Downtown Business Association for booster purposes even while other neighbourhood-based businesses lobby council for a Business Revitalization Zone (BRZ) designation. The BRZ label permits the levy and collection of a particular additional, but modest, local assessment for the purpose of funding (in partnership with the city) themed neighbourhood improvements such as antique street lighting and other ornamentation.

A third type—clientele groups—is concerned with *functionally specific* areas of governing, specifically in areas such as social services, recreation, and leisure, or the provision of affordable housing. As is to be noted, it is not unusual for both of these latter kinds of groups to become a regular part of the business of decision-making at city hall as, in many cases by the early 1990s, they have progressed to the point of standing as fully fledged policy communities. Policy communities, by current definition, are considered to be all those interests, agencies, commentators, and persons who hold an interest in a particular functional area and somehow endeavour to influence the development of policy for it (note Pal 2001: 242-50).

7.1 Institutionalized Policy Communities

By definition, pressure group politics are a selective process of exclusion. All are not invited to join; many are not even invited to play. Necessarily, when a person becomes aware of his or her group attachment, this implies a subconscious and personal public policy agenda if only at the point where one wishes neither to be punished nor discriminated against. What is of real interest to the social scientist are questions about what prods a group to come forth, to become politically involved, and what might underlie the emergence of a particular cluster at any given moment. Compared to the national arena, the interests organized in the municipal system of the Canadian city, even the largest, are still more personally linked to authoritative figures in the process. City politics are local and spatially limited. In this sense then, American-style pluralism has historically been more a myth than a reality in the Canadian city.

In a long tradition, the classification of Canadian interest groups has considered their role in public policy development across categories embedded in some measure of their distance from (or proximity to) the authorities charged with the making of official policy decisions. By the mid-1980s, for a number of observers of the newly emergent neo-conservative state, which was premised on downsized interventions and the contracting out of services remaining in the federal and larger provincial governments, it seemed to be more accurate to categorize the formal expression of policy interest into communities, networks, and stakeholders. That theoretical divergence is not resolved; nonetheless, it remains accurate to characterize it as *the style of influence* at city hall today (cf. Higgins 1986: 268-69). A more recent formulation by Paul Pross, for example, employs this convention even while elaborating it considerably (1992: 92-115).

The classifications range from the institutional, or official, groups along a line to groups immediately and enthusiastically oriented to specific policy issues. Other systems focused on group activities have varied in the detail, but not on this central divergence (Presthus 1973: 67; Van Loon and Whittington 1987: 406-09). The main point is that the institutionalized group is considered to be a part of the ongoing policy system; the issue-oriented group is very much outside the system, and, in this vein, its identity is defined as a mirror image of any official group. The focus of the institutional organization is on longer term policy stability in general alignment with the expectations of their members, and its leaders will ignore small-scale reverses by council as but potholes on the road to more broadly defined territories. The policy issue group usually is possessed of very specific and narrow objectives, often in reaction to policy directions proposed by city administrators. To their leaders, compromise is anathema, and the goal is immediate policy change. They are the agitators.

Issue-oriented groups, especially obvious these days in lifestyle policy areas such as ecology or employment equity, are usually staffed by volunteers and decry their access to the policy system. Through protests, direct action, and publicity stunts for media consumption, these groups seek to challenge and confront authority while hoping, in the process, to educate the public about the virtue of their positions. The official or institutionalized policy groups, such as the local Real Estate Board or Chamber of Commerce, will normally enjoy extensive human and financial resources and exist for more general purposes than political lobbying. For such groups, policy action can be unnecessarily disruptive to the more primary functions of servicing and coordinating membership activities. Their professional staff interact with their counterparts in the civic administration even while their publicly visible leaders will regularly "do lunch" with councillors. While the issue-oriented are demonstrating, official groups expect to be consulted in advance of significant policy changes. They also expect to be represented among council's appointees to its various quasi-autonomous boards, agencies, standing committees, and consultative bodies.

Typical of the institutional group is the local chapter of the provincial motor association. It has among its priorities, and in this order, service to members, sustaining a supportive attitude among city councillors for roadways, and public education about travel safety. It also coordinates public participation in any critical debates surrounding amendments to the city's transportation master plan, especially where those might imply a considerable diversion of limited public funds from roadways into large-scale public transit. An expansive glossary of contemporary concepts associated with interest activity in policy-making has recently been summarized by Leslie Pal (2001: 233-35).

What is of both theoretical and practical interest is that local brokerage-style council activities have been so effectual that some students of city politics, especially in the 1970s, failed to recognize the lobbying activities of "general purpose" or institutional groups, such as the local Board of Trade. Albert Rose, for instance, finds group activity only in the "polemics and pamphleteering" of neighbourhood groups whose activities resulted only in "important contributions to the literature of housing and urban renewal planning" (1972: 168-70). These groups were also, and not coincidentally, the groups least likely to be in agreement with Metro Toronto's policy-making where Kaplan found an "index of agreement" from them of only 18.2 to 100 (1967: 166). Lorimer's critical survey of local process in Winnipeg in the early 1970s (1972) strongly suggested a similar high level of institutionalized interest group agreement and a dearth of "citizen's groups" as well. Axworthy described Winnipeg's local system as "executive dominant ... with a fair amount of consensus and low levels of public or interest-group participation" (Axworthy 1974: 105). Most players inside the policy loop of this period would have been inclined to dismiss neighbourhood leaders as little more than small confederations of quarrelsome blowhards, and they would not yet have had much experience with issue-specific lobbying.

7.1.1 The well-established players

Nearly 40 years ago in their American classic, Banfield and Wilson observed the five important sources for influence over policy direction at city hall: the media, business interests, labour unions, the permanent bureaucracy, and what they identified as "civic" groups (1966: 27). What they were reporting was their perception of the open face of the public, representative governing process of that time just prior to the third reform period. Left unasked were important questions about the urban regime of urban areas, the informal constellation of connections, checks, and commands.

Today there are many more private, city-region policy communities focused on functionally specific areas than there were a generation ago, especially where the policy stakes are very high. From his observations of provincial and national policy-making, Pross defines these activities: "A policy community is that part of a political system that has acquired a dominant voice in determining government decisions in a field of public activity. This is by virtue of its functional responsibility, its vested interests, and its specialized knowledge" (1992: 119). In essence, citizens and public authorities permit the policy community to create public policy in a delegated field. Pross argued further that "Society permits specialized publics to dominate decision-making in sectors of policy where they have competence, interfering only when larger concerns must take precedence, when systemic or technological change within the special public spills over into the larger political arena" (1992: 118-19). A policy community is populated by government agencies, pressure groups, media people, and specific individuals (including academics) with an interest in the issue area.

Still, for the sake of argument, the big five sources of influence over council decision-making identified by Banfield and Wilson provide a useful

Table 7.1: Spending Preference Perceptions of Canadian Municipal Elected Officials (1998)

Actors	Spending Preference	Activity	Council Response
Public Employees	67.88	44.44	36.56
Low-income Groups	65.89	37.89	29.33
Homeowners Groups	46.14	38.11	35
Neighborhood Groups	54.4	34.89	34.89
Civic Groups	53.17	25	24.33
Minority Groups	59.89	28.11	22.11
Taxpayers Association	44.8	34.22	28.44
Business	46.33	47.44	41.44
Local Media	42.47	41.11	26.67
The Elderly	46.38	36.78	38.56
Churches/Religious	50.36	26.11	27
Citizens	39.1	41.44	34.67
Mayor	47.58	65.78	53
City Council	44.06	66.33	60
CAO	50.86	61.78	53.78
City Finance Staff	50.34	61.56	53.89
Department Heads	61.08	61	51.78
Average Scores	*51.09*	*43.2*	*37.68*

Notes:

Spending preferences of participants: 0 spend a lot less ↔ 100 spend a lot more.

How active participants have been: 0 no activity ↔ 100 the most active.

Favourable council response to preferences of participants: 0 almost never ↔ 100 almost always.

Source: FAUI (2002).

shorthand for our discussion. This may be especially so if tempered by the data presented in Table 7.1, the FAUI survey of elected officials in 100 Canadian cities with a population average of 92,057.

7.1.1.1 THE MEDIA

Although discussed in greater detail towards the end of Chapter 8, we may observe here that survey respondents consistently affirm that local and city-region news interests them most in the city's press. A wide variety of other news sources are sought for national and international content. Local radio or television offer little to listeners or viewers in the way of autonomous municipal news reporting, since, for their city hall stories, radio newsreaders in this "convergence age" are dependent upon the reporting of their "sister" dailies. Above all, with the exception of the CBC, all media are themselves in business even as they report on corporate activities and company dealings (Higgins 1986: 299-307). Revenues depend on corporate advertising; the lucrative classified advertising pages are filled by realtors; and week-end newspapers especially are filled by new home-builders' full page advertisements cobbled to spam or puff "lifestyle stories" supportive of their sylvan glade suburban or retro central city condo-loft developments.

Circulation and advertising managers are prominent in local chambers of commerce and their spin-off operations. The local media are indefatigable boosters, whose daily business sections have but a trace more subtlety than their counterparts in the sports sections. There is always an enthusiastically maintained—by month-to-month and year-over-last—record of housing resale costs, number of multiple listings, apartment and commercial vacancy rates, inventory of building permits issued, number of new residential starts, and new business openings (and associated employment). Frequently, "investigative" pieces contrast the community's prowess measured against traditional competitor locales, stories which speak well of local tax rates, user fees, and utility charges. Collectively, editors, columnists, and reporters are neither a lobby nor a policy community, even though individuals may so involve themselves. Nonetheless, journalists still play a prominent role in every city's policy process.

In the perception of Canadian municipal elected officials, as revealed in the survey evidence of Table 7.1, if the media were a policy community in the budgeting process, their specific preferences would tend not to advocate much in the way of increased expenditures. They were also ranked toward the lower end of activity and were seldom listened to (fifteenth among the 17 interest sets). The city hall press gallery appears to have been more fixated with style and symbolic policy issues than with allocative or redistributive matters, more concerned with personality than with principle. Generally, these findings confirm a long-standing hypothesis that the press gallery holds little direct influence over particular policy matters even as its reportage has a cumulative impact on choices taken. The editors and columnists, especially, set a frame-of-reference for decision-takers as to the legitimacy of new policy ideas, demands, or spending plans, providing practical implementation rules for unstated assumptions. In a real sense the media place political culture assumptions into policy play.

7.1.1.2 BUSINESS

In Canadian cities, the local Board of Trade or Chamber of Commerce has been the first of two historic or traditional sources of civic lobbying, the second being ratepayer associations. Especially during the early years of the twentieth century and in the immediate postwar era of the 1950s, membership of most city councils was virtually indistinguishable from a civic policy committee of the local Chamber. Artibise, for instance, has documented the interlocking of Winnipeg's commercial, social, and political elites from 1874 until the General Strike of 1919. Along the way he observes that artisans and working men "were grossly under-represented" (1975: 25-28). Indeed, in some respects, facilitating business enterprise was viewed as the central municipal task during these periods, and the Chamber was understood to be the voice of the community.

Banfield and Wilson discussed the general phenomenon of civic boosterism south of the border and concluded that "Americans, in short, are natural-born civic boosters, and the more influential they are the more powerfully they are expected to boost" (1966: 245-50). Canadian men in business were not at all immune to these siren voices, as Artibise observed of Winnipeg (1975: 23). As an institutional group, the Chamber or Board of Trade exists primarily to provide services to members. Their lobbying activities can still be very impressive. Higgins observed: "Their briefs to municipal council tend to get a receptive audience, they tend to have easy access to the offices of senior local administrators, and they can sometimes be seen mixing business with pleasure by entertaining local officials at lunch in the board of trade's dining room or elsewhere" (1986: 291). Larger businesses outside the policy world of land development tend not to care deeply about what a local council is up to except when it has an impact on the needed infrastructure of roads, water, sewerage, and the protective services. Apart from general support for economic development strategies, their directors and officers have long held, when surveyed, an aversion to overt involvement in city policies. They prefer to operate in the shadows made possible through the collective arrangement of the institutionalized policy player, the Board of Trade or Chamber of Commerce.

The most persistent direct policy pressure emanates from those who have a direct pecuniary stake in outcomes. They are often represented by three organizations. The Urban Development Institute (UDI) usually involves the big players with large tracts under development but also includes local members in related professions (e.g., architects). The Canadian Home Builders Association (CHBA) represents smaller contractors (plumbers, framers, electricians, dry-wallers, and the like) with over six dozen local chapters across

Canada. The third is the Real Estate Board. While there may be small differences in policy timetabling, it is usually these three who work in concert to bring new lands onto the market quickly and, for them, cheaply.

In the typical instance, the objectives of the UDI include sustaining a long-term working relationship with the professional managers of land-use planning and at least a majority, if not all, council members. In Calgary, for instance, shortly following the 1995 municipal elections, the UDI presented its wish-list publicly. It included a request for the city to relax density and dedicated land-use regulations for new developments and to assume the initial costs for the development of basic infrastructure (roadways, lights, piped services) in proposed new neighbourhoods as well as the typical demand "to cut red tape" (*Calgary Herald*, 18 November 1995). In Edmonton, in the same year, the UDI hosted a "get acquainted breakfast" for city councillors within a month of the election, which three-quarters of the council attended. A social democratic member of council observed that the UDI had funded a campaign during the election "which urged the public to vote for pro-development councillors." The councillor observed in response to demands similar to those in Calgary: "They succeeded in electing a pro-growth council and I'm presuming they now want to cash in their chips" (*Edmonton Journal*, 2 February 1996). One of the UDI's better friends on council pointed out to the media that "the UDI folks are vexed at the mounds of paperwork that must be waded through before a subdivision development gets the green light" (*Edmonton Journal*, 30 November 1995). The best surprise is no surprise.

Writing of similar circumstances, Lorimer was sanguine, even if touched by a dash of Marxist paranoia, in his discussion of "The Political Program of the Property Industry" (1972: 65-80), which he said had four aims. The first is to at least protect the current value of property. The second endeavours to maximize the increase of property value over time through, perhaps, restricting the supply of land for specific categories of buildings. The third requires balance with political allies in the construction industry by keeping new construction on the go but not so much as to impinge upon property values. Lastly, integrating the package is a general belief in maintenance of the political and economic status quo by keeping the business of property development exclusively in private hands. In practical terms, this provides protection against any mischievous politician campaign for, say, publicly owned land banks.

The evidence in Table 7.1 reveals that, when asked, Canadian municipal elected officials concede that business interests remained, in the 1990s, the most active, and heeded, of the local players in the municipal budgeting process outside of those in official policy roles. By this evidence, councillors value the business agenda more than that of any other non-official actor.

Only "the elderly" as a group also received a favourable budget response from council at a rate above the average of all potential interests. Even late twentieth-century councils, comprised of more diverse elements, remained susceptible to not-so-subtle business direction.

7.1.1.3 THE PROFESSIONAL CITY ADMINISTRATION

The professional city administration and the more or less permanent quasi-bureaucratic policy networks, like a Social Planning Council or non-profit housing cooperative, play a prominent role in the definition of the single preferred policy option for presentation to senior managers and council. The single preferred policy option is developed within the middle ranks of the bureaucracy, who can couple resources available with first-hand knowledge about the position of clientele groups. It is at this pressure point that lobbyists experienced with the real process of decision-making—those who have practical experience gleaned in either prior employment with the city and its agencies or within a well-institutionalized pressure group—focus their energies. This is also the point at which fundamentally satisficing choices are taken (see the theoretical discussion of this in Chapter 2). As reported in Table 7.1, it is the perception of elected officials that their own department heads seek higher municipal expenditures than public employees and lower income group advocates. Of course, these department heads do not necessarily share the same holistic vision of the budget.

Senior departmental managers play a more enduring role in structuring policy choice than influence over budget choices. The now classic dissection of bureaucratic sabotage of reform programs by administrators tied to past practices carried forward (Lipset 1950: 255-75) has led to a policy science tradition that posits the modern state's relative autonomy from public pressure (note Nordlinger 1981). In the extreme, these ideas develop from the observation that states shape and regulate economies and societies; their governing machinery is supreme. Thus, the state is virtually human and possesses the capacity to realize its own public policy agenda. Howlett and Ramesh summarize this theoretical viewpoint in these terms: "Its autonomy and capacity are based on its staffing by officials with personal and agency interests and ambitions and the fact that it is a sovereign organization with unparalleled financial, personnel, and—in the final instance—coercive resources" (2003: 45). However abstracted from reality, the extreme statist model helps to put into perspective the actual cultural, political, and marketplace limits on even the most benign bureaucracy to surrender its own accountability to the public views that have been given priority through electoral choice. To return to where we began the chapter, the statist theoretical digression reminds us that the non-elected side of the state operation is far more than a neutral arbiter in a pluralist fight for public policy results.

Canadian history provides some proof of the way large-scale bureaucracies operate. Lipset observed that when the "radical" social democrats of the CCF came to power in Saskatchewan in 1944, there was no "housecleaning" of the key civil servants in the province. The reasons varied, but among them were (1) the new ministers were administrative amateurs, (2) their platform had been expressed in generalities and not specific actions, and (3) the top administrators "did their utmost" to persuade the politicians that they would be cooperative (1950: 262-65). The consequences were both predictable and inevitable. Because their job security was interpreted by top deputies as a sign of weakness in the political operation, they felt that traditional policies would also not be threatened. Arguing from the basis of their experience, administrators persuaded the newcomers that change was "not administratively feasible" or would "incur too much opposition." Among themselves, managers exchanged best techniques for controlling ministers. New ideas were trashed because "they had never been tried before or would require revamping the work of a department" (Lipset 1950: 264). Newly elected and innovatively inclined city councillors confront similar difficulties; however, where elections are non-partisan, they cannot call on the support of cabinet colleagues, caucus, or even party policy conventions to help bend the bureaucrats to the political will. In short, the oligarchic conservatism characteristic of any bureaucratic hierarchy, intrinsically inclined to preserve position and policy authority, is a tough mountain for mere city councillors to budge.

Public officials in Canadian cities are neither policy eunuchs nor mindless robots. They are individuals with personal preferences who operate with enormous resources in the policy caverns of centralized and normally *stasis*-grounded state agencies. Observers of the politics surrounding the city's annual budget process can count on witnessing protective behaviours when, driven by perennial conditions of fiscal austerity, department managers, in concert with more narrowly based clientele and their policy communities, offer for political sacrifice universally consumed, "high profile," and well-appreciated programs in order to protect core levels of funding and concomitant prestige. Less critical departments (parks, community services) may offer to purge flower bed plantings, limit amateur hockey ice time availability, and so on. Police, fire, and emergency response departments are more adept; media stories appear magically, but reliably, to coincide with the budget cycle to reveal either an upsurge in street gang battles or a reduction in fire response-time capabilities.

From the evidence in Table 7.1, Canadian municipal elected officials, when asked, believe that they themselves, advised by their senior officials, are the most active *and* influential in determining their cities' spending priorities. Were it statistically reasonable to calculate a rank order correlation between columns two and three, it would confirm the obvious that the administrators are the ones who have the influence and would also hold significance at the 1 per cent level. In other words, mayors and councillors by their own responses say that in making the hard budget choices they actually rely most closely (and by far) upon their chief administrative and financial officers and department heads.

7.1.1.4 LABOUR UNIONS

Except for the recession years after the First World War and during the Great Depression of the 1930s, organized labour has seldom been overtly much involved in any city's ongoing policy processes. As noted in Chapter 6, the local Labour Council usually endorses a slate of candidates considered friends of the union movement, but this is hardly the stuff of institutionalized involvement in the policy process. Indeed, several of today's textbooks make but passing reference to any labour role in Canadian city politics: Tindal and Tindal (2000) make no mention of labour at all, and Graham and Phillips note labour's limited interest in employment equity issues and concern about the use of non-union labour when traditional city services are contracted to private entrepreneurs (1998: 166-67, 210).

Those unions most attentive to general municipal policy remain the ones with employees under public service contracts. There are two main exceptions to this general rule of inattention, and both have reasonably limited objectives. First, the unions in the building trades tend heavily to subscribe to the same economic boosterism propounded by realtors, developers, and electrical or plumbing contractors. Growth means construction which in turn means employment; union and commercial leaders easily collaborate in support of ambitious growth plans (Higgins 1986: 291-92). As an aside, this policy outlook provides an explanation for the increased conservatism of many NDP-affiliated city mayors over their terms in office, as they match city hall policy choices to the immediate economic security of their supporters.

Secondly, the city's own employees are as concerned with protecting departmental base budgets as they are opposed to contracting out to competitive private-sector service providers. By the early 1980s, for instance, the *Toronto Star* reported councillors' perceptions that one of the best lobbies was the firemen's union which invited council members to firemen's dances, dinners, and golf tournaments. One council wage and benefits negotiator observed, "They in general make us feel that the firemen want to work with politicians" (*Edmonton Journal*, 11 November 1980). These days, city unions tend also to be very suspicious of performance review measures drawn from business experience.

They have good reason to be concerned. In American cities since the late 1970s, management strategies deployed in response to fiscal stress included such broad tactics as "across-the-board cuts" (used by 56 per cent) and reduced overtime (53 per cent). From the American evidence, contracting out was the major response by the 1,333 cities surveyed by the International City Management Association in 1982 (Clark 1994b: 214–16). The larger movement of public-sector operations toward use of market-type mecha- nisms was advanced and legitimated in the UK and in American national politics in the 1980s. Current data from the FAUI project based at the University of Chicago (2002), however, reveal that the relative importance among municipalities in Canada of contracting out is used 20 per cent more frequently here than in either of the originating political systems and is today at a level closer to their use in Finland and Israel. Union response is typi- cally reactionary but occasionally successful. In March 2002, for example, Edmonton city council scrapped its "Closing the Gap" performance review of its 43 core programs in the face of concerted opposition from civic unions, substituting "customer-service" surveys and a lobbying effort for provincial funding. It will be noted in Chapter 13 that, during periods of city-region reorganization, public sector unions in Canadian city-regions have demon- strated two absolute goals: their leaders wish first that no jobs be lost and seniority be respected and second that wage scales will rise, following con- solidation, to the highest level among the pre-existing municipalities.

The evidence presented in Table 7.1 reveals that, when asked, Cana- dian municipal elected officials admit that their own employees exhibit the highest spending preferences of the 17 sources of pressure, are the busiest in lobbying for these apart from city managers and the council itself, and are rewarded with a less than average positive response from councillors when the moment of decision comes.

It should be emphasized that, as do other citizens, union members have many personae: as homeowners and parents, sports fanatics and environ- mentalists, and so forth. They thus share in the values of the new political culture discussed elsewhere in this chapter when assessing civic leadership. Still, the occasional interventions noted above and the positions always taken should neither be unexpected nor downplayed when workers are involved with union activities.

7.1.1.5 CIVIC GROUPS

The traditional face of organized civic participation during the twentieth century took the form of the various associations representing citizens in the many neighbourhoods of any city; these will be considered in more detail in section 7.2 below. Although Banfield and Wilson were describing American "good government" groups in their original listing, I would include the traditional ratepayers' (i.e., those paying a property tax on the basis of a council-set mill rate) as well as the more contemporary neighbourhood organizations from the third reform era. The ratepayers' associations have always been the more bourgeois, reflecting their long historical connection with a nineteenth-century concept of local governments being funded by property owners for purely local purposes. They were also a training ground (and self-promotional base) for prospective candidates for city council. Most of these organizations had exhausted their legitimacy and lapsed into mere organizational shells by the late 1960s (note the discussion of the SSSOCCC below).

The old-style ratepayers' associations were gradually usurped by neighbourhood residents' groups after the Second World War (Higgins 1986: 277–82). In Canada's increasingly larger and more socially diverse cities, these groups were defined by place, by the geography of their homes and neighbourhoods. In turn, these boundaries were themselves delineated by residents to reflect the natural self-sorting of citizens into roughly homogenous pockets. In general, then, residents' groups have all had twin goals in the protection, mostly as is, of their streets and in securing modest local improvements like better street lights, sidewalks, and parking arrangements (Kaplan 1982: 164). Residents' groups usually penetrated the city hall policy radar only in hostile reaction to proposed planning changes in their neighbourhoods, such as the building of a convenience store, service station, or halfway house. Councillors, especially in a small ward system of election, were seldom hesitant to accede to demands to "protect property values" by preventing these small-scale spot changes.

During their short period of prominence, more representative residents' groups were mobilized in areas of higher incomes or among the traditionally established minority communities. By the 1990s, however, residents' groups had themselves been replaced in public relevance by issue networks based on lifestyle issues. A new political culture rooted in expanding wealth and knowledge emerged, with group policy expectations grounded in global authority as revealed by such as the "World Values Surveys" (Clark and Hoffmann-Martinot 1998: 10–19, 59–61). While looking for policy innovations in areas like environmentalism, ecology, or personal identities, citizens became less likely to be overly concerned with neighbourhood bike lanes or the placement of parking meters. Even still, city hall planners and their managers continued to exploit the increasingly less representative old leadership as easy sounding boards to validate their community planning exercises.

For purposes of the taxonomy of groups presented above, smaller area geographic groups are seldom if ever institutionalized except perhaps in the kind of public-private partnership that emerges when a community league may build, operate, and maintain a clubhouse and adjacent sports fields or rinks. Generally, though, these groups tend to be more issue-oriented in the style of their operation. Both ratepayers' and residents' groups in Canadian city-regions have become most aggressively involved when neighbourhood interests are threatened. It might be observed that *anyone can be radicalized* should they awaken to find survey stakes in their front yards. In consequence, these associations tend to be seen by officials as noisy, negative, and reactionary, because, in the usual circumstance, they are. Unsurprisingly, given the nature of their involvement, group leaders have tended to be least satisfied with council decisions when surveyed in the context of other process participants.

However, it is also to be remembered from Chapter 6 that non-partisan councils are more easily susceptible than partisan to threats and electoral blackmail on geographically centred issues. To combine non-partisanship with small ward elections is, therefore, extremely conducive to putting priorities on short-term issues as they are defined by neighbourhood leaders. Community organizations, even the officially recognized types such as Winnipeg's RAGs or Montreal's District Advisory Committees, tend not to have had much in the way of long-lasting interest in the development and application of planning policy or even site guidelines.

The many faces of the 1960s reform were well researched by Higgins (1986: 245-54). His "contemporary reform era" was an urban phenomenon in Canada for about 20 years beginning in the mid-1960s. The movement was expressed in a mixed bag of small organizations which had both liberal and socialist ideological roots. Their common target was the existing hierarchy at city hall, which represented what they perceived as a booster business establishment and which they attacked on grounds of structures (the electoral system) and process (i.e., demands to "open up" the policy system to wider, non-official scrutiny). Thus, reformers of this era were decentralists. As Magnusson correctly notes, their model was akin to that of a nineteenth-century community organization: "they were suspicious of public bureaucracies and favoured a dispersal of authority and responsibility among community organizations, co-operatives, and other voluntary agencies" (1983a: 34). They were, of course, strongly resisted by the centralized authority "reformers" whose roots were in the 1900 turn-of-the-century American reform package.

Toronto's Bureau of Municipal Research (1975, 1970) noted a set of group behaviours which correlate with the objective social stratification of members. In short, the lower the status (and incomes) among the members of a group, the more likely it is that the group perspective will be parochial, short-term, and very specific; that is, it will be along the lines of "no half-way house on our street, now or ever!" On the other hand, groups based in higher status neighbourhoods tend to be more confident that city officials will "do the right thing," are prepared to accept a longer time-line for the resolution of conflict, and are possessed of an ability to appreciate city-wide issues. Their leaders are prepared to work with planners and politicians to plot new truck routes or to locate an alternative to a proposed land-fill site. Of course, the new truck route may well go through the same lower income sector which has just received a new garbage-processing facility.

Considering the individuals and groups that have the political resources to be able to challenge city hall well, those who are least dissatisfied tend to be politically the most competent to challenge its premises, structures, and processes. This correlates back to the previous discussion of voting behaviour in Chapters 3 and 5.

According to the data in Table 7.1, Canadian municipal elected officials think that neighbourhood and civic groups expect more spending than the average, but are well below the mean in activity levels and among the least rewarded at budget time. Only organizations representing minorities are seen to have wanted more, to be less active, and were ultimately rewarded less.

7.1.1.6 SUMMARY OF CONCLUSIONS FROM TABLE 7.1

1. Those who are seen to most want council to increase its program spending are public employees, in cahoots with their direct departmental managers. They are considered to be joined in this by organized, but non-institutional, groups representing ordinary residents (low income, neighbourhood, minority, and civic groups). Councillors see themselves as being the least inclined to spend of anyone in the budget loop.

2. In the view of elected officials, the business community and the city's own employees are the only ones who are active in policy busy work at levels above the mean score and outside the officially positioned sources of direct policy influence (the top five rankings). All other non-official groups fall well below the average participation score, although individual citizens are also seen to pay modest attention.

3. Finally, administrative continuity over budget direction appears to be more important and more powerful than any policy pressures from "outside the box." Even business preferences, the next highest ranked on the response

hierarchy after internal budgeting sources, are deeply discounted. Any effective influence from the new policy networks is probably subsumed under the "department head" title in this table.

7.1.2 Reverse pressure and clientelism

The first of two generally symbiotic patterns, or underlying subprocesses, in the city's public policy process ought to be noted here (the second lies in the relationship of the city hall press gallery to persons in authority). Van Loon and Whittington (1986: 409-10) carefully employed the term **reverse pressure group** to describe the important and not infrequent occasions in the federal political system when persons in political authority wish to initiate an important change in policy direction but need a little lobbying to get the ball rolling. In these instances, bureaucrats and, less frequently, elected officials seek both to build more broadly based support for their own policies or programs and to offset and dilute the activities of lobbyists opposed to their preferred course of action.

Whatever the motivation, the policy-maker either feeds resources (financing, technical expertise, insider information about proposals and their timing) to supportive groups or initiates the formation of an appropriate network, so that either of these may play a more effective role in the policy process. These actions may not be entirely altruistic, of course, but self-justifying in the sense that program managers can demonstrate they have deserving clients to serve, which appeal in turn protects their core budgeting and employment. Even by the 1970s, it was estimated that more federal departments had fashioned such supports than had not. Van Loon and Whittington add this notation: "In addition to this function of creating or mobilizing a clientele, they may also be used for communication with an otherwise poorly organized portion of the public, or even to administer some aspects of an agency's program" (1986: 409).

By the 1990s, reverse pressure groups were a prominent fixture in the institutionalized policy processes of Canada's larger cities, normally for the functional areas of parks, recreation, culture, social services, and occasionally public transit. Often the phenomenon was situated in umbrella agencies such as the Social Planning Council or, in western Canada, the local Federation of Community Leagues. Sometimes, different reverse pressure groups worked at cross purposes, revealing that the municipal bureaucracy is not a monolithic juggernaut, but is comprised of subunits with often competitive agendas. This pattern was evident in third reform period neighbourhood struggles against intensified urban redevelopment and freeways. During these policy confrontations, it was often mid-level administrators in the parks and social services departments who acted as "bureaucratic guerillas" by leaking the designs of roadway engineers (and transportation departments) or large developers to potentially affected communities. This provided the latter the time needed to counter the proponents' justifications and to provide informed alternatives to sympathetic councillors.

The idea is closely akin to the general custom of clientelism, a term usually associated with the politics and government of more traditional cultures elsewhere on the globe. Larger cities in North America have witnessed political practices in this tradition nonetheless. By definition, clientelism involves an exchange between mainly elected officials and particular groups in the general population. People in positions of authority (patrons) offer to these groups "mediated and selective access" to public goods and opportunities to which the rest of the people are denied an entrée. The patrons "place themselves or their supporters in positions from which they can divert resources and services in their favour" (Roniger 2004: 2). Clients, as electors, return the favour by working to support their benefactors' electoral prospects. The American boss system of the late nineteenth century was an extreme example of this type of exchange, but Roniger makes a strong case that similar behaviour persists. Why not? The prototype is the relationship of *patrocinium* (the patrician political class) and *clientelae* (their claques) in the classic era of Republican Rome, and patronage is an established practice through all levels of the Canadian federal system. In the latter years of the nineteenth century in Toronto, for instance, "The political, social, and economic life of the community was structured by a complicated pattern of clientelist relations ... structured by ethnic, religious, and fraternal loyalties" (Magnusson 1983b: 97). In Montreal at that time, business leaders pressed for centralized city government not only because it was thought more efficient but also because it would shrink the population of "gratuity seekers" (Kaplan 1982: 149).

A blatant excess of patronage like that decried by the good government reformers opposed to boss rule suggests that certain legitimate boundaries, legally or engrained by culture, have been crossed. Also implied is that principles such as merit and competence, competition for positions and promotion, and transparency in contract tendering have been violated. In its most highly developed form, clientelism provides a corruption of the public service by passing around jobs and handing out contracts and services to those favoured by persons in charge. In current vernacular, it erodes both "entitlements" to public policies and public trust in state institutions. These violations exceed any justifiable need for people in political positions to surround themselves with executive personnel and program managers committed to a similar policy agenda. The difficult balance is that between the need to innovate as signalled by the election of new political leaders and the requirement to protect best current practices and institutional memory within an otherwise highly professional public bureaucracy.

The point here is that clientelism is *not* limited to autocratic, tribal, or emergent democratic communities, nor is it a peculiar cultural pathology. The basic conventions have become bureaucratized in western Europe as well as in North America as particular categories of citizens seek specialized access with restricted public accountability. Larger cities tend to be more susceptible to clientelism because their populations are more diverse, their bureaucracies bigger, and their councils larger and more heterogeneous. Where lobbying efforts are abetted by public officials in order to mobilize the less powerful, this reverse pressure activity may, correctly, be labelled clientelism.

While Roniger argues that clientelist practices are criticized and resented by the usual reformer claque, he concedes that researchers have also found "that sectors benefiting from clientelist brokerage and patronage see it as a pragmatic avenue, useful for advancing in competitive social, economic, and political domains" (2004: 14). If there is any irony here, it is that the world-wide neo-liberal practices of the last generation which have acted to limit state interventions, privatize service sectors and agencies, and limit service provision through unionized operators have, paradoxically, prodded a growth in demands for support and recognition. No city service sector is immune from clientelist pressures.

It is neither irrational nor inappropriate for recipient population groups to award benefactors with votes (and lobbying for base budget on behalf of supportive bureaucrats), especially in a period of stress occasioned by provincial financial cutbacks, privatizing, downloading, and general fiscal austerity. Roniger thoughtfully notes, "The politics of identity and the decline of ideological mobilization can provide a favorable ground for clientelistic articulation" (2004: 13).

Scrupulous analysis of survey data may sustain a case that traditional party and election-focused clientelism as well as "ethnic politics" declined at the end of the twentieth century; this is also the period when a new political culture rooted in individualism and consumption seemed to emerge (Clark and Hoffmann-Martinot 1998: 33, 61-65). The basic problem with this analysis is that it is hard to overlook the obvious perpetuation of overt clientelism in Canada's non-partisan councils and among frontline program administrators. The continuing policy issue arising out of clientelist practices is a lack of transparent accountability for public resources because they are diverted into the policy silos of groups well away from public oversight.

7.1.3 The political regimes hypothesis

The concept of a political regime in Canadian city-regions is considered more fully in the case study at the heart of Chapter 13. Basically grounded in the old power elite school of the community power debates noted in Chapter 1, the concept itself merits short mention here because of its interest in community groups and policy action. In his seminal work on the subject, Clarence Stone (1987, with Heywood Sanders; 1989) argues that informal arrangements, worked out behind the scenes, accomplish better quality policy goals and mediate intergroup friction.

In practical terms, Stone describes how lead actors in the public community in specific instances and acting collectively are able to transcend the divisions of any city-region's numerous specialized policy communities. He does not use the term "governance" but does describe how public office-holders and private interests can work together to make and implement government decisions. He points out that, especially during moments of social and economic pressure, the part of society best positioned to intervene is its less publicly obvious urban regime. The urban regime is *not* itself a pressure group, even though individual leaders of institutional groups will hold prominent positions in the regime; their influence will vary as a particular set of issues warrants.

These arrangements have been particularly useful in the United States where the city-region is carved into multiple municipal governments: Even critics of numerous governments like H.V. Savitch and Ronald Vogel (1996) concede that beneficial public policy may accrue as a consequence of regime efforts if one is prepared to look beyond the formal boundaries and into overall politics. One case study in their volume indicates, for instance, that Pittsburgh is "one of the most fragmented regions in the country" with over 300 governments for only 1.4 million residents; 12 cities are home to less than 1,000 residents. To be comparably governed, Toronto in 2004 would need some 535 units of local administration. And yet, seeing an urban regime behind the scenes, the authors conclude this: "Under the fragmented form, however, lies a unifying net of business elites that ties the region together through public-private partnerships [that] worked for more than half a century to restructure the economy, attract investment, and rebuild the city" (1996: 292).

New opportunities for policy influence by political regimes in city-regions arises out of the decline in electoral clout of traditional, hierarchically structured organizations, a decline that led politicians to seek out wider constituencies. World-wide pressures to level hierarchy in one set of institutions or in one place contribute to pressures, accelerated through the technology of the Internet, to replicate that flattening in other communities and in other aspects of social life. Fluctuating membership loyalties among traditional policy subsystems leads to constant questioning, even about the legitimacy of their own spokespersons. In the growing absence of hierarchical certainty where leaders speak for followers, politicians tend to respond to the immediacy of personal demands in continuous flux. In larger cities, influence over public policy-making is increasingly reduced to the level of individuals and to networks of individual citizens.

For city-regions with fragmented local governments, the increased salience of lifestyle policy issues relevant to the individual, many of which are not costly in economical terms (such as abortion, gay rights, employment equity, and environmental protection), are provided multiple pulpits. The existence of smaller municipalities, be they in Pittsburgh, Atlanta, or Vancouver, imbues "not-in-my-back-yard" (**NIMBY**) behaviour with authority and makes the realization of area-wide issues less likely. The provision of some level of voluntary collective activity requires the political resource of sometimes quite blatant *ad hominem* appeals to authority. Globalization of public policy communities has led both to high levels of emulation from country to country and to complex leadership patterns in policy networks because they are less stable, less coherent, and not established in traditional clientele patterns.

The new political culture described here is stronger in larger cities, partly because they have more powerful print and electronic media which command officials' responsiveness to citizens. In a very important way, these media empower citizens by providing both more information in general and more information about new ways of thinking about public policy issues and solutions (Clark and Hoffman-Martinot 1998: 109, 159–60). In public policy struggles today, even well-informed and attuned managers in public institutions are seldom able to surpass the expertise of outside specialists on their own policy issues. And, even though they have the benefit of popular sanction, councillors will normally find themselves operating at a disadvantage in education and professional training in dealings not only with their administrators but also the new policy movements.

In this general context, urban regimes are important for city-region policy systems for the resources—of expertise, prestige, and capacity for trans-global legitimation of innovative ideas—they command. Their effective behind-the-scenes bargaining for a mixed bag of satisficing opportunities with widely distributed collateral benefits, and occasionally for big-ticket items, means that a vacuum in political leadership for larger goals may partly be compensated for as non-governing coalitions glean sufficient cooperation to make "the system" appear to work.

7.1.4 Associations of municipalities

If only because they exist, associations of municipalities in Canada deserve brief comment. Some years back, a small tangential debate questioned their generic legitimacy as lobbyists in a pluralist democracy in which governments at all levels are to be viewed as "mediators" not pleaders (Feldman and Graham 1979: 26-27). While not much of significance has changed over the past 25 years regarding the relative influence of municipal associations over provincial policies, public permission to be on the intergovernmental playing field is not in question today.

The structure of the Canadian state, with local governments the exclusive responsibility of the provinces, has consistently fragmented the municipal lobbying of other government levels. Approaching the federal government has always proven difficult, normally requiring both provincial permission for any local application of federal initiatives and federal use of its spending power to intervene. In approaching their respective provinces, local governments have been handicapped by their very multiplicity, their variety, and, for much of their history, the very smallness of so many localities. Unlike baseball caps, when it comes to lobbying for provincial policy initiatives, one size has never fit all, and bickering in the ranks nourishes the historic disdain of provincial ministries.

The history of a national association for municipalities dates back to the Great Depression when, during 1935-36, the mayors of Canada's larger cities began to cooperate to petition the federal government for financial assistance in providing for unemployed men (Feldman and Graham 1979: 30). The FCM (Federation of Canadian Municipalities) has over the past few decades had a membership hovering at slightly over 300 individual cities and towns; it is not an association of the municipal organizations in the provinces. Except for the holiday junkets it provides, the attention paid the FCM by members' councillors tends to be tangential. The attention devoted to the organization by citizens is nonexistent.

These days, the FCM's thin veneer of legitimacy is useful as a general purpose instrument for the generic funding concerns (combating crime and the struggle to rebuild roads and sewers) of Canada's bigger cities and as an urban affairs podium for federal politicians who, for reason of the Constitution, believe that they must tread cautiously across the paths of provincial ministers. Provincial truculence has forestalled any return to a tri-level concept of the Canadian state (note Higgins 1986: 112-16). Even a return to a formal tri-level *process* among governments ended after the 1976 Quebec Conference was effectively cancelled by a provincial refusal to participate when an acidic policy statement by the municipalities critiqued their reliance on conditional grants. The statement also demanded a more stable revenue base grounded in access to "growth" taxes (i.e., provincial monies).

In short, by reason of the Constitution, municipalities' federal orientation is weak; equally, by reason of the relative size of the federal taxation base, bigger cities exhibit the greatest interest.

Apart from the FCM, there are 18 associations of municipalities in Canada, usually with two general types of association in each of the provinces to represent the divergent policy interests and financial concerns of different classes of municipalities. One is broadly representative of urban centres, and the other exists for rural municipalities. In British Columbia, Nova Scotia, Newfoundland and Labrador, and Quebec, single organizations had been formed by 2000 (Higgins 1986: 78-79; Graham, Phillips and Maslove 1998: 194). Typically Alberta, in 2002, had both the Alberta Urban Municipalities' Association (AUMA) and the Alberta Association of Municipal Districts and Counties (AAMDC). In the larger provinces, regional associations have also existed from time to time, such that in 1975 Ontario had seven associations of municipalities. In the more unified federations like the Union of British Columbia Municipalities (UBCM), with 179 members in 1997, policy rifts in provincial relations are frequent, because only 33 of the province's municipalities are larger than 25,000 population while half have fewer than 5,000 residents.

Because all councillors as delegates vote at conventions, those representing the smaller municipalities consistently dictate policy and control executive positions. In 1996, the NDP government in British Columbia won public plaudits from the UBCM when it reduced its grants to the larger urban communities while retaining levels for the more numerous smaller ones. Senior Vancouver councillor George Puil (a representative of the very conservative NPA) observed for media benefit that "it's the classic political tactic of divide and conquer. Get municipalities squabbling among themselves so they can't unite and turn their guns on Victoria" (*Vancouver Sun*, 18 October 1997). In Ontario, Tindal and Tindal have noted that "Partly because of its make-up and internal sections, small municipalities tend to dominate the attendance at AMO [Association of Municipalities of Ontario] general meetings and participation on its executive committee" (2000: 244-45). Quite frankly, many big city councillors believe they have better things to do with their time; representatives from the hinterlands relish the socializing and mutual respect of their peers and the once-a-year media limelight for those in executive posts. But the persistent imbalance in "rep-by-pop" within the organizations considerably weakens the overall capacity of municipal associations to advocate on behalf of all.

From this general introduction, three observations arise and ought to be considered more fully.

7.1.4.1 THE PURPOSE AND RESULT OF GENERAL MEETINGS OF MUNICIPAL ASSOCIATIONS

The annual policy and venting sessions of municipal associations tend mostly to be meet-and-greet hoe-downs, with omnibus policy packages that are based on least disagreement accords.

The municipal association's typical policy focus on developing lowest common denominators to build consensus consumes more political resources than the position obtained may merit. If unity is not achieved, then, far too often, associations tend to stand mute. Rather like trade organizations such as the Canadian Federation of Agriculture, which represents everything from pig producers to canola growers in the various federal (and provincial) policy worlds, municipal associations must accommodate every diverse interest incorporated under provincial Local Government Acts. Spatial and sectoral divergences—urban and rural, big and small, cities with large bureaucracies and villages with part-time help—are institutionalized. Where policy differences are structural in nature, as with establishing a basis for transportation grants, more rural suburbs consistently differ from core cities on the dollars per kilometre versus dollar per capita issue, and associations cannot speak. Similar generic differences may emerge concerning provincial initiatives seeking municipal support for social services.

Provincial ministers appear at annual conventions to self-congratulate and to float trial balloons. The usual keynote speech contains a paean to cultural referents; in this case, "local government as the cornerstone of democracy" evokes enthused nods of approval. The more ardent the statement, the more wary member municipalities ought to be about their existing powers, resources, and responsibilities! Provincial officials may consult and often circulate policy thoughts in draft, but they operate under no requirement to take any advice proffered. As an organized group, associations of municipalities are useful, from the provincial government's perspective, as tools to disseminate provincial expectations and decisions. Paul Pross, in discussing the Union of Nova Scotia Municipalities (UNSM), notes the inner dynamic that underlies the motivation of the association's leadership to act as a ministry's voice: it builds legitimacy. "Even though it was hampered by the reluctant support of some members, the UNSM found that an equivalent factor in securing legitimacy was the provincial government's decision to use the organization as a mechanism for the downward transmission of government views to members" (1992: 202). In other words, while originally created to push members' views onto the province, UNSM's central office sustained itself by doing the reverse. It should be added that the acceptance of provincial funding support for organizational business, even partnership planning activities, can be a dangerous practice if autonomous lobbying is ultimately the goal. Similarly, ministers *may* canvass association members about potential appointments to regulatory agencies, but, as always, any order-in-council appointment has more to do with partisan calculations than with specialized regulatory knowledge.

Moreover, these organizations are *not* a means through which ordinary citizens may directly influence public policy-making, partly because the associations are usually unknown as actors and operate well within the attentive public's twilight zone and partly because they are accurately seen to hold little legitimacy when it comes to influencing provincial policies. They are discounted as a contrivance for conventioneers, with their only time in the public eye coming when some local columnist notices the travellers' budgets. At these meetings some distance from their home locales, councillors are unusually immune to the direct public opinion of their electors. Thus, they may feel less inhibited in lobbying provincial officials on measures that could prove locally unpopular such as, in Alberta or British Columbia, pleading for a dramatic increase in the percentage of the electorate required to petition in order to force a referendum. The evasion of accountability occurs when, back home, the collective voice of "the Association" is blamed for the resolution.

Like other "institutional" pressure groups, municipal associations do try to provide a number of practical services to their members, in this case usually in the nature of communications about the impacts of new policies. But beyond a small secretariat, normally not much more than a handful, none of these associations retains much in the way of permanent staff and are always reliant on either volunteers from among already time-stressed elected councillors or officials seconded from larger member municipalities for specific purposes. In all instances concerning public statements affecting local governments, one constant rule is that, like deputy ministers in Ottawa or provincial capitals, permanent officials have been and must be extremely reluctant to comment out of deference to their elected "masters."

Consequently, it is fair to observe that associations are reactionary and predictable; they are not innovative or proactive. In 1996, Quebec's Association of Rural and Regional Municipalities strenuously fought a provincial plan to induce municipal consolidation financially; nonetheless, 103 municipal governments became 49. On rare crisis occasions (almost always fiscal), regional groupings may paper together a common front to lobby their respective provinces. In August 2003, for instance, the Prairie Association of Rural Municipalities met in Regina to seek relief in the aftermath of drought and the "mad cow ordeal," which had reduced their residents' abilities to pay property and education taxes. In Atlantic Canada, Graham, Phillips, and Maslove (1998) have noted that the Atlantic Provinces Information Centre serves municipalities in collective bargaining relations. The GVRD similarly supports its member municipalities in labour relations even though, technically, it is not a municipal association.

7.1.4.2 THE POWER STRUCTURE WITHIN MUNICIPAL ASSOCIATIONS

The serious players have increasingly tended to circumvent the conventional process as big cities (each dominant in individual provinces) and wealthier suburban local governments take the lead. Speaking spatially, provincial capitals are located in central cities and face-to-face get-togethers among staff or between elected politicians can be quickly arranged. Still, over the years, even big cities have found it a daunting challenge to convene some sort of annual formal meeting with MPs, MPPs, or MLAs. Ministers, in particular, avoid such sessions. Importantly, however, Graham, Phillips, and Maslove point out that larger cities have other means to pursue their interests and "There is the clout of a big city mayor and the sophisticated expertise of senior city staff" (1998: 195). Big cities use the stakes tactic in dealing with the federal government, and individual mayors (with senior advisers) will meet first with the regional patronage minister and then with portfolio ministers for specific policies.

Recently, Calgary and Edmonton lobbied the province directly, outside the AUMA, for a percentage of the tax on gasoline which rural municipalities would not receive. A 1999 provincial fuel tax revenue-sharing scheme produced five cents per litre, purportedly to offset persistently declining unconditional grants. Still, the 2001-02 declines in petroleum prices allowed the provincial treasurer to reconsider her largesse by an arbitrary 15 per cent in the 2001 budget; were it necessary, this once again reminded city councillors of their standing as creatures of provincial whimsy. Lobbying restored the claw-back. In late 1998, for another example, the City of Halifax opposed then current provincial thinking on service responsibilities and funding issues for fears that its tax base would be exploited to subsidize the services provided by rural municipalities with weaker tax positions. Despite last-minute quibbles over the shape of the proposals, the UNSM had been a supportive participant throughout the entire process (Tindal and Tindal 2000: 245). In 2003, Edmonton council publicly opposed provincial education equalization on the grounds that it exploited Edmonton residents to subsidize the fiscal shortcomings of rural school boards, but did so only after private channels of persuasion failed.

From St. John's through Toronto and Winnipeg to Vancouver, local tri-level redevelopment cooperation on site-specific projects has emerged since the mid-1970s. In 1999-2000, global pressures associated with the implementation of the Kyoto Accord yielded a federal $125 million endowment fund established through the FCM to assist cities to improve their environmental performance. Still, the biggest cities continue to constitute an autonomous lobby of one on any policy matter (usually fiscally shorted capital works) of genuine significance to their councils.

The twenty-first century opened with a new spin on these old ideas. In this tactic seeking a strategy, Canada's "Big City Mayors," beginning in May 2001 and borrowing from the critical thinking of Jane Jacobs, have constituted a quasi-autonomous caucus nominally within the FCM (Canada's Cities 2003). Known to themselves as the C-5 (Montreal, Toronto, Winnipeg, Calgary, and Vancouver), and complete with web-accessible resources, this cartel of big city officials agreed to lobby first ministers collectively on issues of genuine importance (such as infrastructure renewal) to their urban development. A request "that their respective First Ministers invite them to participate in the next full First Ministers meeting with the Prime Minister, *which must focus on the needs of Canada's city regions*" (Canada's Cities 2003; emphasis added) has thus far, as always, been ignored. Part of the rejection stems from the C-5 demand for "a Model Charter" that would provide "greater autonomy and access to more flexible revenue streams" (Canada's Cities 2003) and part from the fuzzy nature of specific policy expectations beyond the fiscal. A flurry of press releases has not disguised absolute provincial disinterest, and individual cities have necessarily resorted to their own bully pulpits outside the umbrella of association.

7.1.4.3 PROFESSIONAL AND POLICY SPECIALISTS IN THE MUNICIPAL ASSOCIATION

Professionals and policy specialists within the municipal associations have considerable control over legislation not only because of expertise in areas of minutiae, but also due to linkages to similar professionals in the provincial government. Two types of associations exist here—those singled out due to the nature of their municipal employment (clerks, treasurers, assessors), and those who are employed by municipalities due to their professional certifications (planners, engineers, lawyers, social workers). Feldman and Graham note: "Professional associations perform useful training, professional development, research, and information functions for their membership and for municipalities as employers" (1979:16). In many instances, they have been delegated certification responsibilities for the professional qualifications of individual practitioners.

The professional associations of municipal officials (clerks and treasurers, planners, public health officers, recreation lobbies, even roadways engineers) are also active in a policy consultative role. Some years back, Higgins observed that their professional qualifications "in highly specialized areas" gave these associations considerable influence over their particular areas of expertise (1986:80). That proposition remains true. Indeed, these are the very policy networks of which Pross (1992) wrote and to whom much official decision-taking has been delegated. The important point is that their influence is normally hidden hardly permeable by the public, and difficult for local councillors to control even if they chose to try.

7.2 The Policy World of Neighbourhood

The pluralist world of liberal democrats sees a municipal environment in which it is unsurprising that specific neighbourhoods "react" against initiatives approved by their local governments and in which neighbourhood groups are consistently least satisfied with the general direction of local decision-taking. The neighbourhood becomes the last line of defence for individuals. This is so particularly in situations where the activity of such wider area but non-business organized groups as did materialize "seems to have been contained or co-opted far more successfully than in other cities by city hall and the social welfare establishment" (James Lorimer, *Globe and Mail*, 6 August 1971). It has long been understood by critics of Canadian urban democracy that, overall, Canadian local government institutions are not impartial but tend to operate as the very active proponent of the commercial interests of any city's booster class.

The third reform period was characterized by a conflict over policy decisions from divergent urban values. E.E. Schattschneider argues generally that "The role of conflict in [any] political system depends, first, on the morale, self-confidence and security of the individuals and groups who must challenge the dominant groups in the community in order to raise an opposition" (1960: 8). In other words, you won't fight if you are going to be punished, squashed, and doomed from the outset. For citizen groups at the neighbourhood level, assuming their assessment that any battle is not absolutely futile, issues must be chosen wisely so as to be workable. Tactically, the "bad guy" whose policy preferences were causing grief has both to be clearly identifiable and its actions reduced to uncomplicated, understandable, and actionable dimensions.

7.2.1 The traditional ratepayers' associations

During the third reform period, many long-established ratepayer groups in Canadian central cities seemed radical in their new policy demands. In reality, they were much more oriented toward safeguarding the neighbourhood status quo. This urban conservatism rose up largely in response to yuppie (young urban professional) buying preferences and developer response. Magnusson put the mood of the movement succinctly for Toronto: "As conservatives, the new reformers were keen to have as much of the old city preserved as possible—not only the historic centre, but the established residential and even commercial and industrial areas surrounding it" (1983b: 116). J.L. Granatstein, a professor of history and neighbourhood activist, encapsulates this view in his small case study: "But then Marlborough [street] had not wanted much. Our aims were limited. We didn't want the moon; we merely wanted to be left alone" (1971: 118).

Kaplan has documented that neighbourhood groups "intervened in Metro policy-making sporadically but intensely" (1967: 168). In these occasional incursions into governing preserves—policy communities populated by administrative specialists, their major clienteles, and institutionalized general purpose groups like the Board of Trade and Bureau of Municipal Research—the neighbourhood groups were loud, negative, and uncompromising in their reactions. Kaplan's findings show that general purpose group leaders "dismissed the neighbourhood groups as narrow-minded obstructionists who lacked any overall program or concept of the area's needs" (1967: 168). Over the years, neighbourhood associations mobilized in all cities across Canada in all categories of local areas which felt their continuing existence threatened in some large or small way by city hall action. Today, the divide remains as wide as 30 years ago when Fish concluded that there were two fundamentally divergent world views at the heart of the conflict: "The urban values of decentralization, controlled growth, neighbourhood stability, mixed use and mixed income areas were still held largely only by those outside government. Those in control tended to adhere to urban values of centralization, growth, change and single purpose commercial centres" (1981: 95). Now, in the twenty-first century, the local voices most fearful of globalization remain convinced that it will inevitably equate to cultural conformity and that the city will become but one socially uniform suburb with fast food joints and strip malls. Further, they accept as truth that all real political choices will be reached by increasingly remote decision-makers.

In 1968, Toronto's CORRA mobilized a network of groups to confront what they then perceived as a councillors-only policy discussion on a wide range of issues related to urban development. While its membership overlapped considerably with SSSOCCC, CORRA also "not only linked the middle-class organizations with one another, but brought them into contact with community groups being formed in poorer neighbourhoods" (Magnusson 1983b: 115). Fish chronicles the overall solid footing of the growing neighbourhood movement of this period in the new professional middle classes, observing that "Teachers, lawyers, architects, planners and the occasional cleric were in the forefront of Toronto's citizen participation movement" (1981: 96).

For a handful of years following 1967-68, Toronto's policy process included a city-wide force trying to counteract the basic economic objectives of urban developers and mobilized around policy in a coherent manner never quite approximated by the Confederations of Community Leagues in Canada's prairie cities. The corollary was that the Toronto Board of Trade along with the groups associated with larger developers fared less well in their bargaining with city councillors. The Board's general manager observed of the "new parochialism" in 1980 that "Many of the politicians are very conscious of votes that they get from residents who really look at things from a local point of view" (*Edmonton Journal*, 11 November 1980).

Neighbourhood protectionism indeed had a more radical edge in the words and actions of those opposed to the capitalism of large-scale development (Lorimer 1969, 1972). Magnusson noted that these voices added the assessment that "the development industry had effectively captured the agencies that were supposed to regulate it" (1983b: 116). This provided a coherent tinge of radical populism to a dispersed opposition entrenched in conservative values. It further presaged the later emergence of web-wise policy networks, with the now familiar doctrine of "Think globally but act locally," which are based on the extra-community linkages of new social movements to be discussed in Chapter 8. It surprised few observers with any historic sense that leaders among the third period neighbourhood protectionists, such as John Sewell, stood well in the vanguard of those opposed to the Toronto Megacity reforms 30 years later on.

Infrequently in the past, the rubric of ratepayer association has been exploited by politically savvy lobbyists to pervert the policy process. For instance, an array of affected neighbourhoods apparently endorsed the arterial plans for the Spadina Expressway in Toronto in 1962 despite the efforts of others to derail them. Investigations by *Toronto Star* columnist Ron Haggart revealed that the supportive letters written to the city's three dailies were crafted by Irving Paisley, a North York councillor and property insurance agent with a proprietary interest in the planned route. Haggart found that of the over two dozen supportive briefs to the chair of Metro council's roads committee (indicating at least some non-official public support), one-third had been written by the councillor directly and over half had been reproduced (in the required 25 copies) in his downtown office, which also paid almost all of the postage or delivery charges. In reality, the majority represented defunct ratepayers' associations whose nominal existence was sustained by only one or two pliable long-surviving officers (Nowlan and Nowlan 1970: 98-105). In such a way, the "existence" of citizen groups may also be worked to circumvent democratic accountability. Today, even policy networks are susceptible to inflated claims as to whom they represent. It is only the most perceptive councillor (or bureaucrat) who will delve into these tricky questions of representativeness and legitimacy, "tricky" because they query the sacred cow of any group's publicly welcomed participation in the policy process on behalf of "ordinary" residents.

7.2.2 NIMBY and CAVE

The NIMBY phenomenon comes from strenuous neighbourhood antago-nism to such noxious developments as freeways, garbage dumps, or hazard-ous waste sites. NIMBY organizations have been more reactive than the old-style neighbourhood ratepayers' associations that held such sway in the post-1918 civic era. In the last decades of the twentieth century, however, local opposition congealed much more quickly in a variety of citizens' collec-tive behaviours struck to oppose anything that might be considered a threat to personal security, lifestyle, and, more importantly, property values. These threats were perceived to come from both suspect causes like casinos and bars and the more meritorious, such as lower income housing; halfway houses for prisoners, addicts, or the mentally incompetent; and homeless shelters for the young or other outsiders. While less educated persons may express themselves very plainly, even the better informed can engage in genteel dis-criminatory actions and subtle verbalization against any underclass. Clark pinpoints the problem for larger city-regions internationally: "Efforts by the media to make a story *dramatic* or by organized group leaders to *heighten public consciousness* can boomerang in creating exaggerated stereotypes, prompting overly negative *labeling*" (Clark and Hoffmann-Martinot 1998: 40; emphasis in original). The danger for policy-making is that these political pressures are based on media images and not the realities of first-hand experiences.

Within a municipality, the NIMBY experience is a local community's reactive objection to a city's or private developer's plans which the neighbours see as damaging to the quality of life in their immediate world. Residents can be effective precisely because they are the electorate mobilized. Toronto councillor Ying Hope said that one reason large developers may have a hard time in this policy debate is due to their being represented by lawyers "who are overly professional—too much gloss. It doesn't impress me; in fact, it depresses me" (*Edmonton Journal,* 11 November 1980). Gerald Hodge writes that NIMBY has constituted an active and recognized organizational lobbying form since the early postwar period (1991: 370-72; see also McAllister, 1995: 275). Even earlier than this, the wealthier classes in North American cities had exhibited similar proclivities as they sought to enact protective zonings to preserve the exclusivity of their own neighbourhoods such as Tuxedo in Winnipeg, Shaughnessy in Vancouver, and Glenora in Edmonton. Plainly said, NIMBYism today is the status quo mobilized; while there may stand exceptions, generally it does not constitute a display of citizen generosity of spirit in action. Speaking during the euphoria of the early heyday of the "citizen participation" movement in Canada, Fish conceded that "Given the organizing aspects of the citizen participation technique, it would also appear to have limited effectiveness as an instrument of broad policy formation but a high degree of effectiveness in dealing with the particular application of policy in a given project" (1981: 96). However generously appreciated, a NIMBY development more easily prevents than initiates.

In other words, an elegant defence of the block against traffic congestion and possibly diminished property values more commonly fronts an intolerance for group homes (and the like) of any sort (seniors' lodges, youth shelters, addicts' or felons' halfway houses). Proposals for non-traditional churches have also fallen prey to NIMBY assaults. Effective NIMBY organization requires the mobilization of serious political resources of time, social standing, and information, and can abort standard planning processes by either defeating the proposed neighbourhood plan outright or by forcing a political non-decision on the part of local councils in the form of protracted referrals, amendments, and meetings. Non-partisan councillors elected on the basis of neighbourhood wards are the most easily flummoxed by tightly organized and well-heeled NIMBY groups, and no amount of professional planners' intellectual clarity or expertise is ever an even match for elector truculence.

By the 1990s, an emergent public cynicism had led to other new coinages like CAVE (Citizens Against Virtually Everything). Americans are especially fond of such acronyms, in this case descriptive of behaviour and not organizations. David M. Herszenhorn recorded not only NIMBY, but also LULU (Locally Unaccepted Land Use) and continued, "there is Nimtoo, the elected official's retort, 'not in my term of office,' and Nimbl, the budget director's cry, 'not in my bottom line.' Hard-liners can try Niaby, 'not in anybody's backyard'; Nope, 'not on planet earth'; or Banana, 'build absolutely nothing anywhere near anyone'" (*New York Times,* 16 April 2000).

Finally, the smaller local non-partisan councils in a city-region appear to be more easily intimidated by the noise of organized sectoral interests

(Kaplan 1965: 29). Especially is this so in the more particularized life of central cities. As but one example of the power of this recognized pattern of suasion, the Chair of the Toronto Arts Council argued against the proposed Megacity unification because "When we're talking about the ethos that has built an arts community unequalled in the country, and hard to match on the continent, then it's not as simple as looking to eliminate duplication of services" (*Toronto Star*, 10 March 1997). The continuance of a supportive relationship with the central city councillors was much on the mind of their press gallery advocates. It was not more clearly put than by columnist David Lewis Stein: "there is a fear that when there is only one city council giving out money for the arts, small groups will lose out and most of the money will go to the big four [art gallery, opera, ballet, and symphony]" (*Toronto Star*, 6 February 1997). In such a public confrontation, concepts like "citizen engagement" only confuse the reality of a good old-fashioned brawl over political turf.

So, to sum up, although sporadically challenged by neighbourhood or clientelist voices from the street over a specific issue, the policy system of Canadian cities entered the twenty-first century as executive guided, administratively controlled by insiders, and precedent dominated. These activities take place within a public ideology whose limits of tolerance are broadly realigned only periodically and then only incrementally adjusted by the interested minority which chooses to participate in the election process. In the next chapter we turn to a discussion of the impact of new styles in citizen interest and the new policies these embrace to assess the capacity of traditional leadership patterns to adapt honestly, effectively, and responsively.

eight | Social movements, leadership, and the policy agenda

In this chapter we will expand the discussion of interest groups and lobbying to consider important hypothetical and actual roles of **new citizen social movements** in the twenty-first century. Then, we will consider what might be expected by way of needed changes in traditional leadership patterns. We will conclude with a note on the work of the mass media in cities and with a statement on the fundamental issue of conflict of interest.

In a well-known study, *Bowling Alone*, Robert Putnam (2000) observes a collapse in the memberships of traditional associations in the United States. Even as hierarchical organizations in all aspects of social and economic life are being challenged, the nature of the family in western democracies and its extra-familial involvements has also changed significantly. Personal participation simultaneously re-emerges as both disintegrative and recombinant in fluid policy networks of individuals. As will be discussed in relation to new social movements, greater individual anomie has led to forms of selective direct involvement in things that matter to personal lifestyle issues. These behaviours have important consequences for the community "leadership" of public officials in their policy-making efforts, especially when they operate under the gun of competing leaders in the policy networks of new movements.

8.1 Social Movements and Their Agendas

The study of political movements has long been a staple for social scientists interested in provincial and federal politics. Typically the object of inquiry has been those specific social and economic conditions whose occurrence has been sufficiently harsh to cause widespread political dissent from the established party process. Hence, protest movements have been chronicled as emerging from agrarian roots (the Progressives in the 1920s, Social Credit in the 1930s), from radical sources in labour during the first generations of the twentieth century (leading to the founding of the CCF in 1935 and its successor, the NDP, in 1962), and from cultural or regional bases (the PQ, the Reform Party). Especially as the larger parties became more centralized in leaders' offices and the parliamentary wing, they also became more remote from the very specific values and issues that fed movements protesting traditional central government policies. What interested political science in Canada in this pattern were the circumstances that transformed broadly sourced social phenomenon into formal parties.

Here we are more concerned with contemporary social phenomena, and their political voices, which are collectively referred to as new social movements. Their common element is advocacy of democratic decentralization and local accountability. The common condition behind their emergence has been a decline in the relevance of all ideological parties for electors in western democracies as voter education and subsequent policy autonomy has increased.

8.1.1 Social movements and the new urban political culture

One paradox in the politics of post-industrial democracies, Canada included, is that even as voter turnout is everywhere in decline, both the level of political awareness among citizens and issue salience remains high. Vincent Hoffmann-Martinot has elaborated this point, presenting survey evidence which consistently reveals three things: (1) that over three-quarters of respondents believe that local politicians quickly lose touch with electors, (2) that parties are interested only in votes not voters' opinions, and (3) yet that interest in politics has still increased (1998: 198–205). Clark, Lipset, and Rempel have also presented strong evidence that very few in the United States, about one-fifth, can define liberal and conservative ideologies broadly enough so as to be able to base their electoral responses on multiple issues; less than one-tenth offer "tolerably acceptable" definitions (2001: 93). These citizens now vote on the basis of those issues which have been most publicized, which tend to be narrowly framed, and which are the most current. As traditional, broadly sourced neighbourhood groups have declined in importance, except for NIMBY moments, issue networks and new social movements have increased their influence.

There are practical consequences. English statesman Edmund Burke (1729-97) argued in his statement to his "electors of Bristol" that, as representatives, MPs were not mere ambassadors to a national congress but served a wider and more important national interest. More recently, Clark has reported that FAUI international surveys of mayors and councillors included this question, "How often would you estimate that you took a position *against* the dominant opinion of your constituents?" (Clark and Hoffmann-Martinot 1998: 109). He also presented the finding that "Those who did were more likely to be voted out of office or go to jail (most dramatically in Eastern Europe or Italy in the late 1980s and 1990s)" (Clark 2003: 4).

Indeed, the congruence of office-holders' positions with their perceptions of voter preferences has been found to be high only on those issues ranking relatively lowest on the decision-makers' agendas (Gabriel *et al.* 1998: 228-33). In Canadian city-regions, specifically Vancouver and Edmonton, entire suburban city councils have been ousted of late in situations where the populations are roughly homogenous, elections are at-large, and fundamental differences are between traditional boosters and the environmentally-centered growth limits movement. Such dramatic electoral shifts are the result of the political energy of exasperated citizens being focused by a social movement which, even when not organized, remains intellectually coherent. Voters have found the traditional choices among the candidates of organized parties or non-partisan political coalitions so irrelevant, or distant, in municipal elections that they seek out potential representatives whose positions have been crystallized by specific local policy issues even as they are informed by extra-community policy networks.

Social movements as "new" phenomena have been seen by social scientists as international in scope and an urban product of the post-Second World War period. From the Paris riots in May 1968, through the anti-Vietnam war protests in the United States in the early 1970s, the political strength of West German Greens in 1982, the Tiananmen Square demonstration and massacre in 1989 and the fall of the Berlin Wall the same year, to the present-day activism in opposition to economic and cultural globalization and its instruments (like the World Trade Organization), individual citizens have plainly been prepared to set aside traditional policy processes to assert personal voices. Jody Williams spawned an "International Campaign to Ban

Land Mines" which was awarded the Nobel Peace Prize in 1997 for persuading 122 governments to become signatories to a treaty outlawing antipersonnel mines; in short, her movement abandoned governments to bring direct pressure on leadership. In this manner, global pressures have fed a new sort of activism often labelled the new localism, in which Internet communications yield international standards against which local performance can be assessed.

What, then, is meant precisely by the term "new social movement"? Van Loon and Whittington made the valid observation that social movements must be differentiated from both political parties and traditional pressure groups in that they are not organized: "They are informal networks of interaction among a large number of often diverse individuals and groups that have a shared collective identity ..." (1996: 441). They also share a belief that the public policy status quo does not reflect their general set of collective preferences. Susan Phillips offers a better working definition of a social movement as "(a) an informal network of organizations and individuals who, (b) on the basis of a collective identity and shared values, (c) engage in political and/or struggle intended to break or expand the boundaries of the existing system, and (d) undertake collective action designed to affect both state and society" (1999: 373). In other words, a new social movement is a loose association of individuals generally like-minded in a particular arena of public issues, usually without much in the way of formal structure, but united in the search for a greater say in the reformulation of specific policies in this realm. They are drawn together from more narrowly focused policy networks. Many citizens may be supporters or followers in several movements, which undoubtedly explains the survey evidence that their attention to the more shrill of movement leaders' voices is muted. According to Clark and Inglehart, "This leader-follower distinction is often missed by political leaders who deal primarily with group leaders" (1998: 60).

As to organizational form, a small number of summary points should be considered.

1. Social movements are not reverse pressure groups, so purported "movements" partially funded by the state, like the National Action Committee on the Status of Women, are excluded from this category of political activity, as are formally structured non-governmental organizations (NGOs).

2. New social movements have developed their momentum in a political culture of citizens with higher incomes and education and concomitant employments and in a social context in which individualism thrives, leading to an erosion of consensus about values and a rejection of deference to any form of hierarchy.

3. Although the leaders are themselves members of social and economic elites equipped to confront both media and office-holders, volunteers are responsible for mobilizing the essential political resources of time, money, and contacting friends and neighbours. They are the ones who initiate direct mail campaigns and exchange lists of street and e-mail addresses.

4. Organizations and networks within the movement rarely act in isolation and continually struggle with internal hierarchy, but they remain successful as they are quickly able to mobilize citizen coalitions around issues through their own communications networks.

5. Clark observes that the fragmented nature and differentiation around particular issues characteristic of movement activism makes contemporary politicians' jobs very difficult: "people who favor growth controls may or may not be feminists or may or may not favor anti-immigration policy or bicycle paths. Inter-correlations among the different issues are weak. Or Zero. Traditional organized groups decline compared to the past but new ones emerge (like websites, e-mail, list servers ...)" (2003: 5).

6. McAllister contributes the important observation that while the grass-roots environmental movement is both fragmented and focused on several levels of state operations (local, provincial, national, and international), ironically, "'green' interest groups do not always find local public participation the most effective strategy. Some see the devolution of authority to local agencies and interests as a threat to the broader environmental agenda" (1995: 276). What these groups fear, in the local milieu, is such dominant booster agendas for development and employment opportunities among people in authority that citizens have been inoculated against ecological preservation.

It is little wonder that politicians, especially municipal ones, seem so bewildered by policy questions. Their previous ability to write and implement modestly coherent platforms has become obsolescent as old ideas of left and right on the standard ideological spectrum no longer make sense to a public whose concepts are constantly in flux.

In Canada's past, social movements were a harbinger of social upheaval rooted largely in structural economic dislocations. Today, social movements are increasingly focused in the particularism of urban life. Any new group that seeks seriously to make innovations in public policy faces three essential tasks: it must (1) define the problem in coherent public policy terms, (2) devise an alternative choice, and (3) implement a strategy to make the problem's resolution a system priority. There is no need to be "reasonable" in any of this, for the essence of reason in politics is to acknowledge the supremacy of the status quo, and the target of any social movement is precisely to upset the established way of doing things.

8.1.2 Small opportunities, agenda action

How is it possible for ongoing collaboration among otherwise competing elements in urban regimes to persist? Stone located the reason in a patchwork of limited public policy possibilities. Among the less consequential regime adherents, this may very well relate to the "small opportunities" phenomenon which he observed in Atlanta: "most people most of the time are guided, not by a grand vision of how the world might be reformed, but by the pursuit of particular opportunities" (1989: 235). He reminds us that most of the low politics surrounding city hall *are* about small matters on a scale that may actually be realized—such as neighbourhood planning; community-sustained gardens; and volunteer initiatives in the coaching of soccer, hockey, and the like—or even small-scale redistributive initiatives such as food banks or winter clothing drives.

At the wider level of the city-region, new social movements tend to have more precisely defined action objectives than these. Social movements grow out of, and reflect, the social composition of individuals in their communities and, as these are territorially based (i.e., ecological communities), their expectations assume specific policy shape for officials in municipal governments. The demands can often be expressed quite simply: "don't drain the southside wetlands" or "don't spread pesticides or herbicides in neighbourhood parks." Clark and Lipset have effectively argued that, based on surveys of mayors in seven Western countries, fiscally conservative individuals in the new political culture are concerned with lifestyle issues and promote individual freedoms: "even in rallying to a socially liberal agenda, [they] do not act as a self-conscious, united class but usually as voters and members of 'single-issue' groups" (2001: 97, 99).

Many have observed that social movements target specific issues and run with these rather than try to link these policies into an alternative, broadly based, conservative or liberal action program (see, especially, Clark and Goetz 1994: 110-11). Specific items on the new action agenda most likely include some, or all, of the following.

8.1.2.1 GROWTH LIMITS

Activists for and against local growth controls have sprouted since the late 1980s, often led by networks like the Sierra Club. Indeed, the strongest correlation of growth limits propositions in the United States with any variable tested is with high memberships in the Sierra Club (Clark and Goetz 1994: 125-26). Especially in the numerous small quasi-rural suburbs of American city-regions, voting residents have been willing to use the ballot box and direct democracy to preserve the tranquility and sylvan nature they have acquired for themselves. Movements to limit growth are normally found in cities with more youthful and well-educated citizens and leaders, both of whom are usually employed in service sector or high tech industries. This activism leads to multifaceted, and not unselfish, pressures on local governments to control the local development permit process strictly, thus spawning further support for new "rules of the game" that reject intervention from the historically bound vision of strong mayors and the precedent-set views of municipal bureaucrats.

8.1.2.2 ECOLOGY AND ENVIRONMENTALISM

Associated with the above is the wider urban ecology movement, which again targets the existing policy world views of generalist political leadership. Clark summarizes the movement thus: "Since trees cannot speak out, ecologists must speak for them, urging political leaders to defend nature against noxious gases, liquefied chemicals, and physical destruction—or at least protect the persons who would be harmed by these changes in nature" (1998: 54–55). Adherents to the grassroots ecology movement have been disproportionately younger persons, often under legal voting age. Ecological activism finds formal political expression in the Green Party. Its issues are international and salient to voters in Hamburg as well as Burnaby, and it has overridden traditional ties to national, religious, or ethnic communities.

8.1.2.3 FEMINISM

As 1960s radicalism splintered, tension was maintained by more general approaches to the state, such as feminism (Gibbins and Youngman 1996: 126–36). For those women who most closely subscribe to dominant liberal values, the target remains process equality, gaining participatory access in the venues of elections, representation, and full integration into the public sphere. More radical feminists target any and all elements in the perceived patriarchy of the modern industrial state. At its most extreme, such advocates embrace lesbianism as a celebration of the value of femininity over masculinity. It is important to note that all streams of feminism tend to politicize many activities long held to be private matters by mainstream society and that affect the economy, from birthing to absolute pay and employment equity. Having today attained a high degree of public acceptance, if not actual realization, of its primary goals of equity, many of the movement's younger and more active leaders have turned their energies to other more specific policy networks.

8.1.2.4 HUMAN RIGHTS

More individual freedom is intricately entwined in the agendas of new social movements. Advocacy groups in the new political culture accept the extension of rights won for the general population to previously less highly regarded minorities; singly, or in combination, they have thus campaigned for the young and old, the lesbian and gay, new migrants and visibly distinct minorities, nature and animal rights, and so forth. But the force in new social movements also has a dark side. We see this in Europe, for instance, especially in France and Germany, where anti-migrant nationalists like the French New Right and the German neo-Nazis have invested considerable time in developing virtual communities to coordinate their activism. The rise of these movements is a consequence, in part, of the decline of the hierarchically organized socialist parties which had for some time suffused nationalist, anti-immigrant voices in national politics. Nonetheless, in the 1980s local Communist parties in France tried to drive immigrants from their political power bases in low income Paris suburbs by denying access to schools, health care, and public housing (Clark and Lipset 2001: 87). Even purportedly more highly educated citizens than European skinheads can be racial snobs, indulging in discrete discrimination and subtle forms of disassociation that disguise contempt and prolong negative stereotyping. Movements for human rights have at least one common target as they fight against such discrimination.

8.1.2.5 LESS CLIENTELISM AND CORRUPTION

Herman Boschken has observed that the modern upper middle class (UMC) in which many new social movements find their source places considerable value on the socially progressive, quality-of-life, "world-class" image of their city-regions, an image that lends stature to their own lives and reputations. He writes "symbolic considerations including public accoutrements (prominent airport, arts and entertainment, reputable schools, modern mass transit) are more important than economic issues in UMC voting" (2001: 232). Into this grocery cart, and valued for image perhaps more than usefulness, are also tossed items like quality management methods and "best practices," along with "more efficient" government ideals, trustworthy political leadership, and the continual applications of innovative service delivery technologies. Clark argues that, responding to the demands of new movements, younger political leaders have resorted to a populist style by appealing directly to electors through the media rather than through party organizations thus trying to defuse a cynicism grounded in amoral individualism with new public goods like effective public transit, more public spaces, and clean air (2003: 7).

The classic reform elements have been known for a century: "Replacing clientelist contacts with open and transparent government—genuine competitive bids, internet postings of jobs and contracts, stressing 'due process,' the rule of law, honesty, public accountability, mobilizing market forces as a means to cut costs, transcend traditional political cleavages, and engage new sources of talent" (Clark 2003: 8). Openness, new ideas, foreign-sourced evaluations of programs, staff exchanges, and international travel are all aspects of modern administration in an era of direct citizen challenges. In recent years, innovative mayors in Canada, many of them women like Barbara Hall in Toronto and Jan Reimer in Edmonton, seeking inclusion, innovation, and process transparency, set a policy ball rolling that not even their successor retrenchment and 1950s-style mayors (Mel Lastman in Toronto, Bill Smith in Edmonton) could interrupt.

Today, many of these new social movements oriented primarily around municipal politics may coalesce around spot issues directly arising from a generally shared image of their cities that varies considerably and almost in mirror image from the old economic booster package. Interestingly, since he spoke from a developing world locale, Enrique Peñalosa, former Mayor of Bogotá, recently captured the practical application of these feelings rather successfully: "It is frequent that images of high-rises and highways are used to portray a city's advance. In fact, in urban terms, a city is more civilized not when it has highways, but when a child in a *tricycle* is able to move about everywhere with ease and safety." He adds, perhaps too generously, that "The bike path is the only place where people can see themselves as equals. It is the safest place in the city because it creates a kind of solidarity—people help one another" (2002).

8.1.3 New styles of active citizenship

Social change and new economic pressures, especially if rapid, necessarily upset traditional approaches and institutions. Research findings in industrial democracies indicate that even as new movement leaders have become more strident in selling their cause, negotiating with political leadership, and posturing for media consumption, their adherents appear to have become somewhat more tolerant of other groups in society, especially since these followers' status is correlated with higher education and income variables.

The new era is one in which rapidity of change overwhelms traditional institutions, private as well as public, and a new need for a personal connection between leaders and followers, citizens and city hall emerges. Moreover, one consistent and important finding of those observing the policy impacts of modern social movements, especially those which encompass and rely upon highly specialized expertise, is this: "Generalist leaders cannot surpass the specialists on their own issues; their claim to legitimacy is their ability to confront 'the establishment' and fight on any issue" (Clark and Goetz 1994: 110). Capitalizing on both these phenomena, local leaders have necessarily connected to their publics across the past generation through a growing reliance on PPP. In the past such actions have been precipitated by a period of austerity occasioned by a combination of new policy demands, increased servicing costs, reasonably static revenues, and reduced funding support from central governments. Alternatives for human service delivery mechanisms are basically three: they can be contracted to (1) a for-profit private business, (2) a nonprofit volunteer operation or NGO (including local service clubs, neighbourhood groups, or volunteer social agencies), or (3) another unit of government such as a neighbouring municipality or regional special purpose district (Miranda 1994b: 198).

From the American evidence, contracting out was the major response by the 1,333 cities surveyed by the International City Management Association in 1982. The use of contract service providers—such as private project engineers, for example—has become one very common method of reducing permanent municipal staffing rolls. When later FAUI expenditure data are taken into account, careful analysis reveals that savings were least when tasks were out-sourced to for-profit private entrepreneurs, moderately more when with other governments, and only significant when with nonprofit agencies which were able to subsidize operations with volunteers or by piggybacking costs onto other state funding including tax exemptions (Miranda 1994b: 208-10). Canadian findings are unlikely to be dissimilar.

So, the objective of contracting out service delivery is not likely to be cost saving but something other, perhaps the co-option of leaders demanding new policies and service delivery systems, the ensuring of greater sensitivity to specialized needs through volunteers working the privatized operations, or, more basely, the delegation of thorny issues for resolution by the persons themselves seeking state solutions. Those who volunteer and who participate in the co-production of local services tend to be disproportionately correlated with higher socio-economic status. Noblesse oblige issues aside, they tend naturally to work for benefits for their own middle-class—lifestyle enhancing activities along the lines of the "meals-on-wheels" or after-school care approach to preventive social services characteristic of the North American UMC suburb. Still, to involve volunteers directly in service delivery has proven a primary means to engage citizens, to defuse cynicism with traditional mechanisms, and to respond to the local issue demands of new social movements, while simultaneously identifying citizenship roles appropriate for the public demands of the twenty-first century.

8.2 Leadership at City Hall

Setting aside the collective behaviour of social movements, pressure groups, and political parties for the moment, what can be said about the individual leadership of Canadian local political authorities? Interestingly, the direct question of what constitutes effective political leadership in local government for Canada has seldom been given much specific textbook attention. Recently, in *Urban Governance in Canada*, the authors describe only a kind of anonymous, collective "city government" and its ambitious quest for economic development (Graham, Phillips and Maslove 1998: 236). This is not unusual for city studies north of the Rio Grande, and any discussion of the role and power of official leadership at city hall has pretty much been relegated to biography, quick vignettes, and a few final words in obituaries. Few British texts specifically address themselves to the issue because of the role of party and the considerable power of central authority over policy that comes from Westminster. In the UK, local government is more precisely local administration.

The American classics focus on leadership in the context of interest group or political party power, or relative to the type of local government structure such as city manager versus the strong mayor. Stone, for example, begins his discussion of the subject by observing that, in the American context especially, "There is no well developed theory of political leadership ..." He quickly concedes however that "Energetic governance requires more than office holding alone can provide" (1995: 96). So, what might be said about the phenomenon of leadership in the governing of Canadian cities?

8.2.1 The general function of leadership

As a part of the wider social system, politics must provide the general function of leadership. In Canada, the investigation of this function has been largely overlooked, which is curious in that ubiquitous non-partisanship on councils should provide opportunities to observe and assess skilled leadership from either the mayor or permanent administrative chief. The implicit assumption is made that an individual human through determination or an insightful single initiative can make a difference.

An unwritten coda of the non-partisan city council is inclusion of all political forces, barring serious personality differences, and service to an assumed common good of the community overrides whatever small differences may exist. The behaviour of the anti-party Citizens Committee in Edmonton (1934-59) is instructive, for it included prominent gladiators from all political parties at the other levels of the state and even had a CCF mayor, as well as

politically sentient leaders from each of the more powerful ethnic communities. George Betts noted that "There was no reason why, although in different camps at the higher level, they should not pool their experience with
campaigning and electioneering to win the election for the CGA by party
techniques at the municipal level" (Magnusson and Sancton 1983: 266).

For a number of reasons, city councils reward a pattern of very short-
term goals and directly gains-oriented behaviour for councillors, especially
when they are elected through wards. Breadth in problem perception is
institutionally deflated, so the leadership issue tends to be defined as personality. However, as Masson has put it, there is little that is more destruc-
tive to council's legislative agenda than personality politics: "Astute mayors
focus on issues and avoid personality discussions so as not to compromise
their ability to gain support" (1994: 192). The formal rules of the game do
not seem to provide much real scope for a determined leader. However, the
one thing about which there also seems general agreement among scholars
is that a charismatic leader will change the rules. Skilled mayors expand the
authority of the office; the influence of the less able is more likely to implode
quickly into policy stalemate.

The direct election of the Canadian mayor has implications focused on
personality. Kaplan, writing about the formative stages of political culture
in Canadian cities, argued that the city-wide focus on a single personality helped reduce more complex local issues to their bare bones (1982: 74).
Beyond the institutional consequences of personal quirks, according to social
theory the individual leader chosen may come to personify the group and its
social system requirements at a given point in time. In mayors, this can range
from ardent technocrats like Calgary's Al Duerr to rabid idiosyncratics like
Montreal's Pierre Bourque and Toronto's Mel Lastman, to fatuous boosters
like Edmonton's Bill Smith. Of the eight mayors chosen for study by Allan
Levine (1989) only Edmonton's William Hawrelak was genuinely scrofulous
in character and even he presided effectively over the municipal servicing of
a rambunctious growth period. When the personal attributes of a particular
mayor, such as Jean Drapeau as political leader in 1960s Montreal, or the
administrative direction of someone like Al Duerr in 1990s Calgary taps
into the public ethos as political expression, then massive electoral pluralities
will accumulate. This in turn enhances that mayor's informal but powerful personal suasion over the policy choices of the more narrowly focused
councillors elected from wards, but only on identifiably significant issues.
Such personalities seem the exceptional circumstance, however, and not the
general rule.

The idea of leadership has been studied from many perspectives, and,
indeed, more than three score classification systems have been generated over

the last half-century. The general conclusion is that somehow a group leader combines a package of personal traits with a position of authority to identify and achieve collective goals. In a generic sense, leadership may be defined as "a process whereby an individual influences a group of individuals to achieve a common goal" (Northouse 1997: 3). But, in public policy matters there is far more to its exercise than the public selection of, in the cynic's view, the least among the evils presented during elections.

I share Kaplan's appreciation that there are two kinds of leadership required in a political system: (1) effective administrative or managerial guidance that is more than aimless survival and (2) political initiative. Kaplan defines leadership generally, but captures its several components well: "Leadership may be defined as any conscious effort to produce intended outcomes or move resources from one place to another, when those efforts occur within the context of a social system and require some attempt to alter the behaviour of other individuals" (1982: 225).

Administrative leaders are the caretakers of an inherited legacy, and they work through established structures. This distinguishes them from political leaders who are directly associated with, and measured by their success in, creatively adapting policy processes to changing circumstances and building political institutions. Precise distinction between these two necessary styles is often blurred as local politicians over-represent constituents by directly meddling in administrative detail, and senior managers are required to propose adaptive strategies in response to new circumstances of fiscal austerity (Lightbody 1996: 99–101). However, the different manifest direction of each function must remain theoretically distinct if citizens are to understand clearly the leadership phenomenon.

To be precise, the capacity of **political leadership**, a phrase seldom unaccompanied by limiting modifier adverbs, is the ability to engage the political resources of citizens to deploy the power of the state in the enduring struggle of adapting to the natural environment, of reforming dysfunctional historic circumstances to some wiser collective good, or of challenging the power centred in other social and economic institutions effectively. Political leaders may invigorate fresh beliefs, they create new or alter past policy practices, and they are measured by results produced. The one true test of political leadership that reaches beyond passive performance or the rush to stand one step in front of the troops is in the capacity to be genuinely innovative. In this sense, successful introduction of redistributive policies is a concrete test of a leader's abilities: "Promoting change is always difficult because it involves overcoming resistance" (Stone 1995: 106). So, crudely, one might be able to measure the relative capability of any given leader by scoring reallocations from one social group to any other, from rich to poor or, for that matter, *vice versa*.

Most of Canada's big city mayors have been effective as short-term tacticians, but very few have exhibited much in the way of strategic sense. An astute mayor may build public support to limit councillors from sabotaging a program; they are helped a little by their independent city-wide electoral appeal and easier informal access to the city hall **press gallery**. Yet, as Clark and Goetz have recognized, "'Leaders' often follow as much as lead, especially on controversial public policies like supporting or opposing growth" (1994: 134). Such shuffling leadership style was seen often at Vancouver city hall during the freeway controversies of the third reform period at a time when politicians might actually have made a choice but evaded public responsibility for it: "They engaged in 'kite flying,' allowing momentary popular pressures to fill the vacuum of leadership. Or they let their officials bear the brunt of the responsibility" (Leo 1977: 30).

From a comparative and historic vantage, the most intuitive talent of all might well be the creative non-decision. Over time, the more usually effective council leader will be that person who has been able to adapt personal style to various contexts. It will have been learned that not all personalities contribute equally to issue resolution in all circumstances. Abundant social research suggests that the more effective leaders usually possess some combination of five basic personality traits (Northouse 1997: 13-18): (1) intelligence, not as measured by IQ tests, which reveal that few vary greatly from the group mean, but in superior verbal abilities and reasoning; (2) self-confidence in skills and basic competencies; (3) determination as reflected by perseverance and drive; (4) a heightened sense of integrity in the group's eyes for honesty and demonstrated trustworthiness; and (5) a degree of sociability in basic friendliness, outgoing ways, and tactfulness. Having said this, we also understand that even the most able of leaders begins work within the limits of a governing context.

8.2.2 Formal barriers to effective leadership

Barriers to effective performance of administrative guidance and political leadership may exist in the formal arrangement of local governing institutions. Of course, right off the bat we must concede that if the municipal structure itself is heavily dominated by provincial definition and intervention, then it probably does not matter whether or not any given head of council is thought to be powerful. More usually, authority weakness is implied because the mayor of any city is seen only to chair council and is neither a party leader elected by popular convention nor head of a government as are the prime minister and the premiers. The historically sanctioned structural arrangement of council with standing committees supervising quasi-independent permanent departmental managers is conducive to a pattern of rudderless administrative direction, mutually assured. In short, no one position in such a stratarchy of authority is legally empowered to lead.

It is in this general context, writing of the leadership position of the Canadian prime minister some years ago, that R.M. Punnett reminds us that the power of that position rests on four pillars of authority. In his view, the prime minister is the elected leader of the party and subsequently the popular focus of platform attention, (1) has "vast powers of patronage" that extend from cabinet through the senior public service into the judiciary, (2) is the political head of government by constitutional convention, (3) thus controlling the ministry and the timing of elections, and (4) is the link between the governing party and the wider electorate (1977: 19-24). Of these leader's powers and prerogatives, only the last is available to the Canadian head of city council, and the position is very much unlike a prime minister or premier with the party solidarity of caucus behind them. The mayor normally confronts a council comprised of flexible votes who may be swayed by personalities, clientelist payoffs, or low level ideological differences. The municipal reformers of the late nineteenth century indeed left a weak legacy in the constitution of their unique legislative forum.

In the American context, Stone puts it this way: "In judging leadership performance, we should acknowledge structural constraints. No leader has a blank tablet on which to write at will" (1995: 113). Even the latent symbolic possibilities of the mayor's office are cratered by the occupants being guaranteed but one vote on council. Historically, a strong mayor might have been accepted as a source of municipal policy direction, but early in the twentieth century the strong mayor was also equated in the public's eye with boss corruption. As we have seen, the concept of an institutionally weak municipal political executive came to play well in Canadian city halls. Important institutionalized exceptions to this axiom have been mayors of Montreal and the provincially appointed chairs of the Metro councils for Toronto and Winnipeg. However, the essence of leadership lies in overcoming the bitter institutional reality that notwithstanding the city-wide vote for mayor, without partisan discipline on council the potential for informal suasion is short-lived. This is due to councillors' certainty of their own direct, and quite individual, appeals to the voter.

In Canada, Masson has offered that "To exercise leadership while one has few formal powers is truly an art" (1994: 186). Higgins observed that Toronto Mayor W.H. Howland, elected in 1886 as the spokesperson of the temperance movement, could not take effective control of council until the following year's election when he was joined by a majority of like-minded councillors (1986: 236). Nonetheless, most citizen electors in democratic systems expect more from the top than an avid cursing of the darkness. Effective leaders will ordinarily, and intuitively, endeavour to accumulate political capital (that which in business is labelled "good will") which may later be spent on accomplishing change.

An evolved policy system demonstrates both forms of leadership. The managerial leader will consolidate gains from new initiatives and build incrementally upon them, and the political or innovative leader will respond creatively during periods of unanticipated social or economic stress. However, so important are the twin functions of leadership for system maintenance that other social subsystems (such as the permanent bureaucracy or selected interest groups and policy communities) will perform managerial responsibilities should they be unfulfilled and may also perform the political. While the absence of more frequent textbook mention of the importance of Canadian municipal leadership might be assumed to infer a vacuum, it is also probable that we have been overlooking a rather large haystack in the form of continued administrative competence. Just as nature itself abhors a vacuum, one certainty in distributions of political authority is that no power void persists for very long. Some other agency (and it may only be a strategically placed individual) will step forward to expand its own activities to encompass missing possibilities. If the political direction is temporarily missing, the managerial will, under normal conditions, become a more dominant player.

Kaplan's (1982) extended discussion of the inner workings of Metro Toronto's early policy-making is instructive in this regard. In this instance, the fact of indirect elections produced a political deficit at the level of the Metro council, measured in part by councillors' tendency to protect their own municipal electors first with the support of their local bureaucracies. This was compounded by both a continuing institutional rift between core city representatives and those from the suburbs and by persisting divisiveness among the suburban agendas themselves. Such particularized political vision was surmounted only in the person of the appointed Metro Chair from 1953-61, Frederick Gardiner, and he framed council votes carefully. Indeed the tab was impressive when measured. Of 11,539 votes cast during his nine years in office, 81.2 per cent corresponded with his public position; of 579 policy decisions made, 93.4 per cent supported his recommendation, and 33.5 per cent were unanimous. This compared rather favourably with City of Toronto mayors for this period who had four times as many votes in disagreement with their policies (Colton 1980: 99-100).

Almost intuitively, the emptiness in coherent "political" direction for the Metro institution was replaced by a heightened professional administrative push as its department managers met as necessary, almost "as a cabinet," to coordinate programs and to recommend future policy directions to the

Metro chairman (Kaplan 1982: 690). Gardiner's exceptional personal traits provided the particular finesse to render this unusual policy operation publicly palatable. Still, elected politicians have yet to learn the adaptive situational skills that most senior city managers acquire and preserve through institutional memory.

Administrative theories which preserve and protect Canadian local government continuity suppose that the mayor is expected to provide key linkages among council committees, agencies, and department heads. In the ideal of the city manager and commission board models, the head of council puts political constraints on administrators and administrative limitations on council. But the theory is one thing, and the fact of time as the most scarce political resource has brought quite another public reality into play.

8.2.3 Political leadership means innovation

The key test of political leadership is innovation. Political leadership thus means doing something quite new and this "takes great expenditure of energy to produce uncertain, often modest, results ... with a greater likelihood of damage or loss to the actors" (Kaplan 1982: 225). **Political innovation** may be defined as the radical challenge to hierarchy, the existing social and economic order, and established routines. Clark, who has devoted a career to exploring municipal innovation during stressful periods of fiscal austerity, notes that the phenomenon must be more than "new" in the sense of "not tried in this place before" (1994b: 2-3). To him and his team in international comparative studies, creative strategies must respond to specific local conditions. These may be forced by either short-term fiscal exigencies, by immediate political corruption, and sometimes by more fundamental societal change.

What the social scientist must explore is how leadership is related to changing citizen preferences. This entails looking at how leadership is embedded in, and relates to, the activities of policy communities, new social movements, and such organized groups in politics as clients, hierarchical political parties, traditional lobbyists, and professional bureaucrats with an eye to their varying endeavours to adapt and to control public policy.

The standard for modern political leadership as practiced in liberal democracies is what Burns (1978: 18) calls *transactional* behaviour. The heart of the exchange is the vote, and electors reward politicians who have undertaken to meet basic demands, such as the promise not to raise taxes. In its most benign expression, the ambitions of both leaders and followers are attained—the leader is only as powerful as the followers permit. In cases where electoral candidates come from essentially the same socio-economic group, this variable is cancelled out as "a vote-getter"; in campaigns candidates must resort to a very straightforward exchange of votes for amenities (Kaplan 1982: 155). Yet, Burns still argued for "contribution to change" as a significant test for the evaluation of the effectiveness of that leadership (1978: 427).

Effective leadership must adapt to circumvent the established authority lines of organization charts. In Canada we have seen mayors create personal networks from friends, among partisan allies and fund-raisers, and through influential persons within new ethnic communities. It is also important to build independent access into the more established policy communities and by them to the more continuous and important policy networks. Niccolò Machiavelli was the most shrewd assessor of the modern leader's capacity: "The first thing one does to evaluate the wisdom of a ruler is to examine the men that he has around him; and when they are capable and faithful one can always consider him wise ..." (Bondanella 1984: 77). The accomplished leader also comprehends that when power is shared, the sum of one's authority is increased.

Innovative leadership may take the minimal guise of adapting procedural rules, for instance, to produce conflict-of-interest guidelines. It might also change structures, for instance, to wards in elections so that minorities are more likely to win representation, or changing from a Commission Board or Board of Control system to the heightened accountability found in Executive Committee arrangements. Most broadly, it ultimately changes policy itself, for example, to enhance or firm up the social security net. New thinking breeds new policy in the way that environmentalism, as a social and political movement, has led at a minimum to widespread practical recycling and feminism has encouraged equity in employment for much wider sectors of the community. Innovation means the ability to enter into the system new ideas, new means, and new categories of people.

The last decades of the twentieth century were marked by the need for adaptive leadership styles to meet the entry of these new categories. As is to be noted, women, as a group, have asserted their networked presence as local leaders with interesting consequences. Research into gender differences increasingly reveals that gender does make a difference in organizational leadership, and this may hold a greater potency for municipal policy resolution than it does in other legislatures. Women as city managers, for instance, are more likely than their male counterparts to encourage citizen engagement in decision-making, to see themselves as facilitators, and to emphasize communications; they tend more than men to see themselves "in a web" of relations, not at a hierarchy's apex (England 2003: 199).

However, creative political leadership may also work outside the norms because individual leaders are possessed of specific traits. From the evidence, effective leadership style appears to vary with the specific task at hand and the activity, not necessarily the individual; it is much contingent upon a particular setting. After studying Canadian prime ministers, Punnett states that so many varied skills were required that, for any one individual, "it is almost inevitable that he will be found to be deficient in at least one of them" (1977: 28). Generally, an individual who is focused on successful task completion works best when things are under control or just somewhat off-kilter but capable of correction. An individual whose strength is on building relationships tends to be most capable when matters are either in hand or just plain out of control. So it may well be argued that leadership is situational; given a free hand, one would match the leader's personality to the imperatives of the moment and to the abilities of the group to be led. The effective leader is intuitively sufficiently flexible to adapt to differing and fluctuating contexts. The problem at city hall is that councillors, and their mayors, have all usually enjoyed a successful pre-public life career and are thus programmed neither to follow nor to respond.

While some leaders may have an *assigned* position by appointment, others will be *emergent* by some form of election from among the group. The latter are likely to be those persons who command allegiance; the former do not necessarily do so but may possess access to sanctions to command loyalty. The leader is the one who is better and more accurately able to divine followers' motives and power bases than they are themselves (Burns 1978: 20). The key to successful leadership usually lies in being able to motivate followers to adapt their programs by applying modest gratifications and enlarging small opportunities.

It is sometimes claimed that a particular mayor is possessed with an ability to overcome intractability and has considerable personal **charisma**. When genuine, this is an exceptional phenomenon and is an extreme manifestation of what Burns (1978) has labelled *transformational* leadership. A transformational leader such as Mahatma Gandhi has the capacity to excite the imagination of others to heighten their motivation, their morality, and their expectations. In a real sense, followers are empowered by being encouraged to realize their personal potential. This kind of leadership is a direct contrast to the usual transactional leader noted previously.

As Max Weber (1947) observed, charismatic leaders are relatively few. They tend to be more associated with the national, or very important substate regional, political stage. Toronto had two such mayors in William Lyon Mackenzie and W.H. Howland, both of whom have been discussed earlier. Such leaders tend to emerge during prolonged periods of social and economic stress, articulating a vision so inclusive that it appears acceptable as a radical agenda for improvement. Stress arises as the traditional political patterns become somehow incongruous with their own society and economy. One barrier to the appearance of genuinely charismatic mayors in Canada has been that the twentieth-century Canadian municipal reformers so enfeebled the institutional position of head of council that very few could honestly win the label by working only at the level of the city. Several American mayors holding strong institutional positions, such as Rudolph Giuliani of New York (and most large cities in the United States now operate under the strong mayor formula), could be said to have met the charismatic label. Even they have been closely confined to home base.

The overtones of charismatic leadership may be framed ideologically but with a substratum of higher moral calling. The result is public policy as moral crusade, as in last century's temperance, anti-corruption, and anti-crime movements. Often possessed of a resonant oratory, charismatic leaders challenge followers with increased expectations while personally presenting a strongly competent appearance. For Weber the necessary component validating charismatic leadership is followers, and the leaders, in turn, come to validate their social movement followings. Even so, charisma, over and above the important personal elements, may itself be situational and emerges out of broader conditions of social and economic stress.

8.2.4 Change consolidates as hierarchy

Innovation, once successfully performed, quickly becomes the status quo mobilized. Over time, the new leaders and leadership patterns themselves evolve as an hierarchical order, and leaders become policy generalists, emphasizing their learned managerial competence. They then try to direct change from the top down and find it difficult to learn from changes outside their hierarchy. The new leadership pattern becomes first entrenched as the legitimate political order and then the target for future outside challenge as circumstances permit. In public policy political struggles, the now establishment leaders become unable to surpass the expertise of outside specialists on their own policy issues. In any event, outside networks exist, by definition, to fight any kind of establishment structure, in public office or private space, and provide an active breeding ground for new social movements and their leaders. Curiously, the strength of the existing hierarchy appears directly correlated with the potential for social movement challenge.

To win election, a candidate must generally have conformed to a community's political norms, but to accomplish innovation, a political leader will either have to deviate from or dramatically alter them. Thus, the test of effective leadership appears to change *after* innovation has been accomplished. In practical terms this became *the* problem for third period reformers in several Canadian cities. Kaplan put it this way: "Politicians wanted simplified, abbreviated statements; but, to the diagnosticians, this would have involved unforgivable distortions, unacceptable compromises, less than a thorough, accurate discussion of the problem" (1982: 227). The conflict, in these terms, was one between principle and strategy, a confusion of the political and administrative leadership roles. It was also an incongruity which could only for a short time be ameliorated by applying managerial band-aides. Public expectations in the city needed to be shifted from the City Beautiful in planning to broader issues in ecosystem sustainability. In consequence, after innovation, the new leaders' model ought to have focused on shifting community standards; that it did not led ultimately to the collapse of the third reform movement.

The study of effective city hall leadership reveals that it requires at different times and in different places both political innovation (adaptation, transformation) and strong administrative capacities. While leadership is situational, the normal experience in Canadian cities is administrative or caretaking competence. Yet, inattention to basic political fence-mending may lead to a city hall incongruous with its public by keeping people at least one step from the policy process and not being responsive to basic needs in the community for recognition. Pent-up frustrations will lead to social unrest, especially when disagreeable economic conditions release cathartic energies.

Apart from performing the symbolic duties of the position, what behaviour makes any mayor politically successful for a time? To no one's real surprise, all leadership research reveals that the successful leader combines a concern for "product" with careful attention to the people entrusted with attaining it. This latter includes the development of trust and an acknowledgement of personal worth through good working relationships and fair salaries (Northouse 1997: 32–40). In the model smaller city, the effective leader sets an agenda, structures activities so as to achieve it, and nurtures compliance through trust, respect, and consideration. There are enough political rewards for all to share. In bigger cities, a different problem emerges when the mayor's mind wanders and the nature of the leadership changes. Outward mobility to another electoral field is one instance. The problem for mayors, from a strategic perspective, is that there is no longer term, institutionally defined, upward mobility at city hall. No mayor has ever become Canada's prime minister and none, other than George Drew (of Guelph), ever came close. The only mayors as premiers have been Tommy Patullo, Mike Harcourt and Gordon Campbell in British Columbia, Ralph Klein in Alberta, and John Savage in Nova Scotia.

In cities where agenda priorities are more oriented toward administrative effectiveness than ideological engagement, a style that is comfortable with power-sharing and conflict management can be advantageous. To the degree that women as leaders tend to consensus building and are more supportive of all sorts of diversity both in the workplace and in the process of resolving issues (Smith 1997: 209-11), they have a political advantage. Their learned approaches play to the strongly rooted perceptions of local governing as a collective enterprise within a widely subscribed objective public interest. Women in leadership may more easily accomplish more under non-partisanship and its multiple power foci than the personally centred authority necessary in other legislatures with their hierarchy of party and strict caucus discipline. Where issue management is the principal focus of a council, it is better to hear about problems in advance before incipient discord explodes and leadership is reduced to conflict resolution. This job description for a leadership style may form part of the explanation as to why women have enjoyed relatively higher rates of electoral success in municipal politics (Trimble 1995: 93-101).

Finally on this point, E.E. Schattschneider (1960: 141) argued emphatically that a basic requirement of a democracy was a pattern of competing leaders and organizations to define alternatives of public policy so that the public might participate in genuine decision-making. The office of the Canadian mayor may open opportunities for leadership, but it is the personality of the occupant which may (or may not) realize them. It is hard for even informed citizens to keep score as there is no system which judges a mayor's leadership, as in figure skating, for technical merit and artistic impression. The biographical evidence in Canada focuses on those few who made the most of their situations. What this suggests is the corollary that most do not, and that caretakers seldom merit biography.

What we know is that every well-entrenched authority is subject to challenge over time. The trigger of socio-economic stress opens the door to innovative function and even charismatic leadership. To bring this full circle, innovation leads to consolidation of changes, political to administrative leadership, and the seeds for renewal are planted again.

8.3 The Press Gallery and the Life of Ideas

It is not at all coincidental that we should explore the position of the mass media in chapters focused on the lobbying of official decision-makers. This is because the media constitute not only a public and significant means of influence by themselves but also, *sotto voce*, amount to the principal means by which the many publics of the metropolis are massaged and manipulated to form active clusters of public opinion. In thinking about the news we receive, there are two practical limitations to be kept in mind. If it is important to us that broader democratic ideals be realized, then we should scrutinize the relative openness of the communications channels themselves. A second relates to basic questions, some ethical, that should challenge persons in communications media operating as private capital, upon their objectivity and accessibility.

Three points need to be made. First, as communications media are a business it would be surprising if they did not have business objectives. While they do project the culture of a community, they do so through a lens which reflects the basic political and economic ideologies of their ownership. So, as noted previously, the media normally behave as boosters like the Chamber of Commerce with whom their publishers and editors "do lunch." Because they are in business, the media, collectively, follow their communities and seldom lead in setting out policy positions. They are a conservative, not innovative, force in society, closely linked to existing hierarchies and the status quo. The central equation is that advertising yields profits, businesses advertise where there are larger numbers of viewers or readers, and these larger numbers are built through info-tainment that challenges neither cultural precepts nor threaten socio-economic position.

As well, since the significant municipal politics of other major cities are seldom reported in local publications, this vigorous "villaging" in the mass media reinforces another dimension of a vertically integrated media age. The "news," universally similar and with no surprises, is pressed out by a large organization comprising thousands of persons: "The fact that the messages are assembled in an organization, with many persons involved, helps to neutralize the idiosyncrasies of individuals; the messages bear the stamp of the organization" (Siegel 1996: 20). The result is that few citizens, unless they themselves religiously work the Internet, can fashion independent standards from comparative sources against which to measure the local political agenda and the performance of their own city's indigenous political classes. City electors are abandoned by the media to the critical leadership abilities of local cosmopolitans and the UMC elites which we have previously discussed.

For example, Kaplan's analysis of the early years in Metro Toronto policy-making credits the mass media's unity of outlook on the original necessity for intergovernmental reforms in 1953 to the general absence of an ideological spectrum in the city's local politics itself (1967: 170-72). The obvious problem with such analysis is that the observation could equally be sustained where there exists an environment in which such ideologically dissenting elements as did exist were, at the time, denied any visibility or prominence by not being reported in the business booster media. This today represents the concern represented in the phrase "the engineering of consent," and also contributes to acceptance of the view that while many may have a say, none is directly responsible for the final shape of the resultant satisficing, system-sustaining public policy.

8.3.1 A one-way flow in a two-step process

The theory of communications in democratic societies summarizes the process of news communication as a one-way flow in a two-step process. This central hypothesis maintains that since so very few of us witness potentially newsworthy events directly, we are dependent upon the reported *interpretation* of these events by others—a handful, relatively, of editors and reporters—for the "factual basis" upon which we base our own assessments. This is a one-way flow of information in which even the selection of what to convey as news is at the discretion of the press gallery—the public agenda for policy is set by these gatekeepers. "The media exert influence not merely through their choice of certain issues for emphasis in news presentation and editorial comment, but also through the omission of others" (Siegel 1996: 22). Media consumption is not a shared experience for, as is clearly not the case in face-to-face conversation, the structure of the medium provides little opportunity for immediate and direct feedback to newsmakers: "because sender and audience are linked by some medium, no direct contact occurs" (Siegel 1996: 19).

The two-step pillar of the theory is important here. Reporters seeking comment and assessment communicate their understanding of the facts of an event, decision, or policy question to persons in leadership positions in a range of specific, but potentially conflicting, policy communities in the specific policy arena. The assessments of these opinion leaders are, in turn, incorporated into news coverage. In theory, the interested citizen is then provided with both basic data and alternative assessments of the events, decisions, or specific questions. Even from this one-way flow, citizens have been supplied the ammunition to participate as fully and effectively in the policy process as they should subsequently choose.

However, the real practice diverges from theory. For example, in 2002, municipal councillors in Edmonton were presented by their administration with a proposition that would reverse a 20-year fiscal strategy focused on the elimination of long-term debt. The administration intended to borrow $50 million annually to build "necessary" road works, police substations, and so forth. To sustain the debt would result in either increased mill rates or policy substitution choices. Adequate press gallery reporting ought to have included not only a detailed summation of bureaucratic priorities and the immediate reactions of the talking heads on council (the easiest path), but also would have sought and conveyed comment from fiscal conservatives

(Canadian Taxpayers' Federation, Canadian Federation of Independent Business, Chamber of Commerce), from policy communities supportive of infrastructure enhancements (Alberta Motor Association, community leagues in the affected policing subdivisions, building trades unions), from experts or pundits with longer time perspectives (university or college researchers, community historians), and from data banks focused on municipal budgets, such as that established by the Canada West Foundation or CTF. Individual citizens would then have had a short opportunity window in which to have an informed word with their representatives. None of the second part of this hypothetical picture was realized, which is the usual case for the reporting of Canadian city politics.

The practical implications for a healthy locally democratic state are several. If the local political culture is dynamic, characterized as one in which multiple, conflicting policy communities are continuously attentive, energetic, and vocal, then the press gallery has easy access to policy assessments from leaders or spokespersons in a variety of informed but competitive policy communities. Citizens as readers and viewers will in turn gain the means by which they may sort and assess what their city's managers are really up to. If, though, the community political culture tends to the inactive, or is overly deferential to persons in authority, then media coverage may become public relations cheerleaders for city hall. Tindal and Tindal observe, "It can be argued, however, that the media have contributed to the limited public participation in local government by their generally poor performance in providing information about, and promoting understanding of, local government" (2000: 304). In a curious fashion, city hall activities are virtually de-politicized to become the administration of the status quo where the essence of the status quo is not to be questioned and different perspectives on its legitimacy are not voiced.

As far back as the early 1960s, Kaplan noted that the deference accorded persons in authority positions characteristic of Canadian political culture generally had consequences for municipal policy-making in Toronto (1967: 209). He was subsequently to despair over the weak attention paid Metro-level council decisions in these terms: "The only significant source of private influence over metro Council proceedings is the Toronto press [which] is due not so much its pressure on local officials but to its providing clear guidelines for choice in highly fluid policy-making situations" (1972: 222). Overall, it was the press gallery which defined the issues, set the agenda, and structured the alternatives for councillors. In this sense, the press gallery and the editorialists provided an unquestioned ideological rationale for the whole policy-making operation (Kaplan 1967: 179). Where the political culture of municipal political communities is relatively docile, as was argued in Chapter

3, with few ongoing, organized, locally interested pressure groups, then political leadership tends to become preoccupied with their role as technical managers (e.g., the Metropolitan Toronto and Region Transportation Study designs of the 1960s) rather than as political representatives. There is no question that the media play a role in the diminished political responsibility of this culture, an accommodating accomplice seduced by booster sirens.

There are also lingering realities which may be considered problem areas. Consistently, analysis shows that newspapers remain the principal agency shaping public opinion in local politics. Masson very accurately observes: "Local television stations are even more reluctant [than radio] to commit resources to reporting on municipal politics, and when they do, the coverage tends to be in the form of superficial 15-second segments" (1994: 265).

There is very little in the way of proactive issue investigation in any of the mainstream media in the age of corporate convergence. Apart from an occasional spate of interest which follows publicly documented conflicts of interest by well-known personalities, Canadian cities see little policy or personality crusades in the press. This was not always so. In the postwar period, several communities experienced "Clean Up City Hall" campaigns led by the local press. Prominent among these were stories in *Le Devoir* in Montreal against the regime of Mayor Camillien Houde (1944-54) whose blatantly corrupt practices led to a judicial inquiry and the election of its lead investigator, Jean Drapeau, as successor mayor. The *Edmonton Journal* in the late 1950s and mid-1960s campaigned against the ethical (and legal) shortcomings of Mayor William Hawrelak, producing judicial inquiries in both instances, his resignation the first time, and his removal from office the second. Today, newspapers are more interested in reporting the fantasy outcomes of television reality shows than what goes on at city hall.

If there is to be tangible accountability in city politics, the position of the mass media is particularly important because of the general lack of anything approaching adequate widespread competing channels for local information. In the modern urban community, what the ordinary citizen "knows" to be true about public policy, in general terms as opposed to that policy which directly affects them as individuals and stakeholders, is very seldom learned at first hand. Hence, the press gallery of any legislature is important simply through being the conduit of "the facts" by which citizens make personal judgements.

The reporters and editors of the mass media also become an integral part of the political and economic system upon which they report. It is unsurprising that they tend to act to legitimate the established political process locally just as they do in national and substate regional politics (Clement 1975: 270-285; Porter 1965: 216 ff; Miliband 1973: 196-213). Most citizens do not take the time to find out, at first-hand, what councils are up to, nor do we have sufficient access to the clinical data of reports, program evaluations, and budgets to develop our own perspective on particular claims and activities even where we care. So the media provide a sort of shorthand which, if accurate, is sufficient foundation for local democratic accountability. In political life, personal perception is the reality that motivates activity, and any "truth" is relative to what one believes is true or not. So, the essential uniformity of the message emanating from the city hall press gallery no matter how much it may be at odds with realities but because it is consistent overall, validates even dysfunctional institutions and power relationships.

The small number of individuals who comprise the local government press gallery perform a service in the accurate reporting of councillor comments even as they indulge the natural tendency to sanitize remarks from those they like personally. They are very much part of the system on which they report. Reporters on the **city hall beat** tend to lose their "professional" detachment, trading on insider information to become little more than another cog in the city's public relations, tub-thumping machinery.

On balance, and even in the low politics of cities, through their reporting the media work to disseminate "ideas and values which affirm rather than challenge existing patterns of power and privilege …" (Miliband 1973: 211). Speaking of reporters and elections, a jaded and defeated Toronto mayoral candidate Stephen Clarkson observed, that "Some had grown to accept the way the system worked and tended to observe political challenges in the same light as did the incumbents: a threat to the established way of carrying on city business" (Clarkson 1972b: 147). In plainly practical terms, for reporters working closely on a daily basis in a closed system with the same people about whom they are reporting, it becomes easy enough to develop close interpersonal ties; a shorthand political jargon; a shared world view of prospects, limitations and friends and enemies; and a stake in lifeguarding the status quo. In too many locales, this symbiotic claque is abetted by the council's poor record of informative public relations coupled to a proclivity to promote a culture of secrecy in their conduct of city business.

Finally, one mechanism occasionally used by officials and often by candidates to try to circumvent the reporters' web is the **press conference**. Taras assesses this public activity very concisely: "For a strong thinker and debater, the news conference is always an opportunity; for a less able politician it can degenerate into a nightmare" (1988: 40). Even when not a spontaneous media scrum, the live press conference requires quick thinking, adequate knowledge of material (i.e., a "good brief"), and the debater's skill in deflecting the unanticipated query. Most in municipal politics are not so well versed. Effective behaviour is most difficult for those outside the system who have not yet mastered the working shorthand which incumbents and reporters have shared on the job. If the city hall beat is only to be about management detail and administration, then one alien turn of phrase can quickly jeopardize any candidate's otherwise unimpeachable authority.

Further of note here is that, from the gladiator's perspective and in practical terms, an active politician must learn one fundamental rule very quickly: one must never mislead or lie to a reporter. Members of the media will always have the last word. The politician has two options. First is to tell the reporter that one cannot respond completely; politicians are under no obligation to relay everything that they know. No active political gladiator should remark upon any report or document before reading it. The second option is to shut up; political activists too often find themselves in difficulty when they feel compelled to comment for comment's sake.

Rule one of crisis management in politics is that bad facts cannot be made into good facts by any amount of **political spin**. A stage can be built for the facts' presentation, and an appropriate response can be planned. But bad news is effectively that, and political spin inevitably becomes a corkscrew winding downwards.

8.3.2 A small note on ethical applications for the media

There is not much doubt that suburban residents are ill-served by the city-region media since the metropolitan dailies (and electronics) basically ignore them. Their own local operations report only the most banal "news" interspersed among their *raison d'être*, the local business advertisements. Suburban newspapers often operate on a fiscal shoestring; many persist only with *de facto* subsidies: "In return for publishing minutes and notices the council contracts with a weekly newspaper for free distribution to all of its ratepayers" (Masson 1994: 268). The general proclivity of smaller communities' newspapers is to endorse the local notables who are, after all, the folks with whom the staff mingles socially. City-wide, even the larger mainstream media have seldom proven as vigilant in the promulgation and practice of stringent ethical guidelines for their own operations as they have been in prescribing for other professions and, of course, for gladiators in the political life. In the smaller suburban communities that ring city-region core municipalities, the working relationship is even less formal. It is not unknown to see reporters rebuked by politicians for a story that, in the council's assessment, impugns the reputation of the councillors and, by extension, the economic well-being of the community.

Suburban print operations are also very heavily reliant on local advertising as there are few national advertising accounts evident in their pages.

Partly because of this, they are seldom capable of any real separation of editorial, advertising, and print shop functions, since it is usually the same people who must perform all of these tasks. They thus need access to local "authorities" as news sources and advertisers, and so they regularly screen out unfortunate items that question friends' turpitude. It is also natural to overlook occasional malfeasance by councillors themselves such as, perhaps, the addition of a "working lunch" so that a regional policy committee will pay a full, not half, day's *per diem*. A circular general stake in the status quo based on the existing local council-subsidized subscriptions, advertising, and job printing, carries on. In the larger central cities, obvious but probably questionable practices range from the flogging of tickets for the home town sports teams, the promotion of world-class international games and exhibitions and shilling for new stadiums, to the 1950s-style booster jingoism of the business and city sections.

It will be noted, in the context of proposed city-region consolidations, that the suburban press retains the close interpersonal linkages to councils noted above and are linked into a protection network of "community identity." If municipal amalgamation occurs, then their fear is that the easy revenues will dry up. So editors and reporters easily and always indulge in "safe crusades" against consolidations, a measure in tandem with the town council's policies. Otherwise, on a day-to-day basis, media editorial policies are consistently booster since even a small new development may have a significant positive impact on assessment and tax revenues for the town and even new advertising for the paper.

8.3.3 Other notes concerning ethical conduct

A century back, the early beginnings of the study of interest group politics found its roots in muckraking, or journalism focused on uncovering the unholy linkages between office-holders and those seeking state favours (blatant patronage) of one sort or another. Throughout the twentieth century, especially during periods of accelerated urban growth, instances of favouritism, preference, and *quid pro quo* driven public policy were not at all uncommon. This was particularly so in the suburbs ringing the city cores of metropolitan regions; it was in these lands that public watchdogs were few, the local media quiescent and too often complicit, and academic observation either disinterested or oblivious. Siegel argues that the media in smaller centres generally subscribe to the attitude "you have to go along to get along"; further, "Small-town newspapers usually hire only young and inexperienced reporters who seldom know a lot about local government and who may overlook serious problems" (1993: 220). Moreover, as noted, media owners have easily bought into the community notables' broader design to prevent their suburb from "looking bad."

Those who have chronicled questionable practice at city hall have most often done so by illustrative cases usually focused on a single colourful central character like mayors Houde or Drapeau in Montreal, Hays in Calgary, or Hawrelak in Edmonton (see, for example, Lorimer 1972; Gibbons and Rowat 1976; Magnusson and Sancton 1983; Langford and Tupper 1993). That the interested public has not, over the years, been more systemically outraged is perhaps a function of the petty aggrandizement of the public officials when stacked against the overall wealth generated by the economic machine of Canadian urban development.

What might be rightfully considered as wrongdoing in Canadian city politics these days? Perennial ethical dilemmas have hovered round the two issues of the patent manipulation of the land development process by those with a monetary interest in the outcome and the more traditional exploitation of public position for direct personal gain. In 1962, Alan Phillips described 1950s urban Canadian developments: "Breach of trust falls into two classes: 'honest graft' and 'conflict of interest.' The first is most profitable in Quebec, where open political brigandry appears to carry little if any stigma" (1962). In a later publication, he added that when Mayor Jean Drapeau initiated his movement to clear out corruption at Montreal's city hall he spoke of "the complicity of honest people, the silence and inactivity of honest people" (1976: 85, 101). Bryce (1888) had indicted similar behaviours among the American moneyed elite nearly a century earlier. Such marginal behaviours have hardly disappeared into the dustbins of history. In September 2003, a Quebec judge ruled that sufficient evidence of wrongdoing on the part of two councillors in the Montreal suburb of St. Laurent existed to permit a trial on charges of municipal corruption, breach of trust, and defrauding the government; they had accepted a $75,000 kickback involving a real estate zoning (CanWest News Service, 4 September 2003).

More usually, action solutions are related to the precise nature of the transgression, be it honest graft, **spiffs**, or special other peccadilloes.

8.3.3.1 HONEST GRAFT

Over-enthusiastic boosterism occasionally causes some city councillors to become so carried away with civic "progress" that they may equate their own personal wealth accumulation during the official performance of duties with community well-being. Ari Hoogenboom concisely defines honest graft as akin to insider trading on the stock market: "the profit that flowed from advance information on future government action" (1970: 277). Such graft is "honest" only insofar as no money has been directly pilfered out of the city hall treasury. This is an issue quite different from councillors breaking municipal rules without profit in mind. This latter behaviour came to light in Newfoundland in 2000 when over 130 local politicians were to be thrown out of office by the province for failure to pay municipal taxes on time. The new provincial statute and subsequent action came into existence because councillors were reluctant to fire their own members under provisions of the previous statute. Where behaviours are not explicitly governed by the Criminal Code, these practices are now largely regulated by provincial law as conflict of interest under provincial planning, municipal government, or conflict-of-interest acts.

As we have seen, the best Canadian municipal exemplar of honest graft was Edmonton's Mayor William Hawrelak (Lightbody 1993: 207-10). Over the years he was in office, Hawrelak used his position to profit himself, his two brothers-in-law, and sundry business friends and associates. He purchased land for motel development made possible through zoning changes he initiated, he acquired land from the city at deflated prices for future construction, he misled council on the details and kept administrators in the dark, he arranged land swaps with Chrysler for personal profit, and voted in council in contravention of Planning Act provisions. He resigned for "gross misconduct" in 1959 and was "disqualified" from office in 1965 by court order. By the standard of virtually any day or place, he was corrupt.

These are matters which will usually place but one person in conflict with the law and personal conscience. For instance, Winnipeg councillor Dave Brown ran for mayor in the 1992 election, after conflict-of-interest allegations arose concerning his subcontracting firm receiving a contract for which he had lobbied and had voted for in council (Greene and Shugarman 1997: 109). Conflict of interest is "This type of corruption (or potential corruption) [that] does not require a second actor or group of actors, as in the case of patronage, bribery or graft. Conflict of interest is between the actor and the public interest, that is, between a person and a social construct, which may be thought of as 'the whole community.' The rewards for such behaviour go only to one person or group. Thus, there is no transaction process" (Gibbons 1976: 11). Since the 1972 Conflicts of Interest Act in Ontario, the onus is placed on local councillors to declare their "pecuniary" interests on matters coming before councils. In this area, the practical remedy has historically been public censure, and the ballot box is perceived to be the ultimate sanction.

8.3.3.2 SPIFFS

Baksheesh, a tip or present, is essential in dealings with the public officials of many pre-industrial societies. But Canadians have little reason to be smug in this realm, although the practice is discreet and somewhat obscured by the genteel veneer of the collaborators. An open style of grafting occurs when a public official fancies some kind of compensation before providing a service to the public that is reasonably expected from his job, such as the issuance of a building permit or public health inspection certificate. The practice differs from honest graft in that these are the activities of two or more individuals. Essentially, when initiated from the top outward this behaviour is, plainly put, bribery and is now dealt with through the Canadian Criminal Code. Gibbons made the obvious point clear: "Graft, like bribery, can take place only when the political actor has official status, since only an official can grant or withhold the services required" (1976: 11).

Spiffs are a variant of open graft or bribery. "Businessmen are accustomed to giving contracts to friends and relatives. Manufacturers woo purchasing agents with gifts. 'Spiffs'—cash paid to salesmen and store managers for pushing a brand of merchandise—are common practice" (Gibbons 1976: 102). People holding local public office are frequently presented with small gifts as a genuine token for their efforts on behalf of, say, a community league, service club, or other such. A traditional rule-of-thumb for local councillors has been never to accept anything which cannot be eaten, drunk, or smoked in a single day. Canada's most flagrant municipal grafter, Edmonton's Mayor Hawrelak accepted spiffs however when, as mayor, he was retained on the payroll of Loblaws at a "commission" of $20,000 per year while that corporation sought a warehouse site in the city (Lightbody 1993: 208). At the turn of the century, public drunk and cynic Bob Edwards had observed of this sort of behaviour in his *Calgary Eye-Opener* that "Graft is still graft, even if you call it a commission" (Hamilton 1952: 52).

In Chapter 5, we saw two instances of spiff: the Illinois state legislature's poker game disguise and the Ontario York region card games (see page 213). What is important is that supplicants for and suppliers of municipal services could sort things out privately at these games, and, if any favours were exchanged, that process too was private. In an unrelated criminal proceeding against a Metro Toronto councillor in 1992, Greene and Shugarman report the testimony of a major land developer who reported spending around $70,000 a year to "wine and dine" municipal politicians: "He also described his dining of politicians as 'a reward for something that might happen in the future ... He said he was not unique among developers'" (1997: 110).

In the 1950s, Calgary Mayor Don Mackay accepted "a few gifts" which wound up the subject of a judicial inquiry and censure: "From a Montreal financier seeking bus and sewer service for an apartment project—a dishwasher. From a land development company—$1,200 worth of furniture. From the agent of a New York syndicate seeking to buy city land—free flights to Mexico and Hawaii, and two $2,000 'loans,' both written off" (Phillips 1976: 87). The mayor admitted nothing but "lack of judgement." Personal corruption infiltrated even Montreal Mayor Drapeau's "clean government" regime when the investigation of the 1976 Olympics revealed that the country house of the chair of the executive committee had been built for free by a major Olympic contractor (Sancton 1983: 74). In smaller suburbs (Markham), Siegel has reported that the mayor and some officials were able to purchase new subdivision homes at deflated prices; building inspectors later charged that infractions had been ignored by superiors (1993: 228).

Siegel observed that favour is also curried through frequent invitations to private boxes during sporting events, an excellent time to consider the virtue of development proposals. In Edmonton, Mayor Hawrelak attended the 1956 Grey Cup with his grocery friends. He left behind the proposed plans (and traffic patterns) for a new subdivision (Lightbody 1993: 208). In the summer of 2000, several Edmonton councillors accepted the invitation of a major private utility, ATCO, to attend the annual Spruce Meadows equestrian show west of Calgary. During the subsequent public furor, the company's vice-president resigned on the ethical issue, but no councillor admitted any wrongdoing.

To prevent such wrong-doing, all provinces should move by statute the requirement for full and open disclosure of gifts. The 1994 Ontario Local Government Disclosure of Interest Act required local officials not only to disclose assets and to refrain from potential situations placing them in conflict of interest, but also to refuse compromising gifts. The appointment of a municipal commissioner for local conflicts of ethics was also broached but has yet to be acted upon (Greene and Shugarman 1997: 111).

8.3.3.3 OTHER PECCADILLOES

Systemic abuse of powers over patronage in employment and through untendered contracts is now largely reduced in the municipal world except in smaller towns and among the suburbs within larger city-regions (Siegel 1993: 227-28). Influence peddling—the use of one's "good offices" to sway another official's decision on a matter—has seldom been a matter of much concern in Canada's local politics, arguably due to the low stakes in the game. But, in his critique of the apparent symbiotic relationship between "the property industry" (property investors, insurance and real estate agents, property lawyers, architects, contractors and suppliers, building trade unions) and the greater number of elected city politicians, Lorimer presented the case 30 years ago that those involved in property development were able to exercise fairly direct control in a number of ways (1972: 107). They provided dependable financial support for election expenses and nourished a mentality at city hall that growth and development were positive city attributes: "no one should stand in the way of progress."

Quebec's municipal campaigns are today waged under provincial campaign finance legislation; the 1994 municipal election resulted in 212 charges of illegal fund-raising against Vision Montreal, the victorious party, and a fine of $800. In 1988, the *Globe and Mail* reported that three-quarters of municipal campaign contributions in the Greater Toronto Area (GTA) came from the property industry (Greene and Shugarman 1997: 109). The province's legislation now limits donations from a single source to $750 and disclosure of more than $100.

The industry also provides "friendship" which, as in the age of the bosses, may entail carrots in the way of sly advice on property investment or help with their businesses in the property sector. In some instances after a particularly helpful political career, and in the same sense that the retired military gravitate to the gravy of defence contractors, there have also been job prospects for retired mayors or councillors in the realty development, mortgage, or contracting fields (Lightbody 1993: 205). Of course these industries are not only acquiring expertise and insider knowledge, but also persons who have friends on the inside. A few developers prefer the personal touch to the point of directly intervening in council deliberations from the public gallery to ensure that "their" councillors keep the faith and vote correctly (Greene and Shugarman 1997: 109; Lightbody 1993: 206).

Here, the solution is to develop and enforce provincial laws governing municipal campaign finance, to clarify conflict-of-interest provisions, and to provide an ethics commissioner to guide (and, if necessary, to prosecute) local office-holders. Provinces must be extremely cautious about empowering any elected body itself to remove any of its own members from office, even for summary offences. What of individuals who are charged during incidents of civil disobedience to which the council majority does not subscribe? It may also be time to reconsider the recall as a special attribute extolled in rhetoric as that level of governing "closest to the people."

The city today is no longer a new frontier for Canadian politics, one in which raw individualism, reinforced by state patronage and ceaselessly repeated, is a requisite for rapid development. For local governments, the old rules set by British precedent and rooted in widely shared cultural notions of fair play are, plainly put, insufficient. Why is there no registry of lobbyists at any city hall in Canada even if the small problem is the question: who to count?

All of the observations in this section introduce larger questions that must be addressed in city government. They relate to declaring potential conflicts of interest, to defining codes of conduct, to providing an ethical reference point in the form of a public commission, and to modernizing the financing of local elections. Siegel argues persuasively, for instance, that the onus to prosecute councillors for transgression should be removed from individual taxpayers and charged to some sort of quasi-autonomous provincial commission with the authority to resolve disputes and terminate errant behaviour (1993: 229). The court recourse would remain only as a last resort.

Speaking generally, Tupper and Langford maintain that "The problem is the system, not the quality of the officials or the rules that govern their conduct" (1993: 15). Essentially, they argue that the base concept of a broad public interest must be re-invigorated. Phillips presaged this with his note that "Misgovernment of the people is misgovernment by the people. Corrupt politicians are representative. They are only doing what many people would do if they could" (1976: 102). For most Canadian city electors, this is no longer good enough.

PART III

Intergovernmental Issues
and Metropolitan Governing

nine | Relations among governments

Canadian municipal government in the twentieth–first century is still influenced by nineteenth–century practice and law. Not only is the head of city council formally addressed by the Victorian "Your Worship," but the powers assigned by almost all provincial statutes to that role are equally archaic. From the Municipal Corporations (Baldwin) Act of 1849 to the present, Canadian municipal councils have not been much trusted by central governments.

In calling for a "good system of municipal institutions" as a matter of vital importance, Lord Durham in his 1839 Report wrote that "Instead of confiding the whole collection and distribution of all the revenues raised in any country for all general and local purposes to a single representative body, the power of local assessment, and the application of the funds arising from it, should be entrusted to local management" (Craig 1964: 145). As an English politician, Durham understood that little altruism attached to democratic politics, and he knew that the surrender of these revenues would not be "voluntarily made" by representative central governing bodies. Consequently, he argued that the Crown would have to supervise such a division of revenues "until the people should become alive, as most assuredly they almost immediately would be, to the necessity of protecting their local privileges" (Craig 1964: 145). This early statement of the need to raise local funds exclusively for local purposes was affirmed in 1867: the Fathers of Confederation, notwithstanding the underlying imperative to protect cultural distinctions within existing colonial political boundaries, still thought the provinces themselves to be somewhat akin to large local governments, and thus restricted their revenues to direct taxation, while reserving any residual powers to the Canadian national government.

In this chapter, we will examine the distribution of authority between Canada's municipalities and the governments whose wider powers both in territory and in constitutional jurisprudence keeps community-level government subordinate in what European observers have called **central-local relations**.

9.1 Central-Local Intergovernmental Affairs

While it is all well and good to think of the many policy relevant dimensions of society, economy, and ideology that make demands upon Canada's cities in isolation, it must be strongly emphasized that municipalities work their policy processes within the complexities of a hierarchically structured and intergovernmental state. The political economy approach reminds us to observe the impacts upon local decision-makers' autonomy of the many public and private choices taken outside their direct influence (Leo 1995b). Because municipalities appear as well-established structures of authority, however, and because they are both so familiar and considered so legitimate that their current form is thought immutable, there is a tendency for us not to consider just how adaptive the city subsystem can be if subjected to external stress. The apparent inertia perpetuated by some elements within local urban regimes is based on their rough calculations of the benefits of the status quo carried forward. But can it also be said that complexity in the institutions of governing also abets natural drift?

9.1.1 Conditions limiting innovative change

Changes in and to city institutions have seldom been very radical; at least four central premises persist to constrain possibilities.

1. The very nature of adaptive change tends to make it gradual and incremental. The Municipal Corporations (Baldwin) Act (1849) stood in effect in Ontario until the regional government reforms of the 1970s, and even those corrections (albeit affecting about one-third of the provincial population) were hardly "systemic" or a drastic rethinking. The basic form of Quebec's municipalities was established in 1855. Outside Metro Winnipeg, Manitoba's local boundaries were pretty much set in 1902, and the same can be said for rural Saskatchewan since 1909. Until the 1990s, except as has been noted or will be, other provinces have only tinkered with modest institutional overlays upon existing municipalities outside their city-region heartlands.

2. According to section 92.8 of the Constitution, municipalities are the exclusive creatures of the provinces, and there is no constitutional basis whatever for their continuance as autonomous local and democratic entities. Any councillor who argues otherwise is merely posturing for some personal purpose; provincial politicians, usually when in opposition, who propose that this relationship will be genuinely altered through their future benign attentions are uninformed or insincere. In times of financial exigency, or in extreme instances of moral or ethical turpitude, provincial governments have always been prepared to intervene directly as necessary to restore economic confidence in the city or to dismiss the offending local authorities.

3. In this light, the provinces have more than conscientiously preserved their constitutional entitlement over municipalities even when displaying political reluctance to exercise its possibilities. For instance, annexations and amalgamations remain under the powerful scrutiny of various arms' length municipal boards, and municipalities must, by law, balance their annual operating budgets, barring extreme circumstances that may warrant specific exemption by the provincial government. Notwithstanding the statements concerning enhanced municipal autonomy which ministers sometimes make in the artificial enthusiasm of a speech at conventions of municipal officials, no province has ever surrendered its general powers over planning, appeals, and capital borrowing. Indeed, the Alberta cabinet in 1974 unilaterally established Restricted Development Areas around Calgary and Edmonton at the behest of its Environmental Department, at points up to five miles wide (Feldman and Graham 1979: 74-78). Ontario has acted to preserve lands along the Niagara escarpment and the Oak Ridges moraine from urban development, and British Columbia has done the same with respect to agricultural preservation, especially in the lower mainland. No province has ever ceded even symbolic authority to the federal government.

4. All provinces have sustained their prerogatives over the supervision and restriction of local governments. This tradition extends back to the nineteenth century when the central government balanced decentralization to

municipalities (so as to be able to raise funds locally for local public works) with a central control under the pretence of protecting the credit of the municipality. In reality this euphemism then, and now, thinly masked the propertied elite's general worry, which had been reinforced by a misreading of some excesses in the practice of Jacksonian democracy south of the border, that any extension of popular democratic control of the local council into the hands of unpropertied electors would escalate expenditures. They feared that since the financing of municipalities was to come from the property tax, the costs of any local improvements would have to be met directly from the pocketbooks of the small number of local property owners and gentry.

Today the Canadian provinces' central relationship with local governments remains one of "control and guidance." Provincial supervision develops primarily through the departments of Municipal Affairs and Education, although all ministries, especially Transportation and Environment, play some policy role in relation to local administrations. The notion of control has more sensitive political overtones; most provinces have created quasi-independent regulatory agencies to check, curtail, or constrain local initiatives. The existence of agencies in sensitive policy areas such as annexations allows ministers the luxury during question period in the legislature or in press scrums, to refuse other than general hypothetical comment since "the matter is currently before the XYZ board."

In short, even the most recently constituted of Canada's municipal governments are quite distinctly the creatures of provincial ministries, as well as bound by statute structures defined during the period of nineteenth-century liberal political philosophy, which stressed regulation and protection (i.e., a **negative state**). Since structures have not been reformed or altered in their central power relationships radically or systemically, how have they been able to accommodate the many new demands inevitably arising from the stress of modernization?

9.1.2 Local government and the growth of the positive state

Before the emergence of the integrated postmodern service economy, the modernization of Canada was assessed by its degree of urbanization and industrialization. Just 100 years ago, most Canadian municipalities were pretty much self-contained local economic units. Local boundaries were meaningful, and trade was exchanged between manufacturing base, marketplace, and hinterland. Modernization meant that, as individuals lost self-sufficiency, they had to focus on the state to protect them from economic circumstances over which they had no control. As Simmons and McCann point out, "Left to itself, the private sector typically creates a series of economic crises" (2000: 114). That is, populations' needs generally do not vary greatly for health, education, potable water, roads, and so forth, but commerce is cyclical and thus variable. The instruments of the **positive state** became a kind of insurance against the most debilitating consequences of an economic downturn.

So, the positive state had to do more than protect against military invasion, regulate the marketplace, and protect manufacturing through tariff barriers. Even at the municipal level, it was expected to expand beyond paying the constable, paving selected streets, and protecting public health. All levels of the state were expected to minimize individual social and economic distress through a growing packet of interventionist and redistributive public policies. As we observed in Chapter 3, philosophical liberals sought an "equality of opportunity," or level playing field, on which all persons could achieve their personal best in life, while social democrats sought an "equality of condition" by alleviating the most desperate circumstances and raising disadvantaged citizens to a higher state in real life. Even minimalist liberal justifications led to provincial administrative intervention as ministries watched over upgrades made by municipal authorities in service areas (for instance, in social welfare) that had historically been exclusively private community concerns.

Increasingly, city governments in the twentieth century had to devise, and incrementally advance, minimum service standards in response to demands by an increasingly mobile, educated, and observant public. Calculations of this new electoral power led to provincial and federal interest and involvement, by one means or another, within areas that had at one time been exclusive municipal policy bailiwicks like social services and unemployment relief. City governments also had to cope with the bitter reality that the interdependencies of the modern age changed the nature of some state functions from those that one municipality could provide in isolation into matters that involved larger scale regional institutions; the eco-management of watersheds is an obvious case in point.

9.1.3 The permissive and mandatory world

One very practical consequence for central-local relations has been a blurring of the historic (and legal, or *de jure*) distinction between the **permissive** and **mandatory powers** of municipalities. Higgins pointed out that provinces fairly precisely dictate what their local governments may, may not, and must do (1986: 86-93). Local governments across Canada are corporations whose powers are defined by provincial statute law. No matter how large or self-important they may be, municipalities may not pursue innovative policy choices (even if validated by electors' demands or legitimized by the relevant policy community) should the respective province's legislation not reasonably specifically permit them to do so. To lack recourse to statutory authority means that a municipality is open to court challenge for its proposed activity on the grounds of *vires* (i.e., whether or not the action lies within its legislative competence). Debates over the question of whether or not a city government has the jurisdiction to deliver a service contribute much to the appearance that the posturing about the legal ability to undertake an activity is a surrogate for taking that action itself.

The problem is not as silly as it appears. In 1996, the city council in Nanaimo, British Columbia, permitted Rascal Trucking to deposit 15,000 cubic yards of soil on leased lands. Noise and dust fuelled citizen objections to the mound that reached 20 metres high and twice led the council to rescind their permission. Ultimately, city employees removed the mound. Rascal Trucking challenged this action in court, and the provincial Court of Appeal ruled in its favour on grounds that British Columbia's Municipal Government Act (MGA) gave council permission to declare as nuisances only watercourses and "buildings, structures, or erections of any kind." That decision was appealed to the Supreme Court of Canada. In March 2000, the court ruled (7–0) that Nanaimo had the power to act and that council had not behaved in a "patently unreasonable" manner even though the MGA did not specifically refer to "mounds of dirt." Justice Major, speaking for the court, noted, "A pile of dirt does not materialize on its own. It must at least be erected presumably by piling or dumping." The Supreme Court, in developing a doctrine of deference to municipal councils in this instance, warned lower courts generally to defer to local councils on matters within a municipality, expanding presumption of authority to include the "patently unreasonable" test. Justice Major added, "Municipal councillors are elected by the constituents they represent and as such are more conversant with the exigencies of their community than are the courts" (SCR 2000: 343–44). Notwithstanding this decision, consistent past experience suggests that local councils will remain cautious in expanding upon a narrow interpretation of what is permitted by provincial statute.

From the beginning, central authorities have required that substate regions undertake certain governing responsibilities and sustain such specified services at a particular standard. These are *the mandatory or compulsory obligations* of an incorporated local government. In the early years, these functions were largely in the areas of public health (controlling typhoid, for instance) and sanitation, public education, and policing. Today, these compulsory responsibilities of municipalities are typically to be found in reasonably specific provincial statutes like the Public Health Act or Environmental Protection Act.

Additionally, and more importantly as the twentieth century wore on, generalized provincial statutes such as some form of Municipal Government Act in each province *permitted or allowed local units* to do certain things if their councils wished. That is, a municipality might establish a transit system or full-time fire brigade, if it so wanted, but it was under no statutory obligation to do so. Clearly, larger and more complex cities were willing to expand to the full orbit of possible jurisdictions while smaller cities, or suburbs with more particularized (i.e., exclusively upper-middle-class) populations, might choose to provide only a carefully selected few.

While the legal distinction between the mandatory and permissive categories of functions continues to exist, social and economic realities have discounted its authority. Even where a particular government function, such as a package of social services, is an elective choice, all provinces have exerted administrative pressures on localities to establish programs with province-wide standards of performance. Further, sometimes particular interests like the Canadian Home Builders Association, or a specific large developer, may well expect to be issued additional watershed conservation measures over and above traditional roadways, sewers, and street lighting plan provisions. More frequently, it is demand from a policy community, or even the wider public, that pressures councils to explore new activities and to emulate the programs in place in other roughly similar communities. For some time now, the public has not been prisoner to the vision within hometown local boundaries, so innovation means even more than "not tried here before." This outward-looking experience has contributed to progressively incremental upward standardization of service expectations. It is no longer foolish to expect that the standard set for the synchronization of traffic lights in Calgary, Alberta, is that which has already been achieved by Phoenix, Arizona.

Just as the permitted has become expected, some aspects of traditionally mandatory service have become more problematic. Urban municipalities in Canada, for instance, must provide residents with potable water, and now most *must* provide for at least secondary treatment of sewerage. Still, the latter can be a very costly proposition for rapidly growing municipalities, especially those which cannot contract easily with a wider area operation. In short, it is often difficult for provincial authorities to secure voluntary local compliance with mandatory regulations (and specific cases in point exist in British Columbia and Alberta), and yet it is rather inexpedient politically to punish offending councils with fines, dismissal, or imprisonment. Typically in such circumstances, the provinces have resorted to a strategy of bribery, which they have chosen to label "conditional grant programs" through which they offer to pay the cost in order to induce conformity with the law. A larger discussion of this issue follows below.

What citizens now expect of governments in their communities is much different from a century ago. Roads are not built through statute labour, the school is not a one-room multi-grade operation, social welfare is not exclusively a church-sponsored local charity, and, generally, the poor are not left alone to sicken and die. The data on state expenditures clearly reveals that the impact of the positive state since the Second World War has been felt most strongly at the provincial levels of government. Regardless of the party in power and its sustaining ideology, all provincial administrations in the last quarter of the twentieth century increased their spending similarly to satisfy economic and citizen requirements. And city governments have tagged along, putting a local administrative face to the delivery of central regime programs.

It is possible, however, to generalize about adaptations to the patterns of authority in the Canadian state under three general topics which we will next consider separately. These are (1) a realignment in the direct responsibility for specific state functions, (2) an evolution in the arrangements for financing service delivery, and (3) the continuing displacement of traditional structural frameworks.

9.2 Realignment of Central-Local Relations

The remarkable growth in public expectations for state intervention and support across industrialized nations has significantly contributed to a realignment of central-local relations with an eye to moving functional responsibility from the local community to wider area governments. These will presumably be possessed of sufficient resources to deliver specific services more proficiently and to spread the costs more evenly. At the beginning of this century, new localism citizen movements are both a reflection of, and serious reaction to, the contemporary significance of these institutional trends. Indeed, it is the case that certain types of regional governments, most commonly embracing larger city-regions and their more or less proximate hinterlands, have been created by central authorities precisely for the direct purpose of accepting the transfer of one or more local government functions from the municipalities whose boundaries they encompass. While by no means unique even in Canada, the GVRD is a case in point.

9.2.1 Upward shifts of responsibility

In Canada's provinces examples of functional transfers abound. New Brunswick abolished county government in 1967 under its Equal Opportunity program in order to assume responsibility for education, in the process reducing 562 locally accountable school boards to 33. In 1971, the province of Ontario took over assessment of real property, a highly protected local responsibility since the 1840s. In British Columbia, in 1997, functional responsibility for transit and arterial roadways was transferred from the provincial authorities onto the shoulders of the Vancouver city-region's special purpose district, the GVRD.

As positive state entitlements expanded over the course of the twentieth century, matters that were once thought the exclusive obligations of the local community were appropriated by the wider area provincial and federal regimes. Social assistance was once thought a family, church, or local charitable responsibility. The federal government now transfers resources directly to individuals of a certain age, or who are war veterans or students, or who have a specified disability, or who earn insufficient incomes. The provinces, under the tri-level Canada Assistance Plan, have played a considerable role in the design of standards, the administration of program specifics, and financing. Since the Second World War, unemployment insurance has been widely and incrementally adapted as an instrument of federal redistributive policy.

A clear transfer of functional responsibility among governments is unusual. In Canada, it happens most cleanly when regional, or metropolitan, governments are established expressly to accept the vertical shift of responsibility from existing municipalities to a wider area operation. The historical experience has shown that water, sewerage, and transportation (roads and transit) are the logical first choices for such policy action.

More frequently, the policy response to serious demands for state intervention is in some form of partnership arrangement among the levels of government involved; this permits the public representatives of each a say, a veto, and a photo-op. In the 1970s, for example, demands for more easily affordable housing prompted all levels to enter into agreements to assemble properties, to clear (not rehabilitate) slums, and to erect community housing. To some extent still, the three levels of the Canadian state all play major roles in the design and construction of this country's urban transportation networks. However, federal and provincial constitutional posturing in the last quarter of the twentieth century made new, innovative, local urban ambitions very difficult as any positive response by either Liberal or Progressive Conservative national governments was widely considered by at least the larger provinces to be a federal intrusion onto exclusive provincial turf. Still, a critic of some of these earlier tri-level activities notes that the Core Area Initiative in Winnipeg (1982-86) represented a successful tri-level operation inasmuch as new funds became available and the specific programs of differing government departments were coordinated on the problems within a focused geographic territory (Leo 1995b: 36–37).

9.2.2 Instigating a functional shift

It is sometimes the case that central governments take the first steps toward a functional adjustment inadvertently through making a financial investment to upgrade service benchmarks. Like the poorer provinces in Canadian federalism, some municipalities have been unable to provide for higher level performance through relying on their own restrictive taxation bases so that such desirable services are not universally available to all citizens. Specific conditional grant programs have been used by senior governments to help meet policy shortfalls. But in these cases the donor government is not directly administering and at some imprecise moment that funding government can make the choice to stop paying and start playing by assuming direct responsibility for the program. It must be observed that the constitution does not permit the transformation of a financial interest into a functional adjustment from the municipal level to the federal realm. There is no such inhibition between the local and the provincial.

Theoretically, central states can invigorate substate regions by decentralizing service delivery operations through a functional shift from the centre into the hands of citizens at the local community level. Notwithstanding this interesting hypothesis and its occasional successful application elsewhere, the reality in Canada has been that the greater number of important functional transfers have been vertically upward from the local to the wider area central government (usually provincial). The matter of the devolution of transit from the provincial government to GVRD responsibility is the most important recent exception that serves to illustrate the more general rule. That shift might also be understood, in policy terms, as having less to do with an awakening of new lines for formal authority than with an immediate partisan need on the eve of an election to fudge the provincial budget accounts through reallocating bookkeeping accountability for a large incurred public debt.

9.3 Evolution of Financial Arrangements

As was briefly discussed in Chapter 2, the scarcity of many kinds of resources (technological proficiencies, administrative and professionally skilled staff, money) to meet citizen demands constitutes one of the greater tribulations of political life. In the world of city politics, financial capacity appears especially limited, particularly in smaller communities or those with a limited non-residential tax base. Even within the social sciences, the most hard-hearted of apologists for entrepreneurialism recognize that it is by no means pain-less, even under conditions of austerity, to delete continuing policy programs to free resources for new purposes; such programs represent past (and thus policy system processed) and ongoing commitments to policy communities and citizens as clienteles (Osborne and Gaebler 1992: 25–75). A city could, theoretically, eliminate its subsidy to transit for the disabled to free those funds for its animal control division. Even though this scenario is less likely than its reverse, it is still highly improbable that any experienced council would ever put itself into the position of having to make such a choice.

9.3.1 Finding new funds

Municipal councils are not, by law, permitted to run a deficit on current (or operating) expenditures, although they may borrow for capital works. Con-sequently, if Canadian cities are to move beyond the incremental to upgrade existing programs or to undertake new services entirely, and if the taxation pool remains reasonably inelastic, then some kind of financial adjustment has to be made within the intergovernmental system. It is in this sphere of inter-governmental relations that various devices to move money from one level of the state to another are encountered. Money is moved from the federal government to the provinces and from both of these to local governments of all stripes. This activity also provides the most vexing set of perennial prob-lems for intergovernmental bargaining, and over time the financial adjust-ments themselves have become so complex as to obscure any possible direct accountability for success or deficiency in program delivery.

There are only two ways in which **transfer payments** can be made from one jurisdiction to another. In generic terms these may be labelled **conditional** and **unconditional grants**. These specific and general purpose grants from central governments constitute up to 40 per cent of any local government's revenues.

Unconditional grants are, quite simply and as the name implies, transfers of fiscal capacity from a jurisdiction with a more lucrative taxation endow-ment to another level of governing with no strings attached. The money goes directly into the general revenue fund of the recipient government. In federal-provincial relations, equalization payments from the central govern-ment to those provinces and territories meeting the criteria of relative pov-erty in population and taxation base are a prime example of this. Manitoba's budget revenues of $6.4 billion in 2000, for instance, depended upon federal equalization for 18.3 per cent of total income (personal income taxes were 26.3 per cent, and the provincial sales tax yielded another 14.8 per cent). Equalization is not connected to any other federal program (like medicare or, at one time, post-secondary education), and the recipient authorities are not required to initiate any specific activity with the funds. Federal and provincial grants to municipalities in lieu of property taxation (since local governments are unable, constitutionally, to tax any property of the Crown such as military bases) are similar. Since 1997, the federal government has agreed that these particular grants would be precisely what they would have been required to pay had their properties been subject to property taxation. Any grants-in-lieu program operates differently in each province.

Because there are no surprises in the politics of the operation of unconditional grants, they are unquestionably relished by recipient governments and not so well regarded by donors. The reason is simple. The recipient administration can meet demands, enhance programs and services, and win political credit from any expenditure, all without raising taxes or increasing user fees. On the other hand, the donor government must collect the tax resources before they can distribute them; has no hold over how the spending is done; and, since the funds have been pooled in the recipients' general revenues, finds that there is no grand opportunity to glean political glory. There are relatively few unconditional grant programs.

9.3.2 Understanding the roulette of conditional grants

Conditional grants are quite another matter. They appear in many forms and are also known as *shared-cost programs* or *grants-in-aid mechanisms*. Grants with program conditions are a concept inherited from the central Canadian experience of the 19th century (the UK has had such grants since 1835), with the first federal conditional grants dating back to 1900. They will undoubtedly be sustained through the twenty-first.

Although the concept of a tax on the value of real property for local spending purposes originated in the Middle Ages, it has not grown with policy expectations over time. Local own source revenues are nowhere near coincident with expenditure requirements today. Until recently in the UK, for example, one-fifth of the local budget came from fines, fees, licences, and charges; 40 per cent from central grants; and only one-third from property taxes. Whatever the euphemism, the conditional grant formula stipulates that one level of government will financially aid the projects or programs of another *if* specific conditions are met, *if* the program is initiated, and *if* the recipient ponies up a portion of the costs. So, for instance, a province may be willing to pay 90 per cent of costs for an arterial roadway around the urban core if the municipalities concerned agree to build it. If they do not, preferring perhaps to put money into an enhanced transit service, the province will not produce the cash. Or, in the case of sewerage treatment, if municipalities do not build to provincial Environment Department specifications for, say, secondary treatment levels, the respective province will not opt to forgive the capital loans for plants not built to their terms.

Internal choices may thus clash with external funding requirements. Even so, 20 years ago they constituted a larger source of local revenues than property taxation (Higgins 1986: 96). Of the nearly $30 billion now transferred to local governments in Canada from other levels, 98 per cent is from the provinces, and just under 90 per cent of that amount has conditions attached. This means that local priorities are set elsewhere. Just under two-thirds of federal funds to municipalities have been unconditional general grants with no ties to any stipulations, but the ratio of provincial to local conditional funding to general grants is usually about eight to one. Today in Canada, only around 50 per cent of local government revenues derive from the general property tax. Less than 1 per cent comes from permits and licences; at 0.65 per cent of revenues, the purpose of these is clearly control and regulation and not revenue generation.

As an important constitutional footnote, when any municipal government wishes to enter into a federal shared-cost program, it requires both provincial authorization and federal concurrence with working through provincial authorities. Lionel Feldman and Katherine Graham provide a well-documented example of the continuing problems in this area. Calgary and Edmonton solicited federal MSUA financial support for their general plan reviews in 1975. Alberta provincial officials quickly questioned the appropriateness of federal funding for activity directly under Alberta's Planning Act. In January 1977, the cities and the federal minister were informed by the province that it would sign no agreement permitting federal funding of municipal planning: "The reason relates to the question of constitutional pre-eminence and the province's desire not to set a precedent with respect to federal-urban projects" (Feldman and Graham 1979: 73-74). In this case, the province itself provided substitute conditional funds. In Quebec at the same time, the provincial approach was somewhat different. Premier Lévesque informally advised municipal officials that they could certainly accept federal conditional funds such as those contained under the New Employment Expansion and Development program (NEED), even though it was an intrusion into a provincial constitutional realm. But he also indicated that an amount equivalent to any federal contribution would then be deducted from the province's annual general (and unconditional) municipal grants to those municipalities. Notwithstanding provincial obstacles like these, the central government has been able to use its federal **spending power** deployed through Crown agencies, primarily CMHC, to build and transform large parts of Canada's city-region urban landscape.

On the larger matter of the politics of the operation of conditional grants, there are again few surprises for the thoughtful citizen, except possibly as to how their application blurs democratic accountability. There are two rules for this fiscal action. Rule one is that donors like conditional grants for these three reasons.

1. The donor government can establish national or province-wide controls over how programs are to be developed and, by enticing local governments to play along, can, in effect, set provincial standards in areas in which it does not wish to create its own departmental organizations. This was how, for example, the national government was able to ensure that the Canada Health Act provided all Canadians with universal coverage for medical services even though hospitals (section 92.7) are as clearly a provincial responsibility as are saloons (92.9) and municipalities (92.8) (note Van Loon and Whittington 1996: 286–87). It is not to be overlooked that federal and provincial governments also have electoral mandates from the same citizens who vote locally.

In central Canada, provinces as donors were once, and continue to be elsewhere, also ingenious in deploying conditional grants to offset the more odious of the negative policy spillovers which result when decisions made by one municipality's council have detrimental consequences for adjacent communities in larger city-regions. Grants to encourage connections to regional water or sewerage treatment facilities, or to upgrade arterial roadways or transit services, or to comply with the negative assessment consequences of genuine regional planning, or to offset a core city's disproportionate burden in regional policing, community housing, and social service, have all deflected pressures for more radical structural changes.

2. The donor government may take a large share of the political plaudits for projects and programs which are successful. This often assumes the photo-op form when Cheshire-cat-like provincial or federal ministers present "the cheques" to their local counterparts for, for example, building a major sports stadium while standing in some field of mud. Sometimes a symbolic sod-turning follows for local media consumption, the goofiness of the occasion limited only by the public relations' imagination of political aides. Most citizens have noted the laudatory billboards, the largest at any roadway construction site, detailing the percentage of the cost-sharing between province and city and, in the extreme (i.e., in British Columbia) flaunting a full-colour picture of the provincial minister as though it were this individual's personal largesse being distributed.

3. Companion to credit taken is that patron governments are only partly financing and, very importantly, not themselves directly administering

program or project delivery. Consequently, there is always someone else to blame in the unhappy event that a bungle causes the media to assign serious, albeit short-term, front page or electronic lead item attention. As a result, in recent years, no federal or provincial government minister can be held personally accountable if a new city bridge collapses while under construction as part of a shared-cost roadway up-grade. In other circumstances, local officials, in turn, may point back to the funding source for designing inadequate or inappropriate benchmarks for local conditions. Avoidance of *anyone's* direct responsibility while everyone has a comment is one result of complexity in intergovernmental conditional grants. Growing public cynicism with the democratic process is a logical consequence.

9.3.3 Grant recipients: dancing as marionettes

The important corollary here is rule two: recipient governments rather dislike shared-cost programs. Three reasons for this are generally applicable to all conditional intergovernmental transfers.

1. Since the governments which are designing and financing the shared cost programs intend to raise standards for all citizens living within the targeted categories of recipient (i.e., cities, towns, counties, school divisions, etc.), all recipient governments are eligible to participate if the councils decide to put up their end of the funding. But not all potential recipients choose to play, so, in practice, the programs are often not universal in real life application. Some local communities may find that the values entrenched in the central government initiative are not those they wish to apply to their own neighbours, as might be the case in preventive social programs or particular types of recreation grants. Much more frequently, tax-poor local governments find it more difficult to pay their share as their existing short-term and even longer projection budgets are already tightly committed. At the very least, they are faced with extremely difficult substitution choices. Those municipalities which choose not to participate for their own very good reasons do not receive money that those which enter into an agreement do get. Normally, there are *no* substitute funds in lieu of these programs. It is often argued at annual meetings of municipal associations that it is the tax-rich local governments that benefit most from shared cost initiatives because they have more "disposable" resources. Indeed, Canada's largest cities usually now maintain some form of intergovernmental affairs office simply to ensure that no conditional grant opportunity is overlooked.

2. Consequently, the first part of the explanation for these attitudes opposing quasi-compulsory voluntary participation becomes the second gen-

eral objection to conditional grants: their existence influences the priorities which potential recipient governments wish to assign to their own projects and programs. Theoretically, for example, if a municipality were to face two policy alternatives that are equally costly in dollar impact, and the province has a grant scheme that would finance 50 per cent of one and nothing of the other, then that local council would be imprudent, if not fiscally foolish, to prefer the second option over the first. If the provincial transportation grant regulations (as in the case of early 1970s Alberta) supports the construction of freeways and not the operation of public transit, then that province's cities would build thoroughfares and would neither build rapid transit lines nor buy buses. In this case, by changing the regulations to permit a council itself to choose between these options, the province later permitted both Calgary and Edmonton to formalize ambitious light rail transit construction plans by 1978. In local government parlance, this phenomenon is known as "the 50 cent dollar problem"; that is, for 50 cents of own source funds, a council may spend a real amount of one dollar. Even in Canada's wealthier regions, provincial premiers during final choices in the preparation of provincial budgets will direct their treasurers to assign higher priorities to ministers whose portfolios have access to federal matching fund programs so that those federal monies are not lost to the province.

These intentional but usually benign incursions now take the shape, in the 18 months or so leading up to an anticipated federal election, of federal grants for urban "infrastructure." In the observed order of Canadian elections, graders *always* preceded enumerators. At the provincial level, budget documents reveal that highways departments always tend to receive significant infusions of extra money during election years. Federally, immediately after the general election of 1993, a "one time only" infrastructure program of $2 billion was announced for the years 1994 to 1996 as the Liberal platform had promised, if the funds were matched by provinces and municipalities. They were, and this allowed city councils to indulge in the physical plant rehabilitation of almost everything from sewer lines to luxury boxes in the local coliseum; the next federal election followed, in 1997 after the construction. In accountability terms, not only did politicians from all three levels of government indulge in imaginative photo-op moments, but the FCM also took credit for its lobbying game during which it had argued for a $15 billion investment in the renewal of basic physical plant.

Often a major shared cost initiative is announced by the appropriate federal department's minister at the FCM's annual general meeting. In June 2000, the federal prime minister appeared before the FCM to reiterate his government's budget commitment to distribute $2.65 billion over six years on infrastructure spending. The emphasis would be in areas of federally defined priority: environmental clean-up, culture and tourism, afford-able housing, and telecommunications links to more remote communities. Within days, major cities had begun adapting their priorities to fit the new possibilities from dormant plans which had been in forced hibernation dur-ing an austere financial winter.

It is in this general context that local officials, both the elected and their bureaucrats, persistently gripe about being so closely, but surreptitiously, controlled through the regulations surrounding conditional grants that they have become *de facto* extensions of provincial (and federal) public administra-tion. In 1976 the Canadian Federation of Mayors and Municipalities (the FCM's predecessor) argued eloquently for greater local government access to own-source funds and growth taxes (income and corporation). In its lob-bying brief, the organization critiqued the controlling dimension of con-ditional grants regulations: "Democratic accountability is being eroded by a more sinister accountability to bureaucrats, mainly in provincial capitals. This relationship is forced by the municipality's dependence on the system's conditional grants. [This] hidden accountability to masters distant in both miles and mentality destroys the capacity of municipal governments to make their own decisions" (CFMM 1976: 3).

This common complaint was well put by a Calgary councillor in the early 1980s: "I don't care what anyone says, but any time there are strings attached to a grant it erodes autonomy." Another city's manager reported to its council in these terms: "conditional grants are the instruments used to encourage municipalities to implement federal and provincial priorities regardless of the needs perceived by the local government itself" (*Calgary Herald*, 23 September 1987). The Robarts Royal Commission on Metropoli-tan Toronto found similarly that "the lure of subsidization is often enough for local government to change priorities and vary expenditure decisions" (Ontario 1977: Vol. II, 194). In the prelude to the 2004 federal general elec-tion, federal Liberal ministers toyed with trial balloons for cities, such as relinquishing sustainable revenue from the federal share of the gasoline tax, after having earlier agreed to remit the GST paid by municipal governments. What this reveals clearly is that an equilibrium among program need, local resources, provincial and federal mandated priorities, community autonomy, and democratic accountability is still not a balance that has been worked out satisfactorily in Canadian city-regions.

3. The third generic problem concerns both projects and programs. While it is all well and good for a local community to construct new facilities with 50 cent dollars, it is too easy to overlook the ongoing budget costs of mainte-nance and operations which are not included under the project's grants regu-lations. A more serious problem developed during the fiscal austerity "crisis"

of the latter 1990s as Canada's federal and provincial governments endeavoured to balance their budgets partially through terminating, or gradually eroding, ongoing shared-cost program commitments. In short, they bailed out. The 1990s neo-liberal repositioning of authority, especially in Alberta and Ontario, arbitrarily reduced conditional grants and downloaded service commitments onto municipalities and their agencies. The argument offered was that this clarified direct public accountability. Even labelling the exercise as "disentanglement" while showcasing ingenious public relations investigations like the 1996 (Crombie) *Who Does What?* exercise in Ontario (White 1998: 275) did not cover up the revenue shortfalls and did not confuse the leadership in policy networks for much longer than a news clip. Long-established obligations to particular policy communities were shirked by senior level governments, leaving municipal councils holding the bag without new revenue sources being made available. Public accountants may talk excitedly about concepts such as "best locus of responsibility" when they try to describe appropriate levels for positioning governing responsibility (Graham, Phillips, and Maslove 1998: 206), but off the spreadsheet, in the real world of commitments made, fiscal relations are not so easily sorted.

Even unconditional funding is as susceptible to ideological and pragmatically political incursions as these. For one example, in 1996 the NDP government of British Columbia arbitrarily rejigged municipal grants in order to save $113 million as part of a wider election-oriented effort to balance provincial books. The City of Vancouver lost the most in absolute terms, an amount that equalled 2.4 per cent of its total budget; other, more dependent municipalities forecast a 6 per cent cut. The mayor of Fort St. John labelled the action "a breach of trust." The president of the Union of BC Municipalities (179 members) critiqued the retrenchment as a betrayal of an agreement reached in 1993 "that was supposed to give municipal governments more certainty about funding" (*Globe and Mail*, 27 November 1996). To complete the intergovernmental carousel, the provincial minister in turn blamed the federal government for reducing its transfer payments to the province.

For municipal councils the basic snag is that, having been enticed into new areas by the grants, they have generated citizen expectations of service as well as policy communities unwilling to surrender either the innovations or heightened standards of service. In 1994, for instance, Mayor Jan Reimer of Edmonton angrily responded to an unanticipated 14 per cent reduction in the city's social services grant: "I think the city's been blindsided. The province has clearly reneged here." In Calgary, officials facing a similar reduction conceded that "it would be terribly hard to choose which programs to cut," and one referred to the 1982 movie *Sophie's Choice*, in which a concentration camp mother must decide which of her two children

Table 9.1: Types of Fiscal Transfers to Local Governments, in Millions of Dollars

		1976	1986	2002
General grants	Federal	110.9	215.6	484.3
	Provincial	1,139.6	1,703.6	745.0
Conditional grants	Federal	107.3	134.5	405.0
	Provincial	6,376.9	8,110.3	5,261.7

Source: Treff and Perry 2003: 8–14.

would die (*Edmonton Journal*, 30 February 1994). Seven years earlier, the same government's provincial employment minister responded to federal termination of its (90 per cent) share of apprenticeship training by saying, "I have a concern that they get us hooked on a program and then phase out of it" (*Edmonton Journal*, 1 December 1987). Substitute provincial funding had to be arranged, not so hard a political problem in Alberta with its abundant oil and gas revenues as elsewhere.

Generically, then, recipient governments find it just as difficult to offend their electors through terminating their administration of shared-cost programs as donor governments find it electorally profitable to extol their own more balanced books. It is in this limited transactional sense that the muffled accountability game of conditional grants is voter profitable for the central governments of the Canadian state.

9.3.4 The considerable money involved

Having said all this, just how pervasive are conditional grant programs relative to more general and unconditional transfers? Municipalities well know that about 96 per cent of all fiscal transfers to local governments through the last decade or so have come from their provincial governments and are almost equal in total amount to federal to provincial transfers. In Tables 9.1 and 9.2 we see another part of the picture. It is to be noted that while about one-third of federal transfers to the provinces are not conditional and may be deployed for general purposes, provincial transfers to municipalities are in a normal ratio of about eight to one, conditional to untied funding. Where, in any particular, these ratios vary substantially, then questions about that policy choice necessarily follow.

The data in Table 9.2 reveal the "offloading" tendencies of several provinces in the first half of the 1990s, when six provincial governments of all partisan stripes reduced their proportion of contributions to local governing budgets. Alberta reduced transfers by 29 per cent and Saskatchewan by an

Table 9.2: Property Taxes and Governmental Transfers, as a Percentage of Local Government Revenues by Province, 1988, 1996, 2002

Province	Property Taxes			Government Transfers		
	1988	1996	2002	1988	1996	2002
Newfoundland	41.9	50.6	21.8	41.2	30.1	33.5
Prince Edward Island	51.7	63.3	18.2	13.8	9.2	18.2
Nova Scotia	57.9	55.6	40.1	26.3	29.0	28.4
New Brunswick	41.7	51.7	53.8	36.9	25.0	29.5
Quebec	68.8	68.2	41.9	8.8	12.0	12.9
Ontario	41.7	41.7	47.6	31.2	32.4	37.0
Manitoba	44.5	43.1	38.1	26.3	27.9	26.7
Saskatchewan	48.1	52.6	51.8	18.7	12.2	12.4
Alberta	36.3	42.2	29.2	21.9	12.9	14.0
British Columbia	48.1	50.1	31.5	15.1	13.2	13.1
Average	*48.6*	*49.6*	*41.7*	*22.9*	*22.9*	*25.4*

Source: Derived from the Statistics Canada data presented numerically on a financial management system basis by Treff and Perry (2003: Tables 6.3, A.12).

almost identical 28, although the governments in the two provinces were, theoretically, drawn from strongly divergent partisan and ideological traditions (Progressive Conservative and NDP). Since the significant budget reductions of the Harris Progressive Conservative administration in Ontario was not included in these data for the 1996 calculation, it was the considerable *dollar* increase in Quebec which accounts for the constant national average of 23 per cent as a transfers base. By 2002, Ontario still was the transfer king for a number of reasons related to a calculation of political advantage.

At the same time it is virtually impossible, based on their public accounts, to generalize about the relative importance of conditional funding as a budget share in any given year for major Canadian cities across the ten provincial systems. For instance, cities such as Edmonton and Calgary profit considerably from their ownership of utilities like electricity (over and above the usual profits from water and waste). The marked decline in the combination property taxes and transfer payments as a percentage of budget total, in British Columbia and Alberta in particular, is a consequence of sales of "service," fees for services, and investment income. In such a setting, profit from the retailing of electricity reduces in proportionate terms the direct costs of, say, policing. Other cities like Vancouver and Surrey function within a two-tier operation in which major capital and operating expenditures on matters like mass transit and roadway transportation are assumed by the regional authority and paid for by a partial levy against the real property values of lower tier governments. In Montreal during the period of its Urban Community, the 29 municipalities within the regional government also benefited from public safety and sewerage treatment being funded through the regional government.

9.4 Displacement of Traditional Structural Frameworks

Structural adaptation in response to population shifts and a changing economic paradigm has affected both city-region and rural municipality governments in Canada over the past half-century. When speaking of structure in this context, we are primarily talking about changing local government boundaries. Rural local governments have essentially confronted problems of scale, meaning that their boundaries have been expanded by provincial governments in order to build the tax base that will support the purchase of better machinery (for roads maintenance) and modern physical plant (water and sewerage treatment, arenas), as well as the acquisition of more diverse and professionally trained staff (not only for administrative ends, but also in areas of social service and recreational and leisure activities). Since the Alberta County Act (1950), through Ontario's regional government reforms (1969-74), and into the present redefinitions in Quebec and Ontario, provincial governments have tried to redefine form to fit function.

Toward the end of the twentieth century, some 80 major restructurings were initiated by the Ontario Progressive Conservative government, which by June 1998 had forcibly reduced by mergers the number of municipal governments in the province from 815 to 590 (White 1998: 285), including the consolidation of the multiple governments in the Toronto area. If one test of the popular legitimacy of such emphatic reform lies with provincial electors as it is commonly held to be, then the re-election of the Harris government in June 1999 as the first two-term majority Progressive Conservative government in Ontario in 30 years could be argued as a substantial litmus test for approval. It suggests also that traditional community boundaries are much less salient for voters than their elected councillors would have the media believe. Meanwhile, in April 2000, the Quebec government also announced its intention to introduce less radical legislation to collapse the province's existing 1,306 localities, encouraging public compliance through ending provincial subsidies to communities with fewer than 5,000 residents. Consolidation was accomplished, in law, but the government was defeated (for many reasons).

As will be discussed throughout the next few chapters, the many publics of Canadian metropolitan regions have had to confront directly the question of appropriate boundaries. At its heart the problem has been one of coping with population growth which spills over historic community lines. John Meligrana observed that "Recent boundary adjustments continue to be a response to urbanization and are undertaken on the premise of improved growth management through a better match of political jurisdiction with the spaces of urban growth" (1998: 209). In the Canadian provinces incurring the most population growth—British Columbia, Alberta, and Ontario—recent annexations, whether initiated by central cities, developers, or provincial authorities, have principally tried to bring rural fringe lands targeted for development into the ambit of a single political unit. Such an administration would possess, in theory, the authority not only to integrate the various components of service delivery sensibly within its own operations but also place them within the context of a wider, and enforceable, growth management strategy.

The city-region governing issue is one of creating a problem-solving instrument more or less congruent with the metropolitan policy problems associated with large-scale urban expansion. In Canada's city-regions, after initial postwar small-scale annexations and amalgamations quickly proved insufficient, various forms of special purpose districts, regionalized institutions, and two-level metropolitan governments emerged as the next logical step. Yet, and as we will investigate closely, as the particular servicing issues which came with sustained growth continued to escalate, they forced several of Canada's provincial governments to consolidate the authority of all municipalities within their major city-regions. This is known as unitary local government, and for some reformers the rallying cry is simple: "One government for one city."

9.5 Money and the Federal Urban Intervention

9.5.1 Constitutions and conventions

The formal Canadian constitutional rules governing intergovernmental relations are pretty clear on the surface. The Constitution Act 1982 and the British North America Act that preceded it guarantee arenas of functional autonomy for both the federal and provincial realms of government; these are primarily found in sections 91 and 92, respectively, of the acts. In theory, neither realm of governing is to poach on the turf of the other, and the educated citizen ought to be able to determine which level of political authority is to be congratulated or rebuked for services rendered. Yet any student of federal-provincial relations learns quickly that this superficial clarity withered in practice as successions of governments have coped with the evolving economy and modernizing society since the Second World War. Federal-provincial conferences of ministers (in functional areas such as health or justice), advisory committees drawn from deep within the invisible bowels of both tiers' professional bureaucracies, quasi-autonomous but functionally specific regulatory agencies (for instance, in policies affecting the environment, transportation, and communications), informal administrative cooperation, and conditional grant arrangements—all have worked to adapt the Constitution to enable ministries at both "senior" or wider area governing levels to meet the expectations of uncountable policy communities.

To read the Canadian Constitution literally is to expect the governor-general to exercise the powers of absolute monarch, for there is no direct mention of prime minister, party politics, or responsible cabinet government. Constitutional convention, or, as some would have it the "unwritten constitution," gives virtually the force of law to those widely shared popular understandings which inform our political practices and make modern parliamentary government work as well as it does. Political gladiators understand, even as the general population may not, just what constitutes a "vote of confidence" in the House of Commons and why it is so important that the government must win it or face an election. It is also understood that the governor-general today must ask the leader of the largest party in the House, even if it holds only a couple of seats more than the next largest, to form a government and become prime minister. Although this obligation was not always so clear, only being decided in political culture terms by the King-Byng affair of 1926, it is now so accepted a convention as not to be questioned even were a party with fewer seats in the House to have won a significantly larger percentage of the popular vote (as happened in 1979 when the Progressive Conservatives won 136 seats with 36 per cent and the Liberals 114 with 40 per cent of the popular vote).

By the written Constitution, local governments fall clearly under provincial jurisdiction (section 92.8), and there is no constitutional provision for locally accountable, democratically elected municipal autonomy. Even still, by the strong traditions of local democracy and consequent citizen expectations of some type of grassroots government, most municipal officials enjoy an extra-constitutional safeguard against their own quick and easy extermination by any provincial ministry. The practical consequence is that it requires either some overwhelming financial exigency, the grossest form of collective political malfeasance or program mismanagement, or a provincial ministry with a clear ideological direction, or some combination of these, to precipitate any significant reconfiguration of local authority.

9.5.2 The federal incursion

Urban growth sometimes has consequences beyond municipal boundaries, crossing provincial borders—for instance Ottawa-Gatineau and Lloydminster straddle, respectively, the borders of Ontario and Quebec and Saskatchewan and Alberta—or international ones, as Great Lakes water treatment involves, for instance, Michigan and Ontario, and Victoria's raw sewage dumps drift into Seattle Harbour. As a result, the Canadian Constitution has rendered a proactive federal incursion into city affairs a laboured contest indeed. Federal open intervention in an individual city's policies may appear in unusual ways. For example, in July 1999, the federal Department of the Environment officially notified the city of Brandon, on the grasslands of Manitoba, that it would violate the Fisheries Act if it did not augment the waste water treatment the city provided to the discharge from the new Maple Leaf pork processing operation. The concern was based on the department's projections that the ammonia released would exceed the Assiniboine River's ability to absorb the nutrient. Similarly, the pollution of Hamilton's harbour by the surrounding steel-making factories has long vexed the federal environmental policy community without much result. Any federal intervention into municipal affairs can be a treacherous gambit, overridden as it is with so many other tactics in a much broader and continuing constitutional chess match with the provinces.

Tri-level conferences to consider a potential redefinition of tax revenues to make them more appropriate for current expenditure responsibilities have not been scheduled for over 20 years because the provinces have collectively refused to attend any such gathering since 1976 (Feldman and Graham 1979: 46). And, despite their petitions and carping, Canada's municipal governments were not invited to, nor involved directly in, the discussions leading to the patriation of the Constitution in 1982, nor in those which produced the Charlottetown Accord. Indeed, the attorney-general of Saskatchewan informed the FCM general meeting in Regina in June 1981 that entrenching the role of municipalities "might introduce an undesirable nation-wide sameness" (*Globe and Mail*, 9 June 1981). The provinces have remained both guarded and jealous of historic constitutional prerogatives over their municipal subordinates. A decade later, in the spring of 1991, Metro councillors sanctioned a report calling for the city-regions of Toronto, Montreal, and Vancouver "to be recognized and treated as a full and equal partner in the Canadian government system" (*Globe and Mail,* 13 March 1991). No one listened, no one heard, and within six years Metro Toronto council's existence was terminated.

Still, many aspects of federal government policies throughout the twentieth century had considerable consequences for Canada's metropolitan core. Particularly in conjunction with the urbanization following the Second World War, Canadian city-regions were shaped by the often intended decisions of federal departments and agencies, especially the Central (now Canada) Mortgage and Housing Corporation (CMHC) and the National Housing Act. At a minimum the huge financial support for a variety of private and public housing initiatives provided by the federal government through the CMHC placed new pressures on both provinces and cities to plan better. While the provinces had to specify what was expected of communities through their general statutes, the actual planning rules took form via individual municipalities' bylaws.

But federal activities went far beyond this major initiative in housing. When the minister responsible for the creation of MSUA introduced the legislation intended to coordinate and integrate the federal role in 1971, he stated in the House of Commons that, "There are now 112 federal programs involving financing of the urban process, and 131 research programs applying to elements of the urban process. There are 27 departments and agencies which have influence of one degree or another in the cities ..." (Bettison 1975: 280). In the run-up to the creation of MSUA there had been a massive federal intrusion into Canada's urban areas, although it was almost unintended to be such (Higgins 1986: 109ff). This interest had been triggered by the Trudeau government's response to the much headlined "urban crisis" in the United States, the Hellyer (1969) task force on housing, and the Economic Council of Canada's alarmist forecast of the policy consequences of urbanization. At its demise in March 1979, the MSUA had policies but no programs, enemies in federal departments like Transport with large urban-linked activities and especially in federal program agencies like the CMHC, and of course the provinces. It had few supporters other than the politically weak CFMM and its ardent tub-thumping for "their" ministry. As a relative test of institutionalized political recognition, it might be noted that even amateur sports has "its own" federal ministry of state these days.

Why, and how, have policy-makers in central governments been able to carve themselves a role in urban development? Partly this happened because, while the leadership of policy communities is usually rather adept in working the *de jure* authority, citizens facing immediate social or economic problems have no need to be so particular. Their demands for remedy will be focused on that political authority which first becomes, or is most immediately, available. Even unsophisticated demands command some measure of redress as they intensify. In turn, the transactional nature of democratic political leadership enjoins those in elected positions to respond in spite of any constitutional embargo.

Housing, for example, was expected by all to become a priority policy issue in the immediate postwar period. Strictly interpreting the Constitution, section 92 assigns provincial legislatures the *exclusive* power under subsection 92.16 "all Matters of a merely local or private Nature in the Province" and, more precisely in subsection 92.13, to "Property and Civil Rights in the Province." Housing is not only private, but also both property and very local indeed. In short, housing is a provincial legislative mandate, and provincial authorities may, by statute, assign whatever level of effort they choose to their own local communities. Provinces cannot, however, delegate these constitutional powers to the federal government. Nevertheless, even the casual observer is aware of the considerable federal presence in the housing world, mostly as it has been funnelled through the CMHC since its creation as a Crown corporation in 1946. Federal main estimates for 2000 reveal that the CMHC received about $2 billion for its various activities. Since its inception, it has insured home mortgages; since 1992 well over a half-million Canadians have purchased their first homes with such support. From 1949 into the early 1960s, the CMHC also financed ambitious programs of urban renewal through land assembly, slum clearance, and the building of low rental apartments. It acted as an agent for federal social policy by providing housing for seniors, students, and Aboriginal peoples. Its social housing component today focuses primarily on shared–cost, 75 to 25 per cent, federal–provincial initiatives. The CMHC is a major player indeed, insuring 60 per cent of the multiple unit market in 1996 (Treff and Perry 1998: 15.8; Leo 1995: 31, 37; Higgins 1986: 106-09). It continues to administer loans made to local governments under previous policies for water and sewer systems and for neighbourhood improvements.

In housing, as in other policy arenas, the federal government is able to formulate a policy role in a constitutional setting clearly not its own by virtue of the federal spending power. This power means that the federal authorities have the fiscal wherewithal, through superior taxation resources, to be able to tackle the job as they themselves formulate it.

As a rule, any federal constitution will define fairly precisely how the two levels of the state (the centre and the substate regions) may raise money and upon what they may spend it. In Canada, though, the federal power is based on two clauses of section 91 (the federal realm) and subsequent judicial interpretation. In subsection 91.3, the Parliament of Canada is given exclusive power for "The raising of Money by any Mode or System of Taxation," and in 91.1a, it is assigned responsibility for "The Public Debt and Property," and in this context "property" may be thought to include cash itself. The provinces are restricted to direct taxation; municipal governments, as specifically permitted by provincial statutes, are limited to those elements of provincial authority that the province chooses to grant them.

A "watertight compartment" interpretation of sections 91 and 92 regarding exclusive policy functions does not permit either realm of the federated state to make laws within the responsibilities of the other. This is so even were the national government eager to devise fundamental national standards to supersede the existing provincial checkerboard of programs and procedures. However, the need to respond to the devastating impacts of the Great Depression caused federal authorities to refer the question of their capacity to intervene to the Supreme Court which rendered its verdict in 1936. Speaking in dissent (in this instance) Chief, Justice Duff wrote that Parliament could indeed raise money by taxation and dispose of its public property as it saw appropriate. But, importantly, on this latter question of spending, he added: "it is evident that the Dominion may grant sums of money to individuals or organizations, and that the gift may be accompanied by such restrictions and conditions as Parliament may see fit to enact. It would then be open to the proposed recipient to decline the gift—or to accept it subject to such conditions" (SCR 1936: 427, 432; Laskin 1966: 666-67).

In practical terms this means that the constitutional spending power grants to the federal government the legal right to make financial payments to persons or organizations in policy areas for which the federal state does not have the authority to pass legislation. So the federal government offers money for medical care, hospitalization, post-secondary education, and urban renewal, which are all provincial constitutional obligations. The federal authority often sets precise conditions on how its money is to be allocated. The provinces may refuse to participate in such shared-cost programs, of course, and their electors (who naturally are also federal voters) will hold them more or less accountable for missed opportunities, but should they choose to become involved, their own bureaucracies undertake the necessary local regulations and arrangements. These latter may in turn be delegated to universities, hospital boards, and other local governments. The central point is this: as long as the federal government is only financing, and not directly legislating or administering, it has the power to intervene in how the money is spent.

9.5.3 Why municipalities choose to receive conditional money

Three points emerge from this important history lesson. First, even though municipalities operate under a constitutional quarantine from federal influence, as long as there exists the potential for a cut of federal cash, there will be an active interest, especially from municipalities within larger city-regions. It is not to be forgotten that public office-holders in any given space are likely both to know each other personally and, often regardless of party ties, to try to work together on policy possibilities as they troll for the same wary electors. Secondly, the intrusive federal intergovernmental intervention in urban areas is founded on conditional grants. As noted previously, this is an unlikely basis for enduring harmony. Over the past few decades Canada's more decentralist provincial governments, especially Quebec in the 1970s and 1990s and Alberta in the 1980s, have argued the case in constitutional and intergovernmental negotiations that if the federal government has so much money that it can afford to spend in areas of responsibility not its own, then the Constitution should be reformed to enable provinces to meet their obligations in, say, housing and urban infrastructure regeneration without having to rely on federal fiscal interventions. It is also because cities are so suspicious, based on their experience, of what the provinces would actually do with new monies that they, in turn, continue to lobby so openly for the federal presence.

Thirdly, it follows from this that, all things being equal, no level of government would eagerly embrace the role of conditional grant recipient were any other reasonable path available. Two conditions which induce compliance must persist over time: the potential donor authority must possess the necessary taxation resources, and probable recipients must find themselves in chronic need. For Canada, the data in Tables 9.3 and 9.4 reveal that both sides of this equation do exist.

According to Table 9.3, while provincial and federal taxation resources had fattened to meet public policy demands even after the late 1990 neo-liberal belt-tightening, local government revenue sources, in relative terms and before interjurisdictional transfer payments, and as measured as a proportion of the GDP, are significantly more slender than they were nearly 80 years ago. On the other hand, Table 9.4, in presenting expenditures, reveals that while local governments do indeed meet demands for service, they cannot do so without the transfers from the wider area governments. The $33.4 *billion* deficit is only a paper one, since municipalities cannot legally incur a deficit on operating budgets. It is presented here to emphasize the enormity of the shared-cost addiction.

9.6 The Provincial-Municipal Policy Interface

As a form of generic intergovernmental encounter, the provincial-municipal policy interface is not at all similar to the federal-provincial one except insofar as two levels of authority with more, and less, territory are involved. As has been noted, the heart of federal-provincial relations is defined by the

Table 9.3: Revenue as a Percentage of GDP, Excluding Transfers

Governing level	1926	1970	1996	2002
Federal	7.3	14.4	19.3	17.6
Provincial	2.9	11.8	17.6	16.6
Municipal	6.0	4.8	4.7	4.1
Totals	*16.2*	*31.0*	*41.6*	*38.3*

Source: Derived from Treff and Perry 2003: Table B.8.

Table 9.4: Balance Sheet for the Three Realms of Governing, Before Transfers, in Millions of Dollars

Governing level	1926	1970	1996	2002
Federal	+83	+3,216	+11,825	+44,054
Provincial	–8	–734	–3,,143	–9,899
Municipal	–18	–3,639	–29,917	–33,440

Source: Derived from Treff and Perry 2003: Table B.6.

Constitution and its court interpretation. The centre of the legal relationship between any province and its local governments is the indisputable political reality that what a cabinet in Ottawa might want to be able to do to provincial ministers in Quebec City, that government in Quebec *can* do to the city council in Montreal!

9.6.1 Constitutionalism and local government roots

All forms of local government are the creatures of provincial statute law. They are no more and no less. Any provincial ministry is consequently free to create new municipalities, to modify borders and responsibilities, to dismiss locally elected councillors or school trustees, and to alter or abolish all local institutions should it so choose. Furthermore, the Westminster doctrine of **parliamentary supremacy**, which sustains Canadian provincial government, also means that no sitting provincial legislature can bind the hands of any successor legislature because, logically, that second Parliament is also supreme in *its* own time. In plain words, no sitting government can pass such an act as would guarantee in perpetuity the future boundaries, or form, or functions of any local institution within the province. Nor would one ever want to. Unlike the situation in the United States, Canadian local government has no autonomous constitutional or home rule tradition. Nor does the

Canadian Constitution necessarily protect the individual from a legislature operating well within the rule of law. In refusing the appeal by suburban citizens of the Toronto Megacity amalgamation in 1996, Justice J. Borins observed that "In any event, the Charter [of Rights and Freedoms] does not guarantee an individual the right to live his or her life free from government chutzpah or imperiousness" (1997: 24).

Moreover, whereas the federal government works with a single set of ten provinces, each with generally similar operations and responsibilities, and each of which can speak with complete confidence on behalf of the population inhabiting its territory, the provinces do not confront such an array in their own relations with local governments. Without exception, the pattern of governing on the municipal end is structural complexity (of the provinces' making) in which there is literally "a confusion" of subordinate authorities each claiming to be *the* policy representative of a greater, or smaller, or more policy particular segment of the total population. While general purpose municipal governments such as towns, cities, and rural municipalities do exist, these usually function with a variety of regional governing overlays like counties, regional districts, planning commissions, health and hospital authorities, transit boards, or other metropolitan governing instruments. The relative complexity of any province's major city-regions requires special provincial attention as well, particularly when intermunicipal issues are rooted in suspicion of each others' motives and skepticism as to any possible cooperative result. Even more so than on rural terrain, around, under, and on top of the metropolitan municipalities lies a profusion of specialty or boutique governments, often single function, like school divisions or hospital boards and health units, usually without coterminus boundaries, and each staking a claim to citizen support and upon the public purse.

The triple consequences of this organizational muddle seem invariably to be these. First, it is difficult for each province to elaborate public policy for local governments in either general or proactive terms. Generic policies for the "cities" category, for instance, must be so crafted that they may apply equally to those with populations of 10,000 as well as those with upwards of one million residents. Otherwise, they would have to be so precise as to be virtually specific to only one community. Because problems are inevitably intense, issue-specific, locally explicit, short-term, and emerge within the fleeting 3.5 year time-line of provincial electoral horizons, policy response to demands tends traditionally to be stopgap, reactive, and palliative.

Secondly, in the last half of the twentieth century, Canada's major provinces began to undertake specific functional shifts to a variety of new regional bodies which were somewhat congruent with persistent problems, simply because there were too many local governments to permit the coordination of service delivery. The greatest shortcoming occasioned by the addition of any second tier of political authority with certain specific area-wide functions (like transit) to a territory that already has multiple governments is that direct accountability for decisions made becomes even more fragmented and remote. This is especially so where the boards are either indirectly elected (i.e., chosen by the constituent councils from among their membership) or are non-elected citizens appointed by either the province or the existing municipal councils. Various hospital districts, as in Alberta, or regional transit authorities are an example of the latter appointment style, while the old Montreal Urban Community or the GRVD today are examples of the former selection process at work.

The final consequence is that provincial governments tend to decentralize their own operating departments, both by area and by functional specialization, which results in diminished political control from the centre. In short, individual line departments such as Environment, Transportation, Education, and especially Agriculture, operate their own programs, develop their separate organization charts, and interact with local officials in a fashion that Stefan Dupré once described as "splendid isolation" and which is termed the "silo effect" these days. Caroline Andrew also observes that the capacity of provinces to exert coherent leadership over municipalities is heavily compromised by their own patterns of departmentalization (1995: 147).

In provincial-municipal relations the matter of hierarchy is not an issue; municipalities are as provinces dispose in law and regulation. While the idea of hierarchy in the classics is taken from the biblical concept of three orders of angels, local governments are more often dismissed by the provinces in more modern cinematic terms as bumbling comic sidekicks. The attaining of provincial objectives on the national stage, where the federal and provincial governments interact as roughly equal, does not require anything like clarity in provincial intergovernmental relations with local administrations. The development of better policy geared to coherent, comprehensive, city-provincial relations has never been high on any provincial "to do" list.

9.6.2 The application of control and guidance

Since city governments are provincial inventions, it follows that the provinces themselves incur a degree of responsibility for them. All provinces have intervened historically in local affairs well beyond the minimum of setting statutory frameworks. Smaller municipalities especially find themselves under the thumb of provincial administrative supervision, sometimes in a gratefully received "tutelage" association, and even the largest are subject to periodic controls in the realm of finance (for example, in borrowing) and standards of service (such as public health or the quality of potable water). The ubiquitous descriptor phrase for the overall pattern is "control and guidance."

Due to the political sensitivities of elected councillors, *the exercise of control* normally comes through requiring the official approval of boards such as the OMB or similar quasi-autonomous agencies, on matters like annexations and municipal borrowing. But provincial ministers of Municipal Affairs and Education typically reserve the right to exert direct control in unique circumstances. For instance, in May 1985, British Columbia's minister of education sacked the entire Vancouver School Board because they refused to set a budget in conformity with ministry spending limits; the Calgary Board was similarly dismissed in 1999 because internal squabbling among members rendered decisions impossible. Small town municipal councils are periodically dismissed for incompetence, usually under conditions of serious personality clashes or fiscal crisis, and occasionally for abuse of the public trust such as when town councillors repave only the roads leading to their own homes (this happened in Alberta in 2004). In the past, a more frequent occurrence was financial exigency arising from rapid, unanticipated growth which caused a town to seek provincial trusteeship in order to provide the necessary service arrangements; such instances were usually found in single resource towns or among the suburbs of city-regions.

On the other hand, *provincial guidance* comes through the paternal attentions of the Department of Municipal Affairs. In smaller communities, administrative staffs are neither as numerous nor as highly specialized in their professional training as their counterparts in core cities. So, in each province, the Department of Municipal Affairs provides recourse on substantive questions of procedure for local municipal officials as a part of its normal workload. The director of municipal services for one such department on the prairies once observed of the need for this support, "the town secretary in a small town has to deal with the same corporations and developers as in [a large city] ..." (*Edmonton Journal*, 9 December 1981). As recently as 20 years ago, around one-quarter of municipal administrators surveyed had not graduated from high school; even the practical knowledge gleaned from "hands-on" training was diluted by the high turnover rates experienced among officials. This is one reason why ministries publish monthly bulletins, with a title like *Municipal Counselor*, which detail practical tips for good administration and, importantly, include a monthly checklist of due dates and tasks whose completion is required to comply with statutes. Much of this may be statistical reporting, but other important filing dates will include the deadlines for eligibility for provincial matched-cost funding. Even the municipal census head count can be important if any grant is to be awarded on a *per capita* basis. Forgetting can be painful: in the spring of

2000, a new provincial law forced over 130 councillors (including 21 mayors) to relinquish office in Newfoundland because their municipal tax bills were in arrears, albeit in most cases with amounts owing under $100. The Canadian Press reported that the previous statute had only required removal if council had adopted a resolution; this never materialized "mainly because of the close relations councillors share in small towns" (*Globe and Mail*, 23 February 2000).

Nor do provincial ministers always hold their municipal counterparts in high esteem. While the constitutional logistics of federal-provincial relations militate towards meetings at the highest levels, the most publicized being among the prime minister and premiers, the modern politics of executive branch federalism requires at least 1,000 meetings among highest level federal and provincial bureaucrats and their ministers. The situation between local and provincial levels is quite different. While provincial ministers and premiers love to attend the annual general meetings of their province's associations of municipalities, especially if there are new grant programs to be announced, in the ordinary course of affairs those locally elected must work through administrative personnel for provincial counsel and approvals. The dominant provincial standing is continually stipulated, in private and in public, by the day-to-day choice of persons designated to represent it in any negotiations.

9.6.3 Political constraints upon provincial autonomy

From time to time, politicians in active service make self-serving reference to the liberal democratic tradition that a system of locally accountable government is not only an important training ground for democratic citizenship, as J.S. Mill would have it, but also somewhat of a "cornerstone of democracy," as Alexis de Toqueville asserted. Indeed, a North American aspect of this too frequently repeats the latter's claim that even though a nation may establish a free government, it cannot possess the spisrit of liberty without municipal institutions (1946: Vol. I, chapter. 5) Even today he is much quoted by local government politicians and those who wish to appease them. A generation ago, Alberta's Opposition Leader addressed the annual meeting of rural municipalities by outlining his thoughts for a municipal rights protection act which would include access to resource revenues and an end to provincial controls over local planning: "Municipalities are the foundation stones for government, not just in Alberta but across the country" (*Edmonton Journal*, 17 November 1977). Such calculated appeals to the continuing salience of the decentralized politics of municipal governing are as much patronizing as they are disingenuous. This particular leader's own party shortly disappeared, and no fundamental change to provincial-local politics in that province has yet emerged.

Perhaps inevitably, even often accurate observers may be tricked by more official-appearing ministerial pronouncements. For example, also in Alberta but nearly a generation later, Graham and Phillips cited a new minister as authority when he stated that, "The municipalities [have] become a power unto themselves," before they conclude that the new 1995 Municipal Government Act is a "significant departure from tradition ... followed with keen interest by other provinces" (1998: 176-77). The proof is in the pudding, however. The province actually reduced the size of its Municipal Affairs Department by one-third, eliminated regional planning as another cost-cutting measure, required market assessment by local governments, effectively eliminated general grants and reduced shared-cost programs by up to two-thirds, reconstituted but retained the Municipal Government Board, and opened no new growth tax base (natural resources or income) to local governments. It did permit municipalities to license bicycles and to expand their range of user fees. As one on-the-scene observer concluded, "the Alberta government pays homage to local democracy while at the same time carefully maintaining authority by controlling access to fiscal resources and establishing municipal policy guidelines through provincial legislation" (Masson 1994: 19).

Such misreading of public artifice and private reality is not surprising given the cautious cynicism sustaining all provincial leadership when it comes to relations with cities. Manitoba's NDP Premier Ed Schreyer often said one thing while meaning quite another during the consolidation of Winnipeg's municipalities in 1971. For instance, notwithstanding his statements concerning enhanced municipal autonomy after Unicity, the province still retained the existing Municipal Board with its powers over planning, appeals and capital borrowing: "In caucus the Premier had replied to concerns that the province 'was spawning an uncontrollable monster ...' by noting that 'the province retains the purse strings and thus retains controls'" (Lightbody 1978: 500). Well aware that the soon-to-be-elected council for the new Winnipeg Unicity would be won by ideological conservatives, his government was unprepared to surrender its two most potent authority mechanisms, money and the quasi-judicial board. To its credit, the Ontario government with its Toronto unification effective in 1997 chose not to emulate such fictions during public debate.

The importance of this matter of grassroots participation in Canadian local affairs has been previously considered (see Chapter 1). Viewed in the broadest perspective, popular acceptance of a division of power and authority between central and local governments is both a reality and a matter of

degree. Even when a province intends to dissolve one or more local governments, it must proclaim a renaissance of "more effective local democracy"
or use some such similar language. The reality is that grassroots behaviour
is usually reactive, and where it becomes most vociferous and conspicuous
is in community response to structural changes to local boundaries, especially where municipal dissolution is contemplated. Aware of this, provincial authorities do not trumpet contemplated realignments in their election
manifestos.

In his reasons for judgement on the Charter appeal against Toronto
Megacity, Mr. Justice Borins noted that, "I have already found ... that there
is no constitutional requirement on the part of the government to consult
electors prior to the introduction of legislation, nor to be bound by the
majority views of electors as to whether they approve, or disapprove, of
proposed legislation" (1997: 18). In this he was referring to a series of public
relations plebiscite exercises conducted by Toronto's local councils through
mail, email, fax, newspaper coupon, hand delivery, and ballot box which
produced a turnout well under 30 per cent (*Toronto Star*, 4 March 1997).
In reorganization cases like these, public pressure can only emerge after
the decision has been made by cabinet during which process the provincial
government will already have anticipated and evaluated political costs.

Occasionally, though, a response perceived by provincial leaders to
be genuinely representing a popular groundswell may put the brakes to a
province's contemplation of a functional shift away from direct local control (for instance, the assumption of responsibility for education or for the
local social service of community housing). On the other hand, even major
readjustments to fiscal transfers tend to initiate little public attention even
when policy elites are loudly active. This is because such arrangements are
generally too complex where not too obscure to focus grievance, perhaps
an implicit consequence of subconscious intent to smudge direct lines of
accountability.

The real world is always the living practicum for any grand theory of
local democracy. From the evidence of 150 years of local democratic experience in Canada, it appears that municipal governments do have a potential
for providing certain kinds of direct access to authority. They also seem
indispensable for certain public services, even if it is not agreed which ones
these are. The empirical "need" for local structures, though, is far less significant than the widely held public belief in the necessity for some form
of functionally autonomous municipalities. Provincial tinkering with local
governments that can be popularly construed as a violation of "historic"
local democratic units seems to activate a convention that places quite a few
practical limits on provincial legal omni-competence. The result is that,

although legally subordinate status remains, municipal councils do enjoy a far greater potential for innovative initiatives based in their political culture. Sadly, this potential is seldom exercised along any proactive path.

ten | Standing issues in regional governing

The next four chapters focus on **horizontal intergovernmental relations** in Canada's city-regions or, to put it another way, the interactions among types of governments found on a more or less similar plane of formal and functional authority within a specifically defined geographic area. The growing complexities of the transactions among autonomous governing instruments (municipalities, school districts, hospital boards, special districts), in combination with their occasional spectacular failure to establish effective public policies for the region within which they must coexist, has required all four major provinces to intercede with regional policy-implementing devices over the past 50 years. Subsequent incremental tinkering has inevitably led to more drastic interventions.

A genuinely metropolitan Canada emerged roughly a generation following the rapid urban transformation of the United States after the First World War. In Chapter 1, we observed that while the Great Depression leading into the Second World War had subdued urbanization tendencies in Canada, these economic, social, and demographic trends resurfaced with a vengeance towards the end of the war and in the economic recovery which followed. In a sense, the political institutions of Canadian city-regions found themselves faced with policy issues roughly analogous with those previously encountered in the United States 30 years earlier. In hindsight, it is easy to argue that lessons in effective planning, growth management, and political accommodation ought to have been learnt. That they were not assimilated easily or ever (for example, in conceding the emergence of the "donut hole" phenomenon of centre city decay) may only partly be excused by the diffused responsibility for management of urban growth which the Canadian Constitution permits.

The willy-nilly character of governing instruments for the Canadian city-region for the last half of the twentieth century can be attributed to the conflicting mandates of the political authorities directly (provinces and local governments) and indirectly (the federal) responsible. As measured by consistently incremental and reactive policy responses, what is now clear is that no level of political authority seemed able to appreciate the magnitude of what was happening until the avalanche had passed.

For example, towards the end of the Second World War, the federal administration was haunted by the prospect that the postwar recession of 1918 would repeat itself as the voracious industrial demands of Canada's war machine ground down. The influential federal Finance Department's projections, as reflected in the Green Book proposals of 1945, so meshed with Liberal Party re-election ambitions that the powerful Minister of Reconstruction, C.D. Howe, was able to deploy the CMHC as a central instrument of economic policy to administer the National Housing Act (1944). By making new housing more mortgage-affordable for individuals, and later through offering municipal loans for sewage treatment and land assembly schemes, the national state underwrote Canada's suburban diaspora (Higgins 1986: 108-09).

All provincial legislatures of this postwar era functioned under an electoral system with a severe imbalance that rewarded rural electors. There was little in the way of a one-to-one accountability to city electors, a legacy sustained by the perceived relative virtue of the pastoral way of life and justified in practice by the distance rural representatives would have to cover were their constituencies based on any sort of "rep-by-pop" formula. The result was that those legislatures all shared beliefs in a limited, proactive, interventionist role of the state except for the provision of visible improvements to physical infrastructure in the ongoing struggle with a harsh environment. Priorities remained programs of rural electrification and the building and maintenance of provincial (and through a compliant structure of shared-cost programs, rural municipal) roads. As an unintentional policy consequence, however, these continuing upgrades worked to extend the practical commuter-shed of Canadian city-regions.

Also during this period (*c.* 1946-70), local government leaders were consistently classic civic boosters sharing a world view that they must not lose out in any ostensible race to increase their communities' assessment base. In a time during which there seemed to be few if any barriers to sustained economic growth, these three policy directions were singly powerful forces; in combination, they were unstoppable co-conspirators in the spatial expansion of Canadian city-regions.

The experience in the United States ought to have forewarned potentially attentive Canadian policy communities. During the 1920s American cities, which had previously been self-contained and spatially separated from their nearest urban neighbours, now found themselves ringed by populous **satellite suburbs**. In rapid response, governmentally complex metropolitan regions (only hints of which had appeared in the special purpose districts of the late nineteenth century) began to emerge, as did inevitable public policy stresses in providing basic local government functions. Increasingly diverse, but all urban-centred, large-scale population groups had expectations, but the shape of local government had not tracked the new distributions of people. Blue ribbon American reformers grew perplexed: "At first the metropolitan region was perceived as simply another problem in 'social engineering'; if annexation, city-county consolidation, inter-municipal cooperation, or special districts were not feasible 'solutions,' then the more drastic remedy of a fully integrated metropolitan government was required" (Sayre and Polsby 1965: 123-24). But, ultimately, engineering solutions could never be found that could "mend" the socio-political "problem" of the American city-region.

In this chapter, we set the stage with a few particularly relevant environmental issues and social structure and general economic patterns before some initial governmental coping instruments are considered. The central point is that fragmentation of public instruments by local governing boundaries decreases direct accountability to citizens for public policies affecting the wider city-region, even though it may mean heightened responsiveness for smaller matters within the separate units of municipalities. Accountability is further diminished whenever wider area policy pressures force municipalities to delegate specific functions to arms' length local agencies or to single function regional boards.

10.1 Who Manages the Urban Environment?

10.1.1 What is the general problem?

Putting any sort of authoritative boundaries to the modern metropolis in a liberal society has proven virtually impossible given the locational choices which can be made relatively easily by capital (Lightbody 1997: 444-46). For instance, Toronto as a socio-economic urban form will expand whatever political boundaries it possesses as a municipality now as developers and manufacturers look in all directions for more land for their enterprises. Authorities with responsibility for New York City and Paris have struggled for two centuries to give political form to the similar realities of their metropolitan cities. The real limits to the population and economic base in the lower mainland of British Columbia are physical, or topographical, not human mapping demarcations.

Limits to growth through physical expansion of the urban living space can become public policy choices when they focus on the extension of urban servicing in areas such as water and sewerage or roadways. Even where physical boundaries have contained the developed urban space, as with Montreal Island or the prairie agglomerations of Winnipeg or Regina, it has not proven easy to create local government structures which coincide.

During the liberal heyday of the positive state in the immediate postwar period a much wider range of state responsibilities was assumed even as stresses came to bear upon the antiquated system of local government (for example, Ontario's structures in the 1960s, outside Toronto, had not been significantly adjusted after 1849) that had its origins in service as caretaker to a rural, agrarian population. These basic economic and social stresses were centred in the constantly accelerating, overlapping, and complex changes which produced a population concentrated in a small number of very large city-regions. This population explosion paid no heed to municipal boundary lines as it sought affordable housing and secure employment. System overload would not have been unanticipated had provincial governments taken an interest in the future effective governing of these new urban agglomerations.

It will be argued in Chapter 13 that part of the reason behind the audacity of late 1990s metropolitan restructuring in Canada was that successive provincial governments had avoided fundamental reorganization to accommodate new population and economic realities until some form of institutionalized volcanic vent was required to accommodate the pressure. The first, and typical, provincial response in Ontario, Quebec, Alberta, and British Columbia was to avoid basic reorganization of existing general purpose local governments through the tactic of superimposing new layers of patchwork regional operations. Further complicating the matter was that provincial ministries such as Transportation, Social Services, Education, and Environmental Affairs decentralized their operations to realize a city-region focus. Each acted in splendid isolation. One consequence of administrative decentralization, by function or territory, is always a weakening of direct democratic control and accountability.

Still, in urban territories, municipal governing was generally left to its own devices in the struggle to adapt. Even generally well-informed citizens, often including those who were policy specialists and those struggling with a singular grievance, were seldom aware of the complexity of governments which gripped the decentralized city-region. As will be detailed in Chapter 12, the first response by municipalities grappling with the public policy intricacies of an increasingly interdependent city-region society and economy was to try to devise problem-solving instruments whose boundaries in geography and function approximated those of the policy problem.

To examine just how numerous the assorted types of very functionally specific government agencies had become, Toronto's Bureau of Municipal Research (BMR) undertook a calculation shortly after the partial implementation of the Carl Goldenberg recommendations for Metro Toronto in 1965. Except for the consolidation of 13 lower tier general purpose municipalities into six, the changes themselves had been principally incremental in nature, because of the "rationality" of the existing Toronto framework. The BMR chose an expansive definition of what was essential for any instrument to be considered an operational unit of local government. A "government" must be possessed of four characteristics: (1) the territory over which it exercises its jurisdiction must be defined; (2) it must provide at least one, but possibly more, public services through an ongoing formal organization; (3) it must exercise some relative autonomy in reaching decisions; and (4) it must have the capacity to raise funds through fees, charges for services, or taxation. By this definition such an authority need neither be elected nor in any other way be directly accountable to the public it is charged with serving. The BMR found that the "rational" government of Toronto—one area-wide government and six lower tier units of the conventional general purpose sort—was overladen and supplemented by at least 101 other units of governments from 54 boards and 11 commissions to a court, a corporation, and a foundation (DelGuidice and Zacks, 1968). At roughly the same time (1979), a far less populous region, the Edmonton CMA, functioned with at least 50 similar cross-jurisdictional agencies, boards, and committees in addition to its 33 municipalities.

This relegation of functional obligations to numerous quite specific governing agencies within a city-region by municipalities themselves, combined with each province's own departmental decentralizations, produces a recurrent institutional pattern which Stefan Dupré (1968) insightfully tagged "**hyper-fractionalized quasi-subordination.**" This means that authority is fragmented through devolution of functional authority to specialized agencies and that regional "policy," such as it is, will be attained through an attenuated process of limited-stakes consensus-building during which "the buck stops nowhere." One generally observed difficulty is the policy coordination of functional outcomes: Are there schools and fire protection anywhere near the location of proposed new homes, roads, and waterworks, for instance? One further consequence, too little noticed in the busy worlds of fragmented representative governing, is that all of these virtual governments operate within a kind of political twilight (for which there is no sunset) where policies and actions are never subject to even the limited and periodic public accountability that elections may enforce. The continuity in service provision that comes with appointed boards is often declared a virtue, but the debate which ought to be generated by the significance of the policies being considered (for instance, the extension of trunk sewers through, or to, prime agricultural lands) has been surrendered as elected officials give themselves a safety margin by delegating these single responsibilities to a complex of authorities one-step removed.

In this world, no one seems ever directly accountable. In unusually elegant language for an investigating commission, one regional government review in Ontario concluded that: "It is difficult for the expert, let alone the man in the street, to know who is responsible for which service ... or for the general condition of the community. One of the important elements of a properly working representative democracy is to be able to identify [persons responsible] ... and to be able to discern who should be entrusted to continue to exercise judgment in public policy.... It is not going too far to say that activity is so diffused that everyone has a say but no one is responsible, and that even the statutory responsibilities are not in accord with those found in practice" (WALG 1970: 5-6). This situation presents one persistent generic problem in governing for the Canadian city-region.

City-regions are defined variously by their respective national and sub-national governments. In the United States, the Standard Metropolitan Statistical Area (SMSA), which essentially is an urban county of 50,000-plus population, has been employed as a statistical definition since 1960 (Bollens and Schmandt 1982: 4-11). Although the definition was refined in 1983 with four more precise descriptors, the central concept was retained. By 1998 there were 329 census-defined metropolitan areas of one stripe or another in the United States. The complexity of their intergovernmental web is frequently noted, often with approbation: in 1976, the typical SMSA had 84 governments, with special districts (at 30) the most prolific (ACIR 1976: 147). But since each state defines its local governments somewhat differently, there is no common agreement on how many actually exist. The best current estimate by the Governments Division of the American Census Bureau is 87,453, of which 34,683 are special (often single function) districts and authorities. By 1992, the average American metropolitan area with a population of 635,000 had 104 governments: two counties, 24 municipalities, 16 towns or townships, 19 school districts, and 43 special districts (Stephens and Wikstrom 2000: 6-11, 19). Some major metropolitan regions today are very complex indeed, with New York City having 1,716 units of local government and Chicago 1,510.

Table 10.1: Canada's Largest Census Metropolitan Areas and Local Governments in 1996

CMA	Population	Cities	Towns	Villages	MDs	Other	Total	% in Core
Toronto	4,263,757	10	17	0	0	3	30	15.3
Montreal	3,326,510	74	9	15	0	1	99	30.6
Vancouver	1,831,665	11	1	3	6	2	23	28.1
Ottawa-Hull	1,010,498	7	5	5	0	9	26	32.1
Edmonton	862,597	5	9	6	4	9	33	71.4
Calgary	821,628	2	3	2	1	0	8	93.5
Quebec City	671,889	21	10	12	0	1	44	24.9
Winnipeg	667,209	1	0	0	9	0	10	92.7
Hamilton	624,360	3	4	0	0	1	8	51.6
London	398,616	2	0	2	0	7	11	81.7

Source: Statistics Canada 1997.

The Canadian city-region is statistically defined by Statistics Canada as a city-centred region of 100,000 or more population. There are presently 27 of these. While the Canadian CMA is less governmentally fractured than its rough American equivalent, there has not yet been any accurate survey of all its constituent authorities, especially of special purpose districts. The tally of municipal governments in Canada's ten largest CMAs for the federal census of 1996, before the modern consolidation era began, is noted in Table 10.1; school districts are not included. In Ottawa-Hull, the Regional Municipality of Ottawa-Carleton contained five cities, five townships, and one village with a combined 1996 population of 763,426, while the Communauté Urbaine de l'Outaouais was comprised of five cities and had a 1996 population of 247,072. The city-region itself had boundaries roughly the same as the federal government's National Capital Commission (NCC), which was established in 1958 with initial responsibilities for parks and regional park planning. As Caroline Andrew once noted, the presence of the federal government, the interested attention of *two* provinces, and the existence of two regional tiers as well as the two dozen municipalities "all ensure that local politics becomes intergovernmental relations" (1983: 141).

The multiple local governments of complex city-regions, each holding to its own development and servicing agenda, can be said to constitute a diluted system of governing whatever shape it might take at any given time. Many scholars label this a **polycentric metropolitan system** or megalopolis: "Megalopolis has assumed its demographic shape without spawning a political cover" (Savitch and Thomas 1991: 9). The central issue for any reform of metropolitan governing which expects to bring greater overall policy coherence to the polycentric urban system always begins with a focus on more effective land-use planning and its integration with servicing questions.

As will be more fully considered in the next chapter, the demographically defined city-region governed by multiple distinct local governments generates three sorts of policy questions. However they may emerge in public discussion, these boil down to (1) how to coordinate human settlement policies between adjacent communities as well as across the city-region as a whole; (2) how to provide some measure of equity between revenue sources and the need for service expenditures; and (3), importantly, how to establish clear accountability for both present practices and anticipated developments.

Before the 1990s, only Canada's four largest provinces had to address these issues comprehensively in the governmentally separated metropolis and to respond with any type of area-wide instruments. In their initiatives, the policy latitude granted provincial authority by the public was expansive, especially when contrasted with the tight political gateway which restricts American state legislatures. This difference in realizable possibilities is partially conditioned by differing political cultures in our two societies—deference to authority in Canada versus strong egalitarianism in the United States—which sustained a greater collective orientation to the public good in the former rather than the deeply set individualism more characteristic of the latter. In practical policy terms, the Canadian political culture permitted provincial authorities considerable latitude in restructuring and a public acceptance of even wide-ranging adaptations that has been quick to develop after new institutions have been imposed.

10.1.2 The human dimension

The shape of the postwar urbanization of North America, partly fuelled in Canada by federal and provincial urban development policies (see Leo 1995b), in part took the form it did due to "lifestyle refugees" exiting the core city for its suburbs. In a dual migration, those leaving were drawn from the "charter" ethnic communities (i.e., those of British or French origin) and were relatively affluent while those coming in were new immigrants (often visibly distinct).

The public policy problems of this urban diaspora have been most evident in central cities with their need to cope with, for example, English as a second language budgets, or community policing demands, or equity in employment practices. The dispersion of population across a metropolitan region may also have consequences in poor planning activities, wasteful resource usages, and generally bad environmental practices. Such widely deplored activities as urban development pressures on Ontario's Niagara escarpment or the agricultural lands of British Columbia's lower mainland, or even urban encroachment on class 1 and 2 soils within and around Alberta's CMAs have, at the minimum, initiated provincial investigation of city-region policy issues. The consequence of this agenda upgrade, though, has not always been decisive intervention.

Most citizens remain nonplussed by the multiplicity of governing units in the metropolis, and the layering by function or geography has been of less salience than how such institutions contribute to fulfilling lifestyle choices (Williams 1971; Clark 1998b). In the event of any proposed governmental consolidation, these lifestyle perceptions are the basis for ferocious parochialism. Many city-regions in North America also reveal a paradoxical asymmetry in the population with respect to identity. The lower the socio-economic status, the less an individual identifies with the metropolitan city. In short, lower status becomes the most local. On the other hand, community cosmopolitans with prestige occupations and higher incomes have strong extra-community attachments. They are the people who identify the city-region with its core city, and they promote its accomplishments—economic, cultural, professional sports—even when they reside in its suburbs.

One interesting analysis of American suburbs in continuous existence from 1920 to 1960 (Judd 1988: 191) determined that their social and economic mixture had never basically changed. Their original physical design as well as their self-perpetuating ghetto building, of richer as well as poorer residents, worked informally to sort out potentially nonconforming migrants. This idea of social segregation is somewhat akin to John Porter's ideas about Canada's processes of ethnic assimilation and charter groups; he observed that the first group to open up a territory for settlement carefully retained for itself the right to decide what other sorts of people would be allowed to enter (1965: 60).

Since the 1950s, with a few exceptions, the Canadian city-region has not followed the American prototype in permitting the establishment of small, autonomous, and virtually single-purpose cities within metropolitan areas. The home rule tradition abetted efforts not only to resist consolidation but also to fracture urban America further. The Pittsburgh metropolitan area, for instance, has 323 governments serving under 1.5 million people, 12 of which have fewer than 1,000 residents. The St. Louis "functional city" is a metropolitan area of 1.85 million people, covering 12 counties over two states; the core county of St. Louis has one-third of this population but 90 cities within its borders. One of these has 11 residents, another under 100, 21 fewer than 1,000 (Savitch and Vogel 1996: 292, 81). Smaller communities like these can be very specialized communities for industry, medicine, state universities, gambling, or even religion, as in Unity, Michigan (Stephens and Wikstrom 2000: 5).

Sometimes, small-scale municipal structures have been fitted precisely to restrictive ends. In the 1950s, the special-purpose cities of Industry (1957), Dairy Valley (1956), and Rolling Hills (1957) were all carved from the rump of the county of Los Angeles. The first had only 638 residents, 138 of whom were institutionalized in a sanitarium and was zoned exclusively for commercial–industrial ends; the second had 98,586 cows on 12,000 acres of land; the third was geared for one-to-five acre country residential estates whose owners sought to exclude industry and were willing to underwrite the necessary taxation to achieve that end (Bish 1971: 88–89). In 1984, residents in West Hollywood, a predominantly gay community, sought city-hood so as to be able to contract directly for more protection from the county sheriff's department to combat "a 77 per cent increase in violent crime rates" ("Vote Your Democratic Team" campaign brochure).

Specialized communities of this ilk are not, typically, a part of the Canadian CMA experience even though there are industrial examples. The town of Devon, Alberta, for instance, was developed by Imperial Oil to house its workers after its Leduc oil discovery in 1947 when the town of Leduc refused to expand sufficiently quickly. Fort Saskatchewan grew specifically to accommodate workers from the adjacent petrochemical processing operations in the County of Strathcona's "Refinery Row." Kanata, begun in 1966 as a private development new town 16 kilometres west of Ottawa, and with expectations of a high-tech industrial base, was conceived not as a dormitory suburb but an "edge city" with jobs more than equivalent to beds. Specific neighbourhoods within larger Canadian cities have emulated the American practice in placing restrictions on homeowners as a condition of sale. These restrictions include minimum floor areas of homes, a prohibition on front yard fences, and even control of garage door colours. But all these are exceptional cases. More generally, developing suburbs set neighbourhood plans and building codes; their councils control development opportunities. Patterns of exclusion in Canada tend to be more genteel and less heavy-handed than in American gated communities but are no less effective for all that. Permitting only single-family detached dwellings on 50-foot front lots excludes those persons and families in need of more diversified housing who are then forced to settle in core cities, often in territories recently vacated by the new suburbanites.

It should not, then, be surprising to find a strong pattern of social stratification among the municipalities in the polycentric metropolitan area. Examining only city-region average family incomes for towns and cities within CMAs on the eve of city government restructuring, as presented in Table

Table 10.2: Selected City-Region Household Income Disparities in 1996, by Municipalities, Prior to Consolidations (and Winnipeg, 1971)

City-Region	Population	CMA Average	Richest as % of Mean	Richest as % of Poorest
Toronto	4,263,757	$60,110	117	145
Montreal	3,326,510	44,593	316	445
Vancouver	1,831,665	49,553	192	234
Ottawa-Hull	1,010,498	56,760	307	611
Edmonton	862,597	49,908	124	151
Winnipeg	667,209	9,382	350	404
Quebec City	671,889	43,737	186	289

Source: Statistics Canada 1997.

10.2 for instance, reveals the sometimes very considerable disparities between the richest and poorest communities.

10.1.3 The physical plant and natural surroundings

In a dramatic sense, the extension of even the hidden physical infrastructure of sewer and water lines can have a significant impact on the urban topography. For example, the unconstrained land-rush which today constitutes "urban planning" in British Columbia's lower mainland is demonstrably the consequence of permitting intermunicipal tradeoffs in expanding the pipelines. The resulting mutual and continuous assessment expansion, by councils, has perverted all pretense of employing sustainable urban planning precepts. It also illustrates, dramatically, the weakness in any development process where the last word over the central metropolitan planning function is held by councillors in numerous suburban municipalities and their political allies in provincial government.

Although the City Beautiful Movement in Canada, which was based on planning concepts demonstrated at Chicago's World Fair in 1893, worked much good in core cities like Ottawa and Edmonton between the two world wars, it could only plan *within* the confines of particular municipal borders. However, the boundaries of watersheds and wetlands, and their management, are seldom coincident with these, and the negative results of urban expansion quickly became apparent with rapid postwar suburban growth. While time has shown that each watershed has unique characteristics, it has taken longer for policy-makers to realize that one policy approach does not fit all (McAllister 1995: 250-52). Locally specific agencies were needed to transcend local and regional boundaries and to reconcile the divergent policy interests of different provincial (and sometimes federal) departments. Even as local governments remained the most directly accountable to citizens as electors, the requirement for water resource management produced limited pressures for policy delegation to some sort of authority based on a wider territory. Catalogued failures of city planning policies to accomplish more sustainable results compiled by various players in the environmental social movement (for example, the Sierra Club)—assessments patently not limited by artificial town and city lines—have further fuelled heightened expectations by citizens that government should pay attention to these matters.

More generally, the absence of any effective common boundary between policy-making jurisdictions and the policy problems faced in growing metropolitan regions becomes itself an issue when the provision of piped water, sewerage, and, in some instances, drainage and transportation services is on the table. Land without pipes underneath is just mud for any developer interested in capitalizing upon federal and provincial policies supportive of the spatial expansion of the demographic city. With the promise of servicing in the form of regional trunk lines for potable water and sewerage removal, land value increases sufficiently to permit the borrowing approvals for financial investment in new residential neighbourhoods. Advance planning for the arterial roadways and the collector networks which will move prospective residents to future employment around the city-region requires area and neighbourhood planning to begin in earnest.

Issues emerge as each municipality endeavours, on its own, to capture either the largest or the most attractive prospective new developments in order to maximize their community's assessment base even where they don't, in fact, have the basic physical infrastructure available to satisfy developers' requirements. This underlying servicing problem is why the first tentative step toward regional service integration has almost always originated in a seldom romantic, but necessarily cross-boundary and cooperative plan to upgrade water plants and build new sewer lines. For instance, in 1951, the dozen autonomous suburbs of the City of Toronto requested permission from the Ontario Municipal Board to borrow funds sufficient to construct the water facilities that could service more rapid development. This approach followed the city's failed 1950 application for full amalgamation in the region based on its belief that "the suburban councils could not cope with the financial and administrative burdens involved [with massive growth] and that the development of the whole area would be held back as a result" (Magnusson 1983b: 109).

Ultimate control over the livable design of a metropolitan locale comes through the linkage of servicing to planning choices: "If the creation of the master plan for the metropolitan area was seen as the *sine qua non*, then so was the metropolitan authority to establish and police it. The decline in the role has led to the decline in the instrument" (Sharpe 1995a: 2). This has resulted in the feebleness of the planning role in American SMSAs, which today exist without comprehensive city-region governments. Area-wide planning by either a voluntary council of governments or a state-appointed commission without formal powers is ineffective as both are only advisory and, at the same time, are distanced from those officials who are actually responsible for programs and functions. They are policy development instruments without any genuine capacity to implement or enforce.

The Canadian experience with city-region development has been different. Critics of the first Canadian metropolitan governments in Toronto (Rose 1972) and Winnipeg argued along these lines: "While rationality and efficiency were the usual justification for two-level metropolitan government ... in fact the main impact of this reform was to make possible the construction of major public works programs ... which the property industry considered necessary to sustain the kind of urban growth the industry wanted to see ..." (Lorimer 1972: 90). In economics terms, such redistributive policy as did occur at the metropolitan level in the early years of Toronto was from the central core to the suburbs. This facilitated basic municipal infrastructure, not only in terms of arterial roadways but also to replace wells and septic systems with twentieth-century urban waterworks. In the Winnipeg case, the metropolitan emphasis was on roads and bridges. In both cases, metropolitan councils controlled urban development to some extent from the start. But not until well after their statute creation were two-tier metropolitan regimes in Canada able to initiate much in the way of social planning and development.

The few genuine urban consolidations that emerged in the United States required a cathartic hard-servicing crisis to override both local and state legislature resistance to reorganization. The Jacksonville-Duval, Florida, city-county consolidation of 1967 followed revelations of high levels of water and air pollution, inadequate storm water drainage, "dysfunctional" suburban sewer facilities maintained by private developers, discredited schools, and a sheriff's department itself under criminal investigation (Swanson 1996: 232-37). The last straw was the grand jury indictment of 11 officials associated with the city's political machine for police corruption and lax law enforcement, irregularities in purchasing practices, and outright bribery: "Many observers believe that the indictments provided the multiplier factor that put the consolidation referendum over the top" (Bollens and Schmandt 1982: 393). While the groundwork for adaptation was laid by the basic inability of the city-region's governments to provide the fundamental services which are normally taken for granted, to override public resistance grounded in political culture still required an avalanche of policy malfeasance.

10.1.4 The furtive "design" through public choice

The repeatedly demonstrated inability of city-region political leadership in the United States to conclude reorganizational initiatives found academic comfort and legitimacy in a postwar theory usually labelled "public choice." While this idea's central propositions will be more thoroughly considered in Chapter 12, at this point it is enough to note that this theory has been used to justify the governmentally fragmented Canadian CMA by borrowing from the standard American explanation. In a long series of thoughtful essays, for example, Sancton argued the case for the utility of multiple governments in the polycentric metropolis (especially Sancton 1994). The pink glow of this sort of academic vision of the Canadian metropolis was dimmed considerably by the municipal consolidations in Ontario and Quebec CMAs in the 1990s. The reasons for these, plainly put, were that the 1950s American-style governmentally dispersed city-region had been sufficiently revealed to provincial governments to cost more and accomplish less than a more unitary form of city government could provide.

Not all, of course, shared in the belief that absolute measures of these last two variables could be shown to exist; fewer still could establish any accurate accounting for far less tangible, "community values." As will be discussed in Chapter 13, those in power in both of Canada's two largest provinces possessed both the political will and the clear constitutional authority to unify all of their major city-regions for whatever reasons of public policy they saw fit their own circumstances. Before the 1990s, the Canadian record had been notable for its cautious incrementalism, marked only occasionally by spurts of two-level innovation.

The point is that the public choice position was rooted in a North American municipal world whose political logic has long been dominated by American intellectual traditions. Part of the urban legend of the American metropolis is the story of the well-managed local suburb that thrives in its separation from the patronage-ridden, corruption-driven, bureaucratic central city. In a typical, and classic, textbook statement, W.O. Winter claimed the "general excellence" of city government on Chicago's fringes and fretted over the deleterious consequence of any potential amalgamation: "The government of Glencoe, Oak Park, or Evanston is superior, by certain standards, to the government of the city of Chicago … If a metropolitan government were to absorb any of these communities, the very probable result would be deterioration in their governments" (1969: 199).

These assumptions reveal the prescriptive nature of the public choice perspective. Its proponents frequently contend that suburban service delivery costs are less because public bureaucrats are not in a position to exact monopoly charges. Michael Keating makes the obvious rejoinder, however, that suburban taxpayers may, in effect, be better able politically than taxpayers in larger cities to exploit their municipal workforces by, for instance, discouraging unionization. He continues by suggesting that lower costs "might equally reflect the tendency for the American middle classes to retreat into small, homogenous communities which do not face the high costs of areas with more social stress or central place functions, and to provide more services privately" (1995: 125). From the evidence of American experience, contracting out was a major response to fiscal pressures by the 1,333 cities surveyed by the International City Management Association in 1982. When merged with other expenditure data, analysis reveals that savings were least with for-profit private entrepreneurs, moderately more with other governments, and only significant with nonprofit agencies which were able to subsidize operations with volunteers or by piggybacking costs onto other state funding like tax exemptions (Miranda 1994b: 208-10).

So the lifestyle choice so proclaimed by public choice theory has a dark heart, which does not take into account a simple reality: core city decay is not conducive to overall metropolitan prosperity. The metropolitan problem has always been that not every family or citizen is *able* to choose to live in a community which encompasses their exclusive inclinations about how to live well.

The package of suburban municipal services provided in response to each community's demands varies only according to the kinds of residents they themselves have recruited. The services provided restrict the sorts of people who are able to relocate to the suburb which, in turn, reinforces the circle of exclusivity in demand. Suburban communities such as Westmount, Quebec, or St. Albert, Alberta, have lived a variant of the *Field of Dreams* signature slogan with an approach which stipulates, "if you don't build it, they can't come." Not to permit the construction of multi-family residential buildings or lower rent apartments is exclusion. If non-peak hour transit is not provided, shift workers are shut out. Where social services are designed only for middle-class supports (meals-on-wheels, education in crafts, after-school care, etc.), others more dependent must live elsewhere.

The public choice position since Tiebout (1956) has long been that persons with essentially comparable lifestyle preferences will choose to locate in local communities with generally similar expectations. But in the polycentric city-region, not all are equally free to make that location choice.

10.2 Who Delivers What Services?

For the last American political generation of the twentieth century, the major public debate in service delivery increasingly focused on efforts to introduce private entrepreneurial "efficiencies" into public administration. Much celebrated concepts like Total Quality Management, and its exemplar communities like Madison, Wisconsin, replaced more traditional concerns about which public instruments were most appropriate for area-wide service delivery in city-regions. Although much celebrated, and even more frequently quoted, Osborne and Gaebler (1992) did not elaborate much on city-region governing, focusing instead on individual municipalities' economic competence in meeting their own functional obligations. In Canada, suburban resistance to metropolitan unification has never been couched in the terms of accumulating greater city-region proficiency in service delivery but rather on local identity issues; it was widely *assumed* that intra-municipal effectiveness had been accomplished by fringe city councils. Only in retrospective have some academics advanced the proposition that the fractious governing of Canadian city-regions satisfies the lower costs tests of Osborne and Gaebler because of flexibility in their varied localized arrangements (most notably Sancton 1994: 99).

10.2.1 Striving for balance

Regional governments had other objectives set for them, which were intended to contain spillovers in demand, costs, and service use. In theory, those functions that had an impact upon a service area larger than any municipal government would be "regionalized" to a wider area governing unit of some sort. In this way, the problem could be internalized, in economists' terms, by the boundaries of the new institution so that the costs of service provision could be roughly met by revenue generation through taxation, user fees, or some other levy on individuals or the constituent governments. Internalizing is much easier if geographic boundaries are limited by physical features such as the lower mainland for the GVRD, the island of Montreal, or the not-serviced prairie spaces surrounding Regina and Calgary. In each of the major Canadian governing initiatives concerning regional districts (Alberta, British Columbia, Ontario, and Quebec), it is important to bear in mind the corollary to the subordinate constitutional status of municipalities: *the onus for adjustment* and the redefinition of responsibilities rests directly on the shoulders of the respective provinces.

One of the best semi-official considerations of the intricate problem of balance for emergent regions was undertaken in response to municipal demands in Ontario for a review of provincial fiscal and grants structure in 1967. That "taxation and revenue system" appeared to local governments, at least, to present serious difficulties upon the capacity to provide local services equitably and without unfair advantage to a selected, commercially advantaged few. Over the course of their investigations of fiscal stress and the basis for local revenues, Ontario's (Smith) Committee on Taxation came to the conclusion that it was the overall structure of the municipal operation itself which had aggravated the difficult situation presented by population shifts (Ontario 1967: II). The structural features of that system's charter, the Municipal Corporations (Baldwin) Act of 1849, had been touched up across the decades, but its core operating essentials stood unchanged.

The Smith Committee concluded that asymmetry of structure with contemporary functional demands was sufficiently serious that it stepped beyond its terms of reference to recommend a new structure for regional governing across the province. In response, the Province of Ontario acted quickly (as these things go) to fashion new regional municipalities. But while Higgins regarded the new operation as a fundamental or "systemic" change (1986: 198-202), in reality the provincial government only incrementally adapted the two-tier, nineteenth-century county institutions into two-tier twentieth-century ones somewhat better reflective of contemporary social and economic integration.

The argument that rationalized those subsequent reforms is valuable to note. The Smith Committee contended that the objectives of local administration were twofold. First, there was *access*, which they defined as "the most widespread participation possible on the part of all or virtually all individual citizens ... local government is particularly conducive [to access] ... in terms of the capacity to influence public policy decisions and to enforce responsive and responsible administration ... the central reason is that the capacity of government to promote access is in part an *inverse* function of size" (emphasis added). The committee also set an ideal that might fully satisfy the access value in which units of local administration would be "sufficiently small to enable all citizens to participate directly in public affairs" (Ontario 1967: Vol. II, 503); in a very real sense the ideal was the historic New England town meeting style of governing.

The second objective perceived for effective local administration was that of *service* which the committee thought would be the logical outcome of a municipal administration that promoted open access and engaged citizens: "if local government is highly conducive to popular access ... it is also an important service instrument. By service we mean not only the economical discharge of public functions, but the achievement of technical adequacy in due alignment with public needs and desires" (Ontario 1967: Vol II,

503-04). The central problem with achieving this value was that, to some considerable degree, it either conflicted or competed with the attainment of the first, thus limiting the realization of each. This was because service (as defined by the committee) tends to be a *direct* function of size. So, while the most economic provision of a service may imply much larger administrative units, best access is normally accomplished through the smallest units. Best access requires a thorough consultation with all interested citizens and policy networks; on the other hand, the professional provision of quality technology-reliant service is best attained through the operations of an efficient, but closed, bureaucratic hierarchy.

For the Smith Committee, an appropriate balancing of access with service was essential, and the answer lay in a revitalization of the tried and true two-tier form established under the Baldwin Act. The service value could best be met by regionalizing functions that were technologically costly and capital-budget intensive, or that required an array of specialized professional talents. The access value could be satisfied through leaving functions with an immediate impact to existing smaller scale community governments.

In matching theory to the realities on the ground, the committee believed that the establishment of new regions would best be accomplished through the application of five criteria central to any regional governing operation. These were:

1. a sense of the regional community through history, geography, and economy existed and would continue to evolve;

2. the diverse interests in the territory (especially rural versus urban) were roughly in balance and seemed likely so to remain;

3. a proposed region should have a sufficient tax base that it might achieve its own equalization of service levels without constant recourse to the provincial purse;

4. any region should be configured such that region-wide benefits could be accomplished to gain efficiencies as measured in economic terms; and

5. regional boundaries should be cognizant of topography (like watersheds) to encourage intermunicipal cooperation in the discharge of specific large-scale functions.

To the committee's core proposals, provincial ministers added three more before acting—(6) regions could promote participation, (7) boundaries should support provincial departmental decentralization, and (8) any criteria for the lower tier should apply also to the area-wide level—in a move to make the package less costly in political terms (Higgins 1986: 200).

The rhetoric about values came easier than the implementation, since the service value always overshadowed access. Regional government was focused on wider area service upgrades, usually of the physical plant, and important decisions on costly policies consistently underwent a vertical functional shift to regional councils. Because these were not directly elected, thus not directly accountable, any form of consequential public participation quickly became a diminished, not necessary, virtue.

While the Smith Committee contended that new regional boundaries could be developed logically if their five criteria were followed, regionalism in Ontario from 1969 through 1974 was achieved through a consolidation of existing units. The 12 new regions (including Metro Toronto) reduced the number of included lower tier municipalities from 188 to 84. This aggressive consolidation was not attempted in the original construction of the Communauté Urbaine de l'Outaouais or Quebec [City] Urban Community during this same period. Thus, the Smith Committee recommendations differed from the Baldwin Act in two ways: (1) the new regions included all urban areas as lower tier units and (2) the new regional governments (like the first in 1969, Ottawa-Carleton) controlled far more of the area's total municipal spending than the counties ever envisaged. In fact the more urbanized were metropolitan governments along the lines of the Toronto (1954) model. By way of contrast, the parallel regional structures in Quebec at this time had few formal powers apart from traffic regulation, public transportation, and property assessment even though the option for a vertical shift of more serious functions was permitted *if and when* the lower level municipalities ever so wished. There was no rush to do this.

10.2.2 Matching structures to concepts

The central assumptions of the Smith Committee weighed upon other provincial assessments of their own institutions even when unacknowledged (Quebec) or ignored (British Columbia). The questions which underlie studies of public policy-making within Canada's urban concentrations normally concern the many barriers limiting demographically and economically defined cities from redefining their own political institutions. For constitutional reasons, there has been never been a *national* strategy to provide local governments for these citizens. In 1996 Canada's ten largest CMAs had a combined total of just under 300 front-line municipal governments, each with its own servicing and planning operation, and all of the municipalities operated with an autonomous mayor and council and their own more or less public agenda for economic and political development. These were quite exclusive of the uncounted area-wide metropolitan planning and servicing commissions, boards, and agencies that existed to facilitate (as co-depen-dants) a muddling along approach that served as surrogate for genuinely regional policies. In consequence, no one among these institutions had much stake in challenging the institutional status quo.

The first step towards defining practical boundaries to confine municipal policy problems has persistently proven elusive for provincial authorities. While uncovering structural (or institutional) overlap and confusion was reasonably straightforward, it has proven to be quite another matter, until very recently, to devise practicable reforms. It was yet a third level of dif-ficulty to implement these, a question considered in more detail in Chapter 13. Generally, governments forced into contemplating institutional reforms by unanticipated policy developments have attempted to use historical hind-sight to define a "genuine community" basis for a new governing form, a kind of traditional geographic basis for future shared involvement in a huge neighbourhood identity.

This is where somewhat specious academic claims about the appropri-ate scale for locally democratic units come into play. Robert Dahl and E.R. Tufte, for instance, provided data that seemingly substantiated the seminal (for the twentieth century) argument that direct citizen participation beyond the simple act of voting was most probable in units of government no larger than 8,000 persons (1973: 84ff). The claim is specious in that it is based upon a set of assumptions that citizens are *only* likely to be able "to compre-hend" and identify with the personality and issue processes of smaller scale institutions. While this orthodoxy has been maintained by many commu-nity activists and most public choice theorists since the 1960s, and by some among more recent university-based proponents of "identity politics," actual research findings have *not* rendered the association of scale with effective involvement axiomatic.

The difficulty for the provinces has been that most municipal borders in metropolitan regions are not natural in any organic sense. While there may be some history behind some specific locations, and some unpalatable politics behind the emergence of other suburbs, all municipal institutions are the consequence of arbitrarily determined borders. This legal definition of community is necessarily artificial for it stems from the functional delinea-tion of a territory for service delivery. Statisticians might look for workforce or shopping commuter-sheds, and political sociologists could once define a city-centred region on the basis of the delivery pattern of its major metropolitan newspapers, but in this web-based age policy-makers find operational notions of community to be more elusive than ever. At their wisest, provincial governments try to balance territorial scope, functional authority, fiscal competence, and clear accountability. The motivation is usually expressed as a wish to ensure sufficient local technical and operational expertise to provide municipal service at provincially determined minimum standards in rough conformity with the province's assessment of the local public's willingness to pay. Any concerns for the vitality of local democracy have reflected, in the reality of the reforms accomplished, a pretty low priority on all provincial agendas.

As one good example of reform, Ontario, after the serious legislative inquiry of the Smith Committee, undertook a bold rewrite of the statutes defining local and regional (county) governments over the decade after 1968, a policy process only partly disrupted by minority government status from 1972-74. This had the practical effect of reducing the number of lower tier governments; placing two-thirds of the provincial population under some 12 regional authorities; and regionalizing the principal functions of arterial roadways, transit, water and sewerage, police, health, welfare, and, theoretically, regional planning. Direct local control over anything of significance was diminished in the process.

Even where it remains publicly unacknowledged, other provinces have dealt with their urban-centred municipalities by emulating these policies. The vexatious constant, in the absence of significant institutional changes, remained the persistence of well-known city-region problems. For instance, even the minor metropolis of St. John's, Newfoundland, has too many municipalities, averaging one per 10,000 residents. Each of these, except for the core city, is directly dependent upon the province for all sewer, water, and road projects. In late 1990, the City of St. John's pressed the province for amalgamation to capture "homeowners fleeing property taxes by moving to the bedroom communities outside its borders" (*Globe and Mail,* 13 November 1990). The province responded, typically for the time, by promising to study the matter, a policy decision not to decide that directly affirmed the status quo.

Montreal lumbered through the period up to 2000 with 135 local governments, including not only the central island (with 29 cities and the second tier of Montreal Urban Community) but also the suburbs on the south shore of the St. Lawrence River. Throughout this period, the region also produced an impressive array of commissioned studies and reports, all of whose core recommendations were overlooked when structural revamping finally took place. As elsewhere, until its dramatic intervention, provincial involvement came in the form of piecemeal activities, usually in the form of short-term fiscal relief. In June 1997, for example, the Province of Quebec guaranteed $50 million to the City of Montreal, to be collected through taxes on amusements, gas, and electricity, "to compensate [the city] for being surrounded by suburban residents who enjoy its benefits but don't pay it any taxes" (*Globe and Mail*, 26 March 1998).

Other provincial cabinets also backed away from serious restructuring until the latter 1990s with the use of various stop-gap responses to specific problems. This worked to the short-term advantage of the players in the polycentric systems because, as E.E. Schattschneider once observed (1960: 10–11), to raise a conflict to a higher level of government means a loss of control over the matter for directly affected combatants which, in these cases, were *both* suburbs and central cities. Such a consequence was one lesson from the Toronto Megacity debate in 1997 (or Winnipeg Unicity in 1970); once the provincial ministries assumed control of the restructuring agenda, official voices from all municipalities (and many of their constituent citizens' groups) were openly ignored.

In taking on patently necessary changes to existing metropolitan government forms, the policy issues quickly became politically partisan for central authorities and especially for those with only a mild reformist heart. Michael Keating understated considerably when he wrote that "Governments committed to consolidation have always found it extremely difficult to achieve. Change affects the interest of politicians, bureaucrats and residents. It shifts burdens and opportunities and creates fears and uncertainties" (1995: 129). In the face of any reform considered to weaken institutionalized parochialism, suburban councillors, locked in to the political seraglios they have chosen, quickly forge a shrill coalition of the unwilling (Lightbody 1998). However, their arguments are so extremely predictable, they can be easily ignored by determined authorities with a serious reform agenda.

Canadian experience with metropolitan area governing of the two-tier sort began with Toronto in 1953, then Winnipeg in 1961. This short burst of provincial priority interest in city-region governing continued with the Regional Municipality of Ottawa-Carleton in 1969 and ended with the creation of the Montreal Urban Community of that same year. Both domestic and foreign observers saw these institutions, especially the Metro Toronto design, as resolving long-standing issues of accountability and control. In their classic work, Bollens and Schmandt observed that, "The metropolitan government concept is firmly established in the Toronto area," and they described it as "a permanent solution" (1982: 339). More recently, and in the same year that it was disassembled, Metro Toronto institutions were labelled "a jewel" by Katherine Graham and Susan Phillips (1998: 75). The "miracle" of Metro Toronto was much noted from the American side, as in Victor Jones's forward to Albert Rose's analysis of it as constituting "the only truly metropolitan government'" (1972: x). Had anyone cared to take academic notice, each of the other Canadian metropolitan governments would have evoked roughly similar accolades. Norton Long was more cautious when he observed early on that, "the miracle of Toronto became even less miraculous as its metropolitan government turned to social politics and the problems of fiscal redistribution" (1968: 247).

By the end of the century, the heyday of the Canadian two-tier metropolis had ended. In an international and comparative context, Sharpe observed, with regret, that no one really loved metropolitan government and that the model was generally in decline around the world (1995b: 27). But before they went about the fundamental upsetting of vested-interest apple carts, provincial politicians did permit other agencies to step forward with interim policy solutions promising varying degrees of *ad hoc* success.

10.3 Governing by ABCs: City-Region Agencies, Boards, and Commissions

In the last half of the twentieth century, the fragmentation of state operations at all levels of authority had an impact on city-region governing in most Western countries. In the UK, the term QUANGO, for quasi-autonomous non-government organization, is used variously to describe all manner of agencies. Sometimes these are what Canadians would label Crown corporations (like British Rail), but more usually they range from advisory councils to quasi-judicial boards and from coordinating public-sector service delivery to regulating private operations (Byrne 1994). Some QUANGOs are purely promotional, as are Arts or Sports Councils, or are economic development boards. Whatever their purpose, beginning in 1948 these sorts of operations, funded and appointed by the central government, were deployed by Whitehall to provide effective service for wider areas than local government possessed (initially in public transport and land-use planning). Following Margaret Thatcher's Conservative Party election in 1979, the New Right openly and dramatically used this form as a means to remove functions from local authorities, for example, by regionalizing water operations. So QUANGOs have a direct impact on British local government in particular issue areas (Dunleavy 1980: 108-09). The central ministry departments use their influence over these agencies for individual projects, especially where a QUANGO intends to carry out its own development or to regulate private-sector proposals. Some purely local QUANGOs enjoy a symbiotic relationship to local government in that the latter provides funds to a range of voluntary organizations which, in turn, provide services. In North America, the generic term for some similar kinds of activity is **private-public partnership** or PPP.

In Canada, numerous dimensions of this type of activity exist, and we must be careful to differentiate, right off the bat, between provincial statute agencies (like the OMB) and wider area, city-region (but provincially appointed) operations like conservation agencies, housing authorities, or health districts. The provincial decentralization efforts are also to be distinguished from inter-municipal **special purpose districts (SPDs)** which will be discussed in Chapter 11 as they grapple with accountability problems and in Chapter 12 for their effectiveness as tools for service delivery across city-regions.

Provincial decentralization in locally important functional areas (like housing, water conservation or irrigation, or public health), *and* city councils' own penchant to spin away persistently tough and controversial policy choices (parking, property zoning appeals, policing) onto partially autonomous boards found considerable appeal during the twentieth century. This behaviour is justified by reaching back to the idea of the blue-ribbon panels of "expert men" touted by the turn-of-the-century (1900) reform movement. Applied in Jacksonville, Florida, for instance, as part of the effort to restore public confidence in local officials, a set of a half-dozen independent authorities (for electricity, transportation, the port, the downtown, sports, and housing) removed important functions from elected political direction and, in practice, "operated beyond the direct, day-to-day control of the general consolidated government" (Swanson 1996: 237). By standing somewhat removed from the direct turmoil of daily public politics, these non-elected boards, then and there and here and now, are thought able to apply "best practices" or "fundamental principles" that ordinary elected politicians might find it necessary to compromise.

In theory, optimal policy would result, and rules of fairness and equity would prevail. But, as observed in Chapter 4, such local **arms' length authorities** in the form of planning committees, police commissions, parks and library boards, public health authorities, and so on, have also meant that the potential for focused accountability and policy coordination within cities and across city-regions has been persistently fractured. Purely from the perspective of policy innovation, however, functionally specific agencies can be single-minded in their pursuit of best choices and can consequently provide a form of autonomous policy leadership that even the best administrators more closely supervised by council could not.

While the role of these authorities should be considered more fairly in a full discussion of what is expected of local democracy, it *can* be said here that all such authorities operate in a half-light of politics with their policies and actions seldom subject to even the limited and periodic public accountability that elections enforce on representatives. Higgins estimated that in Ontario in 1967 some 3,220 special-purpose bodies existed over and above the 964 municipalities then in place (1986: 145). Today there is no inventory for Canada as a whole, partly because there is no definition common to all provinces (as a statistical measure), partly because municipalities are not all required to publicize the existence of bodies with delegated authority, partly because they are not statute (and occasionally not bylaw) creations, and so forth. It can be estimated that some 6,500 local special purpose bodies now operate within the overall framework of Ontario's local governments, an average of about 15 each, although the City of Toronto alone has at least 75. In small part, this large number reflects definitional differences. However, the greater public policy reality, which mirrors in miniature the experience of complex American city-regions, is that municipal governments have chosen, and are permitted to do so in law and through public inattention, to cope with particularly sticky public policy issue arenas by creating a "government" for that single function. Enthusiastic co-conspirators in this enterprise are both the interested policy community and associated policy networks.

A more significant set of players in the long-term development of Canada's city-regions has been provincial oversight agencies mentioned briefly in Chapter 9 as a means for provincial control of local governments. These include such bodies as the OMB, the Manitoba Municipal Board, or Alberta's Municipal Board. Since provincial domination of municipalities as expressed by the reality of "control" exhibits what political spin-doctors might label "negative optics," that authority is sometimes nuanced through delegation of that power to a **quasi-independent regulatory agency**, (1) which exists outside the formal provincial government structure; (2) whose officers are appointed (often by order-in-council) outside civil service regulations; (3) whose mandate to make policy tends to be restricted to a narrowly defined area of governing functions; and (4) which are subject to quite limited public control although in some cases there may exist a right to appeal decisions to the provincial cabinet (Plunkett and Lightbody 1982: 208-11).

Generically, these agencies claim to provide provincial ministries with a grocery list of advantages beyond diminished accountability. They may be used for cross-jurisdictional service questions, for more "business-like" activities, to recruit more professional personnel, or to gain access to uninhibited expert advice. They may also be used when a provincial government wishes to explore previously uncharted policy territory or to dispense judicial-style decisions expeditiously and without undue costs to the concerned parties. Importantly, they may also remove a contentious subject matter from "political controversy" (Schindeler 1969: 70-76). As to this last, little is more controversial in provincial-municipal relations than the question of separating land from one municipality and attaching it to another. Empires are built in the low politics of municipalities where more than a few councillors readily assign themselves the historical status of great Kublai Khans! Ministers of Municipal Affairs across the country have not been reluctant to avert direct accountability while specific land management cases are "now being heard by the tribunal."

In their general form, Canadian municipal boards have held responsibility for annexations and amalgamations, for appeals on bylaws usually related to specific plans, and for approval of capital borrowings and the imposition of taxes to pay for non–self-liquidating debt instruments. The roots for this provincial oversight in Canada can be traced back to the nineteenth century and the inherent principle of the Baldwin Act that the central government must protect the credit of the municipality out of concern for the rights and privileges of property owners. For the period from 1897 until it was delegated to the Ontario Railway and Municipal Board in 1906, the Provincial Auditor exercised the supervisory power in Ontario. At the height of the Great Depression in 1932, the OMB was established by statute to sustain investor confidence in municipal bond commitments. In a similar vein in Alberta in 1961, the Local Authorities Board was spun out of the jurisdiction of the Board of Public Utilities Commissioners (created in 1915). Its responsibilities were "to inquire into the merit of municipal debentures and to supervise the expenditures once raised, to separate lands from a municipality and to deal with plans for subdivision and annexation" (Plunkett and Lightbody, 1982: 209). Most of the larger provinces have had experience with such arms' length agencies, the only important exception being British Columbia (Plunkett and Betts 1978: 86-87).

Quasi–autonomous agencies are not an exceptional variation of such provincial bureaucratic hybrids as the Office of the Greater Toronto Area (OGTA). This was established in 1988 by the Province of Ontario as a coordinating body to "work with" Metro Toronto and the four regional governments of York, Peel, Durham, and Halton which encircled it. As a provincial bureau to harmonize policies, however, the office had no statutory authority but only limited advisory powers to encourage cooperation in transportation, waste disposal, and, as always, land use planning. The provincial attention was somewhat atypical in having central problems so formally recognized, but with neither a clear mandate nor budget, the OGTA never held status much higher than as an intergovernmental chat room.

As architects of the metropolitan government form in the Canadian CMA, regulatory agencies have figured prominently in both active and more reactive roles. As to the latter, events in Manitoba in 1970 provide one good example of a governing party exerting its authority while skirting direct ministerial accountability. During the internal government caucus debate concerning the advisability of consolidating the municipalities in the Winnipeg CMA, Premier Ed Schreyer responded directly to rural MLA worries that the ministry "was spawning an uncontrollable monster" by saying that the government could leash the new city's finances through the Municipal Board (Lightbody 1978b: 500).

A second example of the use of a quasi-regulatory agency as a policy stalking-horse appeared when, in 1979, the City of Edmonton applied to Alberta's Local Authorities Board for permission to amalgamate with two major suburban municipalities. After extensive hearings, the Board granted this governmental consolidation in 1980, subject only to provincial cabinet consent (Plunkett and Lightbody 1982). It took two years for the province to take the unusual, but shrewdly calculated, partisan political step of overturning the board's controversial order in order to preserve the dormitory communities' autonomy.

More active intervention came from the OMB which originated the proposal for the Metro Toronto form in 1953 when it denied the central city's request for amalgamation with its 12 CMA satellite communities. Suggestive of the close linkages of quasi-independent agencies with the political process, the two-tier recommendation was enacted by the province one month following the OMB's report—an unbelievably short period for the Canadian legislative policy stage! One potent selling point to a tradition-bound conservative administration, within the private corridors of influence, was reference to history and tradition: Metro Toronto was to be the Baldwin Act applied to an urban setting.

Any fair assessment of the role played by provincial regulatory boards in Canadian city-region governmental restructuring should include the note that they do permit the emergence of a highly professional expertise, consistently applied, in often complex and politically controversial policy areas. But this has come at a cost as political leadership with public accountability has diminished.

Over the years, lingering questions and concerns about accountability have focused on three fundamental subjects of importance for citizens. First, and fundamentally, ought boards of appointed officials ever to be permitted to overrule the policy decisions of directly elected local councils and thus erode local authority? This query becomes all too frequently very relevant when the process results in the appointment of party hacks and personal cronies of those in provincial office. Second, whose access is institutionalized in the specialized and *de facto in camera* proceedings, even the language of which is frequently an arcane argot to those for whom it is not an everyday job? Virtually by definition, the existence of an institution dedicated to a particular policy realm creates a policy subsystem with its own particular actors, quasi-professional interests, differentiated means to influence authority, and unique patterns of exclusion. Third, how wide a sweep in the public interest is protected in a process dominated by cartels of parallel interests represented by people in the business, those professionals whose livelihoods depend on positive outcomes, and their provincial and municipal administrative cronies? Boards, especially in entrepreneurial areas, can become virtually self-regulating in the tradition of corporatist political thought in which the delivery of significant activities of the state are devolved into the private sphere of both charitable and for-profit enterprises. It may be expected, and hoped, that future challenges to these virtual closed-shop operations from the past, whose activities were unfettered by citizen curiosity or challenge, might emerge through new citizen movements and policy communities who seek a policy forum and issue veto.

Globalization of knowledge has already begun to play a role in a quite practical form as issue-conscious citizens become willing to oppose the pre-eminence of old-style expertise. The result is a demand for access to information about how policy decisions are made so that the consequences of policy choices in one venue can be shown to be an example of what to copy, or to avoid, in other neighbourhoods and communities.

eleven | Theoretical questions about metropolitan institutions

Despite the distinctive characteristics that render them superficially unique, the larger Canadian CMAs have pretty much developed within a somewhat similar configuration. Typically, the city-region is focused on a well-established core city which is itself anchored in its central business district. Each major Canadian CMA (except Regina) owes its place adjacent to a significant body of water (harbour, lake, navigable river) to an historic need to locate alongside established trading routes. Over time, the central city found itself ringed by both dormitory and industrial satellite suburbs, some mixed and some very specialized to one or the other purpose. Indeed, in some American SMSAs, like St. Louis, suburbs are so specialized as to become not only income but also racially exclusive. This last factor has not been an issue in the politics of the Canadian CMA.

Together, these types of communities, plus the built-up area's urbanizing but still primarily agrarian proximate hinterland, constitute a **metropolitan system**. It must be emphasized that each of these configurations can be substantially different in its own particular composition. Despite this, over the latter part of the twentieth century, almost all North American metropolitan areas progressed toward some type of institutional consolidation due to the persistent emergence, and then recurrence, of three generic problems in city-region public policy. It is the purpose in this chapter to consider the nature of these recurrent matters.

405

Any demographically defined urban region generates specific area-wide problems for public policy. The central issue to be addressed here is what causes these problems to be defined as such priorities that regional public policy processes must endeavour to resolve them. We begin by appreciating that the autonomy of Canadian cities, as governments, is curbed in many ways. First, they are defined by provincial statutes and regulations. Their mandatory and permissive powers are often very restrictively set down by provincial authorities, and these are quite similar across the country regardless of whatever political party is in power provincially. Municipalities are further constrained by a jumble of quasi-autonomous boards, agencies, authorities, QUANGOs, and special districts over and above the activities of, and liaisons with, provincial government departments. As if this were not enough in the way of state overload, many larger urban municipalities have added their own functionally specialized but politically decentralized activities such as parking authorities, planning committees, or library boards. Some of these, like the police commission or public health board, are provincially mandated through legislation. In Chapter 12, we will evaluate how coping with obviously shared functional problems has led many city-region municipalities into mutual cooperative adventures through the creation of specific agencies, labelled special purpose districts (SPDs), to deliver only one service which has area-wide impacts, as in the provision of potable water. Canada's metropolitan area cities have also found themselves locked into history by the artifact of boundary lines on maps.

Political institutions within these boundaries grew in legitimacy over the years. City-regions in the 1950s, splintered in socio-economic terms as populations self-sorted into places of residence and work, were also lumbered with multiple local policy-making instruments. Many of these, for reasons of history, were very small in both geography and population. Regional policy issues, apparently well beyond the competence of these multiple jurisdictions to resolve, initially led good government reformers in a postwar quest for a politically engineered response. In the United States, this assumed the form of pressures toward annexation, city-county consolidation, intermunicipal cooperation through contracting for services, or SPDs. Only well after arrangements which did not threaten any municipality's continued existence or policy authority were understood as insufficient were any more sweeping changes like metropolitan government broached. But seldom in North America, apart from a municipality's pending bankruptcy, could politically engineered solutions be found that were so convincing as to persuade municipal councils voluntarily to surrender their autonomy in order to put right the policy shortcomings of the partitioned city-region. Barring any exogenous intervention, local councils assumed a high enough level of salience with their residents that conviction alone legitimated institutional permanence.

For a short time the multiple local governments within a metropolitan area were thought to operate somewhat like an international structure of autonomous states (Holden 1964). As an analogy, this view saw many resemblances in the degree of legally recognized autonomy, the provision of essential services, competition for economic development, defensive alliances against a threat (usually in the form of the core city), and preservation of territory. The central shortcoming in this approach was that municipalities, and the powers they exercise, operate under borrowed legitimacy from that of a central government; consequently, the citizenship commitment of residents is considerably moderated. Much of what has been said about the structure of other sorts of complex governing instruments may also apply to those in Canada's metropolitan regions. In *The Vertical Mosaic*, for instance, John Porter wrote quite astutely that "it may be speculated that federalism as such has meaning only for politicians and senior public servants who work with the complex machinery that they have set up, as well as for the scholars who provide a continuing commentary on it, but that it has very little real meaning for the bulk of the population" (1965: 384). It is probably also true that the "issues" related to governing metropolitan areas seldom hit home with any real immediacy for most citizens.

Keating, in considering American deliberations over consolidation of city-region political institutions, wrote of "the consensual and technocratic tone of the official debate" (1995: 120), which tended to skirt politically touchy issues concerning taxation equity, social mobility, and greater equality in service provision. The official line focused instead, more obliquely, on service efficiencies and, occasionally, on democratic accountability. Specific problems concerning roadway commuting and differential quality in recreation or social service programs quickly vanish along the public policy route into the arcane argot of equalized assessments, variable tax rates, and bilaterally negotiated contract service arrangements. In all likelihood, real and tangible policy importance exists only for those members of the urban regime who can understand how such questions are directly amenable to political resolution.

Formal organization at a given period in time codifies a structure of bias, to the advantage of those politically dominant at that point, as to who may gain access to, and control over, particular economic resources and political rights. One of the more prescient critics of the governmentally dispersed metropolitan city was Norton Long who once famously observed that "The suburb is the Northern way to insure separate and unequal. It has the advantage of being legal" (1968: 254). In other studies, from the work of Richard Child Hill (1974) to the more contemporary consideration of the idea of a "new localism" by Goetz and Clarke (1993: 5–8), the various distinctive urban roles of the socially differentiated suburb have become a well-documented American phenomena. Also well-recognized is the resistance of municipal councillors and their direct clienteles to any hypothetical form of reorganization that might infringe upon established power bases and relationships: "The sustaining argument of suburban councillors in any governmentally fragmented or polycentric metropolitan system is that there exists great divergence in the social composition of their metropolis which, when codified by the artifact of local boundary, justifies differentiated lifestyle claims" (Lightbody 1999a: 176).

Over time the repetition of these assertions builds urban myths around purported better levels and responsiveness of suburban services and cultivates notions that an authentic community which is distinct within the city-region, and most likely of better quality, is actually alive and kicking. These ideas feed on a nostalgic notion that smaller is better and that a central city lifestyle is a rather pathological existence. In short, arguments against the amalgamation of the various municipalities in city-regions have been entrenched historically in the idea that political boundaries generally encompass communities that are different from the whole in their social and economic status. The arguments are supported by concepts drawn from economic theory that municipalities exist to provide discrete services that can be confined by geography.

To the degree that this may be demonstrably true, as is occasionally the case in the United States, arguments in favour of consolidating governments based on enhanced administrative efficiencies have fallen upon the deaf ears of a populace ingrained with the familiar routines of local communities. Among the Westminster democracies, only governments with a clear ideological bent have been prepared to override belief systems rooted in entrenched neighbourhoods. For example, in the UK in April 1986, the Thatcher Conservatives carried the day for devolution of urban authority away from the Greater London Council by simply abolishing it and the other six metropolitan councils in operation since 1974. In doing this they acted directly on their earlier 1983 White Paper, *Streamlining the Cities*, which had reinforced appeals to a New Right individualist philosophy with a transfer of the metropolitan governments' former powers to existing local boroughs. In Canada, both the strongly social democratic NDP in Manitoba which amalgamated Winnipeg Unicity in 1971, and the genuine whig or neo-liberals of the Harris Progressive Conservatives in Ontario who introduced the Toronto Megacity amalgamation in 1997, were not even startled to find that their ideologically driven reforms were quite similar in consequence even though the start lines were so very different.

The arguments of public choice liberals in North America necessarily seek virtue in the status quo and the conservatism of community preservation. It views the polycentric system as having social and economic differences respected by existing municipal borders so that purely local goods and services are directly responsive to citizen demand. Consequently, the theory produces the rationalization that widely dissimilar government spending patterns for the usual basic municipal services only reflects differing citizen expectations.

It will be argued in Chapter 12 that public choice theorists have justified severe service and financial inequities in the governmentally complex city-region by ignoring the evidence of privilege sheltered by boundaries. Their case averts more serious scrutiny only as it is based upon claims of immediate democratic responsiveness and *overall* economic efficiency. In both the seminal work of American scholars Ostrom, Tiebout, and Warren (1961) and Canadians like Sancton (see, for example, 1994), public choice work has explained that the separation of taxation resources from service requirements, the hallmark of the polycentric system, is simply the logical consequence of social and economic differentiation among distinct municipalities. Normative judgements are not attached to the reality that differentiated population groups must look forward to fewer public goods from local governments with smaller tax bases.

Public choice has not been without its critics in both the United States (see especially Stephens and Wikstrom 2000: 117-21) and Canada (Lightbody 1999a). Any centripetal reform, especially amalgamation, directly confronts that theory's assumptions where it counts: on the streets. The central problem for public choice apart from its failure to address persisting inequities through any sort of redistributive policies is its own economic basis. The fundamental nature of the metropolitan "problem" derives largely from a contrary economic concept of spillovers, in which matching the costs and benefits of public goods cannot fit within the small scale of historic municipal territories.

The generic set of metropolitan policy issues can be more easily stipulated than resolved. Even some of the earlier metropolitan reforms proved unsatisfactory: "Both the Winnipeg and Toronto experience in Canada suggests that these problems may remain so unresolved by even a well devised two-tier format as ultimately to require completed centripetal reform" (Lightbody 1999a: 178). The comparative experience reveals that these general problems may be grouped into three public policy arenas, any one of which may provide the cathartic spark for a reorganization initiative. Very succinctly, these issue areas are:

1. the coordination of specific public policies between and among the metropolitan municipalities;

2. addressing questions of equity in the ability to generate revenues to pay for local services and to ensure rough equality in the levels provided all citizens of the city-region;

3. the matter of establishing clear lines of accountability to the public for the choices either made or not taken.

The basic difficulty in metropolitan governing is the development of problem-solving units of government that bear some rough congruence with the observed policy problems. Both schools—consolidationist and public choice—must come to grips with these three issues in metropolitan area public policy, and it is to some aspects of these to which we will now turn our discussion.

11.1 Coordination of City-Region Public Policies

The failure to coordinate the public policies of the governmentally poly-centric city-region has at least two dimensions. On the one side, decisions made by the various local councils as a legitimate policy response to the demands and expectations of their own residents and businesses may well yield undesirable consequences for adjacent municipalities or the region as a whole. The many governments system in North American city-regions lends itself to competitive land use and transportation planning with unfortunate outcomes. Some public policy economists term these consequences "detrimental spillovers," a confounding problem for the application of public choice theory which may be resolved, slightly, by functionally specific inter-jurisdictional cooperation. Keating, in commenting on the difficulties in relating land use to other policy priorities, assessed the general consequence of the fragmented city-region in these terms: "Policy tends to disintegrate into functionally defined policy communities, each determining its own priorities. There is a denial of territorial community with an ability to take decisions across functional boundaries" (1995: 126).

It is not unusual in these circumstances to notice particular councils engaging in "zoning games" through which they will locate their more noxious businesses and industries (such as cement plants or meat-packing operations) well away, and downwind, from their own prime residential properties. They may find, however, that these are now closely adjacent to homes and neighbourhoods located on the other side of a local government boundary line. Municipal governments, especially of bedroom suburbs whose workers must commute into the central business core, also undertake residential expansion plans without undue worry about the impacts of subsequent traffic on the arterial roadways of the downtown core. These councils are, almost of necessity, most interested in the economic well-being of their own communities and their own residents as electors, but less so about the possibility of any collateral negative results beyond their own frontiers. Intense political competition within suburban polities is reduced, as they become almost closed shops, only to be replaced by even more intense interjurisdictional struggles at the regional level. In the absence of any sort of area–wide authority to be held accountable, injured neighbouring municipalities will find neither a source for redress nor any agency to restrict future incursions.

On this general problem, the Manitoba government in their White Paper, *Proposals for Urban Reorganization in the Greater Winnipeg Area* had this to say:

> #1. There is an imperative need in the Greater Winnipeg area for genuinely effective planning and development of the region as a whole. This has been [made] already abundantly clear by a succession of investigating bodies … that planning and development powers are indivisible. Thus Metro, although it had planning authority, was vested with extremely limited development powers: it was, therefore, largely inhibited in its planning function." (Manitoba 1970: 4)

The other dimension of policy coordination results from concerns with overall city-region public policy integrity. By its very existence as an integrated economic and demographic unit, a metropolitan system spawns specific policy matters. Any city-region must provide water for its residents and remove their sewerage and waste; its arterial roadways must have more or less seamless connections and bridges built. Some measure of city-wide public transportation should exist to move people from their homes to places of work, study, and entertainment. Even on the eve of Toronto Megacity, Enid Slack noted that passengers who wished to cross municipal borders could count on neither fare integration nor service coordination from Metro: "The result is that the transit system is unable to relieve traffic congestion on the roads" (1997: 96). The monitoring and policing of air quality, even the environmental safeguarding of watersheds, today stand as important city hall responsibilities.

This proliferation of local governments, whose boundaries slice the city and dice its delivery of important functions such as these, makes policy development a process of cross-jurisdictional negotiation, barter, and diplomacy.

For instance, geographic boundaries of municipalities today seldom reflect the logic of effective water, sewerage, and drainage provision as they once might have. Seldom, though, does the policy drift become so problematic as to endanger public health as it did when St. John's Public Health officials in the spring of 2002 were required to issue a warning to residents not only to avoid ingesting fish from the harbour but also touching them. This was the predictable outcome of four centuries of dumping raw sewage into the ocean. In general terms, if municipal integration or heightened intergovernmental cooperation fails as a policy instrument for water management, some sort of wider area body with boundaries coincident with watershed will ultimately be required to provide this public good securely.

The potentially and probably conflicting development agendas, land use intentions, and budget priorities of different localities become substantial barriers to policy effectiveness. Before the Toronto 1954 reform, city-region planning ended at each city's borders: "Further problems arose from each municipality acting independently of each other with respect to transportation, land-use and housing" (Slack 1997: 86). In pre-Metro Winnipeg in 1958, for further example, bridges across the rivers which served as municipal borders could not be planned; neither could arterial roadways be planned, financed, or built. More irritating still was the grim reality that a war plan to combat the city-region's killer mosquitoes, which chose not to respect municipal boundaries but rather to ride the winds, could not be devised by the baker's dozen of local governments. Each of these policy areas became a Metro Winnipeg priority in 1961, but even two-tier metropolitan arrangements may not address the issue of coordination sufficiently. A decade later the new Manitoba government made this point: "#2. With control of services divided, and the power to make decisions and carry them out fragmented, the community's human resources are dissipated, and its economic capabilities to a considerable extent squandered" (Manitoba 1970: 4).

Even though the total number of councillors across the city-region will be far larger than in a consolidated operation and thus the talent pool may be somewhat thinner, the governmentally fragmented metropolis does not necessarily instill ineffective political leadership *per se*. What fragmentation does turn out are councillors who must be particularly sensitive to the agendas of their own voters and, in consequence, who have a vision of the urban region that is, necessarily, parochial and self-serving. In plain terms, there exists no "metropolitan voter" who may hold these locally elected councillors accountable.

11.2 Fiscal and Service Equity in the Metropolis

As discussed in the previous chapter, the dispersed metropolitan city resulted from population migration from rural Canada into city-regions generally and from outside Canada into its metropolitan core. The move from the central city into new or revitalized suburbs adjacent to its borders developed as the newly affluent, postwar middle class sought the amenities of the automobile-accessible, detached, single family suburban home. Certainly many were accommodated by more upscale neighbourhoods within central city boundaries. Increasingly, however, moving into a separately incorporated suburban municipality associated physical distance with the psychological move away from the social and economic problems many associated with big city living. This phenomenon also occurred in the UK and, in a greatly more pronounced fashion, the United States. In each instance there were similar ancillary consequences widely observed by, among many, Michael Keating: "This enabled them to escape heavy city taxes, to exclude low cost or public sector housing, and [especially in the United States] to maintain class and racial segregation in their school systems. Central cities, for their part, were left with the burden of central place functions, a low income population, social stress and a depleted tax base" (1995: 120). This experience was just as James Bryce had observed of suburbanization a century previous: "The unfortunate consequence follows, not only that the taxes are heavier for those who remain in the city, but that the philanthropic and political work of the city loses the participation of those who ought to have shared in it" (Bryce 1888: I, 566).

In ideal terms, property taxation is based on a "benefits principle" that equates the tax paid to benefits received; it is not based on an ability-to-pay standard as are income taxes. But specific sorts of industry and manufacturing, especially that which was land intensive, and commerce seeking lower floor rents, further contributed to dispersed growth. As they sought these sorts of marginal gains, both sets of business were enticed by the slightly lower property and business taxes extended by suburbs burdened neither by the upkeep of an aging physical plant infrastructure nor with the provision of the full range of specialized service functions which citizens expect of a mature and diverse city government.

The inevitable consequence of population and economic production shifts across the metropolis were widely varying taxation rates among the many local governments of the governmentally fragmented city-region. The corollary was significant variation in the levels of service the residents of these communities could either expect to receive or that their councils could, or would, provide. Again, the Manitoba White Paper of 1970 was quite clear:

"#3. There is wide disparity in the quality and level of services between one municipality and another—a fact frequently not revealed in the levies made for these services" (Manitoba 1970: 4).

The metropolitan fragmentation of the tax base means that the total resources available to the city-region community are also dispersed. Inevitably, particular municipalities are unable to match the kinds of programs their neighbouring local governments might have. It is usually the case that suburban municipalities with a substantial commercial-industrial assessment base find advantage in both servicing and taxation. For instance, even in late 2001 the suburban communities surrounding Edmonton found budget pressures so modest that it was unnecessary for them to levy a business tax similar to that found in the central city, a circumstance which made their business attraction efforts somewhat easier. Metro Toronto had the highest incidence of taxation on commercial and industrial properties of any region in the GTA. This was evident, too, in Winnipeg:

> #4. The present utilization of the tax base results in an inequitable exploitation of industrial taxation by individual municipalities. Most industries are regional in character. Their work forces are usually drawn from many municipalities and the transportation system which carries their workers between their homes and their jobs similarly spans many municipalities. Yet tax revenues from a given industry accrue to the municipality in which it is located—to the detriment of the areas from which the industry draws its labor force. (Manitoba 1970: 4)

Sometimes political pressures also cascade for councils in the privileged residential suburbs seeking to emulate the discretionary amenities of the well-established core city. For instance, the Edmonton suburb of St. Albert agreed to a proposal in 2002 for a $35 million sports complex, endorsed by the St. Albert Regional Recreational Council, to be built with public funds on 40 acres donated by Landrex developers who intended "to make it the hub of a 300-acre development" (*Edmonton Journal*, 25 June 2002). While the city's population of 60,000 had the second highest average income in Alberta after the resource extraction city of Fort McMurray, the community's assessment base was 88 per cent residential dependent, without the industrial base of Edmonton's other commuting communities. Councillors were in a political squeeze due to their commitment to borrow $40 million to fund an arterial road to connect commuters with the City of Edmonton's ring road. This meant that the 6.2 per cent tax increase to fund a sports debt would have to be in addition to 7 per cent already on the bills for the new road.

The central city is normally the most hard-pressed by both the loss of tax base and by pressures to meet the particular needs of diverse, often stressed citizens whose limited mobility and reliance on specialized services reduces their freedom to choose the community in which to live. The central city council is often forced to become a vocal enthusiast for amalgamation as was St. John's council in 1990 when it described a pattern of suburban residents who exploited core city services and provided little to city-region residents in need, while all the while "fleeing property taxes by moving to the bedroom communities beyond our borders" where they relied on the province for all water, sewer, and road projects (*Globe and Mail*, 13 November 1990).

The underlying point in this must not be obscured. By their very existence, cities as regions generate not only people of wealth but also those who are poor, those who are self-sufficient in many respects but also those who require particular support from community services; city-regions also support the fine arts and complex policing operations. Thus, the central place of any city core provides service to the entire region. Where a single local government is roughly coincident with the built-up city, its one council may provide the complete range of services and charge the resulting tax obligations against the assessment base of the entire city-region. Where the city-region is cleaved into multiple local governments, however, the core city must still service the region, but suburban residents both escape the obligation to pay and reap the service, subsidizing benefits from business assessment within their borders. This is why Manitoba presented argument #5 in its White Paper. "Social ills, and hence social costs, tend to concentrate in the core area. These costs have to be borne almost entirely by taxpayers in the central area, despite the fact that many of the people requiring social services and creating social costs have migrated to the central area from outlying communities" (1970: 5).

Suburbanization, leading into fiscally squeezed variations in service levels, can also intrude into the most traditional central areas of functional responsibility. For example, by late 2001, Vancouver city police reported to council that their resources were "stretched so thin" that the department could no longer dispatch officers to burgled residences unless the crime was still in progress. In contrast the RCMP, policing under contract to suburban municipalities such as Surrey, found that they were still able to investigate all break and enters at residences and businesses, as well as at churches, schools, and construction sites (*Edmonton Journal,* 2 November 2001). Suburban "free riders" exist in this fashion only because they may count on support, on critical occasions, from core city services. The Edmonton suburb of St. Albert, mentioned previously, sustained its policing under contract from the RCMP with only two investigators for all criminal activities from drug trafficking to arson and murder. The focus was on crimes against property and assault, with the inspector ultimately conceding that, "The majority of our drug seizures are from traffic stops." Rather typically, the council only ratified funding for an additional three-person drug unit "because Edmonton's pushers are moving into the city" (*Edmonton Journal*, 24 July 2002).

To repeat, suburbanites escape to home and, in so doing, also escape paying the freight in the city where they work. Dennis R. Judd stipulates this familiar aspect of the central city dilemma in the United States when he notes that suburbanites exploit core city services and take the better jobs while all the while leaving behind those with lower incomes and higher needs for community services. This happens because, as the suburbs select whom they permit to call them home, the central city must become a "receptacle" for all state functions the suburban ring chooses not to perform (1988: 191-92). There should be no real surprise in any of these patterns. Bryce identified the basic difficulty within American city-regions at the end of the last century: "Taxes are usually so much higher in the larger cities than in the country districts or smaller municipalities, that there is a strong tendency for rich men to migrate from the city to its suburbs in order to escape the city collector" (1888: I, 566).

One hundred years later, we still find intra-metropolitan business location choices somewhat influenced by the relative levels of business taxation. The evidence does suggest, however, that, notwithstanding the usual claims by local small business associations, municipal taxation rates hardly ever contribute much to the business choice of one CMA over another. As Slack points out, "The reason for this conclusion is that municipalities in different metropolitan areas are not as close substitutes as municipalities within the same metropolitan area" (1997: 99). Corporate executives are also able to balance marginally higher tax rates against differentials in other costs of core business; higher taxes may simply be judged as reflecting better service levels.

On the other hand, service differentials among the municipalities in the polycentric city-region can work subconsciously, if not intentionally, to benefit the development agendas of businesses already operating within Canada's CMAs. Winnipeg, for instance, prior to unification in 1971 had a number of suburbs operating without resolute building inspections, an "oversight" beneficial at that time and in that context to several quite specific industries. One flaw in the Metro Winnipeg structure (1961-71) was its inability to correct for the continuing compartmentalization of this important activity, and a few suburbs like St. Boniface privately exploited this regulatory failing in its business promotion efforts. Even within a polycentric metropolis, the commercial benefits of locating within a specific municipality so as to be in close proximity to other similar financial service businesses, or technology park agglomerations, or a retail jamboree of big-box stores (as in suburban shopping "power centres") will either offset or balance slightly higher differentials in business tax rates.

Two-tier metropolitan government systems like Canada's, intended exclusively to facilitate the construction of major public works such as waterworks and arterial roadways to permit the more rapid spatial expansion of the city, were never directly intended to address redistributive or equity issues. This is understandable since municipal hard services related to the physical plant (water and sewerage lines, arterial roadways) most easily and measurably satisfy the requirements for economies of scale. Two-tier metropolitan instruments were also subject to prevailing elite beliefs that municipalities are not intended to be redistributive policy instruments. In Winnipeg, for instance, after a decade of metropolitan federation, the central city with roughly half the region's population covered over four-fifths of the area's total municipal spending on public health and 85 per cent of that spent on social welfare. The wealthier the suburban tax base, the more their councils spent on recreation and "culture," in fact, five times more than that spent on welfare charges. Those municipal governments whose assessment bases could most easily support social services were also the most insulated from those policy requests.

At the same time, many suburbs are able to "piggyback" their own operations (like fire protection and secondary schools) onto the base capital investments in the central city. When expenditures were actually analyzed in the Winnipeg case, it was found that the higher the family incomes in a community, the lower that community's property taxes were (Lightbody 1978: 497–99). In a living antithesis to Robin Hood, this divergence had been exacerbated, not ameliorated, during the period of metropolitan government. In 1969 the City of Winnipeg endorsed unification of municipalities because "there has been inequitable exploitation of industrial development while the central city has had to pay for almost all welfare costs of the metro region" (*Winnipeg Tribune*, 2 March 1971).

Social and economic inequity among the residents and their communities in the Canadian metropolis is difficult for any rearrangement of local government—short of unification—to address through public policy. This is partly because a more equitable distribution of tax revenue sources and expenditure obligations runs directly against the reality that the 1960s forms of Canadian metropolitan municipal organization represented, in institutions, the structure of socio-economic bias existing at the moment of their start-up. As basic municipal brick and mortar service providers, area-wide governing instruments were never intended to tackle redistributive policy issues directly. Consequently, and for various reasons including exclusionary planning and zoning practices, municipal borders came to preserve "separate and unequal" communities which, in Canadian city-regions, was best measured by average family incomes (as noted in Chapter 10).

Even well-developed two-tier metropolitan systems could not directly address equity matters, but again that policy arena was never their mandate.

11.3 Public Accountability for Choices Made and Not Taken

The third generally recurrent dilemma of the governmentally fragmented metropolitan centre involves basic questions of democratic accountability. Very simply said, democratic accountability requires that reasonably well-informed citizens ought easily to be able to hold those entrusted with the making of public policy subject both to continuing public scrutiny and to periodic affirmation of their actions. Representative democracy requires that citizens be able, with certainty, to pinpoint persons directly responsible for decisions made in their interest, to applaud when appropriate and to censure as necessary. Even public economists see the need for clarity in the requirement for a tight linkage between money spent and taxes levied: "If there is no accountability in decision-making, there is no incentive to allocate resources efficiently across the competing services" (Slack 1997: 85). In theory, fiscal responsibility develops with "benefits" taxation on those who most directly receive the service. Where transparency in direct accountability is fudged, however, there is likely to be more than inefficiency. Part of the reason for the lower voter turnouts in city politics discussed previously in Chapter 5 is due to the inability of electors to determine with any precision just who in that government supposedly "closest to the people" ought to be accorded further public office-holding based on a *public* policy track record.

Such judgements are not easy to make in the polycentric city-region. For instance, public economists speak of **tax exporting** which occurs when property subject to taxation in one municipality is owned by persons or corporations who live somewhere else (Hobson 1997: 127-29). If businesses under these circumstances are "gouged" by councils in order to provide enhanced services to their own local residents, such behaviour hardly promotes either efficiency or accountability (i.e., taxation without representation). On the other hand, if the tax fields are seen to be greener on the other side of the local fence, a potential migration threat by business to elude "punitive" taxation may cause the council to provide fewer public goods than residents should expect. Here, multiple tax regimens are antithetical to the best social development interests of residents, and, in this case, accountability itself has been exported to non-residents.

One further possibility for trouble with public accountability is that the smaller municipalities within the larger city-region must make deals with the same large residential and commercial developers, but their council-lors have access to fewer permanent administrators than are available in the more complex and professional central city hierarchies and their multiple internal sources of expertise. The councils in suburbs which must rely on privately contracted planning resources seldom directly confront the serious issues of potential conflict of interest that may arise when private-sector planners also have the same developers as clients. Legendary close link-ages between builders and small-town suburban engineers are unique only because they are infrequently reported, less seldom shared with the public than within professional circles. In the 1990s, the Toronto *Globe and Mail* devoted a series of columns to the symbiotic activities of the public engi-neering and private development communities in the York region north of Toronto (see Chapter 5) which revealed the back-scratching behaviour of politicians and developers. The point is that the stakes in land are high, that smaller community administrators may find themselves under less continu-ous scrutiny than those in central city departments, and that in this instance the story was brought into public life by the metropolitan press and not a local community's tabloid.

On the other hand, the small scale "mom and pop" informal admin-istrations of which smaller suburbs are so enamoured may not be profes-sionally equipped to oversee the applications of complex private operations. Additionally, while the metropolitan media frequently observe and report on the far-reaching consequences of central city planning activities, far too frequently similar suburban measures are hidden from, and hence over-looked by, citizens because the suburban press itself is insufficiently staffed. The ownership of suburban papers is also directly tied into local boosterism networks, and their community plumping effort consistently frowns upon any reportage that might bring the town name into disrepute. Advertising revenues are understood to be contingent on growth (and favourable cover-age), and very frequently circulation itself is subsidized by one or another means through the town council itself.

The question of accountability was introduced in the previous chapter where we observed how the multiple governments of Canada's metro-politan areas, appreciating the new interdependencies and urban regional orientations of their residents, once tried to improvise some minimal sort of regional public policy system on their own. This was why the initial response by municipalities across North America to complex policy demands arising from constantly accelerating interactions among diverse business and economic interests, as well as from the divergent populations characteristic of large-scale city-regions, was to create policy-making units more or less congruent with the problems both factors generated. It will be noted in Chapter 12 that metropolitan governing by SPDs is still the dominant form employed in American city-regions.

In Canada, two general sorts of delegated authority followed urban expansion. First, municipalities accelerated the early twentieth-century reform inclination to create their own functionally specific but quasi-autonomous boards and agencies (for parks, police, libraries, and aspects of social services), sometimes under the rhetoric of enhanced citizen "participation" but, more realistically and as previously noted, as either a satisficing policy in appeasement of clientele groups or to feel out safe ground in unprecedented policy terrains.

Secondly, particularly in the earliest part of the last century, specific functions of local government, like the provision of potable water, were seen by virtually all municipal authorities in given city-regions like Winnipeg or Vancouver as being more effectively (and efficiently in a purely economic sense) provided by an area-wide agency. They thus became prepared to delegate those responsibilities to single function agencies created specifically to receive and to implement them. Typically, the management boards of such SPDs were comprised of delegates from the municipalities participating in the programs; this style of appointment of locally elected representatives to functional management boards is called indirect election. In democratic accountability terms, this means that while elected officials from general purpose municipal governments were nominally in charge of the provision of the service, they were one step removed from direct accountability for their activities. As the systems evolved, these elected officials were insulated in their ongoing policy processes from the direct expression of citizen concerns from other than directly affected specific policy communities.

In the provision of water or the construction of regional trunk sewerage lines, for instance, functional SPD boards were more attuned to the expressed agendas of the major developers and contractors whose properties stood to gain in value as the extension of these services made their lands habitable than they were to the more generalized interests of citizens concerned with broader land use or environmental planning practices. To listen to, and hear privately, the technical and market-driven concerns of those business interests most narrowly impacted is seemingly perfectly acceptable behaviour at the SPD board level. But if similar issues affecting the development of new territories had been raised during any city plan amendment process at the very same councillors' home councils, the exclusion of citizen groups and policy networks with more widely cast but no less valid policy interests would be considered absolutely inexcusable and, indeed, in most cases unlawful. Some complex SPD dominant city-regions (in Canada, the GVRD is an excellent model here) further confound the easy access of citizens to their operations through the bizarre practice of holding regular board meetings not at any central board office but rotating them among the constituent municipalities' city halls. Thus, the interested citizen observer, perhaps casually interested in a single agenda item, has first to play hide-and-seek.

The indirect election of SPD board members tends to undermine democratic accountability across city-regions especially when council elections are justifiably waged on wide-ranging but usually, and only, purely local issues and not leadership in the design of the city-region as an entity. So, as twentieth-century Canadian CMAs witnessed a deliberate proliferation of SPDs, which undoubtedly facilitated those regions' more rapid economic and social development, councillors came face-to-face with a "catch-22" proposition. On the one hand, local representatives had to argue for their sensitivity to their city's residents' demands while on the other they were spinning core functional responsibilities off to both their own community's quasi-autonomous agencies and to area-wide SPDs. No intelligent citizen need be conversant with the various strands and nuances of elaborate theories of representative democracy to appreciate the practical problems produced by a fragmented government system with such diffused patterns of responsibility. While everyone appears to have a say, no one ever seems finally accountable, and the growing isolation of modern citizens from their own governing, as noted in Chapter 5, is seen to have an instrumental basis.

Borrowing directly from the SPD tradition, Canada's original upper tier metropolitan councils, except for Winnipeg, were all indirectly elected. Partly in consequence, Harold Kaplan, in the Toronto case, is able to applaud the emergence of a "professionalized, interventionist, 'nonpolitical,' centralized bureaucracy" with rules that would be "neutral, specific, universalistic, and achievement related." Bureaucrats controlled the metropolitan policy agenda: Even were they genuinely interested in Metro Toronto's area-wide policies, the councillors never had a chance: "Almost all of metro's policy initiatives, almost all the intellectual direction and push, was provided by [the administration]" (1982: 690). At the more serious levels of the state, the notion of cabinet government means something quite different. The problem of apparent political inattention emerged because the resource of time is finite. Having to make hard allocation choices about the clock, local councillors found their priorities in service to lie elsewhere—with the people who directly controlled their electoral careers. So, *they* were generally satisfied with a system which both distanced aggrieved electors from metropolitan administrators and maintained, instead, close voter links to the local councils. Only after the fact of its general demise in Canada has a defense of the metropolitan form of two-tier election been constructed by some within the public choice school on the grounds that it was less costly than dual elective bodies (Sancton 2000: 163).

Seldom has the problem of diffuse accountability been more clearly stipulated than in the proposals for metropolitan reform in Winnipeg:

> #7. Many citizens in Greater Winnipeg, faced with the complexities and confused authority of a two tier system of local government, now find themselves unable to focus clearly on the responsible authority. The citizen often knows neither whom to blame for a given situation, to whom to turn for remedy, nor to whom to tender advice if he feels he has a worthwhile idea to offer. The inevitable result is that the citizen begins to feel frustrated, alienated, and hence withdraws from active participation in the community. He is unable, in short, to exercise his full rights of democratic involvement in the level of government theoretically most responsive to his wishes. (Manitoba 1970: 5)

While many may have a say, those who make policy choices are seldom directly accountable, and important aspects of the regional policy process are situated well away from the public spotlight. Such a conclusion brings to mind John Porter's standard critique of Canadian federalism: "A federal system is often seen as a device to decentralize power, but it can also be used as an instrument to acquire and consolidate power, and to maintain economically inefficient and socially out-dated and dysfunctional activities" (1965: 380). Bureaucratic rule prevailed in Metro Toronto and to a lesser degree, due to political party cohesion, in Montreal. In Metro Winnipeg, during 1961-70, pressures to reward suburban life were constant but not always transparent. Ultimately this determined how the budget was directed. Similar to the program choices of Metro Toronto's "cabinet," *most* of Metro Winnipeg's programs were intended to benefit the urbanization of the suburbs even while two-thirds of revenues were generated within Winnipeg's central city boundaries (Kaplan 1982: 552). In a tough twist of fate, these universalist developments later enhanced suburban councillors' capacity to resist centripetal institutional change by deploying their enlarged networks of personal prestige and policy patronage. They could do so because their municipalities had accumulated the trappings of more genuine cities even as their councillors advanced claims for the distinct lifestyle of their communities.

The political problem of the polycentric metropolis is thus simple enough. Even in the two-tier federative form municipal elected officials are seldom in any instrumental position to be brought to account for questions of wider area public policy. In a general assessment of American polycentric arrangements, Professors Wikstrom and Stephens conclude in this fashion: "the public choice alternative results in a bewildering maze of service arrangements incomprehensible to the average voter. This condition serves to undermine accountability to the citizens and local democracy" (2000: 120). To put it another way, and as discussed in Chapter 5, when electors feel that they are not well informed, there exists a general tendency to withdraw from the process.

11.4 Setting the Stage for Reorganization

As did their American counterparts, the governments and politicians with responsibility for the institutions of Canadian metropolitan centres struggled to resolve their modern, specific, public policy issues within a context of fragmented jurisdictions developed in the previous century. Many of these activities, like cooperative SPDs, did work adequately in a patched-up sort of way.

A more troublesome issue than just matching responses to the immediate issues confronting city-region governing was revealed in the wide-ranging critical assessment of Thomas J. Plunkett. Among others, he argued throughout his long teaching and consulting career that the growing institutional complexity of city-regions only made the provision of specific public goods more complicated. He argued consistently that lost in the semi-public negotiations needed to make this growing intergovernmental web work was an emergent reality that complexity itself made planning and control of development for the region, as an entity, virtually impossible. Sancton acknowledged with respect to the pre-Megacity greater Toronto region, "there is no level of government concerned with the city-region as a whole" (1994: 91).

This fundamental shortcoming led to institutional reform efforts from sources in various policy communities, such as specific environmental conservation networks, that tried to have policy elaborated for the city-region in its entirety. Nearing the end of the twentieth century, a wider consensus that the system was not performing as well as it might developed among influential local leaders, most of whom were normally quite casual with their curiosity about municipal affairs. This renewed interest triggered the dramatic governmental consolidations of CMAs in the 1990s.

The record of the early initiatives from policy communities is important since studying it reminds us that three general propositions set the context for the success of both more, and less, ambitious regional governing proposals.

11.4.1 Political history

Comparative research drawn largely from the American experience has confirmed conventional wisdom that there are a number of reliable indicators which provide some guidance as to practical limits for local reorganizations. The *political history* of any metropolitan area sets the general context. The region's age of settlement is important, particularly where older communities are also coincident with a more densely populated territory (Dye 1964: 446). The younger cities of the American southwest, especially, found it easier to expand onto unincorporated and lightly settled lands until roughly the 1960s. One practical consequence is that these city-regions also tend to be characterized by many fewer units of local government than do older metropolitan communities. In Canada this approach, characteristic of newer cities in unoccupied space, has been noted by John Meligrana (1998) with respect to the relatively easier use of the annexation instrument in Alberta and Saskatchewan. In contrast, Vancouver did not extend its boundaries through annexation after 1929, although Calgary moved quickly to amalgamate with its smaller suburbs after the McNally Royal Commission of 1956 so recommended. This stood in marked contrast with Winnipeg City's immobility after the Greater Winnipeg Investigating Commission report in 1958 or the formal codification of all existing local governments' boundaries into the original metropolitan scheme for the Toronto CMA in 1954.

In Canada, the political base of the party holding office provincially has a policy-shaping impact. In Quebec, the Union Nationale, with its largely rural electoral base, was forced to introduce the Montreal Urban Community over its preferred policy of study and delay in order to finance the settlement of the police strike in October 1969. The plan forced island suburbs to subsidize city-region policing and selected public works operations. When in power, provincial Liberals tended to focus their limited attention span for municipal matters onto rural areas. The small town roots of Social Credit in British Columbia flowed into its 1965 policy for 28 regional districts. The GVRD has since operated under the charming fiction that it is not a government because it neither taxes nor is elected directly. In Manitoba, the urban-based NDP produced Winnipeg Unicity in 1971; this was a direct response to the implosion of the two-tier metropolis, which rural and suburban Progressive Conservatives had imposed as a compromise instrument just a decade earlier. Some 25 years later, urban social democrats in Ontario fought to protect the City of Toronto by opposing legislation virtually identical in language and general form to Winnipeg Unicity when a suburban and rural Progressive Conservative government produced Megacity. It would be only moderately cattish to suggest that parochial electoral advantage had any role to play in any of these calculations of the public good. It is finally to be noted that opposition parties in the Canadian provinces have seldom articulated any sort of coherent city-region governing alternative during election campaigns. They understand intuitively that there is no more certain way to lose votes, in the short term, than by threatening to disturb familiar arrangements for local governing.

11.4.2 Degree of divergence in composition

A second set of general conditions appears to set limits on the viability of new ideas for city-region governing. These are related to the degree of divergence in the metropolitan region's composition. Most obvious to even the casual observers is the number of local governments in the system, which Stephens and Wikstrom summarize as the "ecology" of local government (2000: 57–58). Generally, the fewer the institutions, the more probable is the reorganization's success. As will be shown in Chapter 13, the greater the number of bureaucratic institutions, the more likely it is that they will be able to thwart any anticipated loss in status and autonomy. Further to this is the finding that any form of two-level system which relies upon intergovernmental cooperation appears, at least to official participants, to work most effectively when no more than about one-third of the population resides in any one municipality, usually in the core city. Questions related to balanced distributions in public policies, equitable representation, and permanent minority status for one political element (smaller suburbs, for instance) become marginal concerns when all participants are roughly similar in size. Hence, the GVRD or Metro Toronto are, or were, minimally criticized on issues of fairness. But regional governing operations in Hamilton-Wentworth (with 76 per cent of regional population living in the core city), Edmonton (72 per cent), and even Metro Winnipeg (1961) with 50 per cent all failed. The Montreal Urban Community worked as well as it did in considerable measure because to pass a motion required coincident majorities from both the city and suburban blocs.

Population imbalance yields suspicions of motives among elected officials on both sides. The general basis for this, as will also be discussed in further detail in the next chapter, is that suburbs fear their voices will be muted in a central city "revenue grab." On the other side, core city policy networks can be concerned that hard-won (usually social) policy gains may be diluted or lost under the assault of a suburban "regional city" agenda.

This question of regional composition also pays regard to the in-house institutions of existing municipalities. In the United States, reorganization consistently appears the more likely when these internal arrangements of council-management, electoral systems, and delegation of power to the executive are roughly similar among the participating municipalities. This echoes the finding of conditions conducive to emerging federal systems along lines pioneered by K.C. Wheare (1963) and his classic study of federating nation-states. Among the variables he considered crucial to successful federation were geographic contiguity, a previous public policy association in some lower order governing arrangement, and roughly comparable governing structures. That is, liberal democracies were unlikely to become the obliging federative partners of authoritarian regimes.

Translated to the low politics of city-regions, the corresponding governing arrangements (in broad terms) refer to reformed and city manager cities juxtaposed to more traditional communities embracing small wards, political parties, and powerful standing committees. City manager "reformed" cities are consistently more susceptible to the cooperative provision of particular services and less opposed to general consolidation. The probability of unifying reforms is routinely found to be greater where both potential partners are reformed cities whose managerial cluster equate better government reforms with questions of efficiency (Winter 1969: 302). Where one or both of the possible partners weighs heavily toward parties and low-end patronage networks, the significant question becomes one of marginal administrative gains versus absolute losses of personal political power. In the United States, this barrier proved sufficient to derail most consolidations; foot-dragging due to the existence of municipal patronage in Canada merely served to escalate the resolution of local institutional problems from the municipal level onto the provincial agenda.

11.4.3 The social and economic structure

A third very important concern in considering city-region composition is the dimension of *social and economic structure*. In the United States, the factor of race is significant; black leadership, in particular, is acutely sensitive to being "layered under" politically by regional government with the consequence being loss of jobs, access, and programs to redress the persistent dependency of the poor (Stephens and Wikstrom 2000: 56). While this is more clearly a political problem in the United States than in Canada, a second line of inquiry is more problematic. This concerns separation of population in the city-region by municipality, along lines that determine social distance like education, occupation, and wealth. Consistent American experience is that the likelihood of significant metropolitan institutional integration is reduced the wider the differences between central city and suburban populations (Dye 1964: 430–46). Lineberry and Sharkansky made the point axiomatic 30 years ago: "The sharper the socio-economic differences between suburban and central city areas, the smaller is the probability of reform" (1974: 132). Bollens and Schmandt submitted that intergovernmental cooperation had developed most easily among municipalities of roughly equivalent social and economic rank where the policy arena was least directly associated with lifestyle choices such as zoning, social housing, or community renewal (1982: 352–53).

In Canada, as in the United States, suburban lifestyle refugees have exhibited little political support for any initiative destined to close their psychological distancing from the central city. Over time, the suburban communities evolved to enshrine the city-region's socio-economic structure of inequality; the wider the measurable social distance mounts, the greater the intensity of political resistance to most types of integrative instruments. One corollary is also that central cities, calculating the costs of servicing upgrades, have not themselves been overly enthusiastic about absorbing adjacent communities with significantly lower levels of family income and without an off-setting industrial-commercial assessment base.

11.4.5 Political culture

In the UK, Canada, and Australia, where central governments operate through the Westminster model, uncontested authority stands with the government and its ministry. Hence, city-region restructuring was subject to no binding popular referendum in any instance until the Labour proposals for London, UK, in 1997.

This stands in considerable contrast to the American experience. Individual state legislator resistance, with deep roots in the camps, clienteles, and qualms of both suburban autonomists and central city expansionists, is discovered whenever the subject of metropolitan reform has been broached. Since state political structures emulate the separate divisions in authority of the checks and balances of national institutions, this means that the states are not so organized as to be able to undertake the collective action necessary to redesign city-region governments. American reformers of the old school, like Stephens and Wikstrom, stipulate their envy clearly: "Canadian provinces, with the powers of government effectively unified in the legislature under a parliamentary system, have been far more effective in solving the governmental problems of their metropolitan areas" (2000: 127-28). Partly in consequence, the National Municipal League, so powerful a persuasive force in other forms of municipal administration, ultimately admitted failure in trying to devise a universally acceptable framework for metropolitan governing. Whatever it would be, the governing instrument for each metropolitan area would have to evolve individually.

As the consequences for metropolitan change in North America have been so considerable, the distinctive cultural history of the American democratic experience again merits small mention. As that concept's seminal source, S.M. Lipset (1990) has long argued that American democracy was born out of a liberal rebellion and that the "counter-revolution" which established Canada affirmed its attachment to British notions of social hierarchy and deference to authority. The consequence, sustained by their dissimilar political institutions, is that the political cultures of the two national communities have continued in their divergence. American social scientists from the time of de Tocqueville have, for instance, deployed the label "American exceptionalism" to describe the limited political salience of socio-economic class, in contrast with other industrial democracies, as a social and political organizing principle. This more purely bourgeois democracy is one that is both populist and participatory, one which accentuates meritocracy and maximizes libertarianism, one which expects weak but effective governing—of and for the elector behaving and responding as an individual (Lipset 2001: 250–68).

In policy terms, the consequences for American city-region governing have been unmistakably clear-cut. In the nineteenth century, at a time of much smaller scale government than we know today, a consolidation of cities with their surrounding county governments established Boston (1821), Philadelphia (1854), and New York City (1898) in the forms they are known today. In hindsight, to match boundaries for the limited services then needed to those of the service providers was no complex task. But after the Second World War, in the interventionist state era, similar sorts of consolidation initiatives were easiest measured by the few exceptions—Nashville (1962), Jacksonville (1967), and Indianapolis (1969) notably among them—in a very long checklist of failure. While American voters might accept the limited purpose SPD for extended geographic areas, they have resolutely refused to support any greater measures for consolidation no matter whether they live in the central city or its surrounding urbanized pastures.

Precisely because the study of political culture is comparative between and among political communities, it helps us to understand that there are public policy consequences. The American emphasis on individual rights, rather than the more collective orientations of the Canadian community, has consistently buried any ambitious city-region government initiatives in that country.

On the other hand, survey evidence reveals a Canadian community that is still both more elitist and ascriptive than in the United States, even while being less so than in the UK (Lipset 1990). In practical terms, and as will be discussed in the next two chapters, this has meant that initiation of policies for municipal restructuring has been deferred to provincial ministries, and Canadian public acceptance of outcomes is assured. Even where they are stridently opposed, the proposals are not subject to plebiscite. Once enacted, allowing for a short period of adjustment and a tiny whiff of lingering nostalgia for historic arrangements, there has been a rapid adaptation to the new structures by citizens with virtually no expectation for any institutional deconstruction in the future.

twelve | Organizing city governments in the metropolis

It is all well and good to be able to diagnose the problems of the metropolis and to describe them with some measure of accuracy. It is quite another matter, and more difficult, to prescribe a set of realistic solutions. The hardest task lies in the application of any prescription for change. In this chapter it is time to examine the governing alternatives that have been employed and to assess their relative successes. The central policy issue is this: when the councils of the multiple municipalities of the polycentric city-region appear disinclined to coalesce as a single unit, what are the regional governing options to consider? What alternative possibilities exist to provide a means by which public policy can be developed for matters that are of genuine area-wide concern?

Several schools of legitimate academic and applied thinking as to the most appropriate way to structure municipalities exist. At one extreme are **centralists** who argue that a general consolidation of local administrations into one government would reduce if not eliminate the three central problems in metropolitan area governing: (1) manage growth and development, (2) focus accountability in a single mayor and council, and (3) eliminate both service inequalities and taxation inequities. On the extreme other side of the argument stand the more polycentric "who look upon the multiplicity

of local units as the most desirable way of promoting the interests of a pluralistic society by maximizing grassroots control and assuring bureaucratic
responsiveness" (Bollens and Schmandt 1982: 302).

During the late nineteenth and early twentieth centuries in the United
States, annexation was the principal growth mechanism for urban communities. Most northeastern American cities in the nineteenth century were
intended by their civic leadership to be the sole provider of urban services in
what would become metropolitan city-regions. In some cases, most notably
New York City in 1898, annexation was a *de facto* merger of the central city
with its coincident or adjacent counties. What the term annexation normally
means is that some land is separated from the political control of one municipality (which is usually rural) and assigned to another local government's
authority. Both municipalities previously in existence continue to exist even
though one is larger and the other smaller in size. This mechanism was still
widely and easily employed in the western states and prairie Canada until
around the time of the Second World War. Even after the war, over 80 per
cent of Alberta's 259 municipalities extended their boundaries by annexations between 1951 and 1991 as did two-thirds of those in British Columbia
(Meligrana 1998: 186). By contrast, half of Ontario's municipal governments
experienced no annexations through this period, and the process had fallen
into disuse for expansion of a city like Toronto by as early as 1920. By that
time, even though the core city accounted for 74 per cent of the emerging
city-region's population, it already found itself hemmed in by five townships,
four towns, and three incorporated villages.

Even before the Second World War, American metropolitan reformers
were becoming discouraged with more ambitious reorganizational designs.
The early centralists, such as Paul Studenski (1930) and Victor Jones (1942),
argued their case passionately, almost as crusaders. But beginning in the
1950s, as the social sciences moved into the stricter empiricism associated
with behaviouralism, the metropolitan regions the researchers studied looked
increasingly complex, each with its own markedly unique conditions. As an
academic community, their prescriptive uncertainty became more apparent,
until it was somewhat restored through the economic theory of public choice,
which confirmed the status quo. One important hurdle which resisted any
single universal formula for governmental structure and which was never
surmounted in American metropolitan areas was the home rule prescription
of 1900 which conferred constitutional autonomy on municipalities. By the
1960s, this was acknowledged "as an ideological and strategic barrier to metropolitan integration ... Consequently, although the 'social engineers' who
surveyed and recommended solutions for metropolitan reform in the four
decades after 1920 tended to follow a common pattern of prescriptions, no

comprehensive, codified 'Model Metropolitan Charter' achieved acceptance among urban political scientists" (Sayre and Polsby 1965: 124).

Still, after 1970, annexation was still widely used in the United States, primarily among American cities smaller than 50,000 people and largely because annexation was the quickest, least costly way by which development interests could provide urban services to burgeoning suburbs. As a legal instrument annexation differed from amalgamation, which refers to the combination of two or more municipalities into a single unit of government. As will be considered in the next chapter, amalgamation has invariably been a more controversial and hence less probable reorganization path. On the evidence of the Canadian experience, it can seldom be accomplished by municipalities acting alone. Amalgamation most likely occurs when one of the partners is so indebted as to be virtually bankrupt or in such serious need of servicing upgrades that its future continuation is in real doubt. The partner in amalgamation is a municipality with a larger, more balanced assessment base and possessed of some ambition for more orderly city-region development; thus, it is able to view the absorption of the smaller community as more of an incremental cost than a longer term burden. Simply put, the councils of viable municipal governments are never interested in committing instrumental suicide.

For larger metropolitan areas during the latter part of the twentieth century, American reformers turned to an integrative device known as a **city-county consolidation** for which there are no real Canadian parallels. For historic reasons dating back to pre-revolutionary times and the need then to provide for the administration of justice, most American city-region municipalities find themselves existing within the boundaries of wider area counties which themselves have a specific but different public policy mandate. It is not unusual to find that larger metropolitan areas are cleaved by several county jurisdictions. The reformers proposed a city-county merger which would consolidate the operations of a growing central city, its suburbs, and all attendant SPDs into one unit with the already existing but wider area and specialized purpose county government. This took specific shape more or less as the politics of a particular case required.

One general lesson for Canadian observers of these initiatives was that the new "Unigov"—the term used for the 1969 merger of Indianapolis-Marion County—became not only a general metropolitan area governing instrument but also provided minimal local services for the unincorporated territories within its boundaries. This is somewhat akin to regional districts in British Columbia which today, by elimination, are the vehicle for limited services for their unincorporated territories known as "electoral districts." In the United States, the generic problem has been one of equity in that the county government has to use revenues collected from lower tier municipalities and divert those resources to service the residents living on unincorporated lands. The process effectively penalizes the general purpose municipalities. But there, as in Canada, unincorporated "free-riders" have never been enthusiastic in their willingness to pay for the specific services provided even if the costs can be accurately separated out from base county operations. The long history of subsequent failed initiatives in the 1960s, and the only slightly more than a dozen city-county consolidations that came to exist in American SMSAs, meant that reformers had to consider a number of more politically palatable governing alternatives.

During the urbanization of Canada after the Second World War the provincial governments, through their implementation of federal shared-cost programs, largely engaged in the building of comprehensive substate regional infrastructures. While the capacity of provincial systems to challenge federal political pre-eminence was quickly recognized by both scholars and practitioners alike (Black and Cairns 1966), what was not noticed until the last decade or so was that Canadian cities, and many of their larger suburban communities, had also proven capable of growing into substantial and reasonably sophisticated political systems. Just as the provinces were building operations with experienced ministries, fully fledged political party operations, larger scale bureaucracies, and the concomitant networks of policy communities and lobbying by interested parties, so too were many urban municipalities accumulating programs and patronage, administrative prestige, and more mature political skills than the parish pump theatrics ascribed to councillors in the past (about suburban Montreal developments, note Sancton 1979: 248). This situation subsequently became a serious barrier to any city-region institutional reconfigurations considered necessary by core-city reformers.

12.1 Contracting for Public Services

12.1.1 The political culture of public choice

In the decades following the Second World War much of the political economy scholarship focused on city-region governance in the United States sought to devise taxonomies for metropolitan area governing and then to test variables such as economies of scale, service differentiation, and the capacity to meet public consumption requirements effectively (Wrede 1997: 217-20).

Concisely put, classic public choice theory, as grounded in the work of Tiebout (1956) and Ostrom, Warren, and Tiebout (1961), has four central propositions.

1. The modern metropolis has been self-sorting among residents along social and economic lines so as to become a community of communities. The separately incorporated suburb is the policy instrument by which distinctive quarters of one stripe or another are located by institutional means.

2. Polycentrists maintain that a multiplicity of small governments better satisfy the resultant divergent social agendas of citizens through their different expenditure packages. The individual, as a rational citizen consumer of public goods, will choose to live in that community whose package best fulfills his, or her, lifestyle expectations.

3. Importantly, it is believed that the polycentric system is more cost efficient through separating service delivery from its production, either contracting from wider area providers where they exist or entering into mutually exploitive joint-area contracts, employing non-unionized staff or volunteers in governance roles (Keating 1995: 125). The corollary is that the competitive metropolis is able to control for the theorists' supposition that citizens over-consume publicly generated goods and services (Goetz and Clarke 1993: 26).

4. Big cities (through a monopoly on rents) are less efficient as service providers by internalizing the costs of public goods, monopolizing their service production, and entrenching dysfunctional bureaucracy (Lightbody 1999a: 189).

So, public choice grows out of an intellectual tradition and a political culture that emphasize individualism, competition, and utilitarianism: "That is, it holds that the unit of analysis is the self-interested individual and that the public good is no more than the aggregate of individuals' aspirations" (Keating 1995: 123). For economists in this convention, the public finance of the city-region subject to numerous local governments also promotes fiscal responsibility by linking those taxpayers who actually receive the direct service to those who have made the public policy expenditure decision. If one can assume perfect mobility in the population and that the individual choice of residence and corporate preference for location is acutely sensitive to property tax incidence, then, in the desire to keep taxes lower, councils will be at least partially accountable to *potential* residents and business investors (Hobson 1997: 127-29). This may involve "efficiency" of a sort as municipalities across the urban region compete to cut corners, but it also shades and confuses public accountability to produce best policies for current residents even if they are somewhat more costly. The public choice response to such policy, framed in the all-consuming pursuit of efficiency goals, always judges the more costly behaviours negatively for being economically irrational.

Public choice is an economic markets theory of democracy. Being such a theory, it is open to direct challenge from any contrary point of view that sees democracy more as a means by which wider area communities may make a collective determination, through voting majorities or representative institutions, about what constitutes "the good" in public policy. In its heart, public choice as ideology entails a political philosophy that is neo-liberal in its view of society and the individual, while it is conservative in its approach to the institutions of the state. With rare exceptions, to be considered more thoroughly in the next chapter, it has proven compatible with the generally incremental track record of North American city-region institutional adaptation.

As to the evidence, in Canada the academic attack against city-region local government unification has been largely directed at straw men constructed with more words than numbers and using American case studies. Its foremost apologist, Andrew Sancton, politely castigates those who put the case for consolidation: "The efficiency of one-tier comprehensive municipal systems in Canada has tended to be assumed rather than investigated" (Sancton 1994: 33). The problem is that the same charge is standard for those who remain passionate about existing arrangements: the fly in the public choice soup has always been the difficulty in measuring service output and costs. As Keating phrased it succinctly, "In the absence of a controlled experiment, it is possible to measure municipalities only against other municipalities or against their own past performance" (1995: 121). But public policy demands and internal circumstances vary, often considerably, over time and by place. In the absence of absolutely standard units of measurement, to be precise in measuring output has always been difficult. Because there has been no substantive knockout punch it is no copout to observe that the evidence accumulated is conflicting and inconclusive.

The contributions of public choice have been twofold. First, the metropolis governed by polycentric institutions need not be politically chaotic, and incremental changes by municipalities may well be able to address, to some degree, several aspects of the long-standing issues we have described. Second, the evidence, mostly from the United States, is persuasive that economies of scale are unlikely to be realized in all municipal service areas, or each equally, although the capital intensive functions (waterworks, roadways, transit) are the most likely to produce economic efficiencies.

To no one's surprise, the evidence in Canada to date is also that there are considerable costs, some unanticipated, which can be associated with any of the more recent municipal reorganizations (Sancton 1996). In some instances costs were higher than expected after amalgamations due to the consolidation of collective agreements, to unanticipated service upgrades in poorer municipalities, to the standardization of computing services (or communications among the emergency services), and the like. This should not have come as a bolt from the blue since the American evidence consistently revealed that while metropolitan area reorganization was sold initially as an efficiency mechanism, the new governments sought to raise, not reduce, existing service levels. Overall, costs and taxes rose. Even in the polemic *Merger Mania*, for example, a study commissioned by the Montreal suburb of Westmount to buttress its otherwise standard defence against amalgamation, the author acknowledges that the binge-spending of Halifax municipalities before unification—debts that would have to be costed against the new city operation—inflated its eventual budget (Sancton 2000: 90-95). What remains unknown in that, or any other, amalgamation case is what total city-region municipal expenditures might have been at some unspecified future point had consolidation never occurred.

The data which have been accumulated to compare two contrasting city-region systems in Canada that are actually in operational existence do, however, indicate that a unified municipal governing structure is, contrary to public choice conjecture, the one that appears to be the least fiscally extravagant (Lightbody 1998, 1999a).

12.1.2 A case study comparing Calgary and Edmonton

We might employ a case study to examine how well a public choice model of public policy activity actually bears out in the real world of the Canadian city-region. While the full case is presented elsewhere (Lightbody 1999a), the essentials of it can be summarized here.

In 1999, the Calgary CMA had eight municipal governments, but 94 per cent of the population lived within the boundaries of the central city. In contrast, Edmonton was more polycentric in governing, with 33 municipalities of various stripes, and only 71 per cent within the central city; in 1996 its suburbs were expanding their populations while Edmonton itself was relatively static. While this example is not a controlled experiment in any scientific sense, both city-region systems were of similar size. Both lay within one province's political culture, were subject to common legal and regulatory constraints as municipalities, and participated in the same regime concerning fiscal requirements.

The two CMAs of Calgary and Edmonton revealed no statistically significant differences along the usual social dimensions of language, ethnicity, and religion. The measure of average family income across the Calgary CMA, though, was 10.6 per cent higher than for Edmonton. Both central cities attracted families with lower incomes than the CMA average, but in Calgary's case the considerable coincidence of the city's boundaries with its built-up area made the difference, with CMA average inconsequential. Edmonton's middle- to upper-class inner suburbs, however, accommodated families with average incomes 20.7 per cent higher than those in the core city, while its six smaller villages had family incomes 28 per cent lower than the average for the census city-region. The variables that became important to local government in light of these conditions were the extent both of home ownership (rather than renting) and of the business and commercial assessment base. Both factors impinged directly on property taxation. Well over three-quarters of residents in Edmonton's immediately adjacent suburbs were home-owners, although only slightly more than half in the city owned their homes (contrasting with 60 per cent in Calgary).

When 1995-96 municipal expenditures were studied by major functional category (like protection, recreation, transportation, and so on) and against sources of revenues, several central tenets of public choice analysis appeared problematic. Specifically of interest are the following findings (Lightbody, 1999a: 186-90). First, there was some segregation by family income in the more governmentally polycentric city-region of Edmonton; this market was established by the zoning activities and area development plans of the suburban councils which screened prospective residents by family type (i.e., single family residential preferred). The evidence indicates that even these practices did not have the significant effect on the general pattern of councils' spending that public choice would predict. Second, even while segregated somewhat by family income, the suburbs adjacent to Edmonton's boundaries were not significantly distinct in other demographics from suburban neighbourhoods immediately within the city. Further, since the residential tax rates were pretty much the same in all municipalities, and the general distribution of spending among the functional categories did not vary seriously by statistical measures, then what councils did undertake was relegated to matters of servicing style. In other words, the choice within the social services category, for example, was between "meals on wheels" versus more preventive social intervention for families and individuals facing crisis directly. Policing was quite different in suburbs primarily of detached, single-family, owner-occupied homes than in the greatly more variegated core community.

Third, the governmentally polycentric CMA region of Edmonton had higher costs in providing a practically identical package of urban services than the more unitary government of the Calgary CMA. These were calculated to be over $5.00 per capita. One reason for this was the multiple overheads of the numerous governments (Lightbody 1998). Finally, and directly on the question of whether the bureaucratic monopoly of unitary municipal government increases the cost of service delivery, the evidence in 1996 was that Calgary provided the same basic services to 150,000 more residents than

Edmonton and to 94 per cent of its city-region at a per capita cost of $1,487 versus Edmonton's $1,670. All service areas cost significantly more in the city at the heart of the polycentric region and for the region as an entity (Lightbody 1999a: 188–89). Multiplicity was one reason, but the structural fact is that the single city council in Calgary captured both city-region assessment as well as expenditure obligations. Edmonton disproportionately had to accommodate the latter without access to the former. The central point here is that for cities of this population size, a bureaucratic monopoly *did not* foster higher costs in service provision.

It is probable that these findings can be extrapolated to the other governmentally fragmented city-regions of Canada (now, principally, in the lower mainland of British Columbia). Given critical scrutiny buttressed by the hard evidence of actual municipal spending, the public choice governing experiment does not substantiate its theoretical claims.

12.1.3 Contracting for services

Contracting for the provision of municipal services, in its purest form, constitutes the operational face of public choice theory for city-region governing. The approach is premised on the notion that a city-region may experience functional consolidation without having to accomplish much in the way of political consolidation. It is also referred to as the **Lakewood Plan**, a name coined when the City of Lakewood in southern California was incorporated in 1954 as a defensive measure against probable annexation by the neighbouring city of Long Beach. The "plan" aspect refers to the past actions of the surrounding County of Los Angeles which set the stage for easy incorporation (Bollens and Schmandt 1982: 354-55; Bish 1971). The urban agglomeration centred on Los Angeles had come under inexorably accelerating urbanization pressures immediately after the Second World War. In response to demands for development, the county, or area-wide government, expanded and enhanced the range of municipal services it could provide to its constituent lower tier units if so requested.

These days, Los Angeles County offers over 78 services ranging from community planning to rodent control and different levels of policing. This service package is available by contract to the 80 or so front-line general municipal governments, and they may contract for one, or more, or all of the proffered functions. In practice, long-standing incorporated bodies like the City of Los Angeles contract for very little, while newer communities tend towards a more complete bundle. For example, the cities of Industry and Rolling Hills remain comfortable with mostly the county-level services (Bish 1971: 88–89). At the extreme, a community like Lakewood was able to incorporate with only a single employee, the clerk, who was charged with keeping track of the community's contracted functions. Contractual arrangements can technically be ended on 60 days notice, but the reality seems to be considerable stability over time.

From the public choice perspective, a system of government under contractual arrangements performs close to the optimum of economic efficiency because a council, when choosing to make available a service to residents or for property, has basically four alternatives from which to choose.

1. A council might choose to establish its own line department (such as police, fire, or community services) both to produce and to deliver the function in the traditional municipal manner.

2. A council could contract with another municipal (or wider area) government to supply the function. Cities in the Los Angeles County region can, for instance, contract for one among a number of levels for policing with the county sheriff's department. In Canadian CMAs, it has not been at all unusual to find smaller municipalities contracting for specialized (and high overhead) fire protection back-up from the core city's department. It should be clear that such arrangements permit specific sorts of industrial development (petro-chemical for instance) in these communities which could not otherwise proceed without a very costly front-end municipal investment in equipment and personnel. Even a relatively simple metropolitan region such as Edmonton can manage its local governments under an umbrella of such legal partnerships; at the end of 1999 the most accurate available count estimated that there existed over 500 of these bilateral and multilateral instruments.

3. A council can also open specific services to tenders from private contractors; by the 1980s in Canada much local garbage collection was so handled. On occasion a major city's council has contracted only a part of its collection system privately in order to assess the cost-efficiency of its own operations and to impress (or not) its unionized work force.

4. A council may engage in the co-production of a service, as many smaller Canadian municipalities have done. This device was used often during the period of local fiscal austerity associated with recent neo-liberal provincial governments' cutbacks in, and offloading of, government responsibilities. Co-production refers to a variety of PPPs in service delivery, often involving NGOs, in which a municipality diverts staff resources, partial funding, or other subsidy in support of the NGO's taking primary delivery responsibility for a particular specialized service. In federal policy, for instance, the John Howard and Elizabeth Fry Societies have long played a lead role in the integration of parolees into the community. Locally, sports associations manage facilities, service clubs deliver selected kinds of commu-

nity assistance, and community cooperatives run public housing operations. In the United States, a comprehensive survey of 604 cities (1982–88) found that the largest had decreased their direct delivery of services from 56 per cent to 46 per cent. While the level of contracting had not changed (36 per cent), service delivery employing volunteers had increased six-fold (Stephens and Wikstrom 2000: 145). Councils have increasingly deployed various forms of subsidies and tax incentives to initiate or encourage a form of innovation through co-production efforts. Harshly put, volunteerism reduces the labour costs associated with providing programs requiring quasi-professional support. More generously, co-production permits some localities to engage in types of activities that would be too costly to mount if they had to be funded exclusively from the property tax base.

Contracting out was a major response by the 1,333 American cities surveyed by the International City Management Association in 1982 (Clark 1994b: 245). Expenditure data gathered through the international Fiscal Austerity and Urban Innovation project at the University of Chicago revealed that savings were least with for-profit private entrepreneurs, moderately more with other governments, and only significant with nonprofit agencies which were able to subsidize operations with volunteers or by piggybacking costs onto other state funding (Miranda 1994b: 209–10).

Where a polycentric governmental system is fully developed (or mature), all four of the contract elements are expected to be deployed in different combinations by the many municipalities, each of whom is in Darwinian competition with its peers to accumulate plaudits for better management measures. At the same time, the numerous service providers find themselves in performance rivalries with governments and among themselves to win positive economic reviews and the contracts that might follow. Front-line local governments control the quantity of service they provide even though they may exert less influence over the quality of service execution. Where county-level service has proven insensitive to the requirements of specific racial or socio-economic communities, as with policing for instance, several territories in Los Angeles have sought independence to renegotiate county contracts. These actions directly reinforce the arguments of public choice theorists that bureaucratic monopolies tend towards conformity.

The contracting for services approach does not measure up well against the three generic questions for city-region governing raised in Chapter 11. First, the Lakewood Plan appears to encourage a proliferation of municipal governments at the lower tier, thus creating an instrumental problem. The reason for this is that the base start-up costs in the provision of new city services after incorporation are relatively few. Municipalities mushroom, especially in those states like California where incorporation procedures are relatively easy and particularized communities can visualize defining, advancing, and protecting their interests as communities in the form of legitimate municipalities. Some cities, like Industry, have incorporated to avoid the local taxation that would be needed to provide service to residential development. Palos Verdes incorporated to protect its estates from "inappropriate" higher density urban living. Both found county-level contracting sufficient. The possibilities for greater coordination of policies across the entire city-region are limited but may develop through councils of governments, as will be noted below.

Second, the contracting technique is oblivious to concerns over redressing taxation and assessment inequity. It is true, though, that specific services and specializations may be provided, and at lower per unit costs, through economies of scale. But equalization upgrades of services and standards for less affluent communities are not an issue, and the conservative philosophical streak of this approach is underscored by its unwillingness to condone institutional arrangements that are conducive to redistributive policies.

Third, government by contract is governing through negotiation in a realm of bureaucracy and law normally closed to broader public debate, which presents a larger policy problem. While municipal councils are indeed responsible to their own local electors for community services provided, the bilateral nature of contracting negates the probability of any voice for planning for the orderly development and integrated servicing of the city-region in and of itself. As there is no regional control over land use and property development, municipalities retain their capacity to deploy zoning so as to exclude residence by populations discretely targeted. County (or regional) supervisors and officials are both bureaucratic and conscious of their role as service providers always trying to find their position in competition with private-sector providers. Neither role is generally considered conducive to the promotion of citizen engagement, informed debate, or the public resolution of genuine policy differences. When emulated in Alberta's city-regions in the 1990s, in a field such as preventive social services, few outside the affected policy community have been aware of the actual workings of the web of intergovernmental service agreements and contingency plans that support metropolitan area citizens as clients. Outside the much smaller policy networks in areas like family violence, even fewer citizens are knowledgeable about potential policies that can have directly positive impacts upon both clients and service providers.

12.2 Glorifying Councils of Government (COG)

As the British Empire was occasionally able to add to its luster by declaring a military defeat as a victory, so have American scholars of the governmentally fragmented city-region declared that, in and of themselves, complex metropolitan arrangements constitute a functional political system. It is little wonder that, with 117 units of local government now the average number for city-regions, it was natural to turn to theories of international politics to explain interactions and behaviours. One early exponent was Mathew Holden (1964), although Victor Jones (1942) had noted some of the similarities a generation earlier. Municipal boundaries were accepted as artifacts akin to the defensive but static French Maginot fortifications prior to the Second World War: the boundaries were rooted in past experience and maintained at considerable expense against anticipated aggression from any neighbouring community's self-identified need to expand. Borders like these, no matter how entrenched by concrete or political will, are of little utility when faced with new sorts of stress, be they Hitler's panzers in 1940 or today's pressures of global economic integration.

So, victory was declared after the defeat of more substantial reorganizations like city-county consolidations with the application of the SPD system, which will be discussed in the next section. The central weakness with the SPD governing model is in the coordination of intergovernmental policies, and it was early recognized first by the administrators of the multiple autonomous authorities and agencies that discussion, negotiation, bargaining, and cooperation could both make the whole lumbering apparatus operate and forestall more radical (and rational) change. The **Council of Government** (COG) form arose to address this problem. The first COG emerged after more audacious SMSA governing options had been set aside by the Detroit area's Supervisors Inter-County Committee in 1954.

This first COG became a forum for general discussion of common problems in area-wide service provision. It had no power to tax, no autonomous authority structure, and no means to implement choices (if any decisions were actually made) other than through the unilateral action of the participants. Its meetings were congenial, simple, and reasonably informal. The rationale for its existence was two-fold and sustained by its successors and copycat jurisdictions: it met a minimal need for intergovernmental collaboration to respond to urban growth pressures, and it was a response to "a fear that local units were about to lose power to proposed metropolitan governments" (Bollens and Schmandt 1982: 368). This latter fear still sustains the limited interlocal government communication which exists in today's Edmonton region and which defines that city-region's nascent COG activities.

After a decade, only nine COGs existed in American SMSAs, but a dramatic upsurge in the intermunicipal spirit of cooperative endeavour emerged in the mid-1960s coincident with American federal legislation enacting President Lyndon Johnson's War on Poverty. In particular, the Demonstration Cities and Metropolitan Development Act opened a conduit for federal funding (grants, loans) for urban redevelopment initiatives. Regional councils themselves became eligible to receive funds for administration and planning, and, importantly, applications from municipalities for their own direct access to federal funds required the review and approval of an area-wide planning body. This is known as the A-95 process, and COGs were deemed eligible approbation instruments. As a result, the COG quickly became a very popular device, and during the 20 years leading to 1977 most metropolitan planning commissions were converted into COGs. By 1977 well in excess of 600 existed although only two (Minneapolis-St. Paul and Portland, Maine) had the power to tax directly and enforce decisions. Regardless of size, each member municipality, as a rule, exercises the same vote (as in the UN), a mechanism intended at the outset to assuage smaller municipalities' concerns over potential central city dominance.

COG members have organized their own national association and federal lobby group, which is a not-so-subtle reminder of the important federal role in transferring funds to local governments in the United States. Indeed, the model has become so popular that some writers consider them as performing well enough to be considered the ideal model of city-region governing (Osborne and Gaebler 1992: 246–47). Such policy focus as has emerged in activities related to better regional land use planning comes usually in the form of successive studies; they tend not to engage in actual service operations. Although many COGs were critiqued by one wag as "marching and chowder societies" which existed primarily to carve up the federal fiscal turkey, other observers are more generous: "COGs appear to have stimulated considerable interlocal contact and more cooperation than existed previously" (Stephens and Wikstrom 2000: 147). This latter observation applies today to the Edmonton region where there is no federal, and precious little provincial, funding in any case. In the United States, as federal programs evaporated during the Reagan presidency and as funds were diverted to the state governments for local redistribution, the number of COGs has been reduced to slightly more than 500. To survive, these agencies have to seek alternate local funding sources and to uncover a new mission as providers of a limited range of direct technical services.

Only two examples of COGs exist in Canada. The more unadulterated and recent is the Alberta Capital Region Alliance (ACRA) in the Edmonton CMA. This organization, incorporated under the province's Charities

Act, emerged through informal discussions after the province abandoned regional planning commissions during their cost–cutting manoeuvres in 1993. In 1995, 14 of the 19 former planning commission municipal members opted to meet regularly to discuss multi-lateral regional matters. Suburban members' suspicions, based on concerns about Edmonton's past annexation ambitions (Plunkett and Lightbody 1982: 212–13), are revealed by the relatively silly act of omitting the capital city's name from the formal title. Today the commission has a staff of two and relies for funding on voluntary contributions from members, principally the city of Edmonton. Unlike its predecessor planning commission, ACRA provides no direct technical (planning) services to its constituents. It has neither dues nor fees, provides no services, and, should it make any decision, implementation still requires the unilateral actions of individual members. Voting is by municipality, notwithstanding size discrepancies, yet even this measure did not trump the initial reluctance of four municipalities on the city's western fringe to sign on. Policy activities have been minimal, oriented to lowest common denominator agreements for targeted travel for economic development purposes. By 1999, in a further quest for legitimacy, ACRA had obtained an associate member standing in the (American) National Association of Councils of Government. However, it exists as somewhat a protective dike forged from the fear that more radical reorganization lies just over the horizon. The second Canadian COG is the GVRD.

12.2.1 The Greater Vancouver Regional District (GVRD)

The Greater Toronto Services Board, established by the Ontario Progressive Conservative government on 1 January 1999, might be considered something of a COG in that it exists primarily "to provide a forum for promoting better coordination and integration of interregional services in the GTA," and its only operational activity is GO Transit (Tindal and Tindal 2000: 104–05). However, it lacks a minimal legitimacy with municipalities because of its top-down imposition. More energy has been directed into its weighted voting and the quorum requirements than with increasing its planning and implementing authority. Montreal does not have a similar operation even though a metropolitan development commission exists in legislation.

On the other hand, **regional districts** in British Columbia have for some time provided the legislative framework for that province's urban-centred regions to establish a modest COG-style of governing. Although owing their peculiar existence to somewhat unique indigenous circumstances, including the physical landscape which separates population centres widely, in urban areas these frameworks have provided a seemingly practical approach much lauded by Canadian students of public choice. Possibly they find comfort in the provincial government's 1972 assertion that "regional districts were not conceived as a fourth level of government, but are a functional rather than a political amalgamation ..." (cited by Higgins 1986: 218). In an important sense, and whatever the reality, they are COGs because everyone in the political and policy world says they are.

Their history is straightforward. By the mid-1960s, local government organization covered only about 1 per cent of provincial territory, but this included over 80 per cent of the population. Legislation in 1965 set the stage for the creation of 28 regional districts for the whole province, each centred on an urban centre and including its trading hinterland. These bodies came gradually into existence as the minister of municipal affairs issued letters patent after discussions with a variety of interested local parties of his choosing. No municipal boundaries were altered, but most existing SPDs (such as water) were folded into the regional mandates. Each region was different, and, until 1970, municipalities were free to opt out of any regional function they found either uncomfortable or unnecessary. Each region was similar in being managed by a "board of directors" indirectly chosen from the councils of municipalities, but directly elected in those unincorporated territories to which limited municipal service was provided. Those in the province's two most developed CMAs, Victoria and Vancouver, have taken on more operational activity than others in either British Columbia or the United States.

The GVRD has been much beloved of suburban councillors everywhere in Canada as the one example of a viable governing device that might legitimate their municipalities' perpetual existence. It is also popular among those theorists who have consistently protested the desirability of any kind of municipal consolidation anywhere. The most developed essay in this school, *Governing Canada's City-regions* (1994), causes Sancton to characterize the GVRD as "the middle ground between public choice and the traditional approach of the consolidationists" (1994: 99). It is Sancton's belief that this scheme is both "comprehensive in territory and flexible in function" (1994: 100). This assessment is not without its critics but for Sancton the persistence of multiple smaller municipalities allows differentiated and very local citizen expectations to be met by parochial town councils. At the same time, the existence of the regional district structure permits obvious, and specific, wider area functional policy needs (like water, sewerage, drainage) on which there is widespread common agreement.

The GVRD is a singular operation and exists today for a combination of unique conditions that defy replication elsewhere. A partial list of these include the following.

1. The length of the settlement's existence and the history of development is relevant. New Westminster, for example, was founded in 1859 as the capital of the mainland colony and quickly developed a vigorous economy rooted in the timber industry. Vancouver was not incorporated until 1886 as the Pacific terminus for the Canadian Pacific Railway, whose commercial and operational requirements fashioned the original shape of the city. Because the company did not own the land at Port Moody, it extended its line 12 miles to Coal Harbour where the provincial government ceded 6,000 acres of property. Lands essentially expropriated on the south side of the Burrard Inlet from the Musquean Nation and, on the north, from the Squamish Nation were destined to become the heart of the modern City of Vancouver (Gutstein 1975: 11-18), which, alone among municipalities in the province, has its own charter as Chapter 55 of the 1953 British Columbia Statutes. This means that any amendment requires an act of the provincial legislature.

2. The population of the entire CMA plus its proximate commuter-shed is so large that it dominates the political life of the province were one mayor and council ever to speak for it. It is thus politically relevant that some two dozen municipalities exist, enough to confound bilateralism in exploiting development patterns. As a corollary, the distribution of residents among the municipalities prevents a single dominant city heart (it comprises only 28 per cent of the CMA population) or easy permanent coalition of municipal actors. The City of Vancouver underwent its last significant amalgamation over 70 years ago (in 1929), and there has been little in the way of other municipal annexation, amalgamation, or dismemberment across the lower mainland since Langley City incorporated out of its surrounding township in 1951 and the City of White Rock separated from Surrey in 1953. Such stability breeds a comfort zone with a built-in institutional familiarity. For those residents requiring minimal service, the GVRD suffices as the provider to three unincorporated electoral districts.

3. Fiscal imbalance in taxation resources and service requirements has not been so huge as to present a glaring public policy problem. Looking at average family income (1996) among the municipalities, the richest is 192 per cent of the CMA average and 234 per cent of the lowest ranked. While this was greater than that in pre-Megacity Toronto or Edmonton today, it is still far less a variation than the prevailing conditions in Winnipeg (1971) or Montreal (1996). The absence of any sort of redistributive mechanism regionally has not arisen as a significant public policy issue to date.

The absence of any semblance of a metropolitan planning function constitutes a bit of a problem for the public choice tradition, except for those who have no real interest in area-wide general plans. Sancton, for instance, seems genuine in the belief that, "Conceivably, if there is general agreement that regional planning is necessary, it will emerge even without a regional government structure" (1994: 45). But even when planning *was* a GVRD responsibility, and part of the reason that that authority was lifted in the 1983 provincial budget, proper planning practices were held hostage, in true COG-style, to suburban intermunicipal bargaining to facilitate development in support of everyone's assessments. Viewed cynically, regional district authority over water and sewerage access and expansion, without any direct accountability to electors, became a useful adjunct in this overall land rush.

Upon reflection, the COG approach as applied to Canadian city-regions appears to stand as the extraordinary exception that more validates the desirability of centripetal reform than it gives good reason for the existence of its own model. Insofar as it constitutes an area-wide frame of reference, the Canadian COG format may stand as a precursor to more fundamental rethinking of metropolitan government, even as it exists in a state of arrested incrementalism.

12.3 Systemic Reorganization of Institutions

Higgins once used the word "systemic" to describe those changes to the rules and regulations of local governing which widely affect municipalities throughout the province, such as new patterns in functional responsibility or the financial relationship (1986: 173-77). Such changes across the whole system of local-provincial relations are contrasted to those affecting only one city, like a significant boundary adjustment or an amendment of the city's charter (Vancouver) or founding statute (Winnipeg in 1971 or Toronto in 1996). Systemic reorganization happens so infrequently that it may be applied to a single legislative act or to a short, but specific, time period. Modest accomplishments, like regional districts in British Columbia, were the result of generic legislation, while regional communities in Quebec in the 1970s and early 1980s were quite specific to a small handful of urban centres. More ambitiously, Alberta through the 1950s reorganized most municipalities outside its urban centres on the basis of the County Act (1950). On the other hand, regional government reorganization in Ontario from 1969 to 1974, which produced 13 regions whose territories encompassed about two-thirds of Ontario's population, was handled through quite specific city-region legislation.

The possible alternatives from the centripetal to the centrifugal in arrangements for municipal governing are hindered only by the imagination in their stretch from a focus on the core to a focus on the periphery (Savitch and Vogel 1996: 287-99). Extremists in the tradition of the new localism argue the case that the "low" politics of neighbourhood are better able to respond effectively to citizens than any centralized bureaucracy might (Goetz and Clarke 1993: 5-7; Sancton 2000: 163-68). In the mid-range, COGs have been faint-hearted stabs at accommodation, usually in the hope, at most, that an agreement for some sort of city-region planning considerations with limited scope will result. All efforts on the COG model to provide minimal metropolitan governing acknowledge that nothing more substantial can be done in the face of the very real, and zero sum, politics involved.

The American experience is of limited relevance to Canada except for its shortcomings. None of the COG reform packages can be considered systemic with the singular exception of COGs in Virginia, which now find their state funding linked to a lowering of economic disparities between centre cities and their suburbs. On a tangent from this, it is important to note that, in the United States, it is only the least differentiated communities such as Minneapolis-St. Paul that have been able to initiate anything more than modestly incremental centripetal reforms in recent years. The 16-person regional council for that city is further unique in that it is entirely appointed by the state governor.

As to the more advanced centripetal reforms, it has been noted that city-county consolidation was an early favourite of American blue-ribbon reformers. Indeed, the first measures of this kind arrived on the scene early in the nineteenth century, and four of the more significant date back to that time: New Orleans in 1813, Boston in 1821, Philadelphia in 1854, and New York City in 1898. The last was the largest consolidation, embracing four counties and nearly 30 front-line municipalities. The concept came to make superficial sense as a systemic model in service club speeches insofar as the boundaries of about 100 SMSAs were coterminous with county lines. The city-county combination of Honolulu (1907) predated statehood itself and included the entire island of Oahu. In all of these cases, there was an obvious appeal to the use of existing governing structures rather than creating entirely new operations.

All early consolidations were accomplished through state legislatures and did not require direct ratification by electors. But these positive initiatives were overwhelmed by blatant abuses of state-level authority and, in the twentieth century, were usurped by the far more politically powerful systemic reform package of 1900 with its central principle of home rule. This was precisely intended to prevent state intervention into cities' sovereign "rights" to self-governing and became a virtually insurmountable barrier to further consolidation activity. Because of their overtones for economic, social, and political power, such ventures were subsequently, and as a rule, either nullified by state legislators who refused constitutional amendments and enabling legislation or, as a final resort, killed by local voters in plebiscites. Neither core city nor suburban electors were enthusiastic about upsetting their status quo apple carts. Bollens and Schmandt list the 43 major consolidation initiatives defeated by plebiscite from 1950 to 1980 (1982: 316). Only a dozen of these operations exist as twentieth-century inventions in the American SMSAs today, with the most recent being Kansas City with Wyandotte County in 1997.

Generally, the field for systemic reform has been abandoned to the politics of limited imagination and, even when couched in quality management terms, a far more guarded approach to any city-region's institutional status quo. Corporate efficiency now stands paramount, and small governing units are seen as being best able to serve the interests of competition, the marketplace, and citizens choosing as service consumers. Consequently, the failure to annex, amalgamate, or otherwise consolidate the American metropolis since 1978 becomes a retrospective virtue and, with municipalities still continuing to proliferate, a source of theoretical solace (Savitch and Vogel 1996: 11).

Questions concerning the political forces at play during the consolidation of city-region municipalities in Canada will be given specific consideration in the next chapter. Our aim over the next few pages is to consider the centrally important issue of best possible governing by assessing Canadian institutional achievements not only against absolute questions of regional coordination, equity, and accountability, but also alongside American accomplishments.

Comparison here is helpful. One of the most aggressive modern consolidations in the United States is that of Indianapolis with Marion County in 1969 just prior to Winnipeg Unicity. Like Winnipeg, Indianapolis "Unigov" required a specific act of the state legislature, and there was no vote among electors, an unusual American occurrence. Also like Winnipeg, the Marion County city-region was a reasonably small and free-standing metropolis (at about 800,000 people) and not part of any conurbation. There was one major difference between the two: while Winnipeg Unicity amalgamated all previously existing local governments into one, the Unigov operation only merged the core city with its surrounding county. For reasons of political feasibility, there were to be no immediate changes to service delivery or tax structure for the 17 other existing and incorporated suburbs, nine townships, and 11 school districts. Differentials in service and taxing levels remained and were projected into the future. The number of elected officials was not reduced (in contrast with Winnipeg where that number was cut in half, from 112 to 51), although some 50 previously quasi-autonomous agencies were reorganized into six new departments. These have fewer employees than before, but, as in Winnipeg, salary scales followed highest levels. In contrast with Winnipeg Unicity, equity issues in any redistributive sense were largely ignored, and accountability remained diffused even though there were fewer largely unseen agencies. Some measure of policy coordination through the larger departments was achieved, but it has been in very specific functional areas like transportation and public transit.

It must be re-emphasized that barriers entrenched in American political culture not only inhibit centripetal changes but are also so strongly rooted that Americans have had no choice but to turn to more modest alternatives while jettisoning anything that would probably fail. Success has come through governance by contracting for services as discussed above and through SPDs. The lost world seems to be that of formalized metropolitan federations of municipalities. All of these models have found their way into Canadian practice.

12.3.1 Special purpose districts (SPDs)

SPDs have usually been the first step in virtually any polycentric city-region centripetal reorganization. They emerge when the professional administrative staffs of constituent municipalities appreciate that common functional obligations must be provided by all, that there are economies of scale and efficiency which can be realized in particular service areas, and that effectiveness in service delivery can best be realized through a cooperative initiative. The theory is simple. Authority to provide these specific services is delegated from established local councils to some sort of quasi-autonomous agency by means of legally negotiated intermunicipal agreements. In the earliest years of the twentieth century, the piped services were most easily targeted: the Greater Winnipeg Water District was formed in 1913, the Greater Vancouver Sewerage and Drainage District in 1926. Relative success in these operations led to institutional emulation in other hard service areas, notably transit, during the urbanization explosion in the years immediately after the Second World War. For instance, intermunicipal agreements led to the creation of the Greater Winnipeg Transit Commission in 1953. The Toronto Transit Commission (for the period 1923 until 1954) set the precedent when it was set up shortly after the City of Toronto took over the private operation in 1919.

In some instances, provincial authorities have had to act when the councils of even amenable municipalities find the process of delegating functional authority to another body too daunting. In 1946, for example, the Ontario cabinet found it necessary to create (and appoint) a Toronto and Suburban Planning Board for that city-region. It was given the single function of devising a metropolitan plan with which existing municipalities' plans would, theoretically, conform. But its ambitions and legitimacy were sabotaged to varying degrees, most notably in the City of Toronto's 1950 OMB application to amalgamate the entire region under one council.

SPDs can work very well indeed where the service provided is very tangible, such as public transit. The pressures of managing and provisioning for unrelenting population growth make it patently obvious to councillors, as well as their electors, that these individual policy responsibilities can be provided better collectively than by each municipality acting alone. For instance, it would have been patently absurd that there should be two dozen water or sewage treatment plants, one for each locality, on the lower mainland of British Columbia. Given these circumstances of public policy visibility and the need for capital intensive works, the municipalities in a city-region essentially assign their individual responsibility for a specific local service (such as the provision of potable water) to an area-wide body charged with that single responsibility. Where it is necessary to support the construction of major public works, such an organization, because it is independent, in all probability can enjoy better access to financing arrangements and lower borrowing charges.

Success in one area breeds duplication in the policy resolution of others. The average metropolitan area in the United States possessed 43 SPDs in 1992, an increase of 169 per cent over the 16 of 1952, the total number having grown from 2,661 to 13,614. Analysis based on correlations of spending data with public services reveals that SPDs fill a void, essentially stepping in to provide services not offered by state and metropolitan area local governments (Stephens and Wikstrom 2000: 19-20). In some cases SPDs may perform an innovative function for a city-region in the provision of a new initiative (like recycling) that no single municipality alone can, or will, afford to undertake in either dollar or staffing terms. In turn, 90 per cent of these operations undertake a single government function, be it the piped services, fire, libraries, community housing, mass transit, or highways.

The proliferation of SPDs also occurred, more modestly, in Canada. For example, in Winnipeg immediately prior to the introduction of two-tier metropolitan government in 1961, the city-region had 11 such coordinating agencies. In Toronto in the early 1950s, the initial step toward metropolitan federation developed when the city's ring of suburban municipalities applied to the OMB to formalize a joint service area permitting the cooperative provision of certain (water-related) services. Even still, there are often other political considerations afoot. When, in February 1998, the NDP provincial government of British Columbia decided to devolve transit operations in the lower mainland to municipal control, reversing its 1982 decision to shift that function for all districts to BC Transit which had absorbed the earlier Metro Transit Operating Company in 1979 (which looked after transit operations in Victoria and Vancouver), the implementing device was a special district and board within the GVRD general structure (Smith and Oberlander 1998: 395). The new Greater Vancouver Transit Authority (GVTA) was to be managed by a 15-person board, 12 from existing GVRD directors plus three area MLAs to be designated through order-in-council. It is essential to note that the provincial government of this period was no more enamoured of the prospect of a Vancouver metropolitan government than its predecessors, especially one that, by the numbers, would be dominated by conservative suburban members. But the size of the provincial deficit, combined with the pending provincial election, prompted a functional shift that would yield the practical political benefit of offloading debt instruments from provincial books onto those of the GVTA. The new agency was to fund its operations through fares, tolls, fuel taxes, and charges against properties and vehicles within GVRD boundaries.

Over the last generation, the small steps taken to transform the GVRD from COG towards a more genuinely effective metropolitan authority have been in response to continuing difficulties in generating intermunicipal cooperation to link land use planning practices with the economies of hard service provision. The new BC Growth Strategies Act of 1995 addressed this standing issue partially in that it required municipalities to plan regionally and reduce the provincial role to arbitration and conciliation of local differences (Smith and Oberlander 1998: 372, 392). However, the continued weakness is that it remains a consensual model.

When delegating a part of their operational responsibilities to intermunicipal SPDs, councillors will usually designate some or all of their number to serve also as "directors" of these boards or agencies. Such indirect election arguably promotes accountability to the public through the political realm of the designating council. Often complex weighted voting arrangements may accompany the delegated authority to take into account population variations (or differential assessment bases, for instance) among the participating municipalities. For example, in the GVRD setup, the directors have one vote per unit of 20,000 population represented; Vancouver's five directors thus exercise 22 of the total 62 votes (three directors casting four each, and two voting five). In the reality of policy-making, though, board directors have tended to see themselves as making practical decisions among competing administrative alternatives. Under this approach, the service role of municipal government reigns paramount, and the decision style, one step removed from actual council chambers, implies that there is no role for public controversy or direct citizen preference. In their operations, SPD boards consistently tend to diffuse public participation, and attempts to exert broader influence are considered "political" intrusions in highly technical matters.

In short, citizens are discouraged from voicing, say, possible environmental concerns over the extension of trunk water or sewerage lines into previously underdeveloped territories.

This general problem of direct accountability for public policy was evaluated in the previous chapter. The defence is that each municipal service provided is not congruent with municipal boundaries, no two have the same precise definition, so each can be met on its own terms with separate SPDs, separate delegations, and separate territories. This is claimed to be an important advantage for the metropolitan region with multiple smaller municipalities. Sancton also argues that districts can be infinitely flexible in expanding their boundaries to include jurisdictions as functional and local imperatives require (1994: 95–101).

Do SPDs answer the three generic metropolitan area continuing policy questions presented in Chapter 11 (see pages 409-10)? SPDs are intended to coordinate service delivery in their single realm of delegated authority, and they can usually manage these operations in a more cost-effective fashion than is possible were each municipality to follow its own path. They are not, however, designed to coordinate among their separate services or to resolve the political and policy issues that arise from the role of these individual services in the future growth and development of the territory. That is, the extension of water and sewer lines opens lands for residential development which requires schools, roads, and policing. In the United States this policy void has been partly occupied by COGs. Where a COG is not effectively in existence, as in the Canadian CMA of Edmonton, any semblance of regional planning is pretty much cast adrift.

On the question of equity, there is little question that SPDs can deliver specific piped services economically and at lower per unit costs. For instance, the GVRD's water system profitability has for some time partly off-set the costs of other, non-water-related operational areas. But SPDs are not intended to redress fundamental questions related to intermunicipal equity in taxation and service. They are not redistributive policy instruments. In short, each agency has single service responsibility but, due to its singular focus, is never required to make the difficult choices in spending between those for public transit or, for instance, those for waste recycling.

As to public accountability, there seems little question that important issues respecting the pattern of delivery of essential municipal services are removed from direct public scrutiny and reduced to operations and management discussions. Enid Slack makes this point well: "the proliferation of decision-making bodies has 'created a diffuseness of government organizations that is difficult for citizens to understand.' There is no citizen control ... because there is no accountability, there is no direct link between the expenditure decisions made by the special-purpose agencies and the local council that collects property taxes to fund them" (1997: 105-06). As SPDs each exercise considerable autonomy, this raises a general concern that, in the absence of direct accountability, there exist few incentives to value either operational efficiencies or citizen interventions. This basic failure to obtain the necessary policy linkages to facilitate more effective area-wide planning for development ultimately created public policy pressures for some form of general purpose metropolitan instrument in Canada's major city-regions.

12.3.2 Confederations of municipalities

In 1926, Paul Studenski, at the instigation of the American NML, imparted legitimacy to the preferred option for American urban reformers of a federated form of city-region government. This idea held official sway for a long time, although it made little headway in practice. The political and legal obstacles which prevented widespread implementation led to Victor Jones's *Metropolitan Government*, a second powerful argument for dramatic structural change and dismissal of other alternatives as mere stopgaps (1942: 121). The political barriers remained too formidable for words: "The sad history of metropolitan reform is filled with brave efforts of adventurous businessmen armed with the research of political scientists, funded by Ford [Foundation], and supported by the media, that have failed ingloriously" (Long 1968: 246-47).

The American models were based on the Articles of Confederation (1777) which constituted central government for the colonies prior to the drafting of the American Constitution. The two-tier metropolitan model was thus akin to K.C. Wheare's classic notion of a federation. In this form powers are divided in such a way that both an area-wide state and a number of smaller autonomous substates may co-exist while holding "coordinate and independent" authority (1963: 10-13). In both national politics and on the municipal stage, the lower tier units retain their original constitutions, and both levels interact directly with the population. In the United States, one divergence from a more genuine federal community lay in the "confederation" reality that since the national state was the creation of the lower tier federating communities, their congressional delegations would be indirectly elected to it. Thus, until the Seventeenth Amendment was adopted in 1913, state legislatures appointed their two senators to the Congress (after that, senators were elected by the states' citizens). This idea of indirect election was central to all Canadian two-tier metropolitan federations except Winnipeg's.

The one frequently cited instance of the American federative model in operation is the Miami-Dade County "consolidation" in 1957 (Stephens and Wikstrom 2000: 88-95; Bollens and Schmandt 1982: 324-32). That county today, as the result of a 1993 charter amendment, is governed by a board of 13 commissioners plus a strong mayor directly elected by district. The existing 27 municipalities have continued their more "purely local" service delivery operations, and controversy persists between the two levels as to who precisely does what to whom when. Miami–Dade provided the usually standard inventory of area-wide services in expressways, transit, traffic, emergency services communications, public health, parks and recreational areas, air pollution, and even the always hopeful "preparation of a plan for the development of the county" (Stephens and Wikstrom 2000: 90–91). It also delivered municipal functions for its fast developing but unincorporated territories at a discounted cost reluctantly subsidized by county ratepayers. Finally, even as it has nourished a regional perspective on general policy issues, Miami–Dade has also been criticized, in another not uncommon development, for not encompassing the broader three-county metropolitan city-region and thus limiting its geographical borders.

Because the municipal and upper tier regional governments of most Canadian CMAs were essentially amalgamated by the end of the twentieth century, it is tempting to consider their metropolitan federation periods as an evolutionary phase from a polycentric to unitary system. In the specific case of Winnipeg, for example, Tom Axworthy advanced this argument that even though the Metro operation was both disliked and not well understood, "By 1970, people were used to area wide government and Metro had proved that amalgamation was at least technically feasible" (1974: 96). The one great achievement of Metro Winnipeg's ten years, conceded by those working to replace it, apart from over $50 million spent on the construction of roads and bridges, was the "public conception of Winnipeg as an integrated unit" (Brownstone and Plunkett 1983: 32, 62). The integrative theme also courses through and sustains Kaplan's books on metropolitan governance (1967, 1982). But this was *never* the intent of the provincial ministries which imposed the metropolitan structures. The instruments were clearly intended as satisficing public policy to meet the exigencies of a people, period, and place.

To both Canadian and American observers at the time, as we saw in Chapter 10, Metro Toronto in 1954 put paid to long-standing issues of accountability for the physical direction of urban design (transit, freeways, and waterworks) and probably more. Its lightly veiled limitation, as forecast by Long 30 years earlier (1968: 247), was in the area of "social politics and the problems of fiscal redistribution," not the integrated development of hard services in very specific support of the growth machine.

Rather than being the grand experiments of romantic reformist lore, Canadian metropolitan instruments were minimalist interventions for quite specific ends. Change was prompted by the accelerated interdependence of city-region economic communities, institutional incongruity with these, and growing policy elite expectations for structural means through which to respond. The three provincial governments which finally found the pressure too much to avoid were reluctant policy warriors indeed. Ideologically, each of these governments was moderately conservative and resolutely incremental. In their general world view, least was best, and two-tier federation would be the least disruptive intervention that could balance existing arrangements against blatantly obvious wider area requirements. This approach meant several things.

At least in theory, two-tier federation reconciled the conflicting goals of policy "innovation" and familiar patterns. Three regional objectives were economies of scale, minimizing detrimental spillovers, and providing for redistributive policies, which might define geographically larger scale governing units (Slack 1997: 85). But coincidentally, and along the lines of the Smith Committee discussion (Ontario 1967), at least three competing criteria—accessibility to local institutions conforming with lifestyle choices, quick access to local officials, and close public scrutiny leading to accountability—seemed to require considerably smaller units for governing. In the public statements of ministers and provincial officials, the classic argument for two-tier structures was that they accommodated all these conflicting ends. The former targets could be attained at the regional level without sacrificing the latter values, which would be preserved through existing municipalities. If the political art is defining possibilities in impossible circumstances, then designing the "appropriate balance" in the allocation of functions between two metropolitan area municipal tiers was a taxing exercise!

In their initial operations, the first Canadian municipal federations tended only to tack regional physical plant upgrades (like freeways) onto their absorption of long-standing, city-region special districts. In the Winnipeg case, for example, Metro (1961) took over seven SPD operations: the Greater Winnipeg Water District (created in 1913), the Mosquito Abatement Authority (1927), the Greater Winnipeg Sanitary District (1935), the St. James-Winnipeg Airport Commission (1937), the Metropolitan Planning Commission (1948), the Metropolitan Civil Defense Board (1951), and the Greater Winnipeg Transit Commission (1953). These well-developed and highly regarded activities leant immediate legitimacy to the other operations of the new governing level. This provided some initial breathing room against potential critics since the familiar local policy process was disrupted as little as possible, and institutions were not savaged: no existing municipality's boundaries were ever altered in the first two-tier efforts.

What *did* the Canadian metropolitan government do? From his internationally comparative study of metropolitan governments, L.J. Sharpe, the foremost apologist for the formula, has outlined a "comprehensive list of metro functions for an ideal world": master planning; responsibility for arterial roadways, traffic management and public transport, water, sewers, drainage and refuse disposal, police and fire, major recreation and cultural facilities; and housing and environmental protection (1995a: 19). This is a reasonable checklist against which to measure the Canadian experience. The enumeration of the specific powers of the metropolitan governments in Canada, and those of their constituent municipalities, can be compiled with a little effort. That survey need not be replicated at length here (for Toronto, for instance, see Rose 1972: 25-27; Kaplan 1982: 683-736; Higgins 1986: 195-98). Instead, the purpose in Table 12.1 is to provide a general idea about the distribution of functions between the two levels of the Canadian municipal federation within a five city-region comparative setting and to evaluate the evolution of these structures in their own dynamic political environments

In the table, centralization versus decentralizing of a particular governing function is presented numerically. A score of one means that the service is provided by the central or regional authority exclusively, and a score of five represents exclusive local responsibility or the most dispersed governing possibility. The assumption is obvious: governing institutions are no more static than the populations who create them. Nor are all functions of equal importance. The second column (#) endeavours to set a rough three-point weighting scale from one (least important) to three (most) to account for the reality that policing (3) and the provision of potable water (3) are more serious (and usually more costly) matters than the issuance of building permits (1) or operating the zoo (1). The smaller the number of the mean scores for categories, the greater the role of the general government in the provision of that set of functions.

On the basis of the findings presented in Table 12.1, three pertinent points become clear.

1. The area-wide or general governments were focused on providing hard services and became increasingly so over time, even the GVRD where transit became a regional responsibility quite late in the game (1998). Winnipeg was generally the more centralized in the hard service area, although Ottawa-Carleton had by far the lowest score just prior to its unification.

2. The corollary is that the front-line municipalities were focused more directly on human services. All but the GVRD (due to its loss of planning authority in 1983) centralized over time. Winnipeg was the most static system in its functional adjustments over 10 years, Toronto and Ottawa the most dynamic. After a generation in operation, the general government's role in human services was greater than its position in services to physical plant in

Table 12.1: Relative Centralization Index for Selected Two-Tier Operations in Canadian CMAs (1 is city-regional; 5 is local)

City-Region	#	Toronto 1954–96		Winnipeg 1961–71		Montreal 1969–2000		Vancouver 1967–2005		Ottawa 1969–2000	
		1954	*1996*	*1961*	*1971*	*1969*	*2000*	*1967*	*2005*	*1969*	*2000*
Boundary[1]	2	5	3	5	5	5	5	5	5	5	4
Election[2]	3	5	2	1	1	5	5	5	5	5	1
1. Utilities		*6.7*	*5.9*	*4.3*	*4.0*	*6.9*	*6.4*	*6.3*	*6.6*	*7.9*	*2.9*
Arterials	3	1	1	1	1	2	2	4	4	1	1
Water	3	2	2	1	1	2	2	2	2	1	1
Sewerage	3	3	3	1	1	5	4	2	2	2	1
Waste:											
Collection	2	5	5	5	5	5	5	5	5	5	1
Disposal	2	5	2	1	1	2	2	5	5	4	1
Traffic Eng.	2	3	3	3	2	2	2	5	3	5	2
Transit	3	1	1	1	1	1	1	0	2	5	1
2. Human		*6.8*	*4.7*	*7.9*	*7.7*	*6.3*	*5.6*	*7.9*	*8.3*	*7.2*	*5.5*
Reg. Plan[3]	2	3	2	3	2	4	3	3	5	3	2
Dev't Plans	1	4	4	4	3	4	4	5	5	4	3
Police	3	5	1	5	5	1	1	5	5	5	1
Fire	3	5	5	5	5	5	4	5	5	5	5
Public Health	2	3	3	5	5	2	2	5	5	1	1
Reg. Parks[4]	1	3	3	3	3	4	4	4	4	5	5
Zoo	1	5	1	1	1	0	0	5	5	0	0
Recreation	2	4	3	5	5	5	5	5	5	5	5
Libraries	1	5	5	5	5	5	5	5	5	5	5
Housing	2	1	1	5	5	5	4	2	2	5	4
3. Finance		*5.8*	*5.6*	*6.8*	*6.4*	*7.4*	*7.4*	*9.8*	*9.8*	*5.8*	*5.6*
Tax Source	3	5	5	5	5	5	5	5	5	5	5
Borrowing	2	1	1	3	3	5	5	5	5	5	5
Assessment	3	1	1	1	1	1	1	5	5	1	1
Personnel	1	4	3	5	4	4	4	4	4	4	3
Building Permits	1	5	5	5	4	5	5	5	5	5	5
Scores		*166*	*134*	*158*	*149*	*173*	*163*	*197*	*203*	*181*	*114*
Mean		*6.9*	*5.6*	*6.6*	*6.2*	*7.2*	*6.8*	*8.2*	*8.5*	*7.5*	*4.8*

Notes: # Indicates the relative importance of each factor with 1 being the least and 3 the strongest. Scores are the sums of the values of the functions; the range of possible means is from 2.1 (city-region) to 10.6 (local).

1. No local boundary change at initiation is assigned a value of 5.

2. Direct election to regional government is assigned a value of 1; indirect election is assigned a value of 5.

3. Regional Plans are area-wide for entire CMA; Development Plans are for neighbourhoods and communities, and are sometimes called Area Structure Plans.

4. Regional Parks include such large operations as the Toronto Zoo and Winnipeg's Assiniboine Park, which were funded by an area-wide levy.

both the Toronto and Montreal systems.

3. Each system evolved uniquely over its relatively short life span, but all moved toward a greater and significant degree of centralization, except for the GVRD which began, and remains, the CMA with the greatest governmental diaspora of these systems in all three areas of responsibility. Ottawa-Carleton displayed the greatest dynamic over time, while Winnipeg and Montreal were the least varying.

Canadian two-tier metropolitan governments were never the equivalent of nation-state federations imbued with constitutional autonomy, popular legitimacy, and stability. Functions generally agreed to have a regional impact (and whose transfer would thus significantly reduce suburban councils' expenditures) were vertically transferred after the requisite commission of inquiry to legitimate the consensus. For instance, policing in Toronto remained a local service in 1954 but was quickly moved to the Metro level by 1957. The few vertical functional adjustments between levels in the early years provoked little in the way of public outcry. However, because local councils were directly affected, far greater controversy surrounded the issue of the composition of the regional council. It was not until 1988 that the province adjusted Metro Toronto so as to have six mayors plus 28 directly elected councillors; it took 25 years and several commissioners' careers until a special act in 1994 yielded direct elections for the Ottawa-Carleton Region. Relative to Toronto or Ottawa-Carleton, the generally perceived weakness of the Montreal Urban Community, tracked on the bottom line of Table 12.1, was also measured by the nature of elections to senior positions (Sancton 1991: 26-27).

The senior levels in city-region municipal federations were not institutions designed to capture the wider public's imagination through public service directly provided. Outside of concrete, asphalt, and pipes, policy decisions went too easily unnoticed and were thus quickly categorized as inconsequential. These policies generated a politics of limited commitment which weakened Metro's potential to build citizen interest, program involvement, and subsequent loyalty. Disproportionate political energy tended to be directed towards the internal Metro-level integrative processes (Kaplan 1967). Regional planning itself always took far too long to emerge. Comprehensive visions of long-term development were consistently frustrated by suburban sabotage and delay to the point that this function was ultimately destroyed in the GVRD and the Metro form was itself terminated in Winnipeg. Overall, the incremental gravitation to functional centralization at the expense of more equal partnerships in service instruments ultimately set the stage for CMA unification. As Victor Jones correctly predicted 60 years ago, no politically satisfactory and sustainable halfway step has ever existed (1942: 90-91), and Metro would prove to be no exception.

The 1990s amalgamations of municipalities in central Canada in particular were motivated by large provincial cutbacks to equalization grants for municipal governments. This trend to realignment of responsibilities in the larger provinces, sometimes labelled "disentanglement," had direct implications for two-tier regional governments. As provinces centralized responsibilities for financing policies such as education and welfare in their own ministries, traditional municipal matters such as roads and policing become the clear obligation of increasingly larger scale local governments (Hobson 1997: 129-31). This, too, was largely because provincial transfer payments in support of these activities were also "clarified"—which meant significantly reduced. Hobson argues that these moves obviated the need for two-tier regional governments with any sort of marginal redistributive policy ambitions. He maintained that disentanglement and increased user fees created direct links between benefits and costs while it enhanced transparency and responsibility in public finance. Furthermore, disentanglement can build public accountability when specific functional responsibilities are allocated on the basis of reasonable geographic scope and secure fiscal (tax base) capacity . In neither position is there any longer a need for the two-tier municipal governing model.

12.3.3 Why two-tier government had run its term

The shutting down of the two-tier metropolitan operations in the largest Canadian CMAs in the 1990s, just as with Winnipeg in 1971 and always excepting the COG adventure of the GVRD, is due to the failure of those institutions to resolve adequately the three ongoing policy questions raised as issues in Chapter 11. In Winnipeg, equity and accountability matters had been paramount, in Montreal equity was essentially the problem, and in Toronto both accountability and coordination had to be addressed. But, in fairness, the root of these shortcomings in operational, not theoretical, metropolitan institutions was itself fundamental and lay at the heart of the original satisficing policy exercise that had led to the two-tier form. Sharpe notes that by the 1980s, metropolitan governments globally were frail barques in choppy waters; "The harsh truth is that no one really loves metro government and there are precious few sectional interests which have a stake in it" (1995a: 27). The reality in Canada was no different. Moreover, no regional government here was ever born in consequence of some catastrophe in the provision of public services or even public finance to the point that a reservoir of redemptive good will ever existed for the upper tier of the metropolitan federations.

In Canada, the original metropolitan satisficing resulted in three standing conundrums which, by the 1990s, bedeviled, and ultimately flattened, each of the Canadian city-region federations.

12.3.3.1 BALANCING FUNCTIONS AND POLITICAL REPRESENTATION

Sharpe, in stipulating his first "inherent problem" of the metro model, notes that "a metro will always tend to be isolated, squeezed as it is between two probably hostile forces" (1995a: 22). Senior governments may resent a rival; existing municipalities are suspicious of any threat to their traditional powers. Indirect election of the area-wide council, while seen by provincial governments as a central balancing mechanism for city-region interests, also meant that the upper tier would be constituted of representatives from municipal councils which were essentially hostile to that institution's very existence and larger purposes. Central cities were often frustrated in realizing their social policies because they stood at odds with the regional enterprise dominated by suburbs. Caroline Andrew noted early on that under the Regional Municipality of Ottawa-Carleton (RMOC), Ottawa city council "had to contend with a conservative regional government, which has the main financial and administrative responsibility for social services" (1983: 157). The politically thorny reform of direct election of councillors to the Metro Toronto council (1988) and RMOC (1994) ultimately came about far closer to the end of their existence than their outset. Not that direct election can save the institution; Winnipeg's two-tier operation, for example, was riven asunder by the divergent development agendas of the directly elected Metro councillors and local municipal politicians. This achieved the status of a full-scale battle based on suspicions over motives.

One result of indirect election was that power everywhere accrued to those in the policy business who were full-time—the senior administrative officers. Thus, as we emphasized previously, Kaplan has written of Metro Toronto's cabinet, which was not located in the elected political wing but rather in the administrative policy operation. Nowhere, except in Montreal, were partisan political coalitions, or regional political parties, to emerge to define publicly conflicting metropolitan area positions and policies except where alliances of suburban councillors confronted central city aspirations. There was thus little in the way of any coherent election platform differences (or discussion) to grip the public imagination, let alone attention span, about issues in, and accountability for, metropolitan governing.

12.3.3.2 HARD SERVICES TO PROPERTY VERSUS
SOFT SERVICE FOR CITIZEN-ELECTORS

As noted in Chapter 10, and measured in Table 12.1, the first metropolitan experiments in Canada were created to fix policy shortcomings for city-region roads, bridges, water, and sewerage works. The general tier remained oriented to addressing the coordination question by integrating the delivery of hard service functions. Especially in the United States, metropolitan area governments have been "uniformly much more successful" with physical plant than "in dealing with social issues such as fiscal disparities, race relations, open housing, and the location of public, low-income housing in the suburbs" (Harrigan 1993: 358). In Long's (1968) memorable phrase they became "brick and mortar" governments. Initially, even police and fire protection were left to the local levels in Toronto and Winnipeg, and no major community and social services role was projected (beyond Toronto's community housing). Redistributive policies were not an anticipated outcome with one exception: "Two tier government structures, in which the lower-tier municipalities transfer to the upper tier the revenues from a given rate applied to the local tax base, result in an implicit form of equalization" (Hobson 1997: 116). This is an important exception only where the upper tier moves into policy areas beyond upgrades to the regional physical plant.

The Canadian experience is not unique. American metropolitan governments of the federated type "have failed to pass the test or 'pass through the hoop' of serving as innovative and effective redistribution structures for improving the well-being of the less fortunate ... the various metropolitan governments have taken a 'rain check' on the matter of social equity" (Stephens and Wikstrom 2000: 168). To be generous, though, it may be that even in cases where a political will did emerge, the legal authority may not have existed to make changes in public policy with a redistributive objective. Upper tiers are still municipal institutions and, as such, primarily involved in allocative, not redistributive, public policies. In other words, citizens and senior governments share in the perception that responsibility for social equity belongs, in the first instance, to the federal and provincial or state governments.

12.3.3.3 THE COMPROMISE NATURE OF THE FUNCTIONAL
DIVISION BETWEEN TWO LEVELS OF AUTHORITY

Finding a middle ground on service provision was supposed to be a major strength of the metropolitan system, but, as is the case with any federative governing approach, it was also to be its greatest shortcoming and source of conflict. Kaplan was among the first to note that area-wide government for Toronto was possible only because of the application of this central federative notion of balance between the central and the local (1967: 52-55). In two sentences, Higgins discusses what he perceives as the essential strengths of the original Metro Toronto experiment in its shared functional responsibilities. Simultaneously, and unintentionally, he also pinpoints its, and any other, two-tier structure's Achilles' heel when there is functional division between area-wide planning ambitions and local applications (1986: 195). Further, area-wide governments were typically given responsibility for wholesale water and sewerage operations but it was up to the local municipalities to retail these services to residents. Similar observations might be made for the gamut of shared responsibilities.

The weakness is that conflict was integral to the form. Municipalities could frustrate any or all of traffic planning (with neighbourhood buffers and travel restrictions), regional plans (by zoning, building regulations, or the issuance of building permits), arterial roadways (through inadequate connectors and limited parking), and so forth. And, at the outset, the council for the general was comprised of delegates from the specific.

Over time, though, and largely unnoticed by the political gladiators, a regional metamorphosis emerged which was rooted in the social, economic, and public service maturation of the suburbs. Somewhat distinctive local communities sought, as they grew, to replicate the service activities, on the cheap, of other suburbs and the central core itself. At the same time and partly in consequence, the overall metropolitan population itself became more heterogeneous while the various municipalities became more like each other. In short, any need for a continued federative approach to facilitate "divide and provide" services for autonomous suburban municipalities lost its own internal logic. These actions homogenized the populations of Canada's increasingly larger, more fully developed metropolitan regions.

Ultimately, in city-regions across Canada, the federative structure existed without the constraint of specific constitutional legitimacy, dependent upon any given provincial government's political assessments for its survival. The judgement by these authorities that the metropolitan format no longer possessed a mission sufficient to justify its continuance, rather than any immediate concerns with its productivity and effectiveness, was sufficient to spell its end.

12.4 Formal Consolidation

In the United States, city-region municipal consolidation came about only as the end result of a long, controversial, deliberative, pluralist resolution of political debate. The usual objective was the city-county form of consolidation if the preferred option of amalgamation could not be worked, with the star achievements being locations in the south such as Baton Rouge, Nashville-Davison, and Jacksonville-Duval (Stephens and Wikstrom 2000: 68-69). A variety of local governing units continued to exist; although strongly centralized at the regional (or county) level by American standards, they were all rather weakly centripetal institutional results when measured against the Canadian experience where a full and complete merger was the rule.

The amalgamations in Canada proceeded independently of the underlying ideology of the party in power provincially, the major cases being Winnipeg (1971, NDP); Halifax (1996, Liberal); Toronto (1998, Progressive Conservative); and Montreal, Longueuil, Quebec City, Levis, and Hull-Gatineau all through Bill 170, which was introduced into the legislature on 15 November 2000 by the PQ to come into effect 1 January 2002.

One significant difference from the American reorganization history was that each of these occurrences was, publicly, a policy surprise enacted fairly soon after the preceding provincial general election. Neither observers nor candidates had projected that the consolidation of Winnipeg would follow the provincial general election of 1969. Immediately prior to his government's election, NDP leader Ed Schreyer had indicated that he was prepared to set aside his party's long-standing position endorsing amalgamation in order to strengthen the metropolitan government. Even so, the Winnipeg amalgamation came almost out of the blue. Neither was merger specifically proposed for Toronto in provincial party platforms for Ontario's 1995 vote, and a Charter challenge to Bill 103 (Toronto's Megacity) was partly based on the argument that Toronto had not been specifically targeted during the campaign. But the intent of the Harris Progressive Conservative government with respect to municipalities was more clearly presaged in its *Common Sense Revolution* platform than in the other cases. It had stipulated that "We must rationalize the regional and municipal levels to avoid the overlap and duplication that now exists …" (Ontario PC 1994: 14). The reorganizing of Montreal, leave alone the four other city-regions, was a component of no PQ policy platform. It is thus unsurprising that public choice prognostications had been wildly off-base: "As in the United States, complex relationships between ethnic segregation and municipal fragmentation make wholesale municipal consolidation in Montreal all but unthinkable" (Sancton 1995: 144-45).

The conventions of unitary municipal government in Canada have long roots. A century back, the normal approach for central city expansion was through amalgamation with smaller, fiscally weaker communities on its boundaries. Typically, Montreal annexed all or part of 43 adjacent localities between 1883 and 1918, in the process increasing its own territory by more than five times. As with Montreal after the First World War, the much younger city of Edmonton experienced little spatial growth with no annexations from 1917 to 1947. But then, like most other prairie cities except Winnipeg, it expanded rapidly through the annexation and, less so, the amalgamation process, experiencing 20 cases over the period 1947 to its last in 1980. Together these totalled 55,474 acres; during this time also, the city's population quadrupled.

But Alberta, in a curious approach for any province, followed a dual path with respect to the municipal organization of its metropolitan corridor. As a policy response to the growth pressures on its two city-regions that followed the Second World War and the immediate postwar petroleum discoveries, the provincial government established a formal inquiry. The McNally Royal Commission on the Metropolitan Development of Calgary and Edmonton specifically rejected the two-tier forms of Toronto and Vancouver in 1956 and recommended the unitary form instead. However, the province poured money into municipal debt reduction.

The City of Calgary's commission board subsequently pursued a consistently aggressive policy of expansion by amalgamation (three small towns) and annexation up to 1989. Its northern neighbour Edmonton, after the McNally Commission, fell victim to both political intrigue over ex-boundary suburban developments and British decentralist town planning with the consequence that commuter towns began to capture significant residential growth (Lightbody 1999a: 181-84). A 1979-80 amalgamation initiative to institute unitary government fell afoul of provincial partisan calculations. In stark contrast to the pattern in the Edmonton CMA, it should be noted that since 1956 the City of Calgary has also endeavoured to control its urban expansion by specifically rejecting regional servicing agreements and the SPD concept. It has instead had a long-standing policy of not providing services to districts along but outside its borders. By the 1990s, for instance, it only accepted sewerage from the rapidly expanding town of Cochrane and the smaller distant community adjacent to Chestermere Lake. In direct contrast, Edmonton's councils seldom if ever viewed their utilities operations as a tactical arsenal. Consequently, its power, water, and sewerage utilities behaved much like other private corporations with the goal of making money from sales to developments dispersed anywhere and everywhere across the CMA region. In government form, then, as noted in the case study earlier, the two metropolitan regions have evolved quite distinctly.

Unification came about differently in central Canada. All significant aspects of the language in Bill 103 amalgamating Metro Toronto, despite being the baby of the very conservative government of Mike Harris, is identical to that used by the social democratic government of Ed Schreyer which, by Bill 36, created Winnipeg Unicity in 1971. The central substance of Bill 170 to create the unitary municipality on Montreal Island was another carbon copy, not an innovation by the PQ. The tag of party does not seem to define the style of government in this policy realm. Both Toronto (1997) and Montreal (2000) closely emulated Winnipeg (1971) in basic organizational structures and in transition methods. Having privately evaluated that anticipated vigorous opposition would come only from the usual list of suspects, as will be discussed in the next chapter, the government of Ontario, as would Quebec and as had Manitoba before them, pre-emptively launched the unification of the six inner cities of Toronto with a quick first reading of the legislation and expeditious passage with minimal amendment.

Winnipeg's original community committee and ward boundaries followed the boundary lines of the pre-existing suburban municipalities. The Toronto Megacity proposals were modified slightly from the original proposal by increasing the number of councillors to 56 in order to retain the somewhat familiar 28 Metro wards. Each former municipality retained a shadowy existence as a "community council" with limited advisory powers. Montreal combined 28 municipalities into one, but 27 "boroughs" with familiar boundaries were enacted to keep an eye on very local service delivery. In all cases, city councillors also served as the neighbourhood community's official committee. These accommodations were clearly considered as proxies for any substantive alterations to the original unitary plans and to moderate short-term dissent. In the case of Winnipeg, no one, outside of official consultants' circles, had requested these arrangements, and both cabinet and caucus had been divided on the practicality of the concept (Brownstone and Plunkett 1983: 40-44). However, because the precedent exists, it is reasonable to predict that the measures in central Canada will follow the dismal path of Winnipeg's failed Community Committee experiment (Higgins 1986: 269-74; Brownstone and Plunkett 1983: 175-76) and are predestined to collapse in the persistent absence of any more significant powers clearly decentralized by statute means.

Public choice advocates were not the only critics of unitary city-region governing arrangements. Critics from the left, like Warren Magnusson, critiqued early central city efforts to amalgamate, such as Toronto's 1950 application to the OMB to take over all surrounding municipalities in an effort to manage growth more effectively as "imperialistic designs" (1983a: 109). Comparable assaults by ideologically similar opponents were made to Alberta's Local Authorities Board against Edmonton's 1979 application to annex its most immediate suburban neighbours (Plunkett and Lightbody 1982). As will be discussed in the next chapter, such ideological critics (in contrast with more directly self-interested office-holders) had real program concerns in mind in the form of specific social and cultural policy commitments which had been laboriously wrested from central city councils and which they feared might be watered down by the new suburban majorities on any unified council. Such apprehensions were somewhat analogous to the opposition of inner city blacks in American central cities to any centralizing initiative that would dilute their existing power within their communities over, for example, policing.

The creation of Toronto Megacity still means that only 55.9 per cent of that urban region is captured under one government roof. Putting frontiers to the city-region has been a persistent problem for central governments around the world, barring the presence of the natural and topographical constraints which, for instance, defined Oslo by its perimeter of virgin forests (Sharpe 1995b: 18). More usually, the core community has peripheral settlements. Astutely, but whimsically, Magnusson has noted that "The metropolis we would govern is everywhere and nowhere" (1994: 542). One constant complaint of the city-county form in the United States is that it has never encompassed or confined the socio–economic urban agglomeration. From a different ideological perspective, Osborne and Gaebler observed of American cities that "We have outgrown our governments" (1992: 246).

Continuous urbanizing pressures mean that the boundaries of any megacity have always been negotiable, and few have ever been sufficiently comprehensive, territorially, for land use planning and controls to be completely effectual or to be so for very long (Lightbody 1997: 445-46). The Chinese Great Wall could not deny the Mongol barbarian incursion any more than mediaeval walls in Europe were sufficient to confine commercial expansion. Montreal has its island, but that does not constrain its commuter-shed any more effectively than seas of wheat and grass confine Winnipeg, Regina, or Calgary. The GVRD, in various places described by planners as too small or too large to be a realistic city place, is bounded to the west by sea, to the north by rock, and to the south by the international border with the United States. But to the east, it has remained vulnerable to accelerating growth constrained only by the escalating costs of extending services. Policy problems continue to be defined by population and economic growth that spills over local boundaries and commands provincial oversight. For example, the provincial government of Ontario has since 1988 maintained within its senior administration an Office of the Greater Toronto Area (OGTA). Like less formalized but similar initiatives in London (UK), this is a senior bureaucratic attempt to coordinate provincial department efforts and devise broad urban policy coherence. In the Westminster system, policy suggestions from the central authority have a way of becoming something like commandments. However, in both cases it is all a bit slapdash, a rough dike in lieu of a more genuinely palpable policy-making authority.

Outside the ephemeral world of ministerial rhetoric, larger scale municipal amalgamations were always unlikely to constitute short-term, cost-cutting exercises. Service upgrades, staff mergers and buyouts, integration of divergent operating systems and other equipment, and so forth are both one-time and continuing costs. To offer conjecture on the probabilities, we can compare roughly similar city-region communities with different local governing systems, as was done with Calgary and Edmonton earlier in this chapter, to glean an approximate idea of their expenditures and to pinpoint sources of difference. But without a time machine to predict the future or redesign the past, it is impossible to predict what the price tag of an existing fragmented system would have been if current institutions were simply projected forward to respond to the social and economic demands, and supports, of some future time. The new cities of Canada will become what electors will make of them.

12.5 Concluding Note

Recent research initiatives have once again affirmed that the unitary model for city-region governing in the United States correlates positively with variables associated with growth and prosperity. D. Rusk, for instance, writes of cities with elastic boundaries, "cities without suburbs," which have been able to expand aggressively through annexation as being better able to manage growth and to address redistributive issues. Without the ability to expand their territories, and consequently to have the capacity to devise and implement integrating strategies, cities will be ensured futures of economic decline (Rusk 1993: 35). Conversely those city-regions with a dominant local government are also those with a higher incidence of residents who are more educated and professional and have higher incomes. These variables, in turn, are also associated strongly with cities more willing to be innovative in their public management by deploying productivity improvement strategies, frequent fiscal reporting, and precise revenue forecasting (Clark 1998: 160-67). What is not surprising about the annexation tactic is that for 40 years, well before the sun belt against rust belt conceptual dichotomy was in common use, scholars like T.R. Dye (1964) associated ease of annexation with the younger and more professionally managed cities of the American southwest. But, by very large coincidence, these cities (i.e., Houston or San Antonio) are situated in states like Texas which have more relaxed annexation requirements, such as excluding the use of referendums (Harrigan 1993: 348-50).

In a second set of interesting research, Sohrab Abizadeh and John Gray examined the behaviour of politicians in office. They looked at the increase in expenditures in all ten Canadian provinces across 30 different governments, from seven parties, over the period spanning the 26 years from 1960 to 1986. They came to this conclusion: "We find that the provincial political party in power, whether left, right, or centre, has had no statistically significant impact on the level of growth in government spending in any of the ten Canadian provinces." They add that "it may be that parties of the left spend more on visible social programs and public works which attract press attention, while those of the right spend money instead on grants to industry and on contracting out of services" (1992: 520). However, when actually tested, the realities of big spenders and frugal husbandry are rather different from popular perceptions that politicians on the left spend like Santa while those on the right scrimp like Scrooge. Persons holding public office spend to govern, and they expand and contract accounts as their judgement of public expectations and economic circumstances dictates. Of course, this especially holds true at the city level where there are usually no organized political parties, and councillors must make choices as their personal ideologies dictate.

The pattern of the expenditures in any administration becomes its governing "style," and this style may well differ somewhat among the many municipalities of the polycentric city-region. Style issues tend to take over local governing agendas, particularly as they are concerned with licensing requirements, development approvals, modes of policing and bylaw enforcement, the design of social services, and recreational programs. Even where the total budget packet assessed by some neutral measure like per capita outlay does not vary much from one municipality to the next, these small variations in style become very important to residents. Over time, they impart the imprint of a distinctive signature, the mythology of which is embraced by the residents in each municipal barrio.

Because cities determine policy measures of direct importance to personal lifestyles, the existence of multiple municipalities provides some residents in the city-region with what they choose to view as a marginally distinctive subset of public policies. Certainly, neighbourhood councillors argue that they provide what their residents want. So, autonomous cities will devise separate public policy packages, even where the common essential hard services related to water and roads are provided through regional instruments, in response to the expectations of their own residents and business interests. While the cumulative measurable output is similar over time, small observable style differences hold the virtue of a tangible reality. In consequence, the importance of style as public policy substance is that consolidation disputes are not really about technical matters but about values and, thus, exchanging ideals. What we do know about any policy debate is that any attempt to shift the focus onto problems seemingly capable of being resolved in a "technical realm" of service standards becomes, to paraphrase E.E. Schattschneider, a value-neutral way of imposing one's own values.

There has always existed a comforting psychological remoteness in the detached suburb from the perceived social problems and concomitant anxieties attending city life that was noted as far back as James Bryce in 1888. These shared beliefs reach the status of "urban legends," and suburbanization enables a physical distancing from the undesirable traits that certain categories of people are understood to entertain. At one time, this would have been the vice and corruption that immigrant classes brought into public life; perhaps today it is the level of central city crime and the costs of punishment or ameliorative social programs. This is why resolving the small technicality of city-region governing always becomes the most heated of any subject in the low politics lexicon of municipalities. Even where the city-region is demonstrably an integrated urban whole, these beliefs, however detached from reality, have continued to fuel anti-amalgamation forces and fears. Local councillors will represent their constituents' belief systems in hyperbolic overdrive.

Hence, the obvious source of the strongest opposition to late twentieth-century local government consolidations in Canada lay in one fact that is retrospectively very clear: in Montreal in 2002, when 28 municipalities became one, 290 legislators were reduced to 73 positions. Earlier in Toronto in 1998, 106 councillors had but 57 seats to contest; in Winnipeg in 1971, 112 had been cut in half to 50 Unicity seats. The policy process of such unification is explored in the next chapter.

thirteen | The politics of local government reform

This chapter will consider how it is that, virtually unexpectedly, a general model for the rapid modification of city-region government in Canada came to exist, especially since similar initiatives in the United States have conspicuously failed. The specific public policy approach to the amalgamations of the municipal governments of Toronto (effective in January 1998) and Montreal (in 2001) and to other recent provincially initiated adaptations like Ottawa and Hamilton reveals a generally similar, and uniquely Canadian, pattern for changing the municipal institutions with responsibility for governing in the metropolis. At the same time, the sweeping, provincially imposed municipal consolidations came as a particular policy surprise to most citizens of these city-regions. So, we will also explore the behaviours, and the consequences of these behaviours, of selected policy communities during the turmoil of Canada's relatively brief reorganization episodes.

Urbanization of Canada during the period after the Second World War transformed a population that was only half "urban" in 1941 into one 80 per cent so in 2001, making Canada one of the more urbanized countries in the world with over two-thirds of the population concentrated in one of 27 metropolitan centres of 100,000 or more. Elsewhere in the international community, central city and commuting suburb systems like these city-regions have tended to witness increasingly intermeshed commercial activities, with one consequence being heightened levels of social and general economic integration. Canada's unanticipated success in the relatively smooth management of this urbanizing trend contributed to pressures for even more comprehensive regional development strategies. In turn, the demonstrated competence in public management of service delivery within Canadian city-regions has been increasingly believed by lead actors in business and commerce, especially in the services sector, as a marketable advantage in bidding for either private-sector or public-service urban civic works projects. This was a very competitive international market estimated at US$850 billion in 2001. When the fragmented boundaries within city-regions are viewed as no more than needless local inefficiencies, then commercial expectations become an unanticipated, but powerful, exogenous source of pressure on provincial governments for city-region municipal reorganization.

Even where they have contributed by their actions to the financial exigencies of local governments, substate regions (provinces, states) have been somewhat able to insulate themselves from directly negative public pressures. Municipalities, though, find themselves in the front lines. Facing, globally, a time of fiscal restraint and austerity as well as new sets of policy expectations, the municipalities within city-regions have tried to respond with a menu of diverse strategies (Clark 1994b: 213-40). During the neo-liberal period of the last political generation, municipal structures in Canadian city-regions faced challenges to their status quo from consistently accelerating economic sources. Beyond this have been internal pressures from popular, as well as policy community, expectations for emulation of fiscally attractive policies in other municipalities. One effective possibility for exploiting cost efficiencies beyond the reach of most municipalities was the adaptive mechanism of integrating institutions and structures.

In short, the traditionally polycentric institutions of the Canadian CMA were a system facing numerous challenges that questioned their political legitimacy. Of the ten largest Canadian CMAs, half (London, Winnipeg, Calgary, Hamilton, and Ottawa) would become essentially unitary in municipal structure. The Toronto city-region's core was unified, and Quebec's CMAs were variously consolidated by statute in 2000. Of these ten biggest centres then, only the Edmonton area's public officials might join their counterparts in the GVRD in reasonably contemplating a short-term future with some semblance of persisting form as a COG. But even the GVRD is struggling today to integrate and manage the recently devolved operations of regional transit and transportation routes, an exercise which may produce more in the form of municipal consolidations than anyone now publicly anticipates.

The central point sustaining any discussion about a new Canadian model for metropolitan government reform in this chapter is that reorganization is not so much about efficiency or differences in community lifestyles as it is about ideology and political power. The mythology of the distinctive suburban lifestyle, as pronounced by many Canadian suburban councillors, was given the most powerful life and legal shape in the United States. In general consequence, the greatest resistance to any form of centripetal reorganization "is resistance, stemming from disparity—either by affluent suburbs that defensively incorporate or by the sheer demographic and racial disharmony of a region" (Savitch and Vogel 1996: 12). For largely historical reasons, Canadian city-regions have not fragmented into the economically and racially distinctive splinters characteristic of SMSAs. In this admittedly different context, Canadian provinces have recently proven competent, unlike their American state counterparts, to initiate and complete comprehensive city-region municipal consolidations notwithstanding the lifestyle resistance gambit. The question here is why, and how, this northern pattern of decisions came to exist.

13.1 The Role of an Urban Regime

As we have seen, there is no longer much doubt that intellectual legitimacy in the public policy debate between generally centripetal and centrifugal local governing options in Canada has been appropriated by scholarship of the American metropolis, largely by students in the public choice tradition of Tiebout (1956). The underlying strength of this approach, which assumes that all citizens are both rational and perfectly mobile in matching the location of their homes with local service levels and taxation rates, is that governments need not *produce* service in order to *provide* service. Theoretically, multiple local governments within a city-region offer opportunity for diversity in residential and commercial choice, promote efficient and effective competition both among themselves and with private-sector providers, and enhance citizenship opportunities in involvement and co-production of service (Stephens and Wikstrom 2000: 107-21). Case studies in the public choice tradition have also been validated in the public eye by the work of Osborne and Gaebler (1992) whose "reinventing government" considered that any search for efficiencies in the provision of specific services is considered helpful to governments facing conditions of fiscal austerity. In particular, public choice investigations provide evidence, sometimes contradictory, as to which functions are not easily subject to economies of scale (for example, public health, local libraries, even fire protection) and are consequently more efficiently provided by smaller scale municipalities (Bish and Warren 1972; Bish and Ostrom 1973). However, many theorists of this analytic mode completely overlook the regional system's overall failure to govern for the general community and to provide broad support for economic growth and environmental sustainability. These concerns are not always missed by those whose interests are not vested in existing arrangements.

Public choice theory has been beneficial to students of the Canadian city-region in suggesting the powerful but theoretical rationale for the continuance of the governmentally polycentric CMA that is posited largely by both local elected and administrative public officials to whom it has most appeal as a bourgeois defence of the status quo (Sancton 1994). But the benefits from the lower costs associated with co-production of public service are also positively correlated with their location among the higher income groups found most often in Canada's suburbs. Where the theory comes up very short is this: even were all citizens exhaustively informed and thoroughly rational in assessing service delivery, they are not all equally free to relocate into a new municipality within the Canadian metropolis. Moreover, the parochialism entrenched by multiple large neighbourhood governments leaves little room for city-region redistributive public policies to compensate for immobility. This can create new priorities for those policy communities and issue cosmopolitans with a wider regional embrace; however, in the absence of a city-region government, there exists no institution to empower a policy voice for that city-region over and above local self-interest.

Largely because it must draw so much from the pluralist intellectual tradition of American experience, where it represents the individual, the market place, and competition even among public institutions, public choice theory tends to be tangential to what has actually been going on in Canada. It is more concerned with explaining the record of consolidation failures in the United States than anticipating the sources of stress which may initiate more fundamental changes in this country. Because it assumes an anti-hierarchical stance and focuses on eliminating any public-service provider monopoly, this view is blind when avenues permitting collective public policy choices open up.

This is why case studies from the public choice angle provide little practical understanding as to why dramatic provincial interventions into the governing of Canadian city-regions took shape as they did. A better explanatory approach may be found in the work of Clarence Stone. Drawing from his study of private power in Metro Atlanta politics, Stone argued that every metropolitan area is governed by a particular urban regime. While he was careful to differentiate among different foci for regime expression (Stone and Sanders 1987: 286-74), he stated that, in the normal course of events, "Urban regimes are arrangements for acting, for accomplishing policy goals, for managing friction points between groups, for adapting to an exogenous process of social change. These arrangements are informal; they enable public bodies and private interests to function together in making and implementing government decisions" (Stone 1989: 231). For example, one of the more governmentally fragmented American metropolitan areas, Pittsburgh, has over 300 governments serving 1.4 million people in its central county, 12 with less than 1,000 residents. But importantly, as noted by Savitch and Vogel, "Under the fragmented form … lies a unifying net of business elites that ties the region together through public-private partnerships" (1996: 292). The stagnant nature of the municipal form sustained by American political culture is given wider area authority through the overriding machinations of the urban area's regime

In Canada, Sancton has argued that, in the absence of unitary institutions, no political structure can guarantee the result of effective regional planning, hopefully concluding that, "if there is general agreement that regional planning is necessary, it will emerge without a regional government structure" (1994: 45). This is the crucial point, for superfluous complexity in city-region structures weakens the capacity of the region itself to carry out public, public-private, and even private governing decisions without institutional distraction. The absence of integrated policy through area-wide CMA institutions means there is no formal mechanism to legitimize whatever "general agreement" may have been reached by whomever. Public bodies and private interests necessarily try to work to develop and deliver local governing decisions in the municipally polycentric metropolis by establishing limited common objectives, coordinating their activities, and working through their differences. But for the most part, until recently the mechanisms for planning and coordination had to be informal and the important work settled behind the scenes.

Across North America, the urban regime is anchored by the commercial community. Business remains central not only because economic investment is so widely believed necessary to sustain a thriving urban community but also because its leaders normally enjoy easy access to private channels of political influence. The evidence from Canadian experience is that urban regimes are primarily situated in commercial enterprise and its floating coalitions of business interest groups. From time to time, however, successful regimes will become as inclusive of other interests as necessary to realize mutual and cooperative objectives. In short, business interests with wider area economic agendas can become decisive actors in other policy communities.

An urban regime is thus different from any potential sum of metropolitan "governance" policy communities as these were discussed in Chapter 7. It is characterized by a breadth of focus that is both elastic and hard to measure and not by the depth of any specialized policy involvement. Rather, it possesses influence across the many separate policy worlds of each metropolis. The urban regime is differentiated from specific functional policy communities precisely because it is not publicly obvious or exclusively centred in any one public policy area, but still possesses the capacity to exert a strong general control over disruptively centrifugal metropolitan tendencies. At moments of pressing social or economic stress, it is positioned as that one part of the community which *can* intervene for broader purposes.

In Stone's model of activity, the *dominant* players within the urban regime are normally within the private sector and tend to share a generalized strategy for urban development. As Stone himself observed, however, "in practice, private interests are not confined to business figures. Labour-union officials, party functionaries, officers in nonprofit organizations or foundations, and church leaders may also be involved" (1989: 7). Business leaders have been most important not only because of a widely perceived need to encourage economic investment but also because businesses have at their disposal a wide range of politically important resources which, even when apparently dormant, are not totally absent from any policy scene.

Existing local government arrangements in city-regions will generally favour economically dominant groups. That is why they are able to persist. Since the political gladiators primarily operate to broker policy arrangements for this establishment, it is also to be expected that local officials seldom innovate in the interests of those outside their social and economic ambit. It is necessarily left to political authorities from outside the municipal spectrum to upset, radically, the apple carts of often long-standing patterns of institutionalized bias (Miliband 1973: 97). This is why institutional change, when it comes, seems to be so dramatic. Change, to be realized, requires a degree of stress so associated with existing structures as to demonstrate their most anachronistic features.

In the normal course of events, leaders in the urban regime are interested in achievable specific functional accomplishments, such as a realizable network of regional trunk roads. The absence of an overarching metropolitan authority may make things more difficult, but as long as the focus can be on specific and obtainable objectives, this leadership may be content to leave existing institutions well enough alone. Where the urban regime's absence of interest is most noticed, as is usually the case within the polycentric American metropolis, is when the greater interests of the region itself are not represented at any bargaining table. Who, for instance, could be singularly responsible for vitalizing the waterfront of Toronto, the inlets of Vancouver, the archipelago of Montreal? To this question, Stone might answer that "Regimes involve arrangements through which elements of the community are engaged in producing publicly significant results and providing a variety of small opportunities. The latter task often overshadows broader questions and makes it possible for governing coalitions to gain cooperation even though their larger goals enjoy only weak or even unpopular support" (1989: 235). Regimes sacrifice building great castles of grand opportunity in order to see the paving stones laid for the streets that all may walk. Viewed in this light, existing municipal government structures can act only to facilitate urban growth initiated by economic interests as municipalities cannot, as themselves, really do very much to jump-start economic expansion or social transformation.

Based on these observations, it can be concluded that what local municipalities do with respect to planning and development has not necessarily been of great concern to dominant actors within urban regimes in either the United States or Canada. There remains a lingering, almost nineteenth-century belief that municipalities exist for limited local purposes. As long as routine services are provided and planning is conducted at a reasonable level of professionalism, the vagaries and inefficiencies in the network of multiple municipalities may be tolerated. For example, even private service agencies that are partly publicly financed, such as shelters for abused persons, solicit their funds, as well as receive their clientele, without much regard for local boundaries. A well-established urban regime can normally accomplish its broader economic and social objectives by many means other than through traditional governmental forms. However, new spark point initiatives, such as the installation of area-wide fibre optic capacity, may reach beyond the authority of existing institutions which are then understood as being a handbrake on regional development.

Stone's general analysis of the relationship of local power with municipal governing provides an accurate statement of the Canadian city-region circumstance. The generic regime problem of widely dispersed formal authority in the polycentric metropolis is that policy attention is so diverted to very specific functional achievements (and monument building) within local borders that attention to overall city-region capacity does not exist. This sets the general condition required for radical structural innovation.

The policy question of equity within a multiple governments arrangement is generally not a problem for urban regimes. The economic structure of inequality of the governmentally polycentric American SMSA and the social disparity with which it is correlated are the result of an autonomous legality that comes with a virtually perpetual "home rule" constitutional warranty. In Canada, preservation of upper income safe havens lies in the political and not the judicial world. Still, except for the Winnipeg Unicity initiative considered in Chapter 10, even where residential patterns reflecting serious equity issues existed as in the Quebec City and Montreal city-regions before their 2000 reorganization, they have not been much of an issue in and of themselves. In Montreal in particular, Marie-Odile Trépanier notes how stubbornly the wealthier inner suburbs held on to their independence (1993: 70). Equity issues can seldom be directly addressed by any institution in the regional public policy sphere. The topic is not even raised as a priority policy issue in some detailed studies of metropolitan arrangements (Frisken 1993; Trépanier 1993), although it is arguable that Metro Toronto's social housing strategy of dispersal across its region, with the necessary and concomitant community services, did contribute to a rough metropolitan sameness across the boroughs (Frisken 1993: 160). For its urban regime, and except for the nuisance factor of coping with the regulatory regimens of seven jurisdictions, Metro Toronto had pretty much become one city well before the province consolidated its municipal governing institutions.

City-region economic and social conditions change, and their urban regimes are themselves adaptive operations, but postwar Canadian municipal boundaries were usually static. In analytic terms, regime dynamics are mostly concerned with the ways in which pressures for change play against the forces of continuity. In this scenario, dynamic change is usually best worked in private. Since lead actors in urban regimes were seldom perturbed by concerns over equity, it was coordination and accountability problems that lay at the heart of the 1990s political discourse about institutional incongruence with wider objectives.

The important question, to be considered next, is what prompts a provincial government to restructure municipalities. It is only well after the fact, and in the analysis and memoirs of participant-observers, that a pattern of the urban regime's behaviour is clearly recalled as having provided uncompromising support for centripetal government policies (note Brownstone and Plunkett 1983: 30-31).

13.2 Reaching the Decision to Amalgamate City-Regions

It is necessary to look beyond the sudden dramatic bursts of policy theatre surrounding Megacity or Unicity after their most intense moments (and after provincial elections) to set what has been done, and why, into better context. A general model of municipal restructuring for the Canadian metropolis is more widespread than the circumstances of each case, superficially unique, might suggest. At its core, the provincial approach is more

pragmatic than ideological and is brought into play only after the incremental patchwork of bilateral contracting, single purpose districting, or
even two-tier municipal federation has been judged to fail as serviceable for
broader purposes. The earliest federative steps (Toronto in 1954, Winnipeg
in 1961, and Montreal in 1969) established a metropolitan governing capacity for the physical expansion of the spatial city-region. Community leaders,
especially those within the business community, were sufficiently impressed
with the results that they paid virtually no overt attention to the actual process of policy-making at the metropolitan level (Kaplan 1967: 173). In the
normal course of operations where routine services are adequately provided,
the "low politics" of municipalities are usually of insufficient consequence
to command much attention from private-sector players with any cosmopolitan focus. This pattern of inattention changes when an accumulation
of small grievances and nuisance barriers builds pressure for some measure
of change. Because this envelope of small obstructions varies so greatly
from one city-region to the next, municipal politicians are encouraged to
advance the proposition that each regional experience is unique. It is left to
more cosmopolitan actors to differ.

Early structural reforms set the stage for an information-sourced economy
to anticipate institutions even more attentive to that new economy's infrastructure requirements. Such development supported industry clustering, an
urban ecology attractive to a highly skilled and more cosmopolitan labour
pool, and dependable electronic infrastructures. Whatever governing shape
may come, incremental tinkering with existing government forms appears as
incompatible with the new immediacies of governing as rust-belt warehous-
ing capacities were with the development of IT-amenable capabilities.

Social and economic developments in Canadian city-regions have led to
increasingly integrated patterns of work and private relationships over the
past decade and a half. The metropolitan myth of multiple distinct and self-
contained local communities, each self-sufficient and supportive of its own
discrete municipal government, was nowhere sustained by the evidence.
Even still, metropolitan area municipal governments remained reasonably
immune to consolidation until 1996 when, at the dawn of Ontario's unitary
government period, the ten largest CMAs in Canada averaged 30 units of
municipal government, a number halved if Montreal (99) and Quebec City
(44) are excluded. (The actual 1998 Montreal commuter-shed metropolis, for instance, contained at least 135 front-line local governments.) This
governing pattern included neither the secondary tier in half the cases nor
proximate municipalities just outside the CMAs and excluded school divisions, specific multi-lateral functional districts, and any negotiated, quasi-
governmental, intermunicipal service delivery arrangements, which, for

example, in the Edmonton CMA (with 33 municipalities) requires around 500 formal agreements today.

Repeated inability to respond adequately to any one of the three predictable public policy issues which bedevil the polycentric city-region can solidify perceptions that a systemic failure exists, and it is this perception that becomes sufficient to precipitate a more general restructuring initiative. For example, the 6,743,000 residents of Greater London (UK) living in a territory of roughly 616 square miles got by for over a decade with 32 boroughs and the City until 1998. Then, the establishment of New Labour's "government for London" was presented as a pre-emptive policy to coordinate economic activities in the face of perceived threats that European commercial competition would overshadow London on the world stage. There was no deeper ideological motivation for restructuring.

Fragmentation into multiple governing units impedes the emergence of what could be termed a city-region subgovernment that can process routine matters through government agencies and institutionalized lobbies (Pross 1992: 120-11). When local municipal boundaries which have lingered about for no particular reason become grossly inconvenient for service delivery or impede the emergence of a sustained city-region specialized public or policy community pressure can build quickly for change. Garber and Imbroscio cautioned, though, that there is a "possibility that institutional forms create their own logic and weight through continued use" (1996: 598). The possibility does exist as past practice validates existing local government arrangements to the point that public policy potential is so framed by historic precedent as to deny the legitimacy of *any* change. The resolution of wider area policy problems is then distracted by a broader public which is accustomed to the fractured past carried forward and by local councillors whose very positions are at stake should it not be. While some localities persist only for the limited advantages they permit clientele groups like old-style development interests, suburban recreational associations, local chambers of commerce, or even volunteer fire departments, the larger, more powerful pressure militating against the easy emergence of a regional political identity is just how comfortable councillors, and citizens as clients, have become in working within the established frameworks.

Barriers to the formation of greater overt pressure for comprehensive city-region governmental integration can always find a range of plausible explanations. For Montreal, the record of linguistic and cultural diversity sustained the writ of municipal differentiation to the point that these institutions had built sufficiently fully fledged polities as to cause provincial authorities, strongly interventionist in other policy worlds, to avoid blatantly obvious city-region pressure points until 2000. By 1988, the Province of Quebec had even dismantled its own Montreal administrative region, replacing it with five others (Trépanier 1993: 87). Indeed, nearing the turn of the century, the Quebec government initially responded to unfavourable economic circumstances by "softening" their previous support for the Montreal Urban Community to allow it to become a "facilitator" for the most innocuous of technical matters like sewage collection. In consequence, its council evolved into squabbling bastions of local autonomy while suburban councillors tried to redefine it as a weak form of an American-style COG (Trépanier 1993: 102-05). This sorry episode ended with the dramatic introduction of Bill 170 on 15 November 2000.

Other barriers to the evolution of city-region policy instruments are evident elsewhere. Business leadership in the urban regime of the lower mainland of British Columbia easily transferred its external economic development and policy initiatives into the mostly private realm. To realize promotional opportunities required so little from the municipal realm that wider area institutions, primarily the GVRD, came to constitute a caretaker policy tangent. In another instance, the 40 years of rudderless regional drift in the Edmonton CMA was kept afloat by, at various times, lower rates of urban growth, a concomitant absence of servicing pressures, the absence of any critical mass of established corporate head offices, and the spatial distance from the urban core of a number of suburban communities.

The adaptation of structures through some style of tiered metropolitan government reorganization may be adequate for a time in realizing a low-key agenda of public and private policy. Among the less consequential regime adherents such a forum may be geared very well to the "small opportunities" phenomenon which Stone observed in Atlanta (1989: 235). He was careful to note that the non-corporate component of the regime did not exactly represent altruism versus self-interest because altruists also pursue small opportunities such as food banks or arts festivals. One result can be that opponents of systemic reorganization can dampen systemic pressures to adapt with a tactic of partial steps.

These can take curious shape. To achieve more regionally based public policies, a kind of metro-coincident subgovernment emerges through the joint actions of provincial government ministries to deliver public services. A growing awareness of the city-region as a singular community can also develop through their use of PPPs in service co-production. The persisting problem is the tendency for line departments with functional responsibilities in relation to municipalities—such as community services, health, and environment (especially water and sewerage) as well as transport and public works—to each devise its own program activities and regulations, as well as cultivate its own special publics, almost always in impressive isolation from the others. The general consequence for Canadian city-regions before consolidation was a limited potential for any wider area policy community except in piecemeal, reactive, and issue-specific roles. Even today, after significant municipal consolidation, there is still little evidence in any province of any strong central coordinating role such as that played in London by Whitehall's Ministry for the Environment.

While leaders in an urban regime may not be keenly interested in playing the regional "governance game" through existing decentralized structures, there is nothing to prevent more private conversations about rule changes with those who have the power to act. Interventions at the provincial executive level to prompt some measure of institutionally defined regional authority will reflect regime leaders' differing experiences with what changing circumstances require. Paul Pross observed, from the more conventional interest group perspective, somewhat similar behaviour with the wider concerns of potential policy initiators: "The attentive public ... is neither tightly knit nor clearly defined.... Their interest may be keen but not compelling enough to warrant breaking into the inner circle" (1992: 121). "Breaking in" is not the issue here, but what circumstances constitute a compelling need to seize the ear is.

Consistently, a threshold develops at which leaders in a Canadian city-region's urban regime become mutually persuaded that an integration of political authority across the region is necessary to realize opportunities. The stress conducive to this decision has usually been related to negative impacts, as somehow measured by competitive economic development, for which the apparent cause is "anachronistic" structures. In 1971, for example, the Manitoba Association of Architects supported the Unicity initiative, citing concerns with "division in authority ... [and] duplication in jurisdiction" (Manitoba 1971: 842). Because of the "practical focus" nature of this sort of support, significant unification of metropolitan institutions has proceeded independently of the underlying ideology of the political party in provincial power. While the provincial intervention appears bold when it happens, this is only because it is decisive. A requirement for structural change will already have been informally tested for general fit with key elements in the regime's unwritten agenda. An example of such fit is the 1997 survey by the Toronto Board of Trade of its 502 members which found that 65 per cent favoured the municipal merger as announced and only 17 per cent opted for the status quo (*Toronto Star*, 4 March 1997).

In the 1971 Winnipeg case, leaders within the urban regime had been privately dismayed by the tax incentives and forgiveness measures, low-priced serviced lands, and relaxed zoning regulations dealt out by the various suburbs (especially St. Boniface) in a cut-throat competition for commercial and industrial assessment. These concerns were conveyed through intermediaries to several ministers who had themselves served as Winnipeg, suburban, and/or Metro councillors. The result was that the new NDP government could realize its modest redistributive policy goals for their new Unicity on the back of small efficiencies afforded to business leaders. Overall, though, Winnipeg's metropolitan federation (1961-71) imploded because it had been a "system" only through its conflicts, conflicts premised on a general belief held firmly by both tiers that the other had no right to exist (Kaplan 1982: 597-98). Questions concerning core city redevelopment escalated to a level at which any development became impossible, and, by 1969, a nearly unanimous vote for amalgamation by Metro council reflected the private appreciations of its own senior bureaucrats. More importantly, it also represented the public face of the more discreetly conveyed, through private links, less embroidered concerns of leadership within the UDI, Winnipeg Real Estate Board, the Downtown Business Association, and the business editors of the daily newspapers.

When we examine the pattern of interest expression in the next section, clarity in understanding the audience or the decision-making authority to be influenced is paramount. Because of the proclivity in American political culture to resort to plebiscites over local reorganizations, interest aggregation and expression around this policy issue unfold within a fish-bowl atmosphere. Formally organized groups and other policy communities have a clearly specified goal to work toward and tangible mechanisms to wield. On the other hand, the major municipal restructurings in Canada were initiated within the quasi-secrecy of cabinet government institutions where the most effective sources of influence are not necessarily available to the more public of local figures. We may still see the usual leaders in policy communities and formalized interest groups publicly assert their positions on the issue both "for the record" and for the more sanguine purpose of reinforcing their own internal group supports. In the American experience, opinion leaders are most oriented toward influencing and gaining support from their own policy constituencies first. Although emulated, similar endeavours are unlikely to be so productive in Canada in blockading reorganizations once the central decision has been reached within the provincial government. Because of this difference between cultures, and between the structures of state and provincial governments, it is patently incorrect to advance a formula for the feasibility of city-region municipal reorganization across all of North America framed in such fashion that *any* significant local opposition is predestined to derail the initiative (see Smallwood 1972: 266-68). This should have been a lesson easily understood by the suburbs of Toronto and Montreal, or at least learned through the earlier Winnipeg case, unless the instruction had been well watered down by the ministrations of consultants.

What is sometimes lost in the consideration of public policy determination in Canada is the base reality that the faction or group that sways the political judgement of the provincial premier on the most fundamental policy initiatives has, tautologically, commanded the most influence. Not always is the electoral equation paramount; the PQ held only eight of the 30 seats on Montreal Island, the Ontario Progressive Conservatives were strongest in Toronto's (905) suburban ring, and the Manitoba NDP had little but electoral dreams in most of Winnipeg's suburbs. By the persistent evidence in Canada since 1954, metropolitan area municipal consolidation has been forced when, through informal lines of access, private interests have convinced the first minister that a more or less immediate decision is required to accommodate social change and to manage economic growth for a term longer than a single electoral mandate. It is these types of resources which matter. Other individuals, no matter where they are institutionally situated, merely set the stage and define the detail by pointing out small problems within any initiative. The controversy of legitimizing follows in public only *after* the choice has been made.

In the case of Toronto Megacity, suburban representatives in response to constituents' expectations had unintentionally constructed a well-integrated region whose institutions mirrored a rough social and economic unity. Yet the perception lingered among prominent regime members and in the provincial cabinet that the central city council still pandered to quite particularized and probably spoiled clienteles. Such perceptions are easily set in zero sum terms. For example, wire service stories reported Sancton's assessment that the provincial government of Ontario had acted on Megacity as it had because it "thought the city of Toronto was not behaving in a way that would make it clear it was open for business in the way the province of Ontario was open for business" (*Toronto Star*, 2 February 1998). For the intended audience, to be "open" also implied an implementing capability unfettered by dysfunctional municipal boundaries. By early 1999 the Ottawa-Carleton press gallery had been given a similar preliminary spin for reforms proposed there. Describing "a capital mess," Jeffrey Simpson wrote: "The vast majority of the Ottawa region's business community wants one city.... Having small communities competing with each other, and with the regional government, makes no sense to them, and they are right" (*Globe and Mail*, 20 August 1999). John Ibbitson later applied the political calculus underlying Toronto Megacity to the Ottawa setting: "Premier Mike Harris is convinced that the best way to counter leftish downtowners is to yoke them to councils dominated by suburbs" (*Globe and Mail*, 25 September 1999). To have the media frame the target in these terms seemed least likely to cost a governing Progressive Conservative party many votes.

Even so, provincial governments have responded pragmatically to quite powerful private calls for change. The shortcomings of investigations and the recommendations of such reports as the Golden Report (1996) for Toronto, the Louis Bernard proposals (2000) for Montreal, or the pre-Unicity Winnipeg Smellie Commission Report in 1968, are fundamental in that they took place in the public eye, were based on the evidence of self-interested practitioners, and were unlikely to reflect broader understandings that would be active in shaping cabinet views. Even an internal provincial policy, such as the Toronto Centered Region policy, was adopted in 1971 not as a plan but as a "concept," and was sustained over at least three different provincial governments because it seldom anchored precise provincial decisions (Frisken 1993: 171–80) and neither precipitated nor anticipated the consolidation choice in 1997. Political choice still matters, and this is underscored by the inability of the administrative sense of direction contained in the concept to overcome internal structural divisions within the bureaucracy. In the Toronto instance (which had parallels in Montreal) at least ten separate departments possessed their own programs and ambitions in the GTA. Even a potentially powerful public policy force as the OGTA was reduced to a "cooperation and coordination" mission among these and "a large number of local and provincial agencies" (Frisken 1993: 198). The urban regime acts in a private dimension and focuses its energies elsewhere on the one office with an integrated vantage point—that of the premier.

Consequently, as conditions of stress and opportunity converged, and as prodded by their respective communities' urban regimes, provincial governments of right, left, and centre introduced roughly similar major amalgamations to Canadian CMAs even though their public argument is couched in different terms. In all significant regards, the language in Bill 103 amalgamating Metro Toronto in 1997 under the very conservative government of Mike Harris is identical to that used by the social democratic NDP government of Ed Schreyer which, by Bill 36, created Winnipeg Unicity in 1971. The central substance of Bill 170 for Montreal in 2000 is further emulation, not innovation, by the PQ. Party tag is simply irrelevant once in power, and for such "administrative" house-keeping as municipal issues, there is not much need to seek legitimacy by appeals to historic labels. There should be little surprise in this. Once in office, provincial governing coalitions in Canada have been practical rather than ideological; devotion to ideology proves unhelpful in sustaining power. Much like urban regimes themselves, provincial governments have concentrated on building a pattern of small opportunities, reciprocal payoffs, mutual loyalties, and so forth. They become program managers. This behaviour is not unique to Canada. Creating a regional government for London (UK) became a priority for the new Labour government in 1997 due to a decline in that city's international economic positioning. Even a Labour ministry could argue for its reforms in these terms: "The new strategic authority will work to improve London's competitiveness, creating a climate in which business can thrive and a city where people want to live and work" (Deputy Prime Minister, UK, 1997: 2).

Although the ends are pragmatic, the means are often dramatic. When they do act, Canadian provinces have produced restructuring changes in quick, bold, broad strokes. In rejecting the suburban challenge to the Megacity initiative, Justice J. Borins noted, "it was submitted that Bill 103 came as a surprise to most inhabitants of the municipalities as the restructuring of Metro Toronto, and the mode of its governance, were not included specifically in the government's 1995 election platform" (Borins 1997: 9). It might be quibbled that while Toronto had not been specifically targeted, the intent of the Harris government with respect to municipalities was presaged in its Common Sense Revolution platform: "We must rationalize the regional and municipal levels to avoid the overlap and duplication that now exists ..." (Ontario PC 1994: 14). However, the point is that until in office, the party leadership was itself unencumbered by any precise plan, and this was why the response to accumulated nuisance and grievance could be so audacious.

In policy terms, the Winnipeg amalgamation came similarly out of the blue (Lightbody 1978: 498). Immediately prior to his government's election, NDP leader Ed Schreyer had indicated that he was prepared to jettison his party's well-known position endorsing amalgamation in favour of amendments to strengthen the Metro government (Winnipeg *Free Press*, 25 June 1971). Reorganizing Montreal (leave alone the four other city-regions) had not been a component of any PQ policy platform, but, by 1999, Montreal's historic anglophone commercial competitor had its Megacity up and running. For those commercial leaders foremost in the urban regime who were bothered by Montreal's declining economic fortunes when compared to Toronto, and who saw municipal structure as symbolic evidence of languishing competitive status, the moment for intervention was ripe. The dramatic consequence was reminiscent of the sudden emergence of the Montreal Urban Community 30 years earlier in the aftermath of the 1969 Montreal police strike. Being unexpected, all these infrequent but powerful executive interventions overwhelm traditional, thus predictable, resistance that is mostly entrenched in existing public institutions.

Once decided, the cabinet view prevails. Provincial politicians, not particularly concerned about the resolution of cities' internal policy problems one way or the other, formalized the reforms and pushed them to conclusion. What provincial line department bureaucrats preferred in each instance could be endlessly speculated upon, but whatever those choices might have been was simply not crucial to the final calculation.

13.3 Rounding Up the Usual Suspects

The study of Canadian city-regions has produced very little theoretical discussion of the interest group phenomenon at the regional level. Kaplan brushed off such limited overt activity he had observed as being of little relevance to Metro Toronto's official public policy activities (1967: 92). Ever since, published research has pretty much followed suit: Sancton makes but three passing references to business policy agendas in his *Governing Canada's City-Regions* (1994). It was Kaplan's original observation that the absence of formal interest articulation was the consequence of a kind of dissociation between what Metro council had the formal power to accomplish and any broader sort of social issue that was salient to the civic community (1967: 158–59). Still, it was altogether another matter to conclude, as he did, that the absence of overt pressure revealed a broad regional "social consensus" in the social and economic community of Metro Toronto.

There are three other explanations for the traditionally reported low levels of observable wider area interest group activity across Canada.

1. Formal interest groups active in policy formulation in other areas of state responsibility see no legitimate basis to organize on the small scale and transparently caretaking issues of municipal governing even if the issues are raised to some regional level. Defining wider area issues continues to be elusive in the absence of periodically cathartic crises quite specific to the basic services that local governments try to provide.

2. Potential interest gladiators see themselves as generally well-represented among the low-status politicians on municipal councils and in a dominant position among them. Thus, they let the councillors protect the community, broker the deals, and settle scores, since their resources are normally too finite to squander in over-attention to such low-level opportunities.

3. Groups that do hold wider horizons have worked in private to come to accommodations over broader specific ends. Community leaders then transmit these conclusions to those in local officialdom with the authority to write the arrangements into public policy. In a much narrower sense than even this, specific development interests have never hesitated to exploit close personal ties with municipal engineers and town planners to ensure they know about future locations for regional trunk sewers. More benevolent motives may attend the attentions of regional Chambers of Commerce or recreational and social services organizations.

Table 13.1: General Policy Positions of Actors Affected by Proposed Changes to Metropolitan Institutions

Favour Centripetalism	Opposed to Centralizing	Ambiguous, Conflicted
1. Central Chambers of Commerce	1. Suburban business associations	1. n.a.
2. Central city business operations	2. Suburban business concerns	2. n.a
3. Metropolitan print media	3. Suburban press	3. Electronic media
4. Civic reform groups	4. New citizen movements	4. Ethnic minority groups
5. Professional groups	5. Rural organizations	5. Labour unions
6. Central city elected officials	6. Suburban municipality elected officials	6. Political party hierarchies
7. Central city line operations bureaucrats	7. Suburban officials	7. Central professional bureaucrats

Institutional reorganizations, once decided upon, awaken a monster whose behaviours are well understood. The now clichéd phrase, "Round up the usual suspects," reminds us of the absolute predictability of the positions taken, and the persons taking them, during any city-region structural reform. This was the response of Claude Rains's jaded character, Vichy regime Police Inspector Louis Renault in the movie *Casablanca*, whenever an unpleasant incident such as espionage or a murder interfered with the benign tranquility of his administration.

Thirty years ago, Smallwood noted that the relative intensity of reactions of those opposed to institutional change contrasted markedly with the apparently meandering interest of those in favour: "The supporters of reorganization are generally fighting for marginal gains (e.g., incremental increases in powers and finances), while the opponents of reorganization are usually fighting absolute losses (i.e., their very existence as viable entities)" (1972: 336). His list of protagonists in regional reform showed that almost any such *locally organized* initiative was predestined to failure. By focusing only on overt expressions of interest activity, Smallwood summed up the endless needles while failing to notice the haystack. This oversight is understandable since the barriers to the emergence of a city-region policy community, rooted in the self-preservation concerns of the many municipalities, mutes the voice of advocates for area-wide policy resolution by denying them any comparable institutional soapboxes.

A policy initiative for municipal reorganization normally involves only a narrow range of policy communities, formal interest groups, and political actors, organized along the lines set out during the discussion in Chapter 7, whose positions are usually unsurprising. In the normal instance, the alignment of those opposing reorganization has been sufficient to forestall any radical realignment. The veto power of opposing interests is most effectively wielded when local *and* state or provincial governing authorities see themselves only as brokers among competing interests (as in Alberta or British

Columbia today). But when the role of the state is seen to be less neutral—when a political party more clearly defined in ideological terms captures power—city-region institutions being of the "old order" themselves may be seen to represent a priority target. It is in this sense that the vehemence of the opposition actually reinforces the determination of authorities to proceed with their plans.

The political debates over Winnipeg Unicity, Toronto Megacity, or the Montreal merger legislation did not involve unanticipated actors taking unprecedented positions. In Winnipeg, for instance, the provincial government's consultants Meyer Brownstone and T.J. Plunkett retrospectively note of the legislature's committee hearings that "There were no briefs from rate-payers associations, real estate interests, planning groups, companies, labour unions, welfare agencies, or community associations." Their assessment of the Manitoba hearings was that "Apparently the local politicians were the principal ones interested in what was going to happen [13 of the 27 formal presentations]" (1983: 97). Similar hearings over the Toronto Megacity bill, with around 600 formal appearances of 10 minutes each, were easily dismissed by the government as little more than a loosely orchestrated assemblage of directly interested stakeholders. Although interesting as a public relations display, the activities resulted in no policy alteration. The most sympathetic observer could only describe the exercise as "Performative Citizenship" (Boudreau 2000: 60-65; 154-63). In the Montreal committee hearings, the 27 suburban area mayors were collectively allocated 60 minutes to express their views. Their positions bowled no one over.

The comparative North American experience with city-region municipal reorganization reveals that, consistently, the seven distinct categories of interest summarily presented in Table 13.1 will emerge during the public debate (Bollens and Schmandt 1982: 381-88; Harrigan 1993: 360-63; Stephens and Wikstrom 2000: 56-67). The occasional exceptions are sufficiently infrequent that the playbill of principals will be carbon copied from one venue to the next. Initiatives have been based in the "nonpolitical sectors of the community and groups without mass-based support" (Bollens and Schmandt 1982: 382); reaction has found focus in locally elected officials. The specific positions taken by policy communities, organized pressure groups, and other significant actors are also tabulated in Table 13.1. The categorization convention is simple enough. The general rule is simplicity itself in that "the supporters of re-organization are generally fighting for *marginal* gains ..." (Smallwood 1972: 262) while the opposition to institutional change has been characterized as "the status quo mobilized" (Greer 1963: 32).

In the final analysis, the *modus operandi* of American plebiscitary decision-making in local reorganizations mobilizes those with a stake in the outcomes into the ranks of "usual suspects." Almost without exception, individual actors, officials, and groups can be expected to take positions as follows.

13.3.1 Central city business interests

First, it is useful to differentiate between umbrella business organizations such as Boards of Trade or Chambers of Commerce and their component members. Individual member firms are usually motivated to assess reorganization on the basis of their own immediate self-interest. When grouped, however, people in business tend to assume civic boosterism postures which, as previously noted, equate the potential for community growth with civic "progress." In the early weeks of the Toronto amalgamation, that city's authoritative business paper editorialized that "A consensus appears to exist that Metropolitan Toronto should no longer have two levels of government ..." (*Globe and Mail*, 27 February 1997). Chambers of Commerce can be expected to view area-wide governing arrangements for the city-region in symbolic, innovative terms as well as instrumental ones, promoting the impression that their community is progressive, dynamic, and able to implement "state-of-the-art" government. Also as a beneficial consequence, central city business groups can equate reorganization with relieving tax pressures in the core through widening the tax base which sustains their own essential support services. Suburban business associations are much less enthusiastic, especially when amalgamation is the objective. Their standard arguments bubble with abstract quality-of-life assertions and emphasize the uniqueness of their suburb's difference from the overall urban conglomerate.

Central city business interests, represented by either area-specific or function-specific associations, have appeared most able to associate centripetal metropolitan reorganization with direct economic advantage. They perceive municipal consolidation as conducive to the continued vitality of the core city which, in turn, they generally equate with the central business district. In the 1971 Winnipeg case, the president of the Downtown Business Association observed shortly after the release of the government's White Paper that it was "reasonably compatible with what we have in mind" (Brownstone and Plunkett 1983: 57). Real estate and larger development interests, together with their lobbying organizations, such as the UDI, appear the most willing to support a centralized political authority with the power to regulate the supply of serviced land. For Lorimer, the logic was clear: "Booming business conditions help ensure a steady market for all kinds of existing accommodation as well as attracting new city residents who in turn create housing demands" (1972: 67). Arguments demonstrating the greater efficiency and professionalism of large-scale administration will anchor their presentation of self-interest in "good government."

The neighbourhood businesses in the city's fringe communities normally reject these contentions. They, and the firms attracted to the periphery by the less stringent zoning regulations and taxation considerations of suburban municipalities (Nader 1975: 288–90), are less likely to perceive any advantage in financing services within the central city. For them, the two-tier metropolitan formula can be considered a satisficing policy reconciling the necessary physical plant upgrades with instinctive suburban resistance to municipal adaptation to meet evolving socio-economic integration.

13.3.2 The mass media and the suburban press

The character of the mass media apparent in other policy areas noted in Chapter 7 is accentuated during periods of institutional adjustments. Newspapers with a wider area circulation have provided editorial backing and given news support to stories supporting the creation of metropolitan area institutions. They are joined in this focus by the managers of the more substantial electronic media (Greer 1963: 24; Bollens and Schmandt 1982: 383–84; Stephens and Wikstrom 2000: 66). When Greater London, UK, was first introduced to two-tier metropolitan governance in 1963, the metropolitan press was essentially in favour, but their almost absent-minded support and weak leadership was attributed by Smallwood to an orientation to their "national" circulation (1965: 160–67). Media management, in particular, shares the "progress-growth-reform" line dance of related larger regional enterprises; after all, they regularly support other Chamber of Commerce "region as community" initiatives.

In Toronto, the three dailies only opposed the initial creation of the Metro form editorially because of their strong support for unitary government, both before 1954 and into the mid-1960s (Higgins 1986: 196; Rose 1972: 32–33). More typically, Winnipeg's two dailies generally supported the NDP's White Paper in 1970, although the *Tribune* was the more positive. In one editorial endorsing the Megacity consolidation, the generally liberal *Toronto Star* observed, "One of the factors that limits our economic development potential is that too many cities are chasing the same business prospects. Potential investors say they are confused by all this uncoordinated lobbying" (22 February 1997). Reporters on the city hall beat may be a tad more schizophrenic, torn between the stance in the editorial boardroom and their longer term symbiotic relationships with councillors and senior administration under status quo arrangements. The editorial position is the more important for legitimating reorganization concepts.

The suburban press is quite another story, since it too is an integral part of the system upon which it reports. Not only do the managers, editors, and reporters share a village-setting phobia concerning core cities, they assume an editorial stance as guardians of small town virtue. In an environment in which it is highly unlikely that any local paper will investigate the nature of the close linkages between town councils and the authors of desperately sought development deals, it has been correctly observed that "Metropolitan reorganization gives them an opportunity to launch a 'safe' crusade of the type they can rarely afford on local issues for fear of alienating some of their readership" (Bollens and Schmandt 1982: 384). More so than the larger and more professional city operations which have access to national advertising accounts, suburban journals are directly dependent on advertising by local merchants and can easily share their fears for survival, however unreasonable. In an all-too-familiar pattern, marginally profitable suburban newspapers are also often dependent upon local councils for the publication of legal notices or council minutes as paid advertising, subsidized circulations, and job printing contracts. Consequently they feel, as Bollens and Schmandt concluded a generation ago, "a personal stake in keeping the existing governmental system intact" (1982: 384).

13.3.3 Professional groups and middle-class civic groups

Likewise predictably, a variety of other policy communities, formal groups, and official representatives has frequently given loud voice during city-region restructuring as indicated in Table 13.1. Among those usually in favour of more unitary forms of reorganization are middle-class civic reform groups and associations of such professionals as planners, architects, and accountants. Usually in opposition are both rural organizations representing members in partially urbanized but still largely rural suburbs on the fringe of the city-region and those groups that claim to speak for minority communities resident in the central city. In the United States, labour unions have frequently been ambivalent while evaluating the gains and losses probable for themselves and their political allies; Scott Greer suggested that "passive resistance" best characterized their posture while the sums were calculated (1963: 31). Why might all these groups be expected to take their respective positions?

Proponents of consolidation appear to be susceptible to the same civic booster blandishments as central city business interests. Both middle-class civic groups, such as Civic Government Associations, and professional organizations share reform vogues generated through their extra-community lines of communication. Both are well conditioned to endorse the intangible values of "good government" associated with metropolitan reforms.

Frequently, professional groups have played a strategic role in legitimating a reform initiative by virtue of their influential stature (Greer 1963: 26–27; Smallwood 1965: 121–25; Bollens and Schmandt 1982: 382–83). In Toronto, for example, Rose noted the instrumental role of the Bureau of Municipal Research in the early postwar period: "[Their] White Paper was important, not only because it expressed the concern of a civic organization that derived its membership from many leading business and professional enterprises, but also because it was among the first modern statements calling for the development of regional planning and a metropolitan form of government in the Toronto region" (1972: 16). Professional and civic reform groups appear the most likely to try to evaluate structures in the "neutral" terms of mechanical advantages and efficiencies (see, for one example, BMR 1968). However, the legitimation function may be tempered into support for incrementalism since these groups traditionally represent middle-class interests similar to the voting support behind most sitting councillors. So they also have a vested interest to protect, one that may be threatened by any unanticipated innovation through external authority. From time to time, their role of diagnostic expertise is somewhat akin to that of the working press insofar as their résumés may be studded with contract consulting work.

13.3.4 Rural organizations and distinguishable cultural minorities

More consistently opposed to centralizing change in city-regions have been two other communities. First, rural organizations in the peripheral suburbs have argued for protection of a lifestyle which encompasses fewer municipal services, less stringent building codes and enforcement, and more modest levels of property taxation. This is why, to be successfully accomplished, American city-county consolidations have often had to establish different general and urban taxing territories within their boundaries to gain voter acceptance. In these cases, two different taxation levels apply with one supporting the basic general operation and the second applying to those in the more densely populated urban areas who receive the more complete package of city functions. Even with this concession, policy communities with a quasi-rural focus are unlikely to be enthusiastic about any initiative they may interpret as binding them more closely to the central city. A roughly parallel circumstance in Canada is in the system of regional districts in British Columbia which recognizes that rates in the unincorporated electoral districts will not support the same general municipal activities that are supplied elsewhere.

Particularly in the United States, city-region reorganization can be expected to mobilize distinguishable cultural minorities as policy communities with an interest to protect. Black leadership has typically opposed metropolitan governing options for the very practical reason that it dilutes black voting prowess (Harrigan 1993: 359-60). Black leaders quite correctly oppose changes that would replace their community's majority power in the central city with a minority voice in the reaching of regional redistributive public policy decisions such as poverty redress and affirmative employment programs (Stephens, Wikstrom 2000: 56). Even where a guarantee is given, through proactive districting, of roughly proportional representation in the proposed new structures, black politicians have seen area-wide structures as a means "to thwart the hard-won and long-in-coming political influence of blacks by joining the predominantly white electorate of suburbia to that of the core municipality" (Bollens and Schmandt 1982: 387). Indeed, as black and Hispanic political strength increased in core cities, their opposition to regional governments also grew. What must be appreciated is that the reasons run deeper than mere issues of voting strength. As noted in Chapter 1, urban newcomers like southern blacks in the early twentieth century and other visibly distinguishable ethnic minorities later, following the Irish before them, initially exploited the institutions of the central city as a means for wider social and political adjustment into an unfamiliar environment. As the early bosses well understood, eventual control over municipal institutions (like the police force) was a practical way to facilitate upward mobility and integration. Such political control quickly assumed important symbolic legs. Integrated city-region institutions threatened both.

Unlike American cities, Canadian city-regions have *not* been structured in racial terms; one of the few rough parallels might be the anglophone suburbs of Montreal, even though these are synonymous with privilege and not disadvantage. However, for reasons having more to do with an aversion to reopening historic sore points than avoiding clear explication of motivations, the 2000 amalgamation policy debate in Quebec was not couched in equity terms. In a similar vein, the political motivation behind Winnipeg Unicity, never openly laid out by public figures, can partly be understood as being stoked by the lingering memory of the 1919 Winnipeg General Strike and the political cleaving of that community, from that moment forward, along ideological and socio-economic lines. Occasionally, and always unexpectedly, the cultural nuance has overtly entered the Canadian city-region restructuring debate. For instance, during Winnipeg's 1970 reorganization, francophones in the suburb of St. Boniface expressed fears that they would be submerged in the amalgamated city, although the Société Franco-Manitoban ultimately supported the citizen access aspects of the community committee proposals as a better guarantee of the "French fact" than "we have had from the present city council" (*Winnipeg Free Press*, 2 February 1971). The

St. Boniface council, in fact, aggressively opposed the Unicity legislation, but when questioned during legislature hearings, the mayor conceded that although the council had asked for support for their brief from the Société, they had been rebuffed (Manitoba 1971: 226). This was an exceptional instance, however, and issues of citizenship and identity are usually raised in far more genteel terms.

13.3.5 Labour unions

North American labour unions, as traditional public policy communities, have never taken a clear and consistent position during metropolitan government debates. Bollens and Schmandt note only a generally "token" involvement by organized labour in the United States and a lack of consistency in positions taken (1982: 386-87). Greer observed that American labour's "specialized representatives" ranged "for the most part, from cool to frigid with respect to reform" but were usually reluctant to disturb existing political arrangements (1963: 31). Why is this so? On the one hand, by the 1970s between half and two-thirds of union members themselves lived in suburbia, most frequently in unincorporated lands adjacent to the central city where service costs tend to be cheaper (Harrigan 1993: 279). On the other hand, more important policy questions—like the privatization of traditional municipal services—have preoccupied local union leadership who saw any new city-region understanding as an opportunity for elected politicians to jeopardize long-standing collective agreements. This is partly what Smallwood was predicting when he wrote 30 years ago that labour depends upon "localized bargaining" with individual candidates to protect their interests and so "invariably tend to take a rather dim view of such [reform] programs" (1972: 262-63). Behaviour based on such political tradeoffs was to be expected from the non-partisan councils that were normal in Canada's city-regions. Montreal's labour unions endorsed island unification, for instance, only as a last ditch reinforcement for the more subtly expressed concerns of commerce that the municipal region was "falling behind Toronto" (*Montreal Gazette*, 12 December 2000). During reorganizations, this is what Stone meant as "small opportunities."

Local unions can step outside the regime umbrella to stand opposed to changes, especially on the issues of job security, seniority, and pay. During the legislature hearings on Bill 103 concerning Toronto, the President of CUPE (Canadian Union of Public Employees) Local 79 representing both City and Metro workers, argued that the two tier was best: "These complementary levels of government have resulted in a system which balances the needs of all communities and spreads responsibilities in an equitable way"

(*Toronto Star*, 6 March 1997). Fear had been headlined earlier when the president of the Amalgamated Transit Union Local 113 warned at the hearings that council unification would "inevitably" lead to privatization of the system, higher fares, and "deep service cuts" (*Toronto Star*, 25 February 1997). In Winnipeg, CUPE Locals 500 and 555, representing Metro and civic employees in all municipalities but two suburbs, supported unification once assured by the municipal affairs minister hat no jobs would be lost and that salaries across the region would rise to the highest scale (Brownstone and Plunkett 1983: 57; Manitoba 1971: 895). In Montreal, a promise of job "harmonization" that would be heavily influenced by the overwhelming size of Montreal's unionized workforce, plus those unions' long-standing affiliation with the governing PQ, meant that even the imposition of a 15-month strike freeze after the merger did not spark public dissent by labour leadership.

Where organized labour is directly affiliated with a political party, as in the UK, it may be expected to defer to its elected officials for statements on city reorganization. It remains relatively easy for labour to take a back seat in any public debate even where the involvement of unions with party is looser, but still close, as with the NDP in Canada. As there are few unincorporated tax havens in Canadian city-regions, and because suburbs often operate on the cheap through contracting with non-union sources, labour officials are likely to endorse consolidation as a device by which the privileged suburban tax base may not escape the provision of area-wide service even if they are uncertain of the precise calculus of probable gains and losses. In these instances, and especially if adequate guarantees are provided as safeguards for existing unionized staffs, labour leaders will most probably endorse municipal amalgamations. Labour leaders may also be influential associates in the urban regime and supportive of the basic inclination for "necessary" municipal reorganization. This behaviour has been indirectly observed in Canada in the frequent coincidence of interest between labour and business development groups, especially the building trades, on matters of economic expansion (Lorimer 1972: 124-27).

13.3.6 New citizen social movements and political party organizations

During the 1990s political authorities had to anticipate one new development in the constellation of interest group alignments that was not present for the debates 30 years earlier. This was the emergence of new citizen social movements with the capacity to oppose proposed policy changes. The most noteworthy, "Citizens for Local Democracy" (C4LD), appeared during the Toronto Megacity debate (Boudreau 2000). In quick order, and galvanized by a small, dynamic, and focused leadership cadre often at odds with the provincial government on other policy matters, C4LD mobilized loud weekly rallies of up to 1,500 citizens. The leaders' own social activism dated back to citizen struggles against bulldozer urban renewal and corridor expressway penetration into that city's core in the late 1960s. A website set out rules for engagement, links, information and a newsletter, fax and e-mail numbers, and the Ontario government's own electronic form for communicating with the premier's office. The legislature committee hearings were stacked by adherents mobilized through what became sophisticated networks, and it was not uncommon for all 44 speakers in a day to be opposed to the legislation. No public funds were requested, but donations were estimated at $5,500 for each Monday night gathering. Residents' groups, 20 to 50 present at a time with numbers impossible to estimate Metro-wide, met regularly to organize more traditional phone and canvass campaigns. According to veteran city hall columnist Michael Valpy: "Canadians are becoming an undeferential lot, an increasingly sophisticated, cosmopolitan, well-educated and politically engaged electorate unwilling to be pushed around by hierarchical authority" (*Globe and Mail*, 3 February 1997).

Informal networks among a broad range of otherwise divergent groups and, in other situations, widely dissimilar individuals became unified in resistance to the specific policy of municipal amalgamation. They were both easily mobilized and quick to disappear. In Montreal, on 10 December 2000, a mass protest rally of an estimated 40,000 persons convened on René Lévesque Boulevard to march downtown. It was led by the suburban mayors of Westmount and Montreal North following a 1950s-era Town of Mount Royal fire truck (*Montreal Gazette*, 11 December 2000). In Toronto opponents to amalgamation paraded in a reenactment of the 1837 Rebellion and "the size of the march far exceeded the 800 or so pitchfork-bearing reformers who tumbled out of a tavern north of the city to begin their short-lived fight for responsible government 160 years ago." Police estimated that there were 4,000 demonstrators who followed a hay wagon drawn by Percheron horses and carting Toronto's mayor (*Globe and Mail*, 21 February 1997). However, in the end, eloquent advocacy for a "new localism" or for community-based forms of public participation coincident with an assertive "municipal citizenship" turned out to hold little salience for most citizens *after* the radical institutional assault on the historic CMA municipal structure was completed.

More traditionally, political party organizations active in the city-region see themselves as having a stake in the public policy of municipal reorganization. Their positions will be defined both by the stance of traditional rivals and by the probability of electoral gain. In the United States, Edward Banfield concluded 40 years ago that metropolitan government institutions were under Republican control north of the Mason-Dixon Line: "In effect, advocates of consolidation schemes are asking Democrats to give up their control of central cities, or at least to place it in jeopardy" (1957: 85). If anything, the ideology of the American suburb has diverged more starkly from central city values, attitudes, and activities since the 1980s. Conforming to their stereotypes, American suburbs have become significantly less liberal than central cities, and suburban whites are less liberal than city whites on municipal spending (FAUI 2002). There are some differences among suburbs according to socio-economic rank, with poorer communities less adamant about keeping taxes down. Pretty much everywhere, suburbs, regardless of their objective social position, can agree with propositions that "undesirables" should be kept out (Harrigan 1993: 282-88). Excepting the racial overtones of some suburban rhetoric, political parties in the city and suburbs reflect their constituents' world views, and these have clear consequences for positions taken during reorganization debates.

Partisan alignments during the 1965 local government reorganization of London, UK, paralleled those noted above. Leaders in the London Labour Party expressed bitter opposition to the Conservative government's new authority: "They were considerably more interested in protecting an immediate sure thing [i.e., their existing iron grip on the London County Council] than in gambling on potential long-range success with a larger, and more powerful, first tier authority" (Smallwood 1965: 293). The hierarchy of any party based in the central city tends to react negatively to any wider area governing proposals because it fears that the change will weaken its power base in clientelist programs and the rewards of specific patronage networks. As a general rule, positions taken by political party organizations anywhere is directly a consequence of their own patterns of patronage and authority.

In Canada, municipal partisan considerations are superficial. As noted, a suburban dominance of the Toronto Megacity council might have been thought likely to dilute the positions of the few social democrats on the core city's council. No doubt this was viewed by the Ontario government caucus as a beneficial collateral consequence. Indeed, the case might be made that social democrats so strongly opposed Megacity simply because it had been proposed as part of the neo-liberal "revolution" of the Harris government. Their counterparts in Manitoba had, after all, strongly supported virtually identical propositions for Winnipeg Unicity in 1971. However, Unicity was ostensibly designed to achieve the NDP's long-standing equity principles even though, as the cabinet predicted, these came to grief under suburban control of the new council (Lightbody 1978: 498-99, 500-03). In 2000, the PQ had little to lose or gain for policy or party on Montreal Island itself.

13.3.7 Councillors, other elected officials, and public bureaucracies

The final absolutely predictable significant source of explicit lobbying in any municipal reorganization is that from councillors and other elected officials for whom there are tangible costs and benefits. Their behaviour was projected 60 years ago by Victor Jones: "Most of the suburban opposition to integration with the central city seems to be expressed by suburban politicians and suburban publishers, some of whom are subsidized by interests opposed to integration" (1942: 319). Jones did, however, also concede that both groups generally reflected their constituents' general sentiments.

In the twentieth century, Canadian metropolitan areas were governed by any number of autonomous municipalities which made it more difficult for specific urban regimes to coordinate activities for wider area public purposes. Irrespective of place, it was an even more problematic political task for the individual municipal authorities, acting by themselves, to establish an overall focus to city-region public policies. In part this reflected the reality that modern society had became increasingly slivered into a greater number of special personal and institutional roles. Still, governmental polycentricity institutionalized communities, each with their own legitimate and fully fledged political systems, bureaucracies, and clienteles, stood naturally against proposals to overcome dispersed formal authority. Consequently, it should surprise no one that there will always be substantial opposition to local government restructuring from politicians and public officials whose careers are connected to particular municipalities. For instance, as noted in Chapter 12, city-region amalgamations reduced the number of locally elected positions, usually to less than half. Even though councillors may appear blatantly self-interested during reorganization debates, they still have the power to forestall integration in the absence of any substantial outside force. Simply put, in the usual case, dispersed but entrenched political authority will defeat integrative efforts.

Bollens and Schmandt once observed that "Wherever a 'going system' of local government exists, it reacts against radical transformation. If it did not, it could hardly be called a system" (1982: 384). Usually, central city councillors are in favour of a total city-region merger or amalgamation that would not only enlarge their own community's boundaries but also enhance their own political and program powers. Albert Rose, for instance, recorded that Toronto city councillors clamoured for metropolitan area consolidation for the two decades after the Second World War (1972: 23-44). In 2000, Montreal's city council spent $700,000 to lobby the province to advance Mayor Bourque's vision of "One Island, One City." On the other hand, "suburban government officials are … fighting to save their jobs and their very institutional identity" (Smallwood 1972: 262). In Winnipeg, the opposition of virtually all suburban councils to the White Paper advocating Unicity was no surprise; neither was the support given by Winnipeg city council. At most, the suburbs were prepared to concede "preserving the status quo with limited modifications" (Brownstone and Plunkett 1983: 58–61). In defending a geographic identity, suburban councillors also presume an implicit sense of socio-economic differentiation from the central city. However, even where a suburb closely parallels the centre's social structure, its council is unlikely ever to sacrifice assessment and tax advantages in support of centralized government (Kaplan 1967: 45).

Within the public bureaucracies of the city-region the positions on municipal restructuring are normally those set by their elected officials. Suburban bureaucrats have consistently viewed centralization as a threat to their specialized community-based knowledge, seniority, and jobs. Especially in American city-regions, part-time employees and the volunteers in some rural fringe area PPPs (like volunteer fire fighters) are acutely hostile to any amalgamation which threatens their quasi-official standing. That suburban administrators publicly reflect the official position of their councils is hardly surprising. But, even in private consultations, a close rein is held. When the Local Government Boundaries Commission met on 8 May 1970 with the police chiefs of suburban Winnipeg before the Unicity White Paper, each chief was accompanied by a member of his respective council. The internal summary comment of the commission's secretary was, perhaps unintentionally, revealing: "The presence of political representatives tended to make police officials restrict their comments. Police views followed almost identical lines. The briefs that were presented adhered very closely to the views of councils on amalgamation that have already been heard" (LGBC 1970: 76). Central city administrators perceive the efficiencies in centralization and acknowledge that territorial expansion requires their functional expertise. The only caveat here relates to core community size, both integrally and in relation to surrounding communities. In the United States, central city officials in mid-size operations have followed the expected line as long as the reform package includes some nod toward proper city management (Bollens and Schmandt 1982: 384–85).

Comparative experience provides only one anomaly in this configuration. In larger and more complex metropolitan areas, the central city concern both in the United States and Canada has been that political control of programs might shift to the more numerous (and more conservative) citizens of the periphery. Even in 1960s London (UK), professional groups in the city core opposed larger scale service amalgamation "on the grounds that it would have an adverse effect on the discharge of their particular service specialties"

(Smallwood 1965: 294). Consistently, these have been public policies representing a political commitment by the core city but not emulated by suburban councils; cases have included the provision of welfare or community assistance for specialized inner city populations, the commitment to affirmative hiring programs in the protective services, and the continuing public support of high profile arts and cultural organizations.

Central city appointed officials are particularly concerned that professional standards established by past councils will be corroded by an influx of more conservative suburban councillors. In the original 1965 London (UK) reorganization, central city professional groups opposed a regionalized operation, even though it would extend their administrative reach, because it *might* dilute their specialized services. In the 1997 Toronto case, one Public Health Board member argued, likewise, that their "mandate to prevent illness and foster good health could be jeopardized in a larger, amalgamated city ... a lack of local government can lead 'to malaise, illness and disease'" (*Toronto Star*, 4 March 1997). The next day the director of the central Toronto food bank argued that amalgamation would definitely worsen the "losing battle with hunger" (*Toronto Star*, 5 March 1997). Interests who have wrested policy commitments and a cozy working relationship from central city councils, managing in the process to become an institutionalized lobby, especially fear they will lose. For instance, City of Toronto gay and lesbian leaders argued that "Certain communities hold certain values and other communities don't hold the same values, which is fine [but] if we're required to sit at the same table, we will lose those local values" (*Globe and Mail*, 21 February 1997).

13.3.8 Neighbourhood groups and ratepayers' associations

Most conspicuously absent from intervention in the formal public debate process in Canada have been representatives for neighbourhood groups and local ratepayers associations. Of 64 oral presentations (from 22 May to 17 July 1975) to the Royal Commission on Metropolitan Toronto, only 10 were made by ratepayers' and residents' associations; only four of 34 additional briefs were from similar groups (Ontario 1977: Vol. 2). The hearings in 1951-52 prior to Metro Toronto's original enactment were almost exclusively a battle among municipal corporations (Rose 1972: 20-21). In the Winnipeg 1970 Unicity process, the mayors and councils of Winnipeg's suburban communities were most visibly aggressive, leading Tom Axworthy to conclude that "In their attacks upon the White Paper, the mayors of the suburbs only represented themselves ..." (1974: 102). This behaviour followed a pattern set a decade previously. Of the 27 briefs received by the Greater Winnipeg Investigating Commission (1959), all but five were presented by municipal governments.

One problem for traditional associations of ratepayers and residents is that no common view exists either about the amalgamation policy or its importance relative to service delivery issues. A former member of both City of Toronto and Metro Toronto councils, and an established TV commentator, took the pulse "of resident associations across metro" to find that "The general drift is that most of the [well-connected and] better-off communities are split slightly in favour of amalgamation in the belief that, despite a lot of evidence to the contrary, a Megacity will cost less to run and that property taxes will be lower" (Vaughan 1997). A second difficulty for neighbourhoods is that councillors inevitably hoard the spotlight. The third is the widely held belief that well-positioned community leaders have already staked out their claims within the calmer private processes of the urban regime.

13.4 Debate and Resolution

13.4.1 The debate

The lineup of stakeholders opposed to amalgamation is thus entirely predictable and largely irrelevant since the choice will have been taken with this knowledge in hand. The political ministry listens only to whom it wants after its decision is made and consults only to legitimate the process. In Ontario, the 1,200 or so requests to speak before the legislature all-party committee on Bill 103 were ultimately reduced to 600 formal appearances of 10 minutes duration each, and, beyond public relations, these had no impact on the government's legislation. In the committee hearings on Montreal, the 27 suburban mayors were collectively allotted 60 minutes to express their views; there were no surprises. The minister answerable for the 1971 Winnipeg amalgamation once talked with me about positions opposing his government in sentences that may as well have been uttered by his counterparts responsible for Toronto in 1997 or Montreal in 2000: "We knew they [suburban councils] were all opposed; we also knew all their arguments. So, there was no real point in talking"[1] In each case those opposed had already lost in the private corridors of policy determination.

Those supporting municipal integration are usually leaders in the urban regime. As such, they have private access to the senior provincial government, and they generate public policy solutions quite independently of any that may arise in the official worlds of municipal governing. Even though small cartels of municipal officials always appear to hold the upper hand over issues of structural change *in public*, whenever the city-region regime views local boundaries as an impediment to longer range policy ambitions, they possess the separate, and pooled, capabilities to commit the political resources and personal influence to press for change in private ways.

To be effective in accomplishing institutional adaptation, an urban regime does not require media attention. Who was most in the public eye did not derail, delay, or rework the Montreal 2001, Toronto 1998, or the Winnipeg 1971 initiatives. The legitimizing forces played their important role in the less conspicuous world that is the half-light of politics. In other words, such quiet and pragmatic endorsement for wider area governing as the government finds necessary has been supplied away from press gallery scrutiny. The Winnipeg Unicity case was further interesting in that it matched provincial ministers' interests in fiscal and service equity with wider regime concerns for a greater coordination of municipal effort in support of hoped-for urban development. During the public policy process, the Winnipeg Chamber of Commerce encouraged and then with a few small reservations openly endorsed the NDP legislation in 1971 (Manitoba 1971: 830). Ironically, arguments for the continued autonomy of suburban municipalities because they are distinctive local communities have been undermined by their own councils' booster passions. These actions homogenized the larger metropolitan regions as suburban officials sought to emulate the programs and instrumentalities of the core city. Frances Frisken notes that with respect to Toronto by the 1980s, "the six municipalities have become more like each other as the suburbs have become more fully developed and their populations more heterogeneous" (1993: 166).

Opponents of integration make their case in public. They usually have good access to local media by virtue of their positions as community leaders, and the media have their own reasons for publicizing disputes. As the media seek "balanced" expressions for the wider area presentation of the news during reorganization periods, the multiple city hall pulpits create the illusion of more considerable opposition than actually exists. During the Winnipeg reorganization in 1971, for a typical instance, all suburban mayors and councillors, and all their senior bureaucrats, condemned the Unicity legislation with only the councillors in East Kildonan (which had the highest mill rate in the city-region) surfacing occasionally in support of the province. Extensive opposition to amalgamation *seems* to exist even though, as noted in the preceding section, only a relative few with narrowly defined interests are deeply concerned. Legitimacy is somehow attained for these raw politics when the councillors most opposed to structural change operate under a veneer of anti-partyism presumably in contrast to the ideological vision associated with any provincial government.

As well as the new citizen movements discussed above, local notables may also enlist as lead antagonists to change. As reported by the *Globe and*

Mail, "Most of Canada's best known writers [including Michael Ondaatje] live within a few dozen blocks of one another in the City of Toronto, and yesterday a dozen of them gathered to express their dismay at the imminent disappearance of that city" (17 January 1997). A month later, Margaret Atwood foresaw that "evisceration and evacuation" would follow amalgamation: "The movie version will be called 'Exodus'" (*Toronto Star,* 25 February 1997). Such hyperbole spoken before a sympathetic rally is very hard to sustain over the long policy haul, especially once the new structures have a formal existence. The opposition in Canada's best known three unification cases conforms with other models of issue-generated protest by a small number of very self-interested people. In these, the capacity for a small range of individuals to enter into reactive public debate disguised for public (and media) consumption as multiple, differently named, organizations is a well-understood tactic. It should not be confused with any enrichment of the civic culture through the emergence of new movements. While such sham diversity provides different identities for the same interest from different geographic concentrations, it affords much material for media consumption and assists local council lobbying. Policy gladiators at the level of the province are less easily duped than the press gallery, however.

Invariably it is suburban councillors who stand most boldly in the vanguard of the status quo (Lightbody 1998: 33–34). They are also quite prepared to deploy their own community's public purse to sustain dissent against change. Probably injudicious spending kept the City of Toronto case going in 1997; for example, and with no ironic twist, "Taxpayers Against Megacity" with but 12 members and no membership list received a grant of $20,000 from the core city's outlay of $1,665,000 to preserve itself (*Toronto Star,* 29 January and 2 February 1997). Nowhere will suburbs rush to enlist in any consolidation of governments. Sancton (1979) observed a generation ago that language difference, being the principal variable of public significance on Montreal Island, was irrelevant in the face of opposition to virtually any central city plans. Local behaviours were no different in 2000. Linguistic divergence, so important to other policy debates, had little impact on policy differences at the Metro council level where a powerful alliance of suburbs always emerged to oppose Montreal's ambitions. Suburbs anywhere would subscribe to the goals of this loose coalition because "*their leaders* have no desire to lose power over local systems which have proven to be valuable sources of political influence, patronage or even personal profit" (1979: 248; emphasis added). In December 2000, five island suburbs organized referendums that produced a 94 per cent vote opposing amalgamation (*Montreal Gazette,* 21 December 2000). Adhering to the practice of other governments in the Westminster tradition, the Province of Quebec ignored both the vote and the protest march mentioned above. The electorate can be sanguine about council motivations, though: 46 per cent of electors surveyed during the 1997 Toronto reform agreed with the proposition that area mayors "are merely trying to save their jobs" (*Toronto Star*, 2 March 1997).

13.4.2 Resolution

Provinces have learned that opposition during the debate phase of the policy process comes and goes quickly. Once the changes are made, the more quickly and certainly the better, people follow the quiet leadership in the urban regime and adapt to the new framework, find it generally an improvement, and become sufficiently attached that they do not want any reversal. On the evidence, citizen acceptance of new municipal governments is indeed quick to emerge. The former mayor of Bedford became the newest mayor of Halifax (October 2000). The first mayor of Toronto Megacity had served previously in that capacity in North York; the new mayor of Winnipeg Unicity was the old mayor of Winnipeg. Preliminary polling of Toronto residents also suggests an integrative direction. In the spring of 1999, Environics Research reported that 70 per cent of Toronto residents agreed "that they were satisfied with life after amalgamation," and Ekos Research found a consistent proportion in that 66 per cent of those providing an opinion "felt that amalgamation was a success" (Toronto 1999). Even after reducing the number of Ontario municipalities through consolidation from 856 to slightly more than 550, and eliminating some 1,200 locally elected offices in the process, the Harris government was re-elected.

The clearest investigation of the rapid social and political integration of citizens into new municipal systems came five years after the controversial imposition of Winnipeg Unicity. The Taraska Commission appointed to investigate Unicity's performance appeared almost astonished, considering the "abhorrence" and "widespread opposition" which had accompanied the amalgamation initiative, to report that "Perhaps the single most noteworthy 'accomplishment' since the Act was passed is the general acceptance of unification." They note that the over 100 submissions made to them included numerous suggestions for improvements. "But none recommended the abandonment of the unified city, a return to the former two-tiered structure or, for that matter, a return to the pre-Metro situation of multiple autonomous municipalities." In short, there existed a level of acceptance of the new institutions "that would have seemed scarcely credible five years ago" (Taraska 1976: 10). By privately and publicly working the new instruments, the several components of Winnipeg's urban regime had minimized lingering rancour while demonstrating many small and newly realizable opportunities.

Finally, there should be no confusion about the fact that the last word is always held by the provincial cabinet. Subsequent recourse to the courts—as occurred in Toronto on 22 April 1997 with the challenge using the Charter of Rights and Freedoms as pretext, or the threat to do so in Montreal in January 2001—was only an analgesic for those facing instrumental bereavement. It was also a sure sign that the fundamental case had been lost politically.

The public relations plebiscite exercises conducted by Toronto's local councils and described in Chapter 9 put the question "Are you in favour of eliminating [your municipality name] and all other existing municipalities in Metropolitan Toronto and amalgamating them into a Megacity?" (*Toronto Star*, 4 March 1997). Thirty years earlier the Winnipeg suburb of St. James-Assiniboia had proposed a similar area-wide proposition, an idea the NDP provincial government rejected as had Progressive Conservative Premier Roblin of a similar exercise on the Metro question in 1961. Its question was "Are you in favour of the Manitoba Government's 48-man council concept for Greater Winnipeg without knowing what it may cost? OR Would you prefer to keep your own local council and change the representation of the present Greater Winnipeg Metropolitan Council to be delegates from your local council?" (*Winnipeg Free Press*, 6 March 1971).

But there is little cultural support in Canada for direct democracy and local community autonomy. Simply put, the preamble to the Canadian Constitution in which it is stipulated that Canada will have "a Constitution similar in Principle to that of the United Kingdom," combined with the precise provision of section 92.8 which subordinates local governments to provincial statutes, has meant that there is no political tradition sustaining home rule concepts in Canada. Regardless of how eloquently or passionately some citizens voice their beliefs in "grass-roots" democracy, in today's world global economic developments have assigned urban policy issues a prominence that has forced more active attention from central government leaders, more interest in the structural adaptation of city-region governments, and ultimately a process culminating in a wider-area city government.

Note

1. Personal interview with Minister of Urban Affairs Hon. Saul M. Cherniak, 25 August 1975.

PART IV

Canadian Metropolitan Centres
in a World Context

| **fourteen** | The impact of world practices on Canadian metropolitan cities |

There are over 300 city-regions with populations in excess of one million in the world today—six of these are in Canada—and at least 20 with 10 million people. What is interesting to many students of local politics is the degree to which a city-region political culture has become a world commonality even as each city-region remains vulnerable, on its own, to the ebb and flow of global markets, capital shifts, and labour force choices. The divergence in the commonality is one of degree, often expressed through institutions and political practices. Yet, these days, globalization and urbanization are inextricably linked as phenomena, and both are tied into variable but rising tides of consumerism and cut-throat corporate competition.

This chapter is about global interconnectedness and how it has placed new demands on Canada's city governments while simultaneously restricting their ability to respond effectively. Over the past political generation, the historic status quo has been challenged by two sources of innovation in (1) the arrival of new communities from across the world and (2) the evaluation of local public policy on the basis of comparative experience shared in new social movements. (Some of the specific external processes and institutions having a direct impact on decision-makers in Canadian city-regions were introduced in Chapter 1.)

The term "globalization" is an insubstantial tag for a wide number of strands of interconnectedness over political borders that disregards international experiences. In historical perspective, past pan-global events such as the spread of early modern world religions, the vast trading connections of the city-states of mediaeval Europe, or the chartered adventurers' companies of the Age of Empire, helped to shape today's institutions. But over the past two decades, "neo-liberal globalization" has grown to become a dominant concern in public policy. However, the study of global interconnectedness, as such, is not yet an evolved social science theory by which the relations among specific processes and institutions are easily made sense. By the 1990s, the collapse of the Soviet Union had permitted a consolidation of capitalism quickly and globally. This was accompanied for better or worse by an American world hegemony which too easily made "globalization" a synonym for "Americanization." The phenomena described are greater than that. Essentially, globalization consists of three separate but interwoven developments: (1) more widely available rapid transportation modes, (2) publicly accessible and inexpensive means for worldwide communications, and (3) powerful multinational corporations accompanied by international financial markets and regulatory regimes. David Held and Anthony McGrew sum up the possibilities well: "By eroding the constraints of space and time on patterns of social interaction, globalization creates the possibility of new modes of transnational social organization.... Simultaneously, it makes communities in particular locales vulnerable to global conditions or developments, as the events of 11 September, 2001 and its aftermath demonstrate" (2002: 7).

The central questions for Canadian metropolitics taken from this too brief introduction are two. How well did the municipal system manage the external pressures driving urbanization in the twentieth century? Based on this track record, is the municipal system likely to be able to cope well with the further internal fissures and extra-national pressures of the twenty-first century? The general answer to both is "not well," a response conditioned by knowledge that the path ahead is uncharted and not conducive to easy incrementalism even were the civic political leadership unified and skilled. At the same time as the importance of local community as an identity source has become most striking, traditional administrative boundaries of the local town, canton, or borough have become largely irrelevant for the effective expression of these very same identities. Conflict may arise if the spatial city is not as equivalently meaningful to city *users* (guests, visitors, commercial travellers) as to city dwellers. In the city-region of London (UK), for example, the City of Westminster severely restricts parking for tourists even as the new London council struggles to control traffic with motor vehicle entry fees into the central core.

Globalization seems to homogenize important aspects of cities around the world. Beyond the utilitarian demands of the modern functional economy (stadiums, airports, four-star hotels), normally it is the financial district that becomes the first to standardize familiarity and consistency. Such capitulation to capitalism quickly follows as the central shopping zones are led by apparel and other retailers of fashion (sports clothing and footwear) with international labels. Today sameness abounds. One irony in the rapid growth of international tourism has been that the more the middle class travels to explore the exotic, the more the destination itself seeks to emulate home comforts for the visitor. By 2000, for instance, the pyramids on the Giza plateau overlooked the warm glow of American fast food.

14.1 Globalization of the Urban Phenomenon

Demographic historians note that around 5 per cent of people lived an urban life from the Roman to Victorian periods; half the world's population now lives in cities. Within the next generation, the largest world cities, at one time a product of the European Industrial Revolution, will mostly be found in less developed countries in Asia and Africa without the budgets to sustain even minimal local government services. Only four of the world mega-cities (populations of 10 million) are located in First World countries. The World Bank has also projected that, over the next 50 years, 42 new mega-cities will emerge, with only one to be found in the First World (*New York Times*, 23 May 1999). The largest agglomerations are Tokyo (nearly 30 million people), Bombay, Lagos, Dhaka (Bangladesh), and Sao Paulo (Brazil). China plans to manage population growth by shifting peasant migration into 40 large cities of 30 million or more, providing jobs, homes, schools, and other infrastructure. By and large all these cities, excepting Tokyo which has expanded less rapidly, will be characterized by urban sprawl, unemployment, violence and social disorder, and large underclass barrios. While none of these city-regions will develop in Canada, their existence poses both problems and possibilities for any Canadian urban strategy.

Canada's largest city of Toronto, with a population of 2.5 million, is the fifth largest municipality in North America although this does not place it among the largest 30 world cities. The city's website brags that: "The city's governed population is actually more than all the Atlantic provinces combined and is twice that of Manitoba. Only the governments of Canada, British Columbia, Alberta, Ontario and Quebec govern larger populations ..." (<http://city.toronto.on.ca>). While the boast is rooted in fact, the homepage tends to gloss over policy shortcomings in serving the quality of life for neighbourhoods on the city's social and economic fringe. This suggests that the growth of world cities has two general policy ramifications which will apply to Canada. First, there is the question of central government support for the city's position in the world economy. Second, and no less important, there will be intense pressures on established internal governing reflecting a new struggle between external ambitions and internal consequences (such as the reallocation of resources and personnel) in response to redistributive policy demands.

In this new era in which social, economic, and political behaviour increasingly ignores the boundaries of traditional states, place and territory remain important to citizens but are centred in, and anchored by, global city-regions. It is partly in this context that some writers have gone so far as to forecast the general decline of the traditional nation-state. Guido Martinotti of the University of Milano, among many others such as Manuel Castells (1996, 1997), has argued that in the quest for a new and relevant local identity: "In large regions of the world, such as Europe, even national governments appear increasingly inadequate in governing urban systems evermore dependent on an integrated world economy, and often capable to move autonomously on transnational markets" (1999: 1).

Considering populous global city-regions like London, New York, and Tokyo, which centre the financial and services networks of the global economy, raises questions over the future of national sovereignty and the potential disruptions from making "purely local" choices. One broad bundle of issues concerns the quasi-liberal tendency of central governments to decentralize important state functions to cities (often with little financial support) without a concomitant appreciation of how this may hinder the capacity of major cities, as social and economic communities, to participate in competitive global markets. A second set of issues, as we shall discuss, relate to the international migration that has dramatically increased the heterogeneity of the world's larger cities, including those in Canada (Scott *et al.* 2002: 18). Just as Canada's economic developments after the Second World War acted as an urbanizing magnet for the rural underemployed (discussed in the Chapter 1), globalization has drawn the world's poorest to cities. The rich, of course, were and are always with us.

One of the more influential modernizing and urbanizing pressures of the late twentieth-century international community has been mass tourism. Transnational corporations frequently present rapid expansion of the tourism sector as a sure-fire elixir for regional development and sustainable economic expansion as demanded by indigenous boosters among the host country's own commercial claque. Developing nations in nice latitudes, by responding to siren allures of large-scale tourism from advanced economies, can reap benefits. Local development, underfunded in the past, becomes oversubscribed by central authorities to offset tourism's negative impacts, such as disruptions from traffic, noise, garbage, prostitution and drugs, and the like, on social institutions, especially families.

A more equitable (and possibly more democratic) local public economy *can* develop through rent extraction from the renewable resource of tourism. The problem for many less developed countries is that tourism is an urban development. As an industry, tourism requires the skills of urban labour pools and is prepared to enlarge, create, and exploit them. In this sense, the whole business is a fraud presenting sylvan sinew over a skeleton of newly urban populations. It is as John Lea observed in the South Pacific of twentieth-century colonialism through the Cold War to the present: "The result was a form of dependent urbanization that owed little to local conditions and life-styles" (1996: 125).

Canada has not been immune to the demands of tourism. The Japanese tourist boom in the 1980s alerted the Canadian tourism business to the new potential of the Asian marketplace. Recognition of a suddenly affluent middle class in China (estimated in 2003 at about 110 million in a population of 1.4 billion) led to travel industry pressures on Ottawa to act as a facilitator by accelerating official talks between governments originally begun in 1999 as an initiative to curb illegal immigration. The revised priority was to gain for Canada the official designation of "Approved Destination Status," which was attained by the Europeans in 2004 and which has been credited with increasing Chinese tourism to Australia by 30 per cent in 2002-03. Authorization for Canadian travel by all its residents, using only a "tourist exit visa," was awarded by the Chinese government in late January 2005. Central government support for local institutions has been less sure-footed.

14.1.1 World trade and economic development

It is a common error of anti-globalization social movements to conceptualize the United States as an ideological monolith personified by its political, military, and business leadership. This is false. Noam Chomsky (1999), for example, persistently condemned the "more or less continuous aggressive and warlike role" of the United States in pursuit of some sort of global Manifest Destiny. It is really too simplistic to view the United States as "the Roman Empire with air conditioning," as Maurice Duverger once wagged in the 1960s (Pieterse 2004: 78). This is because, as Held and McGrew observe, "it is crucial to recognize the complexity of US domestic politics and the existence of progressive social, political and economic forces seeking to advance a rather different kind of world order from that championed by the Republican right of the political spectrum" (2002: 136). America remains a diverse community socially, economically, and politically, and, as will be considered in a moment, it is exceptionally unresponsive and inequitable with respect to its own least powerful citizens. However, its public ideology is that most widely subscribed to by an admittedly broad centre-right slice of the ideological spectrum.

The sustaining economic ideology behind globalization since the end of the 1970s is commonly known as neo-liberalism. In a passionate deconstruction of "Dixie Capitalism"—the economic unilateralism and political multilateralism of the United States—J.N. Pieterse describes Washington-style global neo-liberalism as deregulation, privatizing of state enterprises, giving market forces free reign, the conversion of tangible assets into more itinerant financial instruments, "and the ideology of lean government." This is the implicit force pushing worldwide for "government on the cheap" by rolling back institutions (often through deploying PPPs), underfunding state capacities, defusing accountability through privatizing state operations, and even depoliticizing NGOs by means of professionalizing their activities and personnel (Pieterse 2004: 1-15). The harsh 1990s provincial cutbacks to long-standing financial support of Canadian city activities is one local application of global orthodoxy, which may win plaudits from Wall Street bond raters but which comes at the price of shorting programs at street level. The political ideology of "public choice" also finds its source in this belief pattern.

It takes no large lens to spot all aspects of this global public ideology at work in the policy-making activities of Canadian city-regions, weakening the very structures and processes its advocates purport to be enhancing. Classic boosterism has, for instance, been redefined to emphasize balanced budgeting; to deploy quality management practices; and, in the absence of opportunities to tilt the playing field with bundles of economic incentives, to act as facilitators with demonstrable sound infrastructure and a distinctively rich local culture.

The apparent irrelevance of historic nation-states in a time of transnational capitalism also assumes that people become "unmoored" from familiar local community docks and are able to move by immigration almost as freely as goods, services, and information (Sassen 1998). This process of disaffiliation and reattachment across the world has yielded two general policy consequences for metropolitan Canada. First, the more successful cities in economic growth terms have oriented towards an external focus so as to capitalize upon the new global interconnectedness; by 2000, for example, all but two provinces exported more to the world than to the rest of the country (Pal 2001: 45-59). Secondly, a declining role for the nation-state in the global economy is perceived by many scholars; even a skeptic such as Saskia Sassen concedes that the emergence of a world urban system lies at the heart of the global grid of financial transactions (1998: 211-13). As national states surrender their ability to protect and regulate domestic markets, the onus in Canada has been on the provinces to overcome local barriers, especially within CMAs, which are seen to limit a more global focus. The *fin-de-siècle* provincial government initiatives to adjust municipal boundaries in Ontario, Quebec, and Nova Scotia are not best explained as providing tools to permit local governments to govern themselves more sagely. Rather, boundary adjustment becomes a means by which provincial governments may achieve "economic rationalization" of structures for their own broader purposes. These may be as simple as trying to balance provincial budgets or to induce local compliance with provincial transportation plans or as complex as devising subregional state structures competent to compete economically on the world stage.

Scott *et al.* note a global tendency for coping with the new reality that cities "in a narrow sense [are] less an appropriate or viable unit of local social organization" to be consolidated: "adjacent units of local political organization [now] search for regionwide coalitions as a means of dealing with the threats and the opportunities of globalization" (2002: 11). The endemic buzzword is "governance," which means a co-option of state, market, and civil society into the "managing of urban areas." The importance of a physical location remains because even the most advanced information industries require concrete processes that are situated in specific places. New service industries in particular further require an agglomeration of specialized, or boutique, service providers, especially since they tend to buy such specialties and no longer produce them in-house (Sassen 1998: 196-205). Hence, the politics and policies governing place remain important. Recent European experience suggests the heightened identity assigned to city-regions by their citizens is crucial because they are not only places of economic growth and opportunity, but also cosmopolitan meeting and market places providing a valued interpersonal counterpoise to transnational power networks.

Another development in the more industrialized world is that the existence of global communities organized around policy issues "simply means" that the low politics of city policy-making becomes more complex. While new possibilities for innovative regulation have been opened as even the largest transnational corporations require local arrangements for their factories, services, and markets, even simple choices in infrastructure and services (roads and sewers, protective and social services) can become lumbered with important normative dimensions. What, for instance, is the public consequence of privatizing the enforcement of environmental standards to quasi-autonomous or non-governmental agencies that may function under the thumb of extra-national corporations? This quickly becomes a quality-of-life issue, since the environment is local in nature, and informed populist citizens are watchful over it

In addition to feeding off the historic booster tactics of subsidized lands and servicing costs packages, companies in new fields of specialized electronic components have created internal pressures on civic governments to provide new and to up-grade traditional services to public infrastructure to meet the market requirements of clean industries. Cities may have to create new categories in land planning, such as the "Special Industrial," category Edmonton introduced in 1999, and find lands to accommodate this. Even conventional research and development parks may no longer fit new requirements. In Edmonton's case, the prospective development was in the semi-conductor industrial field which could not locate in or near areas occupied by medium and heavy industry or any commercial or transportation activity that creates vibrations, airborne contaminants, and heavy or disruptive traffic patterns. Canada's city politicians are well advised to notice research in the United States and western Europe which confirms that "policies devoted to assisting and retaining existing firms are more effective in stimulating local economic growth than are policies committed to capturing inward investment" (Scott *et al.* 2002: 22).

14.1.2 New knowledge elites and pan-national linkages

Political and business leaders in budding global city-regions appear to be pre-occupied with being "competitive" in the new global economy and, just like the old-time boosters, associate sustained growth with the public good. But to be competitive requires a bit more of a community in this century than the last. As Jeanne Wolfe summarizes the "strategy" of recent Canadian federal task forces, the new world requires that "cities must become centres of learning and innovation, with a skilled workforce, good infrastructure, and a highly desirable quality of life, complete with a range of cultural and green space amenities" (2003: 5). The very nature of place itself must change to attract what Richard Florida (2002) has labelled the "Creative Class," those individually mobile persons who value and are able to exploit talent, technology, and tolerance. A local community's "Quality of Life"—its opportunities for cultural, educational, and green space enrichment—has become a tangible asset in establishing its world standing. For example, world business elites these days are more likely to be concerned with advantageous location than about any questions of nationality. Indeed, throughout her various works, Sassen has argued that businessmen have been the first to become "global citizens," a sort of transnational capitalist class (2002: 25). Specific numbers are understandably elusive, but Pal provides data indicating that "The international economy consists of some 60,000 [transnational corporations] with over 500,000 foreign affiliates" which together account for about one-quarter of global production (2001: 49).

Business is not the only global actor. New pan-national social movements (environmental, women's, anti-racist) provide local actors with information, intelligence, *and* heightened legitimacy, thus spurring specific local initiatives focused upon the city-region institutions of their own particular communities. FAUI (2002) data discussed previously in Chapters 7 and 8 reveal that the world's social issues, as distinct from traditional fiscal and economic concerns, have risen in salience considerably. It is entirely probable that networks newly organized in these realms will discover that their common interests lie not with fellow citizens without similar education and access at home but with their own knowledge compatriots abroad. Their shared, urban culture will be that of the diverse lifestyles and middle-class diversions of the new political culture discussed in Chapter 3. Elites of this type used to be labelled community cosmopolitans, persons whose business or professional travel, contacts, and journals caused them to assess local practices and political institutions against those which seemed to perform better in other locales. Individuals engaging in these "politics of identity," largely through new social movements emerging in the late 1970s, uncover political space in their own persons, in environmental causes, and in human rights. Political space shrinks, in a sense, as borders become porous and global concerns are expressed by local action. "Geographical space contracts, as such movements develop ties around the globe, linking the new politics of Canada with those of Third World women, anti-apartheid struggles, Amazonian Indians, and peace and Green activists, East and West" (Jenson 1991: 219).

If the observed agenda of the multi-faceted global culture has any overall coherence at all, it is that populism is the prevailing ideology. The generally craft industry nature of the modern IT economy reinforces an atomistic world-view for citizenship. Persons in a cell phone culture are individually isolated, cannot be found through telephone directory assistance, and have jealously preserved this privacy from even the most aggressive telemarketers. The emergent, globally shared political culture generally correlates most strongly with higher levels of education and income, and with city-regions with higher concentrations of high tech service occupations. This describes precisely those individuals who are most unwilling to be treated as docile "clients" or "subjects" of establishment organizations (Clark 1994a: 27). Any projected "programs" by city-regions today will find issue priorities assigned through networks of individuals on the basis of information conveyed through new communications competencies and not by the organizational hierarchy that has become anathema.

The networked communities of the new world economy evolve on a daily basis, their shape shifting as technology permits, to the point that some demographers now speak of a single, borderless "World City" or "Exopolis" as elites rooted in knowledge are easily able to transcend political boundaries electronically on the Internet (Martinotti 1999: 2–3). So, political boundaries still retain limited value for those municipal office-holders trapped by space, in time, and on function.

Communications based on the Internet have reduced traditional patterns of reliance on the local community as a primary source of information. In turn, these evolving new linkages reduce local communities' abilities to engage residents as citizens (Fenn 2002: 292). Even as public elites now turn to the BBC and CNN on the World Wide Web, print media in Canada's CMAs have become metropolitan (or city-region) in the locus of their reporting, while the electronic media reduce that coverage to sound bites and 60-second news clips. First World local media sources have been largely absorbed by huge conglomerates like Fox or Canwest/Global. One consequence has been erosion in the effectiveness of these media in communicating the decisions of local policy-makers to the local community.

IT is accessible around the world, and although roughly half a billion persons have on-line access, it still remains the advantage of industrialized nations. Nortel Communications estimated, for the Association of Commonwealth Universities, that industrialized countries possessed 84 per cent of the world's mobile phone users, 91 per cent of all fax machines, and 97 per cent of Internet host computers (*Globe and Mail*, 18 August 1998). Network Solutions, Inc., which registers Internet addresses in the United States, reports, for instance, that 84 per cent of new registrants were signed ".com." High-speed network technologies that connect global data sources are thus more accessible to those nations already possessing most other categories of wealth. The long-existing North–South inequality divide has widened as information poverty accumulates. Canadians have the largest Internet penetration rate in the world (428 Internet users per 1,000 population) followed by the Scandinavian countries, the United States (number four), Singapore, and the Antipodes (Held and McGrew 2002: 34).

The global reach of the English language must also be noted. At the start of the twenty-first century, the British Council reported that English was "the international currency of science and technology," and it has become the dominant choice of international commerce (*Times of London*, 3 September 2001). About 85 per cent of international organizations use English as their working language, including 99 per cent of pan-European organizations. Best estimates are that over 80 per cent of home pages are in English. Sixty per cent of all European secondary school students learning modern languages study English. Should these trends continue, the Council estimated, by 2050 half a billion of the world's population will be native English-speakers, a *gain* roughly twice that of all those who speak French.

At the extreme, and quite different from the past, constant connection through electronic communication means that specific individuals can interact simultaneously no matter where they are on this planet, while being oblivious to the burning house of next-door neighbours. What this means for Canadian metropolitan areas is that their global cosmopolitans are isolated from both their underclass neighbours and those outside the policy communities of specific interest to them. They are out of traditional policy-making loops while tightly connected to the new.

14.2 The New Localism

Jane Jacobs's passionate opposition to Toronto Megacity (1997) revealed an irony within the Canadian experience. Although the case was most resonant in Toronto's suburbs, her opposition was based on a misplaced and nostalgic plea for older style of neighbourhood self-government *within* the city even though couched in the new global idiom of localism. As Magnusson reminds us, this new urbanism is animated by the concept of the *polis* from Greek antiquity in which a defined space was required for the practice of democracy: "urbanism as *a way of life* spills out of contained spaces. It deterritorializes, reterritorializes, and deterritorializes again" (2002: 342). The city is redefined as "the locus of identity" in all its forms (gender, ethnicity, occupational, and so forth). For passionate advocates of the new localism, the "low" politics of communities is argued to be more flexible and responsive to evolving international opportunity structures than are centralized bureaucracies (Clarke 1993: 5-7). With charismatic local leadership, community links to cosmopolitan elites, and limited professional guidance, it is believed much can be accomplished through very local initiative.

Sadly, the evidence for new localism victories is less impressive in reality than in appearance. The new localism has a sea anchor in the economic linkages of the international community. In First World countries, it has encouraged co-production of service, an operational fact of life as governments have been forced by fiscal necessity to work with either the private sector or voluntary organizations to plan, produce, and deliver public goods to either a particular sector of the public or to the wider community. In places like Baltimore and Pittsburgh, "in the absence of adequate local government attention to their interests and problems, many low-income groups are now forming into a wide diversity of self-help and community-based organizations, and this trend is no doubt likely to intensify ..." (Scott *et al.* 2002: 20). The usual problems of legitimacy abound as lower income citizens try to emulate the co-production behaviours of their more bourgeois neighbours. Even an apologist like Harvey Molotch concedes that "Neighborhood leaders almost always exaggerate the size of their active constituencies. Their occupational hazard is to make a great deal out of even trivial accomplishments and take credit for gains which would likely have occurred without their efforts" (1988: 39). Traditional city authorities and councillors are seldom comfortable with initiatives of this sort.

What new localism reformers overlook in any debate over city-region consolidations is that what the wider scale metropolitan city facilitates is a vital role for the neighbourhood in the power units of the new economy and society. If a post-industrial metropolitan centre is to attract the competitive attentions, the buying and marketing powers, of conglomerate global interests, it requires a critical mass in size and a determined policy direction. A larger scale for cities thus presents a realistic framework in which to include local neighbourhood voices in the making of decisions that still matter. If there is any irony here, it is that large cities actually make smaller democratic initiatives work.

Finally, comparative evidence suggests that those central governing regimes that are attentive to the agenda of local opinion are strengthened by the process, but also that few central governments are prepared to defer from their own reading of local will when it comes to decentralizing formal decision-making. Those who are prepared to deliver a series of small opportunities, often symbolic, for which others may take the lion's share of the credit, have to live with short-term loss for far larger longer term gain. This is a lesson some transnational corporations have more easily taken to heart than have governments.

14.2.1 Democratic tensions and possible policy initiatives

In sum, new localism is a term used to explain a variety of collective initiatives in economic development and political action at the level of the community; an analogous 1970s term was "neighbourhood government." The revolutionary change in IT that purportedly encourages local action has not automatically opened floodgates of direct democratic participation either in Zimbabwe or Canadian city-regions any more than market capitalism necessarily yields democratic choice in Malaysia, Florida, or Alberta. IT enables boundary crossovers between modes of production as, for instance, when "Masai herdsmen in Kenya now use mobile phones and wireless radio to manage herds" (Pieterse 2004: 92). These activities have emerged more quickly than the incongruence between established authority patterns and easily accessible new knowledge of what is possible (and practised) elsewhere has produced political pressure for autonomous local action.

The older style of international social activism was long term, combining the motivation of applied religious ethics with trade and investment sanctions (as against apartheid in South Africa). It was hard to mobilize people in institutional hierarchies, policies were difficult to explain to mass audiences, the affirmative actions were challenging to sustain over time, and the policy outcome was often indecisive (i.e., a moral victory alone). In this respect, modern pressure from individuals in new social movements with a global focus has led international donor organizations more quickly to suspend aid relief to create a "political opening" for the advent of democratic reforms in addition to, and in support of, the considerable personal courage of local dissidents. One such instance occurred with the suspension in November 1991, of $US 350 million destined for Kenya, pending political reforms in that country. The indigenous pressure came from educated cosmopolitans; as Susan Clarke notes, "[opposition] was centered in the new urban middle class and voiced its discontent through church groups, lawyers' associations, women's groups, and subtle press reportage of 'nonevents'" (1993: 9).

The new form of global activism tends to be more instantaneous and non-hierarchical, such as the late-1990s activism that led to the international land mines treaty. Such individually explicable public policies lend themselves to "virtual pressure" on political authorities to assume leadership roles in a clear issue resolution. Global interconnectivity has politicized a whole new range of issue arenas, new policy networks surrounding them, and, in consequence, closer and immediate international surveillance. The clash between the established order and newer "subaltern" movements which seek change yields a world in which none have the power to determine all business and the politics which matter are those "within and between movements" (Magnusson 1997: 112). Accessible worldwide communications permit NGOs an effective means to organize across boundaries; the assemblies of the new international monetary organizations (World Bank, World Trade Organization, G 8, etc.) provide a public forum for international protest.

There exists populist pressure from the post-industrial world to export improved democratic circumstances abroad to what are categorized in a patronizing fashion as "transforming societies." Knowledge networks can mobilize and move rapidly to pressure their own political authorities to apply targeted sanctions against authoritarian regimes in those countries. The rejection of traditional hierarchy has generated enthusiasm for new localism sorts of collective initiatives at the community level; Held and McGrew succinctly define the objective to be "to establish the conditions necessary to empower people to take control of their own lives and to create communities based on ideas of equality, the common good and harmony with the natural environment" (2002: 112-13). In practical terms, community activists with connections to knowledge compatriots abroad find their political behaviour newly legitimized; this may mitigate oppressive state practices and open windows, at least for local citizens in city-regions (where the world is watching).

Yet, these pressures tend to be in the electronic headlines of the high politics of nation-state restructuring and democratic reform. What seeks attention, and is too seldom addressed by democratizing activism, are the low politics which improve daily lives and which focus on immediate communities and the places (and possibilities) for work. Measures directed toward greater democratization at this level may be of considerable concern for more authoritarian countries not generally of the First World, and both concepts and applications are assuredly thought radical.

In short, even as theorists stress enhanced opportunities for citizens' democratic control, there is a tendency to focus on the roof of the state hierarchy while failing to appreciate the tension which has resulted when genuine self-help and bottom-up initiatives are either frustrated or ignored by entrenched statist elites. The distinctive "pith and substance" of local community evident in cultural singularity, social uniqueness, and even a particular local economy can become central to personal validity in the emerging culture of global sameness. In the 1990s, such traits led to pressures to disintegrate even miniature states, causing, for instance, the island of Nevis (population of 8,902) to break away in 1997 from its federation partner St. Kitts (pop. 32,901), which is only three kilometres away. On the antipode of the world that year, the island of Anjouan rebelled and withdrew from the three-island Republic of Comoros (total population of 528,893), only to be enticed back by force, its own subnational government, and a deal brokered by the Organization of African Unity. There was no comparable organization of city unity to work any such deal during municipal restructuring on the island of Montreal in 2000.

In the First World, local democratic activists may also mobilize in challenges to the "world class" aspirations of some community leaders as the consequences for neighbourhoods become immediate. The benefits of unrestrained economic growth may not be equally accessible to all. Molotch summarizes a familiar critique: "Tenants often end up paying more rent, not less, when their city grows. Job expansion provides the economically marginal little chance of bettering their employment opportunities, because the plums tend to go to migrants with better qualifications." He adds, "Environmental degradation affects everyone, particularly the poor, who tend to live and work nearest the pollution and congestion" (1988: 27). The diversion of resources to provide growth-supportive new infrastructure often leaves citizens the choice of either paying higher taxes or dealing with deterioration in the quality of what they already have. Hallmark sporting events and internationally prestigious expositions may have similar consequences. Of the 1996 Atlanta Olympics, Whitson and MacIntosh observe, "For the poor, however, these same developments mean that many are forced to relocate to suburbs that may be far from their work and their social networks, whereas those who remain must survive in a neighbourhood whose shops and services are now aimed at a different clientele" (1996: 290).

On the other hand, one critic of global impacts concedes a socially positive consequence of globalization in the United States by the late 1990s: the revitalization of the central city as transnational corporations, seeking competitive price advantage, have sought locations downtown. Dianne Pinderhughes notes that competition for space has shifted from suburban edges "for land in closer proximity to large public and private cultural and social institutions [and this has begun] to transform the economic dynamics that had driven down the value of central city properties in the 1960s and 1970s" (2003: 104). Who shares in this value-added exercise remains problematic.

14.2.2 Metropolitan underclass: globalization's probable consequence

One gift from the neo-liberal world about which apologists and critics can agree is that capitalist emulation has raised gross wealth accumulation. The collateral damage has come as the invisible hand of globalization's markets slaps the face of the unionized worker with a pink slip through job exporting to India and China from Organization for Economic Cooperation and Development (OECD) states. Some nations and many nationals have become relatively very rich. Even in Canada, globally linked pressures have shifted the operational foci of economic institutions and their principals. Observers have argued over the extent of this old order destabilization, but the evidence is clear on one point. Today, the greatest relative poverty levels are to be found not within poorer countries but in the most post-industrial. Pieterse reports findings, for instance, that show that the United States has the most unequal distribution of any advanced country in the world, with its poorest fifth today earning less than one-quarter of average incomes; the trend in the UK arches similarly (2004: 66–71). Social democrats like Held and McGrew (2002: 118–36) decry the "globalization of poverty." For Canada's city-regions, the 1990s were a time of consolidation for both family income (growth of 1 per cent) and low-income rates; this had followed a 1980s decade of growth in the former (5 per cent) and decline in the latter.

Apologists writing in the neo-liberal tradition of newspapers like the *Economist* or *Financial Times*, or in reports for the World Bank, try to justify the appalling evidence in ideological terms by blaming either the victims (i.e., those in need of social assistance) for failing in a society characterized by "equality of opportunity" or the failure of their states to integrate their economies quickly enough. They hold that economic globalization is the only sure route out of extreme poverty.

The main point of difference in debates about the question of quantification lies in the distinction between poverty and inequality. Poverty is open and absolute, the term is charged politically, and remedial policy change is demanded by most. On the other hand, inequality is more subtle, perhaps justifiable to some if there is equality of opportunity to balance the scales. As Pieterse puts it so well, "Global inequality is a different kind of theme for it measures not just the condition of the world's majority but the gap, and the growing gap, between them and the prospering minority" (2004: 66). Since 1982, inequality has grown among states; the gap between rich and poor within states has also widened.

The source of the anti-globalization movement's extreme distress, and often violent challenge to the new world order, lies in the inequality map of global deprivation. Measuring the income gap between the richest fifth of the population in the world's richest country and that in the poorest reveals that the ratio has moved from 3 to 1 in 1820 (the Industrial Revolution) to 74 to 1 entering the twenty-first century (Pieterse 2004: 63). Through policies such as trade liberalization and financial deregulation, internationalization has worked to dilute union power, erode wages and benefits, limit workplace regulation, and enforce labour mobility in "a race to the bottom." Increasingly in the global economic era, a permanent underclass has grown as earnings are either static or have declined. What does appear non-debatable is that the extremes of poverty and inequality of wealth have been most closely juxtaposed in the world's larger city-regions.

The census data reveal that in Canadian city-regions, the 1990s were a period in which incomes grew most for already high-income families, while the lower income groups actually lost ground. Citing Hoogvelt (2001), Held and McGrew sum up the scenario, familiar to other locales, in this fashion: "The new global division of labour … divides humanity into elites, the bourgeoisie, the marginalized, and the impoverished, cuts across territorial and cultural boundaries, rearranging the world into the winners and losers of globalization" (2002: 81). Further, in Canada, 35 per cent of recent immigrants into city-regions had low-incomes in 2001, twice the overall average for CMAs and a significant increase from 23 per cent in 1980 (Statistics Canada 2004a: 2). Newcomers who have not migrated with officially recognized and individually acquired skills and knowledge are associated with the lower status workforce by individuals who perceive themselves and their groups as currently advantaged in social and economic terms. As traditional workplace avenues out of relative poverty are closed, social mobility, even across generations, also turns stagnant.

Sadly for cities, alongside grand wealth has come great inequality. Across the city-regions of Canada, low-income numbers actually increased in the 1990s (although only by .5 per cent) in contrast with the 1980s in which the low-income rate had actually declined. Looking specifically at neighbourhoods in the 27 Canadian CMAs, Statistics Canada reported that the gap between the richer and poorer widened in the 1990s although the proportion of the poorer quarters (6 per cent of all) had remained static for 20 years. Incomes increased more in already wealthy neighbourhoods: "This is a reflection of the fact that income grew more quickly among high- than low-income families" (2004a: 1–2). We have not yet reached the state of those Latin American countries which have most fully enlisted in the international neo-liberal crusade. Pieterse cites one observer's assessment: "middle classes are failing and working classes are being 'reproletarianized'.... Meanwhile, the overclass increasingly plants itself behind the high walls of suburban developments, Latin-American plantation style, where private funding, not taxation, covers all services" (2004: 69). A somewhat parallel phenomenon emerges elsewhere as international tourism separates visitors and the amenities for them from the local society. All-inclusive luxury resorts operate as "a world away" from ordinary citizens who are denied access for reasons of wealth, dress, custom, or force. In the South Pacific, Lea writes that urban areas often developed in a dual form he labels a kind of urban apartheid. In these communities, the thread of separation extends back into the colonial period when the expatriates replicated the mother country within one area and nearby indigenous populations coexisted as best they could. Various legal and substantive restrictions (such as dress codes, limitations on building entry) further constrained the urban lives of native citizens (Lea 1996: 127–28).

Capital growth in specific city-regions, and not others, creates national centres of attraction for international migration, resulting in new communities with few collectively shared and inherited customs. Individuals in these new global city-regions must forge social bonds where they work and live. So, in migrant-dependent societies like the Canadian, the greater number of newcomers find themselves relegated to a lower status for a time. For Canada's 1990s arrivals, "the unemployment rate of recent immigrants is much higher than that of the Canadian born, which in turn is higher than that of resident immigrants" (Grant and Sweetman 2004: 11). Earnings follow a similar path. At least initially, this lower economic standing has been aggravated by social differences rooted in skin colour, religion, and custom. In both the Toronto and Vancouver city-regions, increases in low-income rates in the 1990s were mostly concentrated among recent immigrants. Hopefully, there are remedial avenues for social advance with which Canadians have experience, and the political system is not the only means for upward mobility.

The census data show that after 20 years of globalizing the Canadian economy, people with low incomes were more dependent on state transfers and less on earnings than when the period began. At the start of the twenty-first century, low-income individuals relied on transfers for 51.1 per cent of income, an increase of 8.5 per cent from 1980. For Canada, the neo-liberal federal and provincial reconfiguration of "social safety net" programs in the 1990s had a consequence. By the end of that decade, urban low-income inequalities, which had eased a little in the 1980s, had returned to pre-1980 levels. This means that substate regions (cities) increasingly count for policy matters involving redistribution and social justice, especially if democratic practice is to be built outward from the social policy of the streets.

There is, however, also a sad policy rumba at work here as standards for comparison and action have shifted. Domestic inequalities have been explained away by pointing to even worse disparities elsewhere, which evidence can be used to mitigate contemplated poverty reduction strategies by the state. At the same time, any bettering of provincial policies for labour and for ameliorating substandard incomes (e.g., minimum wages) is held in check by implicit threats from capital to beat a quick exit to the competitive, low-wage, small-tax nations portrayed on each night's news.

14.2.3 Assessment of local performance against world standards

One interesting turn in the globalized reality soap opera, or "mediascape," as nefarious as it is subtle, emerges in recent discussions of global communications: "Televised images of extreme poverty in Africa and Asia may work not merely as a compassionate wake-up call but also as a domestic pacifier" (Pieterse 2004: 68). That is, if things are so much worse elsewhere, then our own circumstances cannot be too bad, and so governing continuity remains unthreatened. The standard for comparison changes from absolute to relative.

More positively, modern IT has made it possible to mobilize human resources widely and rapidly. For example, the International Campaign to Ban Landmines (recipient of the 1997 Nobel Peace Prize) was carried to its successful treaty conclusion in Ottawa in December 1997, through the efforts of over 1,000 NGOs in over 60 countries. It had begun in 1992 with only six NGOs and never developed a secretariat, central clearing-house, or formal organization. All members could lobby their own governments as they best saw fit, and only loose lines of communication (facilitated by the Web) sustained momentum.

The use of the Internet and cell phones are individualized actions, but, by simultaneously inserting those activities into a mass of common culture *via* CNN or Al Jazeera networks, isolated individuals are permitted attachment to the metropolitan world wherever there is access. For instance, the Brundtland *Report* (1987) popularized while it elaborated the broad political concept of sustainable development and set the groundwork for the 1992 Earth Summit in Rio de Janeiro. This conference, attended by about 150 heads of state and an estimated 50,000 official observers and citizens, led to a set of proceedings that provided a world stage for the global media; under their glare, the various participants agreed to both a global action plan (Agenda 21), committing to sustainable development, and four related international treaties (UNESCO 2002).

Importantly, the events legitimized social movement pressure on governments to act. Over 150 countries now have some sort of advisory panel to conciliate competing actors and interests in the review of national environmental policies. In Canada, for example, by the 1990s forest industries in British Columbia had been forced into a collaborative planning process for Crown lands (94 per cent of the provincial territory) not by sporadic local environmental blockades and protests but by the growing threat of international product boycotts mounted by a world environmentalist network based in global city-regions. This ultimately produced significant changes in provincial land use: protected areas grew from 5.6 to 12.5 per cent of Crown lands and special management zones went from 0 to 16.4 per cent, while general resource extraction areas shrunk from 91.6 to 67.6 per cent (Gunton, Frame, and Day 2004: 18).

At the local level, over 2,000 cities and towns internationally have created their own local action committees both to operationalize Agenda 21 plans and to assess the current practices of home communities against the world standard. Some, incidentally, keep a particular eye on tourism development since its rapid expansion in a region can hold serious, negative consequences for traditional agriculture.

Energized by attachments to an international community, it is "just citizens" in Canada's cities who have more recently pressed forward with province-wide campaigns to enlarge the number and scope of protected areas sensitive to ecosystem planning and to preserve viable populations of species, even against the designs of rapacious provincial governments like Alberta's. The new language of Agenda 21 has passed through the policy gateway for all levels of our governing, and one consequence for city hall has been significant pressure to force more holistic policy-planning practices upon those who make choices. A second consequence, born out of mounting frustrations with the policy-muddling response of "the system," the avoidance of personal accountability by the usual sort of individual councillor, and the "silo thinking" of traditional administrative units, is reflected directly in growing Green political action in Canada's municipal electoral process.

Citizenship itself may also be valued differently in a global age. City-regions have become, by definition, cosmopolitan not only in attitudes and activities but also in their ethnicities, languages, and religions. Holston has argued that in their struggle for basic human rights at city governing levels, groups rooted in these social distinctions have both exploited non-governmental actors with their commitments to "globalization of democracy and human rights" and have won stronger rights for citizens at the national level (2002: 346). Might the concept of citizenship evolve to be defined as participation in policy-making which empowers, even where newcomers as immigrants are denied the traditional citizenship rights of nationals? Cities will learn first.

Finally, and for bigger cities especially, the evaluation of urban institutions' performance by cosmopolitan actors has increasingly been tied to standards established in other communities with which they are familiar, not necessarily at first hand. Existing standards are indigenous and thus likely to be precedent-driven, traditional, and incremental rather than innovative. Today important questions generated by extra-locally sourced debates can produce fundamental skepticism within local policy communities about the relative effectiveness and performance of current Canadian metropolitics. It is entirely possible that lessons learned from elsewhere may lead away from engrained zero-sum games in public policy and budgeting into endeavours which produce more numerous winners.

14.3 International Cities

In 1899, London was the largest city in the world. A century later, with only one-quarter the population of Tokyo and less than half that of Bombay, Sao Paulo, or Shanghai, this is no longer so. But its international influence persists. British urban planner Peter Hall was among the first to draw attention to "world cities" in 1966. He now defines global cities as post-industrial production sites encompassing international firms who provide and innovate corporate services and finance. Their clout is based on the locational choices of transnational corporations. Global city-regions are a new sort of regionalism variously described as subnational regional social formations or "dense nodes of human labor and communal life" (2002: 60-61). Whatever the terminology, globalization has meant population concentration within a few central nerve centres such that a general system of world city-regions has emerged. In the process, lingering policy problems of urban life, like income inequality, have dramatically worsened.

Any city's Board of Trade will naturally boast about its economic positioning in the glossy promotional brochures and any other propaganda it circulates; those cities and institutions which genuinely are "world class" tend to feel no need to proclaim that standing. A global city-region is more than sheer numbers of people, although size does matter. One problem in comparison is that continent-sized countries (United States, Canada, China, and Brazil) have a natural disadvantage when contrasted with a still state-centred continent like Europe because, as Hall puts it, "Very evidently, this combination of state power, language, and culture creates protected urban systems in a way that more open and uniform systems do not" (2002: 64; see also Sassen 1998: 210). Concentration of focus upon a single national centre, often the capital, establishes an importance that is disproportionate to size. Hall also observes that European city ranking has been enhanced by acknowledged achievement in a singular field such as fashion (Milan), banking (Zurich), or art (Paris).

These days, definition of world city standing has become a matter of shifting focus from placing check marks against a list of likely attributes (such measures as international air travel departures) into setting forth a ranked order positioning established by quantifiable, commerce-related activities. What now distinguishes a global city as a post-industrial corporate services and international finance centre is its place in an established pattern of inter-city transactions and relationships. Quite simply, global cities are distinct for their high concentration of "advanced corporate services" for the highest levels of the transnational world of commerce, those "industries producing the organizational commodities necessary for the implementation and management of global economic systems" (Sassen 1998: 203).

The most ambitious attempt to catalogue and measure city-regions based on their relationships has been undertaken by the Globalization and World Cities Study Group and Network at the University of Loughborough (Taylor *et al.* 1999). They have essentially used three measures: (1) content analysis of the world's leading financial media;(2) assessment of the structure of branch offices of large "producer services" operations, especially law, accounting and advertising; and (3) personnel migration patterns (Hall 2002: 65). For example, the Loughborough group has compiled data on the "international migration of highly skilled and specialized professional and managerial workers" which graphically reveals just how concentrated in New York City, and away from London, the international financial system had become in the 1990s (Hall 2002: 66). Professional migration is an important and interesting measure since it reflects voluntary choice of location in which citizenship in the host country is not sought as an end.

In establishing an "Inventory of World Cities" ranking, the Loughborough group established a score for each city developed from its chosen variables and ranked 122 sites as either Alpha (10 cities), Beta (10), or Gamma (35). The remaining 67 are considered to hold "some evidence" of world city status. There are few surprises: the top four alpha cities are London, Paris, New York, and Tokyo (the list is in Hall 2002: 71). In Canada, Toronto stands as Beta, Montreal a low ranking Gamma, and Vancouver embraces "some evidence" of world city formation akin to Brisbane, Cairo, and Montevideo, but ahead of Hanoi and Tijuana.

The long and short of all this is that while federal policies may mitigate a few negative impacts of global forces on some regions' economic opportunities, there *will* be losers among cities in competition. Canada's economically developed urban centre, based on its global city-region(s), will continue to possess accumulating location advantages over the declining peripheries for the foreseeable future. An appropriate comparable track record might be found in the internationalizing of Australia's economy over the past decade which did little to strengthen or to vitalize its diverse regions (including Melbourne, the former centre of trade and commerce) but rather "contributed to a greater concentration of major economic activities and actors in Sydney" (Sassen 1998: 210).

14.3.1 Questing for "world class" standing

Writing from a Canadian perspective, Patrick Smith and Theodore Cohn (1994, 1995) have provided a thoughtful assessment of the practical steps taken by one of this country's smaller city-regions in its pursuit of a higher international profile. In the process, they provide a still valid crib sheet of "Main Characteristics of an International City" (1994: 655), an idea later elaborated as an "Informational Metropolis" model of a diversified service centre by Thomas Hutton (1998: 20-27). Implicitly all endorse Magnusson's observation: "By definition, a global city or city-region transcends the province or the nation. It exists within a *global* space and competes with other cities or city-regions for economic and cultural advantage" (2002: 339).

Canadian city-regions intent on developing as internationalized centres build best if, up front, they have accumulated inherent advantages quite apart from numbers. For example, geographic location at the epicentre of a subnational urban agglomeration (like Ontario's Golden Horseshoe), or Vancouver's history as an international port, are positive attributes (Hutton 1998). Other beneficial attributes include most of the following: a cosmopolitan population, well-developed international transportation and telecommunications links with probable trading partners, a local presence of world financial institutions (and such local institutions working abroad), significant social interactions with multiple foreign organizations and associations (students, tourism, cultural exchanges), and independently initiated public and private cooperative agreements with other world cities. In dollar terms, however, Canadian cities have spent far more on their own self-promotion to electors than they have ever spent on international programs. Smith and Cohn observe that when they *are* prepared to commit resources, the typical city outreach efforts are spent disproportionately on promoting trade and foreign investment: "Despite the expanding scope of municipal internationalism, the establishment of business and economic linkages probably continues to be the most important diplomatic preoccupation …" (1994: 280).

Formal external relations in the modern era began with "twinning," the linking of one city with another through a specific bilateral protocol. The idea of twinning a municipal government with a sister city in a foreign country has been presented to, and by, councils since the Second World War (the first being Vancouver with Odessa in 1944) as an economical means to accumulate the supposed intangible asset of international status. In Europe the idea gained ground after the war as a way to help reconcile communities from former enemy states, and today there exist around 12,000 such intermunicipal linkages. Most still originate among OECD countries, with France and Germany each having more than 3,000 such agreements. Most have not progressed much beyond the usual start-up exchanges of culture, education, and athletics, but others have evolved to develop into new and previously unexploited trading associations.

Cultural (including educational) exchanges, grounded by an expatriate community, appear to be central to maintaining vibrant partnerships. Cultural festivals and touring exhibitions sustain twinning agreements at the official level, but extended kinship breathes life. Vancouver's twinning with Odessa was initiated by war-fuelled humanitarian compassion, but was nurtured through the Cold War and after by "a cultural link between the Jewish communities in both cities" (Smith and Cohn 1994: 633). Linkages of Edmonton, Calgary, and Vancouver with Harbin, Daqing, and Guangshou, respectively, have gained momentum in a similar manner.

A new development of the last decade has been the growth in exchanges of administrative staff between cities in the industrialized and developing worlds. Councillors are themselves usually quite well aware of the positive aspects of short "good will" personal travel (especially during winter months to warmer climates), but exchanges of permanent staff can be quite another matter. The background for this lies somewhat in population projections.

The World Bank estimates that by the year 2025 there will be 2.5 billion more city dwellers than there are today, and most of this growth will occur in the developing world (*New York Times*, 23 May 1999). Canada's National Round Table on the Environment and Economy put it this way: "cities of the world will need to cope with the rough equivalent of two more 'Chinas' worth of population within one generation" (*Edmonton Journal*, 13 September 2001). Whatever the initiator council's motivation may be, there is a pressing inadequacy in technological competence, logistical know-how, and sheer administrative capability within developing world cities confronted with unrestrained urban growth.

So, there is need for practical assistance. It is estimated that around 2,000 partnership exchanges are currently in place worldwide. In this country, the FCM (1993, 1996) has tub-thumped the "unlimited payoffs" loudly (with funding support for the program from the Canadian International Development Agency) to encourage international partnerships, citing enhanced "global stature" and unlimited personal benefits from cross-cultural exposure for staff, while often adding the carrot of potentially unlimited inter-municipal trade opportunities.

For the professional city staff from Canada involved in such exchanges of information, technology, and knowledge, the benefits are almost exclusively personal and relate to the opportunities to appreciate a distinctively different culture. On the other hand, the negative is the personal sacrifice of professional status. W.E. Hewitt summarizes them in these terms: "[those] most involved ... suffered a barrage of criticism from municipal politicians, fellow employees, and sometimes even from members of the community. The harassment they suffered ultimately led them to abandon work on the accord, leading to feelings of guilt" (1999: 326). For a number of reasons, including those listed above, Canadian city councillors are unlikely to ignore these exercises, however. Many came of age during the socially conscious 1970s and are susceptible to expressed citizen concerns that they "do something" about global problems; others feel an ethical need to provide even modest aid internationally; a few may even want to supplement or erode the intentions of national foreign policy (Hewitt 1999: 314-15). Despite best motivations, councillors are still critiqued by some whenever they travel abroad on "official business," essentially for the cost involved and for ignoring duties at home.

On a different front, in a few instances Canadian cities began to develop nascent foreign policies in the late 1980s, often on ethical questions raised by new social movements as to where to invest and with whom to trade. Some cities began to identify "strategic gateway" city-regions abroad as target markets, normally without the target's knowledge. By the 1960s, American city councils had begun to pass resolutions for sanctuary for Central American political refugees (Hobbs 1994: 72-77). Cities like Berkeley, California declared themselves to be "nuclear free" zones in the 1970s, a municipal "foreign policy" that certainly ran counter to the views of the national administration. Vancouver declared the same in 1987, but federal officials casually dismissed that and any similar such moves by other councils as merely "symbolic," saying that cities should not meddle in national business (Smith and Cohn 1994: 629). Nonetheless, the last decade has been one of rising global interest by citizens, and even smaller cities are routinely expected to align their practices with, say, the Kyoto Accord.

Occasionally, issues of conscience cause internal strife in the form of protests against oppressive regimes abroad. In April 1999, Mayor Andy Wells of St. John's, who was also a member of Amnesty International, protested the Chinese occupation of Tibet by having the flag of Tibet raised over City Hall to protest "Canada's shameless pandering to China for business contracts" during Chinese Premier Zhu Rongji's visit. A few days later in Calgary, Mayor Al Duerr automatically presented a ceremonial white Smithbilt Stetson to the Chinese premier. This prompted small vocal protests led by local Tibetan refugees. Calgary council's intergovernmental affairs committee responded to the protest by developing a "white-hat policy proposal" under which terms the hat "would automatically be given to guests of the federal, provincial or municipal government where a gift is required by protocol" (*National Post*, 18 May 1999). The "non-political" courtesy visit of the Dalai Lama to Ottawa and several other cities in 2004 occasioned no protests, even though the government of China privately expressed its unhappiness.

The Asia-Pacific Economic Leaders' meeting in Vancouver in November 1997 was another matter however. The event became the focus for large demonstrations by a loose international coalition of "anti-imperialist" social movements. A disproportionate and inappropriate police response provoked a public inquiry. Far larger protests attended the G 8 summit in Quebec City in April, 2001 with reports that police fired 900 rubber bullets and used 6,000 cans of tear gas.[1] For the next summit hosting opportunity federal authorities scheduled the locale for Kananaskis wilderness in southwestern Alberta.

Outside the Ontario heartland, city councils tend naturally to reflect their electors' views that their economic destiny abroad is in conflict with the sparse interest of rather distant federal officials who, at their most benign, are believed to be somewhat slow when it comes to providing information to foreigners about local economies. Smith and Cohn have made the valid point that, in a sense, cities as "subnational governments are sovereignty-free actors" not expected by citizens to provide the full gamut of state operations. In this sense, cities can cherry-pick their preferred agenda items "and direct more resources to a select group of preferred goals" (1995: 258). This includes, if they choose, trade and infomercial activities abroad and, for cities distant from the national core, an almost mandatory opportunity to move directly into intermunicipal connections with trading partners.

But, as with larger cities everywhere in Canada, the wider aim of municipal internationalism is to be taken seriously, to be assigned "sufficient legislative authority to allow [them] to participate more constructively in global activities and relationships" (Smith and Cohn 1994: 618). Even though city foreign "policies" have rapidly grown even without any constitutional authority, this disquiet over autonomous status festered behind the 2001 C-5 case for City Charters, discussed previously in Chapter 4. An appropriate federal response, not yet realized, could be that their own government's legitimacy would be strengthened through the simple innovation of incorporating ongoing intermunicipal contacts into more general federal frameworks, premised on the concept that dispersed leadership (or power) ultimately augments the sum of all leadership activity and political authority.

14.3.2 New minorities and the internationalizing of cities

Genuine world cities will develop their own particular culture as they take on global influence. One sign of such globalization is that big cities "are sites of diasporic intersection: many, if not most, nationalities are now global, in the sense that the peoples concerned have spread across the world and established themselves in many different places" (Magnusson 2002: 340). Invariably they centre themselves in urban areas. At one time, Canada and the United States had the most city-regions burgeoning with newcomers from a wide slice of the world's peoples. However, to observe the individuals walking the streets of Toronto or Vancouver these days is no different from what one would see in Sydney, Frankfurt, London, New York, or any other globally ranked city.

Canada's 2001 census reveals that roughly 45 per cent of the total population of immigrants living in Canada is of European origin. Because of open immigration policies and low levels of natural increase, our foreign-born population had grown to 18.4 per cent, the highest proportion since 1941 (17.5 per cent) (2003). The highest levels on record were, by the way, during 1921-31 when just under one-quarter of Canadians (22 per cent) were newcomers, reflecting the massive wave of persons settling during the early part of the century. In comparative terms today, the American proportion was 7.9 per cent, France 6.3, the UK 3.4, and Australia 22 per cent (*Globe and Mail*, 5 November 1997). Of Canada's 27 CMAs, ten have 20 per cent or more foreign-born population; the five Quebec CMAs, not including Ottawa-Hull, were all below this number. Quebec is the only province to wrest immigration control from the federal government with an eye to boosting its francophone majority. In practical terms this has meant openness to visible minorities from countries such as Haiti.

Reports from Statistics Canada point out that 94 per cent of the 2.2 million new arrivals to Canada, from 1991-2001, settled in a city-region, and about three-quarters chose to live in Toronto, Vancouver, and Montreal (2002b). Over three in five foreign-born residents of Canada live in the three largest CMAs; only 30 per cent of Canadians born in this country live there. By 2001, 85 per cent of all immigrants lived in an urban area compared to 56 per cent of native-born Canadians. These data indicate that there has developed a significant and demographic separation as indigenous Canadians have moved to the spatially separated suburb leaving the central city for new arrivals. In the 1990s, just under 60 per cent of all migrants originated in the many countries of Asia. Toronto attracted the highest number of newcomers; by 2001, 41.4 per cent of the population were newcomers, an increase from 38 per cent in 1991. Toronto's racial diversity is unknown elsewhere in the world. Until 1961, almost all of Toronto's immigrants (92 per cent) came from Europe, but today only about one-fifth do. Vancouver has 37.5 per cent foreign-born residents, many of whom were hardly "marginalized" economically having arrived under the aegis of the 1986 Investor Program. Even in Montreal during the 1990s, the immigrant population grew at more than twice the rate of the Canadian-born population. One further demographic note of importance both domestically and for external relations is that the great majority of the 1990s cohort of migrants was from visible minority groups (78 per cent in Toronto, 68 per cent in Montreal, and 83 per cent in Vancouver).

Cities face policy consequences as new arrivals internationalize the metropolitan policy agenda. Newcomers to Canada immediately suffer an "income penalty" partly due to inadequate language skills, non-recognition of credentials earned in origin countries, and the genteel practice of discrimination. At least for an adjustment period, they will require a measure of employment support and access to city social services. Implicitly required is a community commitment to language education and mechanisms to align professional qualifications with Canadian standards. Grant and Sweetman summarize some findings of a special multi-authored collaboration on "The Economics of Immigration and Canada's Cities" by observing that, "immigrants, on average, contribute less in taxes and receive slightly greater public transfers than the Canadian born" (2004: 20). While some policy consequences, like demands for racial equity in employment and culturally aware policing, are obvious and direct, others may not be. For instance, new urban immigrants use public transit: "We find that recent immigrants are much more likely than the Canadian born to use public transit to commute to work, even after controlling for age, gender, income, distance to work, and distance between place of residence and the city centre" (Heisz and Schellenberg 2004: 187). The internationalizing of Canadian city-regions has subsequently increased demand for effective public transit, even in the suburbs.

Recent immigrants are not only attracted to cities where economic advantage is foreseen but also, as in nineteenth-century United States and early twentieth-century Canada, are drawn to same-ethnic enclaves within them. These enclaves (or ghettos) can constitute a source of psychological support and physical protection, yet also spatially separate first-generation new residents in an identity preserve. These cultural islands provide networks for those who speak another language at home, are not university educated, and younger: "Negative effects come from increased strains on urban infrastructure and increased use of health services, income support and other social programs" (McDonald 2004: 91, 82). The 2001 census reveals that 9.7 per cent of recent immigrants (and 11.7 per cent of Aboriginal peoples) lived in low-income city neighbourhoods, a rate higher than Canada's CMA average of 4.4 per cent for all residents (Statistics Canada 2004a). Low-income neighbourhoods in 1980 had recent immigrants as 9.9 per cent of their population; 20 years later, the number had doubled to 19.8 per cent. As the policy picture evolves, it appears that front-line service delivery municipal staff, often out on the streets in response to demands from new communities, will lead in adapting traditional practices to this new environment. Resulting city council initiatives will in turn test new practices and carve new possibilities for citizen-centred public policy. Importantly, then, municipal governments may inadvertently perform the function of innovation within the broader federal political system.

Negative issues will surface with integrative pressures, perhaps in the form of racist tensions and xenophobia. Racially motivated fights have broken out at high school basketball games in Markham and Richmond Hill, as have "swarmings" by both Filipino and Asian youth in Vancouver's suburbs. Individuals socialized into a culture in which *baksheesh*, or tipping for service, is both expected and considered normal behaviour in the conduct of public business have run afoul of Canadian codes of conduct. Some native-born Canadians have escaped into newer suburbs around Toronto like Georgetown or even more rural Orangeville, although strip malls in suburbs which cater to specific Asian tastes have created tensions with local politicians representative of old Anglo-Saxon community ideals. At the extreme, new youth gangs have emerged, based on racial differences and reminiscent of nineteenth-century Irish urban settlement.

As conflicts among new communities over space and recognition issues enter into policy debates, cities will need to complement service delivery with tolerance for new standards in public morality to encompass differing cultural values for matters pertaining to health inspections (like old Chinese kitchens) or, more importantly, with violations of new definitions of civil rights. With the introduction of *Shari'a* for family disputes and even family violence comes hints of the ways in which issues of race relations and civil liberties will change the nature of policing. Cities in the integrative front lines will face further stress on policing brought on by the introduction of old world struggles in the new (as with the Sikhs and Tamils, or between Ulster and Republican Irish) or by drug trafficking within new Latin American, Jamaican, and Vietnamese communities. More broadly, Canadian city governments have had only limited, mostly unprofitable, learned experience in grappling with wider clashes stemming from divergent cultural expectations. This has been especially the case where those views rooted in collective orientations (as among First Nations) collide sharply with the strict individualism of Western European liberalism. We may anticipate that the policy frustrations will only intensify as escalating immigration produces communities with collective traditions, which are not only larger and more affluent, but also better organized.

So, the need for adaptive policies is felt most urgently in the largest Canadian cities, those jurisdictions most coincident with neo-liberal cutbacks in provincial budgeting support over the past decade. Magnusson has noted of globalization's ability to shrink world space that it has meant that "Vancouver is also a centre of the Sikh world, and the Tamil world, and many other worlds" (2002: 340). Caroline Andrew puts this idea just a bit differently when she writes, "Globalization is clearly linked not only to the changes in the heterogeneity of the urban population in Canada, but also to changes in the frequency and intensity of contacts between ethnic groups in Canada and similar groups throughout the world" (1997: 145). They existed before, she hastens to add, but the new global era makes them both more immediate and frequent. In a similar sense, international support from within women's movements in the 1990s also precipitated, and legitimized, local efforts in Canadian cities to connect with and to emulate other cities' programs, such as the Safer Cities Initiatives which linked community policing and social development activities into a coordinated crime prevention action plan.[2]

In Vancouver, especially, the clustering of new arrivals sustains ties to Pacific nation origins. For the wider city-region, this means both that people feel comfortable once they emigrate and that personally meaningful ties persist to most Asian nations for the Vancouver entrepreneurial class. Of importance to Canada is that this generation's new world order tends to relive lessons from great trading city-empires of the past. Like the Medici or Hanseatic League, Hong Kong trading families today, for instance, use relatives abroad, shared language, and cultural ties to build networks and clientelist alliances for economic advantage around and about central state control frameworks. People talk about their life experiences, most freely to friends and relatives, and Andrew makes the point that "Globalization is clearly linked not only to the changes in the heterogeneity of the urban population in Canada, but also to changes in the frequency and intensity of contacts between the ethnic groups in Canada and similar groups throughout the world" (1997: 145). Or, as Yasmeen Abu-Laban cautiously adds, "In global cities, issues surrounding immigration, multiculturalism, and racism have a special resonance and currency that may not be present in other urban locales in Canada" (1997: 83).

In the future, Canada, as a secular society, and like other post-industrial democracies, will be seeking newcomers to replenish a work force that is both aging and not being replaced by natural reproduction. By 2003, 59 countries representing 44 per cent of the people in the world anticipated population declines: Japanese fertility rates have been in decline since the late 1950s, Europe has stood below natural reproduction since the mid-1970s, Canada declined below replacement in 1971 and today faces its lowest reproductive level since data have been collected (Longman 2004). Those nations and communities within nations with the highest fertility rates tend, however, to be the most religious (Christian, Islamic, and Judaic). Among all major industrialized countries, the United States still has the highest reproductive rate, but, still, its birth rates correlate strongly with religious conviction. Surveying future scenarios from this perspective, Phillip Longman asks: "Does this mean that the future belongs to those who believe they are (or who are in fact) commanded by a higher power to procreate? Based on current trends, the answer appears to be yes" (2004: 76-77).

So, if Canada is to invite migrants from among the most devout to replenish its citizenship ranks, then city-region social policy will confront considerable adaptive pressures in accommodating arrivals believing they are God's chosen. It must also be remembered that newcomers of all stripes tend not to be knowledgeable about "the system" and, in many cases, are justifiably fearful of any political authority; the current capacity of city institutions to operate responsively is complicated by existing patterns of underrepresentation (of minorities and women) in positions of both elected and managerial authority. Moreover, generating tolerance for difference which may be met through openness in state hiring, recognition of other countries' professional qualifications, language and schooling, and so forth, is somewhat beyond municipal jurisdiction. Barriers like these can all be targeted. Longman makes the obvious point in a generic way: "decision-making and responsibility are increasingly necessary at lower levels" (2004: 78). What this can mean for Canada's cities is a more genuine devolution of central authority permissive of a localism that can deliver child support, recreation and libraries, and home care, not as universal policies but in a fashion more fitting for the locale. Communities will also have to acknowledge that one consequence of the knowledge-based economy is that children reside with parents longer, even into their childbearing years, as they acquire appropriate skills and credentials, and so they must be prepared to open channels for support.

The slow emergence of a "global civil society" since 1948, bound by covenants and international agreements, monitored by the UN and NGOs, networked human rights activists and progressive political gladiators at all levels of authority in all states, has compelled even the most local of policy-makers to keep an outward eye (Pal 2001: 60-63; Held and McGrew 2002: 102-10; Pieterse 2004: 152-59). While federal and provincial politicians face generalized political pressures to unite families, to respond to refugee claims, and to devise longer term human resources strategies for immigration and settlement, city-region policy-makers confront immediate issues quite literally on their doorsteps. Abu-Laban succinctly lists the policy concerns reported as being of urgent concern to immigrants: "finding affordable housing, accessing health and counseling services, receiving English-language training, dealing with family intergenerational conflict, and finding employment" (1997: 83).

14.3.3 The new game plan to attract investment

In the global city age, the successful promotion of the specific locational advantage of smaller city-regions (especially in instances where national states are perceived as distant, not knowledgeable, or politically unresponsive) appears at least in part contingent upon the emergence of city-region regimes led by the business community. Those which are confined to the business community alone, however, will fail. Experience reveals that the flourishing informal alliances embracing labour, ethnic and cultural communities, the effective leadership in post-secondary education and research, and so forth, have achieved sufficient critical mass and common voice to be heard in a rough, competitive world. But even the best intentioned community leadership in desperate locales can be distracted from strategic plans by the tactics of quick-fix booster shots.

The last decades of the twentieth century, for example, witnessed a sharp growth in international tourism from the industrial world to once remote destinations. While these have increasingly included those offering sustainable environments (through what first came to be known as eco-tourism in Belize and Costa Rica), these were the exceptions. Usually, tourist travel has placed entirely new pressures on the destination local governments as it was expected that popular destinations would replicate the amenities of home. This all-inclusive approach is partly a consequence of the degree to which tourism providers are vertically, and internationally, integrated in their operations. Whitson and MacIntosh report that "Tourism has become one of the most globally integrated of industries, characterized by large hotel chains, tour operators, car rental agencies, and financial services companies (American Express, Visa)" (1996: 284). One unfortunate collateral consequence for the destination is that packages are prepaid in originating countries.

The now familiar lure of hard dollars and the prospects of sustainable employment in depressed economies easily distorts existing casual and community-controlled local development. Decisions once made in town halls become subject to central government initiative and extra-national choices, powers which are increasingly remote and unaccountable to local residents. The expectation that home conveniences are available abroad have extended beyond the reasonable expectations for potable water and sewage treatment, which indigenous residents would enthusiastically embrace, into urban redesign to permit asymmetrical tourist zones. These latter often require expedited development processes for everything from banks and mini-marts to fast food franchises and the logos of recognizable bar names.

It takes no detective eye to discern that Canadian city-regions are not at all immune to similar sorts of "world class" development pressures, albeit applied in a little more incremental fashion. It is usually only at the extreme of "world" athletic competitions (such as the Olympic or Commonwealth Games) that the change to community is so disruptive as to evoke widespread neighbourhood opposition. What should surprise, sadly, is that local councillors are typically astonished by any negative feedback. On the other hand, a more sustainable strategy can be activated as when Vancouver's urban regime began to lobby the new Progressive Conservative federal government immediately after its 1984 election to designate that city "as one of Canada's international banking centres" with a Pacific Rim focus. Opposition to this challenge to its Canadian pre-eminence from Toronto's economic and political leadership served only to dilute the legislation and the competitive advantage Vancouver (and Montreal) had sought (Smith and Cohn 1994: 627). Among the general public, few noticed any immediate local impacts one way or the other.

The wider game plan has changed, and not subtly, with global interconnectivity. For a time after the Great Depression, OECD countries led the state parade in elaborating extensive public health and social security systems to complement more traditional social infrastructure in areas like education, justice, and culture. Macroeconomic strategies grounded in Keynesian theory were applied to sustain economic growth and employment within national borders and, it was believed, to build national unity. Not surprisingly, nations in other world regions mimicked these strategies in the immediate post-colonial period.

However, state autonomy in such efforts has proven ephemeral in the new transnational economy as the old border controls over goods, services, technology, and ideas have grown irrelevant. Held and McGrew make the summary point that "States suffer a further diminution in power because the expansion of transnational forces reduces the control individual governments can exercise over the activities of their citizens and other peoples" (2002: 22). It is pretty much the case that today all states must now develop, and trumpet, market-friendly policies (i.e., the neo-liberal bundle) if they wish to catch the attention of investors.

14.4 Cities and Global Interconnections

After standing to watch the sun set over the rim of Ngorongoro crater in Tanzania, travellers return to their lodge where, if they are curious, sociable, or unlucky, they may make the turn into staff quarters. Here they will find the younger employees, during their off-time, watching the NBA playoffs on satellite TV and, after the game, CNN news reports. This is hardly unusual for an area in which the Masai men, even living in traditional villages on the Serengeti, wear not only their habitual scarlet woven blankets but also Nike runners manufactured by child labour in Southeast Asia. Home world is here, and it is global.

It is as hard to be precise in assessing the overall reach of the pan-global influences of the past generation as it is to measure their direct impacts on city policy-making today. We do know, for instance, that ours is a world of greater prosperity than ever, but also one in which social justice remains the exception and widening economic inequality is unexceptional. We also know that the former is, in the world's public eye, found in global city-regions, the very place in which the latter condition is most extreme. Globalization, with its associated market and information processes, still appears as an integrated but largely unregulated paradigm whose workings upon national and substate city-regions have yet to be played through.

Over the past decade, and using country comparisons both within and among countries, member states of the OECD have increasingly acknowledged the obvious reality that not all regions are equally gifted with development potential (Pieterse 2004: 66–69; Held and McGrew 2002: 84-85;

Keating 2001: 376-79). The ensuing advice has had three components: (1) it is unwise continually to buttress a declining industrial base; (2) specific territories have their own particular advantages whose potential can be maximized; and (3) city-regions for reasons of accessibility, efficient form, mobility, and population skills are normally an appropriate centre for larger territorial development. Yet, for the necessary cost-effective service provisions and infrastructure support to be put into effect remains a local community, and hardly central government, mandate. Sufficient resources are seldom available for all. Ergo, central (federal) governments will have to choose to designate which regions are growth priorities in an international environment, and there will be those that lose out. This becomes the impossible political choice for both levels of community.

The persistent struggle for relative advantage between nations and among regions sustains inequality inasmuch as there is no global institution with the power to enforce a redistribution of world wealth. While trade recipient consumers in post-industrial societies may hope to export their own labour and living standards, these options are hardly those which compel Third World leaders: "These sobering realities lead to the conclusion that it is only within the borders of the state ... that legitimate and effective solutions to the problem of global social injustice can be constructed" (Held and McGrew 2002: 87). While even relatively small national states like Malaysia, but not subordinate city-regions, can influence and shape the free market, global cultural, and anti-hierarchical democratic tendencies of neoliberalism in the short term, this remains more like irrational behaviour than real choice over the long haul.

As to information and cultural dissemination, it was once the case in the aftermath of the Second World War that a sort of single world standard was maintained by, and for, a small, influential, and usually tolerant internationally cosmopolitan elite by the BBC World News or Radio Canada International. Today, far more widely accessible information has collapsed this paradigm, simultaneously creating multiple demands on local authorities for new or better service standards while weakening traditional local elite controls that dampen expectations. This again reminds us that one insidious consequence of the new global model of concentrated media ownership and subsequent centralized convergence of news-gathering activity has been a marked decline in the resources directed to local community. Coverage of city news, community leaders, and public policy debates is seldom remotely adequate. In the developed liberal democracies, local institutional memory of the context for past policy choices is crippled as priorities shift from the serious to the comedic, and the community's news is reduced to entertainment.

While "leaders" in global cities may appear to want to engage in debate with people in international business and global financiers over social futures, redistributive policies, and economic and spatial dislocations, there seems to date little coherence in what consequence might result. Are mayors actually city leaders, and what is the reach of their political authority? Who are they consistently most likely to represent? Will central governments continue to erode the formal authority of the municipal? Is the municipal level more likely to be innovative? But, then again, will such innovation be at the expense of real equity in public policy applications?

Effective self-government means more than political space and partial autonomy; it requires some measure of relative equality, genuine opportunities for self-realization, and a politics beyond the single policy to encompass a range of issues that matter. Genuine debates will most likely be rooted in the neighbourhoods of the world's cities. The municipal has, incredibly, become a major constituency in global politics. Possibly it is time for a network of mayors and councils, pressing for a voice, to be heard by circumventing the nation and moving around it directly onto the international stage.

Notes

1. A complete series of the articles filed by reporters David Pugliese and Jim Bronskill in the *Vancouver Sun* and *National Post* on events, reactions, and consequences is maintained at <http://www.fathers.ca/police_and_human_rights.htm>.

2. Under the leadership of Mayor Jan Reimer in 1992, Edmonton was the first large Canadian city to enlist city hall in an initiating and coordinating role for programs ranging from safe housing and spousal violence intervention teams to neighbourhood crime prevention and youth justice committees. Internationally, information about initiatives is disseminated through the auspices of the United Nations Environment Program (UNEP/GRID) <http://www.grida.no/newsroom.cfm?pressReleaseItemID=529>. For Canada consult <http://www.crime-prevention.org/ncpc>. This is the website of the National Crime Prevention Council.

glossary

administrative leadership: Effective managerial guidance that is more than aimless survival; as caretakers of an inherited political order, administrators work effectively through established structures to consolidate gains from new initiatives and to build incrementally.

amalgamation: The combination of two or more municipalities into a single unit of local government.

annexation: A process by which land is separated from the political control of one municipality (usually rural) and assigned to another local government's authority. Both municipalities continue to exist even though one is larger and the other smaller in size.

arms' length authorities: Once labelled blue-ribbon panels of "expert men," these are formal entities appointed by elected officials to remove a narrow subject range of potentially controversial public policy issues from their own directly political resolution.

assessment: Arcane practice of determining the "actual" or "market" value of property for municipal taxation purposes, differently done in each province so that no similar two properties will be valued in the same way if one moves across the country.

at-large election: A city electoral system by which all positions subject to election will be voted upon by all eligible electors.

board of control: A form of political executive required of larger Ontario cities until 1970. Comprised usually of four controllers elected city-wide, plus the mayor, the board's powers over financial matters could only be defeated by a two-thirds vote of council of which they were also members.

boosterism: The activities of those whose unbridled support for a community's sustained growth is assessed solely by commercial measures. For these people, the role of local government is to support expansion by the community's entrepreneurs at the expense of any and all other objectives (social, cultural, environmental).

boss rule: In the United States, for the century beginning about 1840, city politics were dominated from the top down by a small coalition of ward or borough political party officers often personified by a single, usually non-elected leader or boss.

bourgeois ethic: To Banfield and Wilson (1966), these middle-class ideals define local government as a cooperative search for objective but specific policies to benefit the community as a whole with governing arrangements based on non-partisanship, at-large elections, the city manager, master planning, and metropolitan area government.

boxcar loadings: One measure (a short-hand for manufacturing production) used by the business and commercial sectors of year-to-year economic growth as a test of a productive city administration. Such an approach is closely associated with **boosterism** beliefs.

bylaw: The formal means by which city councils operationalize policy which, like a bill passed through the federal or provincial legislature, requires three readings before being enacted and made law.

cadre party: An organization focused exclusively on the winning of elections by controlling all functions and activities from candidate recruitment through striking the platitudinous platform oriented toward that end.

Census Metropolitan Areas (CMAs): Statistics Canada has defined these for statistical purposes as a built-up central urban core, plus its working day commuter-shed, of 100,000 or more population.

central-local relations: A European phrase used to describe the distribution of formal and political authority between local administration and the wider area state government.

centralists: Those interested in city-regional governing who argue for a general merger of multiple existing municipalities.

charisma: An extreme manifestation of transformational leadership, this phenomenon is relatively rare and occurs when a leader has the capacity to excite the imagination of others, thus heightening their expectations. Charismatic leaders emerge during stressful periods, articulating a comprehensive vision so inclusive of their followers that it appears acceptable as a radical agenda for improvement. The necessary component validating charismatic leadership is followers in what becomes a social movement; the leaders in turn validate these social movements.

citizen-amateur: In city politics, a term describing those people who choose frequently to participate in local policy-making processes by standing for public office, but who resolutely refuse to admit any other political ambition, presumably distancing themselves from any stigma which by implication surrounds those who seek federal or provincial power.

citizen engagement: A contemporary usage to describe non-elected citizen involvement in elements of the policy process, ranging from consultation through to actual partnership with state agencies in the delivery of a specific service.

city-county consolidation: In the United States, this is a means to extend city-level services to its fringe, normally unincorporated, territories. It usually leaves existing municipalities intact and so is akin to a major annexation coincident with the surrounding county's borders.

city hall beat (the): The story assignment for those reporters and columnists given topics in local government and coverage of council proceedings.

city-region: Used as a synonym for a **CMA**. In Canada, this refers to an urban core plus trading hinterland of 100,000 or more people. Although one city is usually the focus, the region may contain many other municipal governments containing the larger part of the population.

clientelism: The reciprocal exchange between mainly elected officials and particular groups in the general population with the former offering selective access to public goods and the latter returning the favour by working to support their benefactors' electoral prospects.

commission board: A form of municipal management introduced into prairie cities early in the twentieth century and employing a small team of professional managers, usually three or four, instead of a single professional; typically, there is one commissioner for hard services, another for social and protective services, and a third for finance, personnel, and long-term planning.

community committees: An idea rooted in American neighbourhood government concepts, intended to decentralize the administration of a few selected services in large unitary municipalities (Winnipeg, Toronto, Montreal) to small, geographically defined council subcommittees presumed more susceptible to direct influence by citizens.

community cosmopolitans: Those individuals whose professional and business links make them aware of new policy developments elsewhere which encourage them to assess local practices against those found in other similar communities.

conditional grant: Sometimes known as a **shared-cost** or grant-in-aid program, this is a generic term to describe one government's partial financial support of another's projects or programs if the donor's requirements are met.

contracting for services: This means that councils are prepared to contract with private-sector service providers to satisfy different functional areas of their mandate.

co-production of service: Public-private partnerships (PPP) in service delivery often involving non-governmental organizations (NGOs) in which a municipality diverts staff resources, partial funding, or other subsidy in support of the NGO's taking primary delivery responsibility for a particular specialized service, reflecting the belief that a municipality need not produce a service in order to provide it

council-committee model: The *modus operandi* of towns and smaller suburban cities, by which a number of permanent committees of councillors provides oversight for the operations of one or two municipal departments, working through the contentious details outside council chambers, and relying on councillors to develop specialized "knowledge" and issue familiarity through long service on particular committees.

Council of Government (COG): The application to metropolitan area governing of a policy coordinating model akin to the United Nations in which sovereign governments exercise full autonomy, and decisions to be implemented require voluntary unilateral action.

Crown charter: Dating to the feudal period, corporate towns (boroughs) formed on the basis of a charter from the Crown which granted these areas the privileges of their own administration, magistrates, and ownership of corporate properties (like town halls).

economic multiplier: Based on statistical modelling, a projection of the net benefits that will accrue to a given community from the investment of public funds to build a facility or to host a major event.

electoral system: The framework for the selection of legislators within representative democracy which determines the size, number, and number of representatives for electoral divisions, and the rules for casting and tabulating votes.

federations of municipalities: A theory for metropolitan governing akin to classic federalism in which powers are divided between an area-wide and smaller autonomous substates (which retain their original constitutions), both levels co-existing while exercising "coordinate and independent" authority directly on the population.

gerrymander: Assuming that past voting behaviours will carry forward, this means the configuring of electoral district boundaries so as to favour one party by spreading its electors in a plurality position across a number of ridings, with the opposition support clustered into a few districts won by large margins.

governance: Originally a term describing the complex relationships among government departments, policy networks, NGOs, and powerful private actors in public policy-making, it has been usurped by neo-liberals to describe the collaborative provision of basic services through the private sector.

grassroots democracy: The generic term for directly participatory policy citizenship, used by political campaigners from all ideological persuasions to imply wide elector support for their positions; contemporary advocates of more direct democracy assert this to describe the forces behind any popular initiative.

home rule: In the Untied States, the granting of autonomy, within state constitutions, to incorporated municipalities. Originally intended to curb the caprice, or indifference, or patronage powers of political partisans in state legislatures over cities' operations, home rule became the single most powerful weapon protecting cities' special status as suburbs surrounding a core city against amalgamation.

honest graft: The profit that flowed to office-holders from advance information on future government actions (no money is directly stolen from the treasury); akin to insider trading on Bay Street today.

horizontal intergovernmental relations: The pattern of interactions in a given area among governments with roughly the same measure of formal and functional authority.

hyper-fractionalized quasi-subordination: Regional governing by devolution of functional authority to multiple functionally specialized agencies, with any coordination of regional policies attained through an ongoing process of **satisficing** and consensus-building.

ideology: A comprehensive, internally consistent association of ideas through which people make sense of the world and which provides both an explanation of existing circumstances and a sense of possible future direction.

incorporation: The forming of an organization with powers stipulated, and restricted, by the Acts of a superior legislative body. Local governments in Canada are incorporated under provincial statutes.

incrementalism: The dominant style in Canadian public policy-making through which much depends on precedent, gradually developing new programs from the established roots of existing political accomplishments.

indirect election: A system in which officials directly elected as councillors to general purpose municipal governments are also delegated to separate boards or agencies where they act autonomously to make public policy choices even though one step removed from direct accountability for those activities.

institutional memory: The shared knowledge of persons and offices within long-established organizations provides common reference points for new ideas and a quick test for the result of similar activities in the past.

iron law of oligarchy: Roberto Michels's (1949) observation that no matter how participatory the founding principles of any well-developed social organization, there is an inherent tendency to hierarchical social control from the clique at the apex of authority.

laissez-faire: A term dating from the eighteenth century meaning "leave to do." It is generally used to describe government policies of limited intervention in society and the economy.

Lakewood Plan: An American term describing the polycentric governing of large city-regions by the use of contracts for services, in the first instance from the county level of government.

left to right spectrum: An easy shorthand to denote the ideology of political gladiators in which the right, or conservative position, represents the more status quo associations, and the left stands for social democratic challenges to existing state redistributive public policies so as to enhance social welfare programs, expand progressive taxation, and increase state intervention in managing the economy.

letterhead Liberals: In non-partisan campaigns, the use of prominent local gladiators from federal parties other than the candidate's to showcase broad appeal, people valued not only for their sage strategic advice and contacts but also for their public relations value.

liberal democracy: A form of democratic institutions based on values of individualism, private property, and economic competition to yield a popular sovereignty based on political equality. These values are explicitly stipulated in the Charter of Rights and Freedoms (1982).

machine politics: The systemic partisan operation whose methodical, highly disciplined hierarchy of authority right to the level of the polling station gave the appearance of a permanent social organization. The machine was focused on winning control of the public treasury; power lay in an ability to control the vote of people who placed less value on it than on what the machine provided in exchange (see also **boss rule**).

mandatory powers: Those responsibilities, or functions, which central authorities require that any incorporated local government undertake at a particular standard; the earliest examples were largely in areas of public health (controlling typhoid) and sanitation, public education, and policing.

mass party: A party focused on principles, tending to be devoted to policy while developing hierarchical and centralized operations.

Megacity: A popular nickname assigned in 1996, by its opponents, to a provincial government initiative for a new structure unifying the City of Toronto, its surrounding suburbs, and the regional metropolitan government.

metropolis: A synonym for a "large city-region," usually the main city and sometimes the capital of a substate region or country.

metropolitan system: A socially and economically integrated urbanized territory focused on a well-developed city core, often including industrially specialized and "lifestyle" suburbs as well as an urbanizing but quasi-rural commuter-shed.

mission statement: Ideally, a concise outline of an organization's broad purpose for existing and a general strategy for realizing more clearly optimal results.

negative state: This seldom used term describes a period that was not the antithesis but a precursor of the positive state, a time during which the principal role of state authorities was to prevent and punish crime and to protect the realm (defence and trade).

neo-conservatism: This post-1980s ideology, sometimes called the "new right," has jettisoned the social conscience of historic conservatism to focus on marketplace economics and is susceptible to the social conservatism of fundamentalist religious leaders sometimes expressed as "family values."

neo-liberalism: A political ideology, grounded in consumerism and free markets; driven by the economic phenomenon of modern capitalism; requiring minimum government interference with markets, social life, and the personal initiative of citizens; this is combined with a belief in the flattening of any collective, hierarchical organizations which seek to coerce the state into social or economic interventions.

new citizen social movements: Fluctuating coalitions of individuals, less formally organized than traditional pressure groups, linked by their shared self-identification at the margins of policy debates (for example, environmentalists, gays and lesbians), who seek through public advocacy to introduce particular policy issues into the mainstream of political debate.

new localism: A term used to explain a variety of both collective (and individual) initiatives in economic development and political action at the level of the community. An analogous 1970s term was "neighbourhood government."

NIMBY (not in my back yard): A local community's reactive objection to policies and plans which the neighbours see as damaging to the quality of life in their immediate vicinity.

nostalgia: Derived from the ancient Greek root *nostos*, or a melancholic longing for the home village, this is a stubborn contemporary belief that the city life is not as worthy as the rural, and, as such, it is evil, debilitating, and corrosive of the soul.

oligarchy: The term comes from Aristotle's six-part taxonomy of governing by one or the many, in their own interest or for the general community. Oligarchy is the government of the city by the few in their own self-interest.

parliamentary supremacy: One principle which sustains Canadian parliamentary government, which means that no sitting legislature can bind the hands of any successor because, logically, that second parliament would be supreme in *its* own time.

particularized community: A community in which social and economic cleavages divide citizens into groups on particular public issues.

partisanship: The active identification by an individual with a party (or cause) which, in turn, and the more strongly it is felt, guides that person's participation in all aspects of political life.

permissive powers: Each province permits local governments to do certain things if the council wishes, but it is under no statutory obligation to do so. Larger cities have been willing to exercise the full orbit of possible jurisdictions while smaller suburbs with more homogenous populations make more selective choices.

Pleasantville: The antithesis of a **metropolis**, Pleasantville is a metaphor for America's embrace of traditional small town family values; the 1998 movie of this name is a perfect allegory for the concept.

policy community: Paul Pross (1992) developed this term to describe specialized publics which are permitted by the general community to dominate decision-making in sectors of policy where they have demonstrated technical or professional competence.

policy slippage: This describes the circumstance when a public policy fails to produce its expected outcome, falls short of optimal objectives, or yields entirely unanticipated consequences.

policy system: While similar to a **political system**, the policy system is focused primarily on all persons, activities, and institutions that work to achieve allocative, redistributive, and prohibitive public policies.

political culture: The pattern of orientations toward political objects held by members of a political community, how people think about political authority, what things they know about it (true or not), and why they feel the way they do about the entire operation.

political efficacy: In politics, the feeling by a person that participation in a particular process will yield positive policy consequences. The antonym is phrased, "You can't fight City Hall!"

political gateway: The inside realm for legitimate political debate over public policy ideas, from a point of radical concept before, to acceptance and conventional state obligation after passage through the gate into the world of incremental upgrades.

political gladiators: Comprising under 5 per cent of the population, these people are those for whom electoral politics constitutes almost a full-time avocation.

political ideology: A coherent structure of beliefs and values which serves to justify a person's position on the economic and social policies of a place or period.

political innovation: Defined here as more than something not tried in this spot before, specifically to encompass the radical challenge to hierarchy, existing social and economic order, and established routines.

political leadership: Innovation in the ability to engage the political resources of citizens to deploy the power of the state in the enduring struggle with the natural environment, dysfunctional historic circumstances, or the power centred in other social and economic institutions.

political pressure group: Any organization which attempts to influence public policies through the application of political resources.

political resources: As defined by Robert Dahl (1961), these may be anything employed to sway the specific choice or the strategies of another individual.

political socialization: The cultural process by which members of a society instill into newcomers to their community (that is, children and immigrants) their collective goals and individual norms for behaviour, especially a set of expectations concerning citizenship and public service.

political spin: The attempt by political tacticians to spread their interpretation of political events among reporters (also known as propaganda).

political system: The complex of public institutions and processes which frames the authoritative allocation of scarce resources and defining values in the community.

polycentric metropolitan system: A **CMA** which has assumed its demographic shape while being governed by multiple municipalities.

populism: Any political movement that subscribes to the idea of empowering "the common man" against the influences of big interests, be they government, labour unions, or large corporations. Populist movements are susceptible to **charismatic** leadership.

positive state: Government institutions are expected to minimize individuals' social and economic stress through widely applied but incrementally developed interventionist and redistributive policies; the state provides a kind of insurance against the excesses of a free market economy.

press conference: A scheduled gathering of the **press gallery** at which time a public personality normally presents a statement and responds to reporters' questions.

press gallery: A generic term used to describe the many reporters and pundits whose particular focus is one realm of government like the provincial legislature or city hall.

private-public partnerships (PPP): This 1990s notion, sometimes called co-production of service, means that government works in partnership with neighbourhood associations, service clubs, private agencies, and even business corporations to provide or maintain a facility or service at lower cost and with a presumed greater sensitivity to consumer need.

procedural ethics: Elected officials are assessed by process rules governing ethical conduct. Conflict-of-interest guidelines become stringently stipulated, not "understood"; their enforcement by the unimpeachable stands open and absolute; and sanctions become swift and severe. The objective is enforced democratic fairness and integrity.

property tax: In Canada, one of the longest standing forms of taxation, this tax is levied as an annual charge by municipalities against the owners of real property with the tax rate, known as the "mill rate," being expressed in dollars (or mills) per $1,000 of assessed value.

public corporation: This nineteenth-century model for local administration, with long British roots, saw it as an incorporated entity under a separate **Crown charter**. This gave local communities a vehicle for governing their own most immediate affairs directly, balancing central authority with municipal necessity.

public ethos: A single dominant pattern of shared beliefs that asserts such dominion over the public mood that it stands alone as the all-legitimating and conventional belief system of a people or period.

public ideology: The general thinking of those groups which are dominant in any society at a given time; if contrasting public opinions are so marginal as not to impinge on **public policy**, then the public ideology becomes "common sense."

public policy: The principal consequence of the workings of the political system, this is the dependent variable which in one way or another all of the social sciences try to explain.

QUANGO: A British term standing for a quasi-autonomous non-governmental agency, describing an appointed body with wider area regulatory, service delivery, service coordinating, quasi-judicial, or promotional mandate.

quasi-independent regulatory agency: A body, existing outside the formal provincial government structure, whose officers are order-in-council appointments with a mandate to make policy within a narrowly defined area of government.

radical libertarianism: A political philosophy of personal autonomy based on a belief in an individual's inalienable rights including the right to own property and oriented to reversing all interventionist and collective policies of the modern state. In extreme statements, taxation is viewed as "forced labour."

regional districts: Created individually by letters patent since legislated by British Columbia in 1965 and intended as a means to provide municipal services to two dozen urban centres and their trading hinterlands; the most developed are the Greater Vancouver RD and the Capital (Victoria) RD.

reverse pressure group: A formal organization created or fed resources by public officials so as to become more effective in directing those officials to policy stances they themselves sought in the first place.

rural angst: Rural residents have been passionate for their own bucolic quasi-agrarian way-of-life, fuelled by further belief that an urban existence is inherently wicked. City dwellers are viewed with a mixture of contempt and suspicion as a policy conspiracy against rural electors (see **nostalgia**).

satellite suburbs: Autonomous municipalities, frequently homogenous in socioeconomic terms, within a **CMA**, whose very being is contingent upon the existence of the core city.

satisficing: Coined by Herbert Simon (1945), this word combines the verbs "to satisfy" and "to suffice" to describe circumstances under which public policy-makers choose to accept merely satisfactory rather than optimum levels of performance and results.

section 92.8: Section 92 of the Constitution Act (1982) establishes that "In each Province the Legislature may exclusively make Laws in relation to Matters coming within the Classes of Subject next … enumerated," and subsection 8 stipulates "Municipal Institutions in the Province."

shared-cost programs: Another type of **conditional grant** which requires that the recipient government or organization will pony up a portion of the costs.

slate-making: A party-like activity in which organized groups such as the Chamber of Commerce vet and publish a list of candidates generally sympathetic to their policy ambitions.

social democrats: A European label for socialist parties that is intended to differentiate their organizations from the totalitarian inclinations of twentieth-century communism while sharing a common origin in Marxist thought. The political objective of an egalitarian society was to be realized through the democratic process while respecting a "mixed" economy.

special purpose districts (SPDs): A method of governing complex **city-regions** as the professional staffs of separate municipalities realize that common services must be provided and that the efficiencies and economies of scale can be realized if authority to provide these is delegated from established local councils to a quasi-autonomous agency by means of legally negotiated intermunicipal agreements.

spending power: Defined in federal constitutions with reasonable precision, this determines how the two levels of the state (the centre and the substate regions) may raise money and upon what they may spend it.

spiffs: A variant of open bribery, where businessmen give contracts to friends and relatives, manufacturers woo purchasing agents with gifts, and store managers are paid cash (spiffs) for pushing a brand of merchandise.

stakeholders: A group of individuals who have identified a common interest in a portion of the more general public interest. They may consider themselves as having a common, sometimes a proprietary, interest in a specific policy arena.

strong mayor: One variant of the 1900 American municipal reform platform which provides the mayor with the powers of Chief Executive, including the power to prepare the budget, appoint senior administration, and, in some cases, to veto council decisions. This system does not exist in Canada.

strong party organization: In American cities such as Boston and Chicago political organizations with roots in the classic machines of the boss era exhibit continuity over time, reward supporters in material and symbolic terms, use an hierarchical organization which promotes personnel from within, and are able to offer candidates for all levels of the state.

task force: A body appointed by governing authorities to focus consideration of quite specific public policy questions. Wide public representation combined with the policy's specialists and an open process leading to consensual findings will usually produce explicit recommendations to be implemented.

tax exporting: A circumstance which occurs when property subject to taxation in one municipality is to be paid by persons or corporations resident elsewhere.

Total Quality Management: Taken from recent efforts to develop a "new public management," the TQM concept implies that the public service should emulate the innovative and cost-conscious practices of private-sector entrepreneurs, including business plans, a customer service orientation, and benchmarks by which to assess performance.

transfer payments: The generic term for a monetary grant from one government jurisdiction to another which may either be entered into the latter's general revenues or have specific spending conditions attached.

underclass: The relatively permanent subsistence-level class, perhaps the population's poorest fifth, of urban residents whose earning power has been eroded but who, no matter how energetic, do not possess the skills to benefit from the new economy.

Unicity: A popular nickname provided by journalists during the policy process in 1971 to the provincial government proposal for a new structure unifying the city of Winnipeg, its surrounding suburbs and the regional metropolitan government.

unitary metropolitan system: The centrist argument for city-region government reform equates greater efficiency and effectiveness with "one government for one city." A Canadian **CMA** could be considered unitary if 85 per cent of its population lived within the core city.

unconditional grant: A transfer of funds from one government with greater taxation resources into the general revenues of another with no strings attached as to how the money may be spent.

urban pathology: The twentieth-century social science endeavour to provide diagnosis and institutional prescription against the malady of city dwelling.

urban regime: Associated with the work of Clarence Stone (1989, 1995), a dominant coalition of institutional elites, differently constituted in each city-region, whose particular access to resources enables public bodies and private interests to function together in making and implementing governing decisions.

veto authority: Some interest clusters within the urban regime, perhaps the Chamber of Commerce, may be said to constitute a veto authority: when their specific support is vital if a political demand is to proceed towards any sort of positive resolution.

weak mayor: Beyond the chairing of council meetings and the *ex officio* right to attend all city committee and board meetings, the mayor's formal power is no greater than that of any other councillor although being elected **at-large** may grant heightened personal prestige.

world city: A large urban agglomeration whose world standing is generally defined by its corporate services sector having achieved pre-eminence in its transnational linkages.

zero-sum game: From games theory, a situation in which there is an absolute winner and loser. For one party to emerge victorious, the other party must lose an equivalent amount.

references

Abizadeh, Sohrab and John Gray. 1992. "Politics and Provincial Government Spending in Canada." *Canadian Public Administration* 35, 4 (Winter): 519-33.

Abu-Laban, Yasmeen. 1997. "Ethnic Politics in a Global Metropolis: The Case of Vancouver." In Thomas 1997, 77-95.

Advisory Commission on Intergovernmental Relations (ACIR). 1976. *Improving Urban America: A Challenge to Federalism*. Washington, DC.

Alinsky, Saul. 1971. *Rules for Radicals: A Practical Primer for Realistic Radicals*. New York: Random House.

Andrew, Caroline. 1983. "Ottawa-Hull." In Magnusson and Sancton 1983, 140-165.

——. 1995. "Provincial-Municipal Relations; Or, Hyper-Fractionalized Quasi-Subordination Revisited." In Lightbody 1995, 137-60.

——. 1997. "Globalization and Local Action." In Thomas 1997, 139-50.

Arnstein, Sherry. 1969. "A Ladder of Citizen Participation." *Journal of the American Institute of Planners* 35, 4 (July): 216-24.

Artibise, Alan F.J. 1975. *Winnipeg: A Social History of Urban Growth, 1874-1914*. Montreal: McGill-Queen's University Press.

Axworthy, Lloyd. 1980. "The Best Laid Plans Oft Go Astray: The Case of Winnipeg." In *Problems of Change in Urban Government*, ed. M.O. Dickerson, S. Drabek, and J.T. Woods. Waterloo, ON: Wilfrid Laurier University Press. 105-23.

Axworthy, Lloyd and Angus Reid. 1979. *Edmonton Area Survey Analysis*. Winnipeg: Institute of Urban Studies, University of Winnipeg.

Axworthy, Thomas. 1974. "Winnipeg Unicity." In *A Look to the North: Canadian Regional Experience*, ed. Guthrie Birkhead. Washington, DC: Advisory Commission on Intergovernmental Relations. 89-108.

Bachrach, Peter. 1967. *The Theory of Democratic Elitism*. Boston, MA: Little, Brown and Company.

Bachrach, Peter and Morton Baratz. 1962. "The Two Faces of Power." *American Political Science Review* LVI, 4 (December): 947-52.

——. 1963. "Decisions and Nondecisions: An Analytical Framework." *American Political Science Review* LVII, 3 (September): 632-42.

Banfield, Edward C. 1957. "The Politics of Metropolitan Area Organization." *Midwest Journal of Political Science* I, 2 (May): 77-91.

Banfield, Edward C. and James Q. Wilson. 1963, 1966. *City Politics*. New York: Alfred A. Knopf, Vintage Books.

Baxter, James. 2003. "Municipal Governments Show the most Leadership, Canadians Believe." *Daily Bulletin*, Kimberley, BC (January 21).

Beazley, Doug. 1999. "Bribery claims aren't news to veteran city hall watchers." *Edmonton Sun*, 24 April.

Bentley, Arthur F. 1908. *The Process of Government*. Chicago, IL: University of Chicago Press.

Bettison, David G. 1975. *The Politics of Canadian Urban*

Development. Edmonton: University of Alberta Press.

Bish, Robert L. 1971. *The Public Economy of Metropolitan Areas.* Chicago, IL: Rand-McNally.

Bish, Robert L. and Vincent Ostrom. 1973. *Understanding Urban Government: Metropolitan Reform Reconsidered.* Washington, DC: American Enterprise Institute for Public Policy Research.

Bish, Robert L. and Robert Warren. 1972. "Scale and Monopoly Problems in Urban Government Services." *Urban Affairs Quarterly* 8 (September): 97-122.

Black, Edwin R. and Alan C. Cairns. 1966. "A Different Perspective on Canadian Federalism." *Canadian Public Administration* 9, 1 (Winter): 27-44.

Bondanella, Peter, ed. 1984. *The Prince* [Niccolò Machiavelli]. Oxford: Oxford University Press.

Bollens, J.C. and H.J. Schmandt. 1982 *The Metropolis: Its People, Politics, and Economic Life.* 4th ed. New York: Harper and Row.

Borins, Justice J. 1997. *In the Ontario Court of Justice* Judgment *re: Challenge to the* City of Toronto Act 1997, S.O. 1997, c. 2.

Boschken, Herman L. 2001. "Upper Middle-Class Politics and Policy Outcomes: Does Class Identity Matter?" In Clark and Lipset, 225-48.

Boudreau, Julie-Anne. 2000. *The Megacity Saga: Democracy and Citizenship in This Global Age.* Montreal: Black Rose Books.

Brownstone, Meyer and T.J. Plunkett. 1983. *Metropolitan Winnipeg: Politics and Reform of Local Government.* Berkeley, CA: University of California Press.

Bryce, James. 1888 [1995]. *The American Commonwealth.* 2 vols, ed. Gary L. McDowell. Indianapolis, IN: The Liberty Fund.

Brundtland, Gro Harlem, ed. 1987. *Our Common Future.* Geneva: World Commission on Environment and Development.

Bulpitt, J.G. 1967. *Party Politics in English Local Government.* London: Longmans, Green.

Bunting, Trudi and Pierre Filion, eds. 1991. *Canadian Cities in Transition.* Toronto: Oxford University Press.

Bureau of Municipal Research (BMR). 1968. *Local Government and the Report of the Ontario Committee on Taxation.* Toronto: BMR.

—. 1970. *Neighbourhood Participation in Local Government.* Toronto: BMR.

—. 1975. *Citizen Participation in Metro Toronto: Climate for Co-operation?* Toronto: BMR.

Burns, James MacGregor. 1978. *Leadership.* New York: Harper and Row.

Byrne, Tony. 1994. *Local Government in Britain.* 6th ed. Harmondsworth, UK: Penguin Books.

Canada's Cities. 2003. <http://www.canadascities.ca/background.htm>.

Canadian Encyclopedia, The. 3 vol. 1985. Edmonton: Hurtig.

Canadian Federation of Mayors and Municipalities (CFMM). 1976. *Puppets on a Shoestring: The Effects on Municipal Government of Canada's System of Public Finance.* Ottawa: CFMM, 28 April.

Canadian Tax Foundation (CTF). 2004. "Tax 101." *Finances of the Nation.* <http://www.ctf.ca>.

Castells, M. 1996. *The Rise of the Network Society.* Oxford: Blackwell.

—. 1997. *The Power of Identity.* Oxford: Blackwell.

Chomsky, Noam. 1999. *The New Military Humanism.* Cambridge, MA: South End Press.

Clark, Terry Nichols. 1994a. "Race and Class versus the New Political Culture." In Clark 1994b, 21-78.

—. 1994b. *Urban Innovation: Creative Strategies for Turbulent Times.* Thousand Oaks, CA: Sage.

—. 1998a. "Assessing the New Political Culture by Comparing Cities Around the World." In Clark and Hoffmann-Martinot 1998, 93-191.

—. 1998b. "Is There Really a New Political Culture: Evidence from Major Historical Developments of Recent Decades." In Clark and Hoffmann-Martinot, 75-92.

—. 2003. "Transforming Political Systems and Political Culture: What Works? Lessons from Bogotá and Cities Around the World." Presented to International Seminar on Bogotá: Political System and Political Culture. Bogotá, Columbia, July 29-31.

Clark, Terry Nichols and Edward G. Goetz. 1994. "The Antigrowth Machine: Can City Governments Control, Limit, or Manage Growth?" In Clark 1994b, 105-45.

Clark, Terry Nichols and Vincent Hoffman-Martinot, eds. 1998. *The New Political Culture.* Boulder, CO: Westview.

Clark, Terry Nichols, and Ronald Inglehart. 1998. "The New Political Culture: Changing Dynamics of Support for the Welfare State and Other Policies in Postindustrial Societies." In Clark and Hoffman-Martinot 1998, 9-72.

Clark, Terry Nichols and Seymour Martin Lipset, eds. 2001. *The Breakdown of Class Politics: A Debate on Post-Industrial Stratficiation.* Washington, DC: Woodrow Wilson Center Press.

Clark, Terry Nichols, Seymour Martin Lipset, and Michael Rempel. 2001. "The Declining Political Significance of Social Class." In Clark and Lipset, eds. 2001, 77-104.

Clarke, Susan E. 1993. "The New Localism: Local Politics in a Global Era." In Goetz and Clarke, 1-21.

Clarkson, Stephen. 1972a. "Barriers to Entry of Political Parties into Toronto Politics." In *Emerging Party Politics in Urban Canada,* ed. J.K. Masson and J.D. Anderson. Toronto: McClelland and Stewart. 158-81.

—. 1972b. *City Lib: Parties and Reform.* Toronto: Hakkert.

Clement, Wallace. 1975. *The Canadian Corporate Elite: An Analysis of Economic Power.* Toronto: McClelland and Stewart.

Colton, Timothy. 1980. *Big Daddy: Frederick G. Gardiner and the Building of Metropolitan Toronto.* Toronto: University of Toronto Press.

Cook, Ramsay. 1979. "A Prairie Progressive." *Saturday Night* (October): 78.

Crawford, Kenneth G. 1954. *Canadian Municipal Government.* Toronto: University of Toronto Press.

Craig, Gerard M., ed. 1964 [1839]. *Lord Durham's Report: An Abridgment of Report on the Affairs of British North America.* Toronto: McClelland and Stewart.

Dahl, Robert. 1961. *Who Governs? Democracy and Power in an American City.* New Haven, CT: Yale University Press.

—. 1967. "The City in the Future of Democracy." *American Political Science Review* LXI, 4 (December): 953-70.

Dahl, R.A. and E.R. Tuft. 1973. *Size and Democracy.* Stanford, CA: Stanford University Press.

DelGuidice, D. and S.M. Zacks. 1968. *The 101 Governments of Metro Toronto.* Toronto: Bureau of Municipal Research.

Deputy Prime Minister, UK. 1997. *New Leadership for London: The Government's Proposals for a Greater London Authority.* London: HMSO (July).

de Tocqueville, Alexis. 1946. [1835]. *Democracy in America.* London: Oxford University Press.

Deutsch, Karl W. 1953. *Nationalism and Social Communication: An Inquiry into the Foundations of Nationality.* Cambridge, MA: MIT Press.

Donnelly, Murray S. 1963. *The Government of Manitoba.* Toronto: University of Toronto Press.

Draper, James A., ed. 1971. *Citizen Participation: Canada.* Toronto: New Press.

Dupré, J. Stefan. 1968. *Intergovernmental Finance in Ontario, a Provincial-level Perspective.* Toronto: Ontario Commission on Taxation, Government of Ontario.

Dunleavy, Patrick. 1980. *Urban Political Analysis.* London: Macmillan.

Duverger, Maurice. 1954. *Political Parties: Their Organization and Activity in the Modern State.* Trans. Barbara North and Robert North. London: Methuen.

Dye, Thomas R. 1964. "Urban Political Integration: Conditions Associated with Annexation in American Cities." *Midwest Journal of Political Science* 8, 4 (November): 430-46.

—. 1972. *Understanding Public Policy.* Englewood Cliffs, NJ: Prentice-Hall.

Easton, David. 1965. *A Systems Analysis of Political Life.* New York: Wiley.

Easton, Robert and Paul Tennant. 1969. "Vancouver Civic Party Leadership: Backgrounds, Attitudes, and Non-Civic Party Affiliations." *BC Studies* 2 (Summer): 19-29.

Edmonton, City of. 2003. "Development of the Current City of Edmonton Process of 'Billing for Dangerous Goods Clean-Up,'" 22 October.

Eldersveld, Samuel. 1964. *Political Parties: A Behavioral Analysis.* Chicago, IL: Rand, McNally.

England, Robert E. 2003. "City Managers and the Urban Bureaucracy." In Pelissero 2003, 196-216.

Faure, Alain. 2003. "Montreal, L'ile laboratoire les politiques publiques à l'épreuve du bien commun urbain." *Canadian Journal of Urban Research* 12, 1 (Summer): 35-57.

Federation of Canadian Municipalities (FCM), Intergovernmental Office. 1993. *Benefits of International Partnerships for Canadian Municipalities.* Ottawa: FCM.

—. 1996. *Two-Way Street: How International Municipal Cooperation Benefits Canadian Municipalities.* Ottawa: FCM.

Feldman, Lionel D. and Katherine A. Graham. 1979. *Bargaining for Cities: Municipalities and Intergovernmental Relations, An Assessment.* Toronto: Institute for Research on Public Policy.

Fenn, W. Michael. 2002. "Emerging Trends in Urban Affairs: A Municipal Manager's View." In *Urban Affairs: Back on the Policy Agenda,* ed. Caroline Andrew, Susan Phillips, and Katherine Graham. Montreal: McGill-Queen's University Press. 289-302.

Ferguson, Jock and Paul Taylor. 1987. "Lawyer grows wealthy on development lobbying."

Toronto *Globe and Mail,* 17 December.

Ferguson, Jock and Paul Taylor. 1988. "Speedy approvals benefit developers." Toronto *Globe and Mail,* 28 October.

Fiscal Austerity and Urban Innovation Project (FAUI). 2002. *International Survey Results.* Data are accessible from Terry Nichols Clark, tnc@spc.uchicago.edu.

Fish, Susan A. 1981. "Winning the Battle and Losing the War in the Fight to Improve Municipal Policy Making." In *Politics and Government of Urban Canada.* 4th ed., ed. Lionel D. Feldman. Toronto: Methuen. 90-101.

Florida, Richard. 2002. *The Rise of the Creative Class: And How It's Transforming Work, Leisure, Community and Everyday Life.* New York: Harper, Collins.

Foss, Krista. 2000. "Canadians at forefront of Web use in schools." Toronto *Globe and Mail,* 11 September.

Francis, Diane. 1999. "People Power makes a comeback via cyberspace: Jesse Ventura broke ground bypassing press." *The Financial Post (National Post),* 14 February.

Frank, 2004. "Ottawa employees rake in the dough." #427, 27 April.

Fraser, James W. 1984. "Mayor John F. Fitzgerald and Boston's Schools, 1905-13." *Historical Journal of Massachusetts,* 12 (June): 117-30.

Frisken, Frances. 1993. "Planning and Servicing the Greater Toronto Area: The Interplay of Provincial and Municipal Interests." In *Metropolitan*

Governance: American/Canadian Intergovernmental Perspectives, ed. Donald N. Rothblatt and Andrew Sancton. Berkeley, CA: Institute of Governmental Studies, University of California. 153-204.

—, ed. 1994. *The Changing Canadian Metropolis.* 2 vols. Berkeley, CA: Institute of Governmental Studies Press.

Gabriel, Oscar, Katja Ahlstich, Frank Brettschneider, and Volker Kunz. 1998. "Transformations in Policy Preferences of Local Officials." In Clark and Hoffmann-Martinot, eds., 219-34.

Garber, Judith A. 1997. "Frameworks of Inquiry: Local Government, Urban Politics, and in Social Movements." In Thomas 1997, 33-46.

Garber, J.A. and D.L. Imbroscio. 1996. "The 'Myth of the North American City' Reconsidered: Local Government Regimes in Canada and the United States." *Urban Affairs Review* 31: 595-624.

Gibbins, Roger and Loleen Youngman. 1996. *Mindscapes: Political Ideologies Towards the 21st Century.* Toronto: McGraw-Hill, Ryerson.

Gibbons, Kenneth M. 1976. "The Political Culture of Corruption in Canada." In *Political Corruption in Canada: Cases, Causes and Cures,* ed. D.C. Rowat and K.M. Gibbons. Toronto: McClelland and Stewart. 231-50.

Gidengil, Elisabeth and Richard Vengroff. 1997. "Representational Gains of Canadian Women or Token Growth? The Case of Quebec's

Municipal Politics." *Canadian Journal of Political Science* XXX, 3 (September): 511–37.

Goetz, Edward G. and Susan E. Clarke, eds. 1993. *The New Localism: Comparative Urban Politics in a Global Era.* Newbury Park, CA: Sage.

Graham, Katherine A., Susan Phillips, and Allan M. Maslove. 1998. *Urban Governance in Canada: Representation, Resources, and Restructuring.* Toronto: Harcourt, Brace.

Graham, K.A. and S.D. Phillips. 1997. "Citizen Engagement: Beyond the Customer Revolution." *Canadian Public Administration* 40, 2 (Summer): 255–73.

———, eds. 1998. *Citizen Engagement: Lessons in Participation from Local Government.* Toronto: Institute of Public Administration of Canada.

Granatstein, J.L. 1971. *Marlborough Marathon: One Street Against a Developer.* Toronto: A.M. Hakkert, James, Lewis and Samuel, Publishers.

Grant, Hugh and Arthur Sweetman. 2004. "Introduction to Economic and Urban Issues in Canadian Immigration Policy." *Canadian Journal of Urban Research* 13, 1 (Summer): 1–24.

Greene, Ian. 1991. "Allegations of Undue Influence in Canadian Politics." In Janet Hiebert, ed., *Political Ethics: A Canadian Perspective.* Volume 12 of the Research Studies for the Royal Commission on Electoral Reform and Party Financing. Toronto: Dundurn, 101–64.

Greene, Ian and Howard Shugarman. 1997. *Honest Politics: Seeking Integrity in Canadian Public Life.* Toronto: James Lorimer.

Greer, Scott. 1963. *Metropolitics: A Study of Political Culture.* New York: John Wiley and Sons.

Griffiths, Curt T. and Simon N. Verdun-Jones. 1994. *Canadian Criminal Justice.* 2nd ed. Toronto: Harcourt, Brace.

Gunton, Thomas, T.M. Frame, and J.C. Day. 2004. "Making Collaboration Work: Lessons from a Success Story in Regional Planning." Presented to the Western Regional Science Association, Wailea (February).

Gutstein, Donald. 1975. *Vancouver, Ltd.* Toronto: James Lorimer.

———. 1983. "Vancouver." In Magnusson and Sancton 1983, 189–221.

Hall, Peter. 2002. "Global City-regions in the Twenty-first Century." In Scott 2002, 59–77.

Hall, Stuart. 1991. "The Local and the Global: Globalization and Identity." In *Culture, Globalization and the World-System: Contemporary Conditions for Representation of Identity,* ed. Anthony D. King. London: Macmillan. 19–40.

Hamilton, Robert M. ed. 1952. *Canadian Quotations and Phrases.* Toronto: McClelland and Stewart.

Harding, Alan. 1995. "Elite Theory and Growth Machines." In Judge, Stoker and Wolman 1995, 35–53.

Harrigan, John J. 1993. *Political Change in the Metropolis.* 5th ed. New York: Harper Collins.

Harris, Nigel. 1971. *Beliefs in Society: The Problem of Ideology.* Harmondsworth, UK: Penguin Books.

Heath, Joseph. 2001. *The Efficient Society: Why Canada is as Close to Utopia as it Gets.* Scarborough: Penguin.

Heisz, Andrew and Logan McLeod. 2004. "Low Income in Census Metropolitan Areas." *Our Diverse Cities* 1 (Spring): 63–71.

Heisz, Andrew and Grant Schellenberg. 2004. "Public Transit Use Among Immigrants." *Canadian Journal of Urban Research* 13, 1 (Summer): 170–91.

Held, David and Anthony McGrew. 2002. *Globalization/Anti-Globalization.* Cambridge: Polity Press, Blackwell.

Herring, E. Pendleton, 1936. *Group Representation Before Congress: Public Administration and the Public Interest.* New York: McGraw-Hill.

Hewitt, W.E. 1999. "The Administrative Impact of International Municipal Cooperation on Canadian Cities and Towns: An Assessment." *Canadian Public Administration* 42, 3 (Fall): 312–30.

Hiebert, Janet, ed. 1991. *Political Ethics: A Canadian Perspective.* Toronto: Dundurn Press for the Royal Commission on Electoral Reform and Party Financing.

Higgins, Donald J.H. 1977. *Urban Canada: Its Government and Politics.* Toronto: Gage.

——. 1986. *Local and Urban Politics in Canada.* Toronto: Gage.

Hill, Richard Child. 1974. "Separate and Unequal: Governmental Inequality in the Metropolis." *American Political Science Review* LXVIII, 4 (December): 1557-68.

Hobbs, Heidi H. 1994. *City Hall Goes Abroad: The Foreign Policy of Local Politics.* Thousand Oaks, CA: Sage.

Hobson, Paul A.R. 1997. "Efficiency, Equity and Accountability Issues in Local Taxation." In *Urban Governance and Finance: A Question of Who Does What*, ed. Paul A.R. Hobson and France St-Hilaire. Montreal: Institute for Research on Public Policy. 113-32.

Hodge, Gerald. 1991. *Planning Canadian Communities: An Introduction to the Principles, Practice, and Participants.* Toronto: Nelson.

Hoffmann-Martinot, Vincent. 1998. "Urban Political Parties: Role and Transformation." In Clark and Hoffmann-Martinot 1998, 195-217.

Holden, Matthew. 1964. "The Governance of the Metropolis as a Problem in Diplomacy." *Journal of Politics* 26, 3 (August): 627-47.

Holston, James. 2002. "Urban Citizenship and Globalization." In Scott 2002, 325-48.

Hoogenboom, Ari. 1970. "Spoilsism and Reformers: Civil Service Reforms and Public Morality." In *Political Corruption: Readings in Comparative Analysis*, ed. A. Heidenheimer. New York: Holt, Rinehart and Winston. 276-83.

Hoogvelt, A. 2001. *Globalization and the Postcolonial World.* 2nd ed. Basingstoke, UK: Palgrave.

Hough, J. 1970. "Voters' Turnout and the Responsiveness of Local Government: The Case of Toronto, 1969." In *Politics: Canada.* 3rd ed., ed. Paul Fox. Toronto: McGraw-Hill, Ryerson. 284-96.

Howlett, Michael and M. Ramesh. 1995. *Studying Public Policy: Policy Cycles and Political Subsystems.* Toronto: Oxford University Press.

——. 2003. *Studying Public Policy: Policy Cycles and Political Subsystems.* 2nd ed. Toronto: Oxford University Press.

Hutton, Thomas A. 1998. *The Transformation of Canada's Pacific Metropolis: A Study of Vancouver.* Montreal: Institute for Research on Public Policy.

Isin, Engin. 1995. "The Origins of Canadian Municipal Government." In Lightbody 1995, 51-91.

Jacobs, Jane. 1997. "Affadavit of Jane Jacobs, O.C." Ontario Court of Justice, General Division, (8 May).

Jenson, Jane. 1991. "Citizenship and Equity: Variations Across Time and in Space." In *Political Ethics: A Canadian Perspective*, ed. Janet Hiebert. Research Study #12. Ottawa: Royal Commission on Electoral Reform and Party Financing, Ministry of Supply and Services. 195-228.

Jones, Victor. 1942. *Metropolitan Government.* Chicago, IL: University of Chicago Press.

Joyce, J.G. and H.A. Hossé. 1970. *Civic Parties in Canada.* Ottawa: CFMM.

Judd, Dennis R. 1988. *The Politics of American Cities: Private Power and Public Policy.* 3rd ed. Boston, MA: Scott, Foresman/Little, Brown.

Judge, David, Gerry Stoker, and Harold Wolman. 1995. *Theories of Urban Politics.* London: Sage.

Kaplan, Harold. 1965. *The Regional City.* Toronto: Canadian Broadcasting Corporation.

——. 1967. *Urban Political Systems: A Functional Analysis of Metro Toronto.* New York: Columbia University Press.

——. 1972. "The Policy Making Process in Metro Toronto." In *Politics and Government of Urban Canada: Selected Readings.* 2nd ed., ed. L.D. Feldman and M.D. Goldrick. Toronto: Methuen. 214-24.

——. 1982. *Reform, Planning, and City Politics: Montreal, Winnipeg, Toronto.* Toronto: University of Toronto Press.

Keating, Michael. 1995. "Size, Efficiency and Democracy: Consolidation, Fragmentation and Public Choice." In Judge, Stoker, and Wolman 1995, 117-34.

——. 2001. "Governing Cities and Regions: Territorial Restructuring in a Global Ages." In Scott 2001, 371-90.

Key, V.O. 1949. *Southern Politics.* New York: Alfred A. Knopf.

Kotler, Milton. 1968. *Neighbourhood Government: The Local*

Foundations of Political Life. New York: Bobbs-Merrill.

Kushner, Joseph, David Siegel, and Hannah Stanwick. 1997. "Ontario Municipal Elections: Voting Trends and Determinants of Electoral Success in a Canadian Province." *Canadian Journal of Political Science* XXX, 3 (September): 539-53.

Kwong, Wendy. 2004. "Health Access and Equity: A Local Perspective." *Our Diverse Cities* 1 (Spring): 107-08.

Langford, John and Allan Tupper, eds. 1993 *Corruption, Character and Conduct: Essays on Canadian Government Ethics.* Toronto: Oxford University Press.

Laskin, Bora. 1966. *Canadian Constitutional Law.* 3rd edition. Toronto: Carswell Co.

Latham, Earl. 1952. "The Group Basis of Politics: Notes for a Theory." *American Political Science Review* 46, 2 (Summer): 376-97.

Lea, John P. 1996. "Tourism, *Realpolitik* and Development in the South Pacific." In *Tourism, Crime and International Security Issues*, ed. A. Pizam and Y. Mansfeld. Chichester, UK: John Wiley. 123-42.

Lee, Eugene. 1960. *The Politics of Nonpartisanship.* Berkeley and Los Angeles, CA: University of California Press.

Leo, Christopher. 1977. *The Politics of Urban Development: Canadian Urban Expressway Disputes.* Toronto: The Institute of Public Administration of Canada.

—. 1995a. "Global Change and Local Politics: Economic Decline and the Local Regime in Edmonton." *Journal of Urban Affairs* 17, 3 (Fall): 277-99.

—. 1995b. "The State in the City: A Political-Economy Perspective on Growth and Decay." In Lightbody 1995, 27-50.

Leo, Christopher and Wilson Brown. 2000. "Slow Growth and Urban Development Policy." *Journal of Urban Affairs* 22, 2: 193-213.

Levine, Allan, ed. 1989. *Your Worship: The Lives of Eight of Canada's Most Unforgettable Mayors.* Toronto: Lorimer.

Lightbody, James. 1978a. "Electoral Reform in Local Government: The Case of Winnipeg." *Canadian Journal of Political Science* XI, 2 (June): 307-32.

—. 1978b. "The Reform of a Metropolitan Government: The Case of Winnipeg, 1971." *Canadian Public Policy* IV, 4 (Autumn): 489-504.

—. 1983. "Edmonton." In Magnusson and Sancton 1983, 255-90.

—. 1989. "'Wild Bill' Hawrelak: 'Let's Get Edmonton Rolling Again.'" In Levine 1989, 30-48.

—. 1993. "Cities: 'The Dilemmas on Our Doorsteps.'" In Langford and Tupper 1993, 197-216.

—., ed. 1995. *Canadian Metropolitics: Governing Our Cities.* Toronto: Copp, Clark.

—. 1996. "An Overview of Planning and Political Problems for Canadian Urban Municipalities in the 1990s." In *Strategic Changes and Organizational Reorientations in Local Government: A Cross-National Perspective*, ed. Nahum Ben-Elia. London: Macmillan. 99-103.

—. 1997a. "City Campaigns on the Cusp and the Edmonton Mayoralty Election of 1992." *Journal of Canadian Studies* XXXII, 1 (Spring): 112-34.

—. 1997b. "A New Perspective on Clothing the Emperor: Canadian Metropolitan Form, Function and Frontiers." *Canadian Public Administration* 40, 3 (Fall): 436-56.

—. 1998. "Council Multiplicity and the Cost of Governance in Canadian Metropolitan Areas." *Canadian Journal of Urban Research* 7, 1 (June): 27-46.

—. 1999a. "Canada's Seraglio Cities: Political Barriers to Regional Government." *Canadian Journal of Sociology* 24, 2 (Summer): 175-91.

—. 1999b. "Finding the Trolls Under Your Bridge: The New Case for Party Politics in Canadian Cities." *Journal of Canadian Studies* 34, 1 (Spring): 172-83.

—. 2003. "Adventures in Adequacy: Recent Developments in the Quest for Better Management Practices in Canadian Municipal Government." *Public Performance and Management Review* 27, 1 (September): 71-87.

Lindblom, Charles. 1959. "The Science of Muddling Through," *Public Administration Review*, 19 (Spring): 79-88.

Lineberry, R.L. and I. Sharkansky. 1974. *Urban Politics and Public Policy.* 2nd ed. New York: Harper and Row.

Lipset, S.M. 1950. *Agrarian Socialism: The Cooperative Commonwealth Federation in Saskatchewan, a Study in Political Sociology*. Berkeley, CA: University of California Press.

—. 1985. "Canada and the United States: The Cultural Dimension." In *Canada and the United States: Enduring Friendship, Persistent Stress*, ed. C.F. Doran and J.H. Sigler. Englewood Cliffs, NJ: Prentice-Hall.

—. 1990. *Continental Divide: The Values and Institutions of the United States and Canada*. New York: Routledge.

—. 2001. "The Decline of Class Ideologies: The End of Political Exceptionalism?" In Clark and Lipset 2001, 249-72.

Local Government Boundaries Commission (LGBC) Manitoba. 1970. *File 4703.* 11 May.

Long, Norton E. 1968. "Political Science and the City." In *Social Science and the City* ed. L.F. Schnore. New York: Praeger. 243-262.

Longman, Phillip. 2004. "The Global Baby Bust." *Foreign Affairs* 83, 3 (May/June): 64-79.

Lorimer, James. 1970. *The Real World of City Politics*. Toronto: James, Lewis and Samuel.

—. 1972. *A Citizen's Guide to City Politics*. Toronto: James, Lewis and Samuel.

—. 1978. *The Developers*. Toronto: Lorimer.

Lowy, Alex and Becky Taylor. 1990. "Executive Development in Canadian Municipalities: Current and Future Perspectives," *Canadian Public Administration* 33, 3 (Fall): 306-21.

MacKay, Robert A. 1929 [1963]. *The Unreformed Senate of Canada,* Revised ed. Toronto: McClelland and Stewart.

Macpherson, C.B. 1953. *Democracy in Alberta: The Theory and Practice of a Quasi-Party System*. Toronto: University of Toronto Press.

Magnusson, Warren. 1983a. "Introduction: The Development of Canadian Urban Government." In Magnusson and Sancton 1983, 3-57.

—. 1983b. "Toronto." In Magnusson and Andrew Sancton 1983, 94-139.

—. 1990. "Regeneration and Quality of Life in Vancouver." In *Leadership and Urban Regeneration: Cities in North America and Europe*, ed. Dennis Judd and Michael Parkinson. Thousand Oaks, CA: Sage, 171-187.

—. 1992. "The Constitutions of Movements vs. the Constitution of the State: Rediscovering the Local as a Site of Global Politics." In *Political Arrangements: Power and the City*, ed. Henri Lustiger-Thaler. Montreal: Black Rose Books.

—. 1994. "Metropolitan Change and Political Disruption: The New Left, the New Right and the Postwar Orthodoxy." In Frisken Vol. 2, 1994, 541-60.

—. 1997. "Globalization, Movements and the Decentered State." In *Organizing Dissent: Contemporary Social Movements in Theory and Practice*, ed. William K. Carroll. Toronto: Garamond. 94-113.

—. 2002. "The City as the Hope of Democracy." In *Urban Affairs: Back on the Policy Agenda*, ed. Caroline Andrew, Susan Phillips, and Katherine Graham. Montreal: McGill-Queen's University Press. 331-44.

Magnusson, Warren and Andrew Sancton, eds. 1983. *City Politics in Canada*. Toronto: University of Toronto Press.

Malcolmson, Patrick and Richard Myers. 2005. *The Canadian Regime: An Introduction to Parliamentary Government in Canada*. 3rd edition. Peterborough: Broadview Press.

Mallory, James R. (1971). *The Structure of Canadian Government*. Toronto: Macmillan.

Manitoba. 1970. *Proposals for Urban Reorganization in the Greater Winnipeg Area*. Winnipeg: Queen's Printer.

Manitoba. 1971. *Transcript of Public Hearings*. Winnipeg: Legislative Assembly, Standing Committee on Municipal Affairs, 14-16 July.

Martinotti, Guido. 1999. "Slow-Growing Cities, A Municipal Perspective." Available from jim.lightbody@ualberta.ca

Masson, Jack. 1975. "Decision-Making Patterns and Floating Coalitions in an Urbsan City Council." *Canadian Journal of Political Science* VIII, 1 (March): 128-37.

Masson, Jack with Edd Lesage, Jr. 1994. *Alberta's Local Governments: Politics and Democracy*. Edmonton, AB: University of Alberta Press.

Masson, Jack K. and James D. Anderson, eds. 1972. *Emerging Party Politics in Urban Canada*.

Toronto: McClelland and Stewart.

McAllister, Mary Louise. 1995. "Local Environmental Politics: Principles in Conflict." In Lightbody 1995, 269-89.

—. 2004. *Governing Ourselves? The Politics of Canadian Communities*. Vancouver: University of British Columbia Press.

McAlpine, Scott and Stan Drabek. 1991. "Decision-Making Coalitions on Non-partisan Councils: A Small City/ Large City Comparison." *Canadian Journal of Political Science* 24, 4 (December): 803-29.

McCloskey, H. 1964. "Consensus and Ideology in American Politics." *American Political Science Review* LVIII, 2 (June): 361-81.

McDonald, James Ted. 2004. "Toronto and Vancouver Bound: The Location Choices of New Canadian Immigrants." *Canadian Journal of Urban Research* 13, 1 (Summer): 85-101.

McKenna, Brian and Susan Purcell. 1980. *Drapeau: Love Him, Hate Him, Fear Him, Admire Him—He's Still the Boss!* Toronto: Clark, Irwin & Co.

McKillop, A.B. 1970. "Citizens and Socialists: The Ethos of Political Winnipeg, 1919-1935." Unpublished M.A. thesis, University of Manitoba.

Meligrana, John. 1998. "Annexation and Urbanization: A Descriptive Aggregate Analysis of Three Canadian Provinces: Ontario, Alberta and British Columbia, 1941 to 1991." *Canadian Journal of Urban Research* VII, 2 (December): 167-217.

Merton, Robert K. 1957. *Social Theory and Social Structure*. Glencoe, IL: The Free Press.

—. 1968. *Social Theory and Social Structure*. New York: Free Press.

Michels, Roberto. 1949. *Political Parties*. Glencoe, IL: The Free Press.

Milbrath, Lester W. 1965. *Political Participation*. Chicago, IL: Rand, McNally.

Miliband, Ralph. 1973. *The State in Capitalist Society*. London: Quartet Books.

Milner, Henry. 1997. "Electoral Systems, Integrated Institutions and Turnout in Local and National Elections: Canada in Comparative Perspective." *Canadian Journal of Political Science* XXX, 1 (March): 89-106.

Miranda, Rowan A. 1994a. "Containing Cleavages: Parties and Other Hierarchies'" In Clark 1994b, 79-101.

—. 1994b. "Contracting Out: A Solution with Limits." In Clark 1994b, 197-212.

Mishler, William C. 1979. *Political Participation in Canada*. Toronto: Macmillan.

Molotch, Harvey. 1976. "The City as a Growth Machine." *American Journal of Sociology* 82, 2 (Spring): 309-55.

Molotch, Harvey. 1988."Strategies and Constraints of Growth Elites. In *Business Elites and Urban Development*, ed. S. Cummings. Albany, NY: State University of New York Press. 25-48.

Morton, W.L. 1967. *Manitoba: A History*. 2nd ed. Toronto: University of Toronto Press.

Munro, W.B. 1929. *American Influences on Canadian Government*. Toronto: Macmillan.

Nader G.A. 1975. *Cities of Canada: Volume I*. Toronto: Macmillan.

Nordlinger, E.A. 1981. *On the Autonomy of the Democratic State*. Cambridge, MA: Harvard University Press.

Northouse, Peter G. 1997. *Leadership: Theory and Practice*. Thousand Oaks, CA: Sage.

Nowlan, David and Nadine Nowlan. 1970. *The Bad Trip: The Untold Story of the Spadina Expressway*. Toronto: new-press, House of Anansi.

Ontario. 1967. *(Smith) Committee on Taxation, Report*. 3 vols. Toronto: Queen's Printer.

— 1977. *(Robarts) Royal Commission on Metropolitan Toronto*. 2 vols. Toronto: Queen's Printer.

Ontario PC. 1994. *The Common Sense Revolution*. Toronto: Progressive Conservative Party (May). http://www.ontariopc.com/feature/csr/csr_text.htm

Osborne, David and Ted Gaebler. 1992. *Reinventing Government: How the Entrepreneurial Spirit is Transforming the Public Sector*. New York: Penguin.

Ostrom, Vincent, Charles M. Tiebout, and Robert Warren. 1961. "The Organization of Government in Metropolitan Areas: A Theoretical Inquiry," *American Political Science Review* LV (December): 831-42.

Pal, Leslie A. 1997. *Beyond Policy Analysis: Public Issue Management in Turbulent Times.* Toronto: ITP Nelson.

—. 2001. *Beyond Policy Analysis: Public Issue Management in Turbulent Times.* 2nd ed. Toronto: ITP Nelson.

Parsons, Talcott. 1971. *The Systems of Modern Societies.* Englewood Cliffs, NJ: Prentice-Hall.

Pateman, Carole. 1970. *Participation and Democratic Theory.* London: Cambridge University Press.

Pelissero, John P., ed. 2003. *Cities, Politics, and Policy: A Comparative Analysis.* Washington, DC: CQ Press.

Peñalosa, Enrique. "Urban Transport and Urban Development." Available at <http:www.worldbank.org/urban/forum2002/docs/penalosa-pres.pdf>.

Phillips, Alan. 1976."Graft in Civic Office." In *Political Corruption in Canada: Cases, Causes and Cures,* eds. D.C. Rowat and K.M. Gibbons. Toronto: McClelland and Stewart. 85-103.

Phillips, S.D. 1999."New Social Movements in Canadian Politics: Past Their Apex?" In *Canadian Politics.* 3rd ed., ed. J.P. Bickerton and A.G. Gagnon. Peterborough, ON: Broadview. 371-91.

Pieterse, Jan Nederveen. 2004. *Globalization or Empire?* London: Routledge.

Pinderhughes, Dianne M. 2003. "Urban Racial and Ethnic Politics." In Pelissero 2003, 97-125.

Pitkin, Hanna F. 1972. *The Concept of Representation.* Berkeley, CA: University of California Press.

Plato. 1985. *The Republic.* Trans. Richard W. Sterling and William C. Scott. New York: W.W. Norton.

Plunkett, T.J. 1968. *Urban Canada and Its Government: A Study of Municipal Organization.* Toronto: Macmillan.

Plunkett, T.J. and G.M. Betts. 1978. *The Management of Canadian Urban Government.* Kingston, ON: Institute of Local Government, Queen's University.

Plunkett, T.J. and James Lightbody. 1982. "Tribunals, Politics, and the Public Interest: The Edmonton Annexation Case." *Canadian Public Policy* VIII, 2 (Spring): 207-21.

Pocklington, Tom and Sara Pocklington. 1993. "Aboriginal Political Ethics." In Langford and Tupper 1993, 42-66.

Porter, John. 1965. *The Vertical Mosaic: An Analysis of Social Class and Power in Canada.* Toronto: University of Toronto Press.

Presthus, Robert. 1973. *Elite Accommodation in Canadian Politics.* Toronto: Macmillan.

Price, Trevor. 1995. "Council-Administration Relations in City Governments." In Lightbody 1995, 193-214.

Pross, Paul. 1992. *Group Politics and Public Policy in Canada.* 2nd ed. Toronto: Oxford University Press.

Punnett, R.M. 1977. *The Prime Minister in Canadian Government and Politics.* Toronto: Macmillan.

Purcell, Susan 1989. "Drapeau the Magnificent." In Levine 1989, 149-74.

Putnam, Robert D. 2000. *Bowling Alone: The Collapse and Revival of American Community.* New York: Simon and Shuster.

Qualter, Terence H. 1970. *The Election Process in Canada.* Toronto: McGraw-Hill.

Rayside, David M. 1989. "Small Town Fragmentation and the Politics of Community." *Journal of Canadian Studies* 24, 1 (Spring): 103-20.

Renner, Tari. 2001. "The Local Government Management Profession at Century's End." *The Municipal Year Book, 2001.* Washington, DC: International City/County Management Association. 35-46.

Riordan, William L. 1903 [1995]. *Plunkitt of Tammany Hall: A Series of Very Plain Talks on Very Practical Politics.* Ed. Peter Quinn. New York: Penguin, Signet.

Roniger, Luis. 2004. "Political Clientelism, Democracy and Market Economy." *Journal of Comparative Politics,* 36, 3 (April): 1-25.

Rose, Albert. 1972. *Governing Metropolitan Toronto: A Social and Political Analysis, 1953-1971.* Berkeley, CA: University of California Press.

Rothblatt, Donald N. and Andrews Sancton, eds. 1998. *American/Canadian Metropolitan Intergovernmental Governance Perspectives Revisited.* Berkeley, CA: Institute of Governmental Studies, University of California.

Rowat, Donald C. 1969. *The Canadian Municipal System: Essays on the Improvement of Local Government.* Toronto: McClelland and Stewart.

Royko, Mike. 1971. *Boss: Richard J. Daley of Chicago.* New York: Dutton.

Rusk, D. 1993. *Cities Without Suburbs.* 2nd ed. Washington, DC: The Woodrow Wilson Center Press.

Safire, William. 1968. *The New Language of Politics.* New York: Random House.

Sancton, Andrew. 1979. "The Impact of Language Differences on Metropolitan Reform in Montreal." *Canadian Public Administration* 22, 2 (Summer): 227-50.

—. 1983. "Montreal." In Magnusson and Sancton 1983, 58-93.

—. 1991. *Local Government Reorganization in Canada Since 1975.* Toronto: Intergovernmental Committee on Urban and Regional Research.

—. 1992. "Canada as a Highly Urbanized Nation: New Implications for Government." *Canadian Public Administration* 35, 3 (Autumn): 281-98.

—. 1994. *Governing Canada's City-Regions: Adapting Form to Function.* Montreal: Institute for Research on Public Policy.

—. 1995. "Metropolitan Government in Montreal." In Sharpe 1995, 131-46.

—. 1996. "Reducing Costs by Consolidating Municipalities: New Brunswick, Nova Scotia and Ontario." *Canadian Public Administration* 39, 3 (Fall): 267-89.

—. 1997. "Affadavit of Andrew B. Sancton." Ontario Court of Justice, General Division, (22 May).

—. 2000. *Merger Mania: The Assault on Local Government.* Westmount, PQ: Price-Patterson Ltd (for the city of Westmount).

Sancton, Andrew and Paul Woolner. 1990. "Full-time Municipal Councillors: A Strategic Challenge for Canadian Urban Government." *Canadian Public Administration* 33, 4 (Winter): 482-505.

Santayana, George. 1905. *The Life of Reason, Vol. 1.* New York: Scribner's.

Sassen, Saskia. 1998. *Globalization and its Discontents.* New York: The New Press.

—., ed. 2002. *Global Networks, Linked Cities.* London and New York: Routledge.

Savitch, H.V. and John Clayton Thomas, eds. 1991. *Big City Politics in Transition.* Newbury Park, CA: Sage.

Savitch, H.V. and Ronald K. Vogel. 1996. *Regional Politics: America in a Post-City Age.* Thousand Oaks, CA: Sage.

Sayre, Wallace S. and Nelson W. Polsby. 1965. "American Political Science and the Study of Urbanization." In *The Study of Urbanization,* ed. P.M. Hauser and L.F. Schnore. New York: Wiley. 115-56.

Schattschneider, E.E. 1960. *The Semi-Sovereign People.* New York: Holt, Rinehart and Winston.

Schindeler, F.F. 1969. *Responsible Government in Ontario.*

Toronto: University of Toronto Press.

Schumpeter, Joseph A. 1943. *Capitalism, Socialism and Democracy.* London: George Allen and Unwin.

Scott, Allen J., ed. 2002. *Global City-Regions: Trends, Theory, Policy.* Oxford: Oxford University Press.

Scott, Allen J., John Agnew, Edward W. Soja, and Michael Storper. 2002. "Global City-Regions." In Scott 2002, 11-30.

Sharpe, L.J. 1981. "Theories of Local Government." In *Politics and Government of Urban Canada.* 4th ed., ed. Lionel D. Feldman. Toronto: Methuen 28-39.

Sharpe, L.J. 1995a. "The Future of Metropolitan Government." In Sharpe 1995b, 11-31.

—., ed. 1995b. *The Government of World Cities: The Future of the Metro Model.* New York: John Wiley & Sons.

—. 1995c. "Is There a Case for Metropolitan Government?" Paper presented to the Urban Regions in a Global Context Conference, Toronto.

Siegel, Arthur. 1996. *Politics and the Media in Canada.* 2nd ed. Toronto: McGraw-Hill, Ryerson.

Siegel, David. 1993. "Small-town Canada." In Langford and Tupper 1993, 217-34.

Simon, Herbert A. 1945. *Administrative Behaviour.* New York: Macmillan.

Simmons, Jim and Larry McCann. 2000. "Growth and Transition in the Canadian Urban System." In *Canadian*

Cities in Transition, 2nd ed., ed. Trudi Bunting and Pierre Filion. Toronto: Oxford. 97-120.

Slack, Enid. 1997. "Finance and Government: The Case of the Greater Toronto Area." In *Urban Governance and Finance: A Question of Who Does What*, ed. Paul A.R. Hobson and France St-Hilaire. Montreal: Institute for Research on Public Policy, 81-111.

Smallwood, Frank. 1965. *Greater London: The Politics of Metropolitan Reform*. Indianapolis, IN: Bobbs-Merrill.

—. 1972. "The Politics of Regional Government." In *Politics and Government of Urban Canada*, 2nd ed., ed. Lionel Feldman and M.D. Goldrick. Toronto: Methuen. 333-43.

Smith, Dayle M. 1997. "Women and Leadership." In *Leadership: Theory and Practice*, ed. Peter G. Northouse. Thousand Oaks, CA: Sage. 204-38.

Smith, Patrick J. 1992. "The Making of a Global City: The Case of Vancouver, 1943-1992." *Canadian Journal of Urban Research* 1 (June): 90-112.

—. 1995. "Governing Metropolitan Change: Public Policy and Governance in Canada's City-Regions." In Lightbody 1995, 161-92.

—. 1998. "More Than One Way Towards Economic Development: Public Participation and Policy-Making in the Vancouver Region." In Graham and Phillips 1998, 49-77.

Smith, Patrick J., and Theodore H. Cohn. 1994. "International Cities and Municipal Paradiplomacy: A Typology for Assessing the Changing Vancouver Metropolis." In Frisken Vol. 2, 613-55.

—. 1995. "Developing Global Cities in the Pacific Northwest: The Cases of Vancouver and Seattle." In *North American Cities and the Global Economy: Challenges and Opportunities*, ed. P.K. Kresl and G. Gappert, Gary. Thousand Oaks, CA: Sage. 251-55.

Smith, Patrick J., and H. Peter Oberlander. 1998. "Restructuring Metropolitan Governance: Greater Vancouver—British Columbia Reforms." In Rothblatt and Sancton 1998, 371-406.

Smith, P.J. 1995. "Urban-Planning Systems for Metropolitan Canada." In Lightbody 1995, 215-39.

Statistics Canada. 1973. *Census*. Catalogue #92-723, Vol. 1, Part 3. Ottawa: Minister of Industry, Trade and Commerce.

—. 1997. *A National Overview: Population and Dwelling Counts*. Catalogue # 93-357XPB. Ottawa: Minister of Industry.

—. 1999. *Census of Canada, 1996*. Dimension series CD-Rom. Ottawa: Ministry of Industry.

—. 2002a. *A National Overview: Population and Dwelling Counts, 2001*. Catalogue #93-360-XPB. Ottawa: Minister of Industry.

—. 2002b. *A National Overview: Population and Dwelling Counts, 2001 Census*. Catalogue #97F0006XCB01007. Ottawa: Minister of Industry.

—. 2002c. *A National Overview: Population and Dwelling Counts, 2001 Census*. Catalogue #97F0010XCB01001. Ottawa: Ministry of Industry, 2002.

—. 2003. *Canada's Ethnocultural Portrait: The Changing Mosaic*. Catalogue # 96-F0030XIE2001008. Ottawa: Minister of Industry.

—. 2004a. *Low Income in Census Metropolitan Areas: Executive Summary*. <http://www.statcan.ca/english/research/89-613-MIE/2004001/summary.htm> (accessed 9/8/2004).

—. 2004b. <http://geoodepot.statscan.ca/Diss/Highlights_e.cfm> (accessed 7/7/2004).

Stephens, G. Ross and Nelson Wikstrom. 2000. *Metropolitan Government and Governance: Theoretical Perspectives, Empirical Analysis, and the Future*. New York: Oxford University Press.

Stinson, Lloyd. 1975. *Political Warriors: Recollections of a Social Democrat*. Winnipeg: Queenston House.

Stone, Clarence. 1989. *Regime Politics: Governing Atlanta, 1946-1988*. Lawrence, KS: University Press of Kansas.

—. 1995. "Political Leadership in Urban Politics." In Judge, Stoker, and Wolman 1995, 96-116.

Stone, Clarence and Heywood Sanders, eds. 1987. *The Politics of Urban Development*. Lawrence: University Press of Kansas.

Studenski, Paul. 1930. *The Government of Metropolitan Areas in the United States*. New

York: The National Municipal League.

Supreme Court [Canada] Records (SCR). 1936; 2000.

Sutherland, Sharon. 1993. "The Canadian Federal Government: Patronage, Unity, Security, and Purity." In Langford and Tupper 1993, 113-50.

Swanson, Bert. 1996. "Jacksonville: Consolidation and Regional Governance." In Savitch and Vogel 1996, 229-52.

Sypnowich, Marcia. 1991. "Promoting Ethical Behaviour for Municipal Councils." *Canadian Public Administration* 34, 1 (Spring): 146-52.

Taras, David. 1988. "Prime Ministers and the Media." In *Prime Ministers and Premiers*, ed. L.A. Pal and David Taras. Scarborough, ON: Prentice-Hall.

Taraska, Peter. 1976. *Report and Recommendations: Committee of Review, City of Winnipeg Act.* Winnipeg: Queen's Printer.

Taylor, J.H. 1974. "Urban Social Organization and Urban Discontent in the 1930s." In *Western Perspectives, I*, ed. David Bercuson. Toronto: Holt, Rinehart and Winston. 33-44.

Taylor, P.J., D.R.F. Walker, and J.V. Beaverstock. 1999. *Introducing GaWC: Researching World City Network Formation.* GaWC Research Bulletin # 6. Loughborough, UK: University of Loughborough, Department of Geography. <http://www.lboro.ac.uk/departments/gy/research/gawc/rb/rb2.html>.

Tennant, Paul. 1980. "Vancouver Politics and the Civic Party System." In *Problems of Change in Urban Government*, ed. M.O. Dickerson, S. Drabek, and J.T. Woods. Waterloo, ON: Wilfrid Laurier University Press. 13-37.

—. 1981. "Vancouver City Politics, 1929-1980." In *Politics and Government of Urban Canada.* 4th ed., ed. Lionel D. Feldman. Toronto: Methuen. 127-47.

Thomas, Timothy. 1995. "When 'They' is 'We': Movements, Municipal Parties, and Participatory Politics." In Lightbody 1995, 115-36.

—., ed. 1997. *The Politics of the City: A Canadian Perspective.* Toronto: Nelson.

Thomlinson, Neil R. 1997. "Gay Concerns and Local Governments." In Thomas 1997, 115-36.

Tiebout, Charles M. 1956. "A Pure Theory of Local Expenditure." *Journal of Political Economy* LXIV (October): 416-24.

Tindal, C. Richard and Susan Nobes Tindal. 1979. *Local Government in Canada.* Toronto: McGraw-Hill.

—. 2000. *Local Government in Canada*, 5th ed. Toronto: ITP Nelson.

Tindal, C. Richard and Susan Nobes Tindal. 2004. *Local Government in Canada.* 6th ed. Toronto: ITP Nelson.

Toronto, City of. 1999. *Building the New City of Toronto: Status Report.* June. <http://city.toronto.on.ca/council/amal_report.1.htm#savings>.

Treff, Karen and David B. Perry. 2004. "Tax 101." *Finances of the Nation: A Review of Expenditures and Revenues of the Federal, Provincial, and Local Governments of Canada, 2003.* Toronto: CTF. <http://www.ctf.ca>.

Trépanier, Marie-Odile. 1993. "Metropolitan Government in the Montreal Area." In Rothblatt and Sancton 1993, 53-110.

Trimble, Linda. 1995. "Politics Where We Live: Women and Cities." In Lightbody 1995, 82-114.

Trimble, Linda., and Jane Arscott. 2003. *Still Counting: Women and Politics Across Canada.* Peterborough, ON: Broadview.

Truman, David B. 1959. "The American System in Crisis." *Political Science Quarterly* (December): 481-97.

—. 1964. *The Governmental Process: Political Interests and Public Opinion.* New York: Alfred A. Knopf.

UNESCO. 2002. <http://www.unesco.org/education/tlsf/theme_a/mod02/uncom02t01bod.htm>.

Van Loon, R.J. and M.S. Whittington. 1996. *Canadian Government and Politics: Institutions and Processes.* 3rd ed. Toronto: McGraw-Hill Ryerson.

Vaughan, Colin. 1997. "Ratepayers' groups gear up for Megacity." Toronto *Globe and Mail*, 3 February.

Villeneuve, Paul and Anne-Marie Séguin. 2000. "Power and Decision-Making in the City: Political Perspectives." In

Canadian Cities in Transition: The Twenty-First Century. 2nd ed., ed. Trudi Bunting and Pierre Filion. Don Mills, ON: Oxford University Press. 544-64.

Waterloo Area Local Government Review (WALG). 1970. *Report.* Toronto: Department of Municipal Affairs.

Weber, Max. 1947. *The Theory of Social and Economic Organization*, Talcott Parsons, ed. (trans. A.M. Henderson, Talcott Parsons). New York: Oxford University Press.

Weimer, David L. and Aidan R. Vining. 1999. *Policy Analysis: Concepts and Practice.* 3rd ed. Upper Saddle River, NJ: Prentice-Hall.

Wheare, Kenneth. 1963. *Federal Government.* 4th ed. London: Oxford University Press.

White, Randall. 1998. *Ontario Since 1985.* Toronto: Eastend-books.

Whitson, David and Donald MacIntosh. 1996. "The Global Circus: International Sport, Tourism, and the Marketing of Cities." *Journal of Sport and Social Issues* 20, 3: 278-95.

Williams, Oliver. 1971. *Metropolitan Political Analysis.* Philadelphia, PA: University of Pennsylvania Press.

Winter, William O. 1969. *The Urban Polity.* New York: Dodd, Mead and Co.

Wolfe, Jeanne M. 2003. "A National Urban Policy for Canada: Prospects and Challenges." Canadian Journal of Urban Research—Canadian Institute of Planners, (Joint Issue): 1-21.

Wrede, Matthias. 1997. "Local Public Goods, Heterogeneous Population, Voluntary Transfers, and Constrained Efficiency Allocations." *The Annals of Regional Science* XXXI, 3 (July): 217-34.

Wright, Gerry and James Lightbody. 1989. "Urban Innovation? Conditions Underpinning the Transformation of Movement into Party: The Case of the Urban Reform Group of Edmonton, Canada." In *New Leaders, Parties and Groups in Local Politics*, ed. H. Baldersheim. Bordeaux: CERVEL Institute. 379-408.

Young, Walter. 1969. *The Anatomy of a Party: The National CCF, 1932-1961.* Toronto: University of Toronto Press.

Zussman, David. 1997. "Do Citizens Trust Their governments?" *Canadian Public Administration* 40, 2 (Summer): 234-54.

index

Index of names

Abu-Laban, Y., 538, 539
Alinsky, S., 124
Andrew, C., 28, 33, 58, 371, 383, 460, 538
Arnstein, S., 59, 121
Artibise, A.F.J., 105, 146, 277
Aristotle, 42, 47, 73, 110
Axworthy, L., 123, 200
Axworthy, T., 274, 454, 501

Bachrach, P., 86, 113, 120
Baldwin, R., 108, 138
Banfield, E.C., 50, 54, 104-05, 178, 183, 185, 198, 274, 277, 497-98
Baratz, M., 86
Betts, G., 138, 149, 166, 314, 402
Bish, R.L., 55, 384, 437, 474
Bollens, J.C., 382, 389, 398, 426, 430, 437, 441, 448, 453, 489, 491, 492, 493, 494, 495, 499, 500
Boudreau, J.A., 489, 496
Brownstone, M., 122, 123, 454, 465, 478, 489, 490, 496, 500
Bryce, J., 49, 52, 62n, 66, 114, 115, 116, 141, 145, 174n, 203, 238, 332, 413, 416, 469
Brundtland, G.H., 527
Bulpitt, J.G., 106
Bunting, T., 57
Burns, J.M., 231, 319-20, 321
Byrne, T., 136, 142, 399

Castells, M., 512
Chomsky, N., 513

Clark, T.N., 104, 126, 131, 133, 224, 242, 244, 248, 252, 253, 256, 282, 283, 288, 290, 300, 304, 305, 306, 307, 308, 309, 310, 311, 312, 316, 319, 385, 439, 467, 472, 517
Clarke, S.E., 408, 433, 447, 519, 521
Clarkson, S., 163, 239, 245, 329
Clement, W., 266, 328
Cohn, T., 530, 531, 533, 534, 540
Colton, T., 318
Crawford, K.G., 48, 56, 106, 142, 144, 147, 149, 185, 186

Dahl, R.A., 69, 75, 76, 120, 265, 396
Decore, L., 242, 252
DelGuidice, D., 381
de Tocqueville, A., 49, 109, 114, 115, 116, 119, 373, 428
Donnelly, M., 225
Doré, J., 125
Drabek, S., 252
Drapeau, J., 68, 107, 124, 166, 241, 246-47, 251, 255, 262n, 332, 335
Draper, J.A., 121
Dunleavy, P., 399
Dupré, S., 371, 381
Duverger, M., 234, 250, 513
Dye, T.R., 67, 100, 424, 426, 467

Easton, D., 71
Easton, R., 235
Eldersveld, S., 54, 227
England, R.E., 147, 148, 320

Faure, A., 233
Filion, P., 57
Feldman, L.D., 291, 296, 343, 353, 364
Fenn, W.M., 162, 518
Fish, S.A., 142, 153, 251, 298, 299
Florida, R., 516
Frisken, F., 57, 478, 485, 503

Gaebler, T., 60-61, 123, 127, 128, 129, 131, 132, 133, 147, 351, 392, 442, 466, 473
Garber, J.A., 58, 60, 62, 480
Gibbins, R., 104, 119, 309
Gidengil, E., 189, 225, 257, 258
Goetz, E.G., 133, 308, 312, 316, 408, 433, 447
Graham, K.A., 34, 38, 60, 124, 190, 206, 247, 250, 281, 291, 292, 295, 296, 343, 353, 358, 364, 374, 398
Granatstein, J.L., 298
Grant, H., 525, 535
Greene, I., 206, 208, 210, 212, 333, 334, 335, 336
Greer, S., 204, 220, 256, 489, 491, 492, 493, 495
Gutstein, D., 100, 143, 158, 214, 267, 445

Hall, P., 528, 529
Hall, S., 131
Harrigan, J.J., 461, 467, 494, 495, 498
Harris, N., 102, 236
Hawrelak, W., 51, 211-12, 216, 217, 241, 247, 251, 314, 328, 333, 334

allocative, 82, 235, 436, 455, 458, 461, 535
delegation, 230, 274, 381
redistributive, 82, 236, 315, 389, 417, 440, 445, 447, 452, 461, 474, 483, 512, 526
symbolic, 84, 172-73, 276, 310, 468, 490, 520
public-private partnerships, 61-62, 127, 284, 312, 400, 438-39, 474, 477, 481, 500, 514, 519-20

quality of life, ideals, 126, 133, 300-01, 512, 516
quasi-autonomous agencies, local, 83, 122, 142-43, 163, 168, 210, 230, 273, 381-82, 400, 401, 406, 515-16
provincial, 83, 271, 294, 337, 343, 344, 372, 374, 401-02, 403
quasi-private service provision, 29, 34, 127, 279, 306, 474
Quebec, 26, 29, 41, 137, 141, 168, 170, 189, 190, 195, 207, 208, 259, 294, 332, 336, 343, 353, 360, 361, 380, 395, 424, 446, 465, 480-81, 504-5
Quebec City, 30, 31, 32, 33, 479
citizens, 533
incorporation, 137, 138, 141
organizational structure, 166, 463
political parties, 250

railways, 141, 142, 207, 445
ratepayers, 138, 254, 271, 283, 299-300, 489, 501-2
recreation, 271, 280, 286
referenda, see plebiscites,
reform movements, 64, 90, 184-85, 198
first, 108, 138, 141, 142
second, 50, 52-55, 110, 141, 142, 144-46, 171, 173, 185, 200, 220, 255, 274, 287, 400
third, 56-57, 120-21, 124, 126-27, 141, 153, 155, 186, 228-29, 245, 249-51, 268, 270, 284-85, 298-300, 497

policies, 47, 90, 122, 249, 322-23, 481-82
regime, theory, 64, 84, 289-90, 475-78, 482, 505-6
urban, 28, 77-78, 131, 187, 245, 475-77, 499, 502
Regina, 141, 186, 205, 237, 380, 392
regional government, 348, 349, 380, 392-95, 431, 444, 501
plans, 354, 388, 389, 475, 481, 511
regulation, 83-4
representation, 30, 36, 43-44, 190-91, 305, 458, 460
electoral, 179-80, 185, 187-88, 469
Residents' Advisory Groups (Winnipeg), 114, 122, 123, 125, 154
revenue, 342, 355, 357, 360, 392
sources, 41, 168, 292, 295, 351-52, 353, 359, 369, 437
predictability of, 41, 169, 295, 352, 358

Saskatchewan, 26, 29, 34, 36, 41, 115, 139, 186, 237, 280, 343, 359
Saskatoon, 129, 142, 158, 185, 186, 205, 237
schooling, see education
self-government,
autonomy, 115, 137-38
concepts, 95, 136
historical roots, 73, 138
services, see by functions
social class, 76, 86, 101, 118, 131, 225, 285, 299, 312, 428, 522-23
segregation by, 80, 86, 185, 197, 385, 415-16, 426, 519, 524-25, 535
Social Credit Party, 43, 205, 245, 424
social services, 34, 36, 82, 86, 347, 355, 358, 391, 436, 535, 536
agencies, 271, 286, 440, 477, 501
socialism, 60, 103-04, 131, 310
socialist initiatives, 102, 226, 408, 465

space,
communities and, 58-59, 283, 379, 406, 466, 517, 523
and political organization, 42, 69, 78, 119-20, 186, 295, 361, 386, 393-94, 396, 417, 439-40, 455, 510-11, 515, 519, 543
special purpose authorities, 77, 362, 370-71, 381-82, 388, 400, 406, 420-21, 441, 444, 449-52
spending, public, 29, 41, 291, 353, 369, 436-37, 453, 498
spillovers, 354, 362, 392, 409, 410-11, 455, 466
stakeholders. 59, 78, 87, 88, 202, 489, 502
suburbs, 213, 332, 335, 419, 491
social separation of, 28, 55, 384-85, 386-87, 391, 407-08, 413, 426-27, 436, 439, 469, 474, 477-78, 495, 536
politics, 38, 198, 200, 204-05, 210, 230, 305, 329-30, 347, 392, 398, 414, 417, 419, 422, 468, 480, 481, 492, 499-500, 504
value systems, 45, 86, 204, 218, 312, 330, 386, 391, 416, 444, 462, 468-69, 473, 490, 498
Surrey, 27, 167, 181, 360, 415
Sydenham, Lord, 108, 138

task forces, 85, 122, 173
taxation, 418, 433, 500
assessment, 168-69, 349, 388, 395, 414
business, 414, 416-17, 490
property, 168-69, 352, 416, 496
TEAM, see Electors Action Movement
Toronto, see also Megacity, Metro Toronto, 26-27, 31, 32, 33, 58, 218, 289, 296, 511, 530
citizens, 51, 287, 526, 535
council, 190, 214, 224, 251, 299, 327
elections, 72, 178, 182, 183, 205, 233, 239, 329